Global Dimensions of
the African Diaspora

Global Dimensions of the African Diaspora

Second Edition

Edited by
Joseph E. Harris

Howard University Press
Washington, D.C., 1993

Digitally printed in Canada on acid-free paper by WEBCOM Ltd.
Production management and project consultation provided by Abram
Hall Alternatives, Inc.

Library of Congress Cataloging-in-Publication Data

Global dimensions of the African diaspora / edited by Joseph E.
    Harris.— 2nd ed.

        p.   cm.
    Includes papers from the First and Second African Diaspora
Studies Institutes.
    Includes bibliographical references and index.
    ISBN 0-88258-149-X (alk. paper)
    1. African diaspora—History—Congresses. 2. Africa—
Civilization—Congresses. 3. Slavery—Africa—History—
Congresses. 4. Blacks—Cultural assimilation—Congresses.
5. Blacks—Race identity—Congresses. 6. Afro-Americans—Africa—
History Congresses.   I. Harris, Joseph E., 1929–   . II. African
Diaspora Studies Institute (lst: 1979: Howard University)
III. African Diaspora Studies Institute (2nd: 1982 : Nairobi, Kenya)
DT16.5.G58 1993
909'.0496—dc20   93-3755
                                                           CIP

Contents

v

Return to the Homeland

Toward a Synthesis

Global Dimensions of
the African Diaspora

15

Introduction

Joseph E. Harris

THE African presence in Asia, Europe, and the Americas is not a recent phenomenon. It was not uncommon in ancient Greece and Rome, and it existed in Arabia and other parts of Asia before the rise of Islam. The development of the international trade in African slaves by the Arabs over fifteen hundred years ago and the much more intensive trade by Europeans and Americans from the fifteenth century made that presence essentially global. Only recently, however, have scholars made serious and sustained efforts to study this subject in its global context.

Although a few diaspora-oriented studies have appeared since the publication of *Global Dimensions of the African Diaspora* in 1982, there still does not exist a single comprehensive text on the global African diaspora. However, St. Clair Drake's two-volume study, *Black Folk Here and There* (Center for Afro-American Studies, UCLA; 1987 and 1990), is a major step forward from the perspectives of history and anthropology. Drake's citations alone are replete with data unearthed from sources long unexplored. In spite of this, there remain insufficient data from too many geographical and disciplinary areas to construct a comprehensive, historical, global synthesis. This volume, which includes new data and perspectives, is designed to advance scholarship toward that more comprehensive approach of the African dispersion and settlement abroad.

The Diaspora as Concept and Method

The African diaspora concept subsumes the following: the global dispersion (voluntary and involuntary) of Africans throughout history; the emergence of a cultural identity abroad based on origin and social condition; and the psychological or physical return to the homeland, Africa. Thus viewed, the African diaspora assumes the character of a

3

dynamic, continuous, and complex phenomenon stretching across time, geography, class, and gender.

The concept of the African diaspora as a mode of study gained momentum from 1965 when the International Congress of African Historians convened in Tanzania and included in its program a session entitled, "The African Abroad or the African Diaspora." Since that time the diaspora has become a recurring theme in UNESCO's multivolume *General History of Africa*, with discrete chapters appearing in several of its volumes. The publication of this series in the major languages of the United Nations and in several African languages virtually assures that the historical relationship between Africans and their descendants abroad will remain a subject not only in history and historiography but in other disciplines as well.

In response to inquiries from Africanists and African Americanists alike, this volume draws a number of essays from *Global Dimensions of the African Diaspora* and includes several new essays on subjects vital to the understanding of the African presence abroad. Thus, these essays provide greater historical and sociopolitical analysis and geographical scope.

This volume reaffirms the black diaspora as an extension of the African heritage. It begins with a section on concept and methodology to provide coherence for teaching and research as well as general understanding of the subject. In analyzing the contradictions in the diaspora, Elliott P. Skinner's chapter draws on the concepts of W. E. B. Du Bois's double consciousness, Everett Stonequist's and E. Franklin Fraziers's marginal man, and the concept of stranger developed by George Simmel, William Shack, and Skinner. George Shepperson follows with a chapter that draws parallels between the African and Jewish diasporas and distinguishes between the relevance of exile and diaspora. The chapter by Joseph E. Harris presents data on the African presence in Asia and provides a framework for a comparative analysis of return movements in West and East Africa. Albert J. Raboteau presents a theoretical framework for comprehending African religious influences in the diaspora and identifies areas for future study. These essays provide a foundation for understanding the origin and development of the diaspora abroad and identify themes pursued in the essays that follow.

Settlement, Identity, and Transformation

The essays in this section concentrate on identity and transformation in the diaspora. That Africans left the continent with an ethnic identity should provoke no debate. However, the critical process of transformation began in Africa with capture and the forced marches to the coast, and accelerated with the Middle Passage as African survival required a greater means of communication and collective action/support. Okon Edet Uya discusses this phenomenon, pointing out that, contrary to many observers, Africans did communicate on board slave ships and that once in the diaspora, African languages and cultures persisted alongside European languages and culture. Indeed, over time the several African traditions and languages formed a synthesis and mixed synthetically with traditions and languages of Europeans, thus facilitating a new African reality in which the African dimension sometimes assumed a different form.

Lawrence W. Levine's essay explores aspects of this phenomenon. He addresses assumptions that have prevented the objective study of African influences on thought and society in the United States and argues against the view that African "survivals" are only those that have remained unchanged from the past. He states that too much focus has been accorded the formative rather than the substantive African continuity in the United States. This characterization also applies to other parts of the diaspora.

Adell Patton's essay confirms that transformation from African to African American did not sever links with the homeland. Blacks in the United States shared with Africans their limited educational resources at Howard University, Meharry Medical School, and other institutions generally, and thus educated not only generations of physicians and medical technicians, but other professionals as well.

Colin Palmer's essay focuses on the African presence in Mexico during the sixteenth and seventeenth centuries. He relates religion, folk medicine, and other aspects of culture to African traditions and reveals both Spanish and Indian influences on African-Mexicans. Roy Simon Bryce-Laporte and Trevor Purcell concentrate their analysis on Jamaican migrations to Costa Rica and the impact of their "Costaricanization." They pursue this subject within the context of the broader socioeconomic arrangements in the American hemisphere and demonstrate the potential for a comparative historical-sociological approach to African diaspora studies. Guerin C. Montilus follows with his essay on the collective memory of Haiti, where African elements are dominant in history and culture, thereby making the country a virtual laboratory for the study of Africa and its diasporic connection.

Far too few scholars have published on the subject of the role black women have played in the link between Africa and its diaspora. Filomena Chioma Steady addresses this important issue as she analyzes the impact of the convergence of race, class, and gender in the diaspora. The theme of race and class is pursued also by Thomas E. Skidmore whose essay analyzes the literature of race relations and identifies and critiques the patterns of black consciousness in twentieth-century Brazil.

No study of identity and transformation in the African diaspora would be complete without the treatment of religion. Angela Jorge's essay on *La madama françesita* explores the continuity of the belief system of the Yoruba and provides a basis for comparative analysis of the adaptation of African religions in the American hemisphere.

Three essays address the African presence in Europe. Folarin Shyllon's essay presents a synthesis of the African experience in Britain and links a number of descendant Africans in Britain to African Americans in the United States. Ibrahima B. Kaké follows with an essay that compares the racial context of blacks in the United States to French-speaking Africans during the twentieth century. He relates the origin of negritude to the Harlem Renaissance and links W. E. B. Du Bois, Marcus Garvey, and George Padmore to French-speaking blacks in Europe. M. W. Kodi's essay examines the influence of diaspora ideas in Zaire when it was under Belgian control. He reveals the interrelationship of W. E. B. Du Bois, Marcus Garvey, and the anticolonial, antiracist movement in Zaire and shows how Belgium, other European powers, and the United States collaborated to prevent "Pan-Negroist activities."

The Arab trade in African slaves represents the first great, sustained dispersal of Africans abroad; yet, too few scholars have published research on this subject. In his chapter on blacks in the Mediterranean, J. O. Hunwick assesses the moral and legal aspects of slavery in Muslim areas, evaluates manumission and the status of freed persons in Muslim society, and raises a number of questions for future study. Joseph E. Harris extends the treatment of Africans in Asia and Muslim lands. His essay surveys the African presence primarily in what today are Iran, Pakistan, and India.

Return to the Homeland

That Africans struggled to escape slavery and return to Africa is well documented. Indeed, the idea of a return is deeply embedded in the traditions of the diaspora. This observation is confirmed by the many return movements during slavery and after freedom. Thousands in fact returned, while others lost their lives in the attempt; still others expressed a desire to return in songs, poems, legends, and myths.

This section concentrates on sustained efforts for a physical return to Africa. The first of these sustained efforts led to the emergence of a significant diaspora settlement in Sierra Leone. Akintola J. G. Wyse traces the main contours of that development and shows how the Krios created a society based on the fusion of African and European cultures. Wyse also portrays Sierra Leone as a hub from which influences from the diaspora continue to spread into other parts of West Africa. Debra Newman Ham's essay focuses on African American women returnees to Liberia. This long-neglected dimension of Liberia's history reveals the critical role of women in the founding of that country and the development of links with the United States.

Several essays assess the image and influence of African Americans in different parts of Africa. Kings M. Phiri identifies a number of Malawians who received their education in the United States, especially at Meharry Medical School; thereby reinforcing Adell Patton's chapter. He also emphasizes the role of black Americans in providing moral and financial support to Malawians and spreading ideas that influenced their political development and that of black South Africans. Kimpianga Mahaniah presents evidence of black American support for the education of Zairean students in the United States; he also stresses the importance of African American missionaries in publicizing the Belgian atrocities in Zaire during the 1890s and the early twentieth century, and the influence of Garvey's *Negro World*, which encouraged political resistance to colonial rule in the 1920s. S. Y. Boadi-Siaw extends the scope of the returnees to Afro-Brazilians in West Africa. He identifies the points of return and shows the relationship between the Brazilian experience and the contributions made in West Africa. He also reveals a "double consciousness" on the part of Afro-Brazilians similar to what Du Bois attributed to United States blacks. Tony Martin ends this section with an essay on Marcus Garvey, the best-known exponent of black pride and return. Martin shows that Garvey's influence was multi-dimensional and spread into far more areas of the black world than previously realized.

This volume appropriately concludes with St. Clair Drake's extensive synthesis of the African diaspora in the Americas. Not only is this a substantive essay, but it shows how Drake moved over the years to arrive at what was the culminating scholarship of his career as Pan-Africanist academic and activist, his two-volume study referred to above.

Although no single study can cover satisfactorily all aspects of the global African presence, this volume presents essays on aspects of the diaspora in Asia, Europe, and the Americas; it addresses issues in the Christian and Muslim worlds; and it includes analyses of societies in several Arabic-, English-, French-, Portuguese-, and Spanish-speaking countries. African, American, and European scholars representing several disciplines have contributed essays applying various concepts and methodologies. The result is a volume that will inform readers and stimulate further research and teaching.

The diaspora, as concept and method, facilitates the evaluation of the presence and impact of Africans dispersed throughout the world. Indeed, that presence remains dynamic as continental Africans continue to migrate to different parts of the world as a result of economic and political oppression as well as famine, the desire for education, and the wish to join their compatriots abroad. Conversely, descendant Africans abroad migrate throughout the diaspora and Africa, providing continuity and facilitating change throughout the world of African peoples and laying the basis for ultimate humanity among all peoples. Indeed, these Africans and their descendants represent a new dimension of the diaspora that no doubt will reinforce the African/diaspora connection. That connection thus remains an evolving phenomenon that undoubtedly will influence the configuration of ideas and action in the world of the twenty-first century.

*The Diaspora
as Concept and
Method*

1
The Dialectic between Diasporas and Homelands

Elliott P. Skinner

R ELATIONS between peoples in diasporas and their ancestral homelands are complex and full of dialectical contradictions. First, there is anger, bitterness, and remorse among the exiles—and often among the people at home—over the weaknesses that permitted the dispersion to occur. Second, there is conflict when the dominant hosts attempt to justify the subordinate status of the exiles, and the latter, in turn, refuse to accept the status thrust on them. Often the dominant groups display contempt for the homelands of their victims, and the latter feel constrained to defend the countries from which they or their ancestors came. Third, there is often an acrimonious debate among the exiles themselves, and between them and their host and ancestral communities, as to whether the exiles should return to their homelands. The issues are as follows: Under what conditions should this return take place, and what are the implications for all concerned? Fourth, if a return does occur, there is frequently a conflict between the returnees and the resident populations. A corollary is the issue of what effect a return will have on those exiles still in the diaspora. Last, the various groups of exiles, their hosts, and the people in the homelands face the problem of what to do once the issues arising from the dispersion have been resolved. This is almost inevitable because human beings adapt to almost any condition in which they find themselves, and they often fear change.

The concept of diaspora, sometimes defined as *galut*—exile or bondage—and as *golah*—a relatively stable community in exile—derives from the historic experience of the Jewish people.[1] In many

11

respects, the plight of the people of African descent, especially those in the New World, is similar to that of the Jews. For analytic purposes, comparative data on these two populations will be presented, as will data on overseas Chinese and Indians and the Irish in America. The following concepts will be discussed: double consciousness, developed by W. E. B. Du Bois;[2] marginal man, developed by Everett Stonequist and treated at length by E. Franklin Frazier;[3] and the "stranger," developed by George Simmel and more recently elaborated on by William Shack and Elliott Skinner.[4]

For a human being—a social animal requiring the ministration of other human beings—to be plucked away from the society into which he or she was born and socialized is traumatic. It is no wonder the Jews taken captive by Nebuchadnezzar sat down and wept by the waters of Babylon when they remembered Zion. They were as disconsolate as their forefathers who were taken captive in Egypt and as their subsequent generation who would be taken captive to Assyria and, even later, as those who were dispersed from Judea by the Romans. The Babylonian exiles would not be comforted. They refused to sing the Lord's songs in a strange land and rejected Jeremiah's suggestion that they adapt to conditions there.[5] Down through the centuries, the Jewish exiles suffered because their homeland was caught up in the imperial politics and wars of major powers (Assyria, Babylon, Egypt, Persia, Greece, Rome, Turkey, and Great Britain) and because of militant messianic movements such as Islam and the Crusades that swept over the area. They were forced to work for alien masters in distant lands while their homeland was plundered and occupied.

Those Africans who were captured and shipped across either the Indian or Atlantic ocean did not go quietly into slavery. West Africans fought valiantly against Antam Goncalvez, who wished to take them to Portugal as curios and slaves. Subsequent captives fought against the loss of their freedom. The slave ships were seething cauldrons of revolt, and occasionally slaves did seize ships and attempt to return to Africa. When this was impossible, many captives preferred death either by starvation, or torture, or drowning. The Africans, too, initially refused to adapt to the new lands. They had to be "broken" before they would accept the transculturating process known as "seasoning." They revolted and ran away as often as the opportunities arose.[6]

Like the Jews, the Africans were victims of powerful imperialism. Western European imperialism had as its major characteristics a will to conquer and control foreign lands; a need for commerce to fuel a developing capitalist industrial system; and a creed that justified converting pagans to Christianity.[7] Africa's misfortune was that it did not have nation-state structures, and although Islam provided some West

African rulers with a rationale for large-scale imperial conquests, most of Africa's polities were small. Africa's other misfortune was that its manpower had achieved that level of agricultural, pastoral, and technical skill that was needed by the Europeans, who were bent on conquering the New World and transforming it into plantations and mines. Further, although historians are still debating how many persons did in fact leave the continent, most parts of the Americas received Africans.[8] Moreover, without the valor, skill, and fertility of these persons, it would have been very difficult indeed for Europeans to subdue, settle, and develop the New World. African labor did much to facilitate the rise of industrial capitalism, and with it European hegemony over the globe.[9]

In marked contrast to the Africans and Jews who were forcibly taken into exile or dispersed, the Indians, Chinese, and Irish expatriated by choice before or during the recent colonial period because of appalling hardships at home. These people came from societies with recognized governments even though these governments were often controlled by outsiders. Thus, members of these diasporalike populations had legal personalities in the international arena with which their hosts were forced to deal. Moreover, they could return home when they had the money to do so or when conditions were propitious.[10]

Peoples in the diaspora develop myths, rationalizations, and theories to explain their plight. In many cases these ideas are created to counter explanations given by their enslavers or their countrymen still at home. The result is often a mass of dialectical contradictions. For example, one major difficulty the Jews faced in their struggle for emancipation was the belief that their exile and suffering were ordained by their god, Yahweh. According to this belief, the Jews were the "chosen people of God," but having transgressed his will, they were scattered among the nations of the earth until their sins were expiated. In the fullness of time, a Messiah would come to crush the other nations of the earth, restore the exiles to Zion, and reign forever. The problem was that the Jews did not know when the true Messiah would come. Meanwhile, even though in exile, they believed that they were carrying out the special mission of God. Their lives had to be exemplary, and they had to exercise care when dealing with the *goyim*, for in the end they had to be prepared to do God's bidding. They continued to extol the virtues of Zion and sing the praises of Jerusalem the Golden.[11]

The dialectical tragedy for the Jews was that the Gentiles who controlled the lands where the Jews lived and labored believed that a Jew, Jesus of Nazareth, was the Christ and the son of the living God. The Christians believed that they were doing God's will by penalizing the Jews for rejecting Jesus the Messiah. They also believed that the conversion of the Jews to Christianity and their return to Zion would herald Christ's second coming. Meanwhile, the Christians considered the Jews as "strangers in the land" and as "enemies within the gates." They segregated them in ghettoes; restricted their economic, social, and political activities; and placed them beyond the Pale. Thus, Jews and Christians were locked into a dialectic in which they had differing views of Jesus the Jew, who was also the Christ of the Christians.

There is no evidence that the early Africans in the diaspora developed any elaborate religious explanations for their dispersal. Later, some Afro-American preachers, and at least one historian, theorized that the exile of some Africans was necessary for the rejuvenation, Christianization, and sociocultural development of Africa.[12] Clearly these ideas derived from the Hebraic tradition. Most diaspora Africans acknowledged a secular reason for their helplessness—insufficient economic, military, and political power in Africa. Some continental Africans, such as the King of Ashanti, justified slave trade as being necessary for the economic development of their countries. Other monarchs, such as the Mani-Congo, complained that military and economic weakness led to the capture and export of their people.[13] In many African villages, the belief arose that those persons sent away as slaves were too ambitious, too bright, too rebellious, or too wicked. Ironically, if these "terrible people" had been kept at home, Africa may not have been conquered and colonized by alien races.

The white Christian enslavers of the Africans developed biological, cultural, and biblical theories rationalizing their deed. Asserting the biological and cultural superiority of white over black, and invoking and misinterpreting the biblical story of the sons of Noah, white Christians insisted that the Africans—the sons of Ham—were ordained to be servants to the whites, the sons of Japhet. "Race" and "culture" then structurally opposed blacks and whites.[14]

Africans in the North American diaspora contested these beliefs. In 1778, one Othello who lived in Maryland, while denouncing the slave trade and defending African peoples, suggested that if the tables were turned, and Africans had crossed the Atlantic, seized American citizens, and sold them as slaves in Africa, "every corner of the globe would reverberate with the sound of African oppression."[15] Olaudah Equiano, an African-born slave, defending Africans, declared:

> Let the polished and haughty European recollect that his ancestors were once, like the Africans, uncivilized and even barbarous. Did nature make them inferior to their sons, and should they too have been slaves? Every rational mind answers, No. Let such reflections as these melt the pride of their superiority into sympathy for the wants and miseries of their noble

brethren and compel them to acknowledge that understanding is not
confined to features or colour.[16]

Afro-Americans, like white Americans, also used the Bible as a
weapon in the ideological struggle. They cited Miriam's change of color
when she objected to Moses's marriage to an Ethiopian as proof that
whiteness was a mark of divine displeasure.[17] Considering themselves
akin to the Hebrews in Egyptian captivity, some Afro-Americans said,
"Let my people go!" Charismatic black leaders such as Denmark Vesey
and Nat Turner sought to destroy their oppressors and to lead their
people to freedom.[18]

Ridiculed and discriminated against, diaspora peoples have engaged
their oppressors in a psychophysical battle for greater freedom. Overseas Indians, often viewed as the "morbid wens of a wretched civilization," reminded their detractors that Indians invented important mathematical and linguistic concepts and built the incomparable Taj Mahal.[19]
The overseas Chinese were often less assertive but never forgot that
their ancient civilization dazzled such Western barbarians as Marco
Polo.[20] Many Irish pilloried the British for causing the potato famine
that drove them or their ancestors away from "the old sod." Not much
given to praising the gallantry of their old Gaellic kings, the Irish
extolled the virtues of Ireland and kept faith in St. Patrick's ability to
help defeat the Orangemen of St. George.[21]

Inevitably the struggle of diaspora populations to emancipate themselves often led many of their leaders to advocate a physical or spiritual
return to their ancestral lands. Uppermost in the minds of those who
wished to return was the desire to achieve true human dignity; to help
or liberate their home communities; and by extension to aid their
compatriots still in the diaspora. Inadvertently they also helped their
host communities rid themselves of unwanted exiles. The problem,
however, was that not all exiles wanted to return and, further, the
ancestral communities weren't always prepared to accept such a return.

Moses allegedly led all the Hebrews out of Egyptian captivity to a
promised land. Taking advantage of Cyrus's victory, both Sheshbazzar
and Ezra were subsequently able to induce some members of the first
and second Babylonian captivities "to return to Jerusalem and rebuild
the Temple of the God of Heavens."[22] The Jewish leaders in the
Roman-induced diaspora had greater difficulty persuading their followers to go up to Zion, partly because Palestine remained under the heel
of conquerors and partly because many Jews already believed the
diaspora was due to God's judgment, and others did not know which
self-proclaimed messiah to trust. Numerous messianic pretenders appeared in the Roman-, Byzantine-, Islamic-, and Turkish-ruled regions

and brought personal and financial disasters to those Jews who followed them. When in 1648 Sabbatai Zevi of Smyrna proclaimed himself the Messiah, for example, his declaration was greeted with jubilation all over the diaspora. People in Hamburg sold their possessions in preparation for departure to the Holy Land, and in London Jews wagered that "within two years Sabbatai would be anointed King of Jerusalem."[23] This, however, was not to be. On 16 September 1666, Sabbatai was summoned before the Turkish sultan to explain his mission. When he arrived in the court, he immediately abandoned his pretensions, renounced his religion, and became a Muslim.

With the rise of the nation-state in Europe, the idea of founding a Jewish state began to compete with the notion that the appearance of a Messiah was necessary for the Jews to return to Zion. In a few cases, attempts were even made to reconcile the two ideas. In 1862, Rabbi Kalischer of Thorn sought to prove that "messianic redemption must be preceded by Jewish rehabilitation in Palestine." Jewish leaders created the "Alliance Israelite Universelle" to protect Jewish rights all over the world and to support attempts at a peaceful colonization of Palestine. Then under the shock of bloody pogroms in Russia and Eastern Europe and discrimination in Western Europe, the Jewish leaders sent pioneers to the Holy Land and founded the Zionist movement. Finally, during World War I, when Great Britain was at war with Turkey, Zionist leaders were able to secure a declaration from Arthur James Balfour, the British secretary of state, which read:

> His Majesty's Government views with favour the establishment in Palestine of a national home for the Jewish people, and will use their best endeavours to facilitate the achievement of this object, it being clearly understood that nothing shall be done which may prejudice the civil and religious rights of existing non-Jewish communities in Palestine or the rights and political status enjoyed by Jews in any other country.[24]

With the Balfour declaration, the Zionists had taken a significant step in helping the Jews in the diaspora and in rehabilitating the status of their homeland. From that time onward, the Jewish return increased, and in 1948, the state of Israel was created. With the promulgation of the "Law of the Return" in 1950, which granted Jews everywhere the right to citizenship in Israel, the exile was officially over, but the diaspora remained.

The dream of returning to Africa was very much in the minds of African-born persons who arrived in the New World at any time during the slave trade.[25] This situation changed somewhat with later generations born in the diaspora, but the push to return to Africa invariably increased when diaspora Africans organized to ameliorate their condition. Through good fortune or pluck, a few of the early exiles drifted back to Africa, but it was Captain Paul Cuffe who, in the late eighteenth century, set the general pattern for New World Africans who attempted an organized return. In 1770, Cuffe, a free black man, fought and lost the battle of taxation without representation with the state of Massachusetts. He continued the effort to improve his own position and that of the other blacks by building a school in 1797. Cuffe wished to raise these people out of "their degraded, destitute, miserable condition." He recognized that:

> [t]he force of prejudice was operating so powerfully against them as to give but little encouragement to hope that they could ever rise to respectability and usefulness, unless it were in a state of society where they would have greater incentives to improvement, and more favorable opportunities than would probably be ever afforded them where the bulk of the population are whites.[26]

Cuffe petitioned the president and Congress for help in executing a plan that he hoped might ultimately prove beneficial to blacks in America and to "brethren of the African race within their native climate."[27] Ironically, his plan to settle some of the disenfranchised freedmen of Massachusetts in Sierra Leone was frustrated by the War of 1812—a war fought by America to affirm the rights of its white citizens.

With the support of the British government, hundreds of Africans from Nova Scotia, from Great Britain, and from captured slave ships were settled in Sierra Leone from 1787 onward. In the 1820s, under the auspices of the American Colonization Society, some two thousand freed Afro-Americans settled in what was to become Liberia. Their motto was "the love of liberty brought us here." Some twenty years later, Dr. Martin R. Delany declared that it was "a great principle of political economy that no people can be free who themselves do not constitute an essential part of the ruling element of the country in which they live."[28] He saw no future for the black man in white America. Realizing that he and other Afro-Americans could enable Africa to advance toward civilization, he went to Nigeria and signed treaties with the Egba giving Afro-Americans the right to settle in western Nigeria.

The wholesale emancipation of Afro-Americans after the Civil War did not halt the black exodus to Africa. Indeed, the failure of the Reconstruction Era appeared to have encouraged the view that Afro-Americans could never achieve true equality in America. Bishop Henry

McNeal Turner of the African Methodist Episcopal (AME) Church declared in December 1895:

> There is no manhood future in the United States for the Negro.... I believe that two or three million of us should return to the land of our ancestors and establish our own nations, civilization, laws, customs, styles of manufacture, and not only give to the world...the benefit of our individuality, but build up social conditions peculiarly our own, and cease to be grumblers, chronic complainers, and a menace to the white man's country, or the country he claims and is bound to dominate.[29]

Emigrationism, far from dead among most Afro-Americans during the early twentieth century, took the form of messianism. On the eve of World War I, Chief Alfred Sam was able to raise $100,000, buy a steamship, and transport a number of Afro-Americans from the midwestern United States to West Africa.[30] Sam's movement failed, but a decade later, Marcus Aurelius Garvey, a Jamaican living in New York, saw in the return to Africa a solution to the Afro-Americans' plight in America as well as an opportunity for New World Africans to liberate their motherland. He was struck by the impotence of the black man and saw the problems of African peoples in global terms. Garvey declared:

Back to Africa

> As far as Negroes are concerned in America we have the problem of lynching, peonage, and dis-enfranchisement. In the West Indies, South and Central America, we have the problem of peonage, serfdom, industrial and political governmental inequality. In Africa we have not only peonage and serfdom, but outright slavery, racial exploitation and alien political monopoly. We cannot allow a continuation of these crimes against our race. As four hundred million men, women, and children worthy of the existence given us by the Divine Creator, we are determined to solve our own problems, by redeeming our "Motherland" Africa from the hands of alien exploiters, and [to] found there a government, a nation of our own, strong enough to lend protection to the members of our race scattered all over the world and to compel the respect of the nations and races of the earth.[31]

While preparing to return to Africa, Garvey waged a vigorous campaign against Afro-American shame in being black and in being of African descent. He created black nobility, Black Cross nurses, and black dolls for little girls; designed an African flag with the colors red, black, and green; and painted black almost all the symbols of Western Christendom.

The emigration strategy of Afro-Americans did not result in the creation of an African state powerful enough to challenge racism in

America. Nevertheless, emigrationism had a profound effect on the psyche of Afro-Americans. Roi Ottley believed that this movement:

> set in motion what was to become the most compelling force in Negro life—race and color consciousness which is today that ephemeral thing that inspires "race loyalty"; the banner to which Negroes rally; the chain that binds them together. It has propelled many a political and social movement and stimulated racial inter-nationalism. It is indeed a philosophy, an ethical standard by which most things are measured and interpreted.[32]

It is important to note that diasporalike populations seldom, if ever, advocated or launched large-scale "return" movements. Although the Chinese, Indians, and Irish maintained an interest in their ancestral lands, and while a few important persons returned and caused significant changes there, the bulk of these people remained where they had emigrated.[33]

The failure of the vast majority of people in the diaspora to return to their homelands when a return was possible represents a major dialectical contradiction. This fact is more socioculturally intriguing when one notes that many of the ideologues who worked hard to rehabilitate their ~~assimilated~~ ancestral lands never thought of returning there. The reason was that the later generation of exiles had adapted to their environment. True, they continued to be persecuted, and even killed, but they had become members of the societies in which they lived; they had a niche in their economies; and they often symbolically served as contrast figures, which enabled their hosts to define the insiders and the outsiders.

The Hebrews were allegedly eager to leave Egypt, but Moses had great difficulty preventing many from returning to what they considered, in retrospect, as the "fleshpots" of Egypt, rather than risk death in the wilderness. Either symbolically or literally, the generation of the exodus was not psychologically prepared to enter the promised land. Even Moses was not permitted to do so. Later in Jewish history, "ten tribes of Israel" were lost during their exile in Syria. The simplest explanation, however, is that these people found conditions propitious enough to assimilate rather than to return to their homeland.

Although many Jews who were deported to Babylon returned to Judea with Sheshbazzar and Ezra, respectively, many did not. Most of the exiles adapted to Babylonian society. They had acquired so much influence and riches that their elders sought permission from the Prophet Ezekiel to erect a temple in Babylon. He objected, prophesized that the "dry bones" in Palestine would one day take on life, and declared that when the time came, "the dispersed were to be gathered back" against their will if the need arose. Ezekiel asserted that unless they were careful, the reluctant returnees would die en route, as in the days of Moses, leaving only their children to return.[34] Nevertheless, by Roman time, millions of Jews still lived in Babylon, and these escaped expulsion from their adopted land. With the Muslim conquest of Palestine (A.D. 636–638), many Jews were free to return to the "land of their fathers," but few did so. Instead, in the wake of the Muslim conquest, new Jewish settlements sprang up in northern Africa and Egypt. Later, during the period of Turkish rule in Palestine, a few of the persecuted and expelled Maranos from Spain sought refuge there. This colony did not attract many Jews from either the western or eastern European diasporas despite persecutions and expulsions from Spain, Portugal, the Netherlands, England, Germany, and Lithuania.

It was only with the rise of modern Zionism, occasioned by violent anti-Semitism in France and numerous pogroms in Eastern Europe, that more than a handful of Jews trickled back to Palestine. Even so, the first group, known as the Bilu, who left Russia to found an agricultural colony in Palestine, "could not accustom themselves to the climate and the hardships of tilling the long-neglected soil; the majority departed, making room for less educated but more hardy colonists.[35] Most Russian Jews who fled the Pale went to the United States. These included Zionists who fervently believed that the solution to the Jewish problem lay in the liberation of Palestine, and the Bundist Socialists, who believed that although the Jews should retain their cultural identity, there was "no reason at all for clinging to the obsolete idea of Jewish nationhood."[36] Some of the children of these exiles, such as Golda Meir, would later go to Palestine, but most remained in the United States.

The conflicts between the returnees and those who remained in the galut were often quite bitter, despite the fact that they both agreed on the major objective: the liberation of the Jewish people. Persons such as Rabbi Ahad Ha-am (1856–1927) believed that the Jewish problem was best solved through "cultural revival and modernization," not a mass exodus to Palestine. Nevertheless, he worked closely with Chaim Weizmann and others to secure the Balfour declaration and later died in Palestine. On the other hand, David Ben-Gurion had no patience with the fervent Zionists in America even though he knew that he could count on them for economic, political, and even military support. He was critical of those who went to Israel "to spend a few days, or sometimes weeks, in the country looking for traditions, rites and a spirit from which most of them have become estranged."[37] Ben-Gurion told the leaders of the Zionist Organization of America in Tel Aviv on 14 July 1963 that "Zionism can be taught in America, but it can be learned only in Israel."[38] For him, the huge American community, two and a half times bigger than the community in Israel, was a shocking anomaly.

This feeling accounts for a great many of the continual misunderstandings that arise between the Israelis and the American Jews.

The vast majority of Africans abroad never seriously considered returning to Africa. Yet, they made up a sizable group of people of African origin who considered themselves *African* and who identified themselves with the entire continent rather than with specific regions, thereby becoming Pan-Africanists. Moreover, they saw their future cultural, economic, political, and social positions as being linked to that of Africa, and they sought the freedom of Africa and of African peoples wherever they existed.[39]

The critical problem for Africans in the North American diaspora was the fate of their fellows still in bondage if the freedmen and their leaders departed. Richard Allen, James Forten, and others accused the American Colonization Society of planning to ship away only the freedmen, leaving the slaves at the mercy of their masters. Some, because they were so concerned that any association with Africa would jeopardize their chances of emancipation in America, advocated dropping the word *Africa* or *African* from the titles of their organizations and suggested that these words be chiseled off the marble of their churches.[40] Alarmed by Cuffe's project and that of the American Colonization Society, members of the free Afro-American community in Philadelphia stoutly refused to leave America and issued the following declaration in January 1817:

> We are NATIVES of this country, we ask only to be treated as well as FOREIGNERS. Not a few of our fathers suffered and bled to purchase its independence; we ask only to be treated as well as those who fought against it. We have toiled to cultivate it, and to raise it to its present prosperous condition; we ask only to share equal privileges with those who come from distant lands, to enjoy the fruits of our labour. Let these moderate requests be granted, and we [will] not go to Africa nor anywhere else to be improved and happy. We cannot doubt the purity of the motives of those persons who deny us these requests, and who would send us to Africa to gain what they might deny us at home.[41]

Underscoring their attachment to America, these free Afro-Americans even denigrated the land from which their forefathers came. Their spokesmen declared that "[w]ithout arts, without science, without a proper knowledge of Government, to cast into the savage wilds of Africa the free people of color seems to use the circuitous route through which they must return to perpetual bondage."[42]

When several decades later Martin Delany started to preach emigrationism, Frederick Douglass denounced the back-to-Africa movement.

He declared:

> We have grown up with this Republic and I see nothing in her character or find nothing in the character of the American people as yet which compels the belief that we must leave the United States.[43]

Douglass believed that the less said about the relationship of the Afro-American to Africa the better off black persons would be:

white folks still identified w/ and claimed Euro countries

> No one idea has given rise to more oppression and persecution toward the colored people of this country than that which makes Africa, not America, their home. It is that wolfish idea that elbows us off the side walk and denies us the right of citizenship.[44]

Frederick Douglass was later to concede that Africa was less the cause of his undoing than the attitude of the white in America. He said:

> I have no love for America, as such; I have no patriotism. I have no country. What country have I? The institutions of this country do not know me, do not recognize me as a man. I am not thought of, spoken of, in any direction, out of the anti-slavery ranks, as a man. I am not thought of, or spoken of, except as a piece of property belonging to some *Christian* slave-holder, and all the religious and political institutions of this country, alike pronounce me a slave and a chattel.[45]

Would emigrating have = 'd ignoring of contributions?

Nevertheless, Frederick Douglass could not wholly embrace emigrationism. He did not believe that those Afro-Americans who were free should abandon those who were still captives. Nor did he believe that his contemporaries should return empty-handed to Africa or ignore the contributions that earlier generations of Afro-Americans had made in building America.

Another reason why many Africans in the diaspora did not wish to return physically to Africa was their growing prejudice toward that continent and its inhabitants. Despised in part because of their African descent, they remained ambivalent about Africa. In contrast to the Jewish situation, in which even anti-Semitic Christians sang of "Jerusalem my happy home/Name ever blessed to me," most Europeans and their descendants viewed Africa as a savage and "dark continent." Blacks felt compelled to rehabilitate Africa and African peoples in their own eyes and in the eyes of the world so that by extension both they and that continent would be saved. They would learn about Africa, help it become free, but not necessarily return there.

From the 1840s to the present, innumerable Afro-Americans wrote tracts and histories extolling their African heritage and urging its study.

Henry Highland Garnett believed that the non-Africans of his day sought to subvert the authenticity of the African:

> By an almost common consent, the modern world seems determined to pilfer Africa of her glory. It was not enough that her children have been scattered over the globe, clothed in the garments of shame—humiliated and oppressed—but her merciless foes weary themselves in plundering the tombs of our renowned sites, and in obliterating their worthy deeds, which were inscribed by fame upon the pages of ancient history.[46]

still true today

Garnett believed that Afro-Americans should spearhead the change in the world's notions about Africa. This sentiment was undoubtedly shared by the young W. E. B. Du Bois who, in 1895, declared that if because of historical reasons the blacks in America were

> in the van of Pan-Negroism, then their destiny is *not* absorption by white Americans. That if in America it is to be proven for the first time in the modern world that not only are Negroes capable of evolving individual men like Toussaint, the Saviour, but are a nation stored with wonderful possibilities of culture, then their destiny is not a servile imitation of Anglo-Saxon culture, but a stalwart originality which shall unswervingly follow Negro ideals.[47] *what were those ideals?*

These sentiments led Du Bois to elaborate on his concept of the Afro-American's double consciousness of both Africa and America. He believed that historical circumstances had presented the Afro-American with a classic dialectical dilemma:

> A longing to attain self-conscious manhood, to merge his double self into a better and truer self. In this merging he wishes neither of the older selves to be lost. He would not Africanize America, for America has too much to teach the world and Africa. He would not bleach his Negro soul in a flood of white Americanism, for he knows that Negro blood has a message for the world. He simply wishes to make it possible for a man to be both Negro and American, without having the doors of opportunity closed roughly in his face.[48]

Those Afro-American missionaries serving in Africa could not keep silent about the injustices meted out to Africans by either church or state and sought help from their fellows in the United States. Bishop Coppin, writing about his experiences in South Africa, declared:

> When we are told that a man in America is denied civil and political rights on account of being a descendant of Africa, we are content to call it unjust, ungodly, but when we are told that an African in Africa is denied civil

privileges because he is an African, we feel that besides being unrighteous and unworthy of our Christian civilization, it is ridiculous in the extreme.[49]

In 1897, the Reverend William H. Sheppard, who served in the Congo Free State, was even tried for sedition when he reported that the Zappo-Zap (Basonge) soldiers supposedly collecting taxes were in fact slave-raiding for the government and in the process were committing atrocities. The missionaries demanded an inquiry, but the Europeans held responsible were not punished. When later the Belgian state took over the Congo, Sheppard, perhaps out of complete identification with the Baluba, declared that he was "no longer of England or America, but of the Kasai." He was acquitted, and in one of his last letters from the field, he pleaded: "So we beg of you that you lift up your eyes and see the fast ripening harvest field, and hear our soul's pleading cry, 'Come over into Macedonia, and help us.'"[50]

Nineteenth-century Afro-American diplomats saw no contradiction in serving the United States and in using their prestige and influence to ameliorate the plight of the Africans. John Henry Smyth, minister resident and consul general to Liberia during the Hayes regime, thought that it was

[his] duty as an American citizen and a Negro, in vindication of the men and women of like descent with [himself] . . . to state some facts explanatory of and in rebuttal of much that has been said, ignorantly, unwisely and unsympathetically, to the detriment of the effort being made at self-government in Liberia, West Africa.[51]

Smyth rejected categorically the notion that he could not be loyal to both Africa and to America:

Race allegiance is compatible with patriotism, with love of the land that gave us birth. . . . Though we are part of this great national whole, we are a distinct and separate part, an alien part racially, and destined to be so by the immutable law of race pride, which is possessed by our white fellow citizens, if not by us. The sentiment, the something stronger than sentiment which makes an English American proud of his connection with Britain, a French American proud of his connection with La Belle France, and a German American fondly attached to the memories of the Fatherland, and all European races of the Aryan descent, has something that partakes of the moral sublime.[52]

In a dispatch sent to the State Department on 2 October 1882, Smyth encouraged the United States to intervene on Liberia's behalf against

Britain's desire to seize Liberian territory and attach it to Sierra Leone. He suggested to one Frelinghuysen:

> If not incompatible with the relation of a foreign mutual friend of England and Liberia, you make such suggestions favorable to the Negro nation's rights as may tend to a final and speedy settlement of the matter in justice and equity to both nations, should you feel called upon to interpose, and your suggested views should be heeded. . . . This, I am advised, is the desire of the [Liberian] President.[53]

Then, in a revealing postscript, Smyth added:

> The civilized Negro in Africa under foreign domination, as the civilized Negro out of Africa under like control, suffers in his liberty, because it has not the element of imperium. "Imperium et Libertas" must be the motto and the practice of the Negro, if he is to have self respect; if he is to merit the respect of others. I hope it may be found in consonance with the foreign policy of our Government to aid Liberia in a retention of her self respect unimpaired, her control of her territory, her prestige which is the consequence of her control.[54]

Despite their commitment to remain in America, twentieth-century Afro-Americans used many of the strategies of their predecessors to attempt to change their lowly status and that of Africa. Prominent among these was Du Bois, who had written in 1899: "The problem of the twentieth century is the problem of the color-line, the relation of the darker to the lighter races of men in Asia and Africa, in America and the islands of the sea."[55] Thus, in 1900 Du Bois agreed to join the black delegates in London attending the Pan-African conference called by Henry Sylvester Williams "to protect Africans from the depredation of the Empire-builders." Du Bois transformed Sylvester Williams's modest conference into a major movement for black liberation and placed the plight of Africa's children in world perspective. He urged the British to give "as soon as practicable, the right of responsible government to the black colonies of Africa and the West Indies"; he proposed that the Congo Free State become "a great central Negro state of the world"; and he appealed to the imperialist powers to respect the territorial integrity and independence of Haiti and Ethiopia. The delegates hoped that the blacks in South Africa would receive more consideration from Britain after the Boer War, and they voiced their concern over the plight of the Afro-Americans who had the "misfortune to live among a people whose laws, traditions and prejudices had been against them for centuries." The delegates resolved that black men everywhere should have justice and equality.[56]

Du Bois was convinced that the roots of World War I lay in the competition among the "civilized nations" for "the right to own and exploit" the darker peoples. He favored black participation in World War I because he saw in the war the seeds of liberation for all the darker peoples:

> This war is an End and also a Beginning. Never again will darker people of the world occupy just the place they have before. Out of this war will rise, sooner or later, an independent China; a self-governing India; an Egypt with representative institutions; an Africa for the Africans, and not merely for business exploitation. Out of this war will rise, too, an American Negro with the right to vote and the right to work and the right to live without insult. These things may not and will not come at once, but they are written in the Stars, and the first step towards them is victory for the armies of the Allies.[57]

Du Bois, as well as William Trotter, an Afro-American journalist in Boston, sought to internationalize the plight of Africa and African peoples at the end of the war. As is well known, the 1919 Pan-African Congress passed a number of resolutions, including one demanding the right for educated blacks in all countries to play an important role in affairs concerning them. The 1921 conference held in London, Brussels, and Paris created concern among the Belgian capitalist elite that the Pan-African Congress was organized by the National Association for the Advancement of Colored People (NAACP) and that its principal participants were paid by the Bolsheviks. The Belgian newspaper, *Neptune*, warned that the association:

> has already organized its propaganda in the lower Congo, and we must not be astonished if some day it causes grave difficulties in the Negro village of Kinshasa, composed of all the ne'er-do-wells of the various tribes of the colony aside from some hundreds of labourers.[58]

Many members of the Afro-American elite, especially the members of the governing board of the NAACP, were impatient with Du Bois and the Pan-African congresses that subsequently took place. They insisted that the real task was to improve the status of the blacks in America. Always the dialectician, Du Bois retorted that these men were parochial—that they did not understand the importance of "internationalism in race problems, and to many of them, it seems quixotic to undertake anything of the sort."[59] He charged that they hesitated to show an interest in Africa, for fear of resurrecting the bogey of the forced repatriation of blacks to Africa. Du Bois was convinced that Afro-Americans could never solve their problem by working only within the context of America. He believed that the source of their difficulty lay in the weakness of Africa and could not be solved apart from the liberation of Africa.

In 1936, Afro-Americans reacted strongly to Italy's attack on Ethiopia. Roi Ottley reported:

> From the beginning the Ethiopian crisis became a fundamental question in Negro life. It was all but impossible for Negro leaders to remain neutral, and the position they took toward the conflict became a fundamental test. The survival of the black nation became the topic of angry debate in poolrooms, barbershops, and taverns.[60]

White Americans wondered that blacks could become so fiercely stirred up by a foreign affair. Blacks in East Harlem fought against their Italian neighbors and saw in Joe Louis's victory over Primo Carnera a vindication for Ethiopia's cause. They attempted to recruit volunteers for the war, organized the United Aid for Ethiopia, and held a mass meeting at Madison Square Garden attended by more than twenty thousand people to raise funds for an Independent Red Cross group for Ethiopia. Writing in *Foreign Affairs* about the interracial implications of the Ethiopian crisis, Du Bois voiced the "lost faith" of blacks "in an appeal for justice from the United States in this war or in any affair that concerned black people."[61] Dr. Willis N. Huggins, in a petition to the League of Nations on Ethiopia's behalf, declared that the Fascist destruction of Ethiopia would imperil world peace, would increase the spread of subversive political theories, and would increase the guilt of hypocritical Christian nations "who yesterday raped Africa and carried millions of her children to be enslaved in the Americas."[62]

Coming as soon as it did after the Ethiopian crisis, many Afro-Americans saw World War II, including the Japanese attack on Pearl Harbor, as retribution for the rape of Ethiopia. Nevertheless, conscious of being American citizens, they enlisted in the war effort. Afro-American leaders attempted to place the role of Afro-American troops in perspective, and pointed out that the interest of African peoples should be considered after the war. Du Bois accused President Roosevelt of ignoring Africa during his "four freedoms" speech in January 1941, and suggested that the Atlantic Charter really pertained to Europe and North America. He warned of disaster unless Africa were seen as an end in itself and not as a continuing means to Europe's ends. Du Bois was scandalized by the contradictions he found at the United Nations' sessions in San Francisco in 1945: Britain wanted a world of free states and democracy while holding in thralldom millions of colonials who had neither freedom nor democracy; Jan Smuts waxed sentimental about holism and humanity, yet considered anyone who viewed the South African blacks as human as whites to be "mad, quite mad"; Secretary of State Robert F. Byrnes arraigned Russia for lacking democracy, yet in his native South Carolina the black majority did not have the right to vote.[63]

Du Bois was, therefore, psychologically prepared to heed a call to organize a Pan-African congress in Manchester in September–October 1945, during which continental Africans assumed the leadership of the Pan-African movement. Du Bois, although then seventy-three years old,

> was by no means a silent spectator at the Fifth Pan-African Congress. He entered into all the discussions and brought to the deliberations a freshness of outlook that greatly influenced the final decisions, the implementation of which is already shaping the future of the African continent.[64]

Moreover, when he returned to America, he again tried to persuade the black elite of the NAACP to work with the Africans in the interest of all black peoples. Recognizing the dialectics of the situation, he declared:

> We American Negroes should know that . . . until Africa is free, the descendants of Africa the world over cannot escape their chains. . . . The NAACP should therefore put in the forefront of its program the freedom of Africa in work and wage, education and health, and the complete abolition of the colonial system.[65]

Despite incredible hardships, many diasporalike populations did not launch movements to return to their ancestral lands, perhaps because they left their countries voluntarily and in search of a better life. The large-scale massacres of overseas Chinese in the Philippines in 1603, 1639, and 1778 did not lead these people to depart. Those who were expelled returned as soon as the climate changed.[66] Likewise, during the 1960s when the Indonesians butchered thousands of Chinese, there was no major exodus. Today, many of the boat people from Vietnam are ethnic Chinese who are reluctant to go to China. Similarly, the Indians who were mistreated in South Africa and in the Caribbean protested but did not develop return movements. Recently, when Indians were expelled from East Africa, they preferred to go to Britain rather than return to their ancestral land. The Irish in America initially encountered a great deal of discrimination but never attempted to return en masse to their homeland. They preferred to remain in the New World.

The common aspect of the Chinese, Indian, and Irish populations with the African diaspora is their effort to ameliorate the condition of their ancestral lands. For example:

> The first activity of the Chinese Revolutionary movement was connected
> with overseas Chinese. Dr. Sun Yat-Sen, who soon became its leader, was
> himself a migrant to Honolulu who acquired his education in Hong Kong.
> From its inception, the revolutionary began to enlist support among the
> overseas Chinese.... They responded with enthusiasm.[67]

Eugene Chen, who once served as foreign minister for Chiang Kai-shek,
was

> reputedly the best brain in the Koumintang.... Small, clever, venomous,
> West-Indian born of part-Negro parentage and Western-educated, in gold-
> rimmed spectacles and white spats, Chen, who could not write Chinese and
> scarcely speak it, was famous for his grandiloquent English and consuming
> hatred of the foreigner.[68]

Later, both the Chinese Nationalists and the Communists sought, and
received, support from the overseas Chinese in their battle to represent
all of China in the international arena.[69]

Indians overseas played an important role in the political process
that freed their homeland from imperial rule. Duffett, Hicks, and Parkin
declared:

> It is significant to recall that it was in relation to the problems of Indians in
> South Africa that Gandhi (who in the early years of this century was a
> successful practising lawyer in Johannesburg) first espoused the cause of
> Indian nationalism. It was in South Africa also that Gandhi, in his efforts to
> bring pressure to bear for the amelioration of the status and condition of the
> Indian immigrants, first developed with considerable success, the technique
> and practice of "satyagraha"—civil disobedience—which has subsequently
> played so important a part in recent Indian political history.[70]

As soon as they secured the right to vote, the Irish in America used
their ballots to affect British rule in Ireland. Then, when they took
political control in America's urban centers, the Irish made life miserable for visiting British dignitaries. The American Irish hailed the
rebellion that broke out in Dublin on Easter Sunday 1916 and vigorously
protested the execution of its defeated leaders. The American Irish were
so angry with Woodrow Wilson's attitude toward their ancestral land
that they voted against him in 1916 as well as in 1920. When in January
1919 the newly elected Irish nationalists proclaimed a republic,

> Eamon De Valera, a survivor of the Easter Rebellion, was elected president
> and promptly sent to the United States to plead for private and official

support. British policy was marked by confusion and reflected a fear of alienating the United States where the Irish cause had received strong Congressional support. As a result, the revolutionary government was free gradually to establish control over most of Ireland.[71]

Today, many Irish-Americans are exercised by the conflict between Northern Ireland and the Republic of Ireland and are attempting to use their influence to resolve it.

An important aspect of the dialectic between peoples in diasporas and their homelands was the difficulty arising whenever a sizable group of the exiles returned home. Although the Hebrews who went to Canaan were not returnees, they conquered and disrupted life in the land their God had promised them. Similarly, no sooner had the Babylonian exiles returned to Palestine than they came into conflict with both the Jewish remnants there and the Samarians. The problem was that the returnees wished to maintain the physical and social integrity of their community. They built a wall around the settlement and repudiated marriages made with outsiders.[72] Last, although the Zionist-inspired return was peaceful initially, conflict broke out with the local Arabs. The subsequent Arab-Israeli wars resulted in the exodus of millions of Palestinians and is the basis for the current conflict between the state of Israel and the Palestine Liberation Organization (PLO).

The changes in the ideologies that facilitated the return to Israel and the exacerbations of the cleavages that had developed when the Jews were still in the diaspora have been serious problems for the returnees. The Israelis still have not resolved the problem of the nature of their state. Some Israelis continue to reject the idea of a secular state and await the Messiah; the result is conflict within the state between religious and secular Jews. Israel is also plagued with tension between the Middle Eastern Jews and the Ashkenazim over the problem of "racial" and "cultural" discrimination. The darker skinned and often Arabic-speaking Israelis charge that despite their demographic majority, they hold an inferior position in Israeli society.[73]

Continental Africans have not always been happy with returnees from the diaspora. Those sizable groups who returned from the New World during the slave period often established political hegemony over the local people. This occurred principally in the Gambia, Sierra Leone, and Liberia. In fact, some of the returned slaves engaged in slavery much to the chagrin of continental Africans and of those in the diaspora.[74] With their European ways, repatriated Africans in these countries, as well as in Togoland, Dahomey, and Nigeria, felt themselves socially and culturally superior to the local Africans. Instead of reassimilating themselves to Africa, the returnees kept apart and considered themselves "Creoles," "Americo-Liberians," "Afro-Brazilians," and the like. This attitude and behavior led African continentals such as J. E. Casely Hayford of the Gold Coast to say about those blacks in America who wished to return to Africa: "[I]t is not so much Afro-Americans we want as Africans."[75] Hayford believed that diaspora Africans should forego their alien ways and readapt to their homeland.

Although many individual repatriates, especially women, did accept life as it was and simply disappeared into the general continental populations, others had difficulty yielding leadership to the continentals. There was conflict between African Methodist Episcopal Church ministers from America and the aspiring leaders of that church in South Africa.[76] Blacks from the French Antilles initially did an excellent job representing the Africans of French Africa in the national Assembly, but they eventually came into conflict with continentals who wished to run their own affairs.[77]

Because few persons from the overseas Chinese, Indian, or Irish populations actually returned to their homelands, there was less conflict in these cases. One suspects, however, that while appreciating the role that foreign-born or foreign-trained brethren played in their liberation struggles, the people at home also resented them.[78]

Populations in diasporas have always been affected by the changes they were able to effect in their ancestral lands. The dilemma is that the exiles often did not know how to deal with these changes. The initial tragedy for the Jews was that for centuries there was no Jewish political entity in Jerusalem to protest when Jews were persecuted in the diaspora. Thus, whenever a pseudomessiah such as Sabbatai Zevi arose and aspired to become "King of the Jews," the exiles rejoiced and were willing to give him their allegiance. The result was that leaders such as Napoleon I, who wished to emancipate the Jews in French territories, were never sure of their loyalty. Would the Jews always be strangers, here today and gone tomorrow, with no loyalty to their hosts but only to their fellows and ancestral land?[79]

To compensate for their lack of a nation-state and to protect their interest, diaspora Jews created civil rights organizations. These ranged from the Alliance Israelite Universelle in Paris to the American Jewish Committee in the United States and their analogues in other countries. Because these organizations did not have an international political personality, they could not deal with anti-Semitism and its results: the pogroms and the Holocaust. The best they could do was appeal to the heads of the countries to save Jews in other countries or provide funds for their aid. When these efforts failed, "international Jewry" was helpless.[80]

The creation of the state of Israel did much for the self-image of Jews in the diasporas and helped to protect and enhance their civil and political rights. For the first time in centuries, Jews had an internationally recognized political structure to defend them even if they lived outside the Jewish state. One result is that the Jews are losing their fear of anti-Semitism by a political state, making assimilation a real possibility. On the other hand, Jews in the diaspora, although insistent on the prerogatives of the state of Israel, ignore the rights of other nation-states to control their citizens when these persons happen to be Jews.

Today, both in the United States and in Israel, Jews are working through their governments to pressure the Soviet Union to ameliorate the condition of Jewish citizens. It so happens that the interests of the Jews in both Israel and the United States coincide. What would happen if these interests did not coincide? Already there is a problem with the Russian Jews. For a variety of reasons, many Soviet Jews refuse to go to Israel when they leave Russia. Obviously, they are attracted to other countries for reasons that have very little to do with their being Jewish, the ostensible reason for the American Jews' interest in them. Israel wants these persons to increase its population and is putting pressure on Jews in the United States to induce America not to grant emigrant status to the repatriates. The interests of the United States in the broad spectrum of human rights, rather than specifically in Jewish rights, may put the American Jews in a bad light if they attempt to side with the state of Israel.

Jews in the diaspora are facing what Georges Friedmann has called the "end of the Jewish people."[81] In other words, it is becoming more difficult for persons to be *Jews* and remain in the diaspora, since Israel exists and claims all Jews as potential citizens. Like Soviet Jews, American and other Jews may have to choose either Israeli citizenship or the citizenship of the state in which they were born or live.

There is now widespread consensus that Du Bois was basically correct when he suggested to the NAACP that an improvement in the future status of the Afro-American would be conditioned by developments in Africa. It is interesting that, although never an emigrationist, Du Bois grew tired of being harassed by a hostile American regime and accepted sanctuary and citizenship in Ghana, where he died and was buried.[82] Meanwhile, the political evolution of Africa greatly influenced the condition of the African people in America. John Hope Franklin suggested that international factors, rather than either presidential urging or pressure from civil rights advocates, induced the U.S. Congress to pass the voting rights acts:

[T]he emergence into independence of the Sub-Saharan nations enormously changed world-wide significance of the American race problem and provided a considerable stimulus to the movement for racial equality in the United States. As Congress began to debate the proposed civil rights bill in the summer of 1957, the diplomatic representatives from Ghana had taken up residence at the United Nations and in Washington. This important fact could not be ignored by responsible members of Congress. It seemed that black men from the Old World had arrived just in time to help redress the racial balance in the New.[83]

The independence of Ghana did revolutionize the thinking of the Afro-Americans about themselves and about their place in America. Ordinary Afro-Americans, seeing toga-clad Ghanaians speaking before the United Nations and being received at the White House, started to reevaluate their relationships to Africa and took great pride in its new status. Then, as more and more African states gained independence, Afro-Americans simultaneously increased their interest in Africa and fought harder for full equality in America.

A number of Afro-Americans recognized the potential contradictions in the new situation. At meetings and conferences, black scholars and men of affairs took a hard look at the realities facing both Africans and Afro-Americans. In a background paper for one such conference, St. Clair Drake pointed to the dialectical factors when he cautioned that both the Africans and the Afro-Americans were still relatively power-less. But whereas the Africans were striving to overcome their weakness by working within the context of new nation-states, and could form alliances with Asians and the Soviet bloc, the Afro-Americans were trying to overcome their powerlessness by acquiring political and eco-nomic power within a "white" nation-state and by participating in the vital decision-making processes of its economic, political, and educa-tional institutions. Nevertheless, Drake believed that the two groups could still cooperate for their mutual benefit. The Africans had to recognize the still peculiar racial situation of the Afro-Americans, and Afro-Americans had to realize that the Pan-African sentiments that were useful in the past were now of necessity taking second place to the welfare of the African states.[84]

The Afro-Americans were often pleased by the African display of racial solidarity. They applauded Jaja Wachuku of Nigeria who, before the fifteenth General Assembly on 13 December 1960, declared:

Anybody who is not prepared to eradicate that humiliation that had been meted out to people of African descent or people of our racial stock cannot claim to be in love with us.[85]

Afro-Americans also cheered when American whites were rebuffed by Africans because of racism in America. In May 1963, Gordon Cooper, unaware that Africans were not as concerned about his dramatic space flight as they were about the Birmingham riots, beamed a message of goodwill to the African heads of state meeting at Addis Ababa as he soared over Africa. Not only was the greeting ignored, but the final communique of the conference included an open letter to the late President John F. Kennedy, which read in part:

> The Negroes who, even while the Conference was in session, have been subjected to the most inhuman treatment, who have been blasted with fire hoses cranked up to such pressure that the water would strip bark off trees, at whom the police have deliberately set snarling dogs, are our own kith and kin. . . . The only offenses which these people have committed are that they are black and that they have demanded the right to be free and to hold their heads up as equal citizens of the United States.[86]

White Americans tried to frustrate any solidarity between Africans in the diaspora and those on the continent for a radical improvement of status of Afro-Americans. A number of self-proclaimed white specialists on Africans and Afro-Americans tried to reassure their fellows that there was no real relationship between Afro-Americans and Africa. One published an article in which he wondered whether, in view of the cultural conflicts that often arose between Afro-Americans and Africans, the two groups could be said to have anything in common. He conveniently forgot that other American ethnic groups often had similar problems with people in the lands of their origin. Another writer cautioned Americans in general against taking too seriously a linkage or alliance between Africans and Afro-Americans. He asserted that the relations between Africans and Americans had always been poor and that an attempt to see a relationship between the two groups could be dangerous for "all concerned—the usually discontented or disenchanted Negro, the natives [sic] and the United States."[87]

Ironically, the very success of the Afro-Americans' relations with Africa led to tensions between them and a new generation of Africans. Many of the Africans who came to the United States in the 1960s expected to encounter violence and hostility in the streets of most American cities. They were also prepared to assert their new national identity to combat the expected prejudice. Instead, they found many American whites eager to meet them. African students and diplomats were received in homes, associations, and neighborhoods that had been closed to Afro-Americans. Sometimes the Africans were encouraged to wear their traditional clothes and to speak their native languages, and they allegedly saw no reason to believe that these requests were not made with the best intentions. Some Africans dated white American women and viewed the stares they received as simple curiosity. Many apparently did not see the stares. Periodically, Africans did find their presence unwelcomed by white Americans who saw only a black man under the exotic robe, and many a policeman found out too late that the black man he had beaten up and taken to the police station for being "cheeky" was carrying a diplomatic passport. Embarrassed "city fathers" often tried to make amends, but Africans recognized the real source of their discomfort: the continuing contempt of white Americans for Afro-Americans.

Out of a sense of frustration, a number of Africans grew to resent Afro-Americans—the innocent cause of their dilemma. A few white researchers reported that a nationwide survey showed that "almost two-thirds of all African (student) visitors indicated either friction or coolness between themselves and American Negroes" and that "African students in the United States find it harder to make friends among American Negroes than among whites."[88] The tragedy is that these white researchers, like most American whites who deal with Africans, tend to ignore (or prefer not to understand) how white behavior affected relations between Africans and Afro-Americans. Interestingly, the report cited above added parenthetically that the Africans said they were treated much better by American whites "after they had identified themselves as Africans rather than American Negroes."[89]

But if the Afro-Americans were puzzled by the relations between the new Africans and white Americans, the Africans at home became suspicious of the new Afro-Americans who started to visit Africa. This suspicion was born of fear that the Afro-Americans might take advantage of their "natural ties" with Africa to work in the interest of white America and to the detriment of Africa. The *Ghanaian Times*, a newspaper noted for its pungent copy, editorialized:

> We in Ghana with open hands and warm hearts welcome into our homes and institutions people of African descent who have come to our country, and theirs certainly, to work, learn and live among us. Our hospitality is their's for the plucking.
> ... But there appears to be emerging from the Negro (American) community in Ghana, and possibly in other parts of Africa, dangerous Afro-American elements who appear to have mortgaged their consciences for neocolonialist dollars and favors in the service of collective imperialism.... Because of their brown, ebony or black skins, these notorious Negro agents of imperialism are easily accepted into our homes and social circles as our own brothers and sisters...."
> *Beware, Brother, for there is an enemy at your doorstep, the Negro student, spiv or technical aid worker who is as equally dangerous as the peaceful-looking white Peace Corps meddler, or white C.I.A. agent or embassy stooge.*[90]

The Ghanaian editor was unduly harsh, but he did clearly spell out a widespread concern among Africans that the Afro-American might attempt to betray the African for the sake of first-class citizenship in America.

On the other hand, the Afro-American remained concerned that the continentals, by refusing to acknowledge the persistence of racism in America, might betray him once again. They became alarmed by Africans who see Afro-Americans as firmly embedded in the capitalist system and, hence, as dangerous to Africa as are the whites. This issue arose at the Pan-African Conference in Dar es Salaam when continentals with a vision of a heavenly but socialist Jerusalem argued that the major issue facing African peoples the world over was *class* and not *race*. They scorned what they considered to be the Afro-Americans' atavistic and reactionary concern with "pigmentation."[91]

Many Afro-Americans concede that the decline of Europe or lessening of white power might be the antithesis to the thesis of racism and cultural chauvinism that attended Europe's control of the globe. Certainly, the retreat of the Captains and the Kings and the political independence of Africa and most of the colonial world have changed relations among the black, brown, white, and yellow peoples in Africa, America, Asia, Europe, and the islands of the seas. Afro-Americans hope that in time they will be able to relate to both Africa and America as authentic human beings and not as the victims of that cruel double consciousness. Their only caveat here is based on the warning of a great socialist who declared that:

[n]o social order ever perished before all the productive forces for which there is room in it have developed; and new, higher relations of production never appear before the material conditions of their existence have matured in the womb of the old society.[92]

In another context, he suggested that the "superstructure" such as race relations, "exercises an influence on production relations and can either delay or accelerate their replacement."[93]

There is an emerging consensus that those diasporalike populations whose homelands have achieved international sovereignty or equality in the world arena will now be assimilated by their hosts or expelled to societies where this process will take place. The reason is that the ancestral homelands of these populations can now insist that they be treated fairly or that their hosts face international sanctions including military force. As far as the overseas Chinese in Southeast Asia are concerned, Williams concludes:

Although ethnic and class animosities exist, the former racial bases of these evils do not seem to be present any longer. Rigid racial exclusiveness, elaborately and legally institutionalized, was brought to Asia by Westerners; now that the bearers of the white man's burden are subdued, it is highly possible that a more relaxed atmosphere will favor assimilation.[94]

The occupational limitations that Chinese in such countries as the United States faced are ending, and the younger generations are beginning to exhibit those complex status characteristics of many other ethnic groups.

The Indians overseas are now interested in finding economic and sociopolitical equality in their host societies. The government of India, while concerned about their fate, has advised the emigres to adapt to life in the diaspora, including the possibility of assimilation, or return home and face perhaps more difficult circumstances.

The Irish outside their homeland, for example, have arrived. People scarcely talk about the sharp social differences between the "shanty Irish" and their "lace-curtain" countrymen. Some of these differences still persist, but both groups are relating more and more to other Americans in the same socioeconomic position and to each other. The ability of the Harvard-trained Kennedys to achieve high political offices in the United States, including the presidency, indicates that the Irish have been assimilated by their hosts.

NOTES

1. Ben Halpern, "Exile: Abstract Condition and Concrete Community" in "Negating the Diaspora: A Symposium," *Jewish Frontier* 47, 10 (December 1979):9.
2. William E. B. Du Bois, *The Souls of Black Folk* (Greenwich, Conn.: Fawcett, 1961), 23.
3. See E. Franklin Frazier's treatment of Everett V. Stonequist, *The Marginal Man* (New York: Scribner's Sons, 1937), in *Race and Culture Contacts in the Modern World* (New York: Alfred A. Knopf, 1957), 311.
4. William H. Shack and Elliott P. Skinner, *Strangers in African Societies* (Berkeley: University of California Press, 1979).
5. Max Margolis and Alexander Marx, *The History of the Jewish People* (New York: Meridian Books, 1958), 114–18.
6. Herbert Aptheker, *Negro Slave Revolts in the United States* (New York: International Publishers, 1939), 86–97.
7. Frazier, *Race and Culture Contacts in the Modern World*, 3–11.
8. Ibid. 74–92.
9. Eric Williams, *Capitalism and Slavery* (Chapel Hill: University of North Carolina Press, 1944), 55 ff.
10. W. E. Duffett, A. R. Hicks, and G. R. Parkin, *India Today: The Background to Indian Nationalism* (New York: John Jay Co., 1942), 50–51; C. P. Fitzgerald, *The Third China: The Chinese Communities in South-East Asia* (London: Angus and Robertson, 1965), 14 ff; Stanford M. Lyman, *Chinese Americans* (New York: Random House, 1974), 59–61; Carl Wittke, *The Irish in America* (Baton Rouge: Louisiana State University Press, 1956).

11. Arthur Hertzberg, ed., *The Zionist Idea* (New York: Meridian Books, 1959), 15–100.
12. George Washington Williams, *History of the Negro Race in America from 1619 to 1800* (New York: Putnam and Sons, 1883).
13. Walter Rodney, *A History of the Upper Guinea Coast 1545–1800* (Oxford: Clarendon Press, 1970), 50 ff; Basil Davidson, *Black Mother: The Years of the African Slave Trade* (Boston: Little, Brown, and Co., 1961), 147 ff.
14. Winthrop Jordan, *White over Black* (Chapel Hill: University of North Carolina Press, 1968), 134 ff.
15. Carter G. Woodson, ed., *Negro Orators and Their Orations* (Washington, D.C.: Associated Publishers, 1925), 23 ff.
16. Olaudah Equiano, "The Interesting Narrative of Olaudah Equiano, or Gustavus, the African," in *Africa Remembered*, ed. Philip Curtin (Madison: University of Wisconsin Press, 1960), 83 ff.
17. Num. 12.
18. Marion De B. Kilson, "An Analysis of Slave Revolts in the United States," in *The Making of Black America*, ed. August Meier and Elliott Rudwick (New York: Atheneum, 1969) 1:165–78; Vincent Harding, "Religion and Resistance among Antebellum Negroes, 1800–1860," in *The Making of Black America*, ed. Meier and Rudwick, 1:179–200.
19. Elliott P. Skinner, "Social Stratification and Ethnic Identification," in *Peoples of the Caribbean*, ed. Michael M. Horowitz (New York: Natural History Press, 1971), 120.
20. Fitzgerald, *The Third China*, 14 ff.
21. Wittke, *The Irish in America*, 117–22.
22. Margolis and Marx, *The History of the Jewish People*, 117.
23. Ibid., 563.
24. Ibid., 730–31.
25. Elliott P. Skinner, ed., *Drums and Shadows: Survival Studies among the Georgia Coastal Negroes* (New York: Doubleday and Co., Anchor Books, 1972), ix–xiv, 6–15 ff.
26. Leslie H. Fisher, Jr., and Benjamin Quarles, *The Negro American: A Documentary History* (Glenview, Ill.: Scott, Foresman Co., 1967), 76–77; see also Joseph E. Harris, *Africans and Their History* (New York: Mentor Books, 1972), 87–93.
27. Fisher and Quarles, 76–77.
28. Victor Ullman, *Martin R. Delany: The Beginnings of Black Nationalism* (Boston: Beacon Press, 1971), 152, 273–74.
29. Henry McNeal Turner in *Addresses and Proceedings of the Congress on Africa, Dec. 13–15. 1895*, ed. J. W. E. Bosen (Atlanta: Gammon Theological Seminary, 1896).
30. William E. Bittle and Gilbert Geis, *The Longest Way Home: Chief Alfred C. Sam's Back-to-Africa Movement* (Detroit: Wayne State University Press, 1964).
31. Amy Jacques Garvey, *Philosophy and Opinions of Marcus Garvey or Africa for the Africans* (London: Frank Cass and Co., 1967), 38–39.
32. Roi Ottley, *New World A-Coming* (Boston: Houghton Mifflin Co., 1943), 68–74.
33. Duffett, Hicks, and Parkin, *India Today*; Fitzgerald, *The Third China*; Lyman, *Chinese Americans*; Shack and Skinner, *Strangers in African Societies*, 243–60.
34. Margolis and Marx, *The History of the Jewish People*, 116.
35. Ibid., 697.
36. Golda Meir, *My Life* (New York: Dell, 1975), 22.
37. Hertzberg, *The Zionist Idea*, 250.
38. Georges Friedmann, *The End of the Jewish People* (New York: Doubleday and Co., 1967), 228.
39. Rayford W. Logan, "The Historical Aspects of Pan-Africanism," *African Forum*, 1 (Summer 1965):90; Elliott P. Skinner, "Afro-Americans and Africa: The Continuing Dialectic" (New York: The Urban Center, Columbia University, 1973).

40. Howard H. Bell, *A Survey of the Negro Convention Movement, 1830–1861* (New York: Arno Press and the New York *Times*, 1969).
41. Woodson, *Negro Orators and Their Orations*, 80–81.
42. Ibid.
43. Ullman, *Martin R. Delany*, 152.
44. Philip S. Foner, *The Life and Writings of Frederick Douglass* (New York: International Publishers, 1950) 2:441–47.
45. Ibid., 1:236.
46. Henry Highland Garnett, *The Past and Present Condition and Destiny of the Colored Race* (Troy, N.Y.: J. C. Kneeland and Co., 1848), 6–12.
47. William E. B. Du Bois, *The Conservation of Races* (Washington, D.C.: American Negro Academy, Occasional Papers, no. 2, 1897).
48. Du Bois, *The Souls of Black Folks*, 17.
49. Bishop I. J. Coppin, "Letters from South Africa" in Hill and Kilson, 247.
50. William H. Sheppard, "Yesterday, Today and Tomorrow in Africa," *Southern Workmen* 39, 8 (August 1910):447.
51. John H. Smyth, "Dispatches from United Ministers to Liberia, 1863–1906" (John H. Smyth to Frelinghuysen, Oct. 2, 1882), in Hill and Kilson, 94–97.
52. Hill and Kilson, 94–97. Adelaide Hill and Martin Kilson, *Apropos of Africa* (Frank Cass: London, 1969), 49–51, 94–97.
53. Ibid.
54. Ibid.
55. Du Bois, *The Souls of Black Folks*, 23.
56. Logan, "The Historical Aspects of Pan-Africanism," 90.
57. William E. B. Du Bois, "The Black Soldier," *Crisis* 16, 2 (1918):60.
58. George Padmore, *Pan-Africanism or Communism* (New York: Doubleday, 1971), 110–12.
59. William E. B. Du Bois, *Dusk of Dawn* (New York: Harcourt, Brace, 1940), 275.
60. Ottley, *New World A-Coming*, 63.
61. William E. B. Du Bois, "The Inter-Racial Implications of the Ethiopian Crisis," *Foreign Affairs* 14, 1 (October 1935):88, 92.
62. Ottley, *New World A-Coming*, 109.
63. Du Bois, *The Souls of Black Folk*, 255.
64. Padmore, *Pan-Africanism or Communism*, 140.
65. Elliott P. Skinner, "African, Afro-American, White American: A Case of Pride and Prejudice," *Freedomways* 15 (Summer 1965):384.
66. Fitzgerald, *The Third China*, 14 ff.
67. Ibid., 20–21.
68. Barbara W. Tuchman, *Stilwell and the American Experience in China, 1911–1945* (New York: Macmillan Co., 1970), 95.
69. Lea E. Williams, *The Future of the Overseas Chinese in Southeast Asia* (New York: McGraw-Hill Book Co., 1966), 51 ff.
70. Duffett, Hicks, and Parkin, *India Today*, 50–51.
71. H. G. Henderson, R. N. Lebow, and J. G. Stoessinger, eds., *Divided Nations in a Divided World* (New York: David McKay Co., 1974), 204.
72. Margolis and Marx, *The History of the Jewish People*, 126–33.
73. Friedmann, *The End of the Jewish People*, 158–71.
74. Christopher Fyfe, *A History of Sierra Leone* (London: Oxford University Press, 1962); Robert G. Weisbord, *Ebony Kinship: Africa, Africans and the Afro-American* (Westport, Conn.: Greenwood Press, 1973).
75. J. E. Casely Hayford, *Gold Coast Native Institutions* (London: Sweet and Maxwell, 1903), 130 ff.

76. George Shepperson, "Negro American Influences on the Emergence of African Nationalism," *Journal of African History* 1, 2 (1960):299–312.
77. Thomas Hodgkin and Ruth Schacter, *French-speaking Africa in Transition* (New York: 1960); Ruth Schacter-Morgenthau, *Political Parties in French-Speaking West Africa* (Oxford: Oxford University Press, 1964).
78. Duffet, Hicks, and Parkin, *India Today*; Lyman, *Chinese Americans*; and Wittke, *The Irish in America.*
79. Margolis and Marx, *The History of the Jewish People*, 612–17; Hayim Greenberg, "Pluralism and Plural Loyalties," *Jewish Frontier* 47, 10 (December 1979):44–48.
80. Friedmann, *The End of the Jewish People*, 221 ff.
81. Ibid.,
82. Skinner, "Afro-Americans and Africa," 25.
83. John Hope Franklin, *From Slavery to Freedom* (New York: Random House, Vintage Books, 1969), 622.
84. St. Clair Drake, "Negro Americans, the African Interest, and Power-Structures in Africa and America" [Paper prepared for the Arden House Conference of ANLC (American Negro Leadership Conference), Harriman, New York, November 23–25, 1962].
85. Skinner, "African, Afro-American, White American," 388–89.
86. Loc. cit., 386.
87. Russell Howe, "Strangers in Africa," *Reporter* (June 22, 1961):34.
88. Skinner, "African, Afro-American, White American," 383.
89. Ibid., 393.
90. Skinner, "Afro-Americans and Africa," 24.
91. Walter Rodney, *Towards the Sixth Pan-African Congress: Aspects of the International Class Struggle in Africa* (Atlanta: Institute of the Black World, Occasional Paper, 1975).
92. Karl Marx, "Preface to a Contribution to the Critique of Political Economy," in *Karl Marx and Frederick Engels: Selected Works* (Moscow: Foreign Languages Publishing House, 1962) 1:362–64.
93. *Fundamentals of Marxism-Leninism* (Moscow: Foreign Languages Publishing House, 1963), 116–25.
94. Williams, *Capitalism and Slavery*, 123–24.

2
African Diaspora: Concept and Context

George Shepperson

AT some time between the mid-1950s and the mid-1960s, the period in which many African states were breaking away from European empires and achieving independence, the expression *African diaspora* began to be used increasingly by writers and thinkers who were concerned with the status and prospects of persons of African descent around the world as well as at home. Who first used this expression, I do not know; and I wish very much that someone would attempt the difficult task of tracing the employment of the Greek word for dispersal —which, until it began to have the adjective *African* or *black* attached to it, was used largely for the scattering abroad of the Jews.[1] This expression had its origins in the period spanned by the First International Congress of Negro Writers and Artists, which was organized by *Présence Africaine* in Paris in 1956 (from which came the important publication two years later, *Africa from the Point of View of American Negro Scholars*) and the International Congress of African Historians held in Dar es Salaam in October 1965. The expression appears prominently at least twice in the proceedings of the 1965 Congress *Emerging Themes of African History:* once in an address by Joseph E. Harris, "Introduction to the African Diaspora," and again in my own address, "The African Abroad or the African Diaspora."[2]

The concept that the expression *African diaspora* serves is, however, of much older origin. It can be argued that something approaching an African diaspora concept appears in the Bible. In the Hebrew Scriptures, Ps. 68:31 asserts for example "Ethiopia shall soon stretch out her hands unto God," and in the Greek Scriptures, Acts 8:26–39 tells the story of

41

the conversion of "a man of Ethiopia, an eunuch of great authority under Candace queen of the Ethiopians." In addition, the distinguished nineteenth-century British historian William Mavor used biblical material in his essay, "The History of the Dispersion of the Jews; of Modern Egypt; and of Other African Nations," which appeared in his *Universal History* in 1802. The Afro-American writer, Robert B. Lewis, also used biblical material in his 1844 volume, *Light and Truth: Collected from the Bible and Ancient and Modern History, Containing the Universal History of the Colored and Indian Race, from the Creation of the World to the Present Time.*

Yet, these examples must surely not be taken as proof that an African diaspora concept is implicit in such historical material. Nevertheless, writers of this kind performed a useful service for the emergence of the African diaspora concept. Whether they knew it or not, they disputed the view that Africa had no place worth considering in world history—and the destruction of this view is an essential element in the study of the African diaspora. The most influential exponent of this view in the nineteenth century was the German philosopher G. W. F. Hegel, who said in his famous lectures in history at Berlin in 1830 and 1831 that Africa was "no historical part of the World"; it had "no movement or development to exhibit"; it was "only on the threshold of the World's History."[3] Hegel's view differed from that of another German historian, A. H. L. Heeren of the Göttingen school. Heeren's work, *Historical Researches into the Politics, Intercourse, and Trade of the Carthaginians, Ethiopians, and Egyptians* (published in English translation in 1854), was used by Afro-American writers of the time to argue against the Hegelian point of view, which held the field for a very long time—and is by no means dead yet.

By the end of the American Civil War and the emancipation of 4.5 million slaves in the United States, one did not have to read the Bible or ancient history to see that Africans played a part in the history of the world. Speaking of what he called "this black stream of humanity" that had poured into America from Africa, Winwood Reade, British traveler in West Africa and author in 1872 of an influential sketch of universal history, *The Martyrdom of Man*, declared that it "has fertilized half a continent with its labour, set a world on fire with its wrongs; it has influenced the progress of commerce, culture and morality in Europe, and transformed a Federation into a nationality."[4] But Reade's opinion about the part played by Africans in the history of the world was not shared by most of his contemporaries. To them, Africa was the *dark continent*, an expression that had been popularized by the publication of Henry Morton Stanley's *Through the Dark Continent* in 1878. Stanley had spent three years in east and central Africa laying the foundations for British domination of the Upper Nile area and for Belgian suzerainty over the Congo. The stage was, in fact, being set for the "scramble" for Africa, a period in which the European powers, with little regard for the views of the Africans, divided up the dark continent in a couple of decades. The debacle of Reconstruction in America followed by the triumph of the "scramble" in Africa was accompanied by a reassertion of white racism.

Against this background, it is not difficult to understand why writers of African descent responded with all the force they could muster. It is to this period that the origin of the African diaspora, with its emphasis on the positive contribution of black men and women to world history, may be traced. William Wells Brown's remarkable book, *The Rising Son; or the Antecedents and Advancement of the Colored Race,* published in Boston in 1876, was typical of several works by Afro-Americans who attempted to sketch the African contribution to world history in defense of their race. William Wells Brown traveled widely, but yet another representative of the African diaspora—Edward Blyden—wandered much farther afield. Born in the Danish West Indies in 1832, Blyden, through his life and writings, did the most to promote the concept of the African diaspora, although, strangely enough, considering his knowledge of biblical and ancient history, he never appears to have used this expression. Blyden lived through the abolition of slavery in the Western Hemisphere, the trauma of Reconstruction in the United States, and the coming of imperialism to Africa, and he died in Sierra Leone in 1912.

The concept of the African diaspora, buttressed by Blyden's formidable learning, his insight into the relations between Christianity and Islam, his experience of several African cultures at home and abroad, and his powerful personality, runs throughout his prolific writings. The concept is displayed most succinctly and forcefully in an address entitled "Ethiopia Stretching out Her Hands unto God: or, Africa's Service to the World," which he delivered in truly peripatetic fashion in May 1880, in Washington, D.C.; Madison, Wisconsin; Chicago; Philadelphia; and New York. If anyone wants a manifesto of the African diaspora, its strength in attacking white prejudice, its weakness in its occasional overemphasis on racial purity, and its stimulus to further research (even today), then surely this eloquent address by Edward Blyden will supply it.

Blyden began his address with a defiant, anti-Hegelian assertion:

Africa is no vast island, separated by an immense ocean from other parts of the globe, and cut off through the ages from the men who have made and influenced the destinies of mankind. She has been closely connected, both as source and nourisher, with some of the most potent influences which have affected for good the history of the world.[5]

Blyden adopted in a Pan-African as well as an international manner, Reade's comment, which I have quoted.[6] Blyden contrasted the roles of whites and blacks around the world: "The Negro is, at the moment, the opposite of the Anglo-Saxon. These everywhere serve the world; these everywhere govern the world."[7] But there are times when he seemed to see these roles reversed, for example, when he makes the proto-Hobbsonian, proto-Leninist statement, "Europe is exhausting itself by over-production."[8] Blyden looked forward to the return of some of the exiles from Africa and their task in the regeneration of the ancestral continent. (Incidentally, the study of back-to-Africa movements is an essential part of the concept of the African diaspora, which loses much of its force if it is limited to dispersal in an outward direction only.)

Blyden always wrote in English, but his birth in the Danish West Indies is a reminder that English was not the only language of the African diaspora. "Edward Blyden will remain, despite his limitations, the first and foremost precursor of *Négritude* and of the *African Personality*," Léopold Sédar Senghor commented.[9]

Senghor's comment, indeed, emphasizes three aspects of the concept of the African diaspora. First, it originated in the English-speaking world, where it received most of its development to date. It contains within itself, to be sure, the idea of negritude; and, if not carefully restricted, the concept of the African diaspora may run into sterile sands of racial mysticism as easily as negritude. The use of the concept of the African diaspora as a framework for the comparative study of all levels of slavery, however, makes the mystical deviation less likely. Second, as a concept that is intrinsically comparative, the study of the African diaspora, although it owes much to Anglophone influences, now has everything to gain by approaches through other languages as well as English; the European languages of the slave trade and the transplanted slave cultures; the relevant Asian languages; the African languages of the slave trade, east as well as west; and the hybrid languages that have resulted from the very complex mingling over several centuries of African and non-African peoples. Third, Senghor's comment serves as a reminder that, although the study of the African diaspora can become very statistical, parts of it are difficult to treat in a mathematical form. Many problems in the history of ideas, through the comparative study of slavery, may be best served by a combination of conventional documentary research methods and improved techniques of oral investigation. In the history of the African diaspora, for example, have dispersal-return concepts emerged in other than English-speaking and French-speaking areas? And, if they have, how do they compare with the ideas of African dispersal abroad and nostalgia for home?

Toward the end of Blyden's life, the concept of the African diaspora was still being used by students of African studies. In the late nineteenth and early twentieth centuries, however, when imperialism in Africa seemed very secure, it did not develop much, perhaps because of the influence of the dominating white cultures. Nevertheless, several writers of African descent pursued it on a modest level. In understanding the importance today of the linguistic factor in the African diaspora, both in the material to be studied and in the horizons and research equipment of the investigator, two Afro-American students of the dispersal of Africans around the world are especially important: William Edward Burghardt Du Bois and Lorenzo Dow Turner. Du Bois, in three of his books, *The Negro* (1915), *Black Folk, Then and Now* (1939), and *The World and Africa* (1947), to the best of my knowledge, never used the expression *African diaspora*; but these three books, and many other elements in his voluminous writings, employ an African diaspora approach. They are based on limited research, as Du Bois, with so many other things to do, was the first to acknowledge; but they indicate the dispersal of African peoples around the world, and they emphasize the importance of this knowledge for black and white people everywhere. Du Bois's strength in these synoptic approaches came not only from his inborn talents but also from the ramifications of his ancestry into a number of key areas of the African diaspora: his Anglo-American upbringing; his Franco-Haitian background; and farther away, the Dutch black Burghardts. Add to this Du Bois's knowledge of German, and it is clear that, for a man of his time, he was well equipped to appreciate the cultural differences within the African diaspora. Significantly, whether by accident or design, the last contribution in Alain Locke's seminal *The New Negro* was an essay Du Bois wrote on the occasion of his first trip to Africa. Of course Du Bois was not a linguist by inclination like that other Afro-American pioneer of the study of the African diaspora, Lorenzo Dow Turner. Turner wrote *Africanisms in the Gullah Dialect* and contributed to the study of the Brazilians of Nigeria.[10]

Between the Blyden era of the study of the African diaspora and the emergence of an explicit concept of it in the 1950s and 1960s, some white students of the African presence in the world helped to keep the subject alive. Three, in an ascending level of importance, were the American travel writer, Willard Price, who published in 1925 a book entitled *The Negro Around the World*, a short study of what he called "the Black Girdle," the world's equatorial belt containing most of the then 140 million people of African descent; Nancy Cunard's hefty anthology, *Negro*, which is by no means Anglophone in its orientation and from which it is still possible to find significant information about many parts of the African diaspora; and, of course, Melville J. Herskovits, whose contributions to the study of the diaspora are collected in his *The New World Negro*.

I have just used, as it is so easy for students of the African diaspora to do, the expression *diaspora*. But the only people who really have the right to use the word *diaspora* without a qualifying adjective are the Jews. Edward Blyden, Alexander Crummell, and other early twentieth-century writers of African descent, as well as some early West African nationalists in English-speaking Africa, were conscious of the parallels of servitude, enforced exile, and a longing to return to the homeland that Africans abroad shared with the Jews. This makes it all the more curious that they never appear to have used the expression *diaspora* in an African context. By the 1960s, their concept had been explicitly termed the *African diaspora*, yet many of the Africanists who now employ the expression seem unaware of the term *diaspora* in Jewish tradition or of its present-day supplementation with the Hebrew words *galut* for "exile" and *tephuztzot* for "dispersal" for the Jewish communities in the world after the establishment of the state of Israel. Some knowledge of Jewish history would help students of Africans abroad to realize that, in the expression "the African diaspora," *diaspora* is used metaphorically. This would prevent its becoming an overrigid, ideologized concept to the detriment of serious and imaginative research. Furthermore, knowledge of Jewish usage enables the appreciation of the voluntary as opposed to the involuntary element in the diaspora of the Jews. In the Jewish tradition, *galut* implies forced dispersion; *diaspora* has always included some element of voluntary exile. Without such a realization, the expression *African diaspora* may be doomed to the study of enforced dispersal only—to slavery. Certainly, slave studies always must form a major part of the historical examination of the African diaspora, but not the only part. Excessive concentration on the western rather than the eastern direction of the African diaspora may be responsible for the concealment of the voluntary element in the dispersal, even in the slave days.

If one wishes to acquire a little working knowledge of Jewish history to enable one to put the expression "African diaspora" into perspective, one has to go beyond the Bible. Yet, the Bible was—and still is in many ways—the major work through which the imagery and, by comparison, the ideas of the concept of the African diaspora have developed. It also contains many more references to Africa, south as well as north of the Sahara, than the average student of African history realizes. Where, however, is one to find a single book that deals in a scholarly fashion with Africa in the Hebrew and Greek scriptures? Such a book would be of immense value to the study of the African diaspora. Here, again, linguistic ability becomes of paramount importance, for a work of this sort would demand a knowledge of ancient Hebrew and Koiné Greek. Without such a book one is subject to the ways modern translators of the Bible, especially of the Old Testament, cope with the problem of a name for "the land of the blacks" or the "Bilad es Sudan." (The King James version tends to use Ethiopia but not uniformly, for in Isa. 11:11, it refers to Cush.) Various modern translations seem to have considerable difficulty in deciding whether Ethiopia, Cush, Nubia, or just Sudan should be employed for biblical references to parts of Africa known to the ancient Hebrews. Perhaps the problem is insoluble, but we will never know until at least one scholarly book on the Bible and Africa is made readily available.

Difficult problems also arise at the other end of the time scale, but they have a way of solving themselves. One example of this is the career of Bandele Omoniyi, one of the minor but by no means insignificant figures in the African diaspora. He was born in Lagos in 1884; in 1906 and 1907 he matriculated at the University of Edinburgh in the Faculty of Medicine listing his nationality as "Yoruba." The political entity known as Nigeria, of course, did not come into existence until 1914. In 1907, Omoniyi wrote three articles in an Edinburgh magazine criticizing British rule in West Africa; the following year he published a book entitled, *A Defence of the Ethiopian Movement*, which did not pass unnoticed.[11] And then Bandele Omoniyi disappeared ... or so, over a decade ago, it seemed to me. I have since discovered that he went to Brazil where he produced in 1912—the year of Blyden's death—a manifesto calling for a Nigerian political league. His aim was "the elevation of the Negro Race ... in his native land and ... throughout the world—an essentially African diasporist aim.[12]

Today, the study of African and Afro-American history is much more sophisticated. But the approach of the modern scholar of this fascinating subject is, as I see it, not all that different: the establishment and investigation of the areas to which the dispersed went and in which their descendants are living; the study of the interaction between these centers and their peripheries, at all possible levels; and the unceasing attempt to integrate these studies into the overall history of humanity. The old African diasporists wanted to see Africans, at home and abroad, past and present, treated as human beings. I cannot believe that, at heart, the aim of the African diasporists of today is different. And from their work I hope will come the still-needed redressing of the balance of world history, not only in the interests of Africans and their descendants but for the whole of humanity.

NOTES

1. Compare the use of the term *Scottish diaspora* by the Beit Professor of the History of the British Empire at the University of Oxford, Sir Reginald Coupland, in his posthumously published, *Welsh and Scottish Nationalism* (London, 1954), 271–81.

2. T. O. Ranger, ed., *Emerging Themes of African History* (Dar es Salaam, 1968); this address was also published in *African Forum*, 2 (1966):76–93. See also George Shepperson, Introduction in Martin L. Kilson and Robert I. Rotberg, eds., *The African Diaspora, Interpretive Essays* (Harvard University Press Cambridge, Mass., 1976), 10. Other works by George Shepperson that deal with aspects of the African diaspora include *Independent African: John Chilembwe and the Origins, Setting and Significance of the Nyasaland Native Rising of 1915* (Edinburgh, 1958) with Thomas Price; "Negro American Influences on the Emergence of African Nationalism," *Journal of African History* (London) 1 (1960):299–313; "External Factors in the Development of African Nationalism, with Particular Reference to British Central Africa," *Phylon* (Atlanta), 22, 3 (1961):207–25; "Pan-Africanism and 'pan-Africanism': Some Historical Notes," *Phylon* (Atlanta), 23, 4 (1962):346–58; "Abolitionism and African Political Thought," *Transition* (Kampala), 3, 12 (1964):22–26; "Ethiopianism: Past and Present," in *Christianity in Tropical Africa*, ed. G. C. Baeta (London: Oxford, 1968), 249–64; Introductions to reprints of James Africanus Beale Horton, *West African Countries and Peoples* (Edinburgh: Oxford University Press, 1969), and Sir Harry Johnston, *The Negro in the New World* (New York: Antheneum, 1969) and William E. B. Du Bois, *The Negro* (New York: Antheneum, 1970): The Afro-American Contribution to African Studies," *Journal of American Studies* (London 8, no. 3, (1975):281–303.

3. Georg Wilhelm Friedrich Hegel, *The Philosophy of History* (New York: Glencoe, 1956), trans. by J. Sibree, Introduction, 99.

4. W. Winwood Reade, *The African Sketch-Book* (London, 1873) 2:511–12.

5. Edward Blyden, *Christianity, Islam and the Negro Race* (Edinburgh: Oxford University Press, 1967), 114.

6. Reade's statement (see note 4) reads:
   He who writes the history of the world must not neglect to observe this stream of black humanity which has poured into America from the Sudan. It has fertilized half a continent with its labour, and set a world on fire with its wrongs; it has influenced the progress of commerce, culture and morality in Europe and transformed a Federation into a nationality.
   Blyden's adaptation of this statement reads:
   He who writes the history of modern civilization will be culpably negligent if he omits to observe and describe the black stream of humanity, which has poured into America from the heart of the Sudan. That stream has fertilized half the Western continent. It has created commerce and influenced its progress. It has affected culture and morality in the Eastern and Western hemispheres, and has been the means of transforming European colonies into a great nationality." (Blyden, *Christianity, Islam and the Negro Race*, 118).

7. Blyden, *Christianity, Islam and the Negro Race*, 120.

8. Ibid., 119.

9. Léopold Sédar Senghor, Foreword in *Selected Letters of Edward Wilmot Blyden*, ed. Hollis R. Lynch (Millwood, N.Y.: Kraus Intl., 1978), xxi.

10. Alaine Locke, *The New Negro* (New York: Antheneum, 1925); Lorenzo Turner, *Africanisms in the Gullah Dialect* (Chicago, 1949); idem. "Some Contacts of Brazilian Ex-Slaves with Nigeria, West Africa," *Journal of Negro History* 27 (January 1942):55–67.

11. Compare James Wells, *Stewart of Lovedale: The Life of James Stewart* (London: Heinemann Pub., 1909), 293. Bandele Omoniyi is here referred to as "His Highness Prince Bandele Omoniyi." See also Shepperson, "External Factors in the Development of African Nationalism," 225.

12. Manifesto. Rua Joao Alfredo, No. 75, Para-Belem, June 14, 1922, Bandele Prince: Public Record Office (London), C.O. 520/120/20105, June 29, 1912, 13.

3

Return Movements to West and East Africa: A Comparative Approach

Joseph E. Harris

THE significant crosscurrents of mutual influence between blacks in the United States and the Caribbean, and among those two areas and Africa, as well as between India and Africa, have very deep historical roots that, from the perspective of the African heritage, form a useful Pan-African approach to the study of blacks throughout the world. The key problems of that approach are, first, to trace the changes that occurred among Africans as they adjusted to varied conditions abroad during the period of slavery, abolition, and after; second, to determine the extent to which African customs and memories survived abroad and in what form; third, to analyze the ways in which the idea of Africa arose and manifested itself in the diaspora and related itself to Africa and Africans; fourth, to assess the nature, extent, and significance of contacts between and within Africa and the areas of the diaspora.

The 1770s and 1780s were critical decades in African diaspora history. The key year was 1787. Its significance was twofold: first, because of European decisions about Africans in Europe and America; second, because of the decisions and actions Africans in the Americas were taking. In 1787 Americans wrote into their constitution a provision that permitted the termination of the slave trade in 1807. The consequences of this act resulted in a more limited source of slaves, a federal subsidy for disposal of slaves liberated on the high seas, and cooperation with the American Colonization Society, which founded Liberia in 1821. In

This piece is an expanded and revised version of an article that appeared in *The African Dispersal* (Boston: Boston University, Afro-American Studies Programs, 1979), Occasional Paper No. 5.

Europe in 1787, a group of English abolitionists completed plans for the resettlement in Africa of Africans residing in England. In the wake of the 1772 decision against slavery in England, some abolitionists believed they could found a society of free labor, develop trade in goods, spread Christianity, and contribute to the abolition of slavery and the slave trade in Africa by settling Africa with unwanted, Christianized Africans. Thus, in 1787 some four hundred Africans left to begin that experiment in Sierra Leone; shortly thereafter they were joined by a group from the United States who came by way of Nova Scotia, Canada. A third group from Jamaica, West Indies, followed a few years later.

It was also in 1787 that Africans in the United States were formally organizing their separate institutions: the church, which became the largest black organization in the country; the African lodges; the African Free Schools; and so on. Not only did all these institutions bear the African label, they also expressed interest in the welfare of Africans. Some of them, notably the churches and schools, became seriously involved in the development of a deepening consciousness of and cooperation with Africans in the Caribbean and Africa.

Between 1820 and 1860 there occurred what is sometimes called the first black renaissance in the United States, a period when blacks expressed themselves and their heritage in literature, art, music, and dance. It was also the era when black schools and churches, in particular, sent representatives to Africa and the Caribbean as teachers and preachers. In 1841 Edward Jones, the first black college graduate in the United States, became president of the recently established Fourah Bay College in Sierra Leone. This and other examples confirmed that a situation had developed in the United States that provided a pool of educated and concerned Africans for work in the diaspora and in Africa at a time when such opportunities were rarely available elsewhere.

Because Sierra Leone's repatriates were from England and the Americas, they valued Western culture and education. They enrolled their children in the several mission schools and sent their sons and daughters to English universities. In fact, the liberated African's desire for Western education, and the missionary's commitment to education to "civilize" Africans, had led to the founding of Fourah Bay College by the Church Missionary Society (CMS) in 1826. In 1876 a connection was established between Fourah Bay and Durham University, thereby bringing university education to Sierra Leone, where it became available to students across West Africa, especially British West Africa. In a very real sense, therefore, Western education, in general, and Fourah Bay College, in particular, distinguished Sierra Leone in Africa and the diaspora.[1]

The very nature of these developments, and the fact that the repatriated Africans had not come from that area originally, provided Sierra Leone with the unique opportunity of spearheading a Pan-African tradition. As the repatriates began migrating throughout West Africa in search of their families, a way back home, opportunities to expand their business interests, or, in the case of some, to spread the faith, they took with them aspects of Western education and culture. Those trained at Fourah Bay College were selected by British missionaries, merchants, and colonial officials to entrench British influence. At the same time, however, there were men like Samuel Crowther, who wrote books in the Nupe and Ibo languages and compiled a Yoruba dictionary; Samuel Johnson, who wrote the valuable *History of the Yorubas*; and Thomas Macaulay, father of Herbert and sometimes known as the father of Nigerian nationalism. These were all either repatriates or their descendants and were graduates of Fourah Bay College. Many other examples could be given to show that although they were sometimes exploited for European purposes, the repatriated Africans still forged links in West Africa that broadened the horizons and expanded the channels of communication of several local societies, and thus facilitated Sierra Leone's role in this early Pan-Africanist tradition before a strong, independent base had emerged.

Sierra Leone's experiment had a significant impact on groups in the United States, although repatriation took a somewhat different course. Africans had on their own, early in the eighteenth century, petitioned for freedom and a return to Africa. But the real black repatriationist was Paul Cuffe, that black shipper who organized groups in the United States and Sierra Leone to assist in his efforts to settle Africans from the United States in that colony. He himself financed the settlement of thirty-eight persons in 1815. Cuffe's efforts and the success of Sierra Leone demonstrated the feasibility of black settlement in Africa. Within a few years, colonization schemes to rid America of free Africans became a serious concern of white Americans.

In the United States slave society, Africans were forbidden to speak their language or practice their religion; free blacks were denied many of the rights of freedom. In addition, with the independence of Haiti in 1804, many slave owners in the United States and the Caribbean referred to that black state as the "Black Menace," which could cause blacks elsewhere to revolt for freedom. For these and other reasons, many ordinary and prominent white Americans joined efforts that resulted in the organization of a society to settle "free" blacks in Africa. This endeavor led to the founding of Liberia.

Liberia's development was similar in several aspects to that of Sierra Leone, but there are some differences. First, although the overall number of Liberian settlers was much smaller than Sierra Leone's, the great majority in Liberia had previously resided in the United States. Second, although most of the Liberian settlers were poor, a significant number of them had been born free, were educated, and had owned property in the United States. Their connections with America were, thus, very real and strong. It is not surprising, therefore, that many of Liberia's institutions were patterned after American ones. In addition to the churches, the University of Liberia helped to prepare Liberians as agents of social change, Western-style, as Fourah Bay College was doing in Sierra Leone. But more than in Sierra Leone, Liberian settlers took greater responsibility for their own physical and social survival, which led to their independence in 1847.

With independence, Liberia became unique in Africa and in the diaspora. Not only was Liberia the result of repatriation of Africans from abroad, it also became the only internationally recognized independent black state in Africa until well into the twentieth century. And precisely because of its unique status and history, Liberia became a symbol of hope for many at home and abroad. The pioneer Liberians viewed their venture as an opportunity to exercise their freedom, and within a few years their leaders envisioned the country as destined to become a "province of freedom" for the uplift of all persons of African ancestry. The Liberian constitution noted that the object of forming the state was "to provide a home for the dispersed and oppressed children of Africa." Even more than the case of Sierra Leone, the Liberian situation facilitated continued close relations with Africans overseas, especially in America. The story here is well known: Joseph Roberts from the United States became the first president; John Russwurm, who cofounded with Samuel Cornish the first Afro-American newspaper in the United States, also founded the first newspaper in Liberia, the *Liberian Herald*; John Day left the United States to become the country's chief justice; and Edward Blyden, from the West Indies, became Liberia's most distinguished citizen, as publisher, diplomat, minister of state, and intellectual.[2]

Although Blyden is well known, he deserves special attention. His efforts on behalf of unity and freedom for Africa ranged across West Africa, as he held posts in Liberia, Sierra Leone, and Nigeria. His popular appeal to persons of African descent was extended to the diaspora and to the indigenous peoples on the continent. Blyden wanted to make Liberia College (the second Western-style college in Africa) one in which African religion, political systems, and other customs could be studied; and in this sense, he became the major proponent of black studies at the national and international levels. Later, he pioneered a synthesis of African and Western culture, a task that he realized would require the dedication and labor of large numbers of educated and skilled Africans from the diaspora. We will never know whether his objectives and the Liberian goals might have been achieved because the thrust of the nineteenth-century colonial rule diverted and delayed those efforts from establishing tangible and lasting ties between Africa and the American diaspora. Marcus Garvey through his Universal Negro Improvement Association, W. E. B. Du Bois and others through the several Pan-African congresses, the Harlem Renaissance, and Negritude movements, and the Nation of Islam (Black Muslims) continued that trend in the twentieth century and had a significant impact on nationalism in West Africa.[3]

The Brazilian returnees to West Africa are discussed in a later essay by Dr. Boadi-Siaw. However, it is important to note here that those returnees came voluntarily from communities in Brazil that had retained Yoruba language and culture. Indeed, other African cultural influences persisted in Brazil. Thus, the Brazilian returnees not only retained much of their Africanity, they could identify with the area to which they returned, unlike the returnees to Sierra Leone and Liberia. To be sure, they had adopted aspects of Portuguese culture and had not escaped the idea of redemption that motivated so many returnees. They regarded themselves as special agents of cultural change and were regarded by some as "half-baked Europeans," but, as Boadi-Siaw notes, they nonetheless combined their European and African ideas and skills and made notable contributions to Ghana, Togo, Benin, and Nigeria.[4]

Let us now examine developments on the other side of the continent, where the Indian Ocean slave trade was many centuries older than that of the Atlantic, and where Africans had been planted at various points in Asia from the Middle East probably as far as China since the first or second century A.D., if not earlier. These are episodes that require more extensive examination by researchers, for by the time of my own research—which focused on the nineteenth century primarily—African communities were already centuries old in India, Turkey, Arabia, Iraq, Iran, Yemen, Pakistan, China, and possibly elsewhere.[5]

In India, for example, frequent references to Africans may be found in records from the thirteenth century. Groups of Africans (referred to in Asia as *Habshis* and *Siddis*) revolted in Bengal, India, during the latter part of the fifteenth century and established control there for a few years before finally suffering defeat. During the sixteenth and seventeenth centuries, Africans in western India, Gujarat in particular, emerged in positions of prominence in military and administrative affairs. One such person was Malik Ambar, sold as a slave in Ethiopia, in Mocha, in Baghdad and finally in India in 1575. Malik Ambar had been taught clerical skills in Arabia and later was placed in important clerical positions in the Deccan. Because of his loyalty and military skills, he eventually became a commander of the slave guard in Ahmadnagar. Malik Ambar commanded a unit of a thousand African soldiers and built auxiliary units of Asians; with these two groups he seized power and emerged as the undisputed leader of the Ahmadnagar area between 1602 and 1626. In this role he prevented the Great Mughuls of Delhi from conquering the Deccan for more than a quarter of a century.[6]

Other groups of Africans became prominent on Janjira Island, some forty miles south of Bombay. They claim descent from Ethiopians and have several legends to support their claim. In any case, it appears that most of these people arrived by way of the Indian Ocean slave trade. By the seventeenth century the community had become large enough and had built a fleet strong enough to command control over the area between Bombay and Goa; they were therefore sought as allies not only by local Indian groups, Mughuls and Marathas, but also by European merchants—Dutch, Portuguese, and British. At various times during the seventeenth and eighteenth centuries the Janjira Africans played one group against the other and received subsidies to keep open the sea lanes around Bombay. However, when the economic and political stakes became higher during the eighteenth century, Britain invaded the island, destroyed the fleet, and declared it a colony in 1834.[7]

A different kind of African community in Asia sprang from the abolitionist campaign of the nineteenth century. Between 1820 and 1873, after the legal abolition of the West African slave trade in 1807, Britain negotiated a series of abolitionist treaties with Asian and African sovereigns. In addition to suppressing the slave trade, the British also pressed for the liberation of slaves on the Asian continent itself—and had a measure of success. Thus, Africans liberated from ships on the seas and those freed on the Asian mainland were channeled to three depots for settlement: Aden in Arabia, Bombay in India, and the Seychelles in the Indian Ocean. These places had long been frequented by Africans, and they attracted others seeking the economic and social security these depots provided during the nineteenth century.[8]

Africans resided in Bombay at least as early as the eighteenth century, when British merchants also engaged in the slave trade to India. Several documents refer to British cruiser commanders complaining about the difficulty of controlling the "Madagascar slaves." The British East India Company purchased, trained, and advertised Africans as contract slaves in the eighteenth century. And in the latter part of the century, an official British abstract listing persons who could be called on to defend Bombay included nearly a thousand Africans.

As a depot for liberated Africans, Bombay received its first allotment in 1835. That year a group of 200 African children came from Karachi and was sent to Bombay's police commissioner to place them among families, in employment, or in charitable institutions. From that time until the 1870s at least, European and Indian families in Bombay requested and received liberated Africans as domestics. In addition, the British navy in India enlisted so many liberated Africans that by the 1850s the government observed that the majority of its seamen were Africans.

Mission stations also accepted liberated Africans in India. The principal stations were the Roman Catholic orphanage at Bandora, the American mission at Poona, and the Church Missionary Society (CMS) African Asylum at Nasik. In these cases the government contributed a monthly allowance for the children's upkeep. Thus, by the time of the Treaty of 1873, the East African slave trade was legally ended. When Bartle Frere recommended the establishment of settlements of liberated Africans on the East African coast, liberated Africans in India were prepared to return and make a meaningful contribution to East Africa.

The CMS mission at Nasik, in particular, was called on to provide the initial group. Nasik had been established in 1854 by the Reverend William Price with initial funds from fines imposed on convicted slave dealers in India. In 1857, the government of India began making annual awards from the public revenues. As a center for liberated African children, its responsibilities included the conduct of a school that taught history, geography, English, arithmetic, and Bible studies; in addition, the girls were trained in sewing and cooking, while the boys were trained as blacksmiths, carpenters, masons, and printers. At that time it was thought that the Africans should be prepared to seek jobs in addition to their missionary work. David Livingstone was one of the staunch supporters of the school. In 1865 he visited the school and returned to Africa with nine of the boys, one of whom was with him when he died.[9]

Now, let us turn to the Kenya connection. In 1874, the CMS sent William Price, who had established the program at Nasik, to organize the station in Mombasa. Prior arrangements had already been undertaken as early as 1864 when William Henry Jones, who had been rescued as a slave and landed at Nasik in 1854, was sent to Mombasa to join Johann Rebmann, the CMS missionary. While on the coast, Jones visited several areas, including Zanzibar, to explore the possibilities of establishing mission stations for the resettlement of liberated Africans. He returned to Bombay in 1871 and appealed to Africans to return to the coast and to Zanzibar under the auspices of the CMS. Clearly, therefore, the movement to return was already in motion when Frere recommended that liberated and captured Africans be repatriated at Mombasa.[10]

The history of Nasik led to the selection of William Price, the former superintendent, to supervise the establishment of the community at

Mombasa, which came to be known as Freretown and was patterned after Nasik. The aims of the CMS project were to form an industrial, Christian settlement of liberated Africans at Freretown and Rabai, and to expand toward Kilimanjaro. To accomplish these objectives, a church and a school were built, and William Jones, Ismael Semler, David George, and their wives, all Africans formerly at the Nasik school, became Price's principal assistants. They were joined later by others from the Bombay area, who, thus, have become known in some quarters as Bombay Africans, Bombay boys, and Nasik boys.[11]

The early settler Africans became pioneers in the Freretown settlement. They helped to set the cultural tone and substance of the community through their leadership roles in the churches, schools, media, trade unions, crafts, and civil service; and neighboring Africans, Europeans, Arabs, and Indians in Kenya viewed the Christian community of Freretown as an influential outpost of Western society.[12]

Freretown poses some contrasts to Sierra Leone and Liberia. First, unlike the two West African examples, Freretown was founded by repatriated Africans who, for the most part, were born in Africa, and who had been away only for up to twenty years before returning. They, therefore, retained much more of their culture, especially language (they spoke Swahili and some of the vernaculars); they also had not been abroad long enough to sever ties with families and friends (indeed, some among them were reunited with members of their families and friends at Freretown and Rabai). In addition, because those who returned came from a mission station apart from Indian society, they had not been exposed to any great extent to the wider Indian community and, therefore, had little reason to identify with it, though several of them had been taught the Hindostani and Gujarati languages.

However, like their West African counterparts in Liberia and Sierra Leone, the Bombay group had had significant exposure to Western cultural values for up to a maximum of twenty years. They were Christians, spoke English, adopted European dress, and acquired skills as blacksmiths, carpenters, masons, and tailors. Some of them gained experience as railroad and dock workers. All of these activities made them attractive potential for European missionaries propagating the faith, for merchants expanding their businesses, for explorers venturing into the interior, and for colonial officials entrenching colonial rule. Thus, some of the repatriated Africans became missionaries who settled widely along the coast, establishing mission stations. The Imperial British East Africa Company (IBEA) and other businesses made use of repatriated Africans as clerks and interpreters, while explorers employed them to accompany caravans into the interior and relied heavily on their accounts of inland societies. William Jones, for example, accompanied Bishop Hannington to Uganda. In addition to returning with news of Hannington's death, Jones also provided valuable information on the state of affairs between the coast and Uganda.

With the establishment of colonial rule, people of Freretown were employed as clerks, interpreters, and advisers in the courts, post office, and other agencies. Indeed, one of the few highly qualified printers, African or otherwise, on the coast in the 1920s was James "Jimmy" Jones, son of William Jones.

No one at Freretown really compares with Blyden of Liberia, but there are some similarities with William Jones. He was an ex-slave who was reared in the Indian mission, where he received a good Western education. Like Blyden, he made several trips from Africa to India to encourage Africans to return to the continent. There seems to be no record of the number who responded to his appeals, but he must be given credit for having been responsible for encouraging some of the several hundred who ultimately joined the community directly from India. In Freretown and Rabai, Jones stimulated pride in Africans and provided a rationale for the responsible involvement of the liberated community on behalf of Africans, especially on the matter of slavery and human dignity. For this stance, Jones was denounced by his fellow European missionaries, but he became a hero to Africans.

Because of their background in a Western setting, the pioneer settlers in Freretown, Sierra Leone, and Liberia identified themselves with European culture and ideas. However, because of the great numbers of other Africans who also accepted Christianity and European ways, intermarriages occurred and—as in Sierra Leone—there emerged the Creole society, which represented a blend of African and European beliefs, languages, cuisine, and so on. This group, thus, became exclusive and achieved the greatest mobility in trade and Western-style professions, where Africans could earn the most money. This also happened in Liberia, where the repatriates believed that theirs was the task of redeeming Africa, which meant a special position for them in the country's affairs. In Liberia the strong impact of American racial denigration of blacks as well as the development of the "providential design" concept caused the "Americo-Liberians" to have a greater commitment to the gradual uplift of the masses than the other areas, especially after independence, which—at least theoretically—provided for greater authority in policy formulation for Liberians. A compulsory educational system to facilitate national integration did emerge in principle in the nineteenth century and slowly proceeded to incorporate other ethnic groups in Western-style activities.

Unlike Liberia, Sierra Leone remained a colony on which Britain placed some priority in Africa. Thus, Creoles received appointments to civil service posts and seats in the executive and legislative councils not only in Sierra Leone but also in other British West African colonies.[13] However, from 1896 when the British declared a colony over the hinterland, Creole fortunes diminished because interior peoples, the Mende and Temne in particular, regarded the Creoles as "black Englishmen."[14] The British then proceeded to limit Creole influence in the colony by restricting the expansion of Christianity in the hinterland and by appointing Englishmen to posts formerly held by the Creoles on the coast. This policy assured greater ethnic particularity.

At the same time, Creole merchants had to compete with European merchants whose presence in Africa increased perceptibly during the last quarter of the nineteenth century. And while the Creole community's influence in Sierra Leone declined during this period, and distrust between them and indigenous Africans increased, one should also note that Creole influence on business, education, journalism, the civil service, and other areas was deeply imprinted in neighboring countries of West Africa. The same imprint was made by Freretownians in Kenya and to lesser degrees in Uganda, Tanganyika and Zanzibar (Tanzania).

In Freretown there developed a generally steadier trend of identification with neighboring peoples than in either Sierra Leone or Liberia at the early stage of growth. This was probably because Freretownians had not been as completely alienated from the area as their West African counterparts had been and thus could more easily understand the indigenous groups. Certainly this was evident in their language. In addition, better preparations had been made for the return to Africa, which may have resulted in part from prior knowledge of the West African experiences. Jones had surveyed the area, and Frere discussed plans and negotiated an agreement with Arabs on the coast, and they readily accepted the idea and eventually benefited from the community's presence in such things as trade, medicine, and education. The Arab School in Mombasa drew on the Freretown community for some of its teachers in the 1920s, 1930s, and later. Freretownians thus served as a social and economic bridge between Africans and Arabs on the coast.[15]

Further, several of the local missionaries tolerated (and some, especially the Africans, welcomed) the presence of their brothers fleeing slavery. In addition, neighboring Africans were attracted to Freretown for education and economic survival, especially during the several famines of the 1880s and 1890s, and for security (particularly those running away from slavery). The close identification of the area with Swahili culture also facilitated the eventual development of closer cohesion among the repatriates, refugees, and indigenous Africans. Very early, therefore, Freretown became a mixture of several ethnic groups,

and although the first settlers were viewed as, and considered themselves, a kind of elite, the fact is that they soon recognized that the
Europeans, Arabs, and Asians did not accord them equality but regarded them as inferior, though a step above indigenous Africans. These
factors had the effect of facilitating a fusion into the larger African
community, a process that continues today.

The Freretown settlers never constituted a large group and were
always dependent not only on the European missionaries but also on
good relations with their neighbors, among whom they missionized and
taught. Indeed, by the turn of the century, the "Bombay group" as a
class had greatly diminished, as they moved to coastal towns and into
the interior, fusing with other groups. Some of them migrated because
of grievances against the white missionaries; others sought economic
opportunities in the towns; still others joined different mission stations.
Today, therefore, the descendants of the first settlers are widely scattered on the coast, with only a few remaining in Freretown proper.

Many of the migrating Freretownians became teachers in various
parts of the country. It is probably no exaggeration to say that most
Africans educated in Kenya prior to World War II were taught by
Freretownians or Freretown-trained teachers, and most Christian
Africans in Kenya probably had close contact with Freretown. The
Freretown Divinity School was the main source of primary and sec-
ondary education in the country until 1931, when it was relocated near
Nairobi at Limuru. This educational and missionary influence was also
spread in neighboring Tanganyika and Zanzibar (Tanzania), and
Uganda; and Freretownians were also among the first pioneering Kenyan
journalists, radio announcers, and trade unionists, especially among the
Africans of Mombasa.

The first national political party among Kenya Africans, KASU/KAU
(Kenya African Study Union/Kenya African Union), was founded by
several repatriates, including Francis Khamisi, the first general secretary; Thomas Mbotela, assistant general secretary and later vice president under Jomo Kenyatta; and "Jimmy" Jeremiah; all from the Freretown tradition. Other leaders then and later received their education
and had close contacts with Freretown. Indeed, the influence of ideas
such as multiracialism, nonviolence, and a constitutional approach to
independence became major objectives of KAU until late 1951, in large
measure because of the impact of these men. It is noteworthy that when
Jomo Kenyatta returned to Kenya in 1947 after many years abroad, his
leadership depended on assistants who knew the country—the Europeans, Africans, and Asians—who could communicate easily in English
and local languages and who had a "national image" to underscore the

national character of the party. The Freretownians met those criteria better than anyone else and emerged as key party leaders until Mau Mau ushered in a more radical approach to replace the moderate, constitutional approach pursued by the repatriates and others.

In conclusion, Sierra Leone, Liberia, and Freretown are examples of an important physical return of African people from the diaspora to Africa, thereby greatly influencing not only their immediate settlements but surrounding societies as well. Whether the repatriates served as teachers or civil servants, doctors or trade unionists, journalists or politicians, they were conveyors of ideas and skills necessary to modernize Africa. Their contribution to the development of managerial skills and conceptual approaches necessary to understand international problems and interrelationships greatly accelerated modern freedom movements and the emergence of a national consciousness in several African states. This is not an argument that these developments would not have occurred without the returnees; it is an argument that they did occur with critical assistance from the diaspora.

The black returnees could not escape the influence of their physical and social environment abroad. That influence not only accounted for the contributions they made as returnees in Africa but also facilitated their continued links with the diaspora. Although their language and life-styles changed and their values and goals were modified, traces of several African languages persist in the Guianas and the islands of the southeastern United States; Yoruba became widely spoken in parts of Brazil; Swahili was planted in India; and Creole emerged in Africa and several diaspora communities. Indeed, evidence of cultural continuity continues to be uncovered, and it is likely that the continuity in substance rather than form is even greater. Without a doubt, therefore, cultural as well as biological links were forged between Africa and the diaspora communities, and those links facilitated a meaningful return to Africa.

Whether in music or literature, social or economic relations, military or political achievements, Africans in the diaspora have been major contributors to their adopted societies, in spite of inhibiting racial prejudices on the part of Euro-Americans. Perhaps the greatest contribution of Africans abroad was labor, which facilitated the accumulation of capital, the advance of technology, the internationalization of banking and insurance, and the general administrative organization, especially in the West, but also in the Persian Gulf region and southern Asia, where much additional research is needed.

In conclusion, Sierra Leone, Liberia, Freretown, and the scattered areas in Ghana, Togo, Benin, and Nigeria are examples of an important physical return. This comparative approach clearly has potential for the reconstruction of the history of Africa and its influence abroad; it also promises to provide a more realistic perspective on the history of Africa as well as the areas in which the African presence was established—Europe, the Americas, and Asia.

NOTES

1. Many sources consider this subject: Christopher Fyfe, *A History of Sierra Leone* (London: Oxford University Press, 1962); John Peterson, *Province of Freedom: A History of Sierra Leone* (Evanston: University of Illinois Press, 1969); Johnson U. J. Asiegbu, *Slavery and the Politics of Liberation, 1787–1861* (New York: Longmans, 1969); Arthur Porter, *Creoledom* (New York, 1963); Leo Spitzer, *The Creoles of Sierra Leone: Responses to Colonialism, 1870–1945* (Madison: University of Wisconsin Press, 1974); Jean H. Kopytoff, *A Preface to Modern Nigeria: The Sierra Leoneans in Yoruba, 1880–1890* (Madison: University of Wisconsin Press, 1965); Kenneth L. Little, "The Significance of the West African Creole for Africanist and Afro-American Studies," *African Affairs* 49, 197 (1950); John D. Hargreaves, "African Colonization in the 19th Century: Liberia and Sierra Leone," *Sierra Leone Studies* 4. See also chapter 20 by Akintola Wyse in this volume.

2. The following are sources on Liberia: Raymond Buell, *Liberia: A Century of Survival, 1847–1947* (Philadelphia, 1947); Merran Fraenkel, *Tribe and Class in Monrovia* (New York: Oxford, 1964); Hollis Lynch, *Edward Wilmot Blyden: Pan Negro Patriot* (London: Oxford University Press, 1967); C. L. Simpson, *The Symbol of Liberia* (London: Oxford University Press, 1961); and several issues of *The Liberian Historical Review*.

3. These developments have received much scholarly and popular attention and do not need extended discussion here, especially since some of the contributors to this volume consider the topic.

4. See S. Y. Boadi-Siaw, pp. 421–439 of this volume.

5. This is a largely unexplored dimension of the African diaspora. Consequently, most of the published sources are those of the author: Joseph E. Harris, *The African Presence in Asia: Consequences of the East African Slave Trade* (Evanston, Ill.: Northwestern University Press, 1971); *Abolition and Repatriation in Kenya* (Historical Association of Kenya, East African Publishing House, Nairobi, Kenya, 1977); "The Black Peoples of Asia," *World Encyclopedia of Black Peoples* (Scholarly Press, 1975); *Recollections of James Juma Mbotela* (East African Publishing House, Nairobi, Kenya, 1977).

6. Harris, *The African Presence in Asia* 87–98; Sheikh Chand, *Malik Ambar* (Hyderabad, 1931) in Urdu; D. R. Seth, "The Life and Times of Malik Ambar," *Islamic Culture: An English Quarterly* 31 (Hyderabad, January 1957); Bena Rasi Prasad Saksena, "Malik Ambar," *Hindustani Academy* 4 (October 1933), in Hindi; M. S. Commissariat, *A History of Gujarat* (Calcutta, 1957); E. Denison Ross, *An Arabic History of Gujarat* (London, 1921).

7. D. R. Banaji, *Bombay and the Siddis* (Bombay, 1933); R. V. Ramdas, "Relations between the Marathas and the Siddis of Janjira" (Ph.D. diss., University of Bombay, n.d.); Harris, *The African Presence in Asia*, 80–87.

8. India, Political Department, "Report on the Emigration of Siddhies of Hyderabad" (December 1882) 1: 110–13; Harris, *The African Presence in Asia*, 99–114.

9. Harris, *Abolition and Repatriation*, 19.

10. Ibid., 20.

11. Ibid., 21.

12. James Juma Mbotela, *The Freeing of the Slaves in East Africa* (London: Oxford, 1956) and in Swahili, *Uhuru wa Watumwa* (London: Oxford, 1934).

13. Kopytoff, *Preface to Modern Nigeria*; I. K. Sundiata, "Creolization on Fernando Po: The Nature of Society," *The African Diaspora: Interpretive Essays* (Cambridge: Harvard University Press, 1976).

14. Akintola Wyse modifies this characterization. See page 357 of this volume.

15. For a fuller discussion of this and the remainder of this section before the conclusion, see Joseph E. Harris, *Repatriates and Refugees in a Colonial Society: The Case of Kenya* (Washington, D.C.: Howard University Press, 1982).

4
African Religions in America: Theoretical Perspectives

Albert J. Raboteau

T HE very word *diaspora*, which figures so prominently in recent deliberations, carries religious connotations, referring, as it does in traditional usage, to the dispersal of the Israelites after the Babylonian captivity. Specifically, *diaspora* was the term applied to those Jews (and later to Jewish Christians) living outside Palestine amid the Gentile societies of the Hellenistic world. In the past few years the word has been extended to refer to the dispersal of Africans, primarily captive to the Atlantic slave trade. Just as the first diaspora spread Judaism around the Mediterranean and also left diaspora Jews in contact with the syncretistic patterns of Hellenism, the second diaspora spread African religion across the Atlantic and brought Africans into contact with the foreign cultures of other Africans, Europeans, and Native Americans. One of the largest population movements in history, the Atlantic slave trade ripped an estimated ten to eleven million Africans from their ancestral homes, societies, and cultures, brutally cutting ethnic and familial ties, the webs of tradition and kinship that support the individual's sense of identity and meaning.[1] The personal dimensions of this human tragedy cannot be calculated. With the diaspora Jews of old, diaspora Africans might well lament: "By the rivers of Babylon we sat down/And there we wept when we remembered Zion."

However, the experiences of capture, enslavement, the "Middle Passage," and "seasoning," traumatic as they were, did not wipe Africa from the memories of the slaves. For some, the memory was so powerful that it led them to kill themselves, confident in the belief that they would be reincarnated in Africa. For the vast majority, African customs, perspectives, and values continued to shape their lives and those of their descendants, a fact I was graphically reminded of when I visited Botanica Yoruba, a religious goods store in a Spanish-speaking section of San Francisco. There I saw emblems sacred to Shango, Eshu-Elegba, Yemanja, Ogun, and Obatala, all major gods of the Yoruba people of Nigeria and Dahomey (Benin). Spread by migration from the Caribbean and Latin America, African beliefs and rituals are alive and well in New York, Miami, Los Angeles, and several other large cities of the United States. The gods of Africans are offered sacrifice and are called on to enter their mediums in possession by people who have never seen Africa. Considering the extent of African-derived religions like candomblé, umbanda, voodoo, and santeria, it is tempting to state that African religion—like Judaism, Christianity, Islam, and Buddhism—has become a world religion. However, objections immediately leap to mind. There is no African religion. Africa is a continent, not a country, with many different peoples of diverse cultures and religions. The religions of certain West and Central African peoples have influenced certain Afro-American societies. The when, why, and how of their influences are still unclear. Even when particular correspondences can be established between a specific African religion and an Afro-American one, they differ significantly from each other in other ways. And Afro-American religions diverge widely among themselves. The exigencies of the slave trade made it impossible for any African society to be transmitted or re-created on the other side of the Atlantic. Because social institutions, the carriers of culture, were demolished, slaves had to develop new ones, which in turn modified traditional cultural life, including religious worship. Culture contact with Europeans, Native Americans, and other Africans in an alien environment resulted in syncretistic changes in belief and practice. The system of slave control in some instances prohibited those African customs, including religious worship, that whites deemed subversive. In some areas, notably British North America, the impact of African religions seems to have been weak in comparison with other areas, at least before recent immigration. Despite all these objections, the fact remains that African myths, symbols, doctrines, rituals, and ethics have spread far beyond their original or classical geographical, linguistic, and ethnic sources to give meaning and direction to the lives of non-African peoples. No discussion of the African diaspora can neglect the religious dimension implied by that word, a dimension at the core of African and Afro-American culture.[2]

Since the beginning of Afro-American studies as field of comparative inquiry in the 1930s and 1940s, scholars have debated the relative influence of Africa on the cultures of Afro-Americans. In its first phase the problem was posed in terms of the dynamics of race relations. In the United States, Melville J. Herskovits's groundbreaking volume, *The Myth of the Negro Past* (1941), was produced as a research monograph for the Gunnar Myrdal study of race relations, which resulted in *American Dilemma* (1944). Meanwhile, in Brazil, *The Masters and the Slaves* (1936), the initial volume of Gilberto Freyre's trilogy on race relations, appeared. Herskovits, a cultural anthropologist, was interested in the subject of culture contact and the process of acculturation. He also was intent on demolishing the "myth of the Negro past," that is, the widely held assumption that black Americans had no cultural history to speak of beyond their rather tenuous hold on Euro-American culture. The Africans' past, according to this myth, was one of savagery and superstition that could not possibly survive contact with the superior culture of Europeans. Herskovits, from his research in Dahomey, knew better. He argued that African cultures were by any standard complex and sophisticated, quite capable of holding their own in contact with European cultures. The African cultural heritage had survived enslavement, and "Africanisms" could be found among United States blacks, especially in their religious life. Cultural differences between blacks and whites, he inferred, were due not to cultural lag on the part of blacks but to different cultural origins, Africa versus Europe. Herskovits recognized that "African survivals" were not as numerous nor as observable among United States blacks as they were among Caribbean or Brazilian blacks, but he maintained, nevertheless, that they were there and proceeded to identify them, sometimes implausibly, but in the main, convincingly.[3]

Herskovits's three major contributions to the developing field of Afro-American studies were, first, his attack on the ethnocentric dismissal of African civilization current in his day; second, his use of a comparative approach to elucidate African influence on black North American culture; and third, his theory that African cultures did not just disappear even in the face of prohibition and persecution. For this discussion the second and third points are extremely important and merit explication below. But first, I would like to note an interpretive problem resulting from the enterprise that Herskovits began. The search for "Africanisms" tends to reify African and Afro-American cultures, as if there were pockets of African cultural "traits" hidden behind or under Euro-American cultural "traits." There is something artificial in the attempt, necessary though it be, to separate out authentic African from other threads in Afro-American culture. Moreover, the search for "survivals" tends to focus attention on the archaic rather than the living, adapting, organic aspect of culture. To be fair, Herskovits himself recognized the adaptive ability of African cultures, but his stress on continuity with Africa has tended to blind others to the significance of discontinuities and to the more subtle possibility of "continuity within discontinuity," as another cultural anthropologist has aptly put it.[4]

The idea, supported by Herskovits's research, that blacks and whites in the United States have different cultural roots that still determine cultural differences between the races turned out to be a powerful heuristic for both scholars and political activists. Some black nationalists defended racial separatism by appealing to cultural differences based on the retention and/or recovery of African culture. Other activists sought black pride in a reclamation of the African heritage. A new generation of scholars, as we will see, began to perceive the autonomy of Afro-American culture as based, in part, on the transmission of African cultures. But others, chief among them the sociologist E. Franklin Frazier, disagreed with Herskovits's schema and argued that in the United States, at least, the African heritage was stripped from slaves by the process of enslavement. Although African religion and culture persisted in Latin America and the Caribbean, they were, according to Frazier, dissipated by the unique character of slavery in the United States. Frazier saw Christianity, not African religion, as the source of social unity and meaning binding together fragmented aggregates of slaves into communities. While he agreed with Herskovits that vestigial "Africanisms" continued in black American folk belief, he thought that even these would be "sloughed off" as the black folk became better educated. For Frazier and other scholars, African culture was not a plausible basis for cultural differentiation between black and white. Africa was a "forgotten memory." Segregation and economic oppression were the principal explanations for the inability of blacks to integrate and assimilate into United States society.[5]

Clearly the question of African cultural influence has had implications for the analysis of race relations in the United States. Conversely, the climate of race relations has influenced the analysis of African influence on Afro-American culture. As I have commented elsewhere, "The ideological conflicts between separatists and integrationists have involved judgments about the survival of African culture in the United States." Those who believed that there was no difference between blacks and whites except skin color tended to stress the discontinuity with Africa and the brutality of the institution that stripped Africans of their culture. Those who believed that black Americans had a separate culture from whites tended to discover the origins of that culture in Africa and to celebrate its transmission by slaves as proof of their resistance. The implication was that the preservation of Africanisms was "good" and that acculturation to European culture—for example, conversion to Christianity—was "bad," though perhaps inevitable.

In the last decade a historiographical revolution in Afro-American history in the United States has moved scholarship beyond the limits of the Africanism versus acculturation debate and its ideological pressures. Historians, such as John Blassingame, George Rawick, Eugene Genovese, Sterling Stuckey, Lawrence Levine, and others, began to use slave narratives, black autobiographies, fugitive slave accounts, and black folklore as sources for the history of slavery. These historians supplemented these "nontraditional" sources with familiar ones—planters' diaries, newspapers, travel and missionary accounts, plantation records —and began to discover the slaves' experience of slavery, taken, as it were, "from the mouths of former slaves." They learned that slaves were not merely victims of a brutal institution but were also actors who molded their own lives, communities, and cultures despite slavery's restrictions. This emphasis on slaves as creative participants in the formation of their culture shifted attention from African "retentions" to a keener appreciation of the active presence of African values in the development of Afro-American culture. In other words, having accepted as a given the integrity and strength of African cultures, they moved the discussion of African influence away from an ahistorical and static model toward a more dynamic and historically specific one. Influenced by anthropology, sociology, ethnography, folklore, and comparative study, they began to think of culture in less reified terms and to speak of African values and African perspectives. Following Herskovits's lead, historians of slave religion attempted to prove the ways in which slaves reinterpreted Christianity according to African values and perspectives.[6]

If race relations set the context and the terms of the initial discussion of the African diaspora, the second and related phase was dominated by comparative study. Again Herskovits, at least in the United States, took the lead. As noted previously, one of his major contributions was the suggestion that black culture in the United States should be considered in comparison with other black cultures in the hemisphere. By placing North American blacks on a spectrum with Caribbean and Latin American blacks, the less obvious aspects of African influence (in the United States) would become clearer in comparison with the more obvious aspects (for example, in Haiti). Besides doing fieldwork in Africa, Herskovits studied black cultures in Haiti, Surinam, and Trinidad, and, to a lesser degree, in Brazil.[7] Given the size of the task, it is not surprising that to date only a few historians have fully taken up the challenge of extended comparison across cultures, although George

Eaton Simpson has done so for *Black Religions in the New World* (1978), and Roger Bastide attempted a similar task in a short study, *African Civilizations in the New World* (1967). Comparisons between two countries, for example, the United States and Brazil, centering on the issues of race relations and perceptions of race, have been more influential, as has the issue of comparative slave systems. One of the most important statements of the comparative approach was Frank Tannenbaum's *Slave and Citizen* (1946), which posed fundamental questions about the differences between slavery in Catholic Latin America and Protestant North America. Although some of Tannenbaum's conclusions have been revised by later scholars, particularly his contention that Catholicism protected the personhood and family of the slave more effectively than Protestantism did, his intuition that the hierarchical structure of the Catholic ethos created a view of slavery and of blacks quite different from the egalitarian ethos of Protestantism in the United States has continued to inspire research and discussion. Following Tannenbaum, Stanley Elkins argued that the absence of a strong, established church in North America removed the one institutional protection that might have defended the rights of the slave as a person. However, the establishment and the legal influence of the Catholic church did not necessarily result in actual protection of slaves on the plantations of Brazil, Haiti, and Cuba, where priests were few and were likely to be in the employ, and under the control, of the masters. A much more complex issue is the contrast between a hierarchical society that tolerates varying degrees of freedom or unfreedom and an egalitarian society that diametrically opposes freedom and slavery as absolute rather than relative states. In a hierarchical society, like Brazil, blacks and mulattoes might be placed on different rungs of the ladder of freedom. In the United States, freedom was identified with whites, and slavery was identified with African ancestry no matter how dark or light the skin.[8]

Whatever the impact of Catholicism versus Protestantism on slave treatment and racial perception, the impact of these two different types of Christianity on the development of Afro-American religions has been widely noted. In Brazil, Cuba, and Haiti, the nature of Catholic piety, including devotion to saints, celebration of feast days, veneration of religious images, and ritual use of material objects, seemed very familiar to Africans who quite understandably identified Ogun with St. George, Eshu-Elegba with St. Peter, the Ibeji with Sts. Cosmas and Damian, and Yemanja with the Blessed Virgin, whereas in Protestant North America, veneration of saints, elaborate festivals, and rituals were all prohibited as Papist idolatry, leaving the slave with little to associate with the religious heritage of Africa. Moreover, the Catholic institution of religious confraternities or brotherhoods offered an opportunity for urban slaves and free blacks to regroup according to "nations," so that in Bahia, for example, Bantu confraternities and Nago (Yoruba) confraternities organized along general ethnic lines. There were no such confraternities in British North America.[9] Undoubtedly, the similarity of Catholic to African piety is one explanation for the transmission of African religion to Latin America, just as the hostility of Protestantism to major features of African piety helps to explain the relative weakness of African religion in North America (until recently). However, this explanation is only partial. Another and probably more important factor has emerged from an analysis of slave distribution in the New World. If Curtin's estimates are accurate, and so far I have seen no questioning of these ratios, the United States imported only about 4 1/2 percent of all the Africans brought to the New World, while Saint Dominigue (Haiti) imported more than 9 percent and Brazil about 38 1/4 percent. Jamaica and Cuba each imported hundreds of thousands more African slaves than did the United States. The United States imported relatively few Africans. Moreover, the slave population in the United States had an amazingly large rate of natural increase. By emancipation in 1865, the slave population had increased to ten times the number imported. In contrast, the slave populations, by the time of emancipation in Haiti (1794) and in the British West Indies (1834), were far smaller than the number of Africans imported. These figures indicate that by the end of the slave trade in 1808, a large majority of slaves in the United States were born in America and had no direct experience of Africa, while in Latin America, the slave population, particularly during "boom" periods, had to be reinforced from Africa. New Africans also reinforced contact with African ways and African cultures. Moreover, the racial ratio was an important factor differentiating North America from the rest of the hemisphere. In the United States, in contrast with the Caribbean, the ratio of blacks to whites was either equal or in favor of the whites, with the exception of lowland South Carolina and Georgia, the precise locale where African influence was most marked. Plantations in the United States were small in size compared with Caribbean plantations, and slaves were dispersed among whites rather than being isolated (lowland South Carolina and Georgia again excepted). Thus the extent of cultural contact and the pressures to acculturate were much greater in the United States than elsewhere in the New World.[10] These demographic factors significantly affected the transmission of African culture, the character of cultural contact between blacks and whites, and the formation of Afro-American cultures.

Comparative study has demonstrated the uniqueness of the United States as a slave colony and has made a start at explaining some of the differences between Afro-American societies and cultures, but it has its limitations. As the field of Afro-American studies has developed, it has entered a third phase, in which it has become more difficult to make comparisons precisely because more is known about each society. Scholars have become increasingly aware of how complex the issues are and how much more needs to be learned about the demography, history, economy, sociology, and ethnography of each slave colony before comparison proves more fruitful. It is more than a question of fact; increased data have called into question the adequacy of traditional interpretation. For example, in the spectrum of black societies in the New World, the Afro-Americans of Surinam were usually placed at the farthest, most African end of the spectrum because their maroon forebears had escaped into the forests, where they were free to "re-create" African institutions without interference from whites. However, as detailed research revealed the historical development of these societies, it has become apparent that the diversity of their African origins required the maroons to create a new syncretistic society that could not perpetuate or copy any single African culture. Furthermore, maroon societies changed over time and were influenced by contact with whites, Native Americans, and slaves. Some customs and styles of art identified at first as African in origin have turned out to be new creations or adaptations of American origin.[11] Similarly, the assumption that African culture was brought by the slaves and then passed down generation by generation to the present or relatively recent past has been called into question by historical research in specific areas. For example, the candomblé centers of Bahia cannot trace their history back to colonial Brazil; they can trace only as far back as the beginning of the nineteenth century. The relatively late migration of liberated Africans strongly influenced Afro-American religions in Trinidad, and the nineteenth-century arrival of Yoruba slaves in Cuba helped to form santeria.[12]

Increasingly, new research has called into question the models of culture contact implicit in most of the discussion of the African diaspora. What does *acculturation* or *syncretism* mean in particular historical contexts? For example, it is commonplace to observe that slaves syncretized African gods with Catholic saints in voodoo, santeria, and candomblé. However, when closely examined in the functioning context of ritual, which has been aptly defined as "belief in action," it is clearly the African religious economy that governs the relationship. It is not St. Barbara or St. George who possess; it is Shango or Ogun. And it is sacrifice, drumming, dancing, and possession that form the liturgical core of these religions, not the parish church, even though the statues, holy water, and candles of the church may figure prominently in the sanctuaries. Juxtaposition rather than blending seems the more correct image for syncretism of this kind. Many scholars have commented on the openness of African religions in Africa and in the Americas to accepting "the gods" of others, whether Europeans, Native Americans, or other Africans. The truth of this observation should not hide another truth: the acceptance is functionally on African terms. A musical analogy may not be out of place. The sources of jazz are amazingly eclectic: European marching bands, classical music, pop tunes, blues, gospel. The forms and styles of jazz are tremendously varied. And yet, whether one is listening to Duke Ellington, Miles Davis, or Charlie Parker, it is jazz. Indeed, musicologists are beginning to emphasize that African influence on Afro-American music should be seen in terms of a basic orientation toward making music. It may be proper to speak of a basic orientation toward "doing" or "living" religion.

The basic image behind the term *culture contact* is "encounter." As Richard Price and Sydney Mintz have remarked, whole cultures do not come into contact; people do. And they do so within certain contexts or frameworks of relationship. The framework of contact between Europeans and Africans in the diaspora was, of course, slavery, a relationship in which the European was dominant. Certainly the slave system set the terms of the relationship, but people have ways of maneuvering within systems. The slaves did just that. With regard to culture contact between slaves and masters in the United States, Herskovits made the extremely important suggestion that European and African cultures did not simply war against one another with either one side or the other winning a victory here and there. Culture contact resulted in reinterpretation. Africans reinterpreted Christianity according to African perspectives and values and reinterpreted African forms in terms of Christian perspectives and values.[13] Similarly, the encounter of individual Africans and Europeans did not leave Europeans unchanged. Freyre, Bastide, and Genovese have all remarked on the influence of African myth, magic, medicine, and folklore on Europeans. Bastide even speaks of the interpenetration of cultures. (Given the history of miscegenation in Brazil, the term is particularly apt.) Undoubtedly, the position, one could say the power, of the black nursemaid within the master's family was one source of such influence.[14] There were others. An account written in 1819 by an antirevivalist minister suggests the possibility that white Christians were being influenced by African liturgical practice in the camp meeting revivals of the United States:

> Here ought to be considered too, a most exceptionable error, which has the tolerance at least of the rulers of our camp meetings. In the *blacks'* quarter,

the coloured people get together, and sing for hours together, short scraps of disjointed affirmations, pledges, or prayers, lengthened out with long repetitious *choruses*. These are all sung in the merry chorus-manner of the southern harvest field, or husking-frolic method, of the slave blacks; and also very greatly like the Indian dances. With every word so sung, they have a sinking of one or other leg of the body alternately; producing an audible sound of the feet at every step, and as manifest as the steps of actual negro dancing in Virginia, etc. If some, in the meantime sit, they strike the sounds alternately on each thigh.... [T]he evil is only occasionally condemned and the example has already visibly affected the religious manners of some whites. From this cause, I have known in some camp meetings from 50 to 60 people crowd into one tent, after the public devotions had closed, and there continue the whole night, singing tune after tune, ... scarce one of which were in our hymn books. Some of these from their nature, (having very long repetition choruses and short scraps of matter) are actually composed as sung and are almost endless.[15]

The fact that Afro-Americans continued to dance in African ways at Christian revivals and prayer meetings in the South of the United States indicates their ability to reinterpret a religion that would seem to be antagonistic to the African religious ethos of their ancestors. Despite what was said previously about its inhospitability, evangelical Protestantism did not prove impossible to relate to African religious behavior. At the core of American revivalism was the experience of conversion, and experience surrounded by ecstatic behavior, the outward manifestation of intense religious emotion. The liturgical core of many African religions is the experience of spirit possession, surrounded by rhythmic drumming, singing, and dancing. It may very well be that slaves linked the two. In both cases ecstatic religious experience in a state of altered consciousness is a basic characteristic of the ritual commerce between the human and the divine. That some Protestant slaves saw Christian conversion in distinctly African terms is suggested by the narrative of a fugitive slave, Henry "Box" Brown, who recalled that when his sister "became anxious to have her soul converted," she "shaved the hair from her head, as many of the slaves thought they could not be converted without doing this."[16] Shaving the head is a common feature of initiation rites for mediums of the gods in West Africa, Brazil, Cuba, and Haiti. Moreover, the counterclockwise, shuffling, rhythmic dance of the Christian slaves' ring shout seems to resemble closely descriptions of religious dance performance elsewhere in the African diaspora and in Africa. More important, however, is the theological orientation behind the dance. The reason for the shout was revealed to an acculturated black Christian bishop, who deemed it, significantly enough, "heathenish" and called it a "Voudoo Dance":

> About this time [1878] I attended a "bush meeting." ... After the sermon they formed a ring, and with coats off sung, clapped their hands and stamped their feet in a most ridiculous and heathenish way. I requested the pastor to go and stop their dancing. At his request they stopped their dancing and clapping of hands, but remained singing and rocking their bodies to and fro. This they did for about fifteen minutes. I then went, and taking their leader by the arm requested him to desist and to sit down and sing in a rational manner. I told him also that it was a heathenish way to worship and disgraceful to themselves, the race, and the Christian name. In that instance they broke up their ring; but would not sit down, and walked sullenly away. After the sermon in the afternoon, having another opportunity of speaking alone to this young leader of the singing and clapping ring, he said: "Sinners won't get converted unless there is a ring." Said I: "You might sing till you fell down dead, and you would fail to convert a single sinner, because nothing but the Spirit of God and the word of God can convert sinners." He replied: "The Spirit of God works upon people in different ways. At camp-meeting there must be a ring here, a ring there, a ring over yonder, or sinners will not get converted." This was his idea, and it is also that of many others. These "Bands" I have had to encounter in many places.... To the most thoughtful ... I usually succeeded in making the "Band" disgusting; but by the ignorant masses ... it was regarded as the essence of religion.[17]

Slaves in the country were commonly identified as least susceptible to African influence; that they considered it meaningful, even necessary, "to dance so that the Spirit will come" is proof of the adaptability of African religious perspectives and of their continuity in the most diverse forms and situations.[18]

There seems today to be a general agreement among scholars of Afro-America from different fields—anthropology, folklore, musicology, history, religious studies, and art history— that the issue of African influence in America should be seen more in terms of the continuity of basic African values, orientation, and perspectives and less in terms of the transportation of specific (identifiable) African customs, practices, or cultural forms, important though these may be. The major difficulty with this enterprise is of course the fact mentioned previously—that Africa is a continent, not a country, and during the lengthy period of the trade, Africans from West, Central, and Southeast Africa were enslaved in the Americas. Afro-Americanists have been preoccupied with West Africa, but Central Africa was at least as important as a source of slaves. Scholars need to gain a more precise knowledge of the prevenience and distribution of slaves, and work is underway in this area. More crucial is the need to know more about African societies in time perspective. Because of increased emphasis on discerning basic African values and perspectives, it is vitally important that Afro-Americanists adequately understand the complexity of African societies and cultures lest their generalizations about West or Central African religious traditions be inadequate or banal. What is needed, in Clifford Geertz's term, is "thick description."

Afro-Americanists have, for the most part, relied on the work of Africanists for descriptions of African societies and for theoretical models to interpret African cultures. Placide Tempels, John Mbiti, and Robin Horton have been among the most influential theorists for Afro-Americanists interested in religion. Tempels's emphasis on the idea of force or power, instead of being, as the fundamental concept in Bantu philosophy, Mbiti's delineation of the foreshortened future and the expanded present in the African sense of time, and Horton's description of the communal personalism of African traditional thought compared with the atomistic individualism of Western science have caught the attention of scholars in America. More recently, Horton's theoretical model for African conversion and an article defining the basic characteristics of a Central African religious tradition by Willy De Craemer, Jan Vansina, and Renée C. Fox have generated interest and discussion in some Americanist circles.[19] Without questioning the adequacy of these interpretations of African philosophies and religions, it does seem that the Americanist has problems in testing their adequacy for his or her purposes without a much greater knowledge of the data on which they are based. The "thick description" that is needed is beginning to emerge in the form of "texts" of African scriptures, prayers, songs, and proverbs of particular peoples. The transcriptions of Ifa verses by Bascom and by Wande Abimbola come readily to mind, as does the volume of ritual prayers of the Anlo collected by Christian R. Gaba.[20] Much more of this type of research needs to be done and published. No less than the sacred texts of other religions, the sacred texts of Africa, even though they be oral—all the more so since they are oral—ought to be collected and studied. Moreover, religious performance, its preservation (on record, film, and tape), its description, and its analysis ought to be a primary focus of researchers interested in African and Afro-American religions. On the Afro-American side, the same task awaits. Pierre Verger did admirable pioneering work in this vein by collecting texts and photographs of liturgical services in Bahia and Brazil.[21] Few have followed his example. Institutions such as the Institute of African Studies at the University of Ife are engaged in such research. There need to be closer ties between African and African diaspora scholars at the institutional level so that exchange may be facilitated. Within the Western Hemisphere as well, contact between colleagues from diverse Afro-American cultures should be more frequent and more regularized. With this type of collaboration, we might move toward a deeper understanding of that African diaspora in which we are involved as scholars and as persons.

NOTES

1. The estimates of slaves brought to the Americas are in Philip D. Curtin, *The Atlantic Slave Trade: A Census* (Madison: University of Wisconsin Press, 1969). He has been criticized for underestimating the size of the trade. See J. E. Inikori, "Measuring the Atlantic Slave Trade," *Journal of African History*, 17, 2 (1976):197–223. See also Herbert S. Klein, *The Middle Passage: Comparative Studies in the Atlantic Slave Trade* (Princeton, N.J.: Princeton University Press, 1978).

2. The literature on African religious influence in the Americas is immense. For Brazil: the classic studies are Nina Rodrigues, *O Animismo Fetichista dos Negros Bahianos* (Rio de Janeiro: Civilizacao Brasileira, 1935); Arthur Ramos, *O Negro Brasileiro*, vol. 1, *Ethnographia Religiosa*, 2d rev. ed. (Rio de Janeiro: Companhia Editora Nacinal, 1940); Edison Carneiro, *Candomblés da Bahia* (Rio de Janeiro: Tecnoprint Grafica, 1957); Roger Bastide, *Le Candomblé de Bahia: Culte Nago* (Paris and The Hague, 1958), *Les Religions Afro-Brésiliennes: Contribution à une Sociologie des Interpénétrations de Civilisations* (Paris: Presses Universitaires de France, 1960), trans. Helen Sebba, *The African Religions of Brazil: Toward a Sociology of the Interpenetration of Civilizations* (Baltimore and London: Johns Hopkins University Press, 1978); Pierre Verger, *Notes sur le Culte des Orisa et Vodun à Bahia la Baie de Tous le Saints, au Bresil et a l'Ancienne Côte des Esclaves en Afrique* (Dakar, Senegal: Memoires de l'Institut Francais d'Afrique Noire, No. 51, 1957). For Cuba: Fernando Ortiz, *Hampa Afro-Cubana: Los Negros Brujos* (Madrid: Editorial-America, 1906); Lydia Cabrera, *El Monte* (Havana: Ediciones CR, 1954). For Haiti: Alfred Metraux, *Voodoo in Haiti* (New York: Schocken Books, 1972); Melville J. Herskovits, *Life in a Haitian Valley* (New York: Alfred A. Knopf, 1937); Maya Deren, *Divine Horseman: The Living Gods of Haiti* (London and New York: Thames & Hudson, 1953). See also William Bascom, *Shango in the New World* (Austin: University of Texas, Occasional Publications, 1972); George Eaton Simpson, *Religious Cults of the Caribbean* (Rio Piedras, Puerto Rico: Institute of Caribbean Studies, University of Puerto Rico, 1970).

3. Melville J. Herskovits, *The Myth of the Negro Past* (Boston: Beacon Press, 1958), xxviii–xxix, 6–9, 15–17, 20–32.

4. See Sally and Richard Price's excellent analysis of "continuity-in-change" in *Afro-American Arts of the Suriname Rain Forest* (Berkeley, Los Angeles, and London: University of California Press, 1980), 204–15.

5. Franklin Frazier, *The Negro Church in America* (New York: Schocken Books, 1964), 1–19; *The Negro Family in the United States* (Chicago: University of Chicago Press, 1966), 3–16; *The Negro in the United States*, rev. ed. (New York: Macmillan, 1957), 3–13.

6. John Blassingame, *The Slave Community* (New York: Oxford University Press, 1972); *Slave Testimony: Two Centuries of Letters, Speeches, Interviews, and Autobiographies* (Baton Rouge: Louisiana State University Press, 1977); George P. Rawick, *The American Slave: A Composite Autobiography*, vol. I, *From Sundown to Sunup: The Making of the Black*

Community (Westport, Conn.: Greenwood, 1972); Eugene D. Genovese, *Roll Jordan, Roll: The World the Slaves Made* (New York: Pantheon, 1974); Lawrence Levine, *Black Culture and Black Consciousness* (New York: Oxford University Press, 1977); Albert J. Raboteau, *Slave Religion: The "Invisible Institution" in the Antebellum South* (New York: Oxford University Press, 1978); Mechal Sobel, *Trabelin' On: The Slave Journey to an Afro-Baptist Faith* (Westport, Conn.: Greenwood Press, 1978).

7. Melville J. Herskovits, *Dahomey: An Ancient West African Kingdom*, 2 vols. (Evanston, Ill.: Northwestern University Press, 1967); *New World Negro* (n.p., Minerva Press, Funk and Wagnalls, 1969); and Frances S. Herskovits, *Trinidad Village* (New York: Alfred A. Knopf, 1947).

8. In addition to the books mentioned, see also Carl Degler, *Neither Black Nor White: Slavery and Race Relations in Brazil and the United States* (New York: Macmillan, 1971).

9. Bastide, *African Religions of Brazil*, 114–25, 260–72.

10. Curtin, *Atlantic Slave Trade*, 88–89; C. Vann Woodward, "Southern Slaves in the World of Thomas Malthus," *American Counterpoint* (Boston: Little, Brown, & Co., 1971), 82–89.

11. Price and Price, 194–215; see also Richard Price, ed., *Maroon Societies: Rebel Slave Communities in the Americas* (Baltimore and London: Johns Hopkins University Press, 1979).

12. Bastide, *Religions Afro-Brésiliennes*, 64; Sidney Mintz and Richard Price, *An Anthropological Approach to the Afro-American Past: A Caribbean Perspective* (Philadelphia: Institute for the Study of Human Issues, 1976), 29; William Bascom, "Yoruba Acculturation in Cuba," *Les Afro-Americains* (Dakar: Mémoires de l'Institut Français d'Afrique Noire, No. 27, 1952), 166–67.

13. Price and Mintz, 4–11.

14. See, for example, Bastide, *African Religions of Brazil*, 67–72.

15. John F. Watson, *Methodist Error or Friendly Christian Advice to Those Methodists Who Indulge in Extravagant Emotions and Bodily Exercises* (Trenton, N.J., 1819), 28–31; see Raboteau, 58–73.

16. Charles Stearns, *Narrative of Henry Box Brown* (Boston: Brown and Stearns, 1849), 18.

17. Daniel Alexander Payne, *Recollections of Seventy Years* (1886; reprinted New York: Arno Press and the New York Times, 1969), 253–55.

18. See Raboteau, 65–87.

19. Placide Tempels, *Bantu Philosophy* (Paris: Présence Africaine, 1959); Robin Horton, "African Traditional Thought and Western Science," Part I, "From Tradition to Science," *Africa* 37, 1 (January 1967):50–71; Part II, "The 'Closed' and 'Open' Predicaments," *Africa* 37, 2 (April 1967):155–87; "On the Rationality of Conversion," Part I, *Africa* 45, 3 (1975):219– 35; Part II, *Africa* 45, 4 (1975):373–98; John S. Mbiti, *African Religions and Philosophy* (New York: Doubleday, 1970); Willy De Craemer, Jan Vansina, Renée C. Fox, "Religious Movements in Central Africa: A Theoretical Study," *Comparative Studies in Society and History* 18, 4 (October 1976):458–75; also influential: E. Bolaji Idowu, Olodumare, *God In Yoruba Belief* (London: Longmans, Green & Co., 1962); Geoffrey Parrinder, *West African Religion*, 2d ed. (New York: Barnes & Noble, 1970). See also Benjamin Ray, *African Religions: Symbol, Ritual, and Community* (Englewood Cliffs, N.J.: Prentice-Hall, 1976). For an intriguing application of Horton, De Craemer, et al., to analyze Jamaican Myalism, see Monica Schuler, *"Alas, Alas, Kongo": A Social History of Indentured African Immigration Into Jamaica, 1841–1865* (Baltimore and London: Johns Hopkins University Press, 1980) and "Afro-American Slave Culture," *Roots and Branches: Current Directions in Slave Studies* (Toronto: Pergamon Press, 1979), 121–37.

20. William Bascom, *Ifa Divination: Communication Between Gods and Men in West Africa* (Bloomington: Indiana University Press, 1969); *Sixteen Cowries: Yoruba Divination from Africa to the New World* (Bloomington and London: Indiana University Press, 1980); Wande Abimbola, *Ifa Divination Poetry* (New York, London, and Lagos: NOK Publishers, 1977); Christian R. Gaba, *Scriptures of An African People: The Sacred Utterances of the Anlo* (New York: NOK Publishers, 1973). Art historians, perhaps because of the material facticity of their discipline, have been much better at "thick description" than scholars in other fields. See, for example, Robert Farris Thompson, *Black Gods and Kings: Yoruba Art at UCLA*, Exhibition Catalogue (Los Angeles and Berkeley: University of California Press, 1971); *African Art in Motion* (Los Angeles and Berkeley: University of California Press, 1974); *For Spirits and Kings: African Art from the Paul and Ruth Tishman Collection*, ed. Susan Vogel (New York: The Metropolitan Museum of Art, 1981).
21. Verger, *Notes*; see also Michel S. Laguerre, *Voodoo Heritage*. Sage Library of Social Research, vol. 98 (Beverly Hills and London, 1980).

Settlement, Identity,
and Transformation

5
The Middle Passage and Personality Change Among Diaspora Africans

Okon Edet Uya

IN a contribution to *Global Dimensions of the African Diaspora* (Howard University Press, 1982), I emphasized the need for a conceptual approach that interprets Afro-American cultural history as the experiences of Africans transported to a New World environment.[1] One argument against this perspective insists that:

> slavery not only physically transplanted the Negro; it cut him off sharply from his cultural roots... and reduced him, so to speak, to a cultural zero.[2]

An important episode in this cultural effacement process, it has been argued, was the Middle Passage. This paper examines slave revolts of the Middle Passage to emphasize that the slaves' experiences during the Middle Passage did not obliterate their culture and humanity.

The explosion of interest in the history of black Americans in the last several years and the search by the black intellectual community for a usable past have contributed immensely to renewed scholarly interest in slave revolts as an index of a black revolutionary tradition. In the attempt to assess the impact of slavery accurately on the personality of black people under the "peculiar institution," scholars of different persuasions have come to see revolts among plantation slaves as a commentary on the humanity of the slaves despite the exigencies of a system that attempted to degrade them and reduce them to mere chattel.[3]

Although interest in revolts among slaves on the plantation has increased, there has been no corresponding attention paid to slave revolts of the Middle Passage. Stanley Elkins, who rescued the Atlantic slave trade and the Middle Passage from relative obscurity, promptly assigned the Middle Passage the dubious distinction of being one of the ultimate sources of psychic shock that combined with the "closed system" of the plantation to reduce black slaves to almost perpetual children. Other scholars have tended to focus attention only on the horrors of the Middle Passage, as demonstrated in the mortality rate in the ships as well as the demography of the slave trade itself.[4]

At first glance, the slave ship seems to offer less chance for a successful slave mutiny than the plantations of the Old South. If one considers the plantation system as a sort of minimal security prison with virtually every white southerner acting as unpaid guard to the permanently marked slave prisoners, the few revolts that were executed seem all the more remarkable. By comparison, a slave ship takes on all the characteristics of a floating Alcatraz or, as some contemporaries described it, a "floating coffin" (tumbeiros). While southern geography and climate militated against the kind of runaway slave communities that flourished in Brazil and elsewhere in the tropics, the ocean provided only the means for ultimate escape—suicide. Again, for the black field hand, because of the efficacy of his prison which was, in reality, the whole South, walls or chains were not needed for security. The slave ship even more effectively denied the captive an avenue of escape. Guards were scarce and always vastly outnumbered on the slavers; consequently, maximum security prevailed for all but a few— women, children, and occasionally the sick.

Stripped entirely naked, the slaves were packed into the stinking holds of the ships so close together that they were forced to sleep on their sides. With manacles on both their hands and feet, the slaves were then linked together by a continuous chain bolted to the floor. Most would spend the entirety of what was often a two- to three-month journey in this position. A few, depending on the mind or mood of the captain, would see the deck and daylight at mealtime or during other specified periods such as the torturously cruel exercise period when the slaves were made to dance in their heavy, cutting shackles.[5]

In the face of such security, a revolt or two would seem astounding; that there were literally hundreds seems incredible. The large number of suicides, mutinies, attempted risings, and other forms of resistance continues to confound historians as additional evidence continually forces upward revision of previous estimates. In 1937, Harvey Wish analyzed published data dealing almost exclusively with British slavers and found the incidence of mutiny for a 150-year period beginning in 1699 to be slightly less than two per year.[6] Wish's findings closely paralleled those of French historian Gaston Martin, whose study of the seaport Nantes, from 1714 to 1744, revealed that revolts occurred on an average of about one every fifteen trips, or just over one and a half per year.[7] Daniel Mannix found more than three hundred references to slave insurrections, including successful attempts by the natives to "cut off" departing slavers.[8] Contemporary evidence, primarily from ship captains and surgeons, corroborates this impressive, if somewhat dry, array of statistics. While they generally give no figures, their emphasis is always on the frequency of revolt. In 1788, Dr. Alexander Falconbridge, ship surgeon, noted that the slaves were "ever upon the watch to take advantage of the least negligence in their oppressors and that insurrections are frequently the consequence[,] which are seldom suppressed without much bloodshed."[9] Captain John Newton echoed Falconbridge both in his *Journal* and later in his perceptive and analytical "Thoughts Upon the African Slave Trade" (1788). Newton survived a half dozen plots to take over his ship during his second voyage to the African coast, not to mention an abortive mutiny by his own crew. The captain did not exaggerate when he affirmed in his log that "in the pursuit of my business, both on board and on shore, I was in deaths often." The slaves on board, he explained, "were . . . frequently plotting insurrections and were sometimes upon the very brink of mischief, but it was always disclosed in time."[10] At the end of that harrowing voyage, Newton wrote that he was "continually alarmed with their almost desperate attempts to make insurrections upon us . . . when most quiet they were always watching for opportunity."[11] Some thirty years later in the antislavery tract noted previously, Captain Newton, then a vigorous abolitionist minister, again commented on the "risk of insurrections." "Seldom a year passes," he claimed, "but we hear of one or more such catastrophes; and we likewise hear, sometimes of Whites and Blacks involved."[12] Hoping to make his indictment of the trade as convincing as possible, the captain then proceeded to measure the extent of insurrection in terms of English lives lost defending the ships:

> Few ships, comparatively, are either blown up, or totally cut off; but some are. Of the rest, I have known some that have lost half their people, and some a larger proportion. I am far from saying, that it is always, or even often thus; but, I believe I shall state the matter sufficiently low, if I suppose, that at least one-fifth part of those who go from England to the coast of Africa, in ships which trade for slaves, never return from hence.[13]

Newton deemed his estimate "to be very moderate," and given the fact that he was including only those revolts that resulted in actual loss of life, one can assume that the total attempted revolts were considerably higher. This, of course, ignores revolts that were crushed during the planning state or at their inception. Newton alone reported nearly a dozen such instances in only three voyages. In sum, black resistance during the Middle Passage was frequent and violent.

The motive behind any slave uprising should be obvious: a people deprived of their freedom will naturally seek to regain it as quickly as possible. Slave masters, in their attempt to justify the institution of slavery, have often denied this explanation and substituted a host of less fundamental but seemingly plausible reasons for slave insubordination and revolt. Historians, in turn, have often taken their testimony at face value, thereby compounding the error. Foremost among these rationalizations is the "good–bad master" dichotomy that places the responsibility for insurrection on the master's ignorance or cruelty in caring for his charges. Thus, excessive whipping, overwork, or poor food were seen as causes of slave insurrections, while strict but judicious discipline, realistic workloads, and adequate diet were looked on as equally good preventives.

Recent histories of the slave trade, based on a wholesale acceptance of testimony from slaver captains, indicate a similar trend. There were, according to these writings, good captains and bad captains, and revolts could be minimized by following certain time-tested guidelines. There were the arguments of the tight packers versus the loose packers, those who swore by ethnic mixing of cargoes, and others who relied on proper treatment of the slaves coupled with twenty-four-hour surveillance to curtail the incidence of revolt. In addition, we have been told that the prime motivating force behind the insurrections was the slaves' fear of being eaten by their captors. Less fantastic theories have also been proposed that relate the incidence of revolt to the proximity of ships to the African shoreline.

If slave captains and surgeons were unable to agree on the reasons for the numerous uprisings, the slaves themselves were less equivocal. Shortly after quelling a revolt on the *Henry* in 1721, Captain Snelgrave queried the subdued Cormantine leaders. When asked what had induced them to mutiny, they quickly responded that Snelgrave was "a great Rogue" to buy them in order to carry them away from their own country, and that they were resolved to gain their liberty if possible. Apparently unconvinced by their explanation, the captain asked them if they had been ill used by the white men, or had wanted for anything the ship afforded. They replied that they had nothing to complain of, but by Snelgrave's own account they were "plotting again and preparing to mutiny" within the week.[14] Few whites involved in the trade were as candid as this, but Dr. Falconbridge observed in 1788 that "very few of the Negroes can so far brook the loss of their liberty, and the hardships they endure, as to bear them with any patience."[15] Writing in the same year, Captain John Newton admitted publicly what every captain must have known and feared privately. "It is always taken for granted," he remarked, "that they will attempt to gain their liberty if possible." For Newton the explanation was simple. "When a hundred and fifty or two hundred stout men are [torn] from their native land[,] . . . it is not to be expected that they will tamely resign themselves to their situation."[16]

Clearly the roots of insurrection went deeper than diet, lash, or fear of being eaten by "those white men with horrible looks, red faces, and long hair."[17] Jean Barbot's contention that tight packing somehow caused more revolts holds true only if that practice was accompanied by a smaller crew and/or poorer surveillance. The sharp increase in the frequency of revolts in the eighteenth century, for example (to the point where profits actually suffered), was due not to tight packing but to the penny-pinching policy of independent traders. These shoestring operators, of whom New Englanders were the most notorious, attempted to shave overhead costs by reducing crew size and thereby trimming their security force.[18]

Many more captains relied on the practice of ethnically mixing their cargoes, reasoning that slaves who could not communicate with each other could not plan or execute a revolt. Obviously, the sheer number of mutinies alone indicates that common desires precluded the need for a common tongue. It would also seem that given such desire, a revolt could be executed with a minimum of hand signals, facial expressions, and so on. Others claimed that the "temper" of certain "tribes" made them more or less suited to slavery and consequently more or less prone to rebellion. But opinions differed, and one man's docile slave was another's mutineer. Thus, Captain Snelgrave laid the blame for his mutiny-plagued second voyage on the Cormantine, a Gold Coast (Ghanaian) "tribe," while Captain Canot held that "tribes" east of the Cape and north of Ghana were more likely to revolt than those of Angola, Benin, or Anguda. Canot no doubt revised his thinking on this matter after putting down a revolt of supposedly docile Anguda aboard the *La Estrella*.[19] Again, security was probably the hidden factor behind such analyses of African "temper." When a captain had good luck with a certain group or mixture of groups, he probably continued to obtain cargoes of similar ethnic composition in order to duplicate his former success. The repeated absence of mutiny was then attributed to the selection process itself rather than to successful security measures, and the advice was then passed along. There were no doubt many others who, like Canot, "could never account" for the mutinies.

In the final analysis, the frequency of revolt depended largely on the ability of the captain and crew to maintain tight surveillance of up to seven hundred captives as well as on the slaves' determination and ability to find a loophole in that security system. Either way, it was a deadly contest of tactics and countertactics: chains, irons, whips, and guns pitted against stamina and ingenuity.

The concern over security matters began with the owners of slavers, who naturally stood to lose the most financially from a revolt, and extended down to the lowest deckhand, whose life depended on a safe passage. In 1625, Isaac Hobhouse and Company, Bristol-based owners of *Dispatch*, issued detailed instructions to Captain William Barry, emphasizing the importance of "a Constant and Careful watch... for the preservation of their Own Lives [the slaves], as well as yours." The captain was advised to "keep'em shackled and hand bolted (so soon as you begin to slave)" and to fix a netting "breast high fore and aft" to prevent their "rising or leaping overboard." Barry was further cautioned that sailors "sleeping in their Watch has [sic] often been fatal and many a good Voyage (which otherwise might [have] been made) entirely ruined."[20]

Security did not slacken once these initial precautions were completed, however, and the "Constant and Careful watch" was taken literally. Captain Jean Barbot claimed that his elaborate security measures, which included armed sentinels placed in the quarterdeck, gun room, and "great cabin" as well as on the "avenues to it," were so successful in keeping the slaves "in awe" that he "did not perceive the least inclination in any of them to revolt, or mutiny."[21] Barbot's captives may have been awed by this ever present display of firearms, but their escape attempts were more likely stymied by another of the shrewd captain's practices:

> We use [sic] to visit them daily, narrowly searching every corner between decks, to see whether they had not found means, to gather any pieces of iron, or wood, or knives, about the ship, not withstanding the great care we take not to leave any tools or nails, or other things in the way; which however, cannot always be exactly observ'd, where so many people are in the narrow compass of a ship.[22]

Barbot's record is exceptional, as were his security precautions. There may indeed have been a kernel of truth in his boast that "if all those who carry slaves duly observ'd them [his precautions], we should not hear of so many revolts as have happen'd."[23] Incidently, Barbot never personally witnessed a revolt during his lifetime.

Others, no doubt, mimicked Barbot's methods, but few achieved his results. Sailors were recruited to run ships not to guard slaves, and they resented, sometimes to the point of mutiny, the extra work that the human cargoes demanded. Such an attitude often resulted in lax security.

Most historians of the slave trade have maintained that mutinies occurred only during the loading process or while the ships were within sight of the African coast.[24] This assertion is based on the assumption that the slaves were stranded once the ships were at sea because of their unfamiliarity with the instruments and techniques of navigation. Many slaves from the African interior, they remind us, had never seen the ocean, let alone a compass or astrolabe. Although there is some evidence to support the argument that slaves revolted only "while they had a Shore to fly to,"[25] most contemporary observers thought otherwise. Most mutinies were neither haphazard nor spontaneous events, but were, in the words of firsthand observer John Newton, "always meditated."[26] Their success, therefore, depended on the slaves' ability to weigh the factors involved and pragmatically determine the best time, place, and tactics for revolt.

Apparently, more revolts occurred on or near the shore, for it was at this time that white manpower was at its lowest level. Typical of the onshore mutiny was one witnessed by William Snelgrave aboard his father's ship, the *Eagle*, in 1704. "At the time of their mutinying," he wrote, "we were in that River, having four hundred of them on board, and not above ten white Men who were able to do Service."[27] Lack of manpower was characteristic of this phase of the slaving operation:

> For several of our Ships' Company were dead, and many more sick; besides, two of our Boats were just then gone with 12 People on Shore to fetch Wood, which lay in sight of the Ship.[28]

Similarly, "most of the crew of twelve were ill when the Sixty Africans on board the ship *Ann* got to the Powder and Arms, and about three O'Clock in the Morning, rose upon the Whites."[29]

The massacre at Old Calabar in 1767 provides another clue as to why the onshore revolt was favored over revolts at sea and why it was more often successful. An account of that uprising in a Liverpool newspaper stressed that the one hundred and thirty-two slaves on board the *Nancy* rose up on a crew whose ranks had been reduced to five by African fever:

> As soon as the natives on shore heard the report of the guns, great numbers of them came off in canoes, and surrounded the vessel, and finding her weakly manned . . . immediately boarded her, took away all the slaves, . . . plundered the vessel of everything on board . . . [and] afterwards split the decks, cut the cables, and set the vessel adrift.[30]

If anything, the slaves' desire for freedom must have increased as the ships sailed farther from the African coast. Thoughts of lost family, friends, and freedom combined with the sweltering stench of the filthy holds to produce a variety of reactions. Olaudah Equiano recalled that he "became so sick and low that [he] was not able to eat, nor had [he] the least desire to taste anything. [He] now wished for the last friend, death to relieve [him]."[31] Others, suffering from similar symptoms, called fixed melancholy by those in the trade, succeeded in meeting Equiano's "last friend" by jumping overboard or through some other suicidal act. Some died of disease, and some were killed for the slightest provocation, as in the case of the woman whose baby's cries had awakened a sleeping sailor.[32] Without doubt, a full crew made mutiny at sea more difficult than on shore, but, as John Atkins duly observed, "There has not been wanting Examples of rising and killing a Ship's Company, distant from Land."[33] Indeed, instances of mutiny have been documented at all stages of the Middle Passage: "four or five days out from Senegal"; "the ninth day out" of Cameroons; "ten days [from] the coast of Guinea"; "100 leagues from the coast"; "three weeks" out of Ayudah; a week from Bermuda; "in sight of the Island Guardaloupe [sic]"; and finally "twice ... before the Sale of them began."[34]

The actual planning and execution of a revolt was, to borrow the word of a contemporary, "ingenious." The spontaneous uprising was rare and generally quickly suppressed. One such revolt aboard the American slaver Nancy in 1807 reveals the futility of such desperate ventures:

> ... as the slaves were messing together one afternoon, the males and females apart, one of the males seized the master as he was pouring molasses into his victuals, whereupon the rest of the males rose and tried to seize Captain Viall, but he escaped from their clutches and with the aid of the crew drove the blacks below after small arms had been given out.[35]

The more typical revolt was planned below decks by one or more leaders; frequently involved a slave, who for some reason had access to the upper decks; and generally had at least one definite objective such as the gaining of the small arms storeroom or weapons chest. There are, unfortunately, no narratives by leaders of these slave rebellions comparable to the Nat Turner's Confessions. Ship captains, however, prided themselves on their ability to recognize and single out for punishment those slaves who had planned or managed revolts. Penalties ranged from whippings to execution, and while the former method was preferred for obvious monetary reasons, the latter was often used to "prevent further Mischiefs."[36] A tribunal of ship commanders recommended the death penalty when Captain Snelgrave presented them with a confession from an insurrectionary, reassuring him that "by publicly executing this Person at the Ship's Fore-Yard Arm, the Negroes on board their Ships would see it; and as they were very much disposed to mutiny, it might prevent them from attempting it."[37] Snelgrave took their advice, and the slave, who had murdered the ship's cooper with a hatchet at the inception of the revolt, was tied to the yardarm, shot to death by ten musketeers, then cut down, decapitated, and thrown overboard. The desired effect was apparently achieved, for the captain later reported that "this struck a sudden Damp upon our Negro-Men, who thought, that, on account of my Profit, I would not have executed him."[38]

The success of most mutinies depended, first, on the slaves' ability to rid themselves of their shackles and chains. Occasionally, a careless crew member provided the means to that end. For example, when one of Captain William Bosman's crew made the mistake of storing a discarded anchor as an anvil, the slaves pounded off their irons and attempted to gain possession of the boat, which they would have done had not Bosman received aid from a nearby English merchantman.[39] More often, the slaves relied on fellow Africans to supply them with tools and weapons. John Newton was spared a mutiny late in his first voyage when a sailor saw "a young man, who has been the whole voyage out of irons, first on account of a large ulcer, and since for his seeming good behaviour, g[i]ve them a large marline spike down the gratings."[40] Twenty slaves freed themselves in the hour before the spike was found.

This key role was most often performed by women, as they were frequently allowed to roam the upper decks unencumbered by chains or shackles. Tomba's revolt, recorded by John Atkins, owed its brief life to an unknown female slave. According to the surgeon, "She brought him [Tomba] word one night that there were no more than five white Men upon the Deck, and they asleep, bringing him a hammer at the same time [and] (all the weapons that she could find) to execute the Treachery."[41] Able to induce only the woman and another male slave to join him, Tomba was soon defeated in the scuffle following his murder of three crew members. The leader received a "Rogues of Dignity" sentence and was whipped, while the anonymous woman was "hoisted up by the Thumbs, whipp'd, and slashed...with knives, before the other slaves till she die[d]."[42] A quick-thinking group of slave women also made possible the dramatic seizure of the *Thomas* in 1797, only days from its destination in Barbados. Discovering that the armor chest had been carelessly left unlocked, they rifled the chest and slipped several armloads of light weapons through the bulkheads to the men below. Most of the officers and crew were either killed or driven overboard with the exception of a half dozen who were retained to guide the ship back to Africa. The slaves' triumph was short-lived, however. Forty-two days after the mutiny, the *Thomas* was recaptured by H. M. Frigate *Thames* and sold at Cape Nicola Mole.[43] In addition, women were often found in the thick of battle once an insurrection had begun. Captain Canot, recounting the uprising aboard the *La Estrella*, noted that "the women in the cabin were not idle. Seconding the male, they rose in a body, and the helmsman was forced to stab several with his knife before he could drive them below again."[44]

The timing of a revolt also determined its success or failure. The onshore revolts described above most often took place when sickness and recruiting duties had made the ship's crews skeletal. At sea, a variety of times were preferred. The revolt aboard the *Thomas* occurred while the crew was at breakfast. The slaves aboard the *La Estrella* rose up on Captain Canot and his distracted crew "as the boatswain's whistle piped all hands to take in sail . . . amid the risk and turmoil of a West Indian squall."[45] There were few moments as tailor-made for revolt as the following reported in the *Boston News Letter*. Finding himself critically shorthanded owing to the sickness of a large part of the crew, Captain Hopkins "was forced to fill the vacancies with able-bodied slaves who promptly released their brothers and attacked the crew."[46] Revolts were most often precipitated at night when the slaves could count on a sleeping crew and dozing guards to facilitate their plans. Captain Barry had, in fact, received sound advice from his owners: "Persons sleeping in their watch . . . [had often] entirely ruin'd . . . many a good voyage" including two of William Snelgrave's,[47] one of Benjamen Clark's,[48] one of Captain Harding's,[49] and one of Captain Williams's,[50] to name only a few.

To list instances of the slaves' ingenuity in trying to free themselves would fill pages. They feigned docility and contentment only to rise on their unsuspecting captors, as on the *La Estrella* where Captain Canot reported that, immediately prior to their rising, "there was so much merriment among the gangs that were allowed to come on deck, that my apprehensions of danger began gradually to wear away."[51] They continually cajoled and outwitted the befuddled crews. Snelgrave asserted that one group of "ringleaders" offered themselves as lifelong servants to one of his black linguists "if he could procure them an ax."[52] One enterprising group play-acted their way right into the captain's cabin. Hamilton Montgomery, one of the few white survivors aboard the *King David*, reported that story to one captain Tarr, who eventually related it to the editor of the *Boston News Letter*:

> The Insurrection was contrived and begun by 15 that had for a considerable time been treated with the same Freedom as the white men, a great many of the latter dying, and encouraged them in the Design. As the Chief of these Slaves spoke very good English, he often convers'd with the Captain in his Cabin, where all the Arms were loaded; and consulting with his Comrades, knowing the small strength of the white men, they at once flew into the Cabin, and secured the Arms in a few minutes, kill'd the Captain and five of the People.[53]

Assessing the ultimate impact of revolts like those described above is a much harder task than bringing them to light and describing their internal dynamics. To judge them by the relatively high failure rate (few of the millions involved escaped slavery in the end) is a futile exercise with little historical value. Nor is there much to be gained by viewing the revolts as individual acts of black ingenuity and courage, although at bottom they certainly were that. It is more important that the Middle Passage be seen as a collective experience. As historian Bryan Edwards observed:

> The Negroes in general are strongly attached to their countrymen, but above all to such of their companions as came in the same ship with them from Africa. This is a striking circumstance; the term ship-mate is understood among them as signifying a relationship of the most enduring nature.[54]

Indeed, a striking feature of the Middle Passage was the development of new ties of kinship during that cruel journey. The common circumstances of the ship led slaves to develop strong attachments to each other regardless of ethnic origin, lineage, or language. This kinship, variously described as *shipmate* in Jamaica, *sippi* in Surinam, *mulongo* in Brazil, *malongue* in Trinidad, and *batiment* in Haiti was not dissimilar to the territorially defined kinship that was widely practiced in Africa. *Shipmate* became synonymous with "brother" and "sister." Orlando Patterson has commented that "so strong were the bond[s] between shipmates [in Jamaica] that sexual intercourse between them was considered incestuous." Shipmates on the plantations "looked upon each other's children mutually as their own." Children called their parents' shipmates "uncle" and "aunt."[55] In Surinam, *sippi*, initially used among those who shared the Middle Passage experience in the same vessel, was later used to describe slaves on the same plantation. Sentiments such as shipmateship softened the harshness of the Middle Passage. The following account by Captain J. G. Stedman cited by Sydney Mintz and

Richard Price demonstrates the significance of such ties for the enslaved African: "All the slaves," Stedman reported, "are led upon the deck ... their hair shaved in different figures of stars, half-moons, etc. which they generally do the one to the other, by the help of a broken bottle and without soap."[56] Mintz and Price themselves comment, "It is hard to imagine a more impressive example of irrepressible cultural vitality than this image of slaves decorating one another's hair in the midst of one of the most dehumanizing experiences in all of history."[57]

The evidence presented here raises serious doubts concerning the validity of Elkins's "psychological" interpretation. The methods and frequency of resistance contradict the notion that the Middle Passage contained one of the earliest of a long series of psychological "shocks" that eventually resulted in making the plantation slave into Sambo. The trip was unquestionably a jarring and brutal experience, both physically and emotionally, and different personalities exhibited different reactions. A few committed suicide; many contemplated it; and an even larger number, probably the majority, strove mightily at the daily task of "keeping themselves together and maintaining a sense of individual and collective identity."[58]

The examples cited in this paper clearly illustrate that the Middle Passage cannot be written off as the beginning of a process that numbed the black slaves' minds and bodies, as Elkins and others would have us believe. Nor is it enough merely to indicate the brutalities meted out to the slaves by ship captains and their crew. Rather, the revolts of the Middle Passage clearly represented conscious intelligent solutions to the familiar problem of survival in an environment that presented few other meaningful alternatives. Rather than acting as a cultural obliterator, the Middle Passage was clearly a bridge through which enslaved Africans found their way into the New World. There is, indeed, nothing in the evidence presented here to suggest that they arrived in their new environment as subhumans, culturally or mentally. As Roger Bastide concluded some years ago:

> The slave ships carried not only men, women and children but also their gods, beliefs, and traditional folklore.[59]

NOTES

1. Okon Edet Uya, "Conceptualizing Afro-American/African Relations: Implications for African Diaspora Studies," in *Global Dimensions of the African Diaspora*, ed. Joseph Harris (Washington, D.C.: Howard University Press, 1982).
2. Alain Locke, *Negro Art: Past and Present* (1936; reprinted New York: Arno Press and the New York Times, 1969).

3. See, for example, Herbert Aptheker, *Nat Turner's Slave Rebellion* (New York: Grove Press, 1966); John Lofton, *Insurrection in South Carolina: The Turbulent World of Denmark Vesey* (Yellow Springs, Ohio: Antioch Press, 1964).

4. Stanley Elkins, *Slavery: A Problem in American Institutional and Intellectual Life* (Chicago: University of Chicago Press, 1959, 1968); Daniel Mannix and Malcolm Cowley, *Black Cargoes: A History of The Atlantic Slave Trade* (New York: Viking Press, 1962); Herbert S. Klein, *The Middle Passage* (Princeton, N.J.: Princeton University Press, 1978); Philip D. Curtin, *Atlantic Slave Trade: A Census* (Madison: University of Wisconsin Press, 1969).

5. See Mannix and Cowley, *Black Cargoes*, especially pp. 113– 17, 121–24. For a contemporary description of the brutalities of the Middle Passage, see *Captain Canot; or Twenty Years of an African Slaver*, ed. Brantz Mayer (1854; reprinted New York: Arno Press and the New York Times, 1968), 102–8.

6. Harvey Wish, "American Slave Insurrections before 1861," *Journal of Negro History*, 22 (1937): 303.

7. Gaston Martin, *Nantes au XVIIIᵉ siècle: l'ere, des Negriers (1714–1744), d'apres des documents inedits* (Paris, 1931), quoted in C. L. R. James, "The Atlantic Slave Trade and Slavery: Some Interpretations of Their Significance in the Development of the United States and the Western World," *Amistad*, ed. John A. Williams and Charles F. Harris (New York: Vintage Books, 1970), 126–27.

8. Mannix and Cowley, *Black Cargoes*, 111.

9. Alexander Falconbridge, "An Account of the Slave Trade on the Coast of Africa," *Economic Pamphlets* (London: J. Phillips. George Yard, Lombard Street, 1788), 30.

10. Newton's remarks are quoted in Gomer Williams, *History of the Liverpool Privateers and Letters of Marque with an Account of the Liverpool Slave Trade* (London, 1897), 511.

11. Bernard Martin and Mark Spurrell, eds., *The Journal of a Slave Trader (John Newton) 1750–1754, with Newton's Thoughts upon the African Slave Trade* (London: The Epworth Press, 1962), 101.

12. Ibid., 102.

13. Ibid.

14. Elizabeth Donnan, *Documents Illustrative of the History of the Slave Trade to America* (Washington, D.C.: Carnegie Institute of Washington, 1935; reprinted New York: Octagon Books, 1965), 11: 354–55.

15. Falconbridge, "An Account of the Slave Trade," 30–32.

16. For Newton's comments, see Martin and Spurrell, *Journal of a Slave Trader*, 103.

17. Judicious use of the lash together with proper care in general are cited by many captains as being conducive to a peaceful voyage but are usually listed along with more believable descriptions of tight security. Captain Snelgrave lists both in Donnan, *Documents*, IV: 354, while Captain Barbot emphasizes the latter in his *Description of the Coasts of North and South Guinea* (London, 1732), 546. The slaves' fear of cannibalism was a real (if only temporary) one as Olaudah Equino's narrative illustrates. See Philip D. Curtin, *Africa Remembered: Narratives by West Africans from the Era of the Slave Trade* (Madison: University of Wisconsin Press, 1967), 92–93. Convincing the slaves that they were to be a labor force and not a supplement to the white man's diet was a job that usually fell to the ship's (black) interpreter. If the slaves doubted his word, there is nothing in the records to prove it.

18. See Donnan, *Documents*, II: xlii, 361n, 431n.

19. For Snelgrave's view see Donnan, *Documents*, II: 354; for Fanot's see Mayers, ed., *Captain Canot*, 272–75.

20 Captain Barry's instructions may be found in Donnan, *Documents*, II: 327–29.

21. Barbot, *Description of the Coasts*, 546.

22. Ibid.

23. Ibid.

24. Hennessy, Mannix, and James all suggest this. See James Pope– Hennessy, *Sins of the Fathers: A Study of the Atlantic Slave Traders 1441–1807* (New York: Knopf 1968), 186; Mannix and Cowley, *Black Cargoes*, 108; and C. L. R. James, "The Atlantic Slave Trade and Slavery," 126–29. These writers were no doubt influenced by an observation of John Newton who once recorded that his slaves "entirely changed their tempers" as the voyage progressed. "I was at first continually alarmed by their almost desperate attempts to make insurrections upon us.... However, from about the end of February they have behaved more like children in one family, than slaves in chains and irons." See Martin and Spurrell, *Journal of a Slave Trader*, 80.

25. The comment is John Atkins's, an eighteenth-century surgeon in the Royal Navy, and is quoted from his "Voyage to Guinea" in Donnan, *Documents*, II: 266. Another who shared his opinion was Thomas Phillips, whose *Journal* is quoted in Mannix and Cowley, *Black Cargoes*, 108.

26. See Newton's "Thoughts upon the African Slave Trade," in Martin and Spurrell, *Journal of a Slave Trader*, 102.

27. See William Snelgrave's "Account of Some Parts of Guinea" (London, 1734), in Donnan, *Documents*, II: 354.

28. Ibid.

29. Item in the *Boston Post Boy*, 13 August 1750, quoted in Donnan, *Documents*, II: 485–86.

30. The newspaper account is quoted in Gomer Williams, *History of the Slave Trade*, 549. For other examples of onshore revolts see Mannix and Cowley, *Black Cargoes*, 109, 158; Donnan, *Documents*, II: 232; Williams, *History of Slave Trade*, 492. After quelling a revolt at sea, Captain Newton remarked that he was thankful it had not been attempted on the coast when "we had often 7 or 8 of our best men out of the ship at a time and the rest busy." See his *Journal*, 55.

31. Curtin, *Africa Remembered*, 93.

32. For a discussion of "fixed melancholy" and suicide, see Falconbridge, "An Account of the Slave Trade," 31; Williams, *History of Slave Trade*, 533, 568, 588–89; Mannix and Cowley, *Black Cargoes*, 117–21.

33. Donnan, *Documents*, II: 281–82.

34. Details of these mutinies can be found in George Francis Dow, *Slave Ships and Slaving* (Salem, Mass.: Marine Research Society, 1927), 207, 272, 360; Williams, *History of the Slave Trade*, 480, 493; Mayer, *Captain Canot*, 272; Donnan, *Documents*, II: 361, 485.

35. Dow, *Slave Ships and Slaving*, 272.

36. For example, see ibid., 84; Hennessy, *Sins of the Fathers*, 79; and Donnan, *Documents* II: 83, 354–55, 338–59, 486.

37. Dow, *Slave Ships Slaving*, 358.

38. Ibid., 358–59. For other examples of barbarous punishment (including a case in which a slave was forced to eat the heart and brain of a co-conspirator before his own execution), see Donnan, *Documents*, II: 266.

39. William Bosman, *A New and Accurate Description of the Coast of Guinea* (London, 1705), quoted in Hennessy, *Sins of the Fathers*, 79.

40. Martin and Spurrell, *Journal of a Slave Trader*, 54–55.

41. John Atkins, *A Voyage to Guinea*, quoted in Donnan, *Documents*, II: 266. John Newton, for one, claimed that "from the women there is no danger of insurrection," although he admitted that he was not speaking "universally."

42. Ibid.

43. Gomer Williams details the mutiny aboard the *Thomas* in *History of the Slave Trade*, 592–93.

44. Mayer, *Captain Canot*, 273.
45. Ibid., 273, 275; Williams, *History of the Slave Trade*, 592.
46. Hennessy quotes the story from the Boston paper in *Sins of the Fathers*, 234. A similar incident in which the slaves aboard the *Brookes* were armed to fight off an American privateer and did not revolt is narrated in Williams, *History of the Slave Trade*, 560–61. Captain Hopkins's foolish move is rivaled by a similar mistake of James Barbot. The latter issued knives to his slaves at mealtime only to have them rise on the crew three days later. See his *Description of the Coast*, quoted in Dow, *Slave Ships and Slaving*.
47. Ibid., 121. Donnan, *Documents*, II: 357.
48. Donnan, *Documents*, III: 486.
49. Ibid., 266.
50. Dow, *Slave Ships and Slaving*, 175.
51. Mayer, *Captain Canot*, 272.
52. Donnan, *Documents*, II: 355.
53. Ibid., 486, quoted from the *Boston News Letter*, 6 September 1750.
54. Quoted in Hennessy, *Sins of the Fathers*.
55. Orlando Patterson, *Sociology of Slavery* (London: Maggibou and Kee Ltd., 1967), 150, 163–64.
56. *An Anthropological Approach to the Afro-American Past: A Caribbean Perspective* (Philadelphia: Institute for the Study of Human Issues, 1976).
57. Ibid., 25.
58. For details see my article, "Life in the Slave Community," *Afro-American Studies*, 1, 3 (1971). See also Eugene Genovese, "American Slaves and Their History," *New York Review of Books* (3 December 1970) and *Roll Jordan Roll: The World the Slaves Made* (New York: Random House, 1974); John Blassingame, *The Slave Community: Plantation Life in the Antebellum South* (New York: Oxford University Press, 1972); and Lawrence W. Levine, *Black Culture and Black Consciousness: Afro-American Thought from Slavery to Freedom* (New York: Oxford University Press, 1977).
59. Roger Bastide, *African Civilizations in the New World* (London: C. Hurst and Company, 1967), 23.

6
African Culture and Slavery in the United States

Lawrence W. Levine

A NUMBER of assumptions have rendered it diffi-cult, until very recently, to seriously pursue and understand the role that African culture has played in the development of thought and society in the United States.

The first of these assumptions is that political and economic subordi-nation leads inevitably to cultural emasculation. The subordinate groups, according to this dictum, become a tabula rasa on which their political and economic superiors can engrave what they will.[1] This tendency to equate political and economic subordination with rapid deculturation has structured scholars' treatments of other groups in America as well, especially the new immigrant groups from eastern and southern Europe and from Asia. But in no instance was their cultural erosion seen to be as thorough as that of the Africans. "Other peoples," the sociologist Robert E. Park wrote, "have lost...much of their cultural heritage. None has been so utterly cut off and estranged from their ancestral land, traditions and people."[2]

At the heart of the belief that the Africans thoroughly lost their culture was the assumption that one could arrange cultures in a neat hierarchy with western Europe at the top and Africa at the bottom. The history of music, Frederick Root told the 1893 International Folk-Lore Congress, was a development "from the formless and untutored sounds of savage people to the refined utterances of our highest civilization." Cultural diffusion, therefore, could proceed in only one irreversible direction: from the top to the bottom, from white to black. Guided by these comfortable evolutionary predispositions, scholars attributed al-

99

most every aspect of Afro-American culture to the influence of Euro-Americans. Distinctive patterns of black speech, for example, even the Gullah and Geechee dialects of the South Carolina and Georgia coasts, were devoid of African linguistic influences. Rather, black speech was "frozen Elizabethan English," the product of the "slovenly and careless" speech that was "the natural result of a savage and primitive people's endeavor to acquire for themselves the highly organized language of a very highly civilized race."[3]

Africa could be so readily excluded from any cultural influence because of still another pervasive assumption. It was believed that the peoples of Africa came from societies marked by a wide variety of languages, religions, customs, and institutions, making it impossible for them to maintain their traditional cultures when they were mixed together indiscriminately in the United States.[4]

These views, in various combinations, affected American scholarship from Emancipation until the mid-twentieth century. They were by no means monolithic, and there were important dissenting voices, especially those of W. E. B. Du Bois and Melville Herskovits. But it has not been until the last decade that important breakthroughs have been made on a wide front. Scholars have come to understand that for all the culturally disintegrating forces present in the United States, there were also factors conducive to the perpetuation of aspects of African culture.

The same environmental conditions that helped to maintain African cultural patterns in the Caribbean and South America were at work in parts of the United States as well. Africans brought with them highly developed agricultural technologies that were far more relevant to the ecology of the Southern colonies than were those of the Europeans. Thus, in South Carolina the stereotype of black dependency on whites was reversed. It was to the Africans that the Europeans looked for advice on the cultivation of rice, indigo, and cotton; the use of such indigenous plants as gourds and the palmetto; and knowledge of the medicinal properties of wild plants, herbs, and roots that either duplicated or resembled those that slaves had been familiar with in Africa. It was the Africans, not the Europeans, who knew how to deal with such native wildlife as the alligator and who had the experience necessary to develop the dugout canoe as the prime means of fishing and transportation.[5]

In addition to economic and environmental factors, there were attitudinal forces working for the continuation of African culture. Whites had an unconscious vested interest in seeing their slaves maintain much of their cultural distinctiveness, since it was far more difficult to justify the enslavement of a kindred folk than of a people whose behavior patterns were sufficiently different to allow one to apply such commonly used epithets as "primitive," "barbaric," "childlike." This was at the root of the protracted controversy over whether the slaves should be converted to Christianity. And long after a substantial percentage of slaves were converted, the whites were often content to see them develop and continue their own forms of religious worship. Charles C. Jones, who devoted much of his life to the conversion of the slaves, admitted in 1842 that those among whom he was spreading the Gospel still "believe in second-sight, in apparitions, charms, witchcraft.... The superstitions brought from Africa have not been wholly laid aside."[6]

This situation, which so pained Jones and his fellow ministers, was far less troubling to many masters who used it to justify their stereotype of uncivilized Africans. "We don't care what they do when their tasks are over," a rice planter asserted in 1828. "We lose sight of them till next day. Their morals and manners are in their own keeping."[7] Thus, slave dancing, with its openly African style of gliding, dragging steps, flexed, fluid bodily position, propulsive rhythm, and concentration on movement outward from the pelvic region, which whites found lewd, was decried by ministers but tolerated and even encouraged by a substantial number of masters.[8]

The reluctance of whites to fully acculturate their slaves was, of course, communicated to the slaves in myriad ways. "I was once whipped," a freedman testified shortly after the Civil War, "because I said to missis, 'My mother sent me.' We were not allowed to call our mammies 'mother.' It made it come too near the way of the white folks."[9] Such attitudes not only allowed slaves to develop their own culture but often enhanced that development. While slave culture was in continual interaction with the white cultures surrounding it, slaves understood that the world of whites, attractive as it might appear at times, offered little but the certainty of arbitrary and perpetual bondage. This understanding threw slaves back on their own cultural world in which the peer group and role models—the significant others—remained black. In slavery, the surest way of attaining those things that would alter life positively, short of escape or rebellion, was not through mindless acculturation to the ways of the whites but through Afro-American culture with its comforting precedents and promises, its strategies and alternative sources of power. It was not until Emancipation and the invasion of the South by five thousand Northern school teachers anxious to prove their long-standing belief that blacks were as inherently capable of freedom as whites, that slaves were exhorted in a massive way to turn their backs on the past and their traditional ways of thought and action. "Our work," one of these teachers wrote, "is just as much a missionary work as if we were in India or China."[10] That this messianic impulse to totally change the traditional ways of blacks had

been largely absent in the slave South helps to explain the distinctiveness and continuity that marked slave culture.

 Finally, and perhaps most important, in this catalog of factors conducive to cultural continuity among Africans and their descendants was
the perpetuation of oral culture in slavery. Historians still have not fully
understood the structural relationship between the slaves' preliterate
world and the culture they created. The Africans from whom the slaves
had descended lived in a world of sound; a world in which the spoken,
chanted, sung, or shouted word was the primary form of communication. This world of sound contrasts dramatically with the world of
vision characteristic of literate Western European cultures in which
ideas are held to be distinct from behavior and verbal thought is
separable from action. In nonliterate societies, such distinctions are not
made. Ideas and words are seen as part of the same reality as the events
to which they refer; words are powerful parts of the real world in their
own right.

It is because they came from such societies, and were not inducted
into the literate world of their white masters, that slaves invested their
songs, tales, and the spoken word in general with the same central
importance they enjoyed in Africa. Their world remained a world of
sound in which words were actions. To speak or sing of the heroes and
exploits of the Old Testament, to relate orally the events that occurred in
dreams or visions, was to give them a substance, a reality, to make them
literally come alive. To learn of the past through the personally related
spoken word was to give the past a contemporary, personal significance
missing from the more compartmentalized sense of time characteristic
of literate societies in which knowledge of the past is derived largely
from the more abstract and detached printed page.[11]

If one is to understand the distinctiveness of slave religion, it is
crucial to understand the intimate relationship between the world of
sound and the world of sacred time and space in which there were no
clear lines between the past and the present, between the sacred and the
secular.[12] This was a world common to the traditional societies of
Africa, and it remained common to the societies created by slaves in the
United States. If the slaves had lost many of the specific religious
ceremonies and almost all of the gods they had known in Africa, they
retained an African world view that became embedded in their form of
Christianity. The God the slaves sang of was neither remote nor abstract
but was as intimate, personal, and immediate as the gods of Africa had
been: "O when I talk I talk wid God," "Mass Jesus is my bosom friend,"
"I'm goin' to walk with [talk with, live with, see] King Jesus by myself,
by myself." The heroes of the Scriptures—"Sister Mary," "Brudder
Jonah," "Brudder Moses," "Brudder Daniel"—were greeted with simi-

lar intimacy and immediacy. In their conversions and ceremonies, slaves often actually saw and conversed with their God. In their counterclockwise religious dance, the "ring about," ecstatic dancers were transformed into participants in historic actions: Joshua's army marching around the walls of Jericho, the children of Israel following Moses out of Egypt. In their songs, such events as the Crucifixion and the Day of Judgment were described with a poetic intensity that transformed singers and listeners into participants: "You'll see de world on fire... see de element a meltin',... see the stars a fallin'... see the moon a bleedin'... see the forked lightning.... Hear the rumblin' thunder... see the righteous marching... see my Jesus coming."

In their varied network of religious folk beliefs, too, slaves perpetuated much of the cosmology that had characterized the African cultures from which they had come. Humans were conceived as part of, not alien to, the Natural Order, attached to the Oneness that bound together all matter, animate and inanimate, all spirits, visible or not. It was necessary to understand the world because one was inexorably linked to it. Thus, survival, happiness, and health depended on being able to read the signs that existed everywhere in the natural world, to understand the visions that recurrently visited one, to commune with the spirits that filled the world.[13]

This discussion of world view helps us to identify a methodological fallacy that has for too long bedeviled scholarship: the preoccupation with the problem of origins. A great deal of energy has been invested in the question of whether a specific song, tale, folk belief, or behavioral practice can be traced directly back to Africa. This question, while interesting and often relevant, has also been misleading and has tended to mask the extent to which African cultural patterns continued to influence and shape the culture of the slaves. Cultural continuities with Africa were not dependent on the importation and perpetuation of specific tales, songs, or folk beliefs in their pure form. In the place that tales, songs, and folk beliefs occupied in the lives of slaves and in the meaning slaves derived from them, they had the clearest resemblances with their African past.

Thus, the fact that few slave songs of satire and derision could be traced back to Africa is not important. Most of these songs, of course, were on-the-spot improvisations using the local immediate context and characters. What is important is that the ubiquitous African practice of using songs of satirical derision as a central mode of expression and a crucial safety valve continued to live on in slavery and continued to afford slaves the same avenues of cultural self-assertion and psychological release it had provided their African ancestors. Similarly, the fact that in slave tales all of the divine and many of the animal tricksters of Africa were lost is far less important than the retention of the trickster tale itself. Despite all of the changes that took place, slaves managed to keep alive the mechanism, so well developed throughout most of Africa, by means of which psychic relief from arbitrary authority could be secured, symbolic assaults on the powerful could be waged, and important lessons about authority relationships could be imparted.[14]

Precisely the same argument can be advanced with regard to expressive style. Despite the fact that many—perhaps most— slave songs were the product of black interaction with whites, the nature of their song style with its overriding antiphony, its group performance, its pervasive functionality, its improvisational character, its strong relationship to dance and bodily movement, remained closer to the musical styles of Africa than to those of Western Europe. Similarly, in their tales, aphorisms, proverbs, anecdotes, and jokes, slaves, following the practices of their African past, encouraged and rewarded verbal improvisation, emphasized group participation, and used the spoken arts functionally to voice criticism as well as to uphold traditional values and group cohesion.[15]

An emphasis on cultural style helps to undercut still another of the assumptions mentioned at the beginning: that the wide variety of languages, religions, and institutions differentiating African societies made it impossible for their peoples to reconstitute a significant semblance of African culture on American soil. Historians are finally learning that culture is more than the sum total of institutions and language. It is also expressed by an emphasis on certain virtues, ideals, manners, modes of hospitality, and outlooks toward the past, present, and future —in short, by a common style of life.[16] One has only to picture the ways in which Western Europeans, with their diversity of languages, religions, and customs, could have reconstituted a common European culture had they been subjected to the same process of enslavement and forced resettlement to understand what in fact the African peoples were able to achieve in the New World.

We have been misled by the scholarly search for "survivals" that embodies the mistaken belief that only those elements of slave culture were African that remained largely unchanged from the African past. Culture is not a fixed, static condition but a process; a product of interaction between the past and the present. The question, as VèVè Clark has put it so well, is not one of survivals but of transformations.[17] The creation of Afro-American culture was not a simple process of radical deculturation followed by forced acculturation. It was, rather, the product of a complex process of syncretism, the nature of which we are only beginning to appreciate. Our understanding of this process has been retarded by the long-standing assumption that the gulf between African and European culture was impossibly wide and virtually unbridgeable. While African slaves were transported to an environment that was unquestionably alien, it was not as invariably alien as we have supposed. For example, nothing in the European musical tradition with which slaves came into contact in America was totally foreign to their own traditions, while a number of important features such as the diatonic scale were held in common and a number of practices such as the lining-out of hymns—the singing of lines in advance and their repetition by others—in Protestant churches and the African practice of antiphonal call-and-response were analogous. Thus, slaves were able to maintain the integrity of their own musical heritage while fusing to it compatible elements of Euro-American music. The same situation held true in the area of folk beliefs. From the seventeenth to the nineteenth centuries, African slaves met large numbers of Euro-American people who believed the universe was populated by spirits and witches, by supernatural omens and signs, by charms and magic, by conjuring and healing; who held beliefs, in short, that the slaves could adopt or adapt without doing essential violence to their own world view. It is within this context that we must understand the point made by a number of folklorists that Afro-American folk beliefs often were more specifically European in form than African. Slaves could absorb so many Euro-American beliefs not because their own African culture had been reduced to a negligible force but because these beliefs fit so easily beside and often in place of their traditional outlooks and convictions and constituted a source of comfort, familiarity, and cultural reinforcement.[18]

Clearly, we have just scratched the surface of this question. We need many studies of such areas as language, material culture, and ethical values. These studies will be aided immensely by perhaps the most important breakthrough by historians: their changed attitude toward the slave folk. Such historians as John Blassingame, Eugene Genovese, Herbert Gutman, Nathan Huggins, Leon Litwack, Leslie Howard Owens, Albert Raboteau, George Rawick, and Peter Wood have pictured the slave folk not as inarticulate, impotent historical ciphers who were continually being acted on by forces over which they had no control, but, rather, as actors in their own right who, to a larger extent than we previously imagined, were able to build a culture, create alternatives, and affect the situation they found themselves in.

To further pursue this crucially important subject we must encourage more active interaction and cooperation between African and American scholars who have much to teach one another.

NOTES

1. Ulrich B. Phillips, the influential early twentieth-century historian of slavery, quoted with approval the antebellum planters' saying that "a negro was what a white man made him." Phillips, *American Negro Slavery* (1918, reprint ed., Baton Rouge: Louisiana State University Press, 1966), 291. Four decades later, the historian Stanley Elkins elaborated on Phillips's judgment to show how slavery had "infantalized" its victims so that not only was the culture they had brought with them destroyed, but even their aspirations were reduced to fantasies of "catfish and watermelons," Elkins, *Slavery* (Chicago: University of Chicago Press, 1959), 136 and passim.

2. Robert E. Park, "The Conflict and Fusion of Cultures with Special Reference to the Negro." *Journal of Negro History* 4 (1919):116–18.

3. Frederick W. Root, "Folk-Music," *International Folk-Lore Congress of World's Columbian Exposition, Chicago, 1893* 1:424–25; Ambrose E. Gonzales, *The Black Border; Gullah Stories of the Carolina Coast* (Columbia, S.C.: The State Company, 1922), 10; John Bennett, "Gullah: A Negro Patois," *South Atlantic Quarterly* 7 (1908):336,338. The folklorist Louise Pound exemplified the belief that cultural diffusion was a one-way street by arguing that the spiritual, "Weeping Mary," could not have originated among the slaves, since her grandmother had learned the song from a white woman who heard it at a white Methodist camp meeting in Hamilton, New York, in the late 1820s. If whites knew the song, Pound was convinced, it must have been they who originated and disseminated it. Louise Pound, "The Ancestry of a 'Negro Spiritual,'" *Modern Language Notes* 33 (1918):442–44.

4. Again, Robert Park stated the position succinctly: "The Negro when he landed in the United States, left behind him almost everything but his dark complexion and his tropical temperament." Robert Park, *Journal of Negro History* 4 (1919):116–18. Like Park, most white scholars in the late nineteenth and early twentieth centuries were driven to deny Africa any vestige of cultural influence. They were willing to credit Africa only with genetic influences, especially in the areas of movement and rhythm. This compulsive myopia, which obviously is revealing of white American cultural needs and predispositions, is worthy of a study of its own.

5. Peter H. Wood. *Black Majority: Negroes in Colonial South Carolina* (New York: Norton, 1974), 55–62, 119–24. See also Charles Winston Joyner, "Slave Folklife on the Waccamaw Neck: Antebellum Black Culture in the South Carolina Low Country" (Ph.D diss., University of Pennsylvania, 1977). Labor requirements in South Carolina and other parts of the South allowed the continuation of African cooperative work practices even within the highly individualistic task system. "It is customary (*and never objected to*)" the planter James Sparkman noted, "for the more active and industrious hands to assist those who are slower and more tardy in finishing their daily tasks." Joyner, "Slave Folklife on the Waccamaw Neck," 44–45.

6. C. C. Jones, *The Religious Instruction of the Negroes in the United States* (1842, reprint ed., New York: Arno, 1969), 127–28.

7. Quoted in Dena J. Epstein, *Sinful Tunes and Spirituals: Black Folk Music to the Civil War* (Urbana: University of Illinois Press, 1977), 193–94.

8. For a discussion of slave dance, see Lawrence W. Levine, *Black Culture and Black Consciousness: Afro-American Folk Thought from Slavery to Freedom* (New York: Oxford, 1977), 16–18, 38; Marshall Stearne and Jean Stearne, *Jazz Dance: The Story of American Vernacular Dance* (New York: Shirmer Books, 1968), chaps 2–4; Lynne Fauley Emery, *Black Dance in the United States from 1619 to 1970* (Palo Alto: Arno, 1972), chaps. 1–5; Benjamin Henry Boneval Latrobe, *Impressions Respecting New Orleans: Diary & Sketches,*

1818–1820 (New York, 1951), 49– 51; Henry William Ravenel, "Recollection of Southern Plantation Life," *Yale Review* 25 (1936):768–69.

9. David Macrae, *The Americans at Home* (1870, reprint ed., New York: 1952), 318.
10. See Henry Lee Swint, *The Northern Teacher in the South, 1862– 1870* (Nashville: Octagon, 1941), and Levine, *Black Culture and Black Consciousness*, chap. 3.
11. J. C. Carothers, "Culture, Psychiatry, and the Written Word." *Psychiatry* (1959):307–20.
12. Mircea Eliade, *The Sacred and the Profane* (New York, 1961). For the importance of the sacred world in Africa, see W. E. Abraham, *The Mind of Africa* (London: 1962), chap. 2; R. S. Rattray, *Religion and Art in Ashanti* (Oxford: 1927); and John S. Mbiti, *African Religions and Philosophies* (Garden City, N.Y.: Doubleday, 1969), chap. 3.
13. Levine, *Black Culture and Black Consciousness*, chap. 1; Albert J. Raboteau, *Slave Religion* (New York; Oxford University Press, 1978); Eugene D. Genovese, *Roll, Jordan, Roll* (New York: Random House, 1974), book 2.
14. Levine, *Black Culture and Black Consciousness*, chaps. 1–2; Theodore Van Dam, "The Influence of the West African Song of Derision in the New World," *African Music* 1 (1954):53–56; William D. Pierson, "'Puttin' Down Ole Massa: African Satire in the New World," in *African Folklore in the New World*, ed. Daniel J. Crowley (Austin: University of Texas Press, 1977), 20–34; Alan Dundes, "African and Afro-American Tales," in ibid., 35–53; William D. Piersen, "An African Background for American Negro Folktales?" *Journal of American Folklore* 84 (1971):201–14.
15. Levine, *Black Culture and Black Consciousness* (Cambridge: Oxford University Press, 1978) chaps. 1–2.
16. Robert Redfield, *The Primitive World and Its Transformations* (Ithaca: Cornell University Press, 1953), 51–53.
17. VèVè Clark, public lecture, Berkeley, Calif., Fall 1973.
18. Richard Alan Waterman, "African Influence on the Music of the Americas" in *Acculturation in the Americas*, ed. Sol Rax (Chicago: University of Chicago Press, 1952), 207–18; Alan P. Merriam, "African Music," in *Continuity and Change in African Cultures*, William R. Bascom and Melville J. Herskovits, eds. (Chicago: University of Chicago Press, 1959), 49–86; Alan P. Merriam, "Music and the Dance," in *The African World*, ed. Robert Lystad (New York: Praeger, 1965), 452–68; Levine, *Black Culture and Black Consciousness*, chap. 1; Keith Thomas, *Religion and the Decline of Magic* (New York: Scribner, 1971); John F. Szwed and Roger D. Abrahams, "After the Myth: Studying Afro-American Cultural Patterns in the Plantation Literature" in *African Folklore in the New World*, ed. Crowley, 65–86.

7

Howard University and Meharry Medical Schools in the Training of African Physicians, 1868–1978

Adell Patton, Jr.

Prior to 1946 the records show repeated epidemics of smallpox at 5–10 year intervals, with a high continuous prevalence in the hinterland of West Africa. The United States Public Health Service Mission in Liberia became actively involved in the 1946–1947 outbreaks. The writer saw 42 cases of smallpox disease in hinterland villages within one day with three deaths during the night. Smallpox disease was so rampant in certain villages that one could observe children four feet tall and children who were three feet tall, but not children in between; and the people would say that was the year that the epidemic came, and all the babies died, causing the gap in the height of the children. . . . Locally trained vaccinators undertook to vaccinate the entire population of Liberia against smallpox in 1946–1948. . . . A 1950–1952 study of records showed less than one dozen cases reported for the entire country.[1]

ALTHOUGH this essay focuses on the medical profession, it should be understood within a historical context of the critical role, especially during the colonial period, of African Americans in providing assistance to Africa in education and other areas of development. Moreover, African American study and teaching of tropical diseases in Africa and the training of African students advanced the development of black American education and institutions. This reciprocity affirms the mutual benefits of the African/African American connection. In his field observations, Hildrus A. Poindexter (M.D., Ph.D., M.S., M.P.H.,

Sc.D.), professor at Howard University and pioneer of tropical medicine in the African diaspora, illustrates the impact of disease in West Africa,[2] commonly referred to as the "white man's grave" in the early nineteenth century. William H. McNeill, however, may have overstated the historical effect of disease on African development as a whole:

> Obviously human attempts to shorten the food chain within the toughest and the most variegated of all natural ecosystems of the earth, the tropical rain forests and adjacent savanna regions of Africa, are still imperfectly successful, and continue to involve exceptionally high costs in the form of exposure to disease. That, more than anything else, is why Africa remained backward [sic] in the development of civilization when compared to temperate lands (or tropical zones like those of Americas), where prevailing ecosystems were less elaborated and correspondingly less inimical to simplication by human action.[3]

But in contrast with the less disastrous relationship of human beings and their environment elsewhere in the world, humans and parasites in Africa have generally had a primary relationship to each other; because humankind originated in Africa, humans and infectious disease developed in competition with each other from the start. Through time, innovations in Western and African medicine have been significant in the reduction of disease on the African continent, and the physician has played no minor role in disease control. In the nineteenth century, Sierra Leone was a unique frontier enclave for the development of the pioneer West African physician. Trained and certified in Edinburgh and London, this elite class of African physicians included John Macaulay (1799), William Ferguson (1814), William Broughton Davies (1858), James Africanus Beale Horton (1859), John Farrell Easmon (1880), and Oguntola Sapara (1895)—to name just a few.[4]

Classification of African Physicians

From a global perspective, the training of the African physician falls into four categories: (1) the African M.D. trained in Western Europe, primarily in Britain and France, prior to and after World War II; (2) the African M.D. trained in the socialist nations of Eastern Europe after World War II; (3) the African M.D. trained in the United States, the Caribbean, and Canada; and (4) the most recent development in African medical education, the African M.D. trained wholly or partially in Africa.[5]

This essay focuses on a segment of the third category—the African M.D. trained in the United States at Howard University and Meharry medical schools. At these institutions, Africans matriculated and fostered links between Afro-Americans and Africa in the development of public health.

Colonial Era and African Physicians

Pseudoscientific racism triumphed with the onset of colonial rule in Africa about 1900. In West Africa, the British reversed an earlier trend of allowing Africans to be trained as medical doctors in Scotland and England. Furthermore, African physicians were paid lower salaries than their counterparts in the colonial service.[6] Because some earlier African protonationalists had been physicians, the British may have sought to discourage further nationalist sentiment by reducing the dominance of African doctors.[7]

In regard to public health in Africa, these developments occurred at an unfavorable time, for colonial rule, with its use of labor-intensive projects in the Cameroon, as a common example, shifted segments of the African population from areas with low malaria prevalence to areas of high prevalence. These newly shifted populations had little resistance to malaria and suffered disproportionately from the ravages of that disease. Wherever these dislocations occurred, the newly arrived populations were at greater risk to disease prevalent in the new environment. Available evidence shows that these migrations and changes in living conditions in the early years of colonization wrought unprecedented rates of mortality and morbidity.[8]

Whatever the motive, discrimination ultimately reduced the numbers of African doctors to those serving the coastal elites and curtailed the extension of scientific public health services to the underprivileged urban and rural population. Because the unhealthiest period in all of African history was between 1890 and 1930,[9] the new shift in colonial policy was detrimental to African health and vitality, a factor that did not go unnoticed by Africans. In 1911, the color bar prompted African doctors to send letters and petitions to the British Advisory Medical and Sanitary Committee. Some British colonial administrators supported them because, as the British medical register showed, those African doctors had received degrees from recognized European medical schools.[10]

Although this political action was to no avail, the issue would not disappear. In 1920, Dr. Herbert Bankole-Bright (M.D. Edinburgh and London School of Tropical Medicine) of Freetown, Sierra Leone, not only used the Accra conference of the National Congress of British West Africa to call for gradual self-government within the British Empire, but also presented research papers on topics of medical and sanitary problems in the British territories of West Africa. In his master's thesis on Dr. Bankole-Bright, Mohammed Bah reports:

> Attacking the colonial administration for residential segregation, Dr. Bankole-Bright called on members to urge the colonial administration to improve the conditions of local doctors. Included in his presentation was a direct attack against the British colonial administration for treating African doctors in a different manner from European expatriate doctors.[11]

Based on these conditions, one can understand how and why Howard University and Meharry medical schools made a unique contribution to the development of public health on the African continent. If Africans with medical aspirations wished to study outside the colonial world, these two institutions were their main source of medical education in the United States.

Black Medical Schools

Seven black medical schools were founded during the post-Civil War era. Howard University Medical School held its first classroom lecture on 5 November 1868. Eight students attended, but the class was opened to all persons without regard to sex or race. Meharry Medical School of Nashville, which opened in 1876 "solely for the education of Negro doctors," was initially designated as the Medical Department of Central Tennessee College (1866) and enrolled eleven students with ex-slave status. To supplement the work of Howard and Meharry, five other medical schools were established from 1882 to 1903. In 1882, Leonard Medical School of Shaw University was founded in Raleigh, and by 1915 it had graduated over five hundred physicians, some of whom came from Liberia, Trinidad, and Jamaica. In 1888, the Louisville National Medical College was founded, followed the next year by the establishment of the Flint Medical College in New Orleans. In the Tennessee mountains, Knoxville Medical College began in 1895, with classrooms located over a funeral parlor. Strange as it may now seem, this location was beneficial to the college, for embalmed specimens were indispensable to pathologists and to students studying anatomy. And finally, the least known of all, Chattanooga (Tennessee) National Medical College came into existence in 1903. However, despite the uncertainties surrounding the foundation of these medical schools, their emergence represented a major transformation in black social-medical history. In the antebellum period, the first black physicians were either "self-taught healers," such as James Still, David Ruggles, and William Wells Brown, or apprentice-trained, such as Martin R. Delany. James McCune Smith presumably had received the M.D. degree abroad at the University of Glasgow as early as 1837. By the end of the antebellum era, there were only three U.S.-educated black physicians with training equivalent to their Sierra Leonean counterparts: David J. Peck (1847, Rush Medical College), John V. Degrasse, and Thomas J. White (1849, Bowdoin College). The latter institution had a medical school at the time whose objective was to prepare blacks for medical service in Liberia.[12]

But despite the motivation and intent of the seven black medical schools in the post-Civil War era, by the early twentieth century the dispensers of philanthropy phased out all but two of those schools. In 1910, the Flexner report on the status of medical education in the United States and Canada appeared under the auspices of the Carnegie Foundation. The report encouraged various foundations to support only approved medical schools and recommended that "Meharry at Nashville and Howard at Washington are worth development—the upbuilding of Howard and Meharry will profit the nation much more than the inadequate maintenance of a large number of schools."[13] The Flexner report had a long-lasting impact on the training of black physicians in predominantly black institutions. For nearly half of the twentieth century, Howard and Meharry were the only historically black institutions accredited to provide medical education. It was not until September 1978, some sixty-eight years after the Flexner report, that the School of Medicine at Morehouse College in Atlanta enrolled twenty-four students as the third predominantly black medical school.[14]

Medical School Curriculum

The curriculum of neither Meharry nor Howard showed significant innovation in the nineteenth century. That both institutions were conceived in an era preceding the pioneer discoveries of the causation of infectious diseases is evident by their earliest views on these diseases. In the graduating class at Meharry in 1878, Lorenzo Dow Key reported a common belief in a discussion on malaria:

> Malaria was derived from two Latin words which means bad air. It is supposed that air in certain portions of this and other countries is filled with germs that are formed by the decomposition of animal and vegetable matter and it is thought by a large number of writers on the subject that persons who inhabit these districts take into their systems during respiration, these germs which enter the circulation.[15]

The medical school at Howard University held classes only in the evening, for daytime classes did not begin until 1910, and with only part-time faculty and without certain basic laboratory facilities or quarters for animal experimentation. For the most part, patients were treated as their ancestors and relatives had treated them—without the benefit of antibiotics or specific drugs. Clinicians instructed the sick to avoid certain types of night air and either purged them with cathartics or induced sweating.[16] On the other hand, the curriculum of Meharry, as shown by Falk and Quaynor-Malm, used textbooks such as Gray's *Anatomy*, Dunglison's *Medical Dictionary*, and Meig's *Diseases of Children* without any reference to John Wesley's *Primitive Physick*. In the words of these researchers, the Meharry curriculum was a "thoroughly Anglo-Saxon white medical one."[17]

Religion and the religious experience were extremely important factors in the daily life of black medical students, black physicians, and their black patients. All Meharry graduates were active Christians, and some were part-time ministers. But the medical education that those students received bore little relationship to the tradition or the reality of the patients they were expected to treat. There was little difference between the Howard curriculum and that of Meharry. Both reflected the acculturation process that denied the existence of a rational medical system in ancient Egypt or Africa that was in fact more than three thousand years old.[18]

However, Howard and Meharry started curriculum innovations in the early decades of the twentieth century in ways more beneficial to the development of medical services in Africa. Many of these changes may have had late nineteenth-century antecedents. Courses in tropical medicine, hygiene, dietetics, and preventive medicine are found in the Howard catalog as early as 1912 and 1914. And in 1922, if not earlier, one finds a department of bacteriology with a course in public health, headed by Professor Algernon Brashear Jackson with Dr. Uriah Daniels, Mr. James Julian, Jr., and Mr. Felix Anderson as supporting faculty.[19] Although Meharry's catalog showed change, it did not show a course listing in tropical medicine or epidemiology until 1922. This is not to say, however, that earlier students may not have been provided with medical knowledge useful in the management of tropical diseases. Further, in 1922, a course in parasitology and clinical microscopy appeared with the following course description: "A brief course in Parasitology is given in conjunction with Bacteriology of the second year of the medical course. The students are made acquainted with the methods of identifying malaria plasmodium and other pathogenic parasites."[20] Although the white administration at Meharry brought significant benefits to medical trainees, the real sensitivity for substantive changes came with the inauguration of a black administration. In 1952, Dr. Harold D. West (Ph.D.) became the first black president of Meharry. And in 1966–1967, Dr. Lloyd Elam (M.D.) became the new college president, continuing the faculty renaissance of his predecessor.[21]

In 1926, Howard University installed Mordecai Wyatt Johnson (S.T.M., D.D.) as its first black president. During the thirty-four years of his administration, Howard University became a center of black scholarship, a black intellectual oasis. In 1929, a dynamic phase of development began in the medical school with the appointment of Dr. Numa P. G. Adams (M.D.) as its first black dean. Dr. Adams embarked on a bold program of institutional and faculty development. With the president's support, he recruited a full-time faculty for the first time. Shortly thereafter, in 1930, Edwin R. Embree, executive secretary of the General Education Board (Rockefeller Foundation), provided grants to Howard and Meharry for training beyond the M.D. degree, and Adams insisted on such training. Hence, Howard's outstanding medical graduates such as M. Wharton Young (M.D.) and W. Montague Cobb (M.D.) went on to obtain the Ph.D. in the basic biomedical sciences. Having joined the medical faculty in 1931 with his M.D. from Harvard, Hildrus A. Poindexter also obtained the Ph.D. (1932) in microbiology and immunology at Columbia University and later continued his studies in tropical medicine there as well as at the University of Puerto Rico.

Ernest E. Just (Ph.D., University of Chicago, 1916) apparently worked in liaison with the medical school before the medical faculty renaissance era and was probably the first Ph.D. to teach in the medical school. He directed most of his better students to enter medicine rather than graduate study because of the unfavorable job market. An outstanding scientist, his professional career included appointments at the University of Chicago, and from 1930 onward he studied at the Kaiser-Wilhelm Institute fur Biologie at Berlin-Dahlem until Nazi Germany brought this activity to a halt. Among numerous other publications, Just published his seminal work, *The Biology of the Cell Surface*, in 1938. Finally, Charles R. Drew (M.D., McGill) joined the faculty in 1935 as instructor in the Department of Pathology, and in 1938 he was instructor in the Department of Surgery. He is best known for his pioneering work in blood plasma.[22]

Curriculum innovation was a natural outgrowth of the new faculty. The *Bulletin* of 1931 shows a course listing in vital statistics and epidemiology. Newer concepts in microbiology and immunology, following the reorganization of the bacteriology department in 1934, were the chief innovations along with animal experimentation and darkfield microscopy. The revised curriculum in public health was a direct result of innovations in the Department of Bacteriology. In 1936, a national survey team rated the medical school at Howard University substantially comparable to six other schools in the integration of microbiology and immunology for medical students.[23]

In the 1930s, African medical students at Howard and Meharry could take advantage of the knowledge about organisms for the prevention and control of diseases. For example, in the presulfonamide drug period, medical treatment was based on trial and error. Quinine was given to patients with fever, digitalis for heart disease, opiates or morphine for people with pain, and calomel for bowel disorders as well as other diseases, such as syphilis, typhoid fever, and even headaches. But the discovery of penicillin in 1928 and its first use in patient care in 1941 opened a new era; yaws, which is morphologically indistinguishable from syphilis, could now be cured quickly, as could pneumonia. Sulfonamides were discovered as far back as 1901, but their clinical use was delayed until 1933. Sulfonamides contained thirty-odd chemical properties useful to combat certain illnesses, such as syphilis and leprosy. With the development of vaccines, immunization could eradicate whooping cough, diphtheria, smallpox, and tetanus. Hookworms, trypanosomiasis (sleeping sickness), malaria, and leprosy could all be prevented or cured with proper medical services. Howard and Meharry now had laboratories where the study of most of these diseases could be undertaken. African physicians had only to apply what they had learned about vectors transmitting disease from the infected to the noninfected. Morbidity and mortality could be greatly reduced.[24]

In another study, Leslie A. Falk distinguishes two major categories of health systems.[25] The first is the "scientific" or "Western system"; the second consists of modalities normally considered beyond the role of accepted medical practice. Examples of so-called scientific systems include medical group practice, free clinics, and health centers that use physician or nurse practitioners, physicians' assistants, and so on. In contrast, the system of modalities includes acupuncture, traditional healers, yoga, transactional analysis, and biofeedback. In retrospect, there is no evidence that either medical school used the modalities category either in its curriculum or as an alternative method of health care. It is only within the past five years that serious attempts have been made by institutions of Western medicine, Howard and Meharry included, to incorporate traditional beliefs and practices in the standard medical curriculum.

Some of the African graduates from Howard and Meharry medical schools made significant contributions in the transfer of medical technology to their respective countries. J. H. Roberts, an Americo-Liberian, was the first Howard M.D. graduate from West Africa in 1876; he entered private practice in Liberia and is believed to be the son of the first Liberian President J. H. Roberts (1848–1856, 1872–1876).[26] Howard produced two other graduates during the latter part of the nineteenth century, but little is known about them.

The records from 1900 to 1960 are more detailed.[27] In 1935, Howard University graduated Dr. Malaku E. Bayan, who became Emperor Haile Selassie's personal physician in the 1930s; in 1942, Dr. David E. Boye-Johnson graduated and became the chief medical officer of Sierra Leone in 1944 and served in other public health capacities. In 1955, Dr. Aderohunmu O. Laja graduated and was posted in the pathology department of the Federal Ministry of Health in Lagos, Nigeria. Dr. Badejo O. Adebonojo also was a 1955 Howard graduate and served as the chief medical officer of the Lagos State Government of Nigeria. And there were other outstanding M.D. African graduates of the 1950s.

But the decade's most outstanding Howard University M.D. graduate was the late Dr. Latunde E. Odeku of Nigeria. (It is said that he and Andrew Young, the former U.S. ambassador to the United Nations, were dormitory roommates at Howard.) Odeku was also a poet, and in 1950, some four years before his graduation, he expressed his appreciation in a poem to Howard University:

> Alma Mater
> Our strength with thee forever rests,
> Our usefulness, our pride;
> Our struggles in the years to come
> Shall beam our deeds and crowns to thee
> In lasting thought of gratitude.[28]

Odeku returned to Nigeria, established the first neurosurgical unit at the University of Ibadan, and became its first head. He performed a wide range of neurosurgical operations with modest facilities.

Meharry produced its share of African medical graduates as well.[29] Ironically, Meharry's initial contribution in the transfer of medical technology in the nineteenth century came not from a graduate of the African continent but from the United States. Dr. Georgia E. L. Patton, an Afro-American, was the first woman graduate of Meharry in 1893. The difficulty women graduates had in obtaining certification from medical associations during this era may account for Dr. Patton's going to Liberia to practice medicine from 1893 to 1895. Illness may have been her nemesis because shortly after 1895, she returned to the United States and settled in Memphis, where she died in 1900.[30] Dr. Poindexter, whose remarks on disease control in Liberia prefaced this essay, reports that Dr. Patton is still remembered among the elders in Liberia.

On the other hand, Meharry had only one graduate of the African continent before 1900—John H. Jones of Liberia. Meharry had a more successful record of producing African graduates between 1900 and 1960. Paradoxically, two of Meharry's best-known graduates prior to 1940 have made little or no contribution in the realm of public health. Daniel Sharpe Malekebu of Malawi arrived in the United States in 1908 with the support of black Baptists in New York and Ohio. He studied in North Carolina and at Selma College in Alabama; in 1917, he graduated as a surgeon from Meharry. All total, Malekebu spent fourteen years in the United States and established links with the medical staff at Meharry, the YMCA, the Baptist leaders, and Dr. Whittier H. Wright of Meharry. Further, he married Flora Ethelwyn, an Afro-American. Back in Malawi in 1926, Malekebu succeeded John Chilembwe (a Yao trained in Virginia by Baptists) as head of the Independent Providence Industrial Mission in Southern Malawi.[31]

Dr. Hastings Kamuzu Banda is now life president of the Republic of Malawi. The African Methodist Episcopal (AME) Church of Johannesburg sponsored Banda's first trip to the United States in 1925. He earned a high school diploma at Wilberforce University, studied at Indiana University, and received the bachelor of philosophy degree from the University of Chicago. His benefactors were black professionals and real estate owners in Ohio and Indiana. Banda was also able to exchange views in the United States with J. R. Rathebe of South Africa and with Dr. A. B. Yuma, who became leader of the African National Congress of South Africa in the late 1920s and early 1930s.[32] After graduating from Meharry in 1936, Banda left the United States but was present to give the commencement address at Meharry in 1977.

Meharry graduated a number of other outstanding African physicians, but insufficient data preclude description of their contribution to the transfer of medical technology and skills. Two other figures, however, must not go unmentioned: first, Joseph Nagbe Togba of Liberia graduated from Meharry in 1944 and became an important figure in the World Health Organization; and second, Henry Nehemiah Cooper, also of Liberia, received the M.D. degree in 1954 and heads the John F. Kennedy Hospital in Monrovia.

Some general conclusions can be drawn from this exploratory distribution model. First, the fact that Liberia provided the earliest medical graduates attests to the Americo-Liberians' long-standing links with the Afro-American community in the United States; some Liberians even attended the Leonard Medical School of Shaw University before it went out of existence in 1915. Second, Nigeria has the largest "pipeline" of graduates that began in the last decade of the colonial period; all of them came from southern Nigeria, for northern Nigeria as a region did not graduate its first M.D. until 1973–1974 at Ahmadu Bello University Medical School, Zaria. Third, none of the influential Malawian graduates attended Howard; Dr. Malekebu, having been the first Malawian graduate from Meharry in 1917, controlled the "pipeline" and influenced subsequent Malawians such as Dr. Banda and others to attend Meharry.

The AME Church sponsored more students at Meharry than at Howard, which had a predominantly Congregationalist orientation in the nineteenth century. The AME Church had a long history of involvement in South Africa, which may account for the greater number of South Africans at Meharry (six) than at Howard (two). Ghanaian students in any significant numbers did not attend either of these institutions until the 1950s; it is likely that Kwame Nkrumah (Lincoln University, Pennsylvania), who became Ghana's first president in the postindependence era, accelerated this trend.

During the colonial period (1900–1960), the African M.D. graduates appear at staggered intervals in the catalogs. This pattern developed partly because, as Donald Segal reports, the colonial governments discriminated against African physicians trained in the United States.[33] Howard University and other U.S. institutions provided premedical ungraduate training for many Africans, who then continued their medical studies at either McGill University in Canada or in Europe because of the exclusionist policy of the colonial era. T. Bello Osagie, a Nigerian graduate of Howard in the early 1950s, obtained his M.D. at McGill because he feared that American credentials would exclude him from certification in Nigeria. The postindependence era marks a departure from this trend and apparently lifted the colonial ban of discrimination against African physicians trained in the United States.

Summary

Howard University and Meharry medical schools have contributed significantly in the training of African physicians since they were founded in the nineteenth century. Howard University Medical School, founded in 1868, and Meharry, established in 1876, were two of seven black medical institutions to emerge in that period. But the Flexner report of 1910 phased out all but Howard and Meharry, which continued to receive philanthropic support. Both institutions appeared at a propitious time, when pseudoscientific racism triumphed with the onset of colonial rule in Africa. At the same time, in West Africa, the British reversed an earlier trend allowing Africans to be trained as physicians at Edinburgh and London, and began to discriminate against African medical doctors trained in the United States.

A factor other than pseudoscientific racism may have been at stake in regard to the new colonial policy. Some earlier nationalists were physicians, and the British may have sought to diminish the domino effect of nationalist sentiment by reducing the number of African doctors, since they represented the dominant elite in the new class formation. The policy change, however, tended to confine the distribution of African doctors to the coastal settlements and restricted the expansion of scientific public health services for the mass of the population living predominantly in the rural and periurban areas.

Howard University Medical School and Meharry Medical School made a unique contribution to the advancement of scientific medicine on the African continent by adding to the pool of British-trained physicians in West Africa who had come initially from Sierra Leone. By the second decade of the twentieth century, these medical schools began to incorporate into their curriculum such innovative courses as tropical medicine, bacteriology, microbiology, animal experimentation, statistical epidemiology and the like. African medical doctors had only to apply these innovations to the development of medical services in their respective countries of origin.

Howard University and Meharry medical schools graduated more African students—about forty-one—between 1960 and 1978 than they did in the sixty years preceding the independence era. This fact confirms that transformation from African to African American neither severed the socio-cultural link with the homeland nor precluded black American involvement in the development of the continent.

NOTES

1. Oral interview with Hildrus A. Poindexter, and his book, *My World of Reality: Autobiography* (Detroit: Balamp Publishers, 1973).
2. The research for this paper was funded by the Department of History, Howard University, Washington, D.C. I extend a special thanks to Hildrus A. Poindexter, M.D., and Calvin H. Sinnette, M.D., both of the Howard University Medical School, who rendered invaluable assistance with revisions and sources. The following persons served as consultants to this project: Joseph E. Harris (Department of History, Howard University); Dean Marion Mann, M.D., and Eleanor I. Franklin, Ph.D., both of Howard University Medical School; Dean Ralph J. Cazort, M.D., and Leslie A. Falk, M.D., Ph.D., both of Meharry Medical School; Michael Winston and the Moorland-Springarn Research Center Staff (especially Betty M. Culpepper), Howard University; Adelola Adeloye, M.D., Ibadan University Medical School, Nigeria; Edward B. Cross, M.D., F.A.C.C., F.A.C.P., Dallas; Steven Feierman and Jan Vansina, both of the University of Wisconsin, Madison; and William A. Dixon, Kentucky State University.
3. William H. McNeill, *Plagues and Peoples* (Garden City, N.Y.: Anchor Press, 1976); see also Gerald W. Hartwig and K. David Patterson, eds., *Disease in African History: An Introductory Survey and Case Studies* (Durham, N.C.: Duke University Press, 1978);

Philip D. Curtin, "Epidemiology and the Slave Trade," *Political Science Quarterly* 83, 2 (June 1968):190–217; Philip D. Curtin, "The White Man's Grave: Image and Reality, 1780–1850," *Journal of British Studies* 1 (1961):94–110; for yellow fever and cholera in the sixteenth centuries see Sekene-Mody Cissoko, "Famines et epidemies à Tombouctou et dans la boucle du niger du XVIe au XVIIIe siécle," *Bulletin de l'I.F.A.N.* 30 ser. B, 3 (1968):806–21; Henry E. Sigerist, *Civilization and Disease* (Ithaca, N.Y.: Cornell University Press, 1943); and Steven Feierman, *Health and Society in Africa: A Working Bibliography* (Waltham, Mass: Crossroads Press, 1979).

4. Adelola Adeloye, *Nigerian Pioneers of Modern Medicine* (Ibadan: Ibadan University Press, 1977); M. C. F. Easmon, "Sierra Leone Doctors," *Sierra Leone Studies* n.s. 6 (1956):81–96.

5. Dr. Calvin H. Sinnette, oral interview on August 15, 1979, at Howard University Medical School; see also Paul E. Steiner, "Medical Education in Trans-Saharan Africa," *Journal of Medical Education* 34, 2 (1959):95–106.

6. E. N. O. Sodeinde to Patton, 23 July 1979; Raymond E. Dumett, "The Campaign against Malaria and the Expansion of Scientific Medical and Sanitary Services in British West Africa, 1898–1910," *African Historical Studies* 1, 2 (1968):191–94; and K. David Patterson, "Disease and Medicine in African History: A Bibliographical Essay," *History in Africa* 1 (1974);147.

7. Eliot Freidson, *Professional Dominance: The Social Structure of Medical Care* (New York: Atherton Press, 1970), xi.

8. Marke W. DeLancey, "Health and Disease on the Plantations of Cameroon, 1884–1939," in *Disease in African History*, ed. Hartwig and Patterson, 153.

9. Hartwig and Patterson, eds., *Disease in African History*, 4.

10. Dumett, "The Campaign against Malaria," 192–93.

11. Mohammed Alpha Bah, "Dr. Herbert C. Bankole-Bright and His Impact on the Growth of Constitutional Government and the Development of Political Parties in Sierra Leone 1924–1957" (M.A. thesis, Department of History, Howard University, 1977), 16–17.

12. Herbert M. Morais, *The History of the Negro in Medicine* (Washington, D.C.: Association for the Study of Negro Life and History, 1967), 21–25, 26–27, 44, 60, 64, 66–69; Abraham Flexner, *Medical Education in the United States and Canada: A Report to the Carnegie Foundation for the Advancement of Teaching* (Merrymount Press: Boston, 1910), 180; and L. A. Falk and N. A. Quaynor-Malm, "Early Afro-American Medical Education in the United States: The Origins of Meharry Medical College in the Nineteenth Century," in *Proceedings of the XXIII Congress of the History of Medicine* (London: Oxford University Press, September 2–9, 1972), 347; James L. Curtis, *Black Medical Schools and Society* (Ann Arbor: University of Michigan Press, 1971), 9–10, 13; Dietrich C. Reitzes, *Negroes and Medicine* (Cambridge: Harvard University Press, 1958); Judith Walzer Leavitt and Ronald L. Numbers, eds., *Sickness and Health in America: Readings in the History of Health in America* (Madison: University of Wisconsin Press, 1980); and Gary King, "The Supply and Distribution of Black Physicians in the United States: 1900–1970," *Western Journal of Black Studies* 4 (1980):21–28.

13. Flexner, *Medical Education in the United States and Canada*, 181.

14. *Morehouse College Bulletin* (Winter 1979): ibid., 20 (Fall 1979):13.

15. Falk and Quaynor-Malm, "Early Afro-American Medical Education," 350.

16. Dr. Hildrus A. Poindexter, oral interview on 23 March 1978 at Howard University Medical School, tape 1, side A; see also Todd L. Savitt, *Medicine and Slavery* (Champaign: University of Illinois Press, 1979).

17. Falk and Quaynor-Malm, "Early Afro-American Medical Education," 350.

18. Henry E. Sigerist, *A History of Medicine* (New York: Oxford University Press, 1961), 310–11.
19. *Howard University Record: Howard University School of Medicine* 13, 4 (June 1918); *Howard University Bulletin* 11, 7 (August 1930):52–53.
20. Meharry *Catalogue* for the years 1876–1921, 1922, and 1924–1925.
21. Leslie A. Falk, "A Century of Service: Meharry Medical College," *Southern Exposure* 6 (1978):17.
22. Poindexter, *My World of Reality*, 99. Michael Winston, oral interview on 21 May 1979 at the Moorland-Spingarn Research Center, Howard University; W. Montague Cobb, "Hildrus Augustus Poindexter, M.D., M.S.P.H., Ph.D., D.Sc., 1901–" *Journal of the National Medical Association* 65, 3 (May 1973):243–247; and Ernest Everett Just, *The Biology of the Cell Surface* (Philadelphia: P. Blakiston, Son and Co., 1939). Mrs. Yvonne Brown supplied useful data on Charles Drew.
23. *Howard University Bulletin: School of Medicine* 11, 3 (October 1931); Poindexter, *My World of Reality*, 116–19; Poindexter, oral interview, tape 1, side A.
24. Louis S. Goodman and Alfred Gilman, eds., *The Pharmacological Basis of Therapeutics* (New York: Macmillan, 1975), 1113, 1130; Poindexter, oral interview, tape 1, sides A and B; Judith S. Mausner and Anita K. Bahn, *Epidemiology: An Introductory Test* (Philadelphia: W. B. Saunders Co., 1974); Hartwig and Patterson, *Disease in African History*.
25. Leslie A. Falk, "Alternate Health Care: Does Medicine Care about It?" The Guthrie Bulletin, Vol. 48, Fall 1968. Available from author.
26. See Tom W. Shick, *Behold the Promised Land: A History of Afro-American Settler Society in Nineteenth Century Liberia* (Baltimore: Johns Hopkins University Press, 1980).
27. For references to Howard University African M.D. graduates see the following: *Directory of Graduates: Howard University—1870–1963*; HU Publications Washington, D.C., 1 July 1965; *Howard University Directory of Graduates, 1870–1976*; White Plains, NY, Bernard C. Harris Pub. Co., 1977. Daniel Smith Lamb, *Howard University Medical Department: A Historical, Biographical and Statistical Souvenir* (Freeport, N.Y.: Books for Libraries Press, 1971), 143, 154, 211, 258; *Howard University Bulletin* 9, 3 (1914); ibid., 10, 4 (1915); ibid., 7, 7 (June 1928); ibid., 12 (February 1933); ibid., 15 (February 1935); ibid., 18, 7 (15 January 1939); *Bulletin College of Medicine 1959–1960*; *Bulletin of Howard University—College of Medicine 1974–1975* (see *Bulletin* for other years not cited); *Howard University Medial Alumni Association Directory*; Easmon, "Sierra Leone Doctors," 81–93; and Penelope Campbell, *Maryland in Africa: The Maryland State Colonization Society 1831–1857* (Urbana: University of Illinois Press, 1971), for medical objectives of the Methodist Episcopal Church at Cape Palmas. See also the official histories of Howard University: Walter Dyson, *Howard University: The Capstone of Negro Education: 1867–1940* (Washington, D.C.: Howard University, 1941); Rayford W. Logan, *Howard University: The First One Hundred Years, 1867–1967* (New York: New York University Press, 1969).
28. E. Latunde Odeku, *Twilight Out of the Night* (Ibadan: University of Ibadan, 1964), 71. I thank Dr. Calvin H. Sinnette for bringing this source to my attention.
29. For other references to Meharry African M.D. graduates see the following: *Meharry—Medical, Dental and Pharmaceutical Departments—Catalogue of 1894–1895* (Nashville, TN: Meharry College, 1895); also catalog of 1900–1901, 1902–1903, 1903–1904, 1905 (missing), 1907–1908, 1914–1915, 1920–1921, 1923–1924, 1924–1925, 1936; *Bulletin of Meharry Medical College 1937*; ibid., 1938; *Meharry Medical College Bulletin* 38, 1–A (July 1941); ibid., 50, 4 (1954); *Meharry Medical College: The Centennial Issue (1876–1976)* Nashville, TN, 1976; and "African Alumni—Meharry Medical College," unpublished report prepared for the author by the Meharry Alumni Office; and Campbell, *Maryland in Africa*.

30. Falk and Quaynor-Malm, "Early Afro-American Medical Education in the United States," 352.

31. Kings Mbacazwa Phiri, "Afro-American Influence in Colonial Malawi to about 1940" (Paper presented at the Diaspora Studies Institute, Howard University, Washington, D.C., August 26–31, 1979), 1–33.

32. Phiri, "Afro-American Influence in Colonial Malawi"; and Richard D. Ralston, "American Episodes in the Making of an African Leader: A Case Study of Alfred B. Xuma (1893–1962)," *International Journal of African Historical Studies* 6, 1 (1973):72–93.

33. Donald Segal, *African Profiles* (Baltimore: Penguin, 1962), 89.

8
Afro-Mexican Culture and Consciousness During the Sixteenth and Seventeenth Centuries

Colin Palmer

THE history of the early African presence in the Western Hemisphere is still largely unknown. Not only have historians not focused their energies on the formative period of black life in the Americas but the documentary evidence becomes less accessible and reliable the further one goes back in time. Yet there can be no doubt that it is critically important to investigate the lives of those blacks who were among the pioneers in the building of the Americas under European rule. It is, of course, ahistorical to make generalizations about black life and culture based entirely or principally on nineteenth-century sources. The black experience in the Americas was never static. It changed in accordance with the circumstances of time and place, the nature of the economies, and the creative responses of peoples of African descent to their environments.

The first African came to the Americas with the Spanish colonizers in 1493. He was a free man.[1] It was not until 1501, however, that the institution of slavery was established in the colonies. In that year, the Spanish monarchs Ferdinand and Isabella authorized the use of black slaves in Hispaniola. In time, slavery would spread to the islands of Cuba, Puerto Rico, and Jamaica as well as to the mainland colonies. Few in number, blacks did not form integral parts of these societies in the first decades of the sixteenth century. The Indians constituted the principal elements of the labor force in these early years.

125

The decline of the Indian population, however, accelerated the demand for African slaves. The demographic catastrophe that the Indians underwent resulted in part from their not having any immunity to the new diseases the Spaniards brought to the Americas. Many Indians also succumbed to Spanish brutality. Consequently, in less than a hundred years after the Spanish Conquest, the indigenous population of the Caribbean islands virtually disappeared. In Central Mexico, the Indian population declined from an estimated 27,000,000 in 1519 to less than 2,000,000 by 1605.[2]

The need for an exploited labor force, consequent on the decline of the Indian population, formed the most compelling reason for the importation of Africans in ever larger numbers to Mexico and to other Spanish colonies. Mexico, or New Spain as it was called, presented the Spaniards with an opportunity to amass large fortunes in silver mining, sugar cultivation, and other agricultural pursuits. Given the disdain with which many Spaniards viewed manual labor and the drastic decline in the size of the Indian population, it was imperative that a new labor force be found if the economic dreams of the colonists were to be realized.

The first Africans who came to Mexico shortly after the Conquest had served previously in Spain and, in varying degrees, had been acculturated to Spanish norms and practices. As the demand for African workers increased, however, they were imported directly from Africa. Known as *bozales*, these individuals had to become Hispanicized in Mexico, although, as will be demonstrated, they were able to preserve much of their African heritage.

Given the present state of research, it is not possible to determine with complete accuracy the number of African slaves who arrived in Mexico during the sixteenth and seventeenth centuries. An examination of the shipping records, however, suggests that as many as 150,000 Africans were imported into Mexico by 1650.[3] The vast majority of these people came roughly between 1570 and 1620, the years that experienced the highest rate of decline of the Indian population. Although blacks never constituted more than two percent of the total population at any one time, they outnumbered the Spaniards from as early as 1570. In that year, there were 14,711 Spaniards, 18,567 black slaves, and 1,400 mulattoes in the colony.

Population figures are more scarce and probably less reliable for the seventeenth century. A few estimates may be cited, particularly for the capital city, but the aforementioned caveat must be borne in mind. In 1612, for example, the traveler Vázquez de Espinosa, who visited Mexico City, reported a population of 50,000 blacks and mulattoes, 15,000 Spaniards, and 80,000 Indians. Thirty-four years later (1646), Diez de la

Calle estimated that there were 30,000 blacks and 20,000 Afro-Mestizos in Mexico. Finally, in 1698, Gemelli Carreri noted that "Mexico City contains about 1,000,000 inhabitants, but the greatest part of them are Blacks and Mulattoes by reason of the vast number of slaves that has [*sic*] been carried thither."[4] A contemporary scholar, Aguirre Beltran, has estimated that the black population of the archbishopric of Mexico, which included Mexico City, amounted to 19,441 in 1646. It is unlikely, given the level of the slave trade and the birth and mortality rates of the slaves that the Afro-Mexican population ever exceeded 50,000 at any time during the seventeenth century.[5]

Although they were a small minority, Afro-Mexicans made a contribution to colonial society that was in inverse proportion to their number. Much of the black contribution, however, was made in an environment where they were defined as property and viewed with a certain degree of hostility. Spaniards were convinced that Afro-Mexicans were "naturally evil," of "bad race," and "bad caste." One viceroy observed that blacks were a "vicious people," and another concluded that mulattoes were "naturally arrogant, audacious and fond of change." One local official added that the slaves were "bellicose, bestial and ferocious."[6]

Viewed essentially in a negative light, blacks were invariably placed at the bottom of the hierarchical society that the Spaniards created. In fact, an individual's race was the primary determinant of his rank in the social structure. In a society that placed a premium on whiteness, the Spaniards were ranked at the top, followed by the mixed groups, and then by the Indians and the blacks. Nonwhites in such a society had to struggle constantly to define themselves as people and to preserve the integrity of their cultural heritage. The Spanish colonizers sought, albeit unsuccessfully, to eradicate many aspects of the culture of the indigenous peoples and to elevate their own to a position of respectability and unquestioned supremacy. Although it is now generally appreciated that the Indians preserved much of their cultural integrity and engaged effectively in acts of cultural resistance, the black struggle to achieve the same end has not been accorded much recognition.[7]

Recent studies of the experiences of slaves in the Americas have demonstrated the remarkable cultural resilience of the peoples of African descent. Obviously, there was much diversity in the responses of the Africans to the variegated cultural milieu of the societies of the New World. Slaves in North America were exposed to the English variant of European culture and so were their counterparts in the British Caribbean. Similarly, blacks in the Spanish Empire were influenced by Iberian culture. Yet it may be argued that Africans, particularly those who lived in colonies with a large Indian population such as Mexico, were influenced culturally more by the Indians with whom they came into daily contact and less by their Spanish masters. In any event, the notion of a completely Hispanicized African cannot be supported by the evidence extant for Mexico or for any other Spanish colony.

Given the disproportionate ratio of black males to females in Mexico, it is not surprising that the men would seek to establish amorous liaisons with Indian women. According to Viceroy Martin Enriquez in 1574, the Indian women were "very weak and very attracted to the negroes and so they prefer them rather than the Indians while the negroes marry them rather than those of their own kind in order to make their children free."[8] The accuracy of the viceroy's interpretation of the reasons for these unions may be doubted, and it may be added that his campaign to end such relationships failed. Known as *zambos*, the progeny of these unions drew their cultural inspiration from their Indian and African parents as well as from the Spaniards. Because zambos were more likely to be reared by their mothers, it may be guessed that they were more influenced and shaped by them culturally.

Available evidence suggests that Afro-Mexicans acquired some of the cultural practices of the Indians. Such was the case, for example, of one slave who was accused by the Inquisition in 1582 of having consumed "the meal that the Indians offered in their idolatries to the gods."[9] Another indication of culture contact between the two peoples was the use of the hallucinatory drug called peyote. The Indians' use of the drug had preceded the arrival of the Spaniards, and the Africans acquired the knowledge of its qualities from them. Although the Holy Office prohibited its use in 1620, this did not deter its devotees. Afro-Mexicans claimed that peyote performed a variety of functions for them, such as curing illnesses, divining the future, and discovering wrongdoers.[10]

Afro-Mexicans were also wont to wear the traditional garb of the Indian cultures, a practice that suggested some degree of acculturation. The Spanish authorities frowned on this development, since they wanted to prevent association between the two peoples. In addition, free blacks who committed crimes had a tendency to disguise themselves as Indians to avoid detection. Consequently, in 1582 the Spaniards made it illegal for black and mulatto women to dress "in the habit of Indian women."[11] The ordinance, however, excused Afro-Mexicans married to Indian men from its purview. The enforcement of this restriction was easier said than done, as successive colonial leaders were to discover.[12]

Not surprisingly, the relationship between the Afro-Mexicans and the Indians was not always amicable. Blacks, particularly those who were free and who possessed physical mobility, entered Indian communities and abused some of the residents. As early as 1538, Friar Francisco de Guzman reported to the Crown that "from the negroes and servants who live on the haciendas, the natives have received and receive notable harm because they take by force what they have in their houses and sometimes their daughters and their wives."[13] Almost a century later, Viceroy Velasco complained that Afro-Mexicans were still entering Indian villages where they "possess more liberty and commit great excesses without punishment."[14]

These and other manifestations of conflict between Indians and Afro-Mexicans reflected the deeper tensions in colonial society. It may be argued that these attacks, in a superficial and socially deviant way, demonstrated some degree of racial consciousness on the part of the blacks, vis à vis other groups. Such occurrences were more fundamentally stark demonstrations of the phenomenon of oppressed groups in society directing their violence and frustrations against one another and not against their common oppressors.

There can be no doubt that African slaves, in varying degrees, also underwent a process of Hispanicization in colonial Mexico. Many of them, particularly the Creoles, spoke Spanish. A few Afro-Mexicans, slave and free, were fortunate enough to be able to read and write in their language. The Spanish Crown also sought to convert the blacks to Catholicism, although the souls of the Indians received far more attention from the church than did those of the blacks. In 1537, however, the Crown ordered that Afro-Mexicans receive religious instruction at appointed times each day.[15] Although the implementation of this order was subject to much variation according to time, place, and the masters' sensitivity to the need for religious instruction for the slaves, many blacks were exposed to the precepts of the Catholic church.

Yet it must be concluded that the attempts to Hispanicize the African were only partially successful. It was precisely in those areas associated with their religious beliefs that blacks were able to manifest a significant and abiding adherence to their traditions. In 1612, for example, a Spanish observer reported that blacks who attended a funeral ceremony "gathered together with barbarous ceremonies and rites used in their nation of origin, and while singing, shouting and dancing, they smothered the corpse with oil and wine and did the same to the grave ... and having also thrown dirt into it they raised one arm in a menacing manner as if they were about to take part in a war or a rebellion."[16] Obviously, such beliefs and practices did not all survive in a pure form but were refashioned and shaped by Catholicism and the Indian religions to which they were exposed.

The records of the Holy Office of the Inquisition are replete with instances of Afro-Mexicans accused of religious deviance. The Holy Office saw itself as the guardian of Spanish morals and religious orthodoxy, and it ferreted out and punished those whom it considered to be religious offenders. In many instances, the Afro-Mexicans were merely engaged in the practice of their religion, which included many precepts that were African in origin. The Holy Office believed that many of these beliefs and practices derived their inspiration from the devil and that this placed the practitioner outside the state of grace. Spaniards who were unfamiliar with the cultures of Africa were likely to conclude that these Afro-Mexicans were either agents of Lucifer or were in league with other evil forces.

Spanish authorities frequently accused Afro-Mexicans of practicing witchcraft and sorcery. It is evident from the records of the trials, however, that the Holy Office did not establish a clear distinction between the two. In Renaissance Europe, witchcraft was considered to be a religious aberration because the witch was deemed to have made a pact with the devil. Sorcery, on the other hand, was seen as a special kind of magic used deliberately and exclusively for malevolent purposes.[17] Contemporary scholars have noted that many African peoples do not view the practice of witchcraft or sorcery as constituting religious aberrations.[18] In the context of sixteenth- and seventeenth-century Mexico, however, many of those blacks accused of sorcery or witchcraft were merely engaging in activities to which they had been accustomed in Africa or had learned from the Indians and even from some Spaniards in Mexico. The Holy Office evidently misunderstood the meaning of these folk beliefs and what could probably be called magico-religious practices.

Afro-Mexicans employed a wide variety of their folk practices to achieve a desired objective. Individuals who wanted to win the affections of a certain person resorted to the carrying of charms that were thought to be quite efficacious in matters of that nature. These objects included sticks, idols, human hair, bones of animals, feathers, and herbs. Some believers applied certain potions to their bodies or to the victim's clothes. Luisa, a slave, reported that she was instructed to apply some powder to her hands so that "the men would love her." The consumption of certain potions also performed a similar objective. Two women, for example, were accused of "giving men ground fingernails in their drinks in order to make the men love them."[19]

Afro-Mexicans also resorted to their folk practices to obtain more humane treatment from their masters. Such was the case of Juan Sebastian, who obtained "a little rue, onion and garlic and, drawing a little blood from his arm, he should mix these things together and he should do this in order that his master should treat him well."[20] Other blacks sought to use their magico-religious practices to divine the future, avenge a wrong, or even detect those who had committed offenses. The efficacy of these practices is, of course, not the issue. Afro-Mexicans used them because they performed useful functions in their lives, responded to felt needs, and reflected their world view.

Africans who escaped to inaccessible parts of Mexico and established settlements or palenques were probably the ones who were most successful in preserving vestiges of their past. In 1591, a community of runaways who lived on a mountain called Coyula were described as living "as if they were actually in Guinea."[21] The most famous of these communities was located in the Orizaba region of Vera Cruz. This settlement had as many as five hundred residents during the late sixteenth and early seventeenth centuries. Led by Yanga, a man who had escaped and preserved his freedom for thirty years, these Africans engaged in various agricultural pursuits and practiced a sexual division of labor similar to that which existed in their African homelands. The women were responsible for agricultural labor, and the men saw to the defense of the community.[22] It may be concluded that these and other runaways were able to replicate African kingdoms on the soil of the Americas.

If Afro-Americans were able to maintain some of their cultural traditions, what of their ability to maintain a family under difficult circumstances? Historians are in general agreement that the Africans who came to the Americas hailed from societies with strong kinship systems. Thus, it is not surprising that they would seek to live in family units in the New World. Herbert Gutman has shown that during the nineteenth century, most North American slaves lived in families with one or two parents present. Given the present state of our knowledge about Afro-Mexicans during the sixteenth and seventeenth centuries, however, it is not possible to make any definitive statements about the nature of their family life.

There are indications, nevertheless, that to some extent Afro-Mexicans were able to establish and maintain families. The Catholic church played an active role in encouraging blacks to marry and not to live in concubinage. There were, to be sure, enormous difficulties to be overcome in order to achieve an objective. The overwhelming numerical preponderance of black males vis à vis females was not conducive to marriage. Some masters opposed the marriages of their slaves, and others broke up such unions when they occurred.[23] Still, recent research suggests that Afro-Mexicans contracted marriage unions whenever the circumstances permitted.

It appears that the majority of blacks tended to marry other blacks or mulattoes during the sixteenth and seventeenth centuries. Data from the ingenio at Tuxtla in 1577 show that of the twenty-seven black men who were married, thirteen chose black female slaves as their wives and fourteen chose Indian and mulatto women.[24] A similar pattern is revealed when one examines the marriage records of the Sagrario Parish, located in Mexico City. During the years 1665–70, 48.6 percent of the blacks who married chose black spouses, and 34.7 percent chose mulattoes. For the period 1694– 96, 35.3 percent of the sixty-eight blacks who got married in that parish selected other blacks, and 51.5 percent chose mulattoes.[25] In his study of the marriage patterns of Afro-Mexicans in the parish of Santa Vera Cruz in Mexico City between 1646 and 1746, Edgar Love found that the priests "married 1,662 couples, of whom one or both parties were persons of African descent."[26]

It may be argued that these statistics relating to formal marriages obscure the real nature of the slaves' family life. Afro-Mexicans, like their counterparts in other societies of the Americas, were more likely to live in common-law marriages than to be legally married. In some societies, such as those in North America, slave marriages had no legal standing. The religious authorities in Mexico attempted to break up such unions but were quite unsuccessful in that enterprise. Black slaves in early colonial Mexico also may have consciously rejected or did not fully understand the deeper meaning of marriage as a Christian sacrament. It is this imperfect understanding or rejection of one of the canons of Catholicism that probably led one slave to conclude that it was "no sin to live in concubinage."[27] The evidence is beginning to suggest that Afro-Mexicans, whether they contracted formal marriages or lived in concubinage, sought to create a family life that gave meaning to their lives and helped them endure the pressures of slavery.

The preceding discussion of aspects of Afro-Mexican culture supports the view that these people created a life for themselves quite unlike that of their Spanish masters. The cultural autonomy that they were able to foster and maintain allowed them to define themselves as a group of people who were different from others in society. Afro-Mexicans never lost their African racial and cultural identity. Indeed, their ability to retain vestiges of the African heritage was a successful manifestation of cultural resistance. In addition, it was the Afro-Mexican's consciousness of themselves as an exploited group that accounted for their participation in various acts of physical resistance throughout the sixteenth and seventeenth centuries.

It is apparent from the available evidence that the black slaves challenged the system that exploited them shortly after their arrival in the colony. This sense of perceived injustice led some slaves to escape as early as 1523, barely four years after the Spaniards first came to Mexico.[28] Known as *cimarrones*, the number of these individuals who withdrew from slavery increased from time to time. Many of these cimarrones established enclaves that served simultaneously as sanctuaries and bases of operations. In 1560, the cimarrones in Pachuca used a cave as their headquarters.[29] Others selected mountainous terrains to construct their settlements. Such secluded and inaccessible areas made it difficult for the colonists to locate and suppress the palenques.

Colonial bureaucrats were unyielding in their attempts to recapture the cimarrones and destroy their settlements. Consequently, military expeditions were dispatched at regular intervals to achieve those objectives. The Spaniards imposed severe penalties on the recaptured cimarrones. In 1590, for example, the viceroy ordered that runaways who absented themselves for more than one night receive 30 lashes. A second offense carried a penalty of 200 lashes and the loss of one ear. A third offense brought 200 lashes and the loss of both ears, and the slave would be hanged if he escaped a fourth time.[30] These measures were largely ineffective as Afro-Mexicans, acting singly or collectively, tried to liberate themselves.

Runaway slaves, in many instances, were able to maintain their freedom. Some successfully eluded recapture by the Spaniards, and others forced the colonial authorities to recognize their freedom. Such was the case of the cimarrones who lived in the Orizaba region of Vera Cruz during the late sixteenth and early seventeenth centuries. These Afro-Mexicans had maintained their freedom for many years, having defeated the Spaniards in several armed confrontations. In 1609, their leader, Yanga, justified their right to be free on the grounds that they had escaped from the "cruelty and treachery of the Spaniards who, without any right, had become owners of their freedom." The Spaniards were unimpressed by such claims and dispatched about four hundred and fifty men to destroy Yanga's settlement. Both sides eventually engaged in combat, but the results were inconclusive. The truce that brought the hostilities to an end recognized the freedom of the cimarrones and gave them their own cabildo, or town council. In return, Yanga agreed to return all future runaways to their masters.[31] It is quite clear that this particular group of cimarrones never compromised on the question of their own freedom and acquired it as a result of their courage and persistence.

The ideology of freedom was also reflected in the actions of those Afro-Mexicans who did not escape but who planned and participated in rebellions. These individuals were no less conscious than the cimarrones were of the injustice of their condition, but they chose to attack the institution of slavery from within. As early as 1537, these slaves organized a rebellion in Mexico City and elected a king. Their plans were revealed, however, and the conspirators were arrested and executed.[32] These and other threats to the social order by the slaves led the viceroy to complain to the Crown in 1553 that "this land is so full of negroes and mestizos that they outnumber the Spaniards greatly. Your Majesty should order that they do not give so many licenses to send negroes because there are in New Spain more than twenty thousand and they are increasing."[33]

The increasingly complex nature of the Mexican economy with its demand for a large exploited labor force coupled with the rapid decline in the Indian population ensured that the viceroy's pleas would fall on deaf ears. In fact, the number of African slaves in the colony continued to grow. Nor did the threat of rebellions diminish. Afro-Mexicans, both slave and free, never ceased to plan ways of destroying a system that kept them in thralldom.

One of the most carefully planned conspiracies occurred in 1608 in Mexico City. Thirty-one conspirators gathered on Christmas Eve to elect a king and queen and to name dukes, courts, princes, and princesses who would assume power after the rebellion succeeded. One of the participants, a mulatto woman, announced that it was only a matter of time until the Spaniards and everyone else would be their [the blacks'] slaves. Her expectations, however, were never realized. The conspiracy was revealed, and the authorities arrested those who were involved.[34] It is important to underscore the point that the participants in the conspiracy represented a coalition of free blacks and mulattoes as well as slaves. If nothing else, its composition demonstrates that both groups, slave and free, identified with each other and shared similar interests.

Slaves and free persons of African descent also made common cause in a conspiracy that occurred in 1611 in Mexico City. On that occasion, fifteen hundred Afro-Mexicans angrily and defiantly marched through the streets, charging that maltreatment had caused the death of a female slave. When the authorities arrested and punished the leaders of this protest demonstration, their peers proceeded to plan a rebellion for the purpose of killing Spaniards. The conspirators duly elected a king and a queen to wield power in a black-controlled Mexico. As was the case with the previous conspiracies, however, the Spaniards got word of the plans and arrested those who were identified as the leaders. Thirty-five Afro-Mexicans were hanged and quartered in the central square of Mexico City for their role in the affair.[35] As horrifying as this spectacle undoubtedly was, it did not deter many Afro-Mexicans from seeking ways to liberate themselves throughout the seventeenth century.

Although much work still remains to be done, the broad contours of Afro-Mexican culture in the sixteenth and seventeenth centuries can be painted. The picture that emerges is that of individuals struggling to adjust to a new cultural milieu under very adverse circumstances and simultaneously retaining elements of their past. In their religious beliefs, their folk practices, and the social organization of their runaway communities, and in a variety of other ways, Afro-Mexicans asserted a degree of cultural independence. Their violent challenges to the institution of slavery meant, in addition, that their spirit remained unbroken. Nor should this be surprising. Afro-Mexicans, like other peoples of African descent in the Western Hemisphere, courageously defined themselves as persons, often in quiet and unspectacular ways, although others in society perceived them as property and treated them as such. Their bodies were enslaved, but these men and women controlled aspects of their lives and being that were beyond the reach of the most persistent of masters.

NOTES

1. A number of writers have suggested that there were pre-Columbian contacts between Africa and the Americas. See Leo Wiener, *Africa and the Discovery of America*, 3 vols. (Philadelphia, 1920–1922).
2. Woodrow Borah and Sheraburne Cook, *The Aboriginal Population of Central Mexico on the Eve of the Spanish Conquest*, Ibero-Americana, no. 45 (Berkeley and Los Angeles, 1963), 4. See also their *Essays in Population History* (Berkeley and Los Angeles: University of California Press, 1971), 115.
3. Consult Colin Palmer, *Slaves of the White God: Blacks in Mexico 1570–1650* (Cambridge: Harvard University Press, 1976), 36.
4. See "Censos de la población del Virreinato de Nueva España en el siglo xvi," *Boletín del Centro de Estudios Americanistas de Sevilla de Indias*, Año vi, nos. 23 and 24 (February–March 1919), 45–46.
5. For these estimates see Antonio Vázquez de Espinosa, *Compendio y descripción de las Indias Occidentales*, ed. Charles Clarke (Washington, 1948), 146; John Francis Gemelli Careri, "A Voyage Round the World," in *A Collection of Voyages and Travels*, ed. A. Churchill, 6 vols. (London, 1745), iv, 508; Juan Díez de la Calle, *Noticias sacras y reales de los imperias de las Indias Occidentales*, 2nd ed. (Mexico, 1932); Gonzalo Aguirre Beltrán, *La poblacion Negra de Mexico*, 2nd ed. (Mexico, 1972), 220.
6. For various characterizations of the African, see Gonzalo Gomez de Cervantes, *La vida económica y social de Nueva España al finalizar el siglo xvi*, ed. Alberto María Carreño (Mexico, 1944), 99; *Actas de Cabildo de la Ciudad de México*, 59 vols. (Mexico, 1889–1919), 13, bk 13, 115; *Instrucciones que los Virreyes de Nueva España dejaron a sus sucesores*, 2 vols. (Mexico, 1869–1873), 1, 259; Archivo General de la Nación, Mexico City, Ramo de Ordenanzas, vol. 2, fols. 36^v–37^v; hereafter AGN Ordenanzas.
7. For an excellent discussion of the Indians of New Spain, see Charles Gibson, *The Aztecs under Spanish Rule: A History of the Indians of the Valley of Mexico, 1519–1810* (Stanford: Stanford University Press, 1964).
8. *Cartas de Indias* (Madrid, 1877), 36.
9. Archivo General de la Nación, Ramo de Inquisicion, vol. 125 exp. 69, in Gonzalo Aguirre Beltrán, "La etnohistoria ye el estudio del Negro en México," in *Acculturation in the Americas*, ed. Sol Tax (1952, reprinted New York: Cooper Square Publishers, 1967), 163.
10. See Archivo General de la Nación, Mexico City, Ramo de Inquisición, vol. 339, fols. 275–276, vol. 342, no. 10; vol. 302, no. 8; hereafter AGN Inquisición.
11. AGN, Ordenanzas, vol. 1, fol. 75.

9

A Lesser-Known Chapter of the African Diaspora: West Indians in Costa Rica, Central America

Roy Simon Bryce-Laporte,
assisted by Trevor Purcell

D
RAWING from Rosenblatt's statistics of 1940, Frank Tannenbaum concluded there are 41 million blacks and mulattoes in North and South America, or approximately fifteen percent of the total population (274 million). He further points out that at some time between the sixteenth and twentieth centuries, every country in the Americas has had a measurable presence of blacks in its population.[1] And even though he later discusses variations in the number, proportion, experience, and status of blacks, Tannenbaum shares with us the nineteenth-century perception by Humboldt:

> From Rio de Janeiro northwards, the coastal stretches of Brazil, French, Dutch, and British Guiana, Venezuela, Colombia on both the Atlantic and the Pacific, Ecuador, and Peru have significant and in certain districts preponderant numbers of people of African origin. This same holds true for both coasts in Central America. If Humboldt's reference is taken in a demographic rather than a political sense, the colonization of the Western Hemisphere has involved the settlement of many thousands of square miles by peoples who come from Africa rather than from Europe, and if we draw an arc from Rio de Janeiro to Washington, D.C., and include the West Indian islands within it, we shall have, in outline, the empire Humboldt talked about.[2]

The plantation system was introduced and gained hegemony at different times in different countries, and it sometimes followed rather than accompanied or preceded slavery. Even so, this system has been the contextual baseline and structural commonality in the experience of blacks throughout the Americas, notwithstanding differences in stages or types of plantations or in statuses among Afro-Americans.[3] As such, the plantation system has affected not only culture but also status, identity, organization, and human relations of all members of society. In political-economic terms, it is generally a rural-agricultural form of domination and exploitation; it is a bureaucratic asymmetrical relationship often among alien subordinate capital and technology, native natural resources or territory, and subordinate alien or native labor; it is also a system for controlling labor and preventing ethnic or status "contamination" of the larger society.

Plantations have exercised indisputable hegemony and extensive determination over every aspect of the lives of blacks. This holds not only for the United States[4] but also for other places in the American side of the diaspora.

Therefore, it is obligatory to analyze plantation societies for two reasons: (1) to obtain a fuller understanding of black communities in the diaspora and (2) to appreciate similarities and differences in historical experiences, sociocultural changes and continuities, and the courses and consequences of these on black people throughout the diaspora as well as in Africa.

The presence of blacks in the greater Central American Isthmus has never been emphasized in social, scientific, or historical literature, even though Belice and Panama are rivaled only by Guyana (formerly British Guiana) in having the highest concentration of blacks and mulattoes on the Central American mainland.

Black presence on the greater Central American Isthmus has always been varied. This is due in part to differences in origin, culture, and degree of nonblack mixture among the blacks and in part to their varying relations to the institutionalization of a dominant plantation system of the area. That kind of system was not present during the period of European colonial slavery; it came later. During the colonial period there were black slaves, but they usually worked at jobs other than those of the plantation, such as lumbering, pearl diving, ranching, cargo bearing, mining, and urban, dock, and domestic work. Even where plantations existed, they did not yet dominate the political economy of these states. The plantation system was exported to the Greater Isthmus from North America in the mid-eighteenth century, sometimes by colonial governments rather than private enterprises.

At various points in history, Americans have flirted with the idea of using the Central American Isthmus as an extension of the southern slave plantation society. In reality, however, plantations on the Isthmus did not use slaves, either black American slaves or Haitian freed men. From the beginning they used very few, if any, natives. Their labor force was supplied by black ex-slaves imported from the West Indies. Thus, as the United States replaced its European predecessor as the dominant colonial force in Central America, it also introduced a second step in the black diaspora—the movement of black free labor to build and maintain plantations in lands alien both to them and to their white superordinate benefactors.[5] Variations developed among the systems and societies of the area, but sufficient similarities emerged to make the case presented in this paper more than an isolated geographic event; as we will see, the similarities have implications for the whole region and indeed for future relations between races, classes, and cultures there.

This paper traces the experience of a group of black people through two historically different plantation systems. This group was forcibly brought from Africa to provide labor for Spanish and English plantations in Jamaica during the sixteenth and seventeenth centuries. By the late eighteenth century, the emancipated descendants of these plantation slaves were recruited by North Americans as labor for construction, cultivation, and maintenance of plantations throughout the Central American Isthmus.

Province of Limon, Costa Rica

The Republic of Costa Rica has long been reputed to be the most homogeneous country in Central America—an almost totally white, Catholic, Castillian country. According to a 1973 census, a population of 1,871,780 inhabits an area of 19,328 square miles. The country has seven provinces, one of which is Limon.

The province of Limon, which embraces the entire Atlantic or Caribbean coast of Costa Rica, falls in the area called *tierra caliente*, or hotlands. The majority of the country's population and most of the other provinces are situated in the *tierra templade*, or temperate lands, better known as the *Meseta Central*, or central plateau. The tropical climate of Limon is hotter and more humid than the temperate central provinces. Limon's agriculture, too, differs from the rest of the country.

By the 1970s, Limon's principal agricultural product was cacao (with some resumption and commercial cultivation of bananas and plantains). Since 1950, Limon has had the smallest population of all the provinces; about a third of its population is black, and a third is English-speaking, each category being the highest among the provinces. It has the highest percentage of consensual unions; and the highest percentage of unidentified tenure as well as squatters. It also has the lowest white population and the fewest Spanish-speaking individuals.[6]

The area was inhabited in pre-Columbian times by the Vicetas and the Huetares, two Carib groups, interspersed by a few Nahua or Aztec settlements. The history of the region between the early sixteenth century and 1821, the year Costa Rica separated from Spain, is one of repeated, futile efforts by the Spaniards to conquer and Christianize the Indians of Talamance and of looting, contraband, and slave raidings by the Zambos (hybrids of runaway Negro slaves and coastal Indians), Moskito Indians, and English buccaneers operating off Jamaica. Until the Jamaicans arrived in the 1870s, Limon was an isolated seaport. Prior to the 1870s, Costa Rica was inhabited by other Negroid groups: slaves who worked the cattle ranches and dyewood plantations in the northeast but who are now largely assimilated into the dominant Hispanic sector, and the *cimarrones* (maroons) who lived off the Atlantic coast and who intermixed with the Moskito Indians of the coast. Neither of these two groups, however, has contributed to the demographic, economic, social, and cultural history of Limon and Costa Rica as have the Jamaicans, who entered the area after 1870 (see Table 1).

Jamaican Migration to Limon and Other Central American Ports

English-speaking blacks from Jamaica entered Costa Rica in the early 1870s and continued to do so in intermittent waves until the late 1920s. Some came from other Central American countries or from Panama, but the majority left Jamaica directly for Costa Rica. The 1950 census shows a steady increase in the Jamaican population of Costa Rica from 1885 to 1927 (see Table 2).

TABLE 1
NEGROES IN COSTA RICA: 1522–1801

Year	Negroes	Mulattoes	Total Population
1522	—	—	27,200 (Indians)
1569	50	170	17,479 (Mixtos)
1611	25	250	15,538 (Mixtos)
1700	154	1291	19,293 (Mixtos)
1720	168	2195	19,437 (Mixtos)
1741	200	3065	24,126 (Mixtos)
1758	62	2937	24,022 (Mixtos)
1778	94	6053	34,212 (Mixtos)
1801	50	8925	52,591 (Mixtos)

Source: Tulio Amador Quiros, *Geografía de Costa Rica* (1934), p. 85, citing Bernardo Thiel in *Revista de Costa Rica en el Siglo XIX*.

TABLE 2
NUMBER OF FOREIGNERS IN COSTA RICA

Nationality	1864	1885	1892	1927	1950
Jamaicans	—	902	754	17,245	No separate record made; included in 7,728 English men
Others	2,753	3,694	5,555	27,095	27,495
Total foreigners	2,753	4,596	6,309	44,340	35,223

Source: Tulio Amador Quiros, *Geografía de Costa Rica* (1934), p. 88–89, citing Pablo Luros, *Aspectos graficos de la Poblacion de Costa Rica.*

George Roberts, a respected Caribbean demographer, points out that in 1885 Jamaican migration to Panama decreased and was redirected to Costa Rica. The same phenomenon recurred in the years from 1914 through 1921.[7] Another source pointed out that Jamaicans were already entering Costa Rica in large numbers in the very early 1870s.[8] Melendez and Duncan established the presence of 766 Jamaicans (which no doubt included other West Indians as well) in Costa Rica by 1872.[9] Jamaicans were drawn to Costa Rica first by the construction of the railroads in the earlier periods and then, from the turn of the century into the 1920s, by the banana plantation operations. Yet, these were not the only major movements of the islanders to the Central American coastland. There was a continual flow of Jamaicans to the Caribbean coast of Central America for almost one hundred years. Between 1,500 and 2,000 Jamaicans were drawn to Panama by the transisthmian railroad, built in response to the California Gold Rush. There was another exodus to Panama in the 1880s, with a peak migration of 24,301 in the year 1885, when workers were recruited for the abortive French Canal project under DeLesseps.[10] The biggest exodus to Panama occurred between 1904 and 1914 when the Americans were constructing the Panama Canal.[11] Panama also drew the last notable movement to Central America when, in the 1930s and 1940s, changes were projected in the canal's structure and World War II created a demand for additional civilian employment.[12] Interspersing these movements to Panama and Costa Rica were comparable large movements to the United States and Cuba, and smaller movements to other Central American countries, plus Haiti, Colombia, Belize, and British Guiana (see Table 3).

In addition to those who went directly to Costa Rica from Jamaica, many went indirectly through other Central American ports. There seem to have been considerable recurrent, temporary, and nomadic migrations, in addition to permanent removals, of Jamaicans from one Central American country to another according to the vicissitudes of labor

TABLE 3
ESTIMATED NET EMIGRATION OF JAMAICANS: 1881–1921

Period	To U.S.A.	To Panama	To Cuba	To Other Areas, Especially C.R.	Total
1881–1891	16,000	17,000		10,000	43,000
1891–1911		26,000			26,000
1911–1921	30,000	2,000	22,000	23,000	77,000

Source: George Roberts, *Population of Jamaica* (Cambridge: Cambridge University Press, 1957).

demand and availability. This seems especially true of Costa Rica and Panama, and between these two and Jamaica itself.[13] Yet, in general, all parishes lost some people to the emigrations; Kingston lost some too, but the heavier losses were in the rural areas.[14]

British Culture in the Western Caribbean

Although Limon appears to be an anomaly compared with the rest of Costa Rica, it is in fact very similar to the Caribbean provinces of other Central American countries. Historically, the distinctive character-istics of Limon, in contrast to the rest of Costa Rica, can be attributed to the English and Jamaican presence in the western Caribbean. In this sense, Limon is just part of the larger cultural whole—distinct from the rest of Costa Rica—that Adams has called the Antillean Negro cultural component of the Africo-Euro-American cultural tradition.[15]

In the early days of conquest and colonization, the Spaniards ne-glected the Atlantic coast except for a few ports and outposts that were used in their travel to the much cherished highlands. This was true of the entire Central American Isthmus. Throughout the seventeenth cen-tury, the English, engaging in a flourishing trade with coastal Indians, claimed, conquered, and colonized many offshore islands.

The period from 1655, when the English occupied Jamaica, to the twentieth century, is marked by a steady expansion and consolidation of British trade and culture in the western Caribbean. Thus, today an almost perfect belt of concentration of no less than 500 thousand people who are English-speaking or for whom English constitutes a *lingua franca*, or a second language, stretches through Mexico and Honduras, to San Blas coast of Panama and all the offshore islands between Central America and Jamaica. The predominating genes are Negroid, but other races are represented. What does this pattern tell us about Limon?

Although many theories are possible,[16] Parsons has suggested the most tenable and applicable framework for understanding Limon:

> There is a feeling of kinship relationship and community of interest which still stretches from Belice and Kingston to Bocas del Toro and Colon, but nationalistic inspired legislation recently has been imposing increasing restraints and restrictions on the normal cultural and commercial relations and mobility of these people of such similar background.[17]

Thus, if Limon appears to be an anomaly within the Costa Rican sociocultural system, it certainly appears normal when conceived as part of the *system* comprising the western Caribbean coastal and insular societies of Central America. All these societies are populated principally by persons who are Jamaicans by either birth, ancestry, or heritage, and for whom neither the island nor its culture can be treated with indifference.

The United Fruit Company and Jamaican Immigrant Labor in Limon

The large-scale presence of Jamaican labor in Costa Rica began with the railroad construction. Because of the harsh climatic conditions of the Atlantic coast, the Keith brothers—American contractors charged with the execution of the project—had difficulties obtaining native or Central American labor and so turned to Jamaican black labor. The railroad soon ran into financial difficulties, and faced with a chaotic and discouraging situation, the Keith brothers decided to introduce the commercial planting of bananas as an adjunct to the railroad construction. This venture marked the beginning of the United Fruit Company.

The Caribbean province of Limon was the most completely controlled area of the country held by the United Fruit Company. By virtue of the Soto-Keith contract, the company was granted

> eight-hundred thousand acres of underdeveloped lands along the railroad line or in any part of the country to be selected by the company ... and two of the lots of national property now measured in the port of Limon, for the construction of wharves, warehouses, and stations—all without reimbursement of any sort.[18]

In addition, it was granted tax exemptions and free importation of all necessary materials. With increased production of bananas on its own land it was able to dismiss all competition and operate as an imperialistic monopoly.[19] It continued, however, to receive bananas from three additional sources: large semi-independent growers; small dependent growers with long-term contracts or leases; and peasants or squatters.[20] The large planters were Europeans and Central and North Americans and mostly white. Yet, even among them, a few Jamaican mulattoes gained prominence.

Extending its powers even into the affairs of the large private growers, the company issued five-year banana contracts that gave it far-reaching powers over the use of the lands.[21] Furthermore, by controlling railway, tram, and shipping lines, the company gained the indisputable role of middleman and controlled the commercial and agricultural activities of even the large, independent farmers.

Leases were limited to the production of fruits agreed on by the company (bananas in the earlier days and cacao and/or abaca in the latter days). They were not permitted to build any physical structure on their rented lands without proper authorization from the company. The company could terminate leases with a thirty-day notice, without obligation to pay indemnity. The company also held the lessee responsible for informing it of any squatters on adjacent lots owned by the company.[22]

In the 1930s, land was cheap, plentiful and fertile for many miles inward to the periphery of the Meseta. Yet, most Jamaicans were neither owners nor homesteaders. Most were squatters or, to be more exact, commuting part-time peasants/part-time laborers.

In accordance with the laws of the country, and with the contract between the company and the government, squatting had some amount of legal protection and strategic utility. From the government's viewpoint, after a squatter had occupied a given piece of land for a certain period of time, he could not be removed and had to be redeemed for the improvements or fixtures he introduced, in the case of any transfer or reclaiming of ownership. Hence, the company had to discover the squatters before he completed the given period. Once the period passed, and if the peasant proved willing, the company would sign an agreement, contract, and/or lease and convert the farmer from an independent peasant-squatter to a dependent small lessee.[23] This benefited the company in two ways: (1) it assured it of another supplier, and (2) it provided the company with the proof it needed to show the government that the land had been cultivated as agreed in the Soto-Keith contract. So that while the squatter theoretically served the government as one way of reducing the hold of the company, in practice he served the company by assuring the retention of the land. The company encouraged laborers to squat on the land that was undesirable for its own operations. It also ejected uncooperative squatters from its land after the legally defined period had passed. This tarantula of a company had undisputed power in the province, even over the peasants who, naturally, were its part- or full-time employees.

Some Jamaicans were the workers who rendered services by contracts and for standardized salaries. In general, there was some overlapping between these workers and the peasants, as many of the former were as much half-peasants or squatters as the latter were half-laborers. The company's hold on its workers was complete—it controlled labor, housing, food, medicine, transportation, and shopping, and even provided churches and schools with part of their operating funds. The company reduced wages, labor or the number of workers at will; it demanded increase in workers' services or improvement in workers' efficiency; it even controlled the spending of its employees by introducing a commissary store and coupon system. Receiving as part of their payment coupons redeemable only at the company's stores, workers were compelled to spend money on expensive items sold by the company store when cheaper models of the same commodities were available at private consumer shops. Many employees in need of cash sold these coupons to nonemployees, even though company statutes forbade the practice. Later, the coupon system was replaced by two other innovations: (1) credit blanks and (2) installment purchases that were less coercive than the coupon system but equally conducive to putting the workers into perpetual debt. Subsequent threats of foreclosure on these debts were then used to "encourage" worker cooperation, dependence, and patronage. It also minimized competition from retail and consumer business held by independent parties in the same way that other measures did against independent private planters.[24]

In its banana days in Limon, the company was indisputably monopolistic, totalitarian, and imperialistic. It controlled railroad, tram, and shipping routes, wharves, stores, and lands. All activities—commercial, political, and social—in Limon province were influenced and controlled by it. The company determined the ultimate location and settlement pattern of every townsite in the province after the 1870s. Puerto Limon, the present provincial capital and leading Atlantic seaport, was built by the company and developed from a remote outpost to the leading commercial port city of the country by 1929. The company created the peculiar population composition and distribution of the province. The company was responsible for the communication pattern that existed between Limon and the rest of the country by virtue of having built and controlled the only land route between the rest of the country and Limon—the railroad. It was responsible for some of the political and government policies in Limon and even the historical development of Limon, which became a province only in 1892.

Aspects of Ethnic Relations, Society, and Culture among Early Jamaican Migrant Laborers

As the project progressed, Jamaicans came to dominate the labor force in all areas: plantations, railroad, shops, stores, and wharves. A few obtained supervisory, skilled, and clerical jobs, and a handful became private planters. As sanitation and salaries improved, more and more native whites and those with mixed blood were attracted, first as temporary laborers, but later as permanent employees. Later, other Caribbean blacks, East Indians (from Jamaica), Chinese, Syrians, Europeans, American blacks, and other Central Americans drifted into what was previously a homogeneously black Jamaican Limon.

The more heterogeneous a society, the greater the cultural contact, conflict, and exchange occurring within it. As a society becomes more heterogeneous, new structural and ecological relations demand new adjustments. Acculturation increasingly shares greater importance with ecological adaptation and structural accommodations in creating change. Although we might expect Limon to exhibit these characteristics of a heterogeneous society, in fact, certain factors seem to have mitigated against the rapid acculturation of the Jamaicans.

Throughout the plantation period, Jamaicans regarded themselves as British—culturally superior to Hispanics, superior even to the Americans. Their inclination, then, was to preserve their cultural superiority. When employers preferred them over Hispanics, mainly because they could communicate in English, this feeling of superiority was reinforced. In addition, they lived and worked as a group, apart from Hispanics,[25] and sustained the rich folkways and mores of the rural Jamaica from whence they had come. During times of labor agitation, the company pursued a policy of divide and rule, and this, too, may have reinforced cultural segregation.

The Jamaicans, by their sheer numerical superiority and by the similarity of Limon's cultural setting to Jamaican culture, probably suffered less from culture shock and nostalgia than other groups. Jamaicans persisted in their unshakable conviction of the superiority of British standards over American and Latin American standards in their hypermotivated insular patriotism and in their dogged intolerance of racial discrimination. Some acculturation may have occurred during the period, but it was minimal among most Jamaicans. Some eventually married or mated with Central American women and resigned themselves to making the land their "home." Still others languished in the dream of making enough money and returning to Jamaica permanently. Among the few acculturated Jamaicans, some held responsible, official positions as local police authorities in their local townsites.

Limon in Transition: Its Economic Abandonment, Decadence and Effects on Jamaicans

Costa Rica reached peak banana production in 1907. By 1913, the province showed its first signs of decline caused by (1) soil exhaustion, (2) banana diseases (Panama disease and Sigatoka), and (3) increasing distances between plantation and ports. Efforts to sustain production failed. The company made a major but not altogether successful effort to save its Atlantic stronghold by introducing cacao. By 1943, the company had to abandon the banana exporting business in the Atlantic. It succeeded, however, in winning the right to transfer its operation to the Pacific but was prohibited by the government from transferring its black Jamaican workers.

The year 1940 was to begin the rapid transformation of Limon into an economically decadent, politically neglected, and socially ostracized province. A few of the Jamaicans went home, but most crossed into Panama to work in the Bocas del Toro banana plantations or in the Canal Zone.[26] The great majority of those who remained in Limon became, if they were not before, half- or full-time peasants, while a few became lessees of the company's abandoned land. Business declined and unemployment skyrocketed. Naturally, the most seriously hit victims were the Jamaicans and their native-born offspring who were unable to follow the company on its western movement as their Latin counterparts were privileged to do. By this time, most of the Central American governments had created laws restricting or preventing the entry of foreign labor, especially Jamaicans and other blacks of non-Latin origin or birth. Costa Rica's position on the issue was not too clear, but the government did intensify the passport and entry requirements partly in response to grass-roots agitation by native laborers opposed to competition from alien workers. It is claimed that Costa Rica at one time even sought to deport unemployed Jamaicans. The Costa Rican labor market was also swamped with surplus labor resources as a result of the continuing drift of natives, Central Americans, and Jamaicans from the islands and from Panama and other Central American countries since late 1910. Now, with the company's abandonment of the province, and with the added momentum of economic deterioration caused by World War II, a drastic adjustment took place among the marooned Jamaican middle groups.

Even when the war had caused the United Fruit Company to reactivate some of its plantations to cultivate abaca for marine cords—once produced in the Philippines—many of the workers at the Bataan plantations were native Costa Ricans. Informants speak of this period in different ways but always emotionally; some speak of how "our people foolishly sold their land in Limon to those Spanish people." Others speak of how "the foolish colored people would hide their children under the bed or say to the policeman that they were sick, rather than send them to school to learn the language of their country." It was in the mid-1930s and mid-1940s that the Limonese began to send or surrender their children to at least a half-day of Spanish school and a half-day of English school.

Nevertheless, the stage was now set; the process of "Costaricanization" was about to begin; and the abandoned, demoralized, but still obstinate Jamaican people were being compelled to yield their culture, identity, and preferential status.

Notwithstanding the prolabor legislative efforts of Socialist, Marxist, and Communist politicians, the majority of Jamaican ancestry in Costa Rica today agree quite readily that until 1948, the lot of the *morenos*[27] continued to be pitiful and discouraging and, further, that Limon was purposefully ignored and ostracized by successive national governments. Today, even some political adherents of the opposition concede that ex-president Figueres deserved credit for having initiated the new favorable attitudes and attentive disposition to the needs of the province and its *morenos*. Many *morenos* joined the Figueres military forces during the 1948 revolution, some even dying in battle. But, this was not without great confusion, crisis, fear, and hesitation for a people who suddenly were being pushed by both sides to do military service for a country that never acknowledged them as citizens before and that they lived in but did not comprehend nor consider their homeland.[28]

In recognition of their historical role and the political and economic potentials of Limonese and their province in the development of a postrevolutionary Costa Rican nation, the victorious Figueres responded to their traditional problems— the unpaved market plaza, the worn streets, the inadequate water supply, and the limited electrical power that had gone unattended ever since the withdrawal of the United Fruit Company. Similar patterns have been observed among all subsequent postrevolutionary governments and political parties of Costa Rica in their efforts to incorporate the province in their respective development schemes and its population as part of their political basis. Since 1948, the *morenos* have seen four of their own as deputy representing Limon in the national legislation. Other *morenos* have been given responsible and ranking posts within the government on all levels—municipal, provincial, and national. Some have even served as members of delegations representing the government in technical or diplomatic affairs, especially to Jamaica. The law against their working on the Pacific coast has long since been repealed, the requirements for citizenship or naturalization are less stringent, and moderate concessions have been obtained from the company. At present there are some signs of improvement, including an oil refinery, a highway to the *Meseta Central*, a black governor, municipal officers, and a small group of professionals and small businessmen. Nevertheless, there is general discontent in the province due to disregard and underdevelopment; among younger blacks there are signs of a growing sense of a discontent regarding racial and white ethnocentric practices in Costa Rica. Such practices and their relationship to growing economic deprivation and slow integration have become the focus of attention by the younger and more mobile segment of the black community.

Incorporation of Afro-Costa Ricans

Ideologically, Costa Rica is a social democratic polity. As such, it seeks to give everyone a voice within a single hierarchical structure and to provide equal opportunity for all. The more recent version of this ideological stance is predicted on the *policlasista* concept introduced by Jose Figueres following the 1948 civil war.[29] According to Figueres, there should be no separation of polity other than by class. This should be viewed not simply as an affirmation of socioeconomic inequality but as a recognition, at least in theory, that inequality founded on factors such as racial or ethnic distinction can be eliminated through the creation of an open opportunity structure. Afro-Costa Ricans, therefore, by becoming citizens, were subject to the benefits of a society based on what appeared to be an egalitarian set of principles. Becoming part of society for them, however, meant not only economic integration but at least partial cultural assimilation requisite for socioeconomic mobility.

Jamaican blacks have certainly made some gains in Costa Rica; however, the opportunity structure is by no means as open as it might seem to the untrained eye or to members of the dominant socioeconomic sector. A number of factors contribute to this. With the opening of a highway from the *Meseta Central* (Central Plateau) in the mid-1970s, a large flow of Hispanics into the Atlantic zone has meant stiff competition for available jobs. Granted, many incoming individuals have moved into agricultural employment that blacks now spurn; blacks, claiming to have undertaken more than their fair share of menial tasks in the United Fruit Company plantations, are attracted to clerical jobs, primarily in the public sector. But even here there is competition, for although employment figures distinguishing race do not exist, the balanced opinion among blacks is that Hispanics are favored in such jobs. A 1978 study revealed that most skilled manual jobs are filled by Hispanics from the *Meseta Central*.[30] The transportation industry, which accounts for some

17.4 percent of economic activity in the region[31] and which formerly employed more blacks than Hispanics (such that it was humorously called *BLAKDEVA* instead of *JAPDEVA, Junta Administrativa Portuaria y Desarrollo de la Vertienta Atlantica*), now employs 2.7 Hispanics for each black. JAPDEVA employs approximately 3,000 workers with a salary ratio of 1.8:2 in favor of Hispanics.[32] Besides JAPDEVA, the only other large employers are the hospital and petroleum processing plant, RECOPE, each employing under 300 workers. Small-scale agriculture accounts for much of the economic activity of blacks; however, numerous factors contribute to the decline: loss of untitled land to Hispanics, the appeal of white collar occupation and emigration of the young in search of nonagricultural jobs. Yet, in spite of what seems an already constrained and static opportunity structure, the region continues to absorb considerable population growth. Between 1963 and 1973 the population skyrocketed from approximately 68,000 to over 122,000, a growth rate that outpaces the national average by 18.2 percent.[33] Much of this population growth reflects the movement of Hispanics from the *Meseta Central*, which has contributed not only to the narrowing of job opportunities for blacks but also to increased competition for cultivable land.

The narrowing of the opportunity structure results, then, from a number of factors: reduced availability of cultivable land, competition between ethnic groups for nonagricultural employment, small quantity of marketable skills among blacks, and, in general, the reduction of economic activity in the region since the departure of the United Fruit Company. The following passage characterizes the region as seen in the mid-1970s:

> Indicative of [the] economic situation of Limon is the fact that its slum population is estimated at 8–10,000, or 19–23% of the population.... The unemployment rate was 9.2 in 1973.... There is an estimated 10.2% underemployment, the greater part of which occurs in the transportation sector.... Despite its distinct economic importance to the nation, Limon has the lowest average salary scale except for the northern zone which is mostly populated by peasant farmers and the Talamaca area which is largely populated by indigenous Indians.
>
> In the field of education Limon is the most disadvantaged area in the country. The percentage of individuals having high school education is approximately 30% below the national average, and the percentage having university education is about 65% below the national average.[34]

Mobility within a class-stratified social system requires that the individual submit to the principles that the dominant segment seeks to impose on the dominated segment. This is achieved primarily through educational systems as well as through the process of social, political, and economic reward and punishment. In Costa Rica, blacks submitted to such a system because they saw that the improvement of their social and economic condition depended on vertical mobility within the wider society. Jamaicans could no longer resist "Spanish" education in the postplantation period as they did when their livelihood depended on the English-speaking plantation system. Spanish education, with all its cultural and ideological trappings, had become their passport to a better life.

Access to the better life so vigorously pursued by these migrants and their descendants has meant the acceptance and integration of Costa Rican culture in areas such as language, national identity, ideology, and color. English, which in the past constituted the main vehicle of social prestige, has now acquired negative prestige value in some quarters. At the same time, Spanish has profoundly influenced the structure and content of English creole. A third-generation migrant does not ask "How old are you?" for example, but "How much years you have?" a Creole translation of the Spanish, *"Cuantos años tiene?"* Few second-generation, fewer third-generation, migrants perceive their national identity as Jamaican (or West Indian). An incident in 1978 illustrates the vigor with which the new identity is assumed: a young male Jamaican visitor to Limon received a severe beating at the hands of two young black Costa Ricans for having made derisive comments about Costa Rica. This transformation is also manifested in the marriage patterns. In the plantation period, blacks in general disdained marriages with Hispanics (since Hispanics were reported as culturally inferior). Nevertheless, a random sample of 217 households in 1978 turned up 6.5 percent mixed marriages. In addition, of the 217 interview respondents, 98 expressed a positive disposition toward interracial alliances. One young black woman expressed a desire to marry a "Spanish man" so that the children will have *piel clarc* (clear skin). Those who reject such unions, however, often do so on the grounds that "Latins naturally discriminate against blacks."

Although many blacks agree that there is racial discrimination in Costa Rica, most claim that in spite of this the opportunity structure is equalitarian—at least for those willing to avail themselves of the economic possibilities. Although this ideological position diverges from the objective reality—especially for blacks—it is nonetheless widely accepted.[35] Many relatively successful blacks have joined the Hispanics in arguing that what is interpreted as racial discrimination is actually social discrimination: blacks who comport themselves properly will gain access not only to economic benefit but to mainstream Costa Rican society. This ideological replacement of manifest racial discrimination with social discrimination is related to the idea of the *policlasista* society and to the solidifying class relations in the black community itself. Far more blacks believe that there is strong status-prestige discrimination among blacks than believe that there is racial discrimination.

Social and economic problems notwithstanding, blacks have experienced a general, though by no means equal, improvement of their condition. Abandoned as they were by the United Fruit Company, with no immediate recourse, blacks responded with gratitude to jurisdictional nationality and the restrained opening of the opportunity structure. Yet, the current situation strongly suggests that this enthusiastic response has, in part, produced the contrary of what was expected. For many, attempts at social and economic advancement have been met with frustration— due to racial discrimination—and identity crises. Consequently, the most mobile blacks have organized themselves and have begun to make demands on the system that contradict the democratic/*policlasista* stance accepted, at least in part, by the majority of the black population. In addition to this upper-echelon group, two other groups have emerged to question the structure and process of black incorporation: a leftist party, *Partido Autentico Limonese,* is headed by black Limonese but supported by Hispanics as well as blacks; a black nationalist group with leftist leanings, AFROSCO, appeared around 1975 but has since faded into political obscurity. Both groups have demanded an end to the structural, racial, and cultural domination of blacks and the economic inequities suffered by the Atlantic region.

None of these groups mentioned has managed to achieve significant and enduring changes for Afro-Costa Ricans. They have, nevertheless, brought to recognition grounds for seriously questioning the claims that Costa Rica achieved a conflict-free process of incorporation. In 1978, for example, the so-called black elite organized a four-day national conference on "the situation of blacks in Costa Rica" that focused on racial discrimination as an obstacle to black advancement. The participants were an unlikely combination: Daniel Oduber, the president of Costa Rica, participated in the inauguration along with a few other national figures; a few members of the Hispanic sector participated in various working sessions. The conference cleared the way for the recognition, at the upper political levels, for the first time, that indeed racial problems beset nonwhites in Costa Rica. But one must wonder what significance for the understanding of New World blacks is held in the fact that such a movement for social and economic liberation was initiated not by the most deprived (nor was there broad support among the black masses) but by blacks who were for the most part incorporated professionals.

That the incorporated element of the black group should head the struggle for equality is not in itself unique; however, the manner in which the problem and its solution was stated and the manner in which it was aired suggest significant differences in interest within the black community itself. The difference in interest resulted in the black elite mobilizing itself around its own interests translated into the interests of the wider black community. This group, having achieved a relatively high social and economic position, is logically in the best position to use its material and educational resources to mobilize a following and to articulate their common problems. The mode of organizing the effort, of conceptualizing and articulating the problems, raises questions as to whether what this process signifies is not the mobilization of ethnicity simultaneously with concealed class interest within the ethnic group. This can be explained by the manner in which the black elite state the problem: Is the problem perceived as pertaining only to the upper levels of the black community or to the entire group? The problem of racial discrimination in Costa Rica, it was explained at the national conference, manifests itself as one in which the instrument of democracy, controlled by whites, permits the black individual merely to approach his goal rather than achieve it. This leads to a process of social and psychological *castracion* (castration), resulting in blacks rejecting their own culture as well as their own group. The problem was thus presented as one of cultural identity, and the solution was phrased in terms of the renunciation of stereotypes underlying the identity crisis. These upper level blacks, then, perceived racial discrimination as the root, and restricted access to economic resources the result, of the identity crisis into which all blacks have been drawn.

Blacks of the lower end of the socioeconomic scale showed little concern about the problem as stated by those in the upper levels. Indeed, only a few were aware of the efforts being made, even fewer understood, and none participated. Yet, the manifestation of social and economic inequities related to racism are most pronounced at this level. Lack of access to cultivable land, unemployment, exploitation by middlemen in the marketing of cacao (their main cash crop), nepotism in access to jobs, and restricted access to higher education are the problems plaguing the peasant and urban proletariat, and they view the solutions accordingly. Among the first generation, and to some extent the second-generation, poor black immigrants, the problem of racial discrimination per se is not given saliency, and the question of identity is rarely, if ever mentioned. On the contrary, reference is frequently made to snobbery, contempt, and outright class discrimination on the part of a segment of the black community referred to by poor blacks as the "upper sects."

Clearly the two strata of blacks view the problem and its solution in distinct ways, based on the aspect that seems to affect them most. The black elite, though positing the problem as one pertaining to all blacks and seeking support accordingly, have conceptualized it in a manner that highlights those aspects affecting their lives: identity and discriminatory stereotypes. Exposure to dominant values and social mobility have rendered these aspects of racial discrimination more problematic for them.[36] Poor blacks, on the other hand, not yet exposed to the collision of consciousness inherent in the discrepancies and conflict in social mobility and the frustration arising from unrealized expectations, see their plight as resting on the absence of the concrete means to satisfy their daily needs as blacks in a white-dominated society.

Examination of the Costa Rican core suggests the emergence of a new form of race relations intimately tied to the nature of development as well as the structure of the society as a whole. With the destruction of the old plantation structure that managed to sustain racial separation while providing basic economic support, Afro-Costa Ricans have become dependent on the main structure of a society wherein their life chances rest on competition, not just with other blacks but also with Hispanics. Two related problems have surfaced: first, Limon, the traditionally black region, has become an economic frontier for Hispanics seeking jobs, land, and other economic opportunities, thereby heightening latent hostilities long hidden by the structure of racial and economic separation. Second, blacks who have attempted mobility have discovered that instead of their expectations and aspirations being met, they are confronted with new forms of racism and value conflicts generated by selective competition of each higher level of mobility. Both these problems may be attributed to the emphasis on social mobility as a solution to racial and economic ills in a structure ill-prepared for mobility of such magnitude and complexity. The stipulation of mobility within an equal-opportunity structure was intended not as a vehicle to facilitate ethnic integration but as the ideal principle for the society as a whole. Its society therefore lacks any provision for resolving the conflicts inherent in such selective competition as occurs in the context of racial plurality.

Summary and Conclusion

The fruit plantation enterprise acquired sweeping powers and even paragovernmental authority through its treaties with the national government. It was chiefly responsible for the ecological, ethnic, social, cultural and even political arrangements that prevailed in the area. This pattern may be seen as a combination of a neocolonial and plural society in which racism was practiced and various non-American laborers were pitted against each other along ethnic and national lines.

The Costa Rican case is unique: it is the only country where Jamaicans (West Indians) were imported on a large scale to work in the American colonial plantation system. The ubiquity and character of the plantation or similar arrangements in the history of the blacks of this hemisphere, the formation of plural societies, and the domination- liberation pattern of New World societies provide a perspective within which to reconsider the New World black experience. The case of the Jamaicans of Costa Rica is but a variety, a mild but nevertheless significant one, of multiple types of relations between contextual and status changes in the comparative experience of transplanted blacks—some of whom were originally imported as slave or free labor of plantation-like production systems in alien-dominated land or territory. In his book *Slaves and Citizens*, Tannenbaum presents what may be a more pertinent and profound thesis that has not received much contemporary attention and critical assessment. It is really his major historical, theoretical and philosophical thesis; it underlies the book and the various other theses for which he has been known and criticized. Tannenbaum states:

> Wherever the law accepted the doctrine of moral personality of the slave and made possible the gradual achievement of freedom implicit in such doctrine, the slave system was abolished peacefully. Where the slave was denied recognition as a moral personality and was, therefore, considered incapable of freedom, the abolition was accomplished by force—that is, by revolution.[37]

Given that change was inevitable, Tannenbaum obviously preferred a peaceful, gradual or legally sponsored change by government or the majority over revolution. He thus attributes an admirable superiority in effectiveness to the benign, paternalistic, legislative processes of Brazil and Latin America versus the tension, violence-ridden rebellions and civil wars that preceded abolition in the United States, British West Indies, and Haiti. Perhaps his thesis is prophetic. Urban rebellions and violent civil rights confrontations that occurred in the United States in the last two decades may be seen as unfinished business that inevitably had to take place given the stubborn attitude of the American society with regard to recognizing the equality of its black, exslave population.

Fanon, in *Black Skin, White Mask*, viewed it quite differently. Standing this interpretation on its head, he predicted that North American blacks will have obtained a more healthy, self-fulfilling and thorough status of equality precisely because of their willingness to engage in bloody conflict or frontal struggles with their dominators for their own equality. Such won equality was superior to the granted emancipation that French blacks and colonials (Haitians excepted) received at the behest of paternalistic legislators of the metropolitan states. Similarly, there are those who question the degree to which West Indian societies failed to have a sense of direction and dynamism because of the absence of collective struggle for independence. Today, many Brazilian and Spanish-American blacks openly question the meaningfulness of their emancipated status and mythical equality. In the process they concede that black Americans have won more significant advances through their sufferings and struggles. Of course, there are the imponderables of the Haitian revolution having represented historically the first and foremost expression of active black liberation from plantation slavery but now constituting one of the most tragic cases of economic exploitation and international domination of blacks by blacks.

These various considerations lead to the need to address certain basic questions in comparative historical sociology of the New World black experience—namely, what is the plight of black labor—all originally imported and viewed as alien—when (1) the plantation system declines or (2) the particular political-economic role of black labor as strangers, natives, middlemen, or a basic labor force no longer benefits the system?

NOTES

1. Frank Tannenbaum, *Slave and Citizen* (New York: Alfred A. Knopf, 1947), 5–6.
2. Ibid, 5–6.
3. Charles Wagley, "Plantation-America: A Cultural Sphere," in *Caribbean Studies: A Symposium*, ed. Vera Rubin, (Seattle: University of Washington Press, 1960), 3–13; E. Franklin Frazier, "Introduction" ibid., v–viii, E. Franklin Frazier, *Race and Culture Contacts in the Modern World* (Boston: Beacon Press, 1967); George Beckford, *Persistent Poverty* (New York: Oxford University Press, 1972).
4. Roy Bryce-Laporte, "The Slave Plantation: Background to Present Conditions of Urban Blacks," in *Race, Change and Urban Society, Urban Affairs Annual Review* vol. 5, ed. Peter Orleans and Russell Ellis (California: Sage Publications, 1971).
5. Bryce-Laporte, "The Slave Plantation," and "Varias Ideas Sobre al Negro de Origen Antillano para los Estudios Afro-Americanos," *Actas del IV Symposium Nacional de Antropologia, Arqueologia y Etnohistoria de Panama* (Panama: Universidad Nacional de Panama y Patrimonia Historico, INAC, 1973).
6. Censo de Pobliacion de Costa Rica, 1973.
7. George Roberts, *Population of Jamaica* (Cambridge, England: Cambridge University Press, 1957), 134–36.
8. Charles Wilson, *Empire in Green and Gold* (Westport, Ct.: Greenwood Press 1947), 45–67.
9. Carlos Melendes and Quince Duncan, *El Negro En Costa Rica* (San Jose, Costa Rica: Editorial Costa Rica, 1972), 117–19.
10. Eisner, 147.
11. Roberts, *Population of Jamaica*, 135–36.
12. George Westerman, "Historical Notes on West Indians on the Isthmus of Panama," *Phylon* 22 (1961):343.

13. R. E. Wood, "The Working Force of the Panama Canal," in *The Panama Canal—An Engineering Treatise*, George W. Goethals, ed. (New York: McGraw-Hill, 1916), 194–99.

14. Roberts, *Population of Jamaica*, 140–41.

15. Richard Adams, "Cultural Components of Central America," *American Anthropologist* 58 (1956).

16. Philip Curtin, *Two Jamaicas* (New York: Atheneum, 1955), 405; Tannenbaum, *Slave and Citizen*, 5–6 (Citing the Negroid empire predicted by Humboldt); and Wagley, "Plantation America: A Cultural Sphere," 5–12.

17. Parsons, 13.

18. Wilson, *Empire in Green and Gold*, 46.

19. Charles D. Kepner, *Social Aspects of the Banana Industry* (New York: Columbia University Press: Studies in History, Economics and Public Law, no. 414, 1936), 39–44.

20. Kepner, *Social Aspects of the Banana Industry*, 92–192; and Charles D. Kepner and J. H. Soothill, *Banana Empire: A Case Study of Economic Imperialism* (New York: Vanguard Press, 1935), 257–58.

21. Kepner and Soothill, *Banana Empire*, 94–95, 257–58.

22. Ibid., 261.

23. Ibid.

24. Ibid., 319–22.

25. Ibid., 168–70.

26. Ibid.

27. The term *Limonese* is generally used to refer to the people of the Limon Province, regardless of origin, color or race. In San Jose, however, it is generally used interchangeably with *morenos*, which means black (or more euphemistically browns).

28. Carlos Melendes and Quince Duncan, *El Negro*, 117–19.

29. Charles C. Ameringer, *Don Pepe: A Political Biography of Jose Figueres of Costa Rica* (Albuquerque: University of New Mexico Press, 1958), 102.

30. El Quipo Cornell-Costa Rica, *El Potencial de los Recarsos Naurales Para el Desarrollo Regional de la Provinica de Limon*, 1973, 15.

31. Ibid., 10.

32. Employment figures calculated from JAPDEVA computer list of employees and salary rates 1978.

33. Censo de Pobliacion, 1973.

34. Trevor Purcell, "Rural and Urban Situation of West Indians in Limon" in *Costa Rica: Race and Regional Dependency*, 19. (The figures on education and salary were computed by the author from the 1973 national census.)

35. Ibid., 7–21.

36. Peter Berger, Brigette Berger and Hansfried Kellner, *The Homeless Mind: Modernization and Consciousness* (New York: Vintage Books, 1974), chap. 5.

37. Frank Tannenbaum, *Slave and Citizen*, vii.

Author's Note: This paper was presented in a different version at the Afro-American Studies Symposium on "The Political Economy of the Black World," University of California at Los Angeles, May 1979.

10
Guinea versus Congo Lands: Aspects of the Collective Memory in Haiti

Guerin C. Montilus

EOPLE live by their traditions and culture structured in secular or ritual stereotyped actions; oral or bodily expressions; and collective representations transmissible through symbols and myths.[1] This is a complex unity involving the dialectical dualism of action and word. Both culminate in the synthesis of myth. Myth refers to the network of explanations and understandings of the community transmitted through language. As Roger Bastide put it, myth is a justification of action or any way of behavior of the community.[2] However, myth comes out of sediment stocked in the matrix of memory of the society. Myth is like a replay of old songs kept preciously in the conscious or unconscious mind of a community and called back at will by individuals.[3] It is the resurgence of the societal thought and consciousness through space and time serving to structure and rebuild experience.[4]

This conjunction of myth and action is helpful in understanding some Haitian behavior, both verbal and acted out. However, in the case of Haitians dragged from the mainland of the West African coast by the slave trade, the roots of this social consciousness or unconsciousness delve far into the dark ages in the foundation of these African traditions through ways of thinking, saying, doing, and feeling. These forms collectively shaped the Haitian mind and reappeared as memories. They constitute a part of Haitian collective memories, a part of Haiti's social heritage.

These memories shaped the behavior of the people and resurged in the myth of transmigration of souls, the use of ritual objects, and a multiplicity of other forms. These memories bridge the gap between the

159

Haitian present and the African past, linking them in such a way as to make each individual consciousness mythically contemporaneous with the past African age. However, are these merely memories or are they mirrors and restorations of the past? Could they be stylizations of the past idealized in the present by the work of resurgence? These questions raise issues about the Haitian collective memory as far as the old African base of Haitian consciousness is concerned.

In moments of solemnity, as a gesture of affirmation, a man of the people would strike his chest and say vigorously:

> Moin minm neg Ginin!
> Me black man from Guinea!

Thus, the speaker intends to specify his place of origin, the coastal region of West Africa bathed by the gulf. Guinea remained for the Haitian community the ideal homeland of brave men, men of character, men of their word. Its inhabitants were men gifted with profound social and human virtues, men of organization, strong in combat, intrepid warriors. The name *Guinea* was coined mythically to symbolize these values.

Discussing the character traits of the slaves from the Gulf of Guinea, Milo Rigaud noticed that they were captured and sold according to some labels.[5] The slaves from the Gold Coast (Ghana), for example, were known for their strong and proud character. Their capture and transportation were very difficult. The Ibo, from eastern Nigeria, were said to be prone to suicide because slavery was unacceptable to their self-concepts. They were difficult to subjugate and required heavy surveillance. Still on the same coast of Guinea, the Arada of Juda, Adja slaves from lower Dahomey (People's Republic of Benin) were feared for their "murderous" character and for their vengeance against their masters. The Adja slaves, however, were respected for their intelligence and their bold enterprise.

The expression *neg Ginin* (black from Guinea) refers to this group of Africans whose reputation for valor was firmly established by the colonial period. Guinea has become the mythical origin of virtue and value, the symbol of certain patterns, standards, and norms. Finally, the name *Guinea* refers not so much to a concrete land as to a mythical place of origin that became an ideal of resistance to slavery, its suffering, and its humiliation. This myth took root in San Domingo, land of oppression and servitude and field of struggle.

In waging war against servility and slavery, the slaves remembered their native land and idealized the heroes who exemplified resistance.

But there was a slipping in the semantic concept of Guinea. It came to include a whole undifferentiated mass of ideas and values united in resistance to the oppressors. Since the time of slavery and the war of independence, from 1791 to 1804, behavioral patterns emerged that followed the Guinea model. It would be a great misunderstanding to take this name as a physical reality in the speaker's mind. The word as a verbal expression has become a part of the entire system of symbolic codification in the Haitian culture. As language it became an act of symbolization.

In this process of changing the physical reality into experienced reality, Guinea land contrasts with the Congo, the Bantu land in Equatorial Africa. A Haitian is insulted to be called *neg Congo* (black from Congo). This is an affront equivalent to racial treason. Historically, the Congo also provided San Domingo with an important population of slaves. The Congo, or the Bantu, however, had been under the influence of the Portuguese since the middle of the fifteenth century and had been exposed to Christianity even before the opening of the slave trade between Africa and America. The Bantu were, therefore, the most vulnerable to Western influences, unlike *neg Ginin*. Milo Rigaud has pointed out that men from the Congo were considered excellent house servants, selected especially because of their gentle nature.[6] This Congo symbiosis with the slave masters enclosed them in the same ostracism. They were thought of as undermining the solidarity essential to liberation existing among the slaves in the fields. The image of the accommodating Congo has become associated with the country itself. No Haitian would want to identify with this land.

This linguistic dichotomy between the two historical native lands metamorphosed into mythical reality sends us back again to the process of symbolization, a process that creates its object. Thus, this popular, mythical view of the Congo did not take into account some of the well-known maroon Congo chiefs. Lamour Derance was a Congo maroon who at night brought his bands of fighters down from the mountains to harass the settlers and put their plantations up for ransom. These resistance heroes probably were associated with and called *neg Ginin*. The process of symbolization could justify this association for the sake of universalization, which is fundamental to myth. In disparaging the Congo, the myth seeks to establish an imperative model not to be imitated.[7] This kind of schematization of the object, which occurs as the human mind elaborates mythical language, can lead one astray and, indeed, distort reality.

Mythical language passed through a certain dissection or dessication before being adopted by the community group as a standard. After this process, the mythical language deserves universal attention because it speaks to all of us of the human condition. This is the way the contrasts between two native lands —Guinea on the one hand, the Congo on the other—had become a part of the treasure of Haitian culture. Both lands created through the test of adversity in the period of slavery have survived as memories in the period of freedom—and as witnesses both of the lost paradise in Africa and of the hell of San Domingo.

Roger Bastide, while analyzing the process of synchretism of religions in the bondage of the New World, has argued that the Dahomeans, the group called *neg Ginin*, were more resistant to Western influences than the Yoruba, who in turn were more resistant than the Bantu, the group of *neg Congo*.[8] Interestingly, the Haitian tradition does not hold the name of the Yoruba among the *neg Ginin* in the mythical language. This is surprising, for the Yoruba shared with the Dahomeans and the Ibo the same geographic area. The Yoruba land was wedged in the same Gulf of Guinea between the Adja land, the group of Dahomeans, and the Ibo country. This historical silence about the Yoruba name in Haitian tradition might come from their median position in terms of acculturation. In this hell of San Domingo, only the flamboyant contrasts seemed to survive when referring to the break of bondage, which was the focal point of interest. There is a part of intransigence in the mythical fossilization of the materials coming from history. The selection is arbitrary and merciless. The Yoruba delivered many secular and religious cultural materials to the Haitian tradition. All that was merged, however, with the heritage of the *neg Ginin* in mere anonymity. The Yoruba did not impress the Haitian mind sufficiently to coin their name in the mythical monument of Haitian tradition.

Underlying this division, the pantheon of Haitian voodoo contracts the spirits or *lwa* called *Ginin* with the spirits or *lwa* called *Congo*. The *lwa Ginin*, as the mythical projection of the *neg Ginin*, are strong, bold, helpful, and efficient. They are the only benevolent mediators in the Haitian pantheon. The *lwa Congo* are thought to be cruel and malevolent. They are not interested in the destiny of the people. So the people have thrown these *lwa Congo* to the bush. They are said to be living there in this non-human habitat thirsting for blood. The dog is the impure sacrificial offering to *lwa Congo*. Remembering the acculturation of the Congo, however, Haitian mythology also ascribed to these *lwa Congo* very gentle and mild dances expressing joy, good humor, and happy life. Their musical rhythms are close to the Western dances. These dances contrast with the strength of the dances of the *lwa Ginin*. Even the ritual drums of the *lwa Congo* are acculturated. They are similar in their structure to the Western drums. They contrast with the drums of the *lwa Ginin*, definitively African in their structure. This antithesis is an extension of the myth of origin in terms of rituals or praxis. Thus, passing from myth to ritual, or language to action, the memories circle about in an impressive and elegant loop.

Some other traditions evolved around the antithetic and mythical concepts of the land of Guinea in contrast to the soil of the Congo. Guinea is also the country where the protecting spirits, or *lwa*, live. An old ritual song of Haitian voodoo complained:

> Nu di lwa rele lwa Sao
> We are calling lwa named lwa Sao
>
> Ki kote u ye?
> Where are you?
>
> Nan Ginin sa bel
> In Guinea it is beautiful
>
> Rele lwa Sao!
> Call lwa Sao!

The word *bel*, beautiful, refers to paradisiac beauty. *Nan Ginin*, Guinea land, is a paradisiac habitat, in contrast to the hell of San Domingo where there was no rest, no peace, no relaxation. It is the earth of exile, the earth of loneliness, as another song bitterly complains:

> Marasa, elu! elu! elu!
> Twins, hell! hell! hell!
>
> Nu Pa gin manman, marasa, elu!
> We haven't a mother, twins, hell!
>
> Nu pas gin papa, marasa, elu!
> We haven't a father, twins, hell!
>
> Nu pas gin fanmi, marasa, elu!
> We have no relatives, twins, hell!

This old song expresses feelings proceeding from a deep and abysmal solitude. The slaves who sang as they worked in the fields surely were referring to the life in the enclosure of the extended family in Africa. In San Domingo they were alone with their slaveholders. This song is a scream of nostalgia for the land of Guinea where the relatives lived. The memory of the family life pained the man in bondage. This song and several similar ones are still the favorite refrain of the Haitian people as they are caught by the storms of economic or health problems. Another song mentions the same anxiety:

> Ogu, Feray o!
> Ogu, lwa of iron!
>
> Nan min ki mun u kite pitit-la yo? (bis)
> To whom did you leave the care of your children?
>
> Le-m rete m-ta rele Ogu Feray o!
> Sometimes I would call Ogu, lwa of iron!

This song shows the *lwa* do not live in the Haitian land. The supplicant questioned the spirit as loneliness and solitude smashed him or her. It is also another aspect of Haitian tradition that the *lwa* live in Guinea. They travel to take care of the people and assist ritual ceremonies, and then they go back home, *Nan Ginin*, in Guinea. The spirits come to Haiti through underground waters, and go back home crossing Haiti from south to north through the sky. A Haitian voodoo priest, who is also a native doctor, recently explained to a visitor that every year one of the two spirits assisting him goes to *Nan Ginin* for a whole year for refresher provisions.[9]

The work of medicine always keeps its strength through this process of periodic journey to Guinea, the natural habitat of the *lwa*. One voodoo ritual consists of calling the *lwa* at the beginning of each ceremony and at the entrance of the enclosure where the ritual is held. People act out their myths. These memories become a part of their everyday life.

Finally, Guinea land is also the paradise where the dead return after their life in exile in San Domingo.[10] The dying thought that they would go back to Guinea, where they left their ancestors' shrines. They came from Guinea. At their death they returned home. Again, the myth of birth circled the loop with the myth of death in a perfect way. Thus, Dessalines, *neg Ginin* and chief general of the 1803 War of Haitian Independence, was quoted as urging his soldiers, also *neg Ginin*, to be brave and to fight without fear. For in the event they died they would go back to Guinea where Toussaint L'Ouverture, already dead, was preparing an army to take revenge on the oppressors. The myth of transmigration of souls to Guinea, *Nan Ginin*, goes back to the early beginnings of Haitian history, when the slaves were first thrown into the hell of San Domingo.

Certain general conclusions about the collective mind of a community come to light in this study of the native land. The historical materials give up their historicity in the process of crystallizing around a theme, a refrain shaping individual memory. Such memories evolve around a theme of general interest. Myth as an explanation of the universe can refer only to aspects of the human condition. Using ancestoral materials, the collective mind works in the existing framework of the human community. This environment explains the survival of memories as a social heritage.[11]

NOTES

1. The following definition is used for the word *myth* in this text: "A myth is a symbolic story (or character) which teaches a lesson and which is fascinating to a human collectivity for which it expresses and clarifies an essential aspect of existence, either by justifying a situation, a characteristic of the human condition, or by proposing an active approach, an example to imitate (or not to imitate), a moral norm or a revolutionary plan." Andre Dabezios, "Ancient and Modern Versions of the Faust Myth," in *Lives of Doctor Faust*, ed. Eric Bockstael, (Detroit: Wayne State University, 1976), 1.

2. Roger Bastide, "Probleme de la memoire collective," in his *Les religions africaines au bresil* (Paris: Presses Universitaires de France, 1960), 334.

3. See especially Maurice Halbwachs, *Les cadres sociaux de la memoire* (Paris: Presses Universitaires de France, 1925).

4. See Maurice Halbwachs, "La memoire collective et le temps," and "La memoire collective et l'espace," in his *La memoire collective*, 2d ed. (Paris: Presses Universitaires de France, 1968), 80–129, 130–67.

5. Milo Riguad, *La tradition voudoo et le voudoo haitien* (Paris: Niclaus Editions, 1953), 46.

6. Ibid.

7. See note 1.

8. Roger Bastide, *Les Ameriques noires* (Paris: Payot, 1967), 138.

9. I thank the Reverend Renald Clerisme, S.M.M., anthropologist, who transmitted this firsthand story orally. He recorded the story in 1978.

10. Rigaud, *La tradition voudoo*, 61.

11. I thank Joanna Montilus for her cogent criticism in the process of the writing of this paper and Dr. Bernard Ortiz de Montellano, associate professor of anthropology, Wayne State University, for his various and fruitful suggestions.

11
Women of Africa and the African Diaspora: Linkages and Influences

Filomina Chioma Steady

THIS essay discusses a much neglected dimension of the African diaspora, namely, the linkages between women in Africa and women in the African diaspora. Indeed, no study of the African diaspora is complete without an analysis of the position, role, and perspective of women. To some extent it can be claimed that the very existence of the African diaspora is due to the strength, resilience, and hard work of the black woman. It is also through her struggle against the myriad historical forces of oppression that she has been able to generate, preserve, and advance the well-being and development of her people. In response to the various institutions of enslavement, colonialism, imperialism, and racism, black women's resistance has taken various forms, ranging from passive resistance to protest movements and direct military confrontations.

The theoretical importance of Marxist analysis of power relations is increasingly being applied to race and gender questions in addition to issues based on class conflict.[1] It is also now fairly well established that the history of the interaction between the black and white races has contributed enormously to the impoverishment of the former and the wealth of the latter. For instance, the importance of slave production in providing the basis for European industrialization and capital accumulation was convincingly demonstrated in Eric Williams's, classic study.[2] Also, in stressing the importance of viewing reproduction as an aspect of production organically linking agricultural communities as reserves of cheap labor to the capitalist economy, the exploitation of colonized countries has been shown to be a significant aspect in the growth and prosperity of capitalism.[3]

What all this amounts to is a situation of superexploitation of anyone who is of the lower class, black, and female. This explains why for the majority of black women survival has been a dominant goal and poverty a way of life. The structural subordination of blacks in general and black women in particular best illustrates how capitalist penetration removes some people from their means of production and from their productive functions on the basis of their race, class, and gender. Thus, the historical and continuing link between Europe and Africa and Europe and the Americas has been central.

The European Connection

The crucial element in the linkages between women in Africa and women in the African diaspora was European not African.[4] It was the rise of European commerce and industry and its overseas development through expansionist capitalism, the slave trade, militarism, and colonialism that gave rise to the African diaspora. Despite convincing evidence of African presence in Europe dating back to the racially unprejudiced classical period,[5] it was the slave trade that accounted for the major dispersal of Africans. In a period of about four hundred years, from the sixteenth to the nineteenth centuries, about fifteen to twenty million slaves were shipped by force and in mass from Africa to Europe and the New World to work primarily on the plantations in the Antilles, the southern United States, and the coastal regions of South America to produce sugar, cotton, coffee, tobacco, rice, spices, and so on.[6] In South America, some slaves worked in mining, ranching, and small-scale industries, and in all slave communities, domestic work was performed by slaves, particularly female slaves. African women worked both in the public sphere of the plantation and in the private domestic sphere of the slavemaster's household.

The devastating effects of the Atlantic slave trade on the African continent and its peoples are only now being fully appreciated despite attempts primarily by American and European scholars to demonstrate African complicity or to make unconvincing links between slavery in Africa and slavery in the New World. Any attempt to justify or modify the brutal effects of the slave trade only conceals an even greater brutality. As one European scholar observes:

> The Atlantic slave trade has therefore now been unequivocally revealed in all its atrocity as a prolonged exploitative device by which millions of Africans were brutalized and dehumanized in order to bring wealth to those who organized it.[7]

Colonial penetration in the eighteenth and nineteenth centuries, notably by Britain, France, Portugal, and Belgium, was primarily for the extraction of vegetable and mineral resources. In the 1860s, as colonialism became a more profitable venture and European empires expanded, slavery was abolished.

For a number of reasons, ranging from racism and disdain at the presence of blacks in England to the emancipation movement and the rise of African nationalism galvanized by political forces such as the Garvey movement in the United States, some Africans were repatriated to Africa in the eighteenth, nineteenth, and early twentieth centuries, primarily to Sierra Leone and Liberia. The repatriated Africans added another dimension to the African diaspora, for in one sense they became the vehicles for the spread of European technology and culture to Africa complete with its ideological underpinnings and class dimensions, and in another sense provided the West with convenient scapegoats through which to disguise European domination.[8] This is particularly true of the Creoles of Sierra Leone, who have often been erroneously presented as the ruling elite. Even the so-called Creole bourgeoisie influence ended much sooner than most scholars have been able to perceive. As Samir Amin perceptively points out:

It was the trading station at Freetown, where the British navy assembled the freed slaves, which stimulated the formation of the "Creole" bourgeoisie which spread along the whole of the western coast in the nineteenth century and filled the role of *comprador* bourgeoisie for British capital. But this class disappeared at the end of the last century, when the British executed their main Creole trading rivals on the pretext that they had taken part in the Temne and Mende revolts.[9]

Imperialism continues to ensure the reproduction of domination through the pervasive control of the economies and institutions of the predominantly black nations of Africa and the Caribbean by Europe and the United States. In the more multiracial societies of the diaspora such as the United States, coastal Latin America, and Europe, particularly England and France, internal forms of racial imperialism are always apparent. These processes create structures of global inequality and domination and ensure the continuation of domination through the reproduction of black cheap labor and the maintenance and creation of subsistence economies to facilitate capital accumulation. In these processes, the labor of the black woman in terms of both production and reproduction has been made indispensable to "capital accumulation on a world scale." The oppression of black women has, to a large measure, ensured the current racial feature in the global structure of inequality and domination. This exploitation of the productive and reproductive labor of black women as well as men has functioned to facilitate the accumulation of capital by white men and women, primarily in Europe and the Americas but also in Africa.

Linkages through Production and Reproduction

To fully appreciate the diasporic linkage, it would be useful to examine women's roles in production in Africa and in the New World. Women's economic activities both in Africa and in the New World have, for the most part, been in the agricultural sector. Their participation in agricultural activity provides an important dimension to the linkage, for the European connection in this linkage has assured the continued exploitation of the African woman. In fact, the ecological environment and mode of production of most black women has been agrarian. It has been estimated that about sixty to eighty percent of the labor in African agriculture is female.[10] Slavery in the New World was largely related to large-scale agriculture in which the black woman from Africa participated fully. After Emancipation, most slaves continued working in the agricultural sector in one form or another. In many regions of the southern United States, the Caribbean, and Latin America today, black women are still involved in agricultural work.[11]

Women in New World Agriculture

The black woman brought from Africa to the New World had an agrarian orientation and for the most part continued working in agriculture. Her status and activities within this new environment were, however, entirely determined by the institution of slavery. Although this varied in various parts of the New World, as a slave the black woman was a piece of property with no decision making or control over her own life. Because there was no sexual division of labor in agricultural production, no separate female spheres of economic activities existed in which women could develop some autonomy. Men and women field workers performed the same tasks during slavery from dawn to dusk under the same dehumanizing conditions. Indeed, the black woman was equal to the black man in terms of her hard labor output and also under the brutality of the slavery system.

Although slave labor was involved in the cultivation of food crops for subsistence needs, and although slaves provisioned themselves to a large extent in the New World colonies, particularly from the late eighteenth century onward, much of the agricultural activity was for commercial purposes.[12] Women as well as men were equally involved in the production of cash crops. Similarly, the initial phases of industrialization, tied to large-scale agriculture, extended male and female slave labor to industrial production. Indeed even child labor was not uncommon, for men, women, and children worked in tobacco, textile, hemp, sugar refining, and rice milling factories. Slave women and children also sometimes worked at heavy industries involving transportation and lumbering.[13]

According to one study of African American social structure, after slavery ended in the United States, blacks became mobile but for the most part stayed within the southern section of the United States, participating in essentially agrarian activities as sharecroppers, plantation workers, or small-scale private farmers.[14] "The social structure did not begin to alter radically until after World War II. At that time, planatation agriculture was becoming mechanized and changing over from cotton to other forms of produce such as cattle, resulting in a further reduction of economic opportunity for Afro-American unskilled workers."[15] Migration of blacks to rural towns, then to rural cities, and ultimately to urban cities in the North became a dominant pattern and continues to the present.

Women in African Agriculture

With regard to agricultural production in Africa, most of the indigenous systems of production required both male and female labor. According to the operating pattern of the sexual division of labor, women acquired a certain degree of autonomy in performing their tasks as well as some decision making pertinent to their specific activities. In general, women grew most of the traditional root crops, vegetables, and spices and were involved in the more continuous and tedious activities such as planting, weeding, watering, harvesting, and scaring off pests. As a result, they spent more time on the farm than men, whose labor usually, but not exclusively, was required for land clearing and ploughing. Basic decisions concerning planting, cultivation, use of implements, disposal of food produced, and the constitution of the family diet were made by women.

In terms of women's access to resources within this traditional pattern, one international report has made the following observation:

> In traditional African production systems, women had clearly defined access rights to land and livestock by virtue of membership in the domestic group. As wives, mothers, sisters and daughters their rights were secure and they controlled food supplies to their families. In agriculturally-based societies

they were largely responsible for the disposal of produce insofar as they contributed substantial labour to the growing of specific food crops and vegetables. In pastoral societies that practised some agriculture, women owned agricultural lands and all the produce accruing from them. Women also had rights to milk and other dairy products, also skins from animals, from which they would make clothing and other leather goods. Animals were allocated to a woman at marriage on the basis of milk needs for children and transport for the family.[16]

The integration of Africa into the world market economy, which began about the sixteenth century, seriously disrupted agricultural patterns of production and social relations, particularly in the sexual division of labor. Colonial penetration exploited both female and male labor in agricultural production. Male labor was divested to the production of commercial crops and the manning of mining and construction industries, while female labor was consolidated in the subsistence and reproductive sectors, which became labor reserves. In most cases the divestment of male labor from household production involved the use of coercion through imposed taxation, compulsory cultivation of cash crops, deliberate importation of staple foods, and forced labor. Wage labor also necessitated the migration of males to urban areas, causing disruption of family life and an increase in the workload of women. The exploitation of the subsistence sector facilitated the accumulation of capital in Europe and the United States.

In discussing what he calls "Africa of the labor reserve," Amin points out that the neglect of subsistence agriculture is a function of the reserve in the colony.[17] The divestment of male labor from subsistence farming to cash-crop production was in response to the need for agricultural raw material by European industries. The wages for male agricultural labor in commercial production were so low that they had to be subsidized by the unpaid family labor of the subsistence economy. In this manner, surplus could be accumulated and expropriated to Europe through industrial conversion of the raw material into manufactured goods. At the same time, Africa also became an important market for these manufactured goods.

The differential integration of women to facilitate capital accumulation resulted in a hierarchical structure that placed women at the lowest level and determined access to employment, training, land, credit, and political authority. Because wage labor received "exchange value," it was ranked higher than the "use value" of subsistence of domestic labor, and women's overall status decreased. In addition, women's rights to land were seriously curtailed because the introduction of cash crops tended to alter land rights from common usufruct rules to individualized patterns of tenure.

> Changes in land tenure from communal to individual ownership have placed barriers to women's access rights in land. This is because individualized ownership of land makes it possible for the registered holder of title to land (who is usually a man) to alienate land and dispose of it as he wishes. Communal ownership of land not only made no provision for individuals to alienate land, it also had built-in rights of use for all those dependent on the land for food, of which women stood to be the most vulnerable group. Individual ownership of land also leads to social differentiation based upon acreage and access to capital and labour. This process in turn discriminates against members of poorer households and therefore affects the capabilities of women in provisioning their families.[18]

Perhaps the most detrimental effect of these changes was in the area of nutrition. Cash-crop production competed with the production of food crops for land, agricultural imports, finance, and labor. The decline in subsistence farming led not only to the adoption of less nutritious foods but also to the importation of food crops, particularly staples.

African agriculture today is in a state of crisis mainly because colonial structures that emphasized the production of cash crops for export at the expense of food crops to facilitate capital accumulation elsewhere are still in operation years after independence. Women still constitute the predominant labor force in food production, often working under extremely difficult conditions and without incentives or access to resources.[19] Disillusionment, despair, fatigue, and lack of alternatives in the rural areas have often led to migration of young women to the cities, where they encounter a new form of deprivation and marginalization instead of the expected improvement in their lives.

Linkages through Industrial Production

Slave labor in the Caribbean and South America and the subsequent colonization of these areas led in no small measure to the economic growth of the British Empire and to the economic prosperity of other European countries such as France, Spain, and Portugal. It also started a process of exploitative industrialization that was consolidated under colonialism and persists in modern times. In this process, raw materials continue to be extracted primarily for export. The bauxite industry in the Caribbean is a case in point. Although the bulk of the world's bauxite outside the Communist bloc, Australia, and Guinea is found in the Caribbean and Latin American countries of Jamaica, Surinam, and

Guyana, the mining, processing, and expropriation of the profits are controlled by European and American companies. Many of the industries processing aluminum are located in the racist economy of the American South,[20] in Canada, and to a lesser extent in Europe, providing jobs for Europeans, Canadians, and Americans.

The pattern of industrialization is one of dependency and external control. "Royalties, licensing fees for parent-firm technology and interest charges on loans from the parent firm are all determined by the parent firm.... [A]lthough a small developing country may be a major supplier of a vital raw material to companies in the United States, that small country has no control over its prices."[21] Within the Caribbean, most of the industries are owned by United States companies, and much of the inflow of technology and equipment is imported from the United States and goes directly to United States industrial operations in the region.

Even when import substitution strategies are adopted in industrialization, many of the raw materials, including crude food grain products, technology, and personnel, are imported from European or American countries. For example, raw materials and intermediate goods in Jamaica, Guyana, and Trinidad amounted to fifty percent of their imports in 1974.[22] This, in fact, is the global pattern for most "Third World" countries. According to figures from the International Bank for Reconstruction and Development, imports from industrialized nations to Third World countries amounted to 123 billion dollars in 1975, and exports from Third World nations to industrialized countries were less than 26 billion dollars.

The new trend of locating export-oriented industries in developing countries is producing the same pattern of dependency through the quest for cheap labor, raw materials, and markets. Female labor has been particularly important here, for not only is it cheaper than male labor but it offers more scope for exploitation with impunity.[23] In Africa, the Caribbean, Latin American, and the United States, the employment of the majority of black women in industry conforms to this pattern. The pattern of external orientation characterizes the industrializing process in much of the Third World. An important aspect of it is that the hierarchical structure created by industry replicates the hierarchical pattern of inequality along the lines of race, class, and sex. Here again the black woman in Africa and from Africa finds herself at the bottom of the industrial ladder. If and when necessary, she has been compelled to become proletarianized as an even cheaper source of labor. This is particularly marked in labor-intensive food-processing, textile, and agro-industries in Caribbean countries such as Jamaica and Haiti; in African countries such as Swaziland, the Ivory Coast, and Senegal; in

Latin American countries such as Brazil; and in southern agricultural areas and northern industrial cities of the United States. Most of these industries have the same pattern. They are labor intensive and environmentally unsafe, offer casual rather than permanent employment and have no legislative protection, collective bargaining opportunities, or child-care and nursing facilities.[24]

Within this industrializing culture has developed a process of urbanization that is producing insurmountable social problems and leading to even greater marginalization of women, particularly black women. In the United States, La Frances Rodgers-Rose has characterized this process as destructive to the black family in that it creates larger numbers of poor single-parent families headed by low-income black women.[25] We see a similar pattern in West Africa creating serious problems of unemployment, slum proliferation, and malnutrition, particularly in women and children.[26] In Brazil, urbanization for the black woman has meant increasing participation in industry as low-paid laborers.[27] A study of the spread of capitalism in Colombia has highlighted the exploitative nature of employment available to black townswomen as laborers in agro-industries.[28] These industries prefer to hire women "because they are more docile and will work for low wages." The work they do not only is tiring but also is extremely harmful to their health, since it involves fumigating plants. Powerful organophosphorus pesticides are often applied by hand, plant by plant, from a small container. The exploitation of these black women workers keeps them at a level that barely ensures survival. "Their earnings barely suffice for basic necessities. Emergencies such as a death, sickness, accidents, or something special for school nearly always require that the family pawn a possession, such as a watch, a pair of pants, a dress, or a bed. The four pawnshops are all owned by whites who live outside the town, and they charge 10% interest a month!"[29] This trend toward impoverishment and marginalization of black women facilitates capital accumulation.

With regard to trading, the preponderance of women in petty trading in urban areas of Africa and the diaspora, particularly in Haiti and Jamaica, is often an aspect of their marginalization rather than an indication of economic success. The majority of women are petty traders, and although they enjoy a measure of independence, they barely make enough for subsistence needs and have little or no access to capital or other resources. Petty trading often represents an internal marketing system that is organically linked to more powerful national as well as international economic forces in the monetarized economy. Women traders are at the mercy of these economic forces, as are indeed most blacks, since direct access to the international market economy is often restricted to whites.

Linkages through the Reproduction of Domination

The imperalistic nature of the world economic system produces gross inequalities between and within nations. This manifests itself not only in the commercialization of agriculture but also in exploitative industrialization, premature urbanization, and the internal marketing system. These processes have had deleterious effects on the majority of black women in Africa and the diaspora in that they have produced and exacerbated multiple oppressions based on class, sex, and race.

Much has been written about the economic and psychoanalytic basis of racism and its past and present manifestations, and the relationship between racism and sexism is increasingly being studied. Within the world economic system, the structural relationships of domination and subordination between social and racial groups ensure the differential reproduction of the labor force along similar lines. Consequently, social inequality, discrimination, exploitation, and oppression of one group by another are reproduced. Women in structurally subordinate racial and social groups have played important roles in the reproduction of structurally dominant social and racial groups as child minders, domestics, wet nurses, and so on. In the reproduction of domination, racism has been an important operating ideology. It ensured structural domination of blacks by placing the majority of black men and women in a position of subordination vis à vis the dominant white group not only in multiracial societies but also within the world economic system.

The black woman's exploitation, in terms of both her fertility and sexuality, has been both racial and sexual, and to a large extent she has been the most vulnerable victim of the ideology of racism. Her fertility has been exploited in reproducing abundant black cheap labor under inhuman conditions and in being the target of imperialist and racist population control policies. At the same time, her sexuality has been exploited with impunity by males of the dominant group and has also served to preserve white female chastity. The result is a double standard of protection and valuation of black women and white women that is still in operation today. It is particularly marked in multiracial "caste" societies where the primacy of racism over sexism is most obvious. In the United States, "the myth of the black rapist" is still very much alive as an aspect of the ideology of racism,[30] and South Africa creates a "fantasy of 'pure' white womanhood, which the black man longs to defile."[31] In the Republic of South Africa, which represents the most extreme form of racism, the position of women is determined by their skin color. "Women in South Africa suffer first and foremost from the disability of apartheid."[32] Whites constitute about one-sixth of the population but own eighty-seven percent of the land.

In the United States, racism operates as the critical factor in the subordination of the majority of blacks regardless of sex. It is "a social system which stresses color or descent from color as one means of sorting people into political, prestige or economic classes for particular purposes."[33] Spatial segregation continues even in the North, where because of southern to northern migration of blacks, distinct black communities have developed within northern cities. These ghettos consist of substandard housing and provide cheap labor for the North. The majority of black men and women work in low-ranking jobs in industry and the professions and as domestic servants and laborers. Despite the existence of a black middle class, economic oppression continues for the majority of blacks through institutional racism and "internal colonialism." Moreover, the black middle class never really escapes the stigma of racism despite claims of the "declining significance of race."[34] Indeed, strong economic and ideological barriers still exist that prevent black mainstream Americans from full entry into white mainstream America.[35]

It was not until the 1960s that the Civil Rights Act (1964) and the reenfranchisement of blacks (1965) were enacted into law. Figures from the U.S. Census Bureau have always revealed a lower socioeconomic level for blacks as a group, and from all indications poverty is on the increase in the United States, affecting far more blacks proportionally than whites. So, although some scholars view class rather than caste as the factor that will increasingly explain African American participation in the American social system,[36] we are still awaiting the effects of the legislative measures of the 1960s in improving living conditions and alleviating racial oppression for the masses of black people in the United States.

In many countries in South America such as Brazil, Guyana, Belize, Colombia, Nicaragua, and Guatemala, black populations also exist with cultural as well as historical, political, and economic linkages to Africa. The majority are descendants of slaves who were taken to South America during the slave trade, or of runaway slaves from the Antilles, or of indentured servants taken to the region after emancipation. Very little is known of these South American blacks except that in some of these countries they are among the marginalized and pauperized segments of the population.

Brazil offers one example of a South American country where there are significant numbers of blacks from Africa. It has often been hailed as a country free of racism. The truth, however, is that Brazil represents a country where racism has remained disguised, in part because of the myth of "racial democracy" and also because of the important role blacks of African descent play in the popular mucumba ritual; in national music, dance, carnival, and religion; and in the general African cultural heritage of Brazil. In areas such as Bahia, African cultural elements have survived almost intact:

> To the Afro-Bahians, Africa is . . . a living reality, whence many of the objects they use in their rituals are imported, where people they know have visited and where other acquaintances live, where their fathers and grandfathers come from.[37]

Despite the African influence, racism has always played an important role in structuring Brazilian society, and the role of the black woman in Brazilian society illustrates the way in which racism still continues to be significant in the reproduction of domination. In an illustrative study by Leila Gonzales, racism continues to be the most serious obstacle to black women in Brazil and is related to the political economy and history of Brazilian society.[38] During slavery, the black woman experienced severe oppression in terms of her labor, her reproductive capacity, and her sexuality. She had to work as hard as male slaves, was forced to increase slave labor through excessive reproduction, and was subjected to sexual exploitation by her slavemasters. The freer sexual life with female slaves resulted in a high degree of miscegenation and created a social category—the mulatto, which is neither black nor white—and in many ways characterizes the complexity, heterogeneity, and ambiguity of Brazilian society.

Slavery was not abolished until 1888 in Brazil, and black slaves outnumbered their white masters. For almost three centuries, Brazil was essentially a black country, with much of its values transmitted through the socialization process that was greatly influenced by the black woman from Africa. The "Black Mother" was the black maid who, as surrogate mother, Africanized Portuguese Brazil by instilling much of her African values and culture in the Portuguese child in her care.[39] According to Gonzales, African culture is among the most dominant unconscious elements of Brazilian society today.

From 1890 on, the government encouraged white immigration to Brazil and banned the immigration of nonwhites in an attempt to "whiten" Brazilian society. By 1930 the whitening process of Brazil became consolidated in the ensuing racial division of labor and space. White immigrants settled in the southern states, had the better paying jobs, and often lived a life of privilege. The heaviest concentration of blacks was in the northeast, particularly in Bahia and Ceara, but today blacks are quite visible in cities in the southwest, such as Rio de Janeiro, Spiritus Santos, and Sao Paulo.

A racial pyramid was created that became reflected in the employment structure, where even today blacks are overrepresented in the lower ranks of industry and in the service professions. Seventy percent of blacks are manual workers with an average income twenty to thirty percent less than whites.[40] The majority of blacks today live in substandard houses known as *favelas*. They are often subject to discrimination and policy persecution, for in Brazil "every black is a potential criminal until you can prove the contrary."[41] Racism, therefore, is an important part of the structure of the Brazilian political economy, which is often monopolistic and exploitative. The myth of Brazil as a "racial democracy" is true only as long as blacks remain in their quarters according to the racial division of space.[42] The black woman is even more oppressed. She is often relegated to the lowest rank of the labor force, participating primarily as a domestic servant or as a laborer in the factories.[43] Among the poorest classes, women are often the heads of households. In some impoverished areas of Brazil the population is made up almost entirely of black women and children.

The racial diversity of Brazilian society creates a racial hierarchy in which the lighter color and the higher social class tend to represent the apex of the social pyramid. One study by Maria Louisa Nunes looks at literary expressions of women of color in Brazilian society with respect to race, class, and sexuality. Nunes believes that male authors, particularly nonwhite writers, usually focus on the sexual aspects of women's lives and are obsessed with the theme of the woman of color as a sex object, because of her low status in Brazilian society. The mulatto woman (of mixed blood) is symbolized as the most desirable sexually and in some ways is the symbol of Brazil itself, in that she represents a synthesis of various elements. However, according to Nunes, there is always an aura of immorality about her, and she is, in the final analysis, a victim of sexual and other forms of exploitation, like all women of color in Brazilian society.[44] Nunes points out that the treatment of the female mulatto by novelist Lima Baretos reveals her ultimate marginality as a woman of color in Brazilian society for, although race and class are inextricably bound together in this society, race is the critical factor in the end.

South Africa, under its system of apartheid, offers extreme examples of the reproduction of domination. Because of the migration of African men to urban and mining areas as cheap sources of labor, the African women's role is reduced to reproducing the cheap African labor force in the homelands.[45] An African woman in South Africa is prevented by law from living with her husband in the cities except under rare circumstances. Female domestic servants, who are predominately black, are prevented from living with their husbands and children in their domestic quarters.[46] The African woman's role as domestic servant is vital in only one respect, namely, the social reproduction of the white privileged class.

Responses

This essay has stressed the linkages between women of Africa and the diaspora that are primarily political and economic and related to the history of European imperialism in shaping the world economic system. Social systems and institutions among blacks have, to some extent, been adaptations to socioeconomic conditions of marginality. This is particularly true of low-income matrifocal households, which are prevalent among poor blacks in Africa and the diaspora because of economic conditions resulting in male migration, male unemployment, underemployment, and, in some cases, wars and excessive imprisonment. Women heading households is not necessarily negative. What is significant here is that these marginalized matrifocal systems represent the separation of subsistence production from capitalist production and accumulation by the capitalist system. In countries surrounding capitalist racist South Africa, such as Swaziland, the ratio of males to females is 1:3 because sixty percent of the adult male population migrates to South Africa to work in the mines.

In several areas of the African diaspora, a larger grouping of kinfolk rather than the isolated nuclear family serves as an important unit of social organization.[47] This may also be an aspect of adaptation, since the larger kin group or extended family serves as a form of social security and insulation against economic hardship. It is also a resource for knowledge in areas of child care, health care, vocational training, religion, folklore, music, and so on. The larger kin group acts as an agent of cultural transmission and socialization, not only for familial and community rules but also for survival in racist societies. In the Caribbean, the importance of the larger kin grouping led some scholars to question conventional definitions of "family" and "household," because it is not unusual in these societies for members of the same "family" to live in different households.[48] The larger kin group then becomes a resource base providing material, moral, and emotional support as well as services extending beyond spatial boundaries.

To a large extent also, these linkages are cultural and reflect an African pattern of social organization in which the minimal social grouping is not the nuclear family but the kin group. Socialization takes place within a kin group rather than a nuclear family content. Lineages are corporate groups determined by descent through males or females or both and have important economic, social, and political functions. Communal values are stressed, and the status of the individual is determined by membership in a particular lineage group. Households can, and often do, consist of members of the extended family and other kin with clearly defined roles, expectations, and obligations. As in the diaspora, this larger kin grouping is an important resource base. This may explain why the extended family persists among blacks in Africa and in the diaspora and has proved intransigent to middle-class values of individualism and nuclear family isolation,[49] even among middle-class blacks. The role of women in ensuring the survival of these kin networks is crucial in view of her position as "mother" in the family and household.

In order to survive and resist oppression, black women had to develop great strength and independence. Ironically, the development of these characteristics was sometimes aided by the very system that exploited black women. For example, as Patterson has pointed out, the nuclear family with the dependence of females on males could hardly exist within the context of slavery because families were frequently separated and male slaves could not assert their authority as husbands and fathers. Furthermore, slavery promoted a form of sexual equality by treating male and female labor power on equal terms:

> Slavery abolished any real social distribution between males and females. The woman was expected to work just as hard, she was indecently exposed and was punished just as severely. In the eyes of the master she was equal to the man as long as her strength was the same as his.[50]

Similarly, postslavery developments, which witnessed the establishment of institutions to support industrialization and the ideological underpinnings of class society, created bourgeois marriage and the nuclear family primarily for white women. Black women were, for the most part, excluded for the bourgeois class and consequently were able to develop a more egalitarian form of marriage with greater tolerance of female autonomy by black men. The study by Sidney W. Mintz of post-Emancipation economic activities among blacks in Haiti and Jamaica is a case in point.[51] When heading a household, as is the norm today in many English-speaking Caribbean countries, women often exercised authority, autonomy, and independence. As a result, matrifocality is not usually viewed in negative terms in the Caribbean.[52]

The systems of slavery in the New World, as well as emancipation and the nature of the incorporation of freed black slaves and citizens as low-ranking wage earners, have mitigated against the establishment of a true Western nuclear family-type structure with the male as breadwinner and the female as housewife dependent on the male. As Rhoda E. Reddock observes for the Caribbean:

> The attempt to impose the western nuclear family on the ex-slave population has to a large degree failed. The ideal still prevailed until at least the 1970s but the material circumstances of the majority of the people prevented this ideal, complete with its male breadwinner from becoming a reality.[53]

Some of the responses of black women to political and economic oppression have been more directly political and confrontational than adaptive or cultural. Women have been involved in protests, boycotts, participation in political movements, and outright military combat.[54] Black women in Africa and in the African diaspora have also participated in liberation struggles against slavery, colonialism, imperialism, institutional racism, and sexism.

History is replete with African heroines and warriors both on the continent and in the diaspora, even though with few exceptions, such as Harriet Tubman, Ida B. Wells, Sojourner Truth, Mary Church Terrell, and Granny Nanny, many remain invisible in history books.[55] Indeed, both black women and men have, until fairly recently, been largely invisible in European and American history. In Brazil the black man and woman have almost disappeared from history textbooks, and mention is made of blacks only as slaves up to 1888 when slavery was abolished.[56]

In many ways the "invisibility" of black men and women is not only literary but also physical. Attempts to ensure the invisibility of blacks have included genocidal acts. These range from unethical and aggressive population control activities aimed at controlling black fertility worldwide to malnutrition and starvation in the South African barren black "homelands," the "dumping grounds for expendable humans." These homelands also provide data to buttress racist ideologies needed for the oppression of blacks:

> The diseases of malnutrition are likely to cause physical or mental stunting —or both—for life, and the children who survive the disasters of such a childhood grow up to reinforce white myths about the limited initiative, intelligence, or work ability of the blacks. But it is official policy that causes the malnutrition.[57]

Conclusion: African Feminism—the Ultimate Linkage

African feminism has developed out of the need to ensure the survival, as well as to resist the oppression, of a people. It is more inclusive on account of the multiple oppression of black women based on race, class, gender, and other culturally defined differences.[58] It has often been fused with other forms of liberation from slavery, colonialism, imperialism, racism, and so on, and is more sensitive to the oppression of black men through the world economic system.

In some ways the development of African feminism has been aided by a number of factors. One of these is the tendency for African societies and societies in the African diaspora to develop "limited" rather than "absolute" patriarchal traditions. In doing so, external political and economic factors have been important to some extent. Among these factors are the limited participation of black men in the public sphere of authority and political power in multiracial societies; high unemployment among black men; the prevalence of female-headed households, and the generally subordinate position of black men and women in the racist world economic system.

Important also are the cultural factors embedded in African traditional value systems and institutions that survived slavery as well as political and economic oppression in Africa and in the diaspora. African societies stress complementary roles for men and women and ensure a certain degree of female autonomy in economic activities. Access to resources is often guaranteed for women, as is access to political power through parallel political institutions.[59] In some societies, women have rights to executive office through inheritance and marriage and, in others, rule conjointly with their sons or brothers.[60]

The cultural tradition of separate male and female spheres of economic activity derived from African social organization and cultural norms has no doubt also facilitated the development of female self-reliance and independence in the diaspora. Mintz has shown how this tradition, particularly as it relates to female trading in West Africa, is likely to have been influential in expressing female autonomy and independence through female trading in the Caribbean countries of Jamaica and Haiti after emancipation.[61]

Above all in Africa, the role of "mother" is central even in patrilineal societies, and the female body is highly valued as a symbol of life and continuity of the group. So important is the role of "mother" that the survival of the African "family" in the diaspora has often been attributed to the mother-child bond.[62] Not even the atrocities of slavery could tarnish this high valuation of motherhood. Motherhood was viewed as a sign of strength rather than weakness and ensured the survival of children through the development of strong mother-child bonds. Whenever African motherhood became debased and abused, as in the excessive reproduction of black slave labor, the black woman from Africa rebelled against the oppressive economic system through acts of infanticide, abortion, and sexual abstinence.

Closely tied to the valuation of motherhood is the valuation of humanity, for African feminism has the potential of ensuring human survival and ending all vestiges of human oppression. It stems from multiple oppressions that structure the current global economy and make poverty, hardship, and despair the way of life for the majority of black women in Africa and in the African diaspora. By way of a concluding statement I can only reiterate what I said in my introductory essay to *The Black Woman Cross-Culturally*. In view of all her multidimensional human struggles, the African woman is indeed the original feminist![63]

NOTES

1. For example, see Bernard M. Magubane, *The Political Economy of Race and Class in South Africa* (New York: Monthly Review Press, 1979); and Zillah R. Eisenstein, *Capitalist Patriarchy and the Case for Socialist Feminism* (New York: Monthly Review Press, 1979).

2. Eric Williams, *Capitalism and Slavery* (Chapel Hill: University of North Carolina Press, 1938, 1966).

3. Claude Meillasoux, "From Production to Reproduction," *Economy and Society* 1 (1972).

4. The devastating effects of European imperialism on the African continent have been amply documented by well-known scholars, such as Samir Amin, *Neocolonialism in West Africa* (New York: Monthly Review Press, 1973); *Imperialism and Unequal Development* (New York: Monthly Review Press, 1977); and Walter Rodney, *How Europe Underdeveloped Africa* (Washington, D.C.: Howard University Press, 1974). Similar processes of domination accounted for the underdevelopment of countries in Latin America as exemplified in the works of scholars such as Andre-Gunder Frank, *Latin America: Underdevelopment or Revolution* (New York: Monthly Review Press, 1969). The underdevelopment of black America by similar processes of internal capital accumulation has been analyzed by Manning Marable, *How Capitalism Underdeveloped Black America* (Boston: Southend Press, 1983), and Angela Y. Davis, *Women, Race and Class* (New York: Vintage Books, 1981), among others.

5. Frank M. Snowden, "Ethiopians and the Graeco-Roman World," in *The African Diaspora: Interpretive Essays*, ed. Martin L. Kilson and Robert I. Rotberg (Cambridge, Mass.: Harvard University Press, 1976).

6. Among the many useful accounts of the transatlantic slave trade are Eric Williams, *Slavery and Capitalism*; Basil Davidson, *Black Mother: The Years of the African Slave Trade*, 4th ed. (Boston: Little, Brown and Co., 1966); Philip D. Curtin, *The Atlantic Slave Trade: A Census* (Madison: University of Wisconsin Press, 1969); John Blassingame, *The Slave Community: Plantation Life in the Antebellum South* (New York: Oxford University Press, 1972); Herbert G. Gutman, *The Black Family in Slavery and Freedom, 1750–1925* (New York: Random House, 1977); and Alex Haley, *Roots* (New York: Doubleday, 1976).

7. Christopher Fyfe, "The Dynamics of African Dispersal," in *The African Diaspora: Interpretive Essays*, ed. Martin L. Kilson and Robert I. Rotberg (Cambridge, Mass.: Harvard University Press, 1976), 58.

8. Studies of the "Creoles" of Sierra Leone by Europeans and Americans, for example, have been dominated by this scapegoat perspective. See Akintola Wyse, "Sierra Leone Creoles: Their History and Historians," *Journal of African Studies*, 4, 2 (1977):228–40

and "Sierra Leone Krios: A Reappraisal," in *Global Dimensions of the African Diaspora,* ed. Joseph E. Harris (Washington, D.C.: Howard University Press, 1982).

9. Samir Amin, *Neocolonialism in West Africa* (New York: Monthly Review Press, 1973), xvi.

10. United Nations Economic Commission for Africa, "Interrelations between the integration of women in development, their situation and population factors in Africa," 1974.

11. For example, Roger Bastide, *Les Ameriques Noires* (Paris: Payot, 1967); Kenneth Bilby and Filomena C. Steady, "Black Women and Survival: A Maroon Case," in *The Black Woman Cross-Culturally,* ed. Filomina Chioma Steady (Cambridge: Schenkman Books, 1981).

12. Richard B. Sheridan, *Sugar and Slavery: An Economic History of the British West Indies, 1623–1775* (Baltimore: Johns Hopkins University Press, 1973).

13. Robert Starobin, *Industrial Slavery in the Old South* (London: Oxford University Press, 1970), 164–65.

14. Marion D. de B. Kilson, "Afro-American Social Structure, 1790–1970," in *The African Diaspora,* ed. Kilson and Rotberg.

15. Ibid., 437.

16. Protein Advisory Group of the United Nations Report (PAG Report), 1977 (New York: United Nations), iv.14.

17. Amin, *Imperialism and Unequal Development.*

18. PAG Report, iv.16.

19. See Shimwaayi Muntemba, "Women as Food Producers and Suppliers in the Twentieth Century: The Case of Zambia," *Development Dialogue* 1–2 (1982):29–50.

20. Norman Girvan, "Bauxite: The Need to Nationalize, Part I," in *The Caribbean Economies: Perspectives on the Social, Political and Economic Conditions* (New York: MSS Information Corporation, 1972).

21. Ransford W. Palmer, *Caribbean Dependence on the United States Economy* (New York: Praeger Publishers, 1979), 41.

22. Ibid., 40.

23. See Filomena C. Steady, "African Women, Industrialization and Another Development: A Global Perspective," *Development Dialogue* 1–2 (1982):51–64.

24. Ibid.

25. La Frances Rodgers-Rose, *The Black Woman* (Beverly Hills: Sage Publications, 1980).

26. Filomena C. Steady, "Urban Malnutrition in West Africa: A Consequence of Abnormal Urbanization and Underdevelopment," in *Towards a Political Economy of Urbanization in Third World Countries,* ed. Helen Safa (New Delhi: Oxford University Press, 1982).

27. Leila Gonzales, "The Black Woman in Brazil." Paper presented at the Dag Hammarskjold/AAWORD Seminar on "Another Development With Women." Daker, June 1982.

28. Anna Rubbo, "The Spread of Capitalism in Rural Colombia: Effects on Poor Women," in *The Black Woman Cross-Culturally,* ed. Steady.

29. Ibid., 586.

30. See Davis, *Women, Race and Class,* chap. 11.

31. Hilda Bernstein, *For Their Triumphs and for Their Tears: Women in Apartheid South Africa* (London: International Defense and Aid Fund, 1978), 59.

32. Ibid., 8.

33. Norman Whitten and John Szweb, *Afro-American Anthropology: Contemporary Perspectives* (New York: The Free Press, 1979), 19.

34. W. J. Wilson, *The Declining Significance of Race: Blacks and Changing American Institutions* (Chicago: University of Chicago Press, 1978).

35. Melvin D. Williams, *On the Street Where I Lived* (New York: Holt, Rinehart and Winston, 1981), 12.
36. Kilson, *The African Diaspora*, 447.
37. Melville J. and Frances S. Herskovits, "The Negroes of Brazil," *Yale Review* 32 (1942):256.
38. Gonzales, "The Black Woman in Brazil."
39. Ibid.
40. Ibid.
41. Ibid.
42. Maria Louisa Nunes, "Images of Women of Color in Brazilian Literature: O. Cortico, Clara Dos Anjos, Gabriela Grano E. Canela, and O. Quinze," in *The Black Woman Cross-Culturally*, ed. Steady.
43. Magubane, *Political Economy of South Africa*; Herbert Sibisi, "How African Women Cope with Migrant Labor in South Africa," *Signs* 3, 1 (Autumn 1977).
44. Nunes, "Images of Women of Color in Brazilian Literature"; Magubane, *Political Economy of South Africa.*
45. Sibisi, "How African Women Cope with Migrant Labor in South Africa."
46. Hilda Bernstein, *For Their Triumphs and for Their Tears*; See also Sibisi, "How African Women Cope."
47. Elmer P. Martin and Joanne M. Martin, *The Black Extended Family* (Chicago: University of Chicago Press, 1978); Harriet McAdoo, "Factors Related to Stability in Upwardly Mobile Black Families," *Journal of Marriage and Family* 40, 4 (1978); Michael G. Smith, *West Indian Family Structure* (Seattle: University of Washington Press, 1962, 1988); Raymond T. Smith, *The Negro Family in British Guyana: Family Structure and Social Status in the Villages* (London: Routledge and Kegan Paul, 1964); and Christine Oppong et al., eds., *Marriage, Family, and Parenthood in West Africa* (Canberra: Australian National University, 1978); Niara Sudarkasa, "Female Employment and Family Organization in West Africa," in *Black Woman Cross-Culturally*, ed. Steady.
48. Nancy Gonzales, "Household and Family in the Caribbean: Some Definitions and Concepts," in *The Black Woman Cross-Culturally*, ed. Steady.
49. Harriet McAdoo, "Factors Related to Stability . . . ," *Journal of Marriage.*
50. Orlando Patterson, *The Sociology of Slavery* (London: Maggibou and Kee, 1967), 167.
51. Sidney W. Mintz, "Economic Role and Cultural Tradition" in *Black Woman Cross-Culturally*, ed. Steady.
52. Personal communication with Rhoda Reddock, December 1983.
53. Rhoda E. Reddock, "Women and Slavery in the Caribbean: A Feminist Perspective," *Latin American Perspectives* 11 (Spring 1984).
54. Judith Van Allen, "Aba Riots or Igbo 'Women's War'?: Ideology, Stratification and the Invisibility of Women," in *Women in Africa*, ed. Nancy Hafkin and Edna Bay (Stanford: Stanford University Press, 1976); Lucille Mathurin, *The Rebel Woman in the British West Indies During Slavery* (Kingston: Africa-Caribbean Publications, 1975); Caroline Ifeka Moller, "Female Militancy and the Colonial Revolt: The Women's War of 1929, Eastern Nigeria," in *Perceiving Women*, ed. Shirley Ardener (London: Malaby Press, 1975); Stephanie Urdang, *Fighting Two Colonialisms: Women in Guinea Bissau* (New York: Monthly Review Press, 1979); Oppong et al., *Marriage, Family, and Parenthood . . .*; and Richard Lapchick, "The Role of Women in the Struggle Against Apartheid in South Africa," in *Black Woman Cross-Culturally*, ed. Steady.
55. With exceptions, such as Elaine Noble, *Beautiful Also Are the Souls of My Black Sisters* (Englewood Cliffs, N.J.: Prentice Hall, 1978) and Davis, *Women, Class and Race.*

56. Gonzales, "Black Woman in Brazil."

57. Hilda Bernstein, *For Their Triumphs and for Their Tears: Women in Apartheid South Africa* (London: International Defense and Aid Fund, 1978), 47.

58. Filomena Chioma Steady, "African Feminism as Humanistic Feminism: A Global Perspective." Paper presented at the Association of Black Women Historians Research Conference, "Women of the African Diaspora," at Howard University, Washington, D.C., June 1983.

59. Kamane Okonjo, "Women's Political Participation in Nigeria," in *Black Woman Cross-Culturally*, ed. Steady.

60. For example, Carol Hoffer, "Mende and Sherbro Women in High Office," *Canadian Journal of African Studies* 6, 2 (1972).

61. Sidney Mintz, "Economic Role and Cultural Tradition," in *Black Woman Cross-Culturally*, ed. Steady.

62. For example, Joyce Ladner, *Tomorrow's Tomorrow* (Garden City, New York: Doubleday, 1971); Rodgers-Rose, *The Black Woman*.

63. Steady, ed., *The Black Woman Cross-Culturally* includes a bibliography compiled by the editor on the black woman in Africa, the United States, and the Caribbean.

12
Race and Class in Brazil: Historical Perspectives*

Thomas E. Skidmore

OUR understanding of modern-day race relations in Brazil rests primarily on research done between 1945 and 1965. To appreciate the context of that work, we need to look at the history of sociology and anthropology in Brazil. Before 1945, both disciplines were in the early stages of development, centered largely in São Paulo, with clusters of researchers in Rio de Janeiro and Bahia. The 1930s had seen an influx of influential foreign scholars, such as Donald Pierson, Roger Bastide, and Emílio Willems. All played important roles in the development of graduate faculties at the University of São Paulo (USP) and the Escola Livre de Sociologia e Política, both in São Paulo.[1] One of the most significant publications of this era was by the United States scholar, Donald Pierson, whose *Negroes in Brazil* remains an outstanding research work on Bahia and the Northeast, although its conclusions are now generally rejected.[2]

With the end of World War II there was a renewed surge of foreign interest that reinforced the efforts of the small community of Brazilian researchers. Prominent among the non-Brazilians were North American anthropologists, especially from Columbia University, and French scholars. Most knowledgeable among the latter was Roger Bastide, who had been in Brazil since 1938 and had already won USP support to begin a large-scale survey research project on race relations of São Paulo. Key Brazilian scholars included Florestan Fernandes (University of São Paulo) and Thales de Azevedo (Federal University of Bahia). Among those who

*Reprinted, with changes, from the *Luso-Brazilian Review* 20, 1 (Summer 1983):104–118, by permission of the author and the publisher. Copyright 1983 by the Board of Regents of the University of Wisconsin System.

distinguished themselves in the study of race relations were Charles Wagley, Marvin Harris, Costa Pinto, René Ribeiro, Oracy Nogueira, Fernando Henrique Cardoso, Octávio Ianni, and Arthur Ramos. We largely owe our present knowledge to these researchers and their collaborators.

Several themes have emerged from this body of scholarship.[3] Most relevant for our purposes is the direct, at times explicit, challenge to the long prevailing view of Brazil as a "racial democracy." In its more extreme form, that belief held that race and skin color make virtually no difference in Brazil. Vianna Moog, a prominent Brazilian writer, has stated, "The highest, most significant and most edifying aspect of our culture is racial brotherhood."[4] If there are few dark-skinned Brazilians at the higher levels of society, it simply reflects past disadvantages— poverty and the lack of education that inevitably accompanied slavery. The belief held by the elite was well stated by the president of the National Congress: "In Brazil, access to society depends upon individual effort, intellectual ability, and merit.... We have all inherited common attributes, and what we are building —socially, economically and politically—proves the correctness of our rejection of the myths of racial superiority."[5] This view holds that if race does play a part in stratification, it is a small part. Brazilians may not give the benefit of the doubt to a darker person, but the frequency is not great enough to alter the fact that Brazil is substantially free of racial discrimination.

How did Brazil reach this supposedly harmonious state? The answer, say believers in its "racial democracy," is to be found in Brazilian history. Almost in spite of themselves, the Portuguese created a multiracial, slave-based society with a large free colored population. Portuguese colonization seemed somehow immune to racial prejudice. In the words of the Congress president, "In our land the three ethnic groups interacted to produce the union of which we are the expression and synthesis."[6] The Portuguese male was crucial in this process. At home he had known the charms of dark-skinned Moorish women, and thus it is not surprising that in the New World he succumbed to the Indian, and later African, women. This trend was reinforced by the absence of women among the Portuguese explorers and colonists. The inevitable outcome was miscegenation.

Most important for future race relations, according to this view, was the fact that Portuguese men had guilty consciences, as well as strong libidos. As a result, they often manumitted the mixed-blood offspring they had sired by their slave women. Affectionate weakness for the illegitimate progeny of miscegenation led directly to the sharp contrast between the fate of people of color in Brazil and the United States. This simplistic idea was well expressed in the 1940s by Waldo Frank, a minor United States literary figure who often traveled to Latin America: "Why is the difference so great between the exploited Negro of Brazil and the exploited Negro of the United States? Because the latter have known lust and greed of their masters; the former, lust and greed no less, but tenderness also."[7]

The belief in "racial democracy," whether it fitted the historical facts or not, has been the operating racial ideal among the Brazilian elite since at least 1920. It accompanies an equally fervent faith in "whitening," the result of the elite's struggle to reconcile Brazil's actual social relations—the absence of a clear line between white and nonwhite—with the doctrines of scientific racism that had penetrated Brazil from abroad. It also implied that the inexorable process of whitening would produce a white (or light tan?) Brazil. Thus, the legacy of the Portuguese libido would "solve" Brazil's race problem. This remained the elite view through World War II—despite the fact that "scientific racism" had become discredited in academic circles by the 1930s.[8]

Elsewhere, the 1930s saw the application of one of history's most vicious racist dogmas, antisemitism. In the aftermath of 1945, Europeans looked abroad for models of interracial peace. Hadn't Brazil for years been disproving the racist shibboleths about miscegenation? In 1950, UNESCO decided to study Brazil's harmonious race relations and share Brazil's secret with the world.[9] International teams of scholars, primarily anthropologists, undertook field research around the country, pursuing common research goals. Such international recognition greatly reinforced the Brazilian elite's belief in their "racial democracy." In fact, however, this and succeeding research raised serious questions about, and partially discredited, this image of Brazilian society.[10]

Other factors were also eroding the image. An important element in the definition of Brazil's "racial democracy" had always been the contrast with the United States.[11] The phenomena of segregation and racial violence, such as urban riots and lynchings, were unknown in Brazil. Even if there had once been onerous barriers to black advancement, Brazil had never been infected with the race hatred so evident in the United States. Whatever the precise explanation for the difference, Brazilians could say that their country had the distinction of representing humanity's best future. Hadn't UNESCO said as much?

But the United States was changing. The Supreme Court decision of 1954 sounded the death knell for racial segregation, and subsequent legislation closed virtually every loophole sought by the die-hard racists. Where once the law had been used to segregate, it was now a force for integration. Both uses assumed a clearly defined biracial society. Both stemmed from the assumption that race is a fundamental, perhaps the most fundamental, characteristic of North Americans.

From the Brazilian viewpoint, it might at first appear that the United States, by finally eliminating legal color bars, was merely catching up to Brazil in the early nineteenth century, when its few color bars, remnants of the colonial era, disappeared. The difference in the United States, however, was the militancy and organization of nonwhites. In the nonviolent resistance movement, led by Southern clergymen such as Martin Luther King, Jr., blacks forcefully claimed their "rights." Brazilian nonwhites had not shown a comparable degree of initiative since final abolition in 1888. United States society, the major point of reference for Brazilians when describing their "racial democracy," had changed in a basic way.

Another shift in the Brazilian elite's foreign points of reference occurred in Africa. There, as in Asia, World War II brought in its wake a cry for decolonization. The remaining empires of Britain, France, Holland, and Belgium were now an unpleasant reminder of the era when white Europeans, using racist language, had taken control of much of today's "Third World." In Africa, the departure of the empires and their ruling whites paved the way for the appearance on the world scene of nations totally governed by blacks. This trend contradicted one of the central assumptions of the Brazilian belief in "whitening": the closer to African origins, the less civilized the person of color. Indeed, faith in "whitening" was based on the assumption that the superior racial element, that is, white, was prevailing. Now Africa had, not white, not even mulatto, but black nations. These new peoples wanted no part of "whitening," a doctrine that assumed assimilation, if not extinction, of African identity. As in the case of United States desegregation, history was removing the very landmarks that had helped anchor the Brazilian elite in its racial beliefs.

Brazil's relations with Africa were further complicated by the fact that Portugal was the last European power to relinquish its African colonies. It was a Brazilian, Gilberto Freyre, who had spelled out the most ambitious doctrine to justify Portuguese colonialism, "Lusotropicalism." He argued that the Portuguese were the only European colonizers to create a new civilization in the tropics, an accomplishment attributable above all to their racial tolerance. The logical conclusion was that the Lusitanian legacy would spare Portugal the anticolonial violence found elsewhere in Africa. Freyre himself remained a staunch defender of Portuguese colonial rule.[12]

Because of Salazar's repressive regime and an enormous per capita investment of resources, the Portuguese government prolonged its rule over Angola and Mozambique into the 1970s. By the time the armed struggle began in Africa, Brazil had a military government that was completely committed to the Salazar policy. Freyre, an enthusiastic adherent to the 1964 "revolution" that installed the military, gained increased publicity for his Lusotropical theories. Meanwhile, government censorship prevented an open debate over Brazil's African policy.

As Salazar finally faded from power in the early 1970s, it was his army officers who pushed for withdrawal from Africa. The peoples of Portuguese Africa won independence, and many whites left. After those events were well underway, Brazil also experienced political change. The Geisel presidency (1974–79) brought an "opening" and the possibility for rethinking Brazil's African interests and policies.

One incident shows how this new relationship can call into question the Brazilian elite's image of their nation's race relations. In 1978 and 1979, Brazil's leading television network, Rede Globo, broadcast a series for children adapted from stories by Monteiro Lobato. Brazilians generally considered it a high-level effort for the children's hour. Angolan television, which is state controlled, decided to take advantage of this Portuguese-language resource by broadcasting the series in early 1979. This set no precedent, as they had shown Globo's version of Jorge Amado's *Gabriela, cravo e canela* with no apparent problems. After seven installments, however, the Angolan television abruptly canceled the children's series. It was "racist," they charged, because blacks were depicted only in inferior positions. Most offensive was the role of Tia Nastácia, the sixty-year-old black cook whom the Angolans thought a caricature. Reaction in Brazil was rapid, and many questions arose. Were the Angolans justified? How should blacks be depicted? Had Lobato's characterization been faithfully rendered in the televised script? What is the true meaning of Tia Nastácia's role in the household?[13] Brazil is undoubtedly in for more such surprises in its cultural relations with Africa. It is not the world Freyre had led the Brazilian elite to expect.

These fundamental changes in Brazil's external points of reference in race relations—the United States and Lusophone Africa—did not produce an immediate rethinking of race relations in Brazil; that began only in the late 1970s. There are several reasons for this.

First, the Brazilian elite tenaciously defended their image of Brazil as a racial democracy. They did it in a number of ways. One was to attack as "un-Brazilian" anyone who raised serious questions about race relations in Brazil. Such a tactic was common among politicians, cultural luminaries, and media controllers. The usual argument was, "The only racial 'problems' in Brazil result from the agitation of those who claim there are problems." An interesting case is the reaction to a small "black is beautiful" movement, primarily in Rio de Janeiro. In August 1976, the prominent Rio daily *Jornal do Brasil* ran a feature story of "black Rio," with photographs of young black men wearing Afro hairstyles and platform shoes. This publicity ignited an angry reaction from readers, who denounced the movement and its coverage by the press. Critics implied that reporting on such "un-Brazilian" groups was itself divisive and unpatriotic. As for the movement, it was branded by many whites as a foreign import, illustrating little more than the "cultural alienation" into which Brazilian blacks could slip.[14]

Such vigilance by the elite cannot suffice to explain the lack of debate. There was a second factor—government repression. After 1965, and especially after 1968, successive military governments closely controlled the media and all public events. They justified repression as necessary to meet the threat of "subversion," which in the early 1970s did include a guerrilla movement. But the military branded as "subversive" not only kidnappers with guns but also social scientists with ideas. That was bound to include academics who had raised questions about Brazil's "racial democracy."

One of the most dramatic cases in point was the purge of the faculty at the University of São Paulo in 1969. Prominent among those social scientists involuntarily retired were Florestan Fernandes and his colleagues Fernando Henrique Cardoso and Octavio Ianni. Given their well-known, although differing, ideological and political views, it is not surprising that they should be targets for a military concerned with "national security." Can it be coincidental, however, that they were also among the handful of Brazil's researchers into race relations? And that, by their research, writing, and teaching, they had raised troubling questions about the realities of Brazilian race relations?[15] The military government frequently intervened to suppress news that contradicted the official image of racial harmony. Under full-scale censorship from 1969 until gradual liberalization began in 1975, television and radio were closely watched. Vigilance was especially intense on the popular television soap operas (*telenovelas*), as well as on samba songs. More often than once, television scripts rejected by the censors touched the subject of race relations.[16]

A similar preoccupation appeared in the censorship of the print media. In 1973 a new journal of opinion, *Argumento*, appeared on the newsstands of São Paulo. It was quickly confiscated by the authorities. On the cover was an African-looking boy and the title of an article comparing postabolition race relations in Brazil and the United States.[17] Although the police gave no explanation, many observers thought the article on race relations had, at least in part, provoked their action. Another example of such moves was the Brazilian government's 1978 decision to bar the Inter-American Foundation from further activity in

Brazil. Brazilian authorities believed that this foundation, financed by United States government-originated funds but operating independently from other United States agencies, was supporting "subversive" Brazilian organizations. Among the groups receiving financing at that time were three black organizations whose stated purpose of "consciousness raising" undoubtedly displeased Brasília.[18]

A third example of government sensitivity to the issue of race relations came in connection with a scholarly conference on blacks in the Americas, scheduled to be held in Bogotá, Colombia, in August 1977. Countries were invited to send delegations, on the usual assumption that each government would finance their delegates' travel. Not so in Brazil. Brasília dragged its feet on the travel authorization until it was too late, and most of the Brazilian delegates missed the meeting.[19]

Another incident that occurred in the late 1960s was the most revealing of all: the decision to omit race from the census of 1970. Opponents of racial identification argued that the language of racial categories, such as *preto, negro, mulato,* and *moreno,* was applied so inconsistently that meaningful data collection would be impossible.[20] No responsible observer would dispute the fact that there is a problem, yet the Census Commission's radical solution of eliminating race altogether precluded the collection of any data by race whatsoever. Undoubtedly, many Commission members who voted for this policy genuinely believed that race could not be studied. In doing so, however, they were reflecting the elite consensus that race was not an independent variable in Brazilian society. Without data, of course, discussion would continue being reduced to the anecdotal level. That is where defenders of Brazil's racial myth have always preferred to operate, dwelling on examples of famous Brazilians whose physical features bore little relation to their station in life.

There was a third factor responsible for muting Brazilian discussion of race relations: the belief by the Left that race is insignificant. Social class is the most fundamental variable, leftists argue, both for studying society and for changing it. Advocates of this view usually dismissed race as a "false issue."[21] Because the Left has remained very strong in the university faculties that produce most Brazilian researchers, its negative attitude toward studying race relations has, ironically, helped contribute to the silence on race sought by the authoritarian government.[22]

In the late 1970s this picture began to change. Attention to race increased, in a small but perceptible fashion. Brazilians of color began to publicly question the myth of racial democracy. With the gradual political opening pursued by the government of President Ernesto Geisel (1974–79), debate emerged into the open.

Other writers have described in detail the rapid growth of a black movement that contradicts everything the predominant myth would have led us to expect. Brazil now has militant groups that may come to rival their most ambitious counterparts of the Frente Negra era in the 1930s. The *abertura democratica* (transition to democracy) has allowed many taboo topics to surface, with race relations high on the list. Dramatic confirmation of this change came in the decision to include race in the 1980 census. Initially, the census authorities wanted to follow the 1970 precedent of omitting race. That created a strong reaction among the staff and the public and led to reconsideration and a reversal of the decision.[23] The less repressive atmosphere surrounding the 1980 decision facilitated the collection of data that, even if not wholly reliable, are the sine qua non for any informed discussion of race relations.

Before discussing the renewed attention to race in Brazil, it is worth noting that a more traditional area of interest has never lacked attention: Afro-Brazilian religion, folklore, and art. Interest here centered on African origins and African survivals. Most familiar are the religious cults of *candomblé* in Bahia and *umbanda* in Rio de Janeiro, both well-known tourist attractions. Included also are the "exotic" costumes and foods identified with Africa. The (adopted) patron saints of this world are Gilberto Freyre and Jorge Amado, writers who have gained much of their fame by showing the Afro-Brazilian contribution to Brazilian culture and national character. Although undoubtedly important and valuable, the study and preservation of Afro-Brazilian beliefs and customs have been politically very safe. It fits perfectly with the elite view that Brazil's historic links to Africa are now essentially quaint. For this reason, the Sociedade de Estudos da Cultura Negra no Brasil (Society for the Study of Black Culture in Brazil) represented no threat to the government or elite figures.[24] Another example was the Semanas Afro-Brasileiras held at the Museum of Modern Art in Rio de Janeiro in 1974.[25] The emphasis of such groups has allowed them to avoid the thorny questions of present-day race relationships among Brazilians.

A significant change that took place in the late 1970s was the promotion of racial consciousness among Brazilians of color. Although some leading activists were researchers, they did not use questionnaires or interview forms. They believed that they knew what the facts were. As people of color, they passionately believed that Brazil's claim to be a racial democracy was a fraud. They wanted Brazilians to know that their country's race relations bore no relation to the idyllic scene praised by the elite and many foreigners. This activist explosion has startled many. Is it possible that a significant "black power" movement is arising in Brazil? The militant tone of these activists is more aggressive than that of any group since the Frente Negra of the 1930s. They repudiate whitening—still Brazil's dominate ideology of race relations —and uphold the virtues of blackness. Most important, they want to provoke Afro-Brazilians into racial consciousness. They want to act against what they see as white exploitation—a line of protest that has been forbidden to people of color for the last forty years.

The new black protest movements can now denounce the conditions that Brazilian scholars have long been documenting. To take one example, Thales de Azevedo, one of the doyens of Brazilian anthropology, has attacked the racial democracy myth by publishing a compilation of cases of racial discrimination as reported in the national press. Carlos A. Hasenbalg's important 1979 monograph used similar sources and carried the analysis of discrimination to the most systematic level possible with the limited data then available.[26]

We seem to be on the threshold of a major debate about the role of race in Brazilian society. Any debate is bounded by the terms by which it is defined. What will be the definitions for the debate on race? What are the questions to be posed? What is the subject to be studied? If it is race relations in the broadest sense, how should we proceed?

Research efforts are needed on all fronts, not least the historical front. Surprising as it might seem, our understanding of the history of Brazilian race relations is extremely uneven. Despite the fame of Gilberto Freyre's writing on Brazil's patriarchal past, and much recent work on slavery by many other scholars, we know all too little about some of the most important features of Brazilian social history. One is the historical experience of free persons of color, both in the colonial era and in the nineteenth century.

In the first half of the 1800s, there was a strong mulatto movement, which even published its own newspapers. An important imperial institution, the Guarda Nacional, had become a vehicle for mulatto mobility. By the 1840s the officer corps included many mulattoes, as they were elected by the predominately colored ranks. This channel of mobility was abruptly closed in 1850, however, when the Crown made officers appointive. The command soon turned markedly whiter.[27]

The questions are obvious: How extensive was this mulatto movement? What were its relationships to other Brazilians of color, slave and free? Why did the Crown abolish the election of officers? Did the political and social elite see a threat from the mulatto movement? How did they rationalize their actions?[28]

The early decades of the twentieth century provided similar questions. How do we explain the assertion of black and mulatto consciousness in the 1920s and 1930s?[29] Just as they had a century earlier, black newspapers appeared, aggressively promoting the cause of the Brazilian of color. Why did they appear in the 1920s, and not immediately after final abolition in 1888? Were there unusual economic circumstances in the 1920s and 1930s? Were they comparable to those of the early nineteenth century?

This twentieth-century movement was snuffed out by the authoritarian coup of 1937. The disbanding of the black and mulatto organizations was hardly surprising, given the fact that the Estado Nôvo government (1937–45) was able to repress all opposition groups. But the return of open government in 1945 did not see the movement reappear, and three decades after 1945 saw nothing comparable to the black and mulatto movements prior to 1937, despite the persistent organizing efforts of a few individuals such as Abdias do Nascimento.[30] That did not come until the late 1970s. Why? Is there a general explanation for the militancy that erupted in the late 1970s, the 1920s to the 1930s, and the 1820s to 1830s and 1840s?

Part of the answer lies in a better understanding of the dynamics of Brazilian socioeconomic history. Most important is a deeper understanding of the role of the free person of color before slavery expired in 1888. Some of the most lasting forms of interracial social behavior must have been established in those years. The scholarly consensus has been that Brazil created a multiracial society, as contrasted to the biracial system in the United States. In his extended comparison of the United States and Brazil, Carl Degler suggested that the "mulatto escape hatch" was the key to the difference.[31] Yet Degler's book, the most thoughtful and exhaustive comparative analysis of race relations in Brazil and the United States gives virtually no hard evidence to support his thesis. The reader searches in vain for historical documentation to show that the person of mixed blood got preferential treatment. How do we know that mulattoes enjoyed mobility? What data such as census records, tax records, and court records confirm such mobility? Degler could not provide such information because the necessary research has only recently begun. The "escape hatch" is a plausible hypothesis, but we await evidence of what actually happened.[32]

One priority area for investigation is relations between whites and persons of color in the labor force. In the United States South, for example, there was a period, roughly 1865 to 1900, when poor whites and newly freed blacks might have made common cause against the old agrarian order. Instead, white politicians successfully got poor whites to focus on the threat of job competition from blacks, rather than the fundamental questions of economic structure. As a result, the Jim Crow system became fixed in the South and the cause of black progress was set back for decades to come.[33]

There are obvious perils in carrying historical comparisons too far. It might well be argued that by the time of the Emancipation Proclamation in the United States there was no possibility for the emergence of a multiracial society. Yet some of the explanations given for the United States case may suggest questions about Brazil. What were the racial attitudes of Brazilian workers? Were they manipulated by employers who used similar techniques to maximize control over the labor force? We know, for example, that racist sentiments helped divide Rio de Janeiro dock workers in the 1910s and 1920s.[34] Did this occur in other sectors? Could such patterns be seen in earlier eras? What effect did these patterns have on subsequent race relations? Such questions are implicit in virtually all our attempts to explain present-day Brazilian race relations.

No amount of subsequent research and documentation, however helpful, will answer all our questions. Just as in the study of race relations in the United States, with its avalanche of monographs, symposia, and syntheses, the questions go too deep and in the end their meaning is too elusive for us to be satisfied with the answers provided by conventional social and economic history. In Brazil also, we will find ourselves drawn toward examining "mentalities," habits of mind, and social beliefs. What is uniquely Brazilian about Brazilian race relations? Does it have anything to do with the now oft-denigrated idea of Brazilian national character? There has been a long and rich debate over the Brazilian's alleged *cordialidade*.[35] Does that idea furnish any clues in our quest to understand how and why Brazil has created its particular form of multiracial society? What about those qualities that anthropologists, sociologists, and political scientists have explored—patrimonialism, paternalism, and clientelism? However slippery these concepts may be for the historian, we must remind ourselves that the most enduring attempt to explain the United States—that of Alexis de Tocqueville—was built around a discussion of precisely these kinds of collective traits.[36]

Our efforts to understand Brazilian race relations will necessarily carry us into the ongoing debate about the nature of Brazilian society. It will thus parallel and perhaps at times coincide with attention to the history of labor relations in Brazil, also inseparably linked to our views about the essence of Brazilian social relations.[37]

We are therefore brought to the elusive relationship between ideas and societies. Seen abstractly, they are socioeconomic structures and ideologies. When viewed historically, they embrace the many realities of human behavior and human thought. We appear to be on the verge of a new burst of inquiry into these realities, and although we may ask new questions and produce new evidence, we will be walking familiar ground.

NOTES

1. For a firsthand description of the early years in the growth of anthropology and sociology, see Florestan Fernandes, *A sociologia no Brasil* (Petrópolis: Ed. Vozes, 1977), especially chapter 8. A useful summary of the most relevant researchers and institutions may be found in Charles Wagley, "Anthropology and Brazilian National Identity," in *Brazil: Anthropological Perspectives*, ed. Maxine L. Margolis and William E. Carter (New York: Columbia University Press, 1979), 1–18.

2. Donald Pierson, *Negroes in Brazil: A Study of Race Contact at Bahia* (Chicago: University of Chicago Press, 1942). It was reprinted with the text unchanged (Carbondale/ Edwardsville: Illinois University Press, 1967), but with a long introduction by Pierson, where he defended his original approach, which had emphasized class as perhaps more important than race in determining social position.

3. An excellent synthesis of present-day scholarly views on Brazilian race relations is John Saunders, "Class, Color and Prejudice: A Brazilian Counterpoint," in *Racial Tensions and National Identity*, ed Ernest Q. Campbell (Nashville: Vanderbilt University Press, 1972), 141–69. Barriers to collective mobility are reviewed in Maria Isaura Pereira de Queiroz, "Coletividades negras: ascensão sócio-econômica dos negros no Brasil e em S. Paulo," *Ciência e cultura* 29, 6 (June 1977):647–63. One of the most successful efforts to place Brazil within a framework of worldwide race relations is Michael Banton, *Race Relations* (London: Tavistock Publications, 1967), 258–82. For an excellent survey which emphasizes the lack of more recent work on race in Brazil, see Pierre-Michel Fontaine, "Research in the Political Economy of Afro-Latin America," *Latin American Research Review* 15, 2 (1980):111–41.

4. Moog spoke these words before the highly prestigious Escola Superior de Guerra. (*Jornal do Brasil*, 3 August 1972.)

5. The remarks were by Senator Petronio Portella, speaking on the International Day for the Elimination of Discrimination. (*O Globo*, 6 April 1977.)

6. This also comes from Senator Petronio Portella's speech, as reported in *Correio Brasiliense*, 6 April 1977.

7. Waldo Frank, *South American Journey* (New York: Duell, Sloan and Pearce, 1943), 50–51.

8. The emergence of the "whitening" ideal is traced in Thomas E. Skidmore, *Black into White* (New York: Oxford University Press, 1974).

9. There is a brief discussion of the UNESCO project, along with citation of the principal sources, in Pierre-Michel Fontaine, "Research in the Political Economy of Afro-Latin America," 124; and in Skidmore, *Black into White*, 215–16.

10. It has been argued that one of the senior Brazilian researchers, Florestan Fernandes, believed from the outset the project would "show that UNESCO was wrong, that the Negro was not equal in Brazil." The source is Fernando Henrique Cardoso, a collaborator in the project, as interviewed in Joseph A. Kahl, *Modernization, Exploitation and Dependency in Latin America* (New Brunswick: Transaction Books, 1976), 131. Looking back on the UNESCO-sponsored research after twenty-five years, Fernandes concluded that "if the study has done nothing else then, it has unmasked the myth of racial democracy in the country." See Fernandes, "The Negro in Brazilian Society: Twenty-Five Years Later," in *Brazil: Anthropological Perspectives*, 100.

11. For a discussion of possible approaches in comparing the United States and Brazil, see Thomas E. Skidmore, "Toward a Comparative Analysis of Race Relations Since Abolition in Brazil and the United States," *Journal of Latin American Studies* 4, 1 (May 1972):1–28.

12. Gilberto Freyre, *O mundo que o Português criòu* (Rio de Janeiro: José Olympio, 1940), and *Aventura e rotina* (Rio de Janeiro: José Olympio, 1953).
13. Ida Lobato, "Fala, Tia Nastácia!" *Folha de São Paulo*, 4 March 1979.
14. The story covered four pages of the widely read "Caderno B," a prized source for publicity on the arts in Brazil. The emotions stirred up by the story can be seen in the letters published in the same paper on 3 August 1976. Ten months later "Black Rio" had supposedly won twenty thousand followers in São Paulo, an alarming development in the eyes of some samba composers. See *Folha de São Paulo*, 11 June 1977.
15. Details on the purges at USP, including a number of contemporary documents, may be found in *O Livro negro da USP: O controle ideológico na universidade* (São Paulo: Ed. Brasiliense, 1979).
16. For a general account of censorship, see Peter T. Johnson, "Academic Press Censorship under Military and Civilian Regimes: The Argentine and Brazilian Cases, 1964–1975," *Luso-Brazilian Review*, 15, 1 (Summer 1978):3–25. Details on censorship of TV programming are given in a long dispatch on race relations in Brazil by *New York Times* correspondent David Vidal in the 5 June 1978 issue.
17. *Argumento*, Ano 1, No. 1 (October 1973). The article was my "O Negro no Brasil e nos Estados Unidos," a translation, without footnotes, of Skidmore "Toward a Comparative Analysis of Race Relations."
18. One of the grants was for an Instituto de Pesquisa das Culturas Negras (Institute for Research of the Black Cultures) "to assist Brazilian black communities to appreciate their own history, to achieve more effective participation in development, and a more just distribution of wealth," *Journal of the Inter-American Foundation* (Summer 1977), 17.
19. Letter to the editor from Sebastião Rodrigues Alves in *Visão*, 28 November 1977; *Versus* (October 1977), 34.
20. A brief discussion of the controversy may be found in Skidmore, *Black into White*, 218. It should be noted that race was included in the 1976 PNAD of the IBGE.
21. A scholar who has offered one of the more subtle approaches emphasizing class is Octávio Ianni. See, for example, his *Escravidão e racismo* (São Paulo: Editora Hucitec, 1978).
22. For a stinging attack on the Brazilian Left because it played into the hands of the "reactionaries" by refusing to see that race is not reducible to class in Brazil, see Abdias do Nascimento, O Negro e o Brasil na década dos 80," *Singular & Plural* (February 1979):28–29.
23. My sources are staff members in the IBGE (Instituto Brasileiro de Geografia e Estatística), who were firsthand observers of these events.
24. SECNEB was founded in 1974. Its publication is *Sárépegbé*, whose first issue appeared dated January/March 1975. A conference on Afro-Brazilian religious syncretism, held in Bahia in 1976, was another example. Some of the papers and discussions were published in *Revista de Cultura: Vozes* 71, 7 (September 1977).
25. Even this group ran into difficulties when they planned a series of public seminars to discuss black culture and Brazilian-African relations. The seminars were vetoed by the authorities, although the art exhibition came off without any problems. Details on the planning and the nature of the exhibits may be found in *Revista de Cultura: Vozes* 71, 9, (November 1977).
26. Thales de Azevedo, *Democracia racial: Ideologia e realidade* (Petrópolis: Editora Vozes, 1975). Carlos A. Hasenbalg, *Discriminação e desigualdades raciais no Brasil* (Rio de Janeiro: Ed. Graal, 1979).
27. The case of the Guarda Nacional is studied in Jeanne Berrance de Castro, *A milícia cidadã: A Guarda Nacional de 1831 a 1850* (São Paulo: Companhia Editora Nacional, 1977). Castro's emphasis on race is disputed in Thomas Flory, "Race and Social

Control in Independent Brazil," *Journal of Latin American Studies* 9, 2 (November 1977):199–224.

28. In "Race and Social Control," his important article on race relations in the three decades after Independence in 1822, Thomas Flory argues that the elite succeeded in obscuring the racial issue in a manner that sounds very modern:

> By 1841 abiding reactionary changes in social attitudes and the structures of authority had taken place in Brazil, and the negative outcomes of the race question was one reason for the changes. Genuine race fear, by definition, could not often be mentioned aloud, while constitutional restrictions and ideology prevented racially exclusive legislation. So in informal attitudes as well as in formal regulation, the race problem shaded into a social problem after 1835, and the full range of reaction was therefore directed at social categories described by behavior and class rather than by skin color.

29. There is no general history of black and/or mulatto movements in modern Brazil, aside from the abolitionist era. That is hardly surprising, since so little research has been done on the subject. The most detailed accounts of the movements of the 1920s and 1930s are in Roger Bastide and Florestan Fernandes, *Brancos e negros em São Paulo* 3d ed. (São Paulo: Companhia Editora Nacional, 1971), 229–68; and Roger Bastide, *Estudos afro-brasileiros* (São Paulo: Editora Perspectiva, 1973), 129–56. Signs of growing interest in this history from "official" cultural quarters could be seen in a June 1977 exhibition on "A imprensa negra em São Paulo, 1918–1965," which received national publicity as in *Isto é*, 22 June 1977. It was organized and sponsored by the Secretaria da Cultura, Ciéncia e Tecnologia of the São Paulo state government.

30. In the Constituent Assembly of 1946, one senator denounced what he saw as widespread racial discrimination. His speech and subsequent efforts, largely unsuccessful, at mobilizing black/mulatto protests are described in Rodrigues Alves, *A ecologia do grupo afro-brasileiro* (Rio de Janeiro: Ministério da Educação e Cultura, 1966). Further details on this period can be found in *O Negro revoltado* ed. Abdias do Nascimento (Rio de Janeiro: Edições GRD, 1968).

31. Carl Degler, *Neither Black nor White: Slavery and Race Relations in Brazil and the United States* (New York: Macmillan, 1971).

32. Among the most important analyses of the fate of the free person of color until 1888 are A. J. R. Russell-Wood, "Colonial Brazil," in *Neither Slave Nor Free*, ed. David W. Cohen and Jack P. Greene (Baltimore: Johns Hopkins University Press, 1972); Herbert S. Klein, "The Colored Freedmen in Brazilian Slave Society," *Journal of Social History* 3, 1 (Fall 1969):30–52. Much valuable information on the patterns of manumission has been published in Stuart B. Schwartz, "The Manumission of Slaves in Colonial Brazil: Bahia, 1684–1745," *Hispanic American Historical Review* 54, 4 (November 1974): 603–35; Luiz R. B. Mott, "Brancos, pardos, pretos e índios em Sergipe: 1825–1830, *Anais de História* 6 (1974):139–84. For evidence of occupational mobility among slaves in Rio (which has great relevance for investigating the mobility of free men of color), see Mary Karasch, "From Porterage to Proprietorship: African Occupations in Rio de Janeiro, 1808–1850," in *Race and Slavery in the Western Hemisphere: Quantitative Studies*, ed. Stanley L. Engerman and Eugene D. Genovese (Princeton: Princeton University Press, 1975). One scholar concluded his recent study of the 1822–50 period thus: "Although the system's blurred distinctions did provide a way for a few mulattoes to rise—a mulatto escape hatch— too many historians have failed to note that the same set of conditions also placed a trapdoor under Brazilians of all colors" (Flory, "Race and Social Control," 224).

33. The classic work describing this process is C. Vann Woodward, *The Strange Career of Jim Crow*, 2d rev. ed. (New York: Oxford University Press, 1966).

34. Sheldon L. Maram, "Anarcho-syndicalism in Brazil," in *Proceedings of Pacific Coast Council on Latin American Studies* 4 (1975):101–16; Maram, "Labor and the Left in Brazil, 1890–1921, A Movement Aborted," *Hispanic American Historical Review* 57, 2 (May 1977):254–72; Maram, "Urban Labor and Social Change in the 1920's," *Luso-Brazilian Review* 16, 2 (Winter 1979):215–223.

35. The best introduction to the historic debate over the essential nature of Brazil's "social personality" is Dante Moreira Leite, *O carácter nacional brasileiro* (São Paulo: Livraria Pioneira Editôra, 1969).

36. Alexis de Tocqueville, *Democracy in America* (Garden City: Anchor-Doubleday, 1969).

37. It cannot be coincidental that the political opening brought a burst of attention to previously taboo topics—race relations and labor relations. I have discussed the latter in a comparative framework in "Workers and Soldiers: Urban Labor Movements and Elite Responses in Twentieth-Century Latin America," in *Elites, Masses, and Modernization in Latin America, 1850–1930*, ed. Virginia Bernhard (Austin: University of Texas Press, 1979).

13
La madama francesita:
A New World Black Spirit

Angela Jorge

FRAY Iñigo Abbad y Lasierra, an eighteenth-century friar, reported in 1782 that some enslaved blacks of Puerto Rico believed that when they died their spirits would find their way back to Africa, where they would be reborn.[1] How many, if any, had their dream realized may never be known. What is known by those who communicate with the spirit world is that there are spirits of deceased Africans, whether enslaved, emancipated, or born free, who describe their arrival in the New World, their life in the New World, and their death in the New World. These spirits, including the spirit of *la madama francesita*, are described by Puerto Rican mediums, or Puerto Ricans who engage in communication with the spirits of the dead, as spirits that *"no son de allá, del África"*—a phrase used by the mediums to distinguish between the spirits of New World Africans and their descendants and the spirits of Africans that appear during séances and communicate with the living in the New World but were never part of the New World black population. This distinction suggests that for the mediums interviewed, the former spirits, including the spirit of la madama francesita, are no longer purely African spirits. Their presence in the New World, including their contact with Europeans and Amerindians, makes them New World Africans or black spirits.

This study is a profile of la madama francesita, which is the term used by Puerto Rican mediums for the spirit of a French-speaking black woman from Martinique that manifests itself during séances, or *veladas*, and other activities related to Puerto Rican spiritism or *la tradición de mesa blanca*. This study is the result of informal interviews conducted during the past decade with Puerto Rican mediums. In addition to interviews, extensive observations were made in spiritist centers (hereafter referred to as *centro* or *centros*) in New York City and in Puerto Rico as well as in séances held in the private homes of these mediums. This study summarizes the responses of the mediums to the following questions that guided the informal interviews and observations:

1. What is Puerto Rican spiritism or *la tradición de mesa blanca*?
2. How is la madama francesita, and what it represents, viewed within Puerto Rican spiritism?
3. What is *el cuadro espiritual*, and how is la madama francesita related to it?
4. What are the symbols of la madama francesita and where, when, and how does that spirit manifest itself?

Two additional questions, considered important because their answers were expected to provide cultural and historical dimensions to the profile of la madama francesita, were also asked of the mediums, but significant responses were not available. Fortunately, in addition to Fray Iñigo Abbay y Lasierra's work, the works of Manuel Alvarez Nazario, Luis M. Díaz Soler, Arturo Morales Carrión, and Raquel Rosario proved invaluable in the effort to find answers to these questions.[2] The two questions, the first and the last discussed in this study respectively, are: (a) what is the historical basis for the presence of la madama francesita in Puerto Rican spiritism? and (b) which symbols used by la madama francesita are related to the religious traditions of the peoples of Africa?

This study of la madama francesita, which has proven to be both exhilarating and frustrating, reflects both an academic and a personal interest. Because I teach a course on ethno-religious traditions, including Puerto Rican spiritism, at the State University of New York/College at Old Westbury, this study is part of a continuing effort to contribute to the increasing acceptance of such traditions as areas of study in higher education. Moreover, as an *Afro-boricua* (Afro-Puerto Rican), whose family traditions include communication with the spirit world, this study represents an effort to understand my family's legacy to my generation. It also represents an effort to learn more about those New World French-speaking black ancestors who are very much a part of who I am today.

Historical Basis for "la madama francesita" in Puerto Rican Spiritism

When I first heard the word *la madama* used by one of the Puerto Rican mediums interviewed in New York City, it was (as it still is) used as a generic term for the spirits of all non-Hispanic Afro-Caribbean women who communicate with the living. Other mediums I subsequently interviewed in New York City used the term in the same manner. Therefore, the special significance given to the word *la madama* by some Puerto Rican mediums in Puerto Rico was unexpected.

One of the mediums interviewed in Puerto Rico said, and rightly so, that the word *la madama* is the Spanish translation of the French word *la madame*. It came into use, according to her, when French-speaking black women from Martinique began to arrive in Puerto Rico. The word was used initially to describe only these women, whether alive or dead. However, it eventually became the generic term used by Puerto Ricans for all non-Hispanic Afro-Caribbean women (it was within this context that I initially learned the word as a child). This change also found its way into Puerto Rican spiritism. Consequently, the expression *la madama francesita* (or *una francesita*), which literally means the "little French *madame*," is now used to distinguish the spirit of the French-speaking black woman from Martinique from the spirit of another non-Hispanic Afro-Caribbean woman, referred to as *la madama*, which manifests itself during a séance. This distinction became the basis for the question, when did the first French-speaking black women from Martinique arrive in Puerto Rico? The answer, unfortunately, could not be obtained through the interviews. A review of the literature, however, allowed for a profile to emerge regarding the arrival of enslaved blacks from Martinique.

Alvarez Nazario reported in his study of the African presence in Puerto Rico that there were approximately eighty runaways from the Danish, Dutch, English, and French Caribbean colonies living in Puerto Rico in 1714.[3] These eighteenth-century runways were a living testimony to the policy established by the Spanish government when, after capturing three enslaved black women and a man who ran away in 1664 from Saint Croix, it decided to emancipate them and future runaways who reached its shore rather than return them to their slavemasters.[4] These and subsequent emancipated runaways living in Puerto Rico were authorized in 1714 to establish their own community on the outskirts of the capital city. They did so, and this community of emancipated blacks eventually became, in 1760, San Mateo de Cangrejos, the beginning of what is today the thriving city of Santurce, Puerto Rico.[5] The founding fathers and mothers of San Mateo de Cangrejos cultivated rice, sweet potatoes, kidney beans, vegetables, and yucca, which became their cash producing crop since they sold foodstuff prepared from yucca. According to Luis Díaz Soler, the seaside San Mateo de Cangrejos could boast of eleven huts and a small church by 1776.[6] Twenty years later, in 1791, the community of emancipated blacks had grown to more than seven hundred inhabitants living in nearly two hundred houses.[7]

The profile of blacks presented by Abbad y Lasierra in 1782 suggests that some of the residents of San Mateo de Cangrejos may have earned a living by bartering their services as *curanderos*, or healers. According to Abbad y Lasierra, blacks had a natural remedy for hectic fever and were the only ones to use the palma Christi, or castor oil plant, which could be used as a purgative, and as a remedy for high fevers and headaches.[8]

In 1765, five years after San Mateo de Cangrejos was founded, runaways were reported to be arriving daily and in larger numbers. Twenty-eight arrived in that year alone from Martinique, which had been colonized by the French in the previous century. During this period, there were also other contingents of French-speaking blacks that entered Puerto Rico. They were essentially enslaved Africans who were purchased by Puerto Rican landowners from French-Caribbean colonies as well as others who arrived with French landowners who immigrated to Puerto Rico. Beginning in 1780, landowners in Puerto Rico were authorized by the Spanish government to purchase enslaved blacks from the French-Caribbean colonies, thus bringing to Puerto Rico French-speaking blacks in the eighteenth century. This practice continued until the 1791 slave revolt in Haiti and the 1793 Spanish war against France. The practice was renewed in the nineteenth century and blacks from Martinique again arrived in Puerto Rico during that century.[9]

A quotation credited to David Turnbull in Díaz Soler's work, reveals that enslaved blacks traveled from Martinique to Puerto Rico during the 1830s in what seems to have been a profitable, clandestine enterprise for white landowners in Martinique. According to Turnbull:

> "When a planter thought for any private reason of his own to get rid of a portion of his people he had only to send them to the gaol of St. Pierre [capital of Martinique], with the statement that they were so many *mauvais sujets* ... and by the first opportunity they were shipped to Porto-Rico, as being the nearest market where a reasonable price could be obtained. The shipments ... were all made at midnight ..."[10]

These midnight shipments suggest that they were part of an ongoing black market in enslaved blacks that was reported a century earlier by Abbad y Lasierra.[11]

In addition to the illegal trade, legitimate transactions took place in the nineteenth century that brought French-speaking blacks from Martinique to Puerto Rico. Morales Carrión, in his study of the slave trade in Puerto Rico from 1820 to 1860, cited a few examples that were, according to him, among the many that corresponded to the arrival of enslaved blacks from the Danish and French Antilles during this period. Specifically, he reported that a resident of Naguabo, which is on the east coast of Puerto Rico, was allowed to bring in ten enslaved Africans from Martinique. Four years later, in 1834, another resident of Naguabo brought two more enslaved Africans from Martinique. The Puerto Rican colonists, however, abruptly lost this source of enslaved blacks from the French Caribbean when slavery was abolished in Martinique on 23 May 1848, one day after a general uprising of the enslaved population.[12]

When Haiti became an independent republic in 1804, and Jean-Jacques Dessalines was reported to have "embarked on a policy of killing the remaining whites," French landowners left the black republic with enslaved blacks who had not joined the revolt of the enslaved black population and resettled in such places as Puerto Rico, where enslavement of blacks would not be abolished until 1873.[13] Raquel Rosario, in her study of French immigration from Saint Domingue (Haiti) and Louisiana to Puerto Rico, reports that between 1802 and 1805 a total of 1,107 people left from Saint Domingue for Puerto Rico, making this the greatest immigration for that three-year period. She also reports that Mayaguez, a Puerto Rican town on the west coast, which already had the largest community of French-speaking immigrants— including immigrants from Martinique—received 307, or the largest concentration of new immigrants. San Juan, the capital city, which is located on the northeastern coast, received the second largest concentration, 102 immigrants. Although Rosario was unable to determine the racial background of 32 percent of the new immigrants, she reported that blacks and descendants of blacks, who totaled 647 of the immigrants, constituted 59 percent, while whites were only 8 percent of the remaining 732 persons. This finding led Rosario to conclude that, contrary to popular belief in Puerto Rico, the immigration from Saint Domingue was primarily the immigration of blacks rather than whites.[14]

Alvarez Nazario reported that another large contingent of French citizens, also accompanied by enslaved blacks, arrived in Puerto Rico between 1815 and 1820. Although he did not indicate how large this immigration actually was, he reported that one hundred French citizens from Martinique and fifty from New Orleans were part of it. Since Alvarez Nazario described these immigrants as *"ciudadanos franceses,"* or French citizens, it may be assumed that the one hundred fifty French-speaking immigrants were white. However, because these French citizens were allowed to enter the country with their enslaved blacks, it may also be assumed that some, if not all, of them were accompanied by such blacks to their new island home. In some instances, the blacks may have been the majority of those who immigrated.[15]

Although the following example from Rosario's study does not confirm that enslaved blacks may have been the majority of immigrants from Louisiana, it confirms that enslaved blacks were part of the immigration. Their presence in this immigration from a French colony strongly suggests that enslaved blacks were probably also part of the immigration of the one hundred *"ciudadanos franceses"* who arrived from Martinique during the same period. Rosario reported that the immigration from Louisiana peaked in 1816 and that 70 enslaved blacks were included in this 1816 immigration, which also included 151 whites with 93 children and 12 women who were classified as wives. While the 1816 immigration from Louisiana did not include a majority of enslaved blacks, the immigrant population of enslaved blacks represented approximately 23 percent. That percentage increased to 32 percent once the 93 white children and 12 wives were eliminated from the total population of 314 immigrants since they usually were not a part of the labor force, unlike black children and women who were enslaved.[16]

While the previous discussion of the historical basis for the presence of la madama francesita in Puerto Rican spiritism does not provide a profile of the gender breakdown, nor of the day-to-day existence and customs of the French-speaking black population in Puerto Rico, it supports the presence of blacks from Martinique among the emancipated and enslaved French-speaking black population living on the island. Moreover, it reveals that as early as 1664, women were among the runaways seeking their freedom who arrived on the island of Puerto Rico. This suggests that women were probably part of the later groups of runaways, including the group of runaways from Martinique in 1765. This discussion also reveals information that confirms the historical basis of la madama francesita as a healer in Puerto Rican spiritism. Blacks in Puerto Rico were not hesitant to use certain plants for healing, such as the palma Christi, nor to be acknowledged as *curanderos* of such maladies as hectic fever by the eighteenth century. Although the mediums interviewed and the literature reviewed did not reveal when la madama francesita first manifested itself and communicated with the living in Puerto Rico, it may be assumed that such an event could have occurred shortly after the first black woman from Martinique who lived in the fledgling 1714 community of blacks died.

Puerto Rican Spiritism
or "la tradicion de mesa blanca"

Puerto Rican spiritism, known either as *el espiritismo* or *la tradición de mesa blanca*, is practiced in every major city of Puerto Rico and in every major enclave of Puerto Ricans living in the United States. The present discussion of Puerto Rican spiritism focuses on four areas: the forms of Puerto Rican spiritism, the general beliefs that govern Puerto Rican spiritism, the books used and their relationship to the séance, and spirit manifestation.

There are two distinct forms to the tradition of Puerto Rican spiritism. The first, the one that I have observed exclusively, is *el espiritismo practico*. It is an eclectic or practical spiritism. During a séance, the followers of this form rely on the teachings of modern spiritism as presented in the works of Allan Kardec, (*nom de plume* of Léon-Dénizarth-Hippolyte Rivail), a nineteenth-century Frenchman who is considered the father of modern spiritism; the guidance provided by benevolent spirits who manifest themselves; the rituals and symbols of Catholicism; and the rituals and symbols associated with the religious traditions of Africans and Amerindians. According to the mediums interviewed, the followers of the second form of Puerto Rican spiritism, known as *el espiritismo científico*, also rely on the teachings of modern spiritism and on the guidance provided by benevolent spirits that manifest themselves. The followers of this form of *la tradicion de mesa blanca*, however, abhor rituals, believing, according to the mediums interviewed, that communication with the spirit world should be purely mental. Mental communication supposedly ensures that only *"espíritus de mucha luz"* or *"espíritus de alta jerarquía,"* meaning spirits that are angels or at least very close to being angels, communicate with the followers of *el espiritismo científico* during séances.

While the aforementioned difference exists, the mediums interviewed maintained that the following elements of the spiritist philosophy discussed in Kardec's books are common to both *el espiritismo practico* and *el espiritismo científico*. These elements are: (a) a belief in spirit communication with the living and that this is ordained by God; (b) a belief in the reincarnation of the soul, or spirit of the individual; (c) a belief in the soul's need to experience many stages of spiritual purification, which may take place on different planets and in different universes before the soul returns to dwell in the house of the Lord; and (d) a belief that all human beings have the ability to be mediums, or conduits for spirit communication. While the séances in which these elements can be witnessed initially followed the practice begun by Allan Kardec, of coming together on Friday evenings with others who believed in spiritism "for the purpose of obtaining from spirits, through writing mediums, instruction on elucidation of truth and duty,"[18] the changing life-style of mediums has resulted in a more flexible schedule in the Puerto Rican community, both on the island and in New York City. Séances are now held any day of the week.

Three works by Kardec are considered the bible of modern spiritism by the mediums interviewed and were used during the séances observed in New York City and in Puerto Rico. The Spanish versions of these works are: *El evangelio sequn el espiritismo* [The gospel according to spiritism], *El libro de los espíritus* [The spirits' book], and *Colección de oraciones escoqidas* [Collection of selected prayers]. The last book, usually referred to as *El colecto* by the mediums, is the bible of the séances. It includes prayers to the guardian angels and to the familial spirits as well as the prayers with which to begin and end (or "close") a séance. A fourth book by Kardec, *El libro de los médiums* [The book of mediums], was used by at least one medium in Puerto Rico. The books are used at the beginning of the séance with great reverence, for they are believed to be divinely inspired through Kardec's communication with *espíritus de mucha luz*. They are distributed by the medium who directs the séance (the host and the medium who directs the séance are not necessarily the same) to the other mediums. On some occasions, some of the books are handed to nonmediums.

Those who hold the books say a silent prayer, generally The Lord's Prayer, before randomly opening a book. The passages that appear are believed to be messages from the spirit world. They may provide a solution to the problem or problems that the person who opened the book has as well as provide information that is directed toward the mediums as a way of continuing their education as mediums by the spirits. The passages are read aloud either by those who hold the books or by the official reader of the group of mediums gathered. Each passage is discussed briefly by the mediums, creating a miniseminar on spiritism and its teachings. During the reading and following the discussion period, the mediums usually experience visions, precognition, thought transmissions, and auditory communication, and trance mediums begin to experience the first tremors, or *fluídos*, associated with trance possession. Once the discussion is over, the mediums share the information they have received from the spirit world when the spirits made themselves manifest.

Perhaps the most interesting of the rituals that may occur during a séance is trance possession. When a trance medium is possessed by a malevolent spirit, an exorcism is performed that includes interrogation of the malevolent spirit to confirm whether or not the spirit is *"de existencia"* or *"una enviación."* When the malevolent spirit is *"de existencia,"* it means that there is a karmic debt with that spirit that needs to be reconciled. That karmic debt may have been incurred in the present incarnation or in one of the previous incarnations. When the malevolent spirit is *"una enviación,"* it means that the energies of the spirit have been used to perform witchcraft against the victim, who is usually present at the séance, but does not have to be. This spirit is interrogated to confirm all the different ways in which its energies have been used against the victim and to have the spirit itself neutralize these negative manifestations. The exorcism ends only after the spirit repents and asks forgiveness and the mediums and their respective spirit guides believe in the sincerity of the request. When they do, the response most frequently heard to the petition for forgiveness at the *centros* visited has been *"Qué Dios te perdone,"* or "May God forgive you."

Possession by benevolent spirits usually occurs when the spirit guides of the mediums wish to speak directly to the gathering or to perform a healing or cleansing ritual. Since the spirits that manifest themselves at a séance that follows the *espiritismo práctico* usually represent a variety of ethnic backgrounds, what happens during a healing or cleansing ritual is usually determined by the ethnic background of the spirit at the time of its physical death. For example, a spirit that identifies its last incarnation as that of an Amerindian will perform healing or cleansing rituals that are associated with the Amerindians. The spirits that manifest themselves, whether benevolent or malevolent, seem to have a definite mission that contributes toward the spiritual development of the individuals gathered at the séance, and that, according to the mediums interviewed, is the primary objective of Puerto Rican spiritism.

Although the séances observed revealed that there are some standard rituals in Puerto Rican spiritism, such as those discussed previously regarding the books used at the beginning of a séance and the exorcism done during trance possession, the messages received from the spirit world, whether visual, auditory, or physical, and the spirits that manifest themselves will determine what actually takes place during the séances. Consequently, each séance differs from the preceding and subsequent ones.

"La madama francesita" Within Puerto Rican Spiritism

Puerto Rican spiritism has its detractors in the Puerto Rican community, both in the United States and in Puerto Rico. There are those who equate Puerto Rican spiritism with *brujería,* or witchcraft, and who attempt to further denigrate it by referring to it as *"cosa de los negros,"* suggesting that it is a folk religious tradition of the descendants of Africans and, consequently, has no value in a civilized society. Within this context, the spirits of Africans and their descendants in the New World, including la madama francesita, are considered to be messengers of the angel of darkness. This attitude, whether intentionally or unintentionally, is suggested in Nestor A. Rodríguez Escudero's statements about several *centros* in Puerto Rico, which are particularly pertinent to what la madama francesita represents and how it is perceived in Puerto Rico.

Rodríguez Escudero reported in his 1978 study of spiritism in Puerto Rico that the primary spirit that manifested itself at a *centro* in Cataño was an Amerindian chief, who represented the ruling class of the precolonial Amerindian community. The gentleman who directed this *centro* was praised by the author as one of the outstanding mediums of Puerto Rico. The medium, with the help of the spirit of the Amerindian chief, was credited with many successful acts of healing. Another *centro*, located in the town of Lares, was "blessed," according to the author, with the presence of the spirit of a Spanish priest. The medium at this *centro*, with the help of the spirit of the Spanish priest, was noted for healing the mentally ill and the sick declared incurable by medical science. He was also known for transforming plain water into red wine, which was distributed to the people who attended séances at the *centro*.[19]

Interestingly, the *centros* where a black doll had been placed on the altar were not praised, although they too may have been *centros* where healing of the mentally ill or sufferers of illnesses that had no medical cure took place. The presence of the *black doll* in these *centros* usually indicates that the spirit that manifests itself at these *centros* is an African or a descendant of Africans. Herein lies a conflict because, according to the mediums interviewed, the black doll, depending on how it is dressed, is a physical symbol of la madama francesita or of any black woman referred to as la madama. For them, the black doll on the altar affirms a continuing link to the past, a continuing link to the knowledge that is the legacy of the past to the present. That past in Puerto Rican culture includes the African, the Amerindian, and the European. To deny any one of them is to falsify the past and to shortchange the present of all the information that can be received from the spirit world.

Ready acceptance of a tricultural heritage, unfortunately, is not generally reflected in the broader society and herein may lie the reluctance of some to accept the presence of the black doll. Rodríguez Escudero considered the *centros* with the black doll as practicing a less than pure Kardecian spiritism because of the admixture of African religious symbols. According to him, the mediums who have an altar with such images incorrectly called themselves mediums since Kardecian spiritism does not include magic, spells, and charms.[20] The willingness to praise *centros* where the spirits of Amerindians and Europeans manifest themselves, but not the *centros* where the presence of a black doll on the altar affirms that the spirits of Africans and their descendants manifest themselves, suggests that Puerto Rican spiritism has not been impervious to racism (and possibly sexism), although spiritism is committed to "destroying the prejudice of sects, castes, and colours," to ensure a better future for mankind.[21] The subtle and not so subtle racism found in Puerto Rican spiritism is discussed by such Afro-Puerto Rican authors as Isabelo Zenón Cruz.[22]

Zenón Cruz, in his study of the black presence in Puerto Rican culture, touched upon religion and maintained that *el espiritismo* in Puerto Rico is generally associated with blacks. He also maintained that Puerto Ricans generally associate witchcraft with the people of Guayama, Santurce (cited earlier in the discussion on the French-speaking blacks in Puerto Rico), and other Puerto Rican towns with a significant black population. A person seeking the help of a medium, according to Zenón Cruz, believes that the black medium is more powerful than the white medium and that success in solving a problem, whatever it may be, is more assured with the assistance of the former than with that of the latter. He also states that the herbs and healing plants prescribed by a black folk healer are considered to be *"más virtuosas,"* or more virtuous, than those prescribed by a white folk healer. He reminds his reader, too, that although the spirits are supposedly above witchcraft, there is a distinction made between *espiritus atrasados*, or spirits that are prone to perform witchcraft, and *espíritus adelantados*, or benevolent spirits who abhor evil.[23] The reader is left to surmise that of the aforementioned types of spirits the *espíritus atrasados* are probably more readily associated with black mediums.

The association with *espíritus atrasados* may possibly fuel a perception that may have its roots in the 1541 burning of blacks in Puerto Rico who were accused of being *brujos*, or witches, by the Spanish Inquisition.[24] The burning of these alleged "witches" suggests that an official and very brutal attempt was made, from the earliest moments of the colonization of Puerto Rico, which had begun thirty-three years earlier, to wipe out the traditional ways in which Africans and their descendants worshiped their God and to affirm that these traditions were the work of the devil. This effort, in a less violent form, has continued into modern times. The detractors of *la tradición of mesa blanca*, in general, and of the altars that have a black doll image representing la madama francesita or the spirit of any of the other non-Hispanic Afro-Caribbean women, in particular, discredit the existence of the spirits of African women and the African traditions that these spirits may share with the living during séances.

The observations of séances held in the *centros* and in the private homes of the mediums interviewed revealed that the use of magic, spells, and charms is not limited to the spirit of la madama francesita and the other New World black spirits that manifest themselves. Whenever the spirit of an Amerindian manifested itself during a séance, it usually recommended the use of tobacco leaves, cigar smoke, ears of multicolored corn, and rituals done in the woods, attributes that are associated with the Amerindian healing tradition. The same was true whenever the spirit of a priest, nun, or Catholic saint manifested itself. This spirit invariably initiated prayers as well as recommended that the person seeking its assistance go to church and listen to a mass, light candles before an image of some saint or before the plaster of Paris image of Christ, and/or say novenas. These too are forms of charms and of magic used in the hopes of effecting some positive change for the individuals who seek the help of any one of the aforementioned spirits. The contradiction in how la madama francesita and what it represents is viewed within Puerto Rican spiritism is in the acceptance of one form of magic, such as converting wine to water, and charms for *centros* viewed as positive, but not in other forms for *centros* viewed as negative.

"La madama francesita" and "el cuadro espiritual"

The mediums interviewed, both in New York City and in Puerto Rico, oftentimes used the expression *el cuadro espiritual*, which literally means "the spiritual picture." It is a picture that can only be seen by *las mediums videntes*, or mediums who can see into the spirit world, because mediums have different ways of communicating with that world. *El cuadro espiritual* reveals the identity of the spirits that accompany an individual. After seeing the spirits and communicating with them, the medium ascertains why they are in the picture. This information is conveyed to the individual who may or may not accept it, depending on the extent of his or her belief in spiritism. The information may also serve as the reason for a special séance or exorcism.

El cuadro espiritual, according to the mediums, always includes the guardian angel that accompanies the individual from birth to death, as well as the passage from death back into the spirit world, and serves as the intuitive voice of the person. This definition is compatible with the one given by the spirits who communicated with Kardec. The role of the guardian angel, which is referred to as a "spirit-protector of high degree" by the spirits in communication with Kardec, is "to lead the object of his protection into the right road, to aid him with his counsels,... "[25] This spirit, moreover, "often follows him after death in the spirit-life, and even in several successive corporeal existences...."[26] Although the mediums interviewed did not speak about the ability of the guardian angel to accompany a particular soul, or spirit, throughout various incarnations, they did speak about evil spirits who seem to accomplish this. The absence of any particular reference to the guardian angel's ability to do the same may be because it is understood that the good spirits can also accompany a soul throughout lifetimes.

The other spirits present in *el cuadro espiritual* include familial spirits. These spirits are the spirits of family members such as a parent, a grandparent, a sibling, and so on. The spirit protectors are a third group, and they include spirits whose mission it is to protect the person from evil and all of its manifestations. The last group of spirits that the mediums make frequent references to is *los espíritus de afinidad*, or spirits of affinity. Among these spirits may be found good or evil spirits, whom Zénon Cruz respectively refers to as *"espíritus adelantados"* and *"espíritus atrasados."* The moral character of the person determines which spirits of affinity are attracted to his or her *cuadro espiritual*. These spirits may also be attracted because they want to help or to hinder the person who is predestined to fulfill a particular life occupation, goal, or mission. Another type of spirit of affinity, according to one of the mediums, is *"un espíritu que afina con un espíritu de tu cuadro,"* or a spirit that has an affinity with one of the spirits in *el cuadro espiritual* of an individual and accompanies that spirit in whatever mission it has set for itself in relation to the individual.

La madama francesita, based on what the mediums have said and on what I have heard during séances, may appear as a guardian angel, a familial spirit, a spirit protector, or as a spirit of affinity in *el cuadro espiritual*. When the spirit of la madama francesita appears as a spirit of affinity, and as such may be a good or evil spirit, it is never perceived as an evil force. Its affinity with a particular individual is usually because that person is predestined to be a gifted medium, a doctor, a teacher, a writer, a scientist, or any of the other life missions that are generally perceived as those that help mankind move forward. The presence of la madama francesita in *el cuadro espiritual* affirms its existence for those who can see the spirit. Moreover, its presence as a guardian angel in *el cuadro espiritual* also affirms that la madama francesita is not a malevolent spirit but rather is *un espíritu de jerarquia*.

Symbols of "la madama francesita" and Its Manifestation

In the *centros* that practice a less than "pure" Kardecian spiritism, as Rodríguez Escudero states, the image of the black doll appears placed on the altar. The black doll, representing la madama francesita or any other spirit of a non-Hispanic Afro-Caribbean woman, is perhaps one of the first symbols associated with la madama francesita. It has been observed not only placed on the altar, as reported by Rodríguez Escudero, but also sitting or standing in various locations in the *centros* and in the private homes of the mediums interviewed. Sometimes it has been placed by the door as a symbolic barrier to any evil force, or spirit, that may seek entrance to the *centro* or home of the medium.

Although the black doll cannot phenotypically represent the deceased French-speaking black woman from Martinique referred to as la madama francesita, the doll's unique dress style announces that it symbolizes la madama francesita and not one of the French-speaking black women who arrived in Puerto Rico during the colonial period from the other French colonies, particularly from Saint Domingue and Louisiana mentioned earlier in this study. This unique dress style, as described by a visitor to Martinique at the turn of the century, has survived with only slight modifications in the *centros* and homes where a black doll representing la madama francesita can be seen:

> Some of these fashions . . . offer beautiful audacities of color contrast, and the full-dress, coiffure, above all, is most striking. It is an immense Madras handkerchief, which is folded about the head with admirable art, like a turban, one bright end, pushed through at the top in front, being left sticking up like a plume. Then this turban, always full of bright canary color, is fastened with golden brooches, one in front and one at either side. As for the remainder of the dress, . . . an embroidered, low cut chemise with sleeves; a skirt or jupe, very long behind, but caught up and fastened in front below the breasts, so as to bring the hem everywhere to a level with the end of the long chemise, and, finally, a foulard or silken kerchief, thrown over the shoulders.[27]

Among the pieces of jewelry used to embellish the aforementioned dress style, Hearn described "immense earrings, . . . a necklace of one or many rows of large, hollow gold beads, called '*collier-choux*'."[28] When the mediums who can see into the spirit world see a spirit dressed in the style described by Hearn, the mediums confirm the presence of la madama francesita. Sometimes, according to one of the mediums interviewed, la madama francesita will allow only the madras turban to be seen, but that, according to her, is enough to confirm for the seeing medium that what she is seeing is la madama francesita.

When the black doll, dressed in a style reminiscent of the style described in 1902, is placed on or in front of the altar in the *centro* or in the home, although the altar may have an array of symbols associated with different religious or healing traditions, this usually means that la madama francesita is the primary spirit guide of the medium. If there is a separate altar for the ancestors, or *los muertos familiares*, the black doll may be placed near this altar, indicating that la madama francesita may be one of the medium's ancestors. Sometimes the black doll can be observed seated on top of a painted or unpainted clay vase, or *tinaja*, which contains its symbols of power. These symbols of power are not universal since different mediums may be asked to place different things in the vase. This "asking" usually takes place when la madama francesita manifests herself and communicates her wishes through a trance medium. It may, however, also take place through dreams, thought transmissions, visions, and intuitive messages. The latter are guided by the reactions experienced by the medium upon seeing particular objects or images. These reactions usually produce a sudden flush of the body, a quickened heart beat, or a déjà vu sensation, recalling a previously forgotten vision or dream message in which the symbol was presented.

Although the symbols of power in the clay vase are rarely, if ever, seen by the public, there are other symbols that are visible and used in cleansing or healing rituals, in divination, and during séances when la madama francesita manifests itself. These symbols include a fan; a piece of red cloth; a large cowrie shell or shells; a stand of nine different colored kerchiefs tied together; a broom; tobacco leaves and other medicinal plants; cigars; over-proof rum; honey; coconuts; sweets made with flour; and *barajas*, or cards, which may or may not be tarot cards. Forces of nature may also be used as symbols. This is particularly true of (a) water, including seawater, river water, rainwater, water from a waterfall, and spring water; (b) fire, including lightning; (c) earth, including damp soil, mud, rocks, sand, and crystals; (d) air, including night breeze, early morning air, and wind; and (e) the sun and moon. La madama francesita may use all or none of the forces of nature during a cleansing or healing ritual. It may also use any force of nature such as fire as a personal symbol that announces the proximity of the spirit during a séance or appears instead of the spirit when it does not manifest itself but, nonetheless, is present. These forces of nature may also be used as *fuerzas espirituales*, or spiritual powers that are added to any of the symbols to strengthen them when they are used as talismans for a person or place. For example, in prescribing how a rock talisman should be prepared, la madama francesita may recommend that the rock be placed outdoors periodically to receive the *fuerzas espirituales* of the rain, of the moon, of the sun, of the morning air, and so on. This supposedly reenergizes the rock and ensures its continuing ability to ward off evil. Because all or none of the aforementioned symbols and forces of nature may be used by la madama francesita once it has manifested itself and "possessed" a medium, it suggests that la madama francesita treats each encounter with the living as a unique experience.

La madama francesita can manifest itself anywhere and at any time. Nevertheless, once a formal relationship has been established between the spirit and the medium, la madama francesita will usually manifest itself in formal settings. These settings are the weekly or monthly séances; the yearly *fiesta para los muertos*, or celebration for the dead; and during the healing, cleansing, and divination rituals that may take place any time, either in the *centro* or in the home of the medium. Natural environments also provide settings in which la madama francesita manifests itself. These natural environments include woods, waterfalls, seashores, rivers, mountains, and grounds round large trees, which are considered sacred.

Although possession of the *casilla*, or human body, that serves as a host for la madama francesita is one of the ways that la madama francesita manifests itself, it is not the only way because all mediums are not trance mediums. "Possession" by la madama francesita can take as many different forms as there are types of mediums—seeing mediums, hearing mediums, writing mediums, talking mediums, dreaming mediums, intuitive mediums, and "sensitive" mediums—to name a few. When the medium has multiple *dones espirituales*, or spiritual gifts, communication between the medium and the spirit may take multiple forms or one form in particular. La madama francesita is given free reign and will use any of a number of symbols associated with it in the *centros* that follow *el espiritismo práctico*. However, in the *centros* in which *el espiritismo científico* is practiced, la madama francesita has been *"educada,"* or "civilized," according to the mediums interviewed. This means that when la madama francesita is allowed to manifest itself in the latter *centros*, none of the symbols is available for its use nor is trance possession permitted because the followers of this form of the Puerto Rican tradition of spiritism are committed to mental communication with the spirit world.

This investigation of what the symbols of la madama francesita are, and where, when, and how that spirit manifests itself revealed that la madama francesita manifests itself in various environments and that its symbols include both forces of nature created by The Almighty and manmade products such as a fan and broom. This spirit can also manifest itself in a variety of ways or choose not to manifest itself at all, but, nonetheless, may announce its presence through an image or vision of a special symbol that represents it. Finally, the interviews revealed the significance of the black dolls placed on the altars of the *centros* that practice a less than traditional Kardecian spiritism. La madama francesita and the black doll that represents its spirit are a link to the past, a link to the presence of Africans and their descendants in colonial Puerto Rico.

Symbols of "la madama francesita" and the Religious Traditions of Africa

Although the mediums interviewed attributed some of the symbols and rituals employed by the *casilla* of la madama francesita as *cosa de los africanos*, or "of the Africans," they were unable to associate any specific symbols or rituals with a particular African people. Consequently, we sought to determine which of the symbols and/or rituals are actually rooted in African traditions and who the African peoples brought from Martinique or the French Antilles to Puerto Rico were. In his discussion of the origins of Africans who arrived in Puerto Rico from other Caribbean colonies, Alvarez Nazario identifies enslaved Yoruba and Ewe peoples from Dahomey as the dominant groups brought to Puerto Rico from Martinique and the other French colonies in the Antilles. Peoples from the Senegambia region, primarily the Wolof and Fula, constituted the second largest concentration of Africans to arrive in Puerto Rico from the French Antilles.[29] Moreover, in discussing Africans from the Sudan, Alvarez Nazario contends that the existence in Puerto Rico of a French Creole litany sung during the *fiesta de cruz* or, feast of the Cross, suggests that Mende people from the French Antilles probably arrived in Puerto Rico in the nineteenth century.[30] Based on this information provided by Alvarez Nazario, we assumed that a review of the religious traditions, or world views, of the Yoruba, Ewe, Wolof, Fula, and Mende peoples would reveal which, if any, of the symbols used by la madama francesita are rooted in African traditions. However, our preliminary review suggested that the symbols of la madama francesita and their relation to the religious traditions of the peoples of Africa require a separate study. The new study is expected to provide information that links the symbols used by la madama francesita in the Puerto Rican *centros* to some, if not all, of the religious traditions of the Yoruba, Ewe, Wolof, Fula, and Mende peoples of mother Africa. While the last question posed at the beginning of this study remains unanswered, the other questions were answered and provided a profile of la madama francesita that confirmed the perception of the Puerto Rican mediums informally interviewed— the perception that la madama francesita is a New World black spirit.

In closing, I wish to thank the Puerto Rican mediums who were so generous with their time and who welcomed me so graciously into their circle of believers in *el espiritismo práctico*. I also wish to thank my family for welcoming my intrusion into the past as I continue to seek answers to the present.

NOTES

1. Fray Agustin Iñigo Abbad Y. Lasierra, *Historia geografica, civil y natural de la Isla de San Juan Bautista de Puerto Rico* [Geographic, civil and natural history of the Island of St. John the Baptist of Puerto Rico] (Rio Piedras, Puerto Rico: Editorial Universitaria, Universidad de Puerto Rico, 1782; 1979), 183.
2. Manuel Alvarez Nazario, *El elemento afronegroide en el espanol de Puerto Rico: Contribucion al estudio del negro en America* [The African element in the Spanish of Puerto Rico:

Contribution to the study of blacks in America] (San Juan, Puerto Rico: Instituto de Cultura Puertorriquena, 1974); Luis M. Diaz Soler, *Historia de la esclavitud negra en Puerto Rico* [History of black slavery in Puerto Rico] (Rio Piedras, Puerto Rico: Editorial Universitaria, Universidad de Puerto Rico, 1981); Arturo Morales Carrion, *Auge y decadencia de la trata negrera en Puerto Rico, 1820–1860* [Rise and decline of the black slave trade in Puerto Rico, 1820–1860] (San Juan, Puerto Rico: Centro de Estudios Avanzados de Puerto Rico y el Caribe, 1978); Raquel Rosario, *Los efectos de la revolución en Saint Dominque y de la venta de la Louisiana en Puerto Rico: Las migraciones en la isla 1791–1848* [The effects of the revolution in Saint Domingue and of the sale of Louisiana in Puerto Rico: Migrations to the island, 1791–1848] (Unpublished Master's thesis, Centro de Estudios Avanzados de Puerto Rico y el Caribe, San Juan, Puerto Rico, 1988).

3. Alvarez Nazario, *El elemento afronegroide*, 62.
4. Ibid.
5. Ibid.
6. Diaz Soler, *Historia de la esclavitud negra*, 236.
7. Alvarez Nazario, *El elemento afronegroide*, 63.
8. Abbad y Lasierra, *Historia geografica*, 244, 249, 253.
9. Alvarez Nazario, *El elemento afronegroide*, 63, 68.
10. Diaz Doler, *Historia de la esclavitud negra*, 118.
11. Abbad y Lasierra, *Historia geografica*, 179.
12. Morales Carrion, *Auge y decadencia*, 41–42, 158.
13. Simon Collier, Harold Blakemore, & Thomas E. Skidmore, eds., *The Cambridge Encyclopedia of Latin America and the Caribbean* (New York: Cambridge University Press, 1985), 205.
14. Raquel Rosario, *Los efectos de la revolucion*, 77, 81, 85, 87.
15. Alvarez Nazario, *El elemento afronegroide*, 68.
16. Raquel Rosario, *Los efectos de la revolucion*, 142.
17. Allan Kardec, *The Spirits' Book: Containing the Principles of Spiritist Doctrine . . .* , trans. Anna Blackwell (Albuquerque, NM: Brotherhood of Life, 1989).
18. Ibid., 12.
19. Nestor A. Rodriguez Escudero, *Historia del espiritismo en Puerto Rico* [History of spiritism in Puerto Rico] (Aguadilla, Puerto Rico: Nestor A Rodriguez Escudero, 1978), 166, 170–71.
20. Ibid., 222.
21. Allan Kardec, *The Spirits' Book*, 325.
22. Isabelo Zenón Cruz, *Narciso descubre su trasero: El negro en la cultura puertorriquena* [Narcisco discovers his rump: The black in Puerto Rican culture], vol. 1, (Humacao, Puerto Rico: Editorial Furidi, 1974).
23. Ibid., 207, 215.
24. Ibid., 207.
25. Allan Kardec, *The Spirits' Book*, 233.
26. Ibid., 233–34.
27. Lafcadio Hearn, "Lafcadio Hearn on the Island and People of Martinique," *National Geographic Magazine*, 13, 6 (1902): 214–16. The quotation was taken from *Two Years in the French West Indies* (New York: Harper & Bros., 1902).
28. Ibid., 215–16.
29. Alvarez Nazario, *El elemento afronegroide*, 71.
30. Ibid., 48.

14
Blacks in Britain: A Historical and Analytical Overview

Folarin Shyllon

A Historiographical Note

BRITISH history has done scant justice to the black presence, which is more than four centuries old, in Britain. Until after World War II, British historians were busy extolling the virtue of their country in abolishing a commerce it had perfected. The *locus classicus* was Sir Reginald Coupland, who, in the second chapter of *The British Anti-Slavery Movement*, discussed the Somerset case (1772) at some length in his sentimental vein, but left out any discussion of the black community that made the case inevitable. He merely used the case to further his thesis that British humanitarianism freed the slave and ended the British slave trade—thus the *suggestio falsi* that "the Somerset Case marks the beginning of the end of Slavery throughout the British Empire. For behind the legal judgement lay the moral judgement."[1]

Dorothy M. George was the first scholar to discuss the black community in Britain. Her episodic and superficial account was given within the context of English xenophobia in eighteenth-century London. While discussing "Jew-baiting," hatred of the French, riots against Irish labor, and factional fights between the Irish and English, Dorothy George highlights the plight of blacks in eighteenth-century London.[2] In his famous book published in 1944, Eric Williams, referring to the black community in eighteenth-century England, commented incisively on the degradation of black humanity.[3] In 1948, Professor Kenneth Little published his pioneering work that combined a sociological study of race relations in Cardiff with a conceptual framework that has influenced subsequent studies.[4] Little's conceptual framework, presented in the second part of his book, breaks a conspiracy of silence by presenting the

223

first scholarly history of blacks in Britain since 1600. J. Jean Hecht's 1954 monograph is a dependable brief account of the social and cultural context of the black community in eighteenth-century England.[5]

In 1972, the West Indian writer and journalist Edward Scobie published the first book to cover the general black experience in Britain from the sixteenth to the twentieth century. Although perilously approaching a "scissors and paste job," this volume adds to our knowledge of black-white relations in Britain.[6]

James Walvin's history of blacks in Britain, covering the same period as Scobie's book, traces the origin of the black community in England and probes the roots of British racism.[7] Shyllon, covering the period from the middle of the sixteenth century to Emancipation, essays an uncompromising history of the black experience in Britain. He not only criticizes British racism and condemns Britain for her crimes against black humanity, but demythologizes British heroes such as William Wilberforce, Samuel Johnson, and Lord Mansfield.[8]

The African presence in Britain can be conveniently divided into five phases. The first phase is from early times to the end of the English Civil War; the second is from the Restoration to the end of slavery in the British Empire (1660–1833); the third is from Emancipation to the beginning of World War I (1834–1914); the penultimate period covers both the world wars and the intervening years (1915–45); and the final period is the post-1945 years.[9]

From Early Times to the English Revolution

Fragmentary accounts of the African presence in Britain date back to Roman times. The Emperor Septimius Severus is reported to have met an African soldier in the Roman garrison stationed on Hadrian's Wall. Irish records suggest that during a Viking raid on Spain and North Africa in 862, a number of Africans were captured and were carried to Dublin, where they were known as "blue men." In 1507, two black ladies occupied respectable positions in the court of King James IV of Scotland.[10] Elizabeth I also employed Africans at her court as entertainers and one as a page. Between 1548 and 1550, one Sir Peter Negro (also called Captain Negro, Pedro Negro, or Petro Negro), obviously a black man, was sent against the Scots with a band of "souldiours Spanierdes." It would seem that Peter Negro's band of mercenaries comprised Africans and mixed-blood men.[11] When John Lok returned from his second voyage to Africa in 1555, he brought back to Britain as part of his cargo five "black slaves, whereof some were tall and strong men and could well agree with our meates and drinkes. The colde moyst doth somewhat offend them."[12] Actually, these Africans were not slaves but linguists who returned to Africa after they had become proficient in the English language. Thus, William Towerson, on his second voyage to Africa in 1556–57, took two Africans with him to act as interpreters. When they got to a place he called Bulle, the blacks there refused to have anything to do with Towerson's company until they saw fellow Africans. "The Negros were very glad of our Negros, and showed them all the friendship they could, when they had told them they were the men taken away being now again brought by us."[13]

Although the five Africans John Lok brought to England in 1555 were not slaves, those Africans who followed them were slaves, and they became the first permanent black settlers in Britain. It is impossible to state precisely when trafficking in black slaves began in Britain, but bearing in mind that the first batch of Africans was purchased in Lisbon for the West Indies in 1510, and that the first African slaves, twenty in number, to be landed in what became the United States arrived in Jamestown in 1619, it would seem safe to say that between these two dates, more than a few African slaves were imported into Britain and were probably disposed of by private arrangements. The first instance discovered so far of blacks treated as articles of commerce in Britain occurred in 1621 in the "Petition of William Bragge to the Honorable Sir Thomas Smith, Knight, and all the Company of the East India and Sommer Islands," wherein "thirteen Negroes or Indian people" were included in his claim for £6,875 from the company.[14] As early as 1569, however, Lord Derby employed a black servant,[15] and the *Mercurius Politicus* of 11 August 1659 contains another example of the employment of black serving boys in Britain:

> A negro-boy, about nine years of age, in a grey serge suit, his hair cut close to his head, was lost on Tuesday last, August 9th at night, in St. Nicholas Lane, London. If anyone can give notice of him to Mr. Thomas Barker at the Sugar Loaf in that Lane, they shall be rewarded for their pains.

The number of Africans in Britain during this first period, or indeed in subsequent periods, is not known. Nonetheless, it can be safely conjectured that the number was in the hundreds rather than thousands and that they lived mostly in London. By 1596, they were sizable enough to cause disquiet in official quarters. For in that year, and again in 1601, it was the "pleasure" of Elizabeth I to command:

> Understanding that there are lately divers blackamoores brought into this realme, of which kinde of people there are allready here too manie, consideringe howe God hath blessed this land with great increase of people of our

owne nation as anie countrie in the world, whereof manie for want of service
and meanes to sett them on worck fall to idleness and to great extremytie
... that those kinde of people should be sent forth of the land.[16]

One Casper Van Senden, a merchant of Lubeck, who had procured
and brought to England eighty-nine British subjects detained as prisoners in Spain and Portugal, was licensed to transport an equal number of
blacks to Spain and Portugal from England. Whereupon, the Lords of
the Privy Council directed all the civil authorities:

> to aide and assist him to take up suche blackamoores as he shall finde within
> this realme with the consent of their masters who doubt not, considering her
> Majesty's good pleasure to have those kinde of people sent out of the lande
> ... shall doe charitably and like Christians rather to be served by their owne
> countrymen than with those kinde of people, will yielde those in their
> possession to him.[17]

The form and tone of Elizabeth's expulsion order and the directive of
the Privy Council prepared the ground for British institutional racism.
The reasons given for the expulsion when presently examined and
related to later British reactions to Africans will confirm the suggestion.
The expulsion was ordered because it was thought that the Africans
threatened the purity of English blood and the livelihood of English
servants. And until today, whenever it is thought that blacks are "too
manie," again and again, forced expulsion of blacks has been used in a
fruitless attempt to keep Britain white. "Those kinde of people" were
also expelled because they were black and because they were not
Christians but "heathens." Here we have the establishment of negative
stereotypes of the African as innately inferior, heathen, black, and,
therefore, evil. Thus, a special stigma was attached to the African's
black color. Elizabeth's order manifests the theory of the intrinsic inferiority of blacks to the so-called whites, and the Privy Council directive
put the theory into practice by actually expelling them from Britain,
thus enshrining the cardinal principle and justification of British racism.
Segregation was necessary and good for the British nation. And racial
discrimination against blacks was elevated to a national and patriotic
duty.

1660–1833

To attempt to keep Britain white in 1596 was a failure as evidenced
by the repeat performance, also a failure, in 1601. Africans had, by 1596,
become too well-entrenched at various levels of English social life to be

reason for
failure of
expulsions.

easily expelled from the country. Some were already free men, while the majority who were slaves had become immune to repatriation by becoming favorites in royal, aristocratic, and wealthy households. Elizabeth herself, as we have seen, owned black slaves. James I and his queen also had black servants, and his wife brought her own black body-servants from Portugal. Already, black servants had become an "index of rank or opulence supreme" that was to become more conspicuous in the eighteenth century, and they enjoyed the protection afforded by the rank or wealth of their owners.[18]

When in 1655, Cromwell captured Jamaica from the Spaniards and the end of the Civil War and the Restoration signaled Britain's whole-hearted participation in the slave trade, the purity of the national bloodstream could not be maintained nor Britain kept white. In addition to Africans coming to Britain directly from Africa, more and more Britons began to import their black servants and slaves from the West Indies and America. By 1772, the year of the Somerset decision, there were probably some ten thousand black people in Britain, and Britain had ceased for good to be a white man's country.

From the middle of the seventeenth century, slavery existed under the eyes of Britons. In London, Bristol, Liverpool, and other major towns, black men, women, and children were sold on the auction blocks. In the streets of London, Bristol, Liverpool, and other major towns, slave-hunters tracked down runaway blacks. In London, the Poultry Compter, a city jail, became the processing cage where recaptured blacks were held pending their sale to eager purchasers who would then ship them back to the plantations. Newspapers from the second half of the seventeenth to the end of the eighteenth century contain scores of "Hue and Cry" advertisements relating to absconding blacks; "For Sale" advertisements by those who wanted to sell their chattels; and "Wanted" advertisements by those who needed young black pages[19] to flaunt as an "index of rank" and whom they could "love" as they did their dogs or long-haired kittens. All the great ladies from the queen of England to the profligate duchess of Kingston had black pages as an additional touch of fashion and social cachet.

The fashion was to attire the pages ornately and fancifully in oriental dress. Hogarth, in the fourth scene of his *Marriage à la mode*, portrayed a turbaned black boy playing with a collection of china ornaments. A scene in *The Harlot's Progress* shows another black boy wearing a turban, jeweled and plumed, and conveying a teapot to his mistress's tea table. An exotically dressed black boy also appears in *Taste in High Life*, *Times of the Day* is depicted by Hogarth with verve and serious fun when he shows a black caressing the bosoms of a young English girl. Hogarth was one of the notable artists of the period who appreciated that the contrast between pink and dark skin enhances the warmth and richness of a portrait. Zeffany was another. His painting of the family of Sir William Young is one of his fine portrayals of black domestics. Zeffany's portrait of Charles the Third, duke of Richmand and Lennox, shows him attended by a black page in splendid and distinctive red and black livery. These and other portrayals[20] created the negative stereotype of the African as a slave, a menial, or a lecher. And Gainsborough's fine portraits of the eighteenth-century letter writer Ignatius Sancho and of Julius Soubsie, the protégé of Kitty Duchess of Queensberry, could not erase this stereotyped conception in art and in life. These stereotyped conceptions remained in spite of the presence and apparent acceptance into British society of transient princes, students, scholars, and such privileged blacks as Ignatius Sancho, Julius Soubsie, Job Ben Solomon the Arabic scholar, the poet Phillis Wheatley, and Francis Barber, Dr. Johnson's faithful servant.[21]

Just as small black boys were the favorites of countesses and duchesses, so were black men the favorites of other women. According to Dr. Johnson, Francis Barber, for example, was "eminent for his success among the girls." Many Britons, however, were not amused. Anglicanus, in the *London Chronicle* in 1764, urged the expulsion of blacks from Britain because, among other reasons, they were "of a race whose mixture with us is disgraceful." Again in 1764 in the same *Chronicle*, F. Freeman stated bluntly: "The further increase of them by all means ought to be discouraged on principles of good policy," since "the mixture of their breed with our own ought by no means to be encouraged, because it cannot be made useful, and besides it is disgraceful." Others, including Edward Long, Samuel Estwick, and James Tobin added their strong objections. The taboo against black men marrying white women was and is a root of British racism.[22]

Slave hunting and kidnapping in the streets of London, Liverpool, and Bristol and the shipment of runaway blacks to the plantations raised the legal problem of the unqualified slavery and bondage of blacks permitted by English law. It also raised an important question: Had a master the legal right to kidnap his runaway slave and return him by force to the West Indies or America?

In 1569, it had been decided that English law would not recognize the status of a slave. The case in question is mentioned in Rushworth's *Historical Collections*, and it is there stated "that in the 11th of Elizabeth, one Cartwright brought a slave from Russia, and would scourge him; for this he was questioned, and it was resolved, that England was too pure an air for Slaves to breathe in." But in 1677, in *Butts* v. *Penny*, it was held that English law would recognize the status of a slave, on the ground that blacks "being usually bought and sold among merchants, as merchandise, and also being infidels, there might be a property in them to maintain trover" (an action for trover is an action to recover value of goods wrongfully detained). In 1694, this decision was followed in *Gelly* v. *Cleve*. In a series of decisions, Chief Justice Sir John Holt of the Court of King's Bench gave no countenance to these two cases when he held that slavery was not a status recognized by the law of England. In *Chamberlain* v. *Harvey*, decided in 1698, Holt held that trespass does not lie for a black. Three years later, in *Smith* v. *Browne and Cooper*, Holt declared that "as soon as a Negro comes into England, he becomes free; one may be a villain in England but not a slave." But in the same case, Mr. Justice Powell was of the opinion that "the Laws of England take no notice of a Negroe." In *Smith* v. *Gould*, decided in 1706, Chief Justice Holt held that "by the common law no man can have a property in another."

Far from clarifying the legal status of black slaves in England, these cases confounded the matter, because the precedents were conflicting. Then, too, there was the infamous *York* v. *Talbot* opinion of 1729, which held that a slave did not become free by coming to Britain; his owner's property in him remained; and finally, baptism did not secure him his freedom. Ultimately, through the persistence of Granville Sharp, Lord Mansfield in 1772, in the famous case of James Somerset, ruled only that a black slave could not forcibly be removed from England and taken back across the Atlantic to slavery. It was not until the Emancipation Act of 1833 that black slaves in England were unequivocally free. The fiat of Lord Mansfield in the Somerset case did not apply in Scotland, which had and still has a separate legal system; it applied only in England and Wales. In Scotland, emancipation came to the slaves in 1778 when, in the case of slave Joseph Knight, the Court of Session ruled after a tedious litigation that slavery was illegal in Scotland, as it could not be recognized under Scots' law.[23]

But neither Mansfield's modest ruling nor the sweeping decision in Knight's case was recognized by Britons. By her order of 1596, Elizabeth I had plainly sanctioned that the Africans had no legal rights that a Briton had to recognize. Indeed, an Elizabethan travel account asserted that Africans were "a people of beastly living, without a God, lawe, religion, or common wealth."[24] African slaves in Britain who tried to become Christians by being baptized were tortured by their Christian owners.[25] Yet, these Africans had been torn away from Africa in British ships, the earliest of which, as if to signify that they were engaged in the most pious expedition, bore the names *Jesus* (owned by Elizabeth herself), *Solomon*, and *John the Baptist*.[26]

The recognition by the Africans that they were "lesser breeds without the Law," as the bard of British imperialism and debasement of darker peoples was to sing, generated group loyalty and group solidarity among the blacks, which was particularly noticeable and successful in the eighteenth century. The blacks established a sort of transplant of African communal life in Britain in order to sustain one another. In Africa, christenings, weddings, and funerals were social occasions. The evidence that we have suggests that the same was true of the black community in Britain.[27] A visitor to the house of Dr. Johnson when Johnson was not at home wrote: "When Francis Barber, his black servant, opened the door to tell me so, a group of his African countrymen were sitting round a fire in the gloomy anti-room; and on their all turning their sooty faces at once to stare at me, they presented a curious spectacle."[28] It was precisely because the Africans realized that they "presented a curious spectacle" to Britons, that they developed their ingroup solidarity. A consciousness of racial affinity and a background of common experience were the principal unifying bonds of the black community. Their blackness had produced in their lives legal, economic, and social discrimination and deprivations. As Philip Thicknesse reported in 1788, "London abounds with an incredible number of ... black men, who have clubs to support those who are out of place."[29] Authors and abolitionists Olaudah Equiano and Ottabah Cugoano were the leaders of the black community in the last quarter of the eighteenth century.

In fact, blacks were dispersed throughout the length and breadth of Great Britain. London, Liverpool, and Bristol as slaving ports were naturally the centers of the black community. But they also lived in Manchester (where Clarkson met fifty blacks at a church), Bedfordshire, Yorkshire, Shropshire, Berkshire, Lincolnshire, Nottinghamshire, Carlisle, Plymouth, Isle of Wight, and Shrewsbury. They were also in Kent, Essex, Sussex, Richmond, Barnstable, Kidderminster, various parts of Scotland, and other towns.[30] These blacks were mostly domestics. A good many were beggars, mendicants, and serenaders.[31] Yet another group was apprenticed to tradesmen and artificers. This group became so many that in 1731, the Corporation of London prohibited the teaching of trades to blacks.[32] Another group, though transient, were sailors.[33] Some joined the British army or navy.[34]

Other blacks, however, were self-employed and able to lead independent lives. John Hanson worked as a joiner in Liverpool.[35] George Bridgetower, friend of Beethoven, was a professional violinist.[36] Ira Aldridge was successful on the stage.[37] Ukawsaw Gronni worked as a navvy, builder, and husbandman.[38] Thanks to the annuity granted him by Dr. Johnson, Francis Barber was able to live independently at Lichfield with his English wife, Betsy. Barber's son Samuel became a preacher of note in the Primitive Methodist sect in Staffordshire.[39] The celebrated

Bill Richmond, after retiring from the ring, ran a boxing academy in St. Martin's Street, Leicester Square. This academy was frequented by Lord Byron. Tom Molineux (Molyneaux), a slave from Virginia, arrived in London penniless in 1809 and was "managed" by Richmond. Jim Johnson and Massa Kendrick were also successful boxers who trained under Bill Richmond. Richmond, who was also said to be a skilled cabinetmaker, finally retired to keep the Horse and Dolphin at Richmond, and married a white woman.[40]

Despite the achievements and contributions of blacks to British society, the British government and Britain's liberal establishment made a concerted attempt in 1786 and 1787 to rid Britain of her black population and make Britain a white man's country. It was the culmination of a campaign that began as early as 1764, when an anonymous correspondent in the *London Chronicle* spoke against the folly of importing blacks into Britain and urged "totally prohibiting the importation of any more of them."[41] Another correspondent in the same *London Chronicle* in 1773 ended his article with the humble hope that "Parliament will provide such remedies as may be adequate to the occasion, by expelling (blacks) now here, ... and by prohibiting the introduction of them in this kingdom for the future; and save the natural beauty of Britons from the Morisco tint."[42]

As a result of the American Revolution, many blacks who had fought on the British side, and who would have been in danger had they remained in America after the successful revolution, were taken to Britain. Most were indigent and begged in the streets of London, soon coming to be known as the black poor. In January 1786 the Committee for the Relief of the Black Poor, made up of bankers, merchants, and members of Parliament, was formed, as the name suggests, to provide the black poor with food, clothing, and shelter. Soon, however, the committee decided that the best way to relieve the black poor permanently was to deport them and rid Britain of this nuisance. The government readily agreed. But out of the approximately ten thousand black people in Britain, less than four hundred ultimately left Britain to form the settlement of Sierra Leone. Spearheaded by Equiano and Cugoano, the majority of blacks, in spite of the tremendous pressure brought to bear on them to leave Britain, refused to leave.[43]

1834–1914

With the abolition of the British slave trade in 1807 and Emancipation in 1833, an epoch ended. The unemployed blacks were the black poor, as they had been in the eighteenth century. But in the nineteenth century, they no longer attracted the special notice or prestige they had enjoyed in the previous century. Blacks "fell" from the position of "grace" they occupied in eighteenth-century British social life.

At Emancipation there were still about ten thousand black people in Britain. The majority married and were absorbed into the white population. Their children are now "white," with no inkling of their African blood and ancestry. The black population was further reduced by the ending of importation of blacks into Britain from the West Indies by slave owners. Those who died were not replaced by any new influx as in the eighteenth century. Nonetheless, American black refugees from slavery helped to maintain the existence of the black community. A distinctively black community remained in Britain after Emancipation, though it was considerably reduced in numbers.

Henry Mayhew, compiling his massive survey of the London poor in the 1850s and 1860s, noticed the decline in the black population when he reported in 1862 that "there are few negro beggars to be seen now." The black poor, he discovered, would sweep crossings, run errands, black boots, clean knives and forks, or dig for a crust and a few pence. Others were domestics; black servants were "seldom read of in police reports, and (were) generally found to give satisfaction to their employers." As with their predecessors and successors, the blacks were willing laborers when white prejudice did not deny them work. Mayhew went into the heart of the matter when he observed: "It is only common fairness to say that negroes seldom, if ever, shirk work. Their only trouble is to obtain it. Those who have seen the many negroes employed in Liverpool will know that they are hard-working, patient, and, too often, underpaid." He noted that whenever they were "out of work they have no scruples, but go into the streets, take off their hats, and beg directly."[44]

The number of black beggars was swelled by black American refugees from slavery who flocked to Britain in the middle of the nineteenth century. In the absence of an active black community, as in the eighteenth century, to sustain these new arrivals, they had little choice but to beg. One group left New York and, on arrival at Liverpool, "begged and got odd jobs." At last they joined a traveling circus as servants, but the grooms treated them so cruelly that they were forced to quit when the circus had moved to a place not a day's walk from London. In London, the reporter's brother took a job cleaning knives and forks at an eating house and finally became the footman of "a great gentleman in Harewood-square." The reporter was less fortunate:

> I do porter's work mostly, but I do anything I can get. I beg more than half the year. I have no regular lodging. I sleep where I can. When I am in luck, I have a bed. It costs me threepence. At some places they don't care to take

a man of colour in. I sometimes get work in Newgate-market, carrying meat, but not often. Ladies give me halfpence oftener than men. The butchers call me "Othello" and ask me why I killed my wife. I have tried to get aboard a ship, but they won't have me. I don't know how old I am, but I know that when we got to London, it was the time the Great Exhibition was about.[45]

Another group of black Americans fared much better. Half a century after Equiano traveled around Britain, selling his autobiography[46] and advancing the cause of abolition of the slave trade and emancipation of black slaves in British colonies, black American abolitionists were transients in Britain campaigning for the emancipation of black slaves in America. In 1811, Paul Cuffe, "an excellent specimen of what freedom and instruction can do for the outcasts of colour," had visited London seeking a grant of land in Sierra Leone for his back-to-Africa endeavors. During his stay of four months, he became personally acquainted with abolitionists Thomas Clarkson, William Wilberforce, and Zachary Macaulay.[47] In 1832, Nathaniel Paul, a clergyman, arrived in Britain. He spoke twice before a Select Committee of the House of Commons that was considering the West India Emancipation Bill.[48] Charles Lenox Remond came to Britain in 1840 and remained in the country for nineteen months, lecturing on slavery, temperance, and race prejudice. Speaking twenty-three evenings out of thirty during one stretch, he kept a crowded schedule. Even though his standard speech ran to two hours, Remond held the attention of his audiences throughout. In recognition of his sustained powers of oratory, Buxton sought to enlist him as a lecturer against slavery and the slave trade.[49]

For the twenty years following Remond's visit, a host of American black leaders and reformers stayed in Britain, the length of stay ranging from six months to five years. These included former slaves turned clergymen, like James W. C. Pennington, Henry Highland Garnet, and Josiah Henson, and also included former slave laypersons such as Frederick Douglass, William Wells Brown, and William and Ellen Craft. To these must be added a complement of freeborn blacks, among them Sarah P. Remond, Martin R. Delany, William G. Allen, and clergymen Alexander Crumwell and William Douglass.

Crumwell, Garnet, Henson, and Pennington each spoke at the annual meeting of the British and Foreign Anti-Slavery Society held in London in 1851. Three months later, these black abolitionists met in London for the dual purpose of celebrating West Indian Emancipation and condemning American slavery. With William Wells Brown in the chair, the large audience included two literary luminaries: Thomas Babington Macaulay and the recently appointed poet laureate, Alfred Tennyson.

Each of these American black leaders had a distinctive, rather remarkable career in Britain. William Wells Brown, whose travels took him to "nearly every town in the kingdom," as he reported, published in 1853 in London *Clotel, or the President's Daughter*—the first black novel. Alexander Crumwell took his B.A. degree from Queen's College Cambridge in 1853 and, with a base at Brixton, began preaching in English churches. The Reverend Henry Highland Garnet so impressed the United Presbyterian Church of Scotland that they sent him to Jamaica as pastor of the Stirling Presbyterian Missionary Church. James W. C. Pennington preached twice at the Queen's Street Chapel in Leeds, a local report characterizing everything about him as "impressive." He toured the length and breadth of Scotland under the auspices of the Glasgow Female Anti-Slavery Society, his tearful tales exciting sympathy and sorrow. Frederick Douglass arrived in Britain in 1845. For twenty months Douglass was hailed and feted everywhere in England, Ireland, and Scotland. Mayors presided over meetings gathered to hear him. A month before he died, Douglass dined with the great abolitionist Thomas Clarkson and spent an evening with the economics statesman John Bright.[50]

> Certainly the mission-bent blacks who crisscrossed the British Isles were most cordially received. Small in number and transients for the most part, they posed no threat to the laboring man or to the purity of the national blood stream. Hence they received that heartiest of welcomes that comes from a love of virtue combined with an absence of apprehension.[51]

The activities of black American abolitionists have been highlighted here at some length because they are usually omitted in accounts of the black experience in nineteenth-century Britain.[52] One writer has described the nineteenth century as a period of disintegration for the black community,[53] and from this perspective it is easy to say nothing positive about them during the period. The same writer discusses black musicians and bandsmen in British regiments and black serenaders, or the so-called "nigger minstrels," but omits the name of Samuel ("Hiawatha") Coleridge-Taylor (1875–1912).

Born at Croydon, where he lived practically all his life and where he died, Samuel Coleridge-Taylor was an associate of the Royal College of Music, professor at Trinity College, Crystal Palace, and Guildhall School of Music, as well as conductor of the Handel Choral Society and the Rochester Choral Society. In 1893, he won a scholarship at the Royal College of Music. Coleridge-Taylor had surrendered his scholarship when, on 11 November 1898, the college produced his "Hiawatha's Wedding Feast" and made him famous.

It had got abroad in some unaccountable and mysterious manner that something of unusual interest was going to happen, and when the time came for the concert the "tin tabernacle" (i.e., the temporary concert hall of the Royal College of Music) was besieged by eager crowds, a large proportion of whom were shut out, but accommodation was found for Sir Arthur Sullivan and other musicians of eminence. Expectation was not disappointed, and "Hiawatha" started on a career which, when confirmed by the production of "The Death of Minnehaha" at the North Staffordshire festival in the following year (1899) and of a final section by the Royal Choral Society in 1900, established it as one of the most universally beloved works of modern English music.[54]

Continuing a tradition that began in the eighteenth century, African students continued to come to Britain for their education. Among them was James Africanus Beale Horton, who, between 1855 and 1859, studied at King's College, the University of London, and Edinburgh University for his medical degrees. He was elected associate of King's College. At Edinburgh University, he became president of the Pathological Society and a member of the Noetic Society of Edinburgh. Also, between 1855 and 1856, William Broughton Davies, who came to Britain with Horton, studied for his medical degree at King's College, London, and the University of St. Andrews. During Horton's attendance at Edinburgh University, at least two black American students studied there: J. Ewing Glasgow and Robert M. Johnson, who publicized the abolitionists' cause.[55] John Mensah Sarbah of the Gold Coast (Ghana) studied law at Lincoln's Inn and was called to the bar in 1887. Joseph Ephraim Casely Hayford, also of Ghana, was called to the bar in 1896. J. Edgarton Shyngle studied at Christ Church, Oxford, but never graduated; in 1888 he was called to the bar as a member of the Inner Temple. Richard Akinwade Savage, also of Nigeria, was at Edinburgh University between 1897 and 1905. He was a member of the Students Representative Council from 1898 to 1900. During the same period, he served as assistant editor of *The Students* and as coeditor of the *Edinburgh University Handbook*.[56] In 1908, Bandele Omoniyi, a Nigerian student at Edinburgh University, wrote the *Defence of the Ethiopian Movement*, justifying the growing African consciousness.[57]

J. R. Archer, mayor of Battersea in London in 1914, wrote in the journal, the *Crisis*, edited by W. E. B. Du Bois, that he feared no man and brooked no insults to the African race to which he was privileged to belong.[58] In Battersea politics, the fearless Archer obviously was successful, sitting on four committees, one of which he was chairman. He was a member of the local board of guardians, a school manager, chairman of a group of school managers, a trustee of various charities, and because of his mother's nationality, a member of the United Irish League.

Finally, it should be noted that in 1877, 1878, 1892, and 1905, Edward Wilmot Blyden was Liberia's ambassador to the Court of St. James. We must not presume, therefore, that the nineteenth century was a period of woes and disintegration and devoid of achievements. It was in 1900 that Henry Sylvester Williams, a Trinidadian barrister practicing in London, convened at Westminster Town Hall the first Pan-African conference.[59] In fact, the nineteenth century was the period when educated Africans began preparing the ground in Britain for the emancipation of Africa in such works as Sarbah's *Fanti Customary Law* (1897); Casely Hayford's *Ethiopia Unbound* (1911) and *The Truth about the West African Land Question* (1913); Blyden's *Christianity, Islam and the Negro Race* (1887) and *A Voice from Bleeding Africa on Behalf of Her Exiled Children* (1856); and Horton's *Political Economy of British Western Africa* (1865) and *West African Countries and Peoples* (1868).

1915–1945

At the outbreak of World War I, a few thousand blacks in Britain formed the permanent black community. Some served as domestics, but the majority were destitute and stranded sailors from the West Indies and West Africa. These out-of-work black sailors concentrated not only in London but also in the dock areas of other British ports, including Cardiff, Liverpool, Bristol, Hull, Exeter, and Glasgow. African students usually stayed in London, where they read for the bar or studied at London University. A few others studied at Cambridge and other universities, including Liverpool.[60] During World War I, several thousand blacks were brought to Britain to do work that would free Britons for combat service. They replaced British merchant seamen transferred to the Royal Navy; they were drafted to black labor battalions, and they worked in munition and chemical factories.

When the war ended, the black community in Britain was quite large, perhaps as numerous as twenty thousand, and with the closing down of war factories they flocked to dockside areas, particularly Cardiff and Liverpool. During the war, black sailors had earned good money in the merchant navy, but with the demobilization of white sailors who had been serving in the Royal Navy, black sailors fell on hard times. Like blacks in other jobs, they were expelled from jobs they had held for years just to make places for demobilized white men,[61] thus foreshadowing today's pattern of "last in and first out."

As in the eighteenth century, the black community was nearly all male. Naturally, whether in Cardiff, Liverpool, or London, they married or consorted with white women. The *Times* (London) of 10 May 1919 pointed out that the war had increased the black men in Liverpool until they then numbered about five thousand. "Many have married Liverpool women, and while it is admitted that some have made good husbands, the intermarriage of black men and white women, not to mention other relationships, has excited much feeling."

Sexual resentment has been a recurrent feature of the experience of blacks in British society, which has always been troubled by the spectacle of familiarity between black men and white women. In 1833, the average Briton went livid with rage at the sight of Ira Aldridge playing Othello with Ellen Tree as Desdemona. On 11 April 1833, the *Times*, the supposed symbol of all that is virtuous and noble in British journalism, expressed the national mood when it moaned: "In the name of common propriety and decency, we protest against an interesting actress and lady-like girl, like Miss Ellen Tree, being subjected to the indignity of being pawed by [Ira Aldridge]." The same national uproar occurred a century later when, in 1930, Dame Peggy Ashcroft played Desdemona to Paul Robeson's Othello.

Resentment at blacks competing for jobs with white workers, and reaction to black men marrying white women, finally erupted into racial violence in 1919. Race riots swept English cities such as Liverpool, Cardiff, Manchester, London, Hull, Barry, and Newton. Reporting the Cardiff riots and continuing the line of argument that justified the murder of blacks by whites, the *Times* of 13 June 1919 biliously said that the black man's "chief failing is his fondness for white women." But "some of the sober-minded men of Cardiff consider that the coloured men are not alone to blame for the disturbances, although, at the same time, they deplore the familiar association between white women and negroes, which is a provocative cause."

The *Times* estimated that there were over a thousand blacks out of work in Cardiff, "and it has to be remembered to their credit that during the war they faced the perils of the submarine campaign with all the gallantry of the British seaman." But the only way the British showed their appreciation was to terrorize, murder, or hound black people out of Britain. Some blacks decided to return home. On 18 June 1919, the *Batanga*, an Elder Dempster ship, sailed for West Africa with 103 blacks from Cardiff and Liverpool. Several Africans who had planned to sail refused to go because, as they put it: "When we got on board [there was] nothing for sitting or sleeping for 250 for a 2–3 week voyage. ... [T]hat's how the Ministry of Shipping rewards the Negro who has risked his lives [sic] for them during the war."[62] Blacks were put in internment camps pending repatriation.[63] By 1921, 627 blacks had been sent out of Britain.[64] The war had been fought in the name of justice and humanity, yet the British saw nothing inhumane or unjust in their treatment of blacks. In the aftermath of that war, Britain—suffering from unemployment and irrational sexual jealousies—made black people scapegoats and brutalized and murdered them with impunity. More sympathy was shown by the courts to the criminals who had murdered or maimed than to their black victims.

The following passage, written in 1932, has well summed up British racism in the years between the wars:

> Today race prejudice has become so widespread in England, not only against the coloured workers—Negro, Arab and Indian seamen—but the chauvinist monster has directed its venom against coloured intellectuals and the petty bourgeoisie. We have heard of several cases where coloured middle-class people such as Roland Hayes, Paul Robeson and other professionals have been refused admittance into hotels and other public places. Even in academic circles race prejudice is making strong inroads. Coloured medical students are more and more experiencing the greatest difficulty in conducting their clinical studies. The excuse given is that white women object to coloured doctors attending to them. Everybody knows that this is just another lie. For there are many coloured physicians with long-established practices in white communities throughout the United Kingdom. The real truth of the matter is that the University authorities are the very ones who, in order to cater to the prejudices of the British capitalist class and get donations from them, clandestinely spread race hatred among the patients by making the vilest insinuations about the coloured students behind their backs.[65]

However, World War I marked the beginning of the end of British domination of blacks. That war exploded the myth of white supremacy, and in the 1920s and 1930s, black protest organizations were formed in Britain to plan the overthrow of British rule in Africa and the West Indies. Dr. Harold Moody led the League of Coloured Peoples (LCP), which in 1936 reported that the home life of the discarded blacks had been reduced to subsistence level.[66] The blacks became outcasts and were looked on by the white unions as being responsible for keeping white seamen out of work, and lowering their standard of living.

West African students formed the West African Students' Union (WASU), whose chief object was "to encourage sound and scientific study of African history, laws, customs and institutions with a view to preserving the African identity as well as to proving the Africans as a people evolving progressively to a higher order." As C. L. R. James put it, "From their own self-generated and independent being and motion ... Africa and Africans move towards an integrated humanity."[67]

Between 1912 and 1921, Duse Mohamed Ali, the remarkable Sudanese-Egyptian Africanist, crusading journalist, editor, political campaigner and organizer, and businessman, made 158 Fleet Street not only the place of the publication of *African Times and Orient Review* and *African Orient Review* but also the informal headquarters of the Pan-African movement. Duffield, who in his monumental study has rescued from historical oblivion the contribution of Duse Mohamed Ali to the rise of the Pan-African movement, has concluded that Duse Mohamed Ali, who died in Nigeria in 1945, was "an embodiment of some of the forces of change developing within human society in his era." M.I.5, Scotland Yard, and the Colonial Office constantly trailed "the well known agitator" who was concerned at the seat of British Imperial power with national independence and human dignity and rights for blacks. The *African Times and Orient Review* exposed scandals in colonial administration, including the Zaria whippings or Zaria incident, which occurred in northern Nigeria when third-class Resident Laing gave Africans severe thrashings with his walking stick because they failed to salute and prostrate themselves as he passed a field where they were playing football.[68]

Another paper that played the same role as the *African Times and Orient Review* was the *African Telegraph*, published in London by the wealthy Sierra Leonean businessman John Eldred Taylor, who maintained a "rather expensive suite of offices in the City." In 1918, the *African Telegraph* reported that a colonial officer, one Fitzpatrick, had been responsible for the public flogging of women in 1914 in northern Nigeria. In 1919, Fitzpatrick brought action for libel against Taylor. Though losing the case and ordered to pay crushing damages of £400 plus costs to Fitzpatrick, Taylor won the moral victory. For the trial made it clear that the flogging had taken place and gave a perfect platform from which to attack the entire Lugardian judicial system. The *African Telegraph* showed as much concern for the fate of the black man in Britain, subject to the vicious race riots of 1919, as for the fate of his brothers in Africa. The paper vigorously attacked these outrages, as it systematically exposed all instances of official brutality in British West Africa. In Pan-African circles in 1919, John Eldred Taylor was the man of the year.[69]

It was during the years between the world wars that black students first constituted a high proportion among the black community.[70] A black leadership emerged, brought up on works such as *Ethiopia Unbound* (1911) and *Philosophy and Opinions of Marcus Garvey or Africa for Africans* (1923). Eminent West Indians George Padmore and C. L. R. James collaborated with African students, including the greatest of them all, Kwame Nkrumah. The Rubicon was crossed at the 1945 Manchester

Pan-African congress. In the words of Aimé Césaire, "from the depths of slavery" black men "set themselves up as judges."[71] "Away with racism! Away with colonialism! Away with barbarism! The fruit of the poisonous tree of British racism. If not before, certainly now, British (as well as European) colonialism was already a dying colonialism." Listen to Césaire again: "The colonialists may kill ... torture in Madagascar, imprison in Black Africa, crack down in the West Indies. Henceforth the colonized know that they have an advantage over them. They know that their temporary 'masters' are lying. Therefore that their masters are weak."[72]

Post-1945

World War II again brought to Britain several thousand blacks who served in the armed forces and British war industries. But as soon as the war ended blacks again were most unwelcome. World War II had been fought in order to defeat Hitler's racism, but postwar Britain was barbarized by the naked and undisguised racism of the British government and people toward black people. In 1948, blacks were again terrorized in Liverpool. The following year, white mobs attacked blacks in Deptford, London. In 1954, it was the turn of Camden Town, again in London. Four years later, major race riots occurred in various parts of London, first in Nottingham and then in Notting Hill. But the rise of Nkrumah in what was then the Gold Coast after World War II, and the birth of a new country with the symbolic name of Ghana on 6 March 1957 was the dawn of a new age for black people all over the world. The blacks in Britain as well as those in America, the West Indies, and Africa were going to demand their rights. Blacks in Britain who fought, or whose parents had fought in two British wars to secure the world for freedom, democracy, and humanity, became militant. Unable to realize that they had created the black backlash, Britons started blaming the victims of their individual and institutional racism. Myths grew up like mushrooms. The blacks are lazy and indolent and live off the dole. They are immoral. They breed like rabbits. They are deviant. They are maladjusted. They are inferior. In short, everything black was hideous. Britons forgot the thousands of black men who perished in two world wars in the defense of their empire, and thousands more who as honest, hard-working laborers—sailors, clergymen, messengers, clerks, nurses, doctors, singers, actors, sportsmen—sustained and enriched British society. In a word, they forgot that blacks are people.

The first political demands for legislation to control black immigration came in 1954 from Cyril Osborne and Norman Pannell, both conservative members of Parliament.[73] Paul Foot and others have written ably on immigration and race in British politics. The first Commonwealth Immigrants Act was passed in 1962, another in 1968, and another in 1971. Each act further restricted the already difficult entry of blacks into Britain. On the other hand, the first Race Relations Act was passed in 1965, another in 1968, and another in 1976. Each half-heartedly and with severe limitations sought to give blacks the right to obtain legal redress when discriminated against. The race laws were initiated by a white executive, passed by a white legislature, and interpreted by a white judiciary. They were laws made by whites to protect themselves from their innate racism. The shame, folly, hypocrisy, and deception of this carrot-and-stick approach to British racism were exposed by Bernard Levin in his column in the *Times* of 10 April 1973:

> A wholly contradictory dual approach ... has bedevilled our race relations for more than a dozen years, and that consists of the pretence that it is possible to combine on the one hand increasing restrictions on the numbers of coloured immigrants allowed in, together with continuous talk of the "problems" and difficulties" that this "wave" (or even "invasion" or "assault") has caused, and on the other hand a call for fair and equal treatment of the coloured minority. This is not a plea for a return to the "open door" policy. But if you behave and talk as though a black man were some kind of virus that must be kept out of the body politic as far as possible, and discussed in terms of the ill effects it is having as it multiplies in the national blood stream, together with calls for the production and use of more powerful antibiotics to counter its dire effects, then it is the shabbiest hypocrisy to preach racial harmony at the same time, for the two themes are totally, and obviously, incompatible.
>
> This, if you like, is the real deception, the real concealment, the real cowardice, the real failure of successive governments. But there are no votes in saying so.

On 9 March 1970, the Registrar General produced for the first time quarterly birth-rate figures in England divided according to the origin of parents. All the news media concentrated on birth rates among "immigrants"—a euphemism for "blacks." The news coverage produced fantastic notions about "black hordes" that threaten to "swamp" the natives of Britain. The *Daily Express* had a page-one banner headline: "Immigrant Births Shock." The *Mirror*'s back page story was headlined, "Birth-rate for Immigrants is Higher." The *Evening Standard* front page headline read, "London Tops Immigrant Babies League." The *Times* headlined its front page, "One Child in Eight Born to Immigrants." The newspapers, the BBC, and of course the inevitable "experts" on race relations were talking of black babies as if they were things and not innocent children.

This reaction to the births of innocent babies is a true index of British racism, which regards black children as vermin to be destroyed. And a perfectly legal method has been devised for their mental and psychological destruction. Black children are being placed daily in the schools for the "educationally subnormal" (ESN), where "death at an early age" is the fate of each child. Once a child is classified as being educationally subnormal, he is removed from the ordinary school and placed in a "special" school where he is given a different type of education, with more emphasis on basic activities like reading and writing. But the schoolchild is left behind his old classmates in the important matters of a good general education. Black children are wrongly classified because their background and culture are different from those of the teachers and education authorities, or because they are thought to pose behavior problems, which are dealt with by simply removing the children from a normal school. But the child who has been wrongly classified loses formative educational years. His intellectual growth is stunted, and he will never realize his full potential. He has died at an early age.[74]

The race industry has been growing, as has the rank of race professionals since 1958, when the Institute of Race Relations was founded. In 1971, Gus John wrote:

> The race relations industry gets through thousands of pounds every year, the CRC alone manages to spend £400,000. Departments to *study the immigrants* spring up like mushrooms, financed by trusts and foundations. Yet the only relationship most of them have with black groups is that of visitors to a zoo. Their findings are never meant to enable the deprived to take action.... The hard fact is that despite the various departments of the race relations industry the black man continues to live daily with the knowledge that he is being confirmed more and more as a second-class citizen.[75]

White controlled and manned, the race relations industry is based on the assumption that whites know what is good for blacks, who cannot be trusted to run themselves. Two well-known examples are the collapse of Campaign Against Racial Discrimination (CARD), when blacks sought to control an organization meant to fight for their rights,[76] and the disappearance of foundation money from the Institute of Race Relations, when blacks insisted in 1972 that it should stop managing racism for the British establishment.[77] White *liberals* have always been prepared to tolerate black people as long as they can use them to publicize their own humanitarianism. When black people cease to be pliable and titillating and assert their rights as human beings, the change in relationship is always very perceptible—friends today, enemies tomorrow. Yet, most race "experts" are cynics and hypocrites without any good will toward black people. The legal adviser to the defunct Race Relations Board once felt sure that there would be more racial conflict in Britain—an attitude that was bound to bring a lot more business for his firm. Most white liberals today, like their eighteenth-century precursors, see in the misery, oppression, and repression of fellow human beings a way for their own advancements.

Conclusion

Blacks have been bought and brought, recruited, or invited to Britain. Yet, each successive generation suffered and suffers legal, economic, and social deprivation because of its blackness. When Britain needed blacks as chattels or as an index of rank, or to fight her wars or to power her industries, she never hesitated to import them. But as soon as blacks were no longer needed, Britain never scrupled to disown them. Blacks were expelled from Britain in 1596, 1601, 1787, and 1919. The size of the black population had nothing to do with this recurrent pattern of expulsion from Britain. The truth is that expulsion occurred whenever British capitalism no longer needed blacks. As Walvin put it: "When economic need demanded black labour, Britain was eager to house black workers; once the need had passed, Britain was unwilling to contemplate the full consequences of black settlement."[78] Gus John went to the heart of the matter when, also commenting on the post-World War II period, he wrote:

> Black people were recruited and came to Britain in the post-war years to staff the run-down and undermanned industries of this country. We came with false hopes and misguided notions nurtured for the most part by the Colonialists' teaching of the great land Britain was and its preparedness to extend its open arms to its needy and deserving subjects whose own lands it had systematically left underdeveloped.
> What we were not taught was that racism was endemic to British society and had been its greatest economic weapon for hundreds of years, and that Britain was no more ready to welcome Blacks with respect and human dignity than were Nazis the Jews.[79]

Black men marrying white women, and the supposed threat to white working people posed by black people, have been responsible for morbid racial prejudice against blacks. Social Darwinism, the empire, and colonialism have also nurtured and sustained British racism. If blacks are given equal job opportunities with whites, it is then not possible to maintain the inferiority and incapacity of blacks. If black men marry white women, it is no longer possible to maintain the

Englishman's racist civilization. "How then is it possible to maintain as the one stern creed in the policy of the Empire the eternal supremacy of the white over black?"[80] asked an English writer in 1917, who certainly was expressing the view of the average Englishman.

Racism has been the British way of life ever since the first blacks settled in Britain. Thus, in 1589, Hakluyt described as slaves, free black men brought by John Lok to Britain in 1555. The African from the outset was stigmatized as an inferior race fit only to be a slave. The black community of the eighteenth century successfully resisted British racism. They were successful because of their solidarity as black people and not as Africans, Afro-West Indians, or Afro-Americans. No matter where they had been born, they acted in concert as "sons of Africa," conscious of the common experience that their blackness had produced in their lives. Since the 1960s, blacks in Britain have rejected the British definitions of their past, present, and future. The fight to exorcise racism from their lives has begun in earnest.

Racism is not the only British way of life. First, the "noble savage" has, of course, always had a niche in British hearts. Elizabeth I, as we have seen, owned blacks. Doubtless she treated them well. But that did not stop her from ordering the expulsion of all black people in Britain in 1596 and 1601. This illustrates the proposition that whites may tolerate individual Africans, but they hate them as a race. The black ladies honored at the court of King James IV of Scotland must be viewed in this context. In modern parlance, they are tokens. Then, too, there have always been Britons who genuinely believed in the dignity and worth of the human person. Sons and daughters of Africa and lovers of humanity will always remember them with gratitude. But multiply the generous tradition a millionfold, and it still remains a drop in the ocean of inherent British racism that has always governed and regulated black existence in Britain. It should be clear by now that there is not, and never has been, a black problem in Britain, but a white problem. When whites, for example, object to blacks moving into a particular street or district, it is those whites who manifest such a poverty of respect for humanity who have a problem that cries aloud for solving. And to say otherwise is to blame the victim.

Listen to Aimé Césaire again: "A civilization that proves incapable of solving the problems it creates is a decadent civilization."[81]

NOTES

1. Reginald Coupland, *The British Anti-Slavery Movement* (London: Oxford, 1933), 55. Coupland devotes twenty-one pages to this chapter, headed "The Abolition of Slavery

in the British Isles," but treats the black community in Britain in less than half a page (p. 44).

2. Dorothy M. George, *London Life in the Eighteenth Century* (Harmondsworth: Penguin Books, 1966), 139–43.

3. Eric Williams, *Capitalism and Slavery*. (Chapel Hill: Russell Publishers, Inc. 1944; reprinted London: Oxford University Press, 1964), 44–45.

4. Kenneth Little, *Negroes in Britain: A Study of Racial Relations in English Society* (London: Oxford University Press, 1948). Other studies used included Eyo Bassey Ndem, "Negro Immigrants in Manchester," (M.A. thesis, University of Manchester, 1953); St. Clair Drake, "Value Systems, Social Structures and Race Relations in the British Isles," (Ph.D. diss. University of Chicago, 1954); Michael Banton, *The Coloured Quarter* (London: Oxford University Press, 1955); idem, *White and Coloured* (London: Oxford University Press, 1959); James Wickenden, *Colour Prejudice in Britain* (London: Oxford University Press for the Institute of Race Relations, 1958); Anthony Richmond, *Colour Prejudice in Britain: A Study of West Indian Workers in Liverpool, 1942–51* (London: Oxford University Press, 1954); A. Chater, *Race Relations in Britain* (London: Oxford University Press for the Institute of Race Relations, 1966); Sheila Patterson, *Dark Strangers* (London: Oxford University Press, 1963); idem, *Immigration and Race Relations in Britain 1960–1967* (London: Oxford University Press for the Institute of Race Relations, 1969); W. W. Daniel, *Racial Discrimination in England* (Harmondsworth: Penguin Books, 1968); Paul Foot, *Immigration and Race in British Politics* (Harmondsworth: Penguin Books, 1965); Bob Hepple, *Race, Jobs and the Law in Britain* (Harmondsworth: Penguin Books, 1968); Anthony Lester and Geoffrey Bindman, *Race and Law* (Harmondsworth: Penguin Books, 1972); Dilip Hiro, *Black British: White British* (London: Oxford University Press, 1971); Chris Mullard, *Black Britain* (London: Oxford University Press, 1973); Ann Dummett, *A Portrait of English Racism* (Harmondsworth: Penguin Books, 1973); Nicholas Deakin, *Colour, Citizenship and British Society* (London: Oxford University Press, 1970); E. J. B. Rose and Associates, *Colour and Citizenship* (London: Oxford University Press for the Institute of Race Relations, 1969); Political and Economic Planning, *Racial Discrimination in Britain* (London: Oxford University Press, 1967); John Rex and Robert Moore, *Race Community and Conflict: A Study of Sparkbrook* (London: Oxford University Press for the Institute of Race Relations, 1967); Daniel Lawrence, *Black Migrants, White Natives: A Study of Race Relations in Nottingham* (Cambridge: Harvard University Press, 1974); Michael J. Hill and Ruth M. Issachroff, *Community Action and Race Relations* (London: Oxford University Press for the Institute of Race Relations, 1971); Gus John and Derek Humphry, *Because They're Black* (Harmondsworth: Penguin Books, 1971); Derek Humphry and Gus John, *Police Power and Black People* (London: Oxford University Press, 1972); John Lambert, *Crime, Police and Race Relations: A Study in Birmingham* (London: Oxford University Press for the Institute of Race Relations, 1970); Paul Hartman and Charles Husband, *Racism and the Mass Media* (London: Davis-Poynter, 1974).

5. J. Jean Hecht, *Continental and Colonial Servants in Eighteenth Century England* (Northampton, Mass.: Yale Press, 1954).

6. Edward Scobie, *Black Britannia: A History of Blacks in Britain* (Chicago: Johnson Publishing Co., 1972).

7. James Walvin, *Black and White: The Negro and English Society, 1555–1945* (London 1973); idem, *The Black Presence: A Documentary History of the Negro in England, 1555–1860* (London: Oxford University Press, 1971).

8. The amount of space devoted to each period has been determined by the length of the period and material presently available.

9. Folarin Shyllon, *Black People in Britain, 1555-1833* (London: Oxford University Press for the Institute of Race Relations, 1977); idem, *Black Slaves in Britain* (London: Oxford University Press for the Institute of Race Relations, 1974).

10. Paul Edwards and James Walvin, "Africans in Britain, 1500-1800," in Martin L. Kilson and Robert I. Rotberg, *The African Diaspora: Interpretive Essays* (Cambridge, Mass.: Harvard University Press, 1976), 172-204.

11. John Roche Dasent, ed., *Acts of the Privy Council of England*, n. s. 11, 1547-50 (London: Oxford University Press, 1890), 183, 261, 275, 279, 419, 427-28.

12. Richard Hakluyt, *The Principal Navigations, Voyages, Traffiques and Discoveries of the English Nation*, 12 vols. (Glasgow: Glasgow University Press, 1903) 6: 176.

13. Ibid., 6: 217.

14. *Notes and Queries*, 3d ser. 11 (1 November 1862):345-46.

15. Walvin, *Black and White*, 7.

16. John Roche Dasent, ed., *Acts of the Privy Council of England*, n. s. 26, 1596-97 (London, 1902), 16-17.

17. Ibid., 20.

18. Walvin, *Black and White*, 8-9; Shyllon, *Black People in Britain*, 10-11.

19. For slave advertisements see Shyllon, *Black Slaves in Britain*, 5-11.

20. Others include Van Dyck's portrait of Henrietta of Lorraine, Mignard's Duchess of Portsmouth, and the collar-wearing slave of James Drummond, fifth Earl and second Tituler Duke of Perth.

21. Shyllon, *Black People in Britain*, 15-16, 38-65; Walvin, *Black and White*, 11, 38-43.

22. *London Chronicle* 16 (September 29-October 2, 1964):317; *London Chronicle* 17 (October 19-22, 1765):387; Edward Bollan, *Britannia Libera* (London, 1772), 47; Edward Long, *Candid Reflections upon the Judgement Lately Awarded by the Court of King's Bench* (London, 1772), 46, 48-9; James Tobin, *Cursory Remarks* (London, 1785), 118n.

23. David Brion Davis, *The Problem of Slavery in the Age of Revolution, 1770-1823* (Ithica: Cornell University Press, 1975), 471-501; Shyllon, *Black Slaves in Britain*, 24-47, 50-4, 82-124, 177-83; Walvin, *Black and White*, 105-33.

24. Hakluyt, *The Principal Navigations*, 6:167.

25. Shyllon, *Black People in Britain*, 18-20.

26. William Howitt, *Colonization and Christianity* (London, 1838), 503.

27. Ibid., 75, 81.

28. A. L. Reade, *Johnsonian Gleanings: The Life of Francis Barber* (London, 1912), 15.

29. Quoted in Cedric Dover, *Hell in the Sunshine* (London, 1943), 159.

30. Paul Edwards and James Walvin, "Africans in Britain, 1500-1800," 184-88.

31. Shyllon, *Black People in Britain*, 161-63.

32. Ibid., 84-85.

33. Ibid., 32-33, 160; Walvin, *Black and White*, 48, 202-3, 212.

34. Shyllon, *Black People in Britain*, 76, 159, 163.

35. Ibid., 78; Walvin, *Black and White*, 56.

36. Shyllon, *Black People in Britain*, 204-11.

37. Ibid.

38. Ibid., 169-71.

39. Ibid., 179-86.

40. Edwards and Walvin, "Africans in Britain, 1500-1800," 194; Walvin, *Black and White*, 72; Shyllon, *Black People in Britain*, 164n.

41. *London Chronicle* 16 (September 29-October 2, 1764):317; *London Chronicle* 18 (October 19-22, 1765):387.

42. *London Chronicle* 33 (March 13-16, 1773):250.

43. Shyllon, *Black People in Britain*, 117–58; Walvin, *Black and White*, 145–52.

44. Henry Mayhew, *London Labour and the London Poor*, 4 vols. (London, 1861–62) 4:425.

45. Ibid., 4:425–26.

46. *The Interesting Narrative of the Life of Olaudah Equiano, or Gustavus Vassa, the African*, 2 vols. (London, 1789).

47. Benjamin Quarles, *Black Abolitionists* (New York: Oxford University Press, 1969), 129.

48. Ibid., 130.

49. Ibid., 132.

50. Ibid., 133–41.

51. Ibid., 136.

52. Both Little and Walvin omit them.

53. Walvin, *Black and White*, 189–99. Passages in chapter 12, "Disintegration: Black Society in the Nineteenth Century," disprove his disintegration claim.

54. Quoted from *Musical Times*, October 1912 in *Dictionary of National Biography s.v.* Samuel Coleridge-Taylor; W. C. Berwick Sayers, *Samuel Coleridge-Taylor, Musician: His Life and Letters* (London: Oxford, 1915).

55. Christopher Fyfe, *Africanus Horton, 1835–1883: West African Scientist and Patriot* (New York: Oxford University Press, 1972), 80–86.

56. J. Ayodele Langley, *Pan-Africanism and Nationalism in West Africa: 1900–1945: A Study in Ideology and Social Classes* (Oxford: Clarendon Press, 1973), 189–90.

57. Ibid., 31.

58. Ian Duffield, "Duse Mohamed Ali and the Development of Pan Africanism, 1866–1945" (Ph.D., diss., Edinburgh University, 1971), 535; J. R. Archer, *Crisis* (January 1914):120.

59. Langley, *Pan-Africanism and Nationalism in West Africa*, 27.

60. Little, *Negroes in Britain*, 172.

61. "The ending of the war meant demobilization of large numbers of white seamen who had been serving in the Navy as minesweepers. With their return to the trade ... the shipowners and shipmasters took the line 'our own people first,' with the result that quite soon there were about 1200 coloured men out of work in the port." Little, *Negroes in Britain*, 57, 62–3.

62. Roy May and Robin Cohen, "Interaction between Race and Colonialism: A Case Study of the Liverpool Race Riots of 1919," *Race and Class* 16 (1974):111–26.

63. *Times* (London), 13 June 1919.

64. Walvin, *Black and White*, 208.

65. Nancy Cunard, ed., *Negro: Anthology Made by M. Cunard* (London, 1934), 555. Quoted from *The Negro Worker*, March 1932.

66. Little, *Negroes in Britain*, 78.

67. C. L. R. James, *The Black Jacobins: Toussaint L'Ouverture and the San Domingo Revolution*, 2d ed. (New York: Vintage Books, 1963), 402.

68. Duffield, "Duse Mohamed Ali and the Development of Pan-Africanism," 5:182–185, 269, 321–34, 379–85, 554, 784–87.

69. Ibid., 175–76, 189, 544–46.

70. The students included J. B. Danquah, Jomo Kenyatta, Louis Mbanefo, Pela Sowande, Adetokunbo Ademola, Obafemi Awolowo, Julius Ojo Cole, Oluwole Alakija, E. O. Assafu-Ajaye, Ansa Koi, J. W. de Graft Johnson, Ladipo Solanke, Kofo Moore, and Kobina Sokyi.

71. Aimé Césaire, *Discourse on Colonialism*, trans. John Pinkham (New York: Monthly Review Press, 1972), 10.

72. Ibid., 10, 40.

73. Paul Foot, *The Rise of Enoch Powell: An Examination of Enoch Powell's Attitude to Immigration and Race* (Harmondsworth, Penguin Books, 1969), 31.

74. "Our ESN Children," *Race Today* 5, 4:109–14; Bernard Coard, *How the West Indian Child Is Made Educationally Subnormal in the British School System* (London: New Beacon, 1971).
75. Humphry and John, *Because They Are Black*, 176.
76. Benjamin W. Heinemann, Jr., *The Politics of the Powerless: A Study of the Campaign against Racial Discrimination* (London: Oxford University Press for the Institute of Race Relations, 1972). This is a white man's view and should be read between the lines. On this, see Marion Glean's review of the book, "Whatever Happened to CARD?" *Race Today* 5, 1 (January 1975):13–15.
77. A. Sivananda, *Race and Resistance: The IRR Story* (London, 1974).
78. Walvin, *Black and White*, 212.
79. Humphry and John, *Police Power and Black People*, 209.
80. Quoted in J. A. Rogers, *Sex and Race*, 2 vols. (New York: H. M. Rogers, 1940) 1:207.
81. Césaire, *Discourse on Colonialism*, 9.

15

The Impact of Afro-Americans on French-Speaking Black Africans, 1919–45

Ibrahima B. Kaké

B ETWEEN the years 1919 and 1945, the world underwent significant changes at both political and social levels. The masses and the elite[1] of black peoples in Africa and the diaspora became more aware of their exploitation. Black Africans and Afro-Americans met, after more than three centuries of separation, when the United States intervened in World War I and black American soldiers mixed with the colonial troops (1917–19). United States intervention in World War II further consolidated this contact. On the other hand, the period from 1919 to 1945 coincided with the colonial buildup and the rise of emancipation movements. Afro-Americans and black Africans became conscious of their common destiny having its roots in a multifaceted oppression.

This essay examines the role of the pioneers of the emancipation movement of black Americans and highlights their impact on the French-speaking black Africans living in Paris.

A Common Destiny

Despite their long years of separation, both black Americans and Africans share a common destiny. Both were victims of ruthless exploitation and oppression, and remain in the vanguard of the struggle for freedom. The African slaves were violently uprooted from their native lands and were excluded on their arrival in America from white society on account of their servitude and their color. And yet to survive and continue in this new land, they had to adjust to Western civilization —the language, habits, techniques, and beliefs of their masters. However, they did not abandon their ways of thinking and reacting as Africans. They maintained certain religious and magical practices that captivated the imagination of many observers in the New World. In their new form of speech, they kept linguistic expressions and intonations that were African, thereby giving their culture a special flavor.

Segregated life for blacks in the United States is well known. It should be emphasized, however, that blacks developed and maintained their own associations for social and cultural survival—the churches, lodges, schools, and so on. Thus, although they were segregated from the wider society and limited in their ability to achieve full citizenship, they socialized their communities for the long struggle that unfolded.

The plight of French-speaking Africans is much less well known. By 1919, for example, the political conquest of black Africa was virtually a *fait accompli*. El Haj Omar, the leader of resistance on the Senegal River since 1864, had been defeated; in 1898 Almamy Samori in the western Sudan was captured and sent into exile to the Gabonese island of Ogooe; in 1900 Rabah, the Sudanese Jugurtha in the Lake Chad region, was killed at Kousseri in northern Cameroon. While some resistance continued throughout the colonial period, none was successful in preventing the establishment of European control.

At the politico-administrative level, all power in the colonies belonged to the French government and its representatives: governors-general, governors, administrators, and so on. Africans did not have a right to vote, nor did they have freedom to live where they chose or to manage their own affairs. French civil servants were entrusted with extensive means to enforce their will: prisons, fines, and summary corporal punishment. The Africans were required to pay head and hut taxes. In addition, they were subjected to forced labor—in effect, slave labor.[2]

At the cultural level, colonizers zealously imposed their values on the African. They established a few schools to train badly needed subservient cadres (trading post or administrative clerks). The young Africans enrolled in these schools were given a rudimentary education, designed to inculcate contempt for their culture and peoples, along with admiration for and submission to the white man. In the Belgian Congo, education was left almost entirely to the missionaries. In Cameroon and in French Equatorial Africa, the secular French Republic, until World War II, entrusted the missionaries with the essential duties of education and rewarded them with subsidies.

In the French colonies, the authorities, in keeping with their avowed hostility toward any element of the African culture, formally prohibited the use of African languages in school. African youngsters had to learn to read and write French. Under these circumstances, education during the colonial period was not effective.

Both the white and black communities coexisted in the towns, which was the major means of contact. And yet, the structure of these colonial towns, such as Medina in Dakar, Treichville in Abidjan, and Potopoto in Brazzaville, symbolized segregation, leading geographers to speak of them as "double-faceted." In his excellent work, *Sociologie des brazza-villes noires*,[3] George Balandier emphasized that Brazzavilles Noires (black Brazzavilles) occupied a dejected position in comparison with the white township. Between them there was a no man's land hardly touched by the recent expansions of the capital.

French citizenship was required for any African to live in the white township. And French citizenship was obtainable only in certain circumstances well defined by the law. For instance, an 1872 decree stated that Africans could enjoy full citizenship rights if they were born in one of the four communes of Senegal: Dakar, Saint Louis, Rufisque, or Gorée. This privilege was also extended to all those who were holders of the two parts of the baccalaureate.[4] This latter requirement was difficult to fulfill at a time when only a few privileged persons could go to France and complete the rudimentary type of education they received in the secondary institutions in Africa. The third category of Africans who could become French citizens were those who married French women. They were indeed rare because black men had serious misgivings about white women, and white women despised black men. Assimilation hardly touched the mass of black Africans.

In Guinea, Africans who were touched by Western culture can be divided into four major categories according to the distinctions made by the Malinke of my country:

1. The Toubaboulamo. *Toubab* means the white man, in this case the Frenchman, and the suffix *lamo* means to be educated. The Toubaboulamo are therefore all those who are educated like the whites. Included in this category are the junior "native" civil servants within the colonial administration.
2. The Toubaboudim. This refers etymologically to the sons of the Toubaboulamo. It includes not only the sons of civil servants but also the mulattoes.
3. The Toubaboufelamo. This term refers to those who keep close to the white man but who had no formal education, including the domestics, or "boys" as they were commonly referred to in Africa, and the war veterans who bivouacked in Africa during the two world wars.

4. The Toubabounim. This pejorative term refers to the townspeople with small means who clumsily imitated the white man.

In French-speaking Africa, the Toubaboulamo, the only ones with some rudiments of formal education, were commonly referred to as *evolués*. They made up the first cohort of African nationalists.

Following World War I, these evolués increased their resistance to the colonial establishment. As early as 1917, George Hardy, inspector general of education in French colonial Africa, underscored the fact that many metropolitans were convinced that formal education in Africa was creating social misfits. Formal education, Hardy said, further encouraged black African pretensions, which were already exaggerated and rebellious. In fact, the evolués had contempt for ancestral traditions. Their only goal was to become closer to the white man, whose culture they had assimilated. The white man, however, kept them at a distance. As a result, they were torn between the Western and African cultures and became strangers in their own countries.

In French-speaking Africa, literary works began to promote the return of African values. The leader of this literary trend was a West Indian, René Maran, whose work, *Batouala*, was awarded the Goncourt Academy Prize in 1921.

This, indeed, marked the beginnings of a literature of protest that culminated in the Negritude movement, with Léopold Sédar Senghor, Jean Price-Mars, Aimé Césaire, and Léon Gontran Damas as its spokespersons. Negritude, in its beginnings, however, was simply an extension of the Harlem Renaissance in the United States and the Haitian literary movement of the 1920s. Between the American "trunk" and the Parisian "shoot," there was, naturally, the mediation of the Haitian Renaissance.

In the United States, Afro-Americans were not satisfied with fighting only for their own political liberation. Through the efforts of their leaders, such as W. E. B. Du Bois and Marcus Garvey, and also during the Pan-African congresses organized during this period, they revindicated the same rights for their brothers in Africa and elsewhere.

Du Bois's and Garvey's Action Programs

In 1916, the Jamaican Marcus Garvey capitalized on black bitterness and founded the Universal Negro Improvement Association (UNIA) in New York. Basically, in addition to promoting black pride and advocating economic development, it supported a return-to-Africa movement on the grounds that blacks could never expect to gain their rights from white Americans. This new organization created enormous enthusiasm, which was, unfortunately, dampened by World War I. In 1920, the organization reasserted itself, adding to its ranks numerous war veterans who were disgruntled by the treatment they received during the hostilities. This, along with the fact that in France they were accorded more respect than in the United States, accounted for the new wave of discontent.[5]

Garvey took advantage of this situation. In his journal, the *Negro World*, he exposed the underlying reasons for this discontent. His propaganda schemes bore fruit as masses of new partisans joined his movement. Garvey dreamed of extending UNIA's influence to Africa. In fact, he sought to transplant its headquarters to Liberia. However, the United States, with Western European support, aborted this effort. Garvey's "Declaration of Black Peoples' Rights in the World," which contained twelve commandments, fifty-four articles, and a hymn in honor of Ethiopia, was cautiously but widely circulated among the blacks who were under Belgian, French, and British domination.[6] In Europe some looked on it as a magnificent protest against colonialism. However, French-speaking black intellectuals such as Blaise Diagne, the *deputé*[7] from Senegal and the only African parliamentarian, denounced Garveyism. He reaffirmed his attachment to France and declared his resolute support for a policy of association.

Garvey's movement left few traces among the blacks of the continent after it had aroused some support in South Africa, in some towns in the Belgian Congo, and in numerous centers on the west coast of Africa. Its failure stood as a clear indication of the gap created by education and adoption of Western culture among people of the same race subjected to different influences by destiny.

Garveyism was not understood by illiterate African farmers. Even in America, Garvey's ideas were rejected by the black clergy from all denominations. Indeed, the members of the black clergy refuted the idea of war against the "religion of the white man," as preached by Garvey. According to Garvey, this religion would be impracticable for blacks, forced as they were "to believe in a white God, a white Christ, and even white Angels." What he wanted instead was a purely black religion with a God made in its own image.

The black clergy was not the only group to oppose Garvey's doctrine: Du Bois and Robert Moton, leaders of the two most important contemporary black movements, endorsed politico-philosophical ideas antithetical to Garvey's. Moton was the successor of the work of Booker T. Washington, whose major action program was the gradual emancipation of blacks through work, vocational training, and patient adaptation to the modalities of white civilization. Du Bois, who was more radical in his views, opposed vehemently the ideas of gradual evolution and adaptation advocated by Moton. To him, the salvation of the black race meant complete emancipation and full political and economic equality with whites. Both men, however, were opposed to Garveyism, which preached black pride and complete economic independence along with social and political equality.

Following World War I, the black race could hardly stand aloof from the great world issues then being debated daily at the Paris Peace Conference. Of all the nations and races waiting for decisions greatly affecting the future of the world, the most anxious were those nations that until then had been kept on the periphery of world affairs and those races that had been the victims of racial prejudice. No one was surprised that the black societies capitalized on these circumstances by establishing a common program for their revindication and by informing the world and the organizers of the League of Nations about their interests.

This was the message conveyed at the Pan-African congress convened on 21 February 1919 by W. E. B. Du Bois, Blaise Diagne, and Gratien Candace from Martinique. The participants, belonging to different nationalities yet sharing the same ethnic background, were demanding on their own behalf and on behalf of their brothers and sisters —not the right to form a nation—but assurances of justice within their respective nations.

By using *Pan-African*, the organizers of the congress sought to indicate that all blacks scattered around the world came not only from the same ethnic background but also from the same geographical background. By *Pan-African*, they encompassed those who claimed kinship with Africa by virtue of their ancestral origins, no matter where they now lived, what their nationalities were, or what quantity of African blood they had in their veins. The congress, in deliberating on the names of its members and all the groups of the African race, could rightfully bestow on itself the title of Pan-African congress.

The organizing committee was made up of three members who were citizens of states that, either in their colonies or on their own soil, ruled the greatest number of people of the African race: France, Great Britain, and the United States. Blaise Diagne, the deputy from Senegal, represented French Africans; M. E. F. Fredericks, an attorney from Sierra Leone, represented British Africans; Dr. W. E. B. Du Bois represented the Africans of the United States.

The congress itself assembled twenty delegates, Africans or of African descent, representing the major groupings of blacks scattered on the surface of the earth. These delegates were important personalities who engaged in interesting debates deserving some attention. For instance, in the closing session, a vote was taken on a motion with the following preamble:

> The Congress expresses the wish that the allied and associated governments establish an international code of laws for the protection of the natives and that a secretariat be attached to the League of Nations to see to it that these laws are applied.[8]

The blacks of the world were demanding that from that point on, Africans and peoples of African descent be governed according to certain principles of equality and justice.

In contrast to the Paris Pan-African congress, the congress held in London in the same year had a purely political bent. The major issue there was the demand that Wilson's principle of self-determination be applied to black Africans as well as to the rest of the world.

In the following year, on 20 August 1920, Garvey organized a Pan-African congress in New York. Almost three thousand elected delegates attended from all parts of the globe. On the opening day, fifty thousand blacks paraded in New York City streets, wearing the black, red, and green badge. (Black represented their skin, red their blood, and green their hopes.) Flags floating on the wind displayed their hopes: "One God, One Aim, One Destiny;" "Africa Must Be Free;" "Africa a Nation, One and Indivisible." Several speeches were made, but Garvey's was the most resounding. "The time has come when the entire African continent will be claimed as the motherland of black peoples," he declared.

From the most moderate to the most radical, Afro-Americans shared in this will to liberate Africa. On 10 November 1917, the newspaper *Survey* carried the following lines by Dr. Du Bois:

> The modern world can hardly dream of keeping 200 million people in bondage, even if they are Blacks. If it were to try it, it would pay dearly for it. We must begin to liberate Africa through this war, if we are to avoid this experience. Africa is under the hands of black troops trained by white officers. These troops saved France. They conquered German Africa. Along with Black Americans, they were helpful in saving Belgium. The least Europe could do, by way of making up for this terrible page of history written between the years 1441 and 1861, would be to see to it that a great free Central African state, consisting of German East Africa and the Belgian Congo, be set up.

The Pan-African congresses were held successively in 1921 in London, Brussels, and Paris; in 1923 in London and Lisbon; and in 1927 in New York. A fifth congress was held in Tunis. Each developed the same theme of equality and justice.

To what extent did the ideas discussed in these various congresses infiltrate the European colonies in black Africa, and the French colonies in particular? It is at this point that we must examine the impact of Afro-Americans on African nationalists who, for the most part, were Paris residents at that time.

African Nationalists and the Afro-American School

Many students of the Pan-African movement continue to hold the view that it was only after World War II that the Pan-African ideology, born within the ranks of the African members of the diaspora, managed to reach French-speaking Africans. Nothing could be further from the truth. French-speaking Africans had established contacts with Afro-American nationalists in the days following the outbreak of World War I. Although such contacts were few, their impact, nevertheless, commands our attention today.

As early as 1906, a Senegalese named Moussa Mangoumbe, with the blessing of Booker T. Washington, already sought to promote understanding among blacks of the diaspora. And after World War I, relations between Afro-Americans and French-speaking Africans entered their most fecund period. Although the affected French-speaking Africans lived mostly in Paris, they maintained contacts on the African soil. Three persons are particularly good examples: Kodjo Touvalou-Houénou, a Dahomean (Benin); Lamine Senghor, a Senegalese; and Tiémoho Garan Kouyaté, a Sudanese (Malian).

Kodjo Touvalou-Houénou was the son of a rich merchant of Cotonou (Benin). He was awarded the medal of honor during World War I, and after the war, he was admitted to the bar in Paris. He had established close contact with both the International Communist Movement and Marcus Garvey.

One evening, however, he was expelled from a Montmartre night club in Paris by merrymaking white Americans. Infuriated by this odious insult, he became rebellious and later created the Ligue Universelle pour la Defense de la Race Noire (Universal League for the Defense of the Black Race). He paid a long visit to Harlem, where he intermingled with blacks whose racial consciousness was strong, and he established contact with Garvey. On 19 August 1924, at the Congress of the Universal Association for the Advancement of the Black Race in New York, he delivered a moving speech in which he said:

> When a while ago you were up and vibrant, acclaiming me with a great ovation, you were not addressing this homage to me. You were paying homage to the queen of martyrs, ... the suffering, the soreful, but always

the radiant and prestigious Africa. She is raising her head again after centuries of subjugation to a shameless plundering and after disastrous wars instigated by European bandits whose only goal was getting slaves. All these were indelible crimes committed under the false pretense of [a] civilizing mission and of the stupid dogma of the supremacy of the white race. Conscious of her genius and destiny, Africa wants now to rejuvenate herself.... .

The American society with its democratic pretensions but whose imperialism is being asserted from day to day has scoffed at you, persecuted and secluded you like plague-stricken people. Every day, it disgraces and humiliates you.... .

Your association, Mr. President [Marcus Garvey], is the Zionism of the Black Race. In being radical, it has the advantage of stating in precise and definite terms the problem, to trace the broad and luminous road which must lead us to salvation. ...

The black race presents significant groupings in the entire world; these groupings must be allowed to contribute to the work of redemption according to their methods, disciplines, resources and activities. In keeping with this goal of diversity in action, we have created in Paris the *Ligue Universelle pour la Defense de la Race Noire*.... .

It is the Capital of France. France shares with Britain almost all the population of Africa. Paris is six hours from London and Brussels. It is closer to New York than any other European capital; it is the artistic and intellectual center of the world; it is also the diplomatic capital and the capital of the great innovating ideas.[9]

Touvalou-Houénou ended his speech with these words: "Long live all the Blacks and Africa."

His visit with Garvey was a greater determining factor in his commitment to the struggle for the liberation of Africa. He returned to Paris with the idea of liberating Dahomey. At this time strikes began in French West Africa, and Touvalou-Houénou was accused of being the instigator. The Parisian newspapers launched virulent attacks against his private life. Attempts were made to discredit him for daring to speak in Parisian circles of freedom for colonial blacks. Returning to Africa, he continued the struggle against the French presence. He was arrested on a warrant issued by the court of Cotonou and died a few years later, in 1936, in Dakar. His memory will live for a long time in the minds of second-generation Dahomean nationalists.

The second important African nationalist was Lamine Senghor, who was born in Keolack (Senegal) in 1889 to Serer parents. At the beginning of World War I, he was recruited as a rifleman and did his military service in France (1915–19). His superior officers reported that he had distinguished himself as courageous and loyal. For refusing to take part in the mutiny by Senegalese riflemen in Frejus, he was awarded the

French military decoration. In 1919, he was demobilized and returned to Senegal. In 1922, he returned to Paris and took courses at the Sorbonne. He also began to develop an interest in politics and became a member of the emerging French Communist Party. At the same time, he became a member of the league.

Along with Kouyaté and a certain Dr. Sejous, Lamine Senghor vehemently criticized Blaise Diagne's assimilationist policies. In the aftermath of Touvalou-Houénou's arrest, he assumed leadership of the league. The league's newspaper, *La Race Nègre*, was the main voice of all the black Parisian political groups. It published supportive articles on Afro-American organizations, including the NAACP, the League for Equal Rights (Boston), the Association of John Brown (Philadelphia), and especially Garvey's movement. It also reproduced Garvey's poem, "Africa for the African." *La Race Nègre* condemned colonialism and stressed racial equality, while all of Garvey's activities were reported with the greatest degree of support.

Afro-Americans, on their end, expressed support for Lamine Senghor's movement. In 1927, an Afro-American newspaper noted the interest of the French-speaking black intellectuals in American affairs in these terms:

> Just like the most enlightened Africans, the members of this group [of the League] were being inspired by American Blacks. It is encouraging to learn that an intellectual ferment exists among the French blacks and that revolt is roaring in the colonies. Discontent has already reached the half-way mark. The Africans who are conscious must liberate Africa themselves. Yet we can encourage them reaching this goal, by overcoming all the obstacles surrounding us.[10]

Lamine Senghor stood out from the members of this group on account of the virulence of his writings against colonialism.

In March 1927, Senghor was arrested in Cannes and sent to jail in Draguignan. Protests poured in from everywhere, even from some French members of Parliament, increasing concomitantly his stature and influence as a staunch supporter of the Pan-African movement. From then on, his activities were strictly monitored by the police until his death in that same year.

Following Senghor's death, a more militant team took over, with the Sudanese Tiémoko Garan Kouyaté as leader. Kouyaté was born in Segou (Mali) on 27 April 1902. He attended the famous Ecole Normale William Ponty[11] (Gorée-Senegal) and served two years as headmaster in the Ivory Coast before he won a scholarship for further training at the Teachers's College of Aix-en-Province. Later, he joined both the Committee for the Defense of the Black Race created in Paris by Lamine Senghor and, like Lamine Senghor, the French Communist Party, which drew him to Moscow in 1929. While he was there, the Soviets promised him financial aid, but on his return to Paris, Kouyaté came into conflict with Communist leaders whose orders he refused to follow. As a result, all financial help from the party was suspended. Kouyaté collaborated with George Padmore (the Trinidadian Pan-Africanist) on the editorial board of the *Black Worker*, published first in Hamburg, then in Copenhagen. He sought the assistance of American black organizations and sent a letter to Du Bois, which was intercepted by the French police. The letter, according to Langley, contradicts the myth of nonparticipation of French-speaking blacks in Pan-African movements:

> The League has as its major goal the political, economic, moral and intellectual emancipation of the entire black race. At issue here are two major objectives: (1) to use all possible honorable means to achieve independence in the French and British colonial territories and (2) to establish a Great Black State in Black Africa.[12]

For two years beginning in 1930, the impact of the Afro-American Pan-Africanists was evident in the pages of *La Race Nègre*, which featured news from Haiti and North and South America as showpieces of the world struggle by peoples of color. In 1930, following an internal crisis, the Ligue de la Defense de la Race Noire split into two factions, and Emile Faure, a Senegalese engineer and a descendant of Samori Touré, became its president. Forced into a minority position, Kouyaté decided to create his own newspaper, *Le Cri des Negres* (the *Black Cry*), in May 1931, and succeeded in clandestinely smuggling it into the colonies. It was at this time, in fact, that Kouyaté managed, under Padmore's influence, to get the African students in Paris interested in both Afro-American and Pan-African affairs. Padmore wrote to Du Bois in 1934 that the black question had been debated during a Paris conference organized by Kouyaté:

> This was the most serious political debate I have ever witnessed in an exclusively black setting. The participants in the Conference decided to convene a Congress to deal with the issue of world unity of black peoples. Their major goal was to formulate a program of action which would allow for the realization of Black Unity. I also took this opportunity to inform these young Blacks about your work with the NAACP and your working ties with the Pan-African movement.[13]

This was certainly the decisive turning point in the history of the Ligue de la Defense de la Race Noire, which after 1934 distanced itself from the Communists.

Italian aggression against Ethiopia and the rise of fascism in Europe served as catalysts to blacks to strip themselves of whatever illusions they had about European civilization. The league preached the return to Africanity and, in a long editorial, condemned European education and the sterile intellectualism of European civilization it regarded as the black man's enemy. It looked on the Italian aggression against Ethiopia as a conflict between whites and blacks.

At the time of the Front Populaire in 1936–37, nationalists' hopes for a liberalization of colonial policy were quickly shattered. In spite of laws voted at the time concerning trade unions and political parties, the administration, in fact, was determined not to tolerate any form of nationalism or any liberation movements inside France or in the colonies. In 1937, the league was suspended and its president, Emile Faure, was sent into exile in the Sahara until the end of the war. Kouyaté chose to collaborate for a while with the Front Populaire government but was finally executed by the Germans during the occupation, under circumstances not yet clearly defined. Kouyaté was among the last African nationalists of the interwar period.

To the triumvirate just discussed could be added the name of the nationalist Louis Hunkarin, a Dahomean. Along with Blaise Diagne and W. E. B. Du Bois, Hunkarin participated in the second Pan-African congress, which was held in London, Brussels, and Paris in August and September 1921. This former headmaster came to France on the coattails of Blaise Diagne. While there, he severed his ties with the Senegalese deputy and began agitating for African independence under the probable influence of Afro-Americans. He was sent to jail and into exile until the end of World War II.

Conclusion

French-speaking African nationalists and Afro-Americans, separated for centuries, were bred in different sociopolitical contexts. However, they were finally brought together by their shared experience of suffering and exploitation. Their serious relations, which started during World War I, increased during the interwar period, despite numerous obstacles: administrative, political, and, in particular, cultural. Very few French-speaking Africans understood English and, with the exception of French-speaking Antilleans, most Afro-Americans did not speak French.

Nationalist and Pan-African ideas were first launched in America at the end of the nineteenth century, being assimilated very quickly, nevertheless, by a small circle of African intellectuals who were Paris residents whose influence would be almost insignificant in Africa. The effective dissemination of nationalist and Pan-African ideas among French-speaking intellectuals did not occur until the end of World War II, although the earlier period did prepare the way for the later era.

In 1947, under the direction of Alioune Diop, the journal *Presence Africaine* was founded within the context of the great awakening of (political) consciousness for liberation. This journal, which was read by almost all the French-speaking intellectual elite, contributed significantly to the understanding by the African public of the work and activities of American blacks and West Indians. From then on, the bridge between the scattered sons of Ham would never be cut.

NOTES

1. Those who had the most assimilated Western culture but who did not necessarily constitute the true elite.
2. Ibrahima B. Kaké, "La Francisation de l'afrique noire, 1914–1945: Ses Limites," *L'Information Historique* 4 (September–October 1966):145.
3. George Balandier, *Sociologie des brazzavilles noire* (Paris: A. Colin, 1955), 275.
4. The baccalaureat is the competitive examination closing the secondary school years.
5. The French always had better regard for American blacks than for the black Africans.
6. Henri Labouret, "Le Mouvement," 319.
7. A representative to the French National Assembly.
8. Maurice Delafosse, "Le Congres Pan-Africain," *Renseignements Coloniaux* (1919) provides a detailed account of the meeting.
9. Prince Kodjo Touvalou-Houénou, "Coeur de la race noire," *Les Continents* (October 1, 1924).
10. Cited by J. Ayodele Langley, *Pan-Africanism and Nationalism in West Africa, 1900–1945* (Oxford, 1973), 307.
11. A teachers' college of high repute in colonial French-speaking Africa.
12. Langley, *Pan-Africanism,* 312.
13. Letter from Padmore to Du Bois, cited by Robert Hooker in *Black Revolutionary: George Padmore's Path from Communism to Pan-Africanism* (New York: Praeger, 1967), 34–40.

16

The 1921 Pan-African Congress at Brussels: A Background to Belgian Pressures

M. W. Kodi

THE Brussels session of the 1921 Pan-African Congress took place under the long and threatening shadow of Marcus Garvey and the overbearing pressures of the Belgian Ministry of the Colonies, business concerns, and newspapers.[1] The vicious campaign launched by the Belgian press against the congress made Garvey the main issue of the session and allowed his specter to haunt the participants. Belgian pressures were so strong and their exploitation of the differences among the participants so astute that they not only virtually dictated the resolutions of the session but also dampened the radical trend adopted by the congress in London. As J. Ayodele Langley argues, W. E. B. Du Bois's Pan-African crusade "never recovered its *élan* after Brussels."[2] This is what turned the Brussels session into an interesting and important episode in the history of Pan-Africanism and makes it imperative that we investigate the factors that exacerbated Belgian xenophobic fears at this juncture and contributed to the misapprehension of the aims and political connections of the Pan-African Congress.

Most writers have rightly attributed Belgian suspicion of the motives of the congress and its links with Garvey's Universal Negro Improvement Association (UNIA) to Belgian fears of disruption in the Congo and to generally hostile Belgian attitudes toward foreigners, especially the Americans and the British. My argument in this essay is that the seemingly paranoid reaction of the Belgian colonial authorities and business circles to Marcus Garvey and to the Pan-African Congress was a culmination of a number of events that occurred in the Belgian colony during the ten months that preceded the Brussels session. In fact,

Garveyites had been discovered not only in Kinshasa but also as far inland as Coquilhatville; Simon Kimbangu's movement was thought to be inspired by Garveyites in collusion with American and British Protestant missionaries in the Lower Congo; and an outspoken Congolese intellectual, Paul Panda Farnana, had been identified by influential Belgian newspapers as a Garveyist agitator and as the possible mastermind of Kimbangu's movement. Panda helped organize the congress and introduced W. E. B. Du Bois to the colonial authorities in Brussels. So, by the time the congress was convened in September 1921, the colonial authorities in Brussels and Boma (then capital of the Congo) had gathered a great deal of information from the United States, Great Britain, and France that convinced them that African Americans, led by Marcus Garvey, were bent on overthrowing European rule in Africa, and especially in the Belgian Congo. Furthermore, Panda's collaboration with Du Bois in the organization of the congress was, in Belgian eyes, the confirmation of the Garveyist and, therefore, disruptive nature of the congress.

The period of Panda's most intensive political activism was the early 1920s, which coincided with, and was linked by the Belgian colonial administration to, the spread of Garvey's ideas into Central Africa and the birth of Kimbanguism. An outline of Panda's life before 1920 will shed some light on his later activities and conflicts with the Belgian colonial establishment.

Paul Panda Farnana, 1888–1920[3]

"Mfumu" (chief) Panda was born in the Congo, in Nzemba (near Banana) around 1888.[4] According to Du Bois, a Belgian colonial official took Panda to Belgium when he was five years old and gave him to his maiden sister, who brought him up as her own child, sent him to school, and "defended against the criticism of her friends his right to university training. She was his mother, his friend."[5] After graduating from secondary school in Brussels, he studied agronomy and received an engineering degree from l'Ecole d'Horticulture d'Etat at Vilvorde. He then took special courses in "colonial agriculture" and was awarded a "praiseful" certificate by the same institution of higher learning. After he attended a commercial and consular school in the Belgian town of Mons, Panda continued his training in agriculture at the Ecole Supérieure d'Agriculture Coloniale at Nogent-sur-Marne and was awarded a certificate.[6]

After completing his rather impressive studies, Panda decided to return to his native Congo, and he worked at the Eala botanic garden near the present town of Mbandaka in the Equateur Province for two years. Before leaving the Congo on 22 January 1914 for another leave in Belgium, he was appointed and served for three weeks as a colonial administrator (*chef territorial*) in the Lower Congo.[7]

His leave of absence from the colonial service was supposed to last six months but was extended because of poor health. Meanwhile, World War I broke out and Belgium was invaded by German troops. Panda felt duty-bound to defend Belgium, his "fatherland." In August 1914, he joined a special unit of 330 former colonial officials (Corps des Volontaires Congolais) and took part in the defense of the town of Namur.[8]

World War I was a turning point in Panda's life, an eye-opening and revolutionizing experience, as it was for many blacks who fought for their colonial masters in the "War to Make the World Safe for Democracy." He, like many other Congolese, had enthusiastically joined Belgian troops in order to protect Belgium, a country he thought to be his own. To Congolese soldiers who had fought the Germans in the eastern region of the Congo, in Tanganyika, Cameroon, and Rhodesia, the end of the war brought bitter disappointment. While Belgian war veterans enjoyed various benefits, their Congolese counterparts were denied them and continued to be considered second-class citizens; they were barred from any participation in the government of their country. Even the "traditional" chiefs were divested of their authority over their own people by one of the most overbearing colonial administrations in Africa.[9]

To defend their interests and fight against these injustices, the small Congolese community in Belgium founded an association called Union Congolaise: Société de secours et de développement moral et intellectuel de la race Congolaise (Congolese Union: The Society for Help and Moral and Intellectual Development of the Congolese Race) and Panda, the most educated Congolese in Belgium, was elected president. It was in his capacity as the representative of this association that Panda attended the 1920 National Colonial Congress (Congrès National Colonial), the first of several meetings that were convened in Brussels to discuss Belgian colonial policy. His message to the Congress was, "Africa needs educated men of its own race."[10] He demanded that Africans be given access to higher education and that educated Africans be promoted to higher echelons of the colonial administration. He warned that unless Africans' education and material progress were encouraged, revolution would grow in the Congo. In his own words:

In a letter of protest that I sent to the Permanent Commission on Colonization of the Colonial Council this year, I expressed the wish to see my compatriots participate in the politics and administration of the colony[,] and

I suggested the creation of a council in charge of indigenous affairs. In fact, in the Congo, the indigenous man is represented nowhere in the various councils of the Colony. The indigenous communities have been preserved[,] but the relations with the local government are especially selfish: tax collection, police, collaboration for hygiene.... in order to be civilizing, colonization must, therefore, use the services of the chief and his entourage.[11]

In most colonial capitals this reformist message would not have elicited any extraordinary reactions, but in Brussels it produced an unprecedented surge of protest in the colonial press that heaped abuse on the Congolese spokesman. While the Belgians were debating Panda's subversive advocacy of equal rights for the Congolese, some other developments were taking place in the Congo, which proved to be more threatening than Panda's rhetoric.

Garveyist Activities in the Congo and Belgian Reactions

In December 1920, the Belgian Ministry of the Colonies received some alarming news from Martin Rutten, the vice governor-general of the Congo. Rutten sent to the Ministry a copy of a letter written to the attorney general in charge of Equateur Province by a Belgian magistrate in the small town of Lisala. According to the letter, the magistrate had learned from two Englishmen employed by the SEDEC trading company that a Gold Coast clerk named Wilson, employed by the Société des Cultures de Mongagnia (Yakata)[12] had traveled to Lisala to show a subversive letter to a Robertson, a clerk from Accra employed by SEDEC.

The letter announced the creation of an important company called "the Black Star Line Limited" with headquarters in New York City. The company's aim was to free Africa. The letter stated that this company had organized black Americans and could provoke their uprising throughout the United States. The writer of the letter, a delegate of the Black Star Line in Dakar, whose initials were F. W. H.,[13] announced his arrival in the Belgian Congo in December 1920, in order to introduce and organize the movement. The letter also stated that the Zulu, the Zanzibari, and other "Arabized" people of East Africa had promised to join the movement.[14]

In his own letter, to which the magistrate's letter was attached, the vice governor-general informed the minister of the colonies that he had ordered the attorney general to investigate the matter and had informed the governors-general of French Equatorial and West Africa about the incident. Furthermore, he asked the minister to check whether there were any relations between the Black Star Line and the Phelps-Stokes Fund, whose representatives were to visit the Belgian Congo in a few months.[15]

The evidence of the spread of Marcus Garvey's message in the Congo caused much apprehension among the Belgians. In their usual manner, they overreacted. The minister of the colonies, through the minister of foreign affairs, asked the Belgian ambassador to the United States to investigate the Black Star Line and send him a full report on its activities.[16] At that time (December 1920) the Belgian Ministry of the Colonies did not make any connections between the Black Star Line and Marcus Garvey, who had interested them earlier in the year and on whose activities they had been trying to collect information.

The interest of the Ministry of the Colonies in Marcus Garvey had been triggered in August 1920 by the announcement of the first International Convention of Negroes Congress that was held in New York. The following month, the minister of the colonies asked his colleague in charge of foreign affairs to secure detailed information on the congress from the Belgian ambassador in Washington, D.C. From the first pieces of information he received about Garvey,[17] the minister noticed that the Black Star Line corresponded with the shipping company founded by Marcus Garvey. This spurred his interest even further, and he requested from the minister more details on Garvey and the company.[18]

In a report on Garvey and his activities, dated 9 February 1921, the Belgian ambassador to the United States advised the minister to refuse African Americans entry into the Congo lest they contaminate the Congolese with their Pan-African ideas. He confirmed that the Black Star Line had been founded by Marcus Garvey and denied any links between Garvey's organization and the Phelps-Stokes Fund. The secretary-general of the fund, contacted by the ambassador, had provided him with detailed information on Garvey.[19]

The minister rejected the envoy's advice to keep black Americans out of the Congo because, he feared, the American government would protest against the measure. However, he ordered the ambassador to secure clearance from his office prior to issuing visas to black Americans. At the same time, the governor-general of the Congo was instructed to keep watch on and inform the ministry about all black Americans entering the colony and to deport all those who would organize movements against the European occupation of Africa.[20]

The interest of the Ministry of the Colonies in Garvey was deepened further when Dr. Thomas Jesse Jones, head of the Phelps-Stokes Fund commission that toured the Congo in 1920–21, warned the governor-general of the Belgian Congo against the dangers that the distribution of Garvey's publication, the *Negro World*, could represent for colonial interests in the Congo. Impressed by this warning, the secretary-general of the ministry asked the minister of foreign affairs to make arrangements with the Belgian ambassador in Washington, D.C., for procurement of a few issues of this journal.[21] On 18 May 1921, the Belgian ambassador sent to the Ministry of Foreign Affairs the first of several batches of the *Negro World*, issues that were regularly transferred to the Ministry of the Colonies for the following several years. Moreover, "considering the interest of this weekly publication," the envoy subscribed to it.[22]

Belgian reaction was not limited to watching Garvey's activities in the United States. In fact, the colonial government's almost pathological fear of Garvey led it to alert other colonial governments in Africa to the menace of Pan-African ideas and to urge them and the United States government to cooperate in fighting Garvey and limiting the impact of his intrigues by sharing information. Indeed, the Belgian minister of foreign affairs instructed the Belgian ambassador to France to inform his counterpart in the French government that an association had been founded in New York, whose aim was to encourage Africans to rise against European rule.

The French minister of foreign affairs, who did not know anything about the previously mentioned association, asked his colleague in charge of the colonies and the French ambassador to the United States to inform him about it, and he promised to share whatever information he could gather with his Belgian colleague.[23] A few weeks later the Belgian minister of the colonies requested his colleague in the Ministry of Foreign Affairs to send a report on Garveyist activities in the Congo to the British ambassador to Belgium, and to instruct the latter to inform his government.[24] At the end of April 1921, a few weeks after the Kimbanguist movement had started in the Congo, a further step toward full collaboration of colonial powers against the Pan-African movement was taken by the Belgian Ministry of the Colonies when it insisted that the minister of foreign affairs should explicitly propose to other colonial governments that they should help each other against Pan-Africanist activities.[25]

Although the available archival documents do not give any clues to the response of the British government to Belgian propositions for a coalition of colonial powers against Pan-African activities in Africa, they do show that the French exchanged information with the Belgians. On 16 April 1921, for example, the Belgian ambassador to France notified his minister of foreign affairs that, according to the report of the French General Consul in New York, the Black Star Line "seems to be of little importance. Its commercial activity is almost insignificant because it owns only one ship. It seems that it is mostly a means for serving the ambitions of its president, Marcus Garvey, of [the] black race."[26] It did not seem to the General Consul that "the Black Star Line was a very dangerous association for the security of our colonies in Africa. Nevertheless, it will be good to watch its activities."[27]

In June 1921, while the Belgians were trying to arrest Simon Kimbangu, and W. E. B. Du Bois was making arrangements for the Pan-African Congress at Brussels, the Belgians started collaborating with the United States government to suppress Garvey's movement. Here are the circumstances that led to this collaboration, in the words of the Belgian ambassador to the United States:

> In my report dated 16 May, no. 1142/409, I had the honor of informing you the Belgian Minister of Foreign Affairs that I had decided to subscribe to the "Negro World." To avoid that the King's Embassy be counted among the readers of this journal, who are recruited here almost exclusively in the black population, I made sure I instructed our chancellor, Mr. Van Crombrugge, to subscribe to it in his own name.
>
> A secret police agent of the United States government came by the chancellery this afternoon in order to obtain information on the character and the relations of the person who, having subscribed to the "Negro World," belonged to the staff of the Embassy. It was easy for me to make him understand that my chancellor had acted under my direction and that it was as an individual that I wanted to know about Marcus Garvey's activities, in order to avoid that his propaganda in Africa eventually spreads to the territory of our colony. This agent, whose address and telephone number I kept, told me that he was happy to notice that our interest coincided with that of the American Government, which had charged him very specially to watch the relationships that could be formed between Marcus Garvey and his followers, on one hand, and extremist German and Bolshevik elements, on the other hand, in the United States. He promised to inform me, as much as possible, about the result of his observations and, when that happens, I will not fail to notify you about the information that I will receive from him and that may interest you.[28]

Apparently, the mission of this American agent from the Department of Justice was to watch the UNIA's activities in the United States and in other parts of the world. In fact, in June 1921, he went to the Belgian embassy in Washington, D.C., to inquire about some agitation that, according to the American press, had taken place in an American company in the Congo and involved black Americans and a newspaper that incited blacks to revolt.[29]

In a coded telegram, based on the information that he had received from his colleague, the Belgian minister of foreign affairs denied that there had been any trouble in the Congo, but he confirmed that some

Congolese had been caught with copies of the *Negro World*.[30] Not satisfied with this brief message, the U.S. Justice Department agent asked for details: the name of the American company involved in the *Negro World* affair. According to the Belgian ambassador to Washington, D.C., "he [the United States agent] would like to try to find out how the *Negro World* wound up in our colony and, eventually, to look for the troublemakers whose influence could, from this country, spread to Africa."[31] The reply given by the minister of foreign affairs reveals that Wilson's deportation from the Congo did not stop Garveyist activities in the Belgian colony and that the Congolese elite had heard Garvey's message by 1921. Furthermore, it confirms my earlier suggestion of Garveyist activities and influence in Central Africa:[32]

> I am honored to inform you that no American subject is especially impli-
> cated in the *Negro World* affair. We have only noticed that some Blacks of
> our colony, living in Kinshassa [*sic*], had received this journal through some
> Negroes from Senegal.[33]

Thus, the interest of the Belgian government in Garvey, the UNIA, and the Black Star Line was provoked in August 1920 by the announcement of the UNIA's first Congress of the Negro Peoples. The minister of the colonies sought details on this congress, which he received only in December of the same year, after the colonial administration had discovered Garveyist activities in the Equateur Province of the colony. The increasingly panicky Belgian minister of the colonies alerted the other colonial powers to the dangers of the spread of Pan-Africanist ideas into the colonies. He thus started collaborating with all the colonial powers against Garvey and the Pan-African movement. However, the expulsion of Wilson, the Sierra Leonean who was thought to be the main Garveyist agent in the Congo, did not stem Pan-African influence in the Congo, as copies of the *Negro World* were found in Congolese hands in Kinshasa. So, by the end of 1920 and the beginning of 1921, the Congolese population of Kinshasa, Matadi (the main Congolese port), and Boma had received some Garveyist propaganda. These events shaped the attitudes of the alarmed Belgian government and colonial administration toward Garvey's movement and, in general, toward the Pan-African movement. Although most colonial governments did not perceive Garveyism as a serious threat, the Belgians were convinced that Garvey was out to wreck their African empire.

Another development that affected Panda's political career contributed to the hardening of the Belgian position against Pan-African ideas and wiped out W. E. B. Du Bois's chances of holding a peaceful congress in Brussels was the beginning of Simon Kimbangu's messianic movement in the Congo in 1921. Kimbanguism, so the Belgians thought, was inspired by Panda and Garvey in collusion with American and British missionaries, and possibly with the blessing of the American government.

Kimbanguism as "Pure Garveyism"

The messianic movement that came to be known as Kimbanguism had a considerable appeal to Africans in the Belgian and French Congos and in Angola. Its potential as a nationalist and anticolonial movement was recognized by Belgian colonial officials, businessmen, and missionaries from its very inception. In their attempts to explain the origins of Kimbanguism, the Belgians saw clear signs of Pan-African and more specifically, Garveyist inspiration. *Congo*, a periodical published by the Belgian Ministry of the Colonies, expressed this in very clear terms.

> The territorial administration in charge of watching the visionary had the impression that he wanted to create a religion that corresponded to Black mentality.
> This so-called religion mixed elements of protestantism with the external practices of witchcraft. This is *pure Garveyism*.
> Marcus Garvey also teaches that European religions do not adapt themselves to the psychology of the Black man, and he endeavors to create a "Negro religion"[34] (author's emphasis).

My goal is not to retrace the history of Kimbanguism[35] but rather to explore the likelihood of Garveyist influences in this Congolese messianic movement and to assess the contribution that this made to negative Belgian attitudes toward Pan-Africanism. A short biographical sketch of the founder of Kimbanguism will help place the movement in its proper historical context.[36] Simon Kimbangu was born in the 1880s[37] in the village of Nkamba near Ngombe Lutete, a major British Baptist mission and the center of Protestant activities in the Lower Congo. After attending the missionary school at Ngombe Lutete, he was baptized in 1915 and taught there for a short time. He then returned to Nkamba, where he worked as an evangelist.

In 1918, several nights in a row, Kimbangu heard what he thought was Jesus Christ's voice calling and telling him that he had been chosen to preach and convert his unfaithful brethren. Every time, however, Kimbangu's wife heard him reply that he was not trained enough to shoulder such a heavy responsibility. According to the explanation given by his followers, Kimbangu finally decided to run away from

Jesus' call, and he traveled to Kinshasa in search of work. He was employed in various places, but in 1920 economic difficulties forced him to return to Nkamba, where he resumed his farming activities.[38]

On 6 April 1921, Kimbangu prayed and healed a bedridden and seriously ill woman in the neighboring village of Ngombe Kinsuka. This marked the beginning of Kimbangu's career as a "prophet" and of his religious movement. The news of the healing spread rapidly throughout the Lower Congo and soon reached the major urban centers in the area, Kinshasa, Léopoldville, and Matadi, and the neighboring French Congo and northern Angola. Kimbangu is said to have resurrected a child and a woman and to have cured a blind woman thereafter.[39] Soon, people flocked to Nkamba in the thousands to heal their sick relatives or just to see and hear the new prophet (ngunza). Laborers abandoned their work to travel to Nkamba and thus forced some of the largest employers, such as the Kinshasa-Matadi railways and Huileries du Congo Belge, to close down; European housewives had to make do without their "boys." Protestant as well as Catholic churches were deserted, as the Congolese craved to hear the refreshing message of the powerful prophet of Nkamba. This, as will be discussed later, caused a great deal of concern among missionaries, European businessmen, and Belgian colonial officials.[40]

Brimming with charisma, Kimbangu demanded of his followers that they reject "fetishes" and advised them not to partake in "licentious" dances and polygamy.[41] He told them that the Lord was near and that salvation could be gotten only through faith in Jesus Christ and through repentance. He insisted on the repayment of evil with good, obedience to those in authority, and loving one's enemies.[42] He attempted to translate Christianity in terms that were readily understandable by his Kongo followers, without rejecting Kongo religion wholesale, as missionaries had been trying for centuries. As Georges Balandier has aptly explained, by destroying magical statues (mikisi), Kimbangu brought remedy in a society where social and economic disturbances resulting from colonization had caused a considerable increase of magical practices and sorcery.[43]

The religious role that Kimbangu claimed was very important in Kongo society and had far-reaching political implications. In fact, Kongo people believe that prophets "are reborn with the gift 'to see what is, and foresee what is to come.' On such people the Mukongo rely for help in a world which is made up largely of untoward events, of masks, deceptions, and frustrations."[44] Even Kimbangu's bitterest enemies have acknowledged that the fact that he had a large following, in spite of his antagonism toward some of the most sensitive aspects of Kongo culture, was quite an impressive accomplishment. Kimbangu demonstrated his prestige and charisma among his countrymen and the appeal of the movement he had launched.[45]

As early as 26 April 1921, Léon Morel, the Nkamba territorial administrator, wrote a report, in which he pointed out that Kimbangu had not committed any crime for which he could be indicted. He warned that Kimbangu might have the intention, however, of creating a new church and getting a large enough following to organize an uprising of the Kongolese against colonial rule. He also saw the possibility of an epidemic starting in Nkamba, if the large gatherings were allowed to continue. Nevertheless, he urged the colonial administration not to arrest Kimbangu, as this would increase his popularity.[46]

Fearing adverse effects on their activities, Catholic missionaries and European businessmen pressured the colonial administration to act against the new religion and its "misguided" preachers. On 11 May 1921, Léon Morel was ordered by his superiors to visit Nkamba and verify the allegations of subversion made by businessmen and Catholic priests. He witnessed some healing that he attributed to "the influence of religious fanaticism and Kimbangu's moral power."[47] He went on, in his subsequent report, to pinpoint the main characteristics of Kimbanguism:

> Kimbangu wants to found a religion which contains the characteristics of Protestantism but with the addition of practices taken from fetishism (i.e. Kongo religion).[48]

He concluded by warning against the potential dangers that the new religion represented:

> Everyone can readily see that the religions of Europe are completely shot through with abstractions and in no way correspond to the mentality of the African, who longs for tangible facts and protection. Kimbangu's teaching suits him because it is supported by palpable facts.
> It is, therefore, necessary to oppose Kimbangu since he has a tendency towards Pan-Africanism. The natives will say, "We have found the God of the Blacks, the religion which suits the African."[49]

So, just a few weeks after Kimbangu had started preaching, the colonial administration denounced the Pan-African tendencies that the movement displayed, and clearly saw its disruptive potential.

May 1921 saw the rapid spread of Kimbangu's new religion, thanks to the zeal of his twelve "apostles," who were commissioned to appoint local "prophets" in their respective areas. The local prophets were, in turn, empowered to heal, preach, and baptize, and collect funds from converts. These funds were then bought to Kimbangu, who more and more was called *mvuluzi* (savior) by his followers.[50]

At this juncture, a large number of self-appointed "prophets," claiming to be Kimbanguists, started roaming all over Kongo country and began to preach their own versions of Kimbangu's message. The Nkamba man's warning of the imminent coming of the Lord was construed to mean that no food should be produced, that no taxes should be paid to the colonial administration, that the Congolese should no longer work for the whites, that the ancestors would resuscitate when the whites would leave the Congo, and that the fire of heaven would consume all the whites. These "prophets" and their followers destroyed and burnt several Catholic churches and threatened those Congolese who remained faithful to the Protestant or Catholic churches.[51]

Thus, by the beginning of June 1921, Kimbangu's religious movement was considered by the Europeans as a clearly antiwhite phenomenon that could organize a mass uprising against the Europeans in the Congo. To prevent this from happening, on 6 June 1921 the colonial administration, under increasing Catholic pressures, ordered Morel to arrest Kimbangu and his assistants. Taking advantage of the confusion resulting from a confrontation between the territorial official's armed escort and people assembled in Nkamba, Kimbangu and his assistants escaped and for several months eluded the colonial troops. To most Congolese, this was irrefutable proof of Kimbangu's God-given superior powers and of his divine mission to be the prophet of the black people.[52] The unsuccessful manhunt launched by the Belgians increased Kimbangu's prestige and reinforced the antiwhite tendencies of his movement:

> Once the leaders had been threatened with arrest and removed from the people, there was no way for the unstructured movement to be channelled in an orthodox direction. And by alienating thousands of African Christians from the mission churches, the Government's action ensured a large following for the prophet leaders who had begun to express anti-white sentiments, bringing suddenly to the surface any latent discontent and generating a political thrust which may well have been the start of the long haul towards independence.[53]

Kimbangu and his assistants continued to preach underground, and rumors had it that they traveled as far as Kinshasa, where they had a large following. To facilitate the search for the fugitives by the colonial army, on 12 August 1921, a state of emergency was declared in the districts of Luozi and Thysville, the areas of the Lower Congo most affected by Kimbangu's movement. This measure, however, was unsuccessful. Finally, on 12 September 1921, Kimbangu and his assistants went back to Nkamba and surrendered to the Belgian administrator.[54]

On 3 October 1921, a court martial sitting in Thysville found Kimbangu guilty of hostility toward the whites and of sedition. He was sentenced to death, and his codefendants were sentenced to exile in remote areas of the Belgian Congo. A Protestant missionary who worked in the area at that time recorded the reaction of the Congolese people:

> After the arrests, the natives were restive. We could see the clash of colour. A racial consciousness and unity seemed to develop through the movement. The natives were made deeply conscious of the white man's domination. There was resentment in their hearts.[55]

From its very inception, Kimbanguism was seen by the Belgian administration, the Catholic clergy, and European businessmen as a dangerous nationalist and antiwhite movement influenced by and having connections with Garveyist intellectuals in Kinshasa and with Paul Panda Farnana. Some authors have rejected these accusations as unfounded and as typical of Belgian paranoia and proclivity to blame outsiders for any disturbances that occurred in their colony.[56] It is true that the Belgians throughout the colonial period feared that other world powers, especially the Anglo-Saxons, envied their "model" colony and would not hesitate, through their missions and companies, to manipulate the Congolese to achieve their ends.[57] In the particular case of Kimbanguism, however, there is more than enough evidence to show that Belgian fears of Pan-Africanist influences on the Congolese elite and Kimbangu were unfounded. Sure signs of Garveyist inroads into the Belgian Congo alarmed the Belgian authorities and made them nervous and suspicious of anything that smacked of Pan-Africanism. A short analysis of Kinshasa, the most dynamic urban center with the highest concentration of African intellectuals in the Congo in the 1920s, will reveal the conditions that favored the spread of the radical political ideas that had an impact on Kimbangu and the religious movement that he founded.

Kinshasa, because of its geographical location at the end of both the Matadi-Kinshasa railroad and the navigable section of the Congo River, became a major trading center and saw an accelerated development after World War I. Large numbers of Congolese, affected by the drastic decrease in the prices of the raw materials they produced, flocked to Kinshasa and, thus, helped solve the labor crisis created by new industries, especially in the construction sector. Many were also attracted by the fame that the town, called Kin-Malebo of Poto Moindo (Black

Europe), had acquired as a place where fortunes could be easily made and where European goods were readily available.

In 1921–22, about twenty thousand people inhabited the African section of this rigidly segregated town.[58] Most of the Africans were unskilled laborers; the literate section of this population was made up of about five hundred Congolese and one thousand West Africans. The latter held responsible posts in companies and, as the most literate blacks, served as a reference group for the rest of the Africans.[59] Unfortunately, not much is known about the activities of this elite, but we know that they socialized in a select bar,[60] where their discussions of politics may have taken place. Many of them subscribed to European newspapers such as *Libre Parole*, *L'Humanité*, and *Action Francaise*, and they also read the *Negro World*.[61] The West Africans, who were from Nigeria, Sierra Leone, the Gold Coast, Senegal, and Dahomey (now Benin), received the *Negro World* from their home countries where Garveyists were already quite active.[62]

Life in Kinshasa was rather difficult for the Congolese, for the laborers as well as for their educated brethren. Salaries were rather low, and the cost of living was exorbitant; many workers were forced to steal in order to survive.[63] To make matters worse, the European businessmen in Kinshasa had created an employers' syndicate that standardized and imposed the terms of service on the unorganized Congolese workers, thus eliminating competition for scarce labor. They also imposed their views on the colonial administration and controlled the two most influential newspapers in the Congo, *L'Avenir Colonial Belge* and *Le Progrès Colonial*.[64]

Literate Congolese endured debasement, social abuse, and the thwarting of their ambitions. In an attempt to improve the lot of the Congolese, they formed, under the leadership of André Yengo, an underground organization called "Congomen."[65] The English name of this organization is an indication of the close relations that existed between the Congolese elite and their English-speaking West African counterparts, and of the prestige that the latter enjoyed among the Congolese. The small size of the African elite, the prestige enjoyed by the West Africans among the Congolese, and the closeness of the relations among the elite facilitated the communication of ideas, including Garveyism, from the more educated West Africans to the Congolese. Furthermore, the high proportion of literate people within the relatively small African population allowed easy politicization of the illiterate masses. This is confirmed by an astonished Belgian visitor to Kinshasa who was told by his uneducated Congolese servant that he was looking forward to the day when the whites would be chased from the Congo.[66] By December 1920, when the Belgian colonial authorities discovered

Garveyist activities in Coquilhatville, hundred of miles up the Congo River from Kinshasa, Garvey's message had been heard by the African elite in Kinshasa and had seeped down to the Congolese workers.

Kimbangu lived in Kinshasa between 1918 and 1920, as mentioned previously, and had certainly heard the political ideas propounded by his educated countrymen and the West Africans. His close relations with André Yengo, the leader of "Congomen," were revealed when the Belgian colonial administration discovered the link that existed between Kimbangu and the Congolese intellectuals in Kinshasa, and decided to arrest and interrogate the leaders of the "Congomen" association. The authorities revealed that the association was in close contact with Kimbangu and collected money that was sent to the prophet. It became clear also that the intellectuals wanted to found a Congolese national church because, "for many years, the Blacks have given large amounts of money to missionaries and also because the latter did not allow them to control the use of this money."[67] Yengo's own explanation of his association's motives betrays West African inspiration: "[T]he Senegalese have their marabouts but the French leave them alone."[68] Furthermore, Yengo asked the magistrate who was interrogating him to release him so that he could go and convince Kimbangu (who was then in hiding after the unsuccessful attempt to arrest him in Nkamba) to surrender to the Belgian colonial administration.[69] It is quite clear from this that Yengo had to be quite close to the prophet to know his secret hiding place.

Kimbangu had a large and well-organized following in Kinshasa. In fact, even after the leaders of the Congomen had been arrested, the local branch of Kimbangu's church continued to hold daily meetings. Furthermore, persistent rumors were circulated in Kinshasa that the Kongo people would drive the Belgians out of the Congo in the near future.[70]

Even though it is difficult to document some authors' assertion that Kimbangu met a black American in Kinshasa between 1918 and 1920,[71] one can argue convincingly that Garvey's message, passed on to Kimbangu through West Africans and the Congolese elite of Kinshasa, had a significant impact on the creed of Kimbanguism. The similarities between the gospel of Garvey's African Orthodox Church and Kimbanguism are so fundamental that they cannot be dismissed as mere coincidences.[72] The first, and rather general, similarity lay in the endeavor by both Garvey and Kimbangu to fight against white domination by creating religions that were more meaningful to blacks. Maurice Dekobra summarized the main tenets of Garvey's religion in an article that was published in *Congo* shortly after Kimbangu founded his religious movement:

> According to him [Garvey], white men's religion does not suit Blacks, because one must be as stupid as a nigger [sic] to believe in a white God, in a white Messiah, in white angels and in a white paradise! ... Garvey's thesis is to offer Blacks a black religion with a creator taking their own image as model. ... That is, a Black God. He goes to war against white missionaries who have only been "the emissaries of slave-traders and poisoners of the black race."[73]

The two religions were also similar in the political overtones that characterized their preaching: the imminent demise of the white rulers was a persistent leitmotif in the gospels of Kimbanguism and Garveyism. A third area in which resemblance could be noticed between the two movements was, according to Efraim Andersson, the colors of the banner used by both Kimbanguists and Garvey's followers.[74]

The political message of Kimbanguism showed definite signs of Garveyist influence. Although Wyatt MacGaffey has tried to give a metaphysical explanation of the frequent references by Kimbanguists of black Americans as the liberators of the Congolese people from the yoke of Belgian colonialism, evidence shows that Kimbangu's following referred not to imaginary saviors but to black American Garveyists. This hymn documents the fact that the Kimbanguists were concerned not only about supernatural issues but also about the liberation of the Congo from Belgian colonialism, with the assistance of black Americans:

> If the King of the Americans comes
> To restore the King,
> The chiefs of this world shall pass away.
> If the King of Americans comes,
> The troubles of this world shall pass away.
> If the King of Americans comes,
> The King of the blacks will return.[75]

The Kimbanguists clearly remember the historical context in which this hymn was written. They report that when Kimbangu was exiled to Elisabethville, he told his followers, "I will not leave you comfortless; I will pray to the Father, and he shall give you another Comforter."[76] The message of the hymn is straightforward: Kimbangu promised to have somebody sent—a human being, not a spirit—who would continue his work; he would ask God to send the "King of the Americans":—a sure reference to Marcus Garvey—who would restore the Old Kingdom of the Kongo, after the Belgians had been chased from the Congo. Furthermore, this was the first time that the Congolese referred to black Americans as their redemptors from colonial rule.[77] Thereafter, rumors of the impending arrival of black American saviors were repeated in 1930–35 and during World War II.[78]

The Kimbanguists' concern with liberation in "this world" and their reference to Garveyist black Americans are confirmed by this prophecy dating from 1921:

> Pray to your brethren who were sold in the ivory and rubber to the country of the Americans. The Lord will send them to this country to teach crafts and give skills surpassing those of the whites.[79]

Even Wyatt MacGaffey, in spite of his ethnological lucubrations, pointed out the Kimbanguists' political goal:

> Even though you need an aeroplane to reach it, the other world is not far from here—but just over the hill, as it were—and the heavenly kingdom, Mbanza Kongo, is to be established on this earth, in Kongo.[80]

This plainly shows that Kimbanguism had two concomitant goals: the salvation of the soul and the liberation of the Congo from Belgian colonialism. From the very beginning, Kimbanguist prophets communicated their political message and urged their followers to engage in antiwhite activities. On 24 May 1921, two missionaries of the Baptist Missionary Society (BMS) visited a village near Kibentele (Lower Congo), where they heard a prophet, who had destroyed a Roman Catholic church, advise his followers not to pay taxes. In another village, Ntemo, in the same area, they ran into prophetesses who were preaching about "the fire of heaven which would fall on whites" and who recommended to their people not to pay taxes.[81] So, from its inception, Kimbanguism was a political and antiwhite movement.

The frequent mention by Kimbanguists of a ship that would sail up the Congo River to save the Congolese is another proof of Garveyist influence.[82] The news of the formation of the Black Star Line had also reached Central Africa by 1921 and struck the imagination of the Congolese. This aspect of the Kimbanguist message and the evidence presented previously confirm the argument that Garvey's ideas had gained ground in the Congo by 1921 and deeply influenced Kimbangu's movement. According to the Belgian mass media, further political inspiration for Kimbanguists emanated from Congolese circles in Belgium.

The Garvey-Panda-Kimbangu Connection

As discussed earlier, Paul Panda Farnana drew a great deal of attention and fire in 1920 when he demanded equal rights for the Congolese and participation by his countrymen in the administration of the Belgian Congo. On the heels of the 1920 Congrès National Colonial, the Belgian mass media, especially the two Kinshasa newspapers (*Le Progrès Colonial* and *L'Avenir Colonial Belge*), launched a campaign, the aim of which was to destroy Panda politically by showing that he was a dangerous and ambitious agitator. Well before the beginning of Kimbangu's religious movement, he was accused of having contacts with Marcus Garvey and of planning to overthrow Belgian rule. Later, when the Kimbanguists started preaching against white overrule, he was identified as an l'éminence grise of the prophets and of their intellectual allies in Kinshasa and other parts of the Congo. In the next few pages, I will examine the various accusations made by Belgian newspapers against Panda, to determine if they were based on fact, and I will analyze how the press contributed to the shaping of inimical Belgian attitudes toward Pan-Africanism and the 1921 Pan-African congress.

The first allegation of a Garvey-Panda connection was made on 30 January 1921 by *L'Avenir Colonial Belge*, in response to Panda's declarations at the 1920 Congrès National Colonial and his interview with a Belgian newspaper, *La Dernière Heure*. Panda was suspected of being one of the Congolese delegates who, according to the *Daily Mail* participated in the 1920 UNIA congress in New York. In a calculated move aimed at showing how dangerous Garvey and his followers (and, by association, Panda) were, this excerpt from Garvey's speech to the congress was quoted:

> Africa remains the patrimony of the Blacks. . . . Time has come for them to reconquer their native land, to proclaim its independence.
>
> The moment is favorable. In all the regions of the African territory, the whites have spread, within the reach of our hands, the arms that they used to tear each other during the war and which they have taught us to use. If they refuse to evacuate our plains, our forests, our fields, we will declare war on them and we will stop fighting only after having thrown every single one of them to the sea. We are the number; we will be the might and we have the right on our side. If need be, we will make alliances that can open the ways to freedom. Maybe the blacks, the secular victims of white greed, could count on Lenin's and Trotsky's assistance.[83]

In conclusion, the author of this article asked Panda whether he was not among the participants to this congress, "those liberators" who wanted to poison Europeans or chase them out of Africa. He also inquired whether Panda did not entertain "that criminal idea" of ridding the Congolese of European domination.[84] This text must have made quite an impression on the Belgians, who still strongly believed that the Congolese were just one step above animals on the evolutionary scale. Echoing *L'Avenir Colonial Belge, Congo* concluded that Panda's ideas had a Pan-Africanist bias.[85]

Panda's statement to the newspapers and his speeches in conferences were extremely well documented and, for a long time, Belgian newsmen wondered how he received so much detailed and accurate information on events and developments in the Congo. On 20 March 1921, just a little over two weeks before Kimbangu founded his new religion, *L'Avenir Colonial Belge* revealed that it had finally uncovered the network through which Panda received information from the Congo. Just by chance, the newspaper reported, a European traveling from Kinshasa to Matadi found in his houseservant's luggage an envelope addressed to Paul Panda Farnana. The envelope contained several documents and was to be carried to Europe by a Congolese sailor.

The sender of the documents, Henry Emmanuel John, told Panda, in the covering letter, that all the literate Congolese closely followed Panda's activities in Belgium and begged him to continue raising issues pertaining to the Congo. He promised to inform Panda about everything that occurred in the Congo, and mentioned that he had a brother in Brussels, a John Balomba.[86] In view of the small size of the African population in Kinshasa in 1920–21, and especially of its literate component, it can be safely surmised that Henry E. John was in close contact with André Yengo and other literate Africans. This is confirmed by the fact that he knew and therefore could tell Panda what the "civilized" Congolese thought of his activities. He thus served as the liaison between Panda's Union Congolaise and the Congomen. Besides, Kimpianga Mahaniah II asserts that Henry E. John later served as Kimbangu's secretary.[87] This, then, confirms Belgian apprehensions of a Panda-Yengo-Kimbangu connection.

According to *L'Avenir Colonial Belge*, Henry E. John had studied in a Baptist mission in his native Lower Congo. He was so fluent in English that he was easily confused for a West African, and in 1921 he was working for Omnium Africain. Ferdinand Beco (who is also referred to as Louis Farnana), Panda's brother, wrote regularly to the president of Union Congolaise and also may have given information of a political character to his brother. He had studied in Belgium and was chief of the Lukala train station in the Lower Congo.[88]

L'Avenir Colonial Belge also alerted the Belgian government to the black revolt being prepared by the well-organized Congomen and "black Americans" working for an industrial firm in Kinshasa and regular readers of the *Negro World*. Furthermore, the newspaper identified Panda as the leader of the "liberation movement of the black race" and urged the Belgian government to "shut him up."[89] Since May 1921, *L'Avenir Colonial Belge* had published several reports on Kimbangu and his movement. On 17 July 1921, while Kimbangu was in hiding, the paper announced that André Yengo and other blacks had been arrested two days earlier and that Kimbanguism had spread to all the major towns in the Lower Congo. It also revealed that there was a connection between Marcus Garvey, Panda Farnana, Kimbangu, and Henry E. John.[90] A few weeks later, *Le Progrès Colonial* alleged that Panda was the mentor of Kimbangu and his followers.[91]

As the date of the Pan-African Congress meeting at Brussels drew near, the Belgian press intensified its campaign against Pan-Africanism and Panda. It even attacked, several times, Paul Otlet and Henri Lafontaine, the two Belgian liberals who were helping organize the congress in Brussels. In an attempt to explain the goals of Pan-Africanism and thus allay the fears of the Belgian public, Panda Farnana wrote an article (before the congress), which was published in *L'Avenir Colonial Belge* several days after the Pan-African meeting was held in Brussels. In this article, Panda extolled the merits of Marcus Garvey's activities and defended the back-to-Africa movement:

> [Y]ou will learn that a Pan-African Congress, the goal of which is precisely the plain recognition of the absolute equality of races, will take place at the beginning of September in London, Brussels (at *Palais Mondial*) and in Paris. Intellectuals of the black race will be heard there.
>
> Anyway, read the biographical notes of scholars and famous men of African blood in *The Universal Negro Almanac*, West 135th Street, New York City. This is precisely the address of the association founded by the Afro-American Moses, your nightmare, whose energetic and humanitarian action has been brought to my attention.... Anyway, Afro-Americans' desire [to return to Africa] is legitimate.
>
> ...United as at a battle front, the intellectuals of the black race will collaborate for the moral and intellectual development of autochthonous Africans.[92]

Jubilating over Panda's admiration of Marcus Garvey, the most feared enemy of Belgian colonialism, the editor of *L'Avenir Colonial Belge* could not resist the temptation to deal a *coup de grâce* to Panda's political career:

> You admire Mr. Marcus Garvey, your Moses, as you call him; we, therefore, would like to know to what extent his tendencies are yours.
>
> If you consider him as your leader, do you also accept, as being the expression of your ideas, the remarks that he made in August 1920 at the meeting of the International Negro Conference, and that he addressed to his disciples, of whom you are one?

Time has come for the forty million of blacks to claim Africa, not to ask England, France, Belgium, Italy: "Why are you here"? but to order them to get out.

If you answer in the affirmative, be frank enough to say that you belong to Marcus Garvey's religion, that you share his views and the goal that he is pursuing.[93]

Faced with increasing pressure by the mass media and by his liberal Belgian friends, Panda vainly tried to deny any connection with Marcus Garvey and even tried to take *L'Avenir Colonial Belge* to court for having smeared and discredited the Pan-African Congress, its organizers, and Panda himself, by linking them to Marcus Garvey.[94] However, the campaign launched by *L'Avenir Colonial Belge* and *Le Progrès Colonial* against Panda was showing success by the beginning of August 1921;[95] even the metropolitan press was by then convinced that Panda was a dangerous Garveyite, whose goal was to destroy the Belgian colony with the help of black Americans led by Marcus Garvey. The Belgian public then believed that Panda's Garveyist ideas had played an important role in the formation of the Congomen association and in the birth of Kimbanguism. By August 1921, a few days before the Pan-African Congress meeting in Brussels, the link between Garvey, Panda, Yengo and his Congomen, and Kimbangu was a threatening reality for the Belgian public. There was no doubt in Belgian minds that Panda, through his efficient network of informers and followers throughout the Congo, was the mentor of the disturbances that had rocked the Congo, and especially of the uprising that was being prepared in the African section of Kinshasa, where the Congolese had allegedly organized in military units and had some armaments.[96]

Thus, when the Pan-African Congress met in Brussels and the public was informed of Panda's active participation in it, the Belgians could see the congress only as a gathering of dangerous agitators who, like their leader Marcus Garvey, were bent on freeing Africa from European rule. The differences between Marcus Garvey and W. E. B. Du Bois were not known to most Belgian newsmen, let alone to the Belgian public. After all, as the influential *Le Progrès Colonial* wrote;

There is nobody who does not know that the pan-negro movement is mostly the result of the campaign carried out by Marcus Garvey.[97]

Fearing that the congress might take some radical stance against Belgian colonialism and that the text of such a resolution might reach the Congo (where Kimbangu was still at large and making more and more converts, and from where news reports of an imminent popular uprising were being received), the Belgian press, business concerns, and the Ministry of the Colonies brought so much pressure to bear on the congress that only a mild resolution, the one proposed by Paul Otlet, came out of the meeting. Through Blaise Diagne's skillful maneuvers the London declaration was not adopted. *L'Avenir Colonial Belge*, *Le Progrès Colonial*, and the interests that they defended had scored a major victory over the Pan-African movement and Paul Panda Farnana, its advocate in Belgium and the Congo.

Conclusion

Using some of the sources pertaining to Pan-Africanism in the Congo that have not been fully exploited (that is, Belgian newspapers) and those that have not been used at all (the archives of the Belgian Ministry of Foreign Affairs), I have shown that Belgian apprehensions about Pan-African influence in the Congo, although exaggerated at times by their obsessive fear of external meddling in their colony, were founded on fact. The fortuitous discovery of Garveyist activities in the Congo at the end of 1920, Paul Panda Farnana's vocal advocacy of equal rights for his countrymen, and Kimbangu's radical gospel frightened the Belgians so much that they began to seek information about these movements. Through information gathered in the Congo and in the United States, they discovered that there were links among these various movements. My argument, contrary to what some authors have asserted so far, is that Pan-Africanism (especially Garveyism) had a profound influence on Kimbangu and his movement, on Paul Panda Farnana, and on other Congolese intellectuals.

The vicious campaign launched by the Belgian press against Pan-Africanism and Panda heightened the fears of the Belgian business and government circles. By the time the Pan-African Congress met in Brussels, the Belgian government was so alarmed that it had to exert pressure on the congress not to pass radical resolutions. In fact, it could be of no comfort to the Belgian Ministry of the Colonies to reflect that an anticolonial declaration by the congress could fuel disturbances in the Congo, where the radical and well-organized Congomen and Kimbangu had struck a responsive chord among their downtrodden countrymen and were threatening to provoke an uprising of the Congolese masses.

Thus, it was not only because of their fears of foreigners (especially the Anglo-Saxons) that the Belgian public and government suspected the Pan-African Congress, but also because of events and developments in the Congo that clearly betrayed Pan-Africanist inspiration.

NOTES

1. See, for instance, W. E. B. Du Bois, "The Negro Mind Reaches Out," in Alain Locke, *The New Negro, 1925* (New York: Antheneum, 1969) 413; George Padmore, *Pan-Africanism or Communism* (Garden City, N.Y.: Anchor Books, 1972), 110; Imanuel Geiss, *The Pan-African Movement: A History of Pan-Africanism in America, Europe and Africa* (New York: Africana Publishing Co., 1974), 245–46; Irene Diggs, "Du Bois and the Pan-African Congresses," *A Current Bibliography on African Affairs* V, 2 (new series, 1972), 138–44; John Henrik Clarke and Amy Jacques Garvey, *Marcus Garvey and the Vision of Africa* (New York: Vintage Books, 1974), 97–99; J. Ayodele Langley, *Pan-Africanism and Nationalism in West Africa, 1900–1945* (Oxford: Clarendon Press, 1973), 78–82.
2. Langley, *Pan-Africanism*, 82.
3. The only known biography of Paul Panda Farnana is the sketchy notice written by Coosemans in 1952. This notice does not do justice to Panda's political activities. See M. Coosemans, "Panda Farnana (M'Fumu Paul)," *Biographie Coloniale Belge*, III (Brussels: Institut Colonial Belge, 1952), columns 668–69.
4. Ibid., column 668.
5. W. E. B. Du Bois, "The Negro Mind Reaches Out," 390.
6. Coosemans, "Panda," column 668.
7. Ibid.
8. Ibid., column 669.
9. For critical discussion of Belgian colonial policy in this period, see R. de Briey, "Notre politique sociale au Congo," *Congo* IV, 4 (1923):439–48; P. Henry, "La politique indigène au Congo belge," *Congo* IV, 4 (1923):526; Paul Salkin, *Etudes africaines* (Brussels: F. Larcier, 1920); G. Van der Kerken, *Les sociétés bantoues du Congo belge et les problèmes de politique indigène* (Brussels: E. Bruylant, 1920).
10. M. de Mey, "M'Fumu Panda nous écrit ... ," *L'Avenir Colonial Belge* (11 September 1921) 3.
11. Anonymous, "Politique indigène. Collaboration belge et indigène. Les idées et les opinions de M. Panda Farnana," *Le Progrès Colonial* (4 August 1921):6.
12. The information given about Wilson's identity by most authors is erroneous. He was a Sierra Leonean, not a black American, and was not employed by the African and Eastern Trade Corporation, as it is said in "Le Garvéyisme dans notre colonie," *Congo* I, 4 (April 1922):570. This study mistakenly identifies him as a black American leader of a Congolese political group in Kinshasa. See Damaso Feci, "Vie cachée et vie publique de Simon Kimbangu selon la littérature coloniale et missionnaire belge," in *Les Cahiers du CEDAF* 9–10 (1972):27–28.
13. He has been identified as Francis Webber, an employee of Grace Bros. in Dakar. Webber and other Sierra Leoneans were actively preaching Garveyism in Senegal in the early 1920s. The Freetown branch of the UNIA was established in March 1920. See J. Ayodele Langley, "Marcus Garvey and African Nationalism," *Race* XI, 2 (1969):163.
14. Letter no. 1629 of 5 October 1920 from the "Procureur du Roi" in Lisala to the "Procureur du Roi" in Coquilhatville, Dossier AF. 1–17: *Congo-Etats-Unis d'Amérique*, Archives du Ministère des Affaires Etrangères et de la Coopération Internationale (AMAE), Brussels.
15. Vice-governor Rutten's letter of 2 November 1920 to the minister of the colonies, ibid.
16. Minister of the colonies to minister of foreign affairs, 24 December 1920, ibid.
17. Minister of foreign affairs to minister of the colonies, letter no. 13254 of 13 December 1920, ibid.
18. Minister of the colonies to minister of foreign affairs, 24 December 1920, ibid.

19. Belgian ambassador in Washington, D.C., to minister of foreign affairs, no. 357/113, ibid.
20. Minister of the colonies to minister of foreign affairs, 4 April 1921, ibid.
21. Secretary-general, Ministry of the Colonies, to minister of foreign affairs, 30 February 1921, ibid.
22. Belgian ambassador in Washington, D.C., to minister of foreign affairs, no. 1142/409, ibid. The subscription was renewed several times. See, for instance, minister of the colonies to minister of foreign affairs, 4 July 1922. no 436.
23. Belgian ambassador to France to Belgian minister of foreign affairs, 28 January 1921, ibid.
24. Minister of the colonies to minister of foreign affairs, 23 April 1921, Dossier AF. 1–26: *Congo-Grande-Bretagne (1917–27)*, AMAE.
25. Minister of the colonies to minister of foreign affairs, 30 April 1921, ibid.
26. Belgian ambassador to France to Belgian minister of foreign affairs, 16 April 1921, Dossier AF. 1–17.
27. French general consul in New York to French ambassador in Washington, D.C., 17 March 1921, ibid.
28. Belgian ambassador in Washington, D.C., to Belgian minister of foreign affairs, 7 June 1921, ibid.
29. Belgian ambassador in Washington, D.C., to Belgian minister of foreign affairs, 20 June 1921, ibid.
30. Belgian minister of foreign affairs, to Belgian ambassador in Washington, D.C., 23 June 1921, ibid.
31. Belgian ambassador in Washington, D.C., to Belgian minister of foreign affairs, 29 June 1921, ibid.
32. Muzong Kodi, "Garveyism and Kimbanguism: Belgian Reactions to a Messianic Movement in the Congo," *The Pan-Africanist* (Program of African Studies, Northwestern University), 3 (December 1971):1–8.
33. Minister of foreign affairs to ambassador in Washington, D.C., 5 August 1921, Dossier AF. 1–17.
34. Anonymous, "Le garvéyisme en action dans notre colonie," *Congo* II, 4 (November 1921):575.
35. See, for instance, Marie-Louise Martin, *Kimbangu, an African Prophet and His Church* (Oxford: Basil Blackwell, 1975); Cecilia Irvine, "The Birth of the Kimbanguist Movement in Bas-Zaire 1921," *Journal of Religion in Africa* VI, 1 (1974):23–76.
36. Marie-Louise Martin has written a very sympathetic (but, at times, uncritical) biography of Kimbangu. See her *Kimbangu*, 37–64.
37. Around 1881, according to J. Van Wing, "Le Kibangisme vu par un témoin," *Zaire* XII, 6 (1958):566. Marie-Louise Martin gives the date of 1889. See her *Kimbangu*, 37–64.
38. Martin, *Kimbangu*, 45.
39. Charles Gillis, *Kimbangu: fondateur d'eglise* (Brussels: Editions de la Librairie Encyclopedique, 1960), 24–25.
40. Jules Chome, *La passion de Simon Kimbangu: 1921–1951* (Brussels: Les Amis de Présence Africaine, 1959), 22.
41. Van Wing, Le Kibangisme," 568.
42. Martin, *Kimbangu*, 48–49.
43. Georges Balandier, *Sociologie actuelle de l'Afrique noire* (Paris: Presses Universitaires de France, 1955, 428–29.
44. Wyatt MacGaffey, "Kongo and the King of the Americans," *Journal of Modern African Studies* VI, 2 (1968):173.
45. See, for instance, Van Wing, "Le Kibangisme," 570.

46. Martin, *Kimbangu*, 52–53.
47. D. Desanti, "The Golden Anniversary of Kibanguism," *Continent 2000* 19 (April 1970):7.
48. Martin, *Kimbangu*, 57.
49. Ibid.
50. Van Wing, "Le Kibangisme," 571–72.
51. Irvine, "The Birth of the Kimbanguist Movement," 40–41; Van Wing, "Le Kibangisme," 572; Anonymous, "Le garveyisme en action," 575.
52. Martin, *Kimbangu*, 58; Van Wing, "Le Kibangisme," 578.
53. Irvine, "The Birth of the Kimbanguist Movement," 28–29.
54. Ibid., 55.
55. Ibid., 58.
56. Read, for instance, MacGaffey, "Kongo and the King of the Americans," 175.
57. Chalux, *Un an au Congo Belge* (Brussels: Librairie Albert Dewit, 1925), 144–47; Pierre Daye, *L'empire colonial belge* (Brussels: Editions du "Soir," 1923), 606–608; Raymond L. Buell, *The Native Problem in Africa*, vol. 2, (London: Frank Cass and Co. Ltd., 1965, reprint), 473–77; Bogumil Jewsiewicki, "La contestation sociale et la naissance du prolétariat au Zaire au cours de la première moitié du XXe siècle," *Canadian Journal of African Studies* X, 1 (1976):48.
58. Daye, *L'empire*, 164.
59. Jan Vansina, "Histoire du Congo, 1908–1960" (unpublished manuscript, n.d.), 19, 42; Kitambala, "Le Garvéyisme," *Notre Colonie*, 8 (May 1921):107.
60. Daye, *L'empire*, 207.
61. Ibid., 224.
62. Langley, "Marcus Garvey," 163, 168–69; R. L. Okonkwo, "The Garvey Movement in British West Africa," *Journal of African History* XXI, 1 (1980):107, 109, 111–12.
63. Daye, *L'empire*, 164, 209; Office Colonial, Ministère des Colonies, "Congo-Kasai: situation économique pendant l'année 1920," *Congo* II, 3 (1921):463.
64. Chalux, *Un an*, 142; Daye, *L'empire*, 163; Feci, "Vie Cachée," 20–21.
65. Kitambala, "Le Garvéyisme," 107.
66. Daye, *L'empire*, 215.
67. Anonymous, "Le Garvéyism en action," 576.
68. Ibid.
69. Ibid.; Jeanne Maquet-Tombu, *Le Siècle marche ... Vie du Chef congolais Lutunu* (Brussels: Office de Publicité, n.d.), 142; Buell, *The Native Problem*, 603.
70. Irvine, "The Birth of the Kimbanguist Movement," 1.
71. Maquet-Tombu, *Le Siècle marche*, 199; Feci, "Vie cachée," 27.
72. For a study of these resemblances, read Efraim Andersson, *Messianic Popular Movements in the Lower Congo* (Uppsala: Studia Ethnographica Upsalensia, XIV, 1958), 255.
73. "Le mouvement pan-nègre," *Congo* I, 5 (1921), 774.
74. Andersson, *Messianic Popular Movements*, 255.
75. MacGaffey, "Kongo and the King of the Americans," 176.
76. Ibid.
77. Andersson, *Messianic Popular Movements*, 255.
78. Van Wing, "Le Kibangisme," 600; Jewsiewicki, "La contestation," 57.
79. MacGaffey, "Kongo and the King of the Americans," 177, fn. 3.
80. Ibid., 179.
81. Irvine, "The Birth of the Kimbanguist Movement," 40–41. This contradicts Efraim Andersson's assertion in *Messianic Popular Movements* that the antiwhite element in Kimbanguism appeared late, 254.
82. Andersson, *Messianic Popular Movements*, 255.

83. Anonymous, "Panda exagère," *L'Avenir Colonial Belge* 30 (January 1921):9.
84. Ibid.
85. Anonymous, "Le panafricanisme," *Congo* I, 1 (January 1921):274.
86. Anonymous, "Comment et par qui Panda Farnana est renseigné," *L'Avenir Colonial Belge* 12 (20 March 1921), 1, 5.
87. Kimpianga Mahaniah II, "The Background of Prophetic Movements in the Belgian Congo" (Unpublished Ph.D. thesis, Temple University, Philadelphia, 1975), 244.
88. Anonymous, "Comment et par qui Panda Farnana est renseigné. Un curieux correspondant," *L'Avenir Colonial Belge* 15 (27 March 1921), 1; Ibid., 12 (20 March 1921), 5.
89. Ibid., 1.
90. See *L'Avenir Colonial Belge*, 17 July 1921; and *Le Progrès Colonial*, 21 July 1921.
91. Anonymous, "Politique indigène," *Le Progrès Colonial* 4 (August 1921):6.
92. M. De Mey, "M'Fumu Panda nous écrit ... ," *L'Avenir Colonial Belge* (11 September 1921):3.
93. Ibid., 3, 5.
94. Arthur Bronz, "Panda Farnana nous poursuit. Le M'Fu ... Mu réclame 10.000 francs a 'L'Avenir Colonial Belge,'" *L'Avenir Colonial Belge* 46 (13 November 1921):1.
95. Anonymous, "Les menées de l'indésirable Panda Farnana en Belgique," *L'Avenir Colonial Belge* (7 August 1921):5.
96. Général Wangermée, "La révolte de Kinshasa," *Notre Colonie* 11 (August 1921):160, 162.
97. Anonymous, "Son Excellence Marcus Garvey," *Le Progrès Colonial* 31 (18 August 1921):9.

17
African Slaves
in the Mediterranean World:
A Neglected Aspect
of the African Diaspora*

J. O. Hunwick

THE enormous interest the African diaspora in the Americas has generated has obscured an equally significant forced migration of Africans from their homelands to alien societies—that vast exodus of enslaved human beings to the lands of the Mediterranean, the Middle East, and South Asia that took place after the establishment of an Islamic world empire in the seventh and eighth centuries of the Christian era. Beginning some eight centuries before the transatlantic slave trade, and not ending until several decades after the latter was halted, the movement of slaves across the Sahara, up the Nile valley and the Red Sea, and across the Indian Ocean to the Persian Gulf and India, probably accounted for the uprooting of as many Africans from their societies as did the transatlantic trade.[1]

Yet, to date, this phenomenon has stimulated little interest among either historians of Africa, historians of the Islamic world or those concerned more broadly with diaspora studies. Joseph Harris's study of the role of African slaves in India remains the only monograph to deal with the problem from the perspective of a receiving society,[2] while the Mediterranean and Near Eastern dimensions of the problem have been relegated to a handful of articles and papers, most of which deal with the trade in slaves rather than the more interesting (and in many ways

*Reprinted, with changes, from *The Human Commodity: Perspectives on the Trans-Saharan Slave Trade* (London: Frank Cass & Co., 1992) by permission of the author and publisher.

more pertinent) question of the fate of these slaves in the societies that received them.[3]

The aim of this essay is, therefore, to introduce scholars of the diaspora to a hitherto neglected aspect of the global phenomenon in the hope that this will stimulate interest and further research into the many problems it poses. Any such general account is bound to be superficial, covering as it does such a large area and such a long time span. Nor can it be anything else until a great deal of fundamental research has been undertaken on specific aspects of the question, exploring the archival records, the travel accounts and other literary sources and carefully collecting and analyzing oral evidence in the field. Such studies will, inevitably, go beyond a study of the institution of slavery to examine the social role and economic status of freed slaves, their degree of social mobility, their cultural assimilation (or lack of it), questions of color and racial prejudice, and so on, both in historical perspective and in the contemporary world. Some of these matters are referred to in the present essay which will concentrate on the Mediterranean basin and allow itself a generous Braudelian interpretation so as to include both the Saharan lands and the Arabian peninsula.

Moral and Legal Aspects of Slavery in Islam

As in most of the ancient world, slavery was an accepted fact of life in Arabia at the rise of Islam in the early seventh century. The best confirmation of this is to be found in the many references to slaves in the Qur'ān, where they are often referred to by the euphemism "necks" (riqāb, sing. raqaba), or frequently, as a metonymy for concubines, "those whom your right hands possess."[4] Some of these slaves were undoubtedly of African origin—Ethiopians or persons of part Ethiopian descent—for we have references to a few who fought in the Prophet's battles and one of the first Muslims (and the first muezzin in Islam) was the Ethiopian freedman Bilāl.[5]

In pre-Islamic Arabia, contrary to the legal position under Islam, the child of the slave mother and a free father remained a slave. Several such persons achieved fame as poets and, as a group, these poets of African descent were known to the ancient Arab critics as "the crows of the Arabs." All accounts of them include 'Antara b. Shaddād, recognized as a poet of the first rank, and some also include Shanfarā and Ta'abbata Sharran, both classified among the "stallions" (fuḥūl) of poetic art.[6] In the early centuries of Islam there were many poets of part African ancestry,[7] but by the third century of Islam such persons had become rare—no doubt an indication of a decline in the status of the black freedman in the central Islamic world.

The Qur'ān says nothing of the process or reasons for enslavement but assumes the existence of the institution of slavery and enunciates precepts and injunctions aimed at mitigating the condition and encourages manumission. The Arabian patriarchal attitude toward slaves finds its reflection in a verse of the Qur'ān that mentions them in the same breath as parents, kinsmen, and orphans and enjoins the believer to treat all of these categories with kindness (*iḥsān*).[8] The freeing of slaves is an act of piety which God will reward, and funds in the public alms chest may be used to help a slave buy his freedom. Various lesser sins, such as accidental homicide or the breaking of an oath, may be expiated by freeing a slave and masters are enjoined to enter into written contracts with their slaves to allow them to purchase their freedom by installments.[9]

These injunctions were strengthened by sayings of (or attributed to) the Prophet Muḥammad. Whether the following saying is authentic or not matters little, since it sums up the Muslim pious ideal for the master-slave relationship:

> Fear God in the matter of your slaves. Feed them with what you eat and clothe them with what you wear and do not give them work beyond their capacity. Those whom you like, retain, and those whom you dislike, sell. Do not cause pain to God's creation. He caused you to own them and had He so wished he would have caused them to own you.[10]

These praiseworthy precepts no doubt did much to alleviate the condition of slaves in Muslim society, although we can scarcely suppose that these precepts were universally applied. Within private households where master and slave lived in close proximity they probably were to a great extent, especially in the case of the female concubine who had borne her master a child. In larger establishments, palaces, or armies, or where the slave was used as a means of production, these precepts were no doubt generally ignored. The situation of a slave soldier in particular could rapidly lead to his degradation as he lost personal rapport with a patron, leading to the turbulence and violence that often seem to have characterized slave troops.

These remarks, of course, apply equally to white, black, brown, or yellow slaves, for slaves of many different origins from Asia, Europe, and Africa were imported into the Mediterranean basin at various times in the long history of Islam. The laws of Islam as elaborated by the jurists of the first three centuries of Islam took full cognizance of the institution of slavery, without recognizing any distinctions based on color or ethnic origin. The law made distinctions only between slave and free, and between Muslim and non-Muslim. According to the strict letter of the law, a person could be enslaved only if he/she were a non-Muslim whose people had no pact (*'ahd*) with the Muslims and had been taken captive in a *jihād* launched after a rejection of the summons to Islam. The nineteenth-century Moroccan historian al-Nāṣiri, in a vigorous polemic against his fellow countrymen who assumed that merely to be black and come from sub-Saharan Africa was a sufficient reason for enslavement, summarized the position in the course of his argument:

> The basic condition of the human being is freedom. . . . The reason in Holy Law which existed in the time of the Prophet and the pious forefathers for enslaving people—namely being captured in a *jihād* which has the object of making the Word of God supreme and bringing men to His religion—does not exist in these days.[11]

Thus, strange as it may seem in the light of what actually happened in Islamic history, neither the purchase of a slave from non-Muslims, nor seizure by raiding or kidnapping was a lawful method of obtaining a slave. In fact, after the conquests of the first century of Islam, the most common method of obtaining slaves was by purchase through the long tentacles of the Muslim trading network that reached up to the Baltic in the north and down to Mozambique in the south, while in the east it stretched to China and Indonesia, and in the west to the Niger and Senegal rivers. In Africa, slaves were generally obtained by purchase from sub-Saharan rulers who were, at least nominally, Muslims. They, in turn, obtained them by raiding neighboring non-Muslim (and sometimes Muslim) peoples, often organizing such raids specifically to pay for goods they had selected from North African caravans.[12] Nomadic Saharan tribes, especially the Tuareg, engaged in kidnapping.[13]

Once within the Islamic system, a slave remained a slave until released from bondage by his master, as did his children born of a union with another slave. However, if a slave woman married her master (or, in the much less common case, a man his mistress), she had first to be freed, since there is incompatibility between ownership and marital or blood relationship. For the same reason, children born of concubines were free, since a man could not own his own child. The slave mother was automatically enfranchised on her master's death.[14] Becoming a Muslim (as almost all slaves, apart from some Jews and Christians, did) did not of itself bring enfranchisement; had it done so, the system would have collapsed overnight. Freedom could, however, be purchased. Many European Christians enslaved by North African corsairs were ransomed by their co-religionists. Any slave could enter into a

contract of conditional manumission (*mukātaba*) with his master, stipu-
lating that he would be free after the payment of a particular sum. Such
a slave would then be given permission to earn money on his own
account while still serving his master until the stipulated sum had been
saved up.[15] Generally, the last payment was waived in part and the
master would give the freedman a sum of money to enable him to
establish himself independently.[16] Even then, the master-slave bond
was not completely severed. The freedman remained in clientship (*wala'*)
to his former master who could inherit from him if he died without
heirs.[17] Clientship also provided a social context for the freedman,
providing him with an ersatz family, with a family name, and even, in
time, a fictive lineage.

Within the Islamic legal framework, slaves had both rights and
disabilities, and these varied slightly among the four Sunni schools of
law. In legal terms the slave was an item of property, to be bought and
sold and to be compensated for in case of injury or death. Once the
contract of purchase had been signed and sealed, the master had rights
over the physical person of the slave and whatever the slave owned
(unless this were excluded in the contract), including children whom a
female slave had borne or subsequently bore from anyone other than
her master.[18] A master might chastise his slave, but if he did the slave
serious injury he was bound to free him.[19] However, on the principle of
"the slave for the slave and the free for the free"[20] the owner could not
be put to death for killing his slave. Although a master had a right to
sexual relations with his female slave (but not with his wife's slave), he
could not, in accordance with Qur'ānic prohibition, compel her to
prostitution.[21]

Although legally a "thing," the slave's humanity was recognized by
the law. In some cases he was treated like a free man; in others he was
treated like half a free man; and in yet other cases he was excused
obligations or excluded from offices which might devolve on a free man.
Thus, for apostacy the slave, like the free man, was liable to the death
penalty, and likewise his right hand could be amputated if he were
convicted of theft. On the other hand, the slave's penalty for adultery
was only fifty lashes, whereas that of a free man who had never married
was one hundred lashes; the free man who had married (*al-muhsan*) was
to be stoned to death. Except under Mālikī law, a slave could marry
only two wives, instead of the four permitted to a free man, and was not
permitted to take a concubine since he could not own another person.
He was not legally obliged to attend the communal Friday prayer or to
observe the fifth pillar of Islam, the pilgrimage to Mecca. He could,
however, meet both obligations with his master's permission. He did
not have to pay the annual alms tax (*al-zakāt*) since he owned nothing,

and the alms payable at the end of Ramadān (*zakāt al-fiṭr*) was paid for him by his master. He could not be officially appointed to any religious office, though he was not debarred from leading men in prayer on a casual basis.[22]

In the medieval period, at any rate, there was in the towns and cities an official who, as one of his tasks, oversaw many legal and quasi-legal matters relating to slaves. The *muḥtasib* was the overseer of public markets who inspected weights and measures, ensured that commodities were not adulterated or sold short, kept the streets clean and clear of obstructions, and acted also as the guardian of public morals, preventing wine from being openly sold or consumed and men and women from contravening the locally accepted norms of public decency in dress or conduct.[23] He not only kept an eye on the slave dealers and their transactions (more on this follows), but he had to ensure that masters fed and clothed their slaves adequately, did not impose on them tasks beyond their strength, and allowed them a rest in the heat of the afternoon.[24] Admittedly, most of what we know about this office so far is derived from the theoretical literature—manuals of moralization and advice to the *muḥtasib*—but the existence of such manuals shows that Muslim society did set itself standards in such matters. The warnings given by them to the *muḥtasib* about what to be on the look out for also reveal some of the deceptions practiced by slave traders and throw light on the general conditions of slaves. The literature of legal opinions (*fatāwi*) is also useful in this respect and has so far been little exploited for the study of slavery.

The Trading of Slaves

During the period before the mid-nineteenth century in the Muslim world, slaves of many and varied origins poured into the Mediterranean basin and the Near East. Many were purchased by sultans and princes to serve in their armies, to act as bodyguards, and to staff their palaces. Among the rest of the population it was generally only the middle and upper bourgeoisie—government servants, teachers, merchants and the like—who could afford the expense of purchasing a slave. There were, of course, cheap as well as expensive slaves, the black male (unless an Ethiopian, a eunuch or in possession of some outstanding skills) generally being among the cheapest. Thus, in certain times and places when supply was abundant and prices consequently lower than normal, artisans, tradesmen, and even peasants might be able to afford such a purchase. Although the majority of the population in the areas under consideration was Muslim, slave owning was not confined to them.

Jews and Christians, though legally second-class citizens in the lands of Islam, were permitted to own domestic slaves,[25] although they could not own slaves who had converted to Islam. It was also possible in Islamic law to own a slave jointly with one or more other persons. Joint ownership most frequently came about through the precise require-ments of Islamic inheritance law, although there was nothing to stop two individuals sharing in the price of a slave, if neither alone could afford the slave, and then apportioning his labor. In the case of a female slave, neither owner would have rights of concubinage.

In the first century of Islam, slaves were acquired by the Arabs during the period of the great Islamic conquests that expanded the borders of the Dār al-Islām—the abode of Islam—westward as far as the River Douro in northern Spain, eastward to the Indus valley, and northward to the River Oxus. The conquered people, however, soon began to adopt Islam en masse, and it became necessary to look farther afield for sources of slaves. The jurists, basing their views on the reality of the situation, declared that what lay beyond the Dār al-Islām was Dār al-Ḥarb—the abode of war—of which the Muslims should attempt to gain control by agreement or by force and incorporate in the Dār al-Islām. Although the Qur'ān and the Traditions of the Prophet give no support and the jurists are silent on the issue, it became commonly accepted that because the peoples of the Dār al-Ḥarb were non-Muslims and hence liable to be attacked in a *jihād*, they were also all potential slaves.[26] Hence, any of them the Muslims could lay hands on, whether by actual *jihād* (probably the least common method), by raiding on sea or land, or by purchase, could be taken as slaves.

The Muslims of the Mediterranean basin obtained slaves from all three continents of the Old World.[27] One source was from Europe, notably the populations of central and northern Europe and the west of what was the Soviet Union. These were the so-called Slavs (*saqāliba*), obtained largely through the agency of Jewish and Christian merchants and purchased by Muslims at certain northern Mediterranean seaports and through the ports of the Black Sea. This source dried up by the twelfth century as Europe began to emerge from its Dark Ages, but piratical activity by North African corsairs along the northern shores of the Mediterranean and the Atlantic coasts of Europe continued to the end of the eighteenth century. A second important source of slaves was Central Asia, the home of diverse nomadic tribes speaking Turkic languages. These warrior slaves were in great demand from the middle of the ninth century, when the caliphs of Baghdad first began recruiting forces of Turkish guards to form a buffer between themselves and their regular Arab and Persian troops. Later, the great Mamlūk dynasty of Egypt (1250–1517) was to derive its sultans and all its senior officers of state from, at first, Central Asian slaves (Turkic and Mongol tribes) and later from Circassian slaves from the Caucasus. Indeed, their very name —Mamlūk—means "possessed" in Arabic.

The third great human reservoir, and the one that mainly concerns us in this paper, was sub-Saharan Africa, which was one of the first to be drawn on and the last to dry up. The Nile Valley and the Red Sea provided relatively easy channels of communication between the Mediterranean region and certain areas of the continent. The conquest of Egypt soon brought the Arabs into direct contact with Africans in the Nubian kingdoms that bordered Upper Egypt. An agreement was soon made with the Nubians that in exchange for the annual tribute of 360 slaves the Muslims would leave the Christian Nubians in peace.[28] The name given to this agreement, the baqt, appears to be an arabicization of the Greek pakton (or Latin pactum); thus the Arabs would merely have become heirs to an arrangement that had been in existence for a long time. Up the Red Sea came slaves from Ethiopia, the Horn of Africa, and the East African coast; slaves from these regions were also taken to ports of the Persian Gulf, and some were reexported from there to India.[29] From newly established towns in North Africa, Arab and Berber merchants soon discovered routes leading across the Sahara to the polities of the Sahelian belt. The primary lure there was gold from the western Sudanic regions, but from a very early period slaves also formed a significant item in the trade, especially along the central Sudanic route via the Fazzān to Kanem, just to the north of Lake Chad, for this region produced no gold. The slaves were provided by local rulers. At first, only non-Muslims were engaged in the slave trade, but from the eleventh century onward, Muslims increasingly exchanged slaves they had taken in raids and wars for a wide variety of Mediterranean goods.[30] Barbary horses were among the more valuable commodities imported into the Sahel. They were typically bartered for slaves in the ratio of ten to fifteen slaves (depending on age and sex) for one horse.[31] The trans-Saharan slave trade diminished in the nineteenth century as the North African states, one by one (beginning with the French in Algeria after 1830), abolished first the trade in and then the ownership of slaves, though slaves were still clandestinely brought across Benghazi via the Tibesti and Kufra as late as 1910.[32] Among the Tuareg in central Sahara a form of slavery existed until at least the 1950s.[33]

When the slave-dealer (commonly known as a jallāb, "importer"—or nakhkhās—"goader/cattle dealer") brought his human merchandise to a commercial center within the Dār al-Islām, he handed them over to a broker (dallāl) who either put them up for sale in a public slave market or, if they were more highly prized, arranged for their sale privately. The brokers were also responsible for slave resales, for during this period of captivity a slave might be sold many times over. The *muḥtasib* had to keep a close eye on brokers and ensure that certain stipulations were observed.[34] Among these were that the broker know to whom a slave was being sold and record the slave's name and description (important in case the slave turned out to be a free man or stolen property); the broker also had to find out any conditions imposed at first sale and ensure that no Muslim slave was sold to a non-Muslim. A male slave might be inspected above the navel and below the knees; the purchaser of a female slave might see only her hands and her face (in fact, African slaves were often much more scantily clad), but if women were present and the buyer took the slave girl to his house with them, he might see her entire body in their presence. A woman who had children under the age of seven could not be separated from them. The purchaser was allowed a period of three days' trial with his new slave before the deal was ratified. If he found defects in a slave that were not apparent at the time of sale, he could return the merchandise. Not surprisingly, brokers had a considerable stock of artifices for making their female slaves look more attractive. A twelfth-century Spanish manual for the *muḥtasib* describes the cosmetic treatment given to black girls:

> They anoint their faces, their arms and legs with oil of violets and perfume to improve their appearance. They blacken their hair with oil of myrtle, oil of fresh walnut and poppy oil and wash it with a decoction of myrobalan. They make the hair curl tightly with [extract of] lotus, myrtle and azerderac. They remove body odour by making a paste of white lead and rose-water which they make into tablets and store inside a rose until it dries out.[35]

The same author also warns against the wiles of slave brokers who take advantage of the trial period allowed by law to hire out slave girls clandestinely for prostitution.

By the time the African slave reached the slave market in North Africa or the Middle East, he or she was already a nominal Muslim. The slave-dealers themselves ensured this by having male slaves circumcised when necessary and giving both male and female slaves Arabic names. These names were often peculiar to slaves and tended to have meanings that were redolent of happiness, good fortune, and favor from God: for males, Khayr Allāh (goodness of God), Jār Allāh ("neighbor" of God), Kāfār (camphor), 'Anbar (ambergris), Murjān (gem); for females, Umm al-khayr (mother of goodness), Bakhīta (fortunate), Mabrūka (blessed), Maḥbūba (beloved), Sa'īda (happy), Za'farān (saffron), etc. Under more pious masters favorite slaves were taught to pray and read the Qur'ān; on the other hand, some (perhaps many) retained their original religious and cosmological beliefs and gave an Islamic veneer (sometimes very thin) to ceremonies that derived from their African past.[36]

Most large towns in the Islamic Mediterranean world had a special hall or courtyard within their market area devoted to the sale of slaves.[37] The Dutch scholar C. Snouck Hurgronje, who spent the year 1884–85 in Mecca, describes the slave market there:

> All kinds of African slaves were obtainable in large quantities through the brokers. The slaves of both sexes exposed in the slave market (a large hall near the mosque gate called Bab Derebeyah) are partly fresh arrivals and partly offered for sale by masters who no longer need them. On the benches near the wall sit girls and women, the adults lightly veiled: before them sit or stand on the ground male slaves of riper years; in the middle play dozens of children. Some slave-brokers converse on their living merchandise. One of the spectators is giving special attention to a small black boy. The broker charged with the sale of this boy calls him up and shows his teeth and tongue and meanwhile praises his style and skill. If the customer is a sensible man he now addresses the slave himself, for no slave deceives a person who might ever become his master about his own merits. ... The broker does not delay to show the part of the boy's body where he has small-pox marks (the surest innoculation against recurrence).... If the customer is still doubtful he goes to a doctor who examines slaves for money. If he is very pious he has recourse to what is called *istikhāra*, that is he leaves the choice to God by performing certain religious ceremonies and then going to sleep and letting the decision depend on his dreams, or if he is superstitious, he goes to a divinely illuminated sheikh or to a sand-diviner. Before the deal is closed, the customer asks the slave: "Are you willing to serve me?" ... [for] no one would buy a male slave against his will, and still less a female slave against her will.[38]

Because the sale of a slave was a binding contract in law, the purchaser had to take great care that he was not duped. As the preceding passage points out, there were special doctors who examined slaves to spot physical defects or tell-tale signs of debilitating diseases. Some of them wrote treatises on the examination process (*al-taqlib*), while the tenth-century Christian physician of Baghdad, Ibn Butlān, in his treatise also included sections giving the current wisdom on the qualities and dispositions of slaves of various ethnic origins as well as a warning against the wiles of the brokers.[39]

As mentioned previously, the purchaser had (as with other merchandise) a period of three days in which to uncover hidden defects. In the case of a woman destined to be a concubine, the law demanded that she undergo a period of waiting to determine if she were pregnant (*istibrā'*).[40]

She was to be kept in the household of a trustworthy third party until she menstruated, unless she were sold while actually menstruating, but this precaution was usually ignored.

Slave Occupations in the Islamic Mediterranean World

Al-Saqaṭi, whose manual for the *muḥtasib* has already been alluded to, summed up the principal occupations for male slaves as follows:

In regard to males, Indians and Nubians are suitable for looking after property and persons, Zanj and Armenians are good for heavy labor and service which is rewarded, while Turk and Slavs are suitable for war and acts of bravery.[41]

His categories—domestic and commercial service, unskilled labor (both agricultural and industrial), and soldiering—do, in fact, represent the three major types of occupation to which male slaves were put in the Mediterranean world. Contrary to his ethnic typecasting, however, we find that African slaves served in all three of his categories. Although any statistical basis for such an assertion is lacking, it is probably safe to say that over the eleven or twelve centuries of the African slave experience in the Islamic Mediterranean, most of such slaves were used in the domestic and commercial spheres and fewer were used in the industrial and agricultural spheres. Military service absorbed large numbers only in specific times and places.

Female slaves were reserved for domestic tasks: cooking, cleaning, washing, waiting on the ladies of the house, acting as nursemaids or wet-nurses for their children and, if they were the property of one of the males of the household, sharing the bed of their master as and when he desired. There was a generally recognized "pecking order" for female slaves and a stereotyping of their qualities and abilities.[42] In nineteenth-century Egypt (and other times and places roughly reflect its preferences) white females were at the top of the hierarchy and often married their masters or their masters' sons. Next came the Ethiopian women (*habashiyyāt*—usually Oromo [Galla][43]) who were too proud to serve white women and were usually concubines of middle-class males and did only minor household chores. At the bottom of the list were the African women other than Ethiopians who did heavier household chores and were concubines of lower middle-class males. They were reckoned to be too proud to serve Ethiopians, but were willing to serve white women.[44]

The situation in nineteenth-century Mecca was evidently somewhat similar. According to Snouck Hurgronje, non-Ethiopian African women (presumably mainly East Africans and southern and western Sudanese) were considered the strongest of African women and were used for housework in the kitchen or the living rooms, though sometimes also as concubines. Ethiopian women, who were generally considered to have more delicate constitutions, were reserved mainly for concubinage and were highly prized by Meccan males. The same observer goes on:

> If the ordinary Mekkan followed his inclination [rather than his social obligations], he would unite himself only to Abyssinians. ... The aim of the Abyssinian woman is a lasting connection with a Mekkan to whom she, if her good intellectual and moral gifts have not been spoilt by her upbringing, becomes a true life companion. ... The well brought up Abyssinian women are excellent housekeepers, modest, unpretending women, and they put all their good qualities at the service of their lord. The high esteem in which they are held by Mekkan men is most clearly shown in the many cases in which an Abyssinian woman has borne him from five to twelve children, and the children are the best pledge of the continuance of their parents' happiness. As mother of one or more Mekkans she belongs to Mekkan society as a virtually free member, though nominally her slavery continues.[45]

Lane paints a rather similar picture of domestic bliss involving Ethiopian women and Egyptian males in the earlier years of the nineteenth century and points out that the situation of a concubine who has borne her master children was, indeed, more secure than that of a free wife, for the latter could be divorced unilaterally, whereas the slave mother could not be sold or given away and was free on her master's death.[46] Concubinage thus provided a means of integration into society for both the woman and her children, lineage rather than skin color being the principal determinant of social status.

Concubinage and a settled domestic life were, however, not necessarily the lot of all female slaves. Those who were taken into the harems of large households, even if they were maintained in a state of physical well-being, were, with the exception of passing favorites, treated merely as objects of physical pleasure who might see their master but rarely and could have had little feeling of attachment. Those who did not produce at least one child were liable to be sold, while those whose attractions had diminished through childbearing would find themselves no longer in their master's favor unless they had unusual intellectual or musical talents. In the big harems of Turkish officials, all concubines except the favorites of the hour were subject to the tyranny of their keepers, the black eunuchs, who compensated for their robbed masculinity by bullying and cajoling the females under their command.[47]

Nor, of course, were all female slaves taken as concubines. Some were not considered attractive enough for the role and were destined to a lifetime of household drudgery. Even this was not the worst that could happen to a female slave. Although there is no clear indication of how common it was for such women to be prostituted, the fact that writers on *ḥisba* warn the *muḥtasib* to be on the watch for it, indicates that it cannot have been uncommon. At the hands of a slave dealer, prostitution was but a passing, though inevitable degrading, experience. Among the Ibāḍis of Jabal Nafūsa in Libya in the twelfth century, however, it seems to have been a regular practice,[48] while in Egypt in the nineteenth century the *ghawāzī*—popular singers, dancers and prostitutes—sometimes kept their own African female slaves, the profits of whose prostitution they took for themselves.[49] Reports from the Sudan in the same century also indicate that slave prostitution was not uncommon.[50]

As indicated previously, male slaves were also used for domestic tasks and to assist their master in his commercial dealings or other means of livelihood. In a society where there was normally a rigid partitioning between those areas of the house where the females lived and worked and those that might be used only by the male members of the household and their guests, it was necessary to have males (either slaves or servants—the latter more rare) to look after the public and private rooms, to prepare the master's pipe and coffee, and to attend to the needs of master and guests for refreshments. Slaves also had the task of attending to horses or donkeys and, in the richer households of nineteenth-century Egypt, to carriages. They normally accompanied their master when he rode out, clearing the way for him in the narrow, crowded streets, defending him against aggressors or thieves, and taking charge of his mount at his destination. They were also sent out independently to carry messages, to make purchases in the market, and to fetch goods needed for the master's business. In the households of rulers or other eminent persons (*a'yān*) there might be scores of male slaves, including a number of eunuchs, whose tasks were highly specialized and whose positions were fixed according to a strict hierarchy.

Some interesting glimpses of the condition of the African slave in medieval Egyptian society are afforded us by the scattered entries in the great biographical dictionary of the fifteenth century compiled by al-Sakhāwī.[51] The period he was writing of was, of course, one dominated by men of slave origin, though the reigning Mamlūks were of white, Circassian origin. Nevertheless, it is likely that, in general, a slave origin might have been an advantage rather than a disadvantage. The main rungs of the ruling estate were filled by Circassian Mamlūks as were most subordinate positions in the households of the sultan and the emirs. Some of the latter positions (as well as positions in the households of great Egyptian merchants) were filled by African slaves, mainly Ethiopians, about one third of whom were eunuchs. Many of these rose quite rapidly to positions of responsibility within the sultan's household or in the households of related families; but often just as rapidly they were dismissed or banished on their master's whim, or because he suspected them of embezzlement or other malfeasance. One such Ethiopian became a customs collector for the port of Jeddah, another (a eunuch) was made governor of Aden, and a third (also a eunuch) was sent on a mission to his home country, though he was subsequently removed from office as commander of the Sultan's Mamlūks (*muqaddam al-mamālik*) and banished.[52] More fortunate Ethiopians retained enough of the wealth they gained through office to retire comfortably, to pursue the Islamic sciences, and to build mosque colleges (*madrasa*). Those belonging to merchants were often allowed to trade and travel in their own right. One, who was freed by his master, combined commercial acumen with piety and learning and on his former master's death married his widow.[53]

Another major use to which male black slaves were put was military service. On the one hand they were used in the militia or bodyguards of petty rulers, and on the other hand they often formed a distinct corps in the professional armies of North Africa and Egypt. Slave soldiers were a common phenomenon in the Islamic world, at least during the sixteenth century when the Ottomans established themselves in the Levant, Egypt, and much of North Africa. In the eastern provinces of the Islamic empire these were mainly Turks recruited from the nomadic peoples of Central Asia. In Egypt, too, Turkish troops were commonly used from the late ninth century until the mid-fourteenth century, when they finally ceded to Circassians, while free "Turks" (often, in fact, Greeks, Bosnians, Albanians or other south-east European peoples) made up the military during the Ottoman period (1517–1798). Black slave troops were first introduced into Egypt during the period of the Turkish governor, Aḥmad b. Ṭūlūn (868–84) and a special quarter was built for them in the barrack town established for foreign troops. In the following century, the Ikhshīdids, successors to the Ṭūlūnids, also employed black troops, while under their successors, the Fāṭimids (969–1171), large battalions of black troops were raised to counterbalance the powerful Berber and Turkish contingents. There were many violent clashes between these three great military divisions, and on several occasions the Turks and Berbers united against the Africans. In the final and greatest clash, which took place in 1169, an estimated fifty thousand black troops fought valiantly against their hostile colleagues in arms before being defeated and driven out of Cairo to seek refuge in southern Egypt. The Fāṭimids' successors, the Ayyūbids, did not revive the tradition of using black troops and, indeed, it was not until the early nineteenth century under Muḥammad 'Alī that they were used again.[54]

In North Africa and Andalusia both African and European slave troops were used, the Africans being called by the generic name *sūdān* ("blacks") and the Europeans by the generic name *ṣaqāliba* ("Slavs"), with use of the latter dying out by the twelfth century. Black troops were first used under the Aghlabid dynasty of Ifrīqiya (roughly modern Tunisia) in the ninth century, possibly from very early in their reign, though this has been disputed.[55] The need here, as with Turks in Baghdad and blacks in Egypt at a similar period, was to counteract the potentially rebellious tendencies of local troops by creating a corps that had no local attachments and was made up of men who owed their very existence to the ruler and hence whose loyalty could be counted on. The Aghlabids' successors, the Fāṭimids, first slaughtered the blacks who had served the Aghlabids and then raised another corps of blacks who would have no loyalty but to them. When the Fāṭimids removed the seat of their dynasty to Cairo in 969, their lieutenants in Ifrīqiya, the Zīrids, continued to use black slave troops and, on occasion, we find these troops becoming involved in dynastic struggles.[56] After the Hilālian migration in the mid-eleventh century black troops appear to have been little used; the Hilālī Arabs quickly took over their role, hiring their services to any party that offered them the opportunity for enrichment.

In the "farther Maghrib" (*al-maghrib al-aqṣā*—roughly modern Morocco), black troops are not in evidence until the reign of the Almoravid ruler Yūsuf b. Tāshfīn (1061–1106) who established a bodyguard of some two thousand, as well as a corps of European slave troops recruited in Spain.[57] The Almoravids' successors, the Almohads, also made use of black troops to a limited extent.[58] The most intensive use of black troops— indeed, the supreme example of the use of such troops in the Mediterranean world—came in the reign of the second 'Alawid sultan, Mūlāy Ismā'īl (1672–1727), himself the son of a black concubine.[59] Early in his reign he decided to create an exclusively black slave army that would constitute the instrument of his very personal rule. A small black slave corps had been formed some eighty years earlier from slaves brought back from Timbuktu following the conquest of the Middle Niger by troops of the Sa'dian sultan al-Manṣūr in 1591.[60] Early in his reign Mūlāy Ismā'īl ordered the seizure of all male blacks in his kingdom, whether slave or free, including "naturalized" blacks known as *ḥarāṭīn* who lived in regions bordering the Sahara and occupied a serflike position vis à vis the Arab and Berber tribes.[61] The blacks thus rounded up were subsequently augmented by expeditions into the Sahara and, no doubt, by the direct conduit of the trans-Saharan slave trade.

Tsma'il also looked to the natural process of reproduction to maintain his army and to provide his household with the services it required. He set up a training and reproductive program tailored to his precise needs. In some ways this resembled the Mamlūk system in Egypt in the period 1250–1517, as may be seen from this account by al-Nāṣirī:

> In the year 1100/1689 the sultan ordered those slaves to bring him all their sons and daughters over the age of ten. When they were brought he divided up the girls among the matrons ('arīfāt) of his household—one group per palace—to be educated and taught good manners. He divided the boys up among the builders and carpenters and other craftsmen to serve them and work with them and sent others to drive donkeys and to learn how to ride them. A year later they were transferred to driving mules which carried bricks, tiles, wood, etc., and after a further year they were transferred to the service of the central palace to make prefabricated blocks. The following year they were transferred to the first rank among the soldiery and were given uniforms and trained in the martial arts. After a further year they were given horses which they had to ride bareback and bring out to the arena to learn how to handle them. In the last year of their training, when they had mastered their mounts, they were given saddles to ride on and were taught how to charge and withdraw, how to be skilful in thrusting with lances and how to hurl javelins from on horseback. After this they were enrolled in the army of active service. Then he brought forth the girls who had come with them earlier and married one to each of them, giving each man ten *mithqāl-s* [of gold] as dowry for his bride and each girl five *mithqāl-s* for her trousseau. One of their older male relatives would be given charge of them and he would be given sufficient funds to build a house for him and huts for his companions. Then he would send them off to join the army after their names had been recorded in the army register.[62]

Ismā'il thus created a self-perpetuating black slave army which may have numbered as many as one hundred and fifty thousand men at its height.[63] Following his death they became king makers during the next thirty years, enthroning and deposing during the period no less than seven of Ismā'il's estimated five hundred sons. When, finally, in 1737 a stronger ruler, Mūlāy Muḥammad III, came to the throne, he recruited an Arab army and dispersed the black regiments, some of whom were then enslaved by the Arab soldiers. A small number of those who remained in Morocco were reintegrated into the 'Alawid army at the end of the eighteenth century, while as late as the 1880s a 5,000-strong army of black slaves served the ruler of the small independent principality of Īligh in southern Morocco.[64]

males ③   The third category of employment for black male slaves, and the one which is encountered least in the sources, is agricultural and industrial labor. It is difficult to say just how widespread the use of slave labor in these sectors of production was, since our sources, both Arab and European concern themselves chiefly with urban rather than rural conditions. One thing seems clear, however; plantation-style slavery, such as was the norm in the New World, was not common in the Mediterranean world. When the Arabs conquered the Near East and North Africa in the seventh century, they were not pushing into vast tracts of virgin land. They were taking control either of lands unsuitable for cultivation—such as deserts and mountains—or of agricultural lands of relatively limited extent that had been cultivated by indigenous populations for centuries. As nomads, the Arabs had little interest in settling on the land (and were, indeed, banned from so doing by the Caliph 'Umar) and adopted the more realistic policy of leaving the land in the hands of its owners and taxing them on its produce. Landowning was generally on a peasant smallholding basis (even estates—*iqtā'āt*— were conglomerations of smallholdings rather than united agricultural terrains) and there were few areas where crops suitable to large-scale production (for example, cotton, rice, sugar, dates) could be grown. It is, however, precisely in those areas where such nonperishable (and hence "exportable") produce could be grown that we do find evidence of plantation slavery. Sugar, for example, was being produced with the help of slave labor in the Ahwāz province of western Persia in the late ninth century.[65] Slaves from this area joined in the great Zanj revolt when slaves of East African origin who were clearing marshlands for cultivation in southern Iraq defied the forces of the 'Abbāsid caliphate for a full fifteen years from 868 to 883.[66] In the tenth century we also hear of large numbers of slaves being employed in the date groves of al-Ahsā' in the northeast Arabian peninsula near Bahrain,[67] and in Saharan oases where date growing forms an important source of revenue, slaves were commonly used, both in date production and for cultivating grain and vegetables. In nineteenth-century Egypt, when there was a high world demand for cotton and the supply of slaves from the Sudan was abundant, slave labor was used for a period to boost production.[68] Saharan nomads, "Moors" in the west, and Tuareg in the central Sahara, have traditionally made use of black slave labor for herding flocks, hewing wood, drawing water, and as a general work force in their encampments. Slave labor was also used in working the salt pans of Taghāza and later Taodeni in the western Sahara[69] (modern Mali), in the extraction and smelting of copper at Tegidda (modern Niger)[70] and in exploitation of the gold mines of Wadi 'Allāqi in Egyptian Nubia until the mines became exhausted in the fourteenth century.[71]

There remains one aspect of slavery in the Mediterranean Muslim world that has only so far been referred to in passing and to which, despite its distasteful nature, fuller reference must now be made: the eunuch (*tawāshī*, or, euphemistically, *khādim*—"servant," *fatā*—"young man," *aghā*—"chief," or *ustādh*—"teacher").[72] Although the maintenance of large harems by Muslim potentates undoubtedly encouraged castration of male slaves, it had not been unknown in earlier cultures. It was practiced in ancient Persia and medieval China, for example. The practice seems to have been unknown, however, in ancient Arabia and does not appear in the Islamic Mediterranean until well into the second century of Islam. Early Muslims seem to have revolted against this practice and other abuses of slaves, for a saying was put into the mouth of the Prophet: "Whoever kills a slave, him will we kill. Whoever cuts off the nose of a slave, his nose will we cut off; and whoever castrates a slave, him also shall we castrate."[73] In fact, although Muslims were quite prepared to make use of eunuchs and to pay very high prices to obtain them, Muslims of the Mediterranean lands at any rate were generally scrupulous about observing the prohibition on mutilation themselves.[74] Thus European slaves destined for sale as eunuchs in the Muslim lands of the Mediterranean in the Middle Ages were operated on at Prague or Verdun;[75] those coming from central Asia were operated on in Khārazm close to the Caspian Sea; and those from southern Russia were operated on in Armenia.[76] In Africa, eunuchs were produced in several different locations. For a long time Ethiopia was a provider of eunuchs;[77] all eunuchs mentioned by al-Sakhāwī in his biographical dictionary of fifteenth century Egypt bear the *nisba al-Ḥabashī*, though this term probably referred to a wider geographical area than present-day Ethiopia. Eunuchs were also produced, at least from the seventeenth century onwards, in Baghirmi, a nominally Muslim state to the southeast of Lake Chad.[78] From there they were sent across the Sahara to the Libyan coast or to Egypt, many crossing the Mediterranean to join service in the Ottoman sultan's harem; others were sent with pilgrim caravans to serve in the mosque of the Ka'ba in Mecca or in the Prophet's mosque in Medina. Some eunuchs may also have reached the Mediterranean world from distant Nupe, since this kingdom is said to have begun sending eunuchs to Kano in the fifteenth century.[79] Morocco, too, must have had a source of its own, since Mūlāy Ismā'īl is said to have owned upward of two thousand eunuchs; though whether their source was in West Africa or somewhere in Morocco cannot be definitely ascertained.[80] There was also in the early nineteenth century (and no doubt before this) an operating center in Egypt itself, though it was run by Christians, not by Muslims. At the monastery of Deir al-Jandala near Abu Tig in Upper Egypt, some two to three hundred eunuchs were produced annually by monks who, despite their alleged skills, could not, apparently, prevent two out of every three operated on from dying.[81] As previously observed, it was service in the harems of rulers and rich notables that created the demand for eunuchs. Once in such a position, the eunuch could acquire considerable power, since he alone knew the intimate secrets of the household. The great harem of the Ottoman sultan in Istanbul was policed entirely by black eunuchs from the beginning of the seventeenth century. The status and power of the chief eunuch (the *Kislar Agha*) has been described by Penzer in his classic account of the harem:

> He became commander of the corps of *baltaji* or halberdiers, held the rank of Pasha with three tails, was confidential messenger between the Sultan and the Grand Vizier, was alone entitled to have both eunuchs and girls as slaves, was allotted as many as three hundred horses for his personal use, could alone approach the Sultan at all times of day and night, and was described as "the most illustrious of the officers who approach his August Person, and worthy of the confidence of monarchs and of sovereigns," was the most feared, and consequently the most bribed, official of the Ottoman Empire.[82]

Not only did eunuchs acquire power by virtue of the positions they held, but rulers often deliberately chose them for confidential positions that involved stewardship of money or property because the eunuch had no family whose loyalty might challenge his loyalty to his master, and no sons to whom he might think of bequeathing wealth or whose interests at court he might seek to promote. This did not necessarily stop eunuchs from acquiring wealth by fair means and foul, for in the absence of virility the most tangible evidence they could provide of their self-worth was the rich clothes they wore, the fine horses they rode, the elegant dwellings they lived in, or the mosque colleges they endowed.[83]

It might be thought that their mutilated physical state (which revealed itself publicly through lack of secondary sexual characteristics and other physical peculiarities) would have made them objects of general derision, but this does not seem to have been the case. On the contrary, perhaps because they belonged to the most powerful households and always appeared in public richly dressed and finely mounted, they were held in awe by the common man. Perhaps, too, their rare and anomalous status enshrouded them in an air of mystery. The Swiss traveller Burckhardt, who visited Medina in 1829, described the function and status of the black eunuchs there, the leader of whom (*shaykh al-ḥaram*) was a former Kislar Agha:

The police of the mosque [of the Prophet], the office of washing the Hedjra [an inner covered court] and the whole of the building, of lighting the lamps, etc., etc., is entrusted to the care of forty or fifty eunuchs, who have an establishment similar to that of the eunuchs of the Beitulla [the Ka'ba] at Mekka; but they are persons of greater consequence here; they are more richly dressed, though in the same costume; usually wear fine Cashmere shawls, and gowns of the best Indian silk stuffs, and assume airs of great importance. When they pass through the Bazar, everybody hastens to kiss their hands; and they exercise considerable influence in the internal affairs of the town. They have large stipends, which are annually sent from Constantinople by the Syrian Hadj caravan; they also share in all donations made to the mosque, and they expect presents from every rich hadjy, besides what they take as fees from visitors to the Hedjra. They live together in one of the best quarters of Medina, to the eastward of the mosque, and their houses are said to be furnished in a more costly manner than any others in the town. The adults are all married to black or Abyssinian slaves. ... The eunuch of the mosque would be highly affronted if he were so termed by any person. Their usual title is Aga. Their chief takes the title of Highness, or Sadetkon [sa'ādatkum], like a Pasha or the Sherif of Mecca.[84]

It is a curious irony that while the female slave's best chance of a life of ease and respect was through the exploitation of her female sexuality as a concubine and ultimately as a mother, the male slave's surest road to prosperity and power lay in having his own sexuality sacrificed through a transformation whose physical and emotional pain can better be imagined than described.

Manumission and the Lot of the Freed Slave

As already observed, Islamic ethics encouraged the manumission of slaves, while Islamic law provided the juristic framework within which the injunctions of the Qur'ān and Hadith could find practical expression. There were several ways in which a slave might obtain his freedom. First, the master might free his slave as an act of piety at any time, and masters did evidently celebrate important family events, such as marriages and deaths by acts of manumission.[85] According to Morell, writing of Algeria in the 1850s, "scrupulous Musselmans think themselves bound to offer liberty after nine years' good service, because it is thought that after that time they have paid their value in labour."[86] Manumission at the expiry of a given term, or on repayment of the slave's value, was also common. The slave could enter into a written contract with his master (kitāba) to buy his freedom in installments, and after this had been agreed on he could not be disposed of. He was generally then granted the status of a ma'dhūn—one "granted permission" to conduct business on his own behalf. Slaves also commonly obtained their freedom on their master's death, either by the master writing this condition into his will (as part of the one-third of his estate not subject to formal division) or, in the case of a concubine who had borne him a child (the so-called *umm walad*), by the automatic process of enfranchisement that such a status guaranteed her on her master's death. The *umm walad* and the slave who had been promised freedom on his master's death (*al-mudabbar*) could not be disposed of thereafter, since they were already conditionally free.[87] When a master freed a slave during his lifetime he was under an unwritten obligation to see that the freedman was able to establish himself independently. In nineteenth-century Egypt, a freed slave was given a sum of money equivalent to about half of his replacement value to set himself up in a craft or trade.[88] A female slave would not be freed unless she could be found a marriage partner, in which case the master acted as her marriage guardian (*wali*).

Although manumission meant that the former slave henceforth enjoyed all the rights and privileges of a free-born person (as well, of course, as his liabilities and responsibilities), he nevertheless remained in thrall to his former status through the institution of clientship (*walā'*).[89] This was a two-edged weapon. On the one hand, he enjoyed a link with the family that had roots in the society and a social position within it. Thus, however distantly, the freedman vicariously enjoyed something of the social status of his former master and might use the "family name" (*nisba*), while his descendants might adopt a fictive genealogy that integrated them into the family line. A similar process took place in the first century of Islam when non-Arabs (*mawāli*) who converted to Islam had to become clients of Arab tribes and eventually made the tribal *nisbas* their own. On the other hand, this link with the former owning family had its liabilities, since under certain circumstances the former master might have the right to share in a freedman's estate. If the freedman died without heirs, the former master inherited his entire estate. If he was married but without children, his wife inherited one-fourth of the estate, and the former master inherited the remaining three-fourths. In the case of a married female slave without children, the husband and her former master inherited equal shares of her estate. If the former master was dead, the three-fourths or one-half of the estate in the two cases mentioned previously went to the Public Treasury (*bayt al-māl*).[90]

This brings us to what is, perhaps, the most interesting question—or series of questions—with respect to Africans in the Mediterranean world. What became of the millions of Africans who were taken as slaves into the Mediterranean domains of Islam over the centuries? Is it the case that, in Bernard Lewis's words, "[T]here is nothing in the Arab, Persian and Turkish lands that resembles the great black and mulatto populations of North and South America"?[91] There are two answers to this. First, it is true in the sense that there do not appear to be any massive concentrations of blacks, no ghettoes, no visible struggles for civil rights, etc. Yet, the evidence presented below and that contained in the writings of others would suggest that, at least in regard to North Africa and Arabia, the slave trade may have left behind a not inconsiderable residuum. If this is so, then it must therefore be asked whether it is the lack of contemporary visibility of such populations that makes it seem that they do not exist. A possible answer to this may be that descendants of freed slaves occupy such lowly rungs on the socio-economic ladder that they are quite marginalized both socially and physically.[92] Dispersal or confinement to remoter suburbs and rural villages would likely result in lack of social coherence and, combined with a depressed social and economic status, make it the more difficult for social protest to emerge and attention to be focused.

If, on the contrary, there is no residuum, at least in certain Mediterranean lands into which black slaves were formerly imported, then this raises some very interesting questions. Lewis offers two suggestions for the absence of large black populations: first, the high proportion of eunuchs among black males; second, the high death rate and low birth rate among slaves. The first suggestion seems to me unlikely, given the very high price of eunuchs[93] and the restricted call for their specific services (such as guardians of harems in large households). The second suggestion is more plausible, if we are to judge by the data presented by Walz for nineteenth-century Egypt. If, as now seems to be the case at least for the nineteenth century, female slaves imported outnumbered males by perhaps as much as 2:1, then it is little surprise if black populations were unable to maintain themselves. A fair proportion of the females would have been integrated into households in receiving societies through concubinage, and their offspring would have been biracial and succeeding generations perhaps more genetically mixed. Those women who did not become concubines but remained in service may not have been allowed to marry, or perhaps only to marry when they were manumitted at an age already past that of child-bearing. Male slaves may have had little chance to marry, or at least to marry women young enough to bear children. Additionally, as both Lewis and Walz point out, epidemic diseases often carried off a disproportionate percentage of the slave population because of their lower standard of health care compared with the free population and their genetic unpreparedness for diseases not prevalent in their lands of origin.[94] An alternate hypothesis would be that there are no large identifiable black populations because there has been successful social integration including intermarriage. If this is so, one would like to understand better the particular social dynamics that brought this about.

It is important to stress, however, that there is simply not enough (not *nearly* enough) data at our disposal at present to make any general statements about the existence or size of residual black communities in the Mediterranean world, or the extent to which freed slaves and their descendants have been integrated into host societies, or have remained separate, endogamous, and unequal. It is equally important to stress that such questions must be looked at on a culture by culture, community by community, case by case, basis and no assumptions made based on single cases or single cultures, much less on the assumption that the egalitarian principles of Islam were automatically put into practice in former slave-owning societies.

To date little work has been done on such questions, but they clearly offer a very rich field for the historian and the sociologist. Without trying to offer any answers, however, it may be instructive to conclude this survey of the Mediterranean dimension of the black diaspora by looking briefly at two contrasting images of former African slaves in the Mediterranean world: first, the image that appears in the writings of nineteenth-century European travellers in the Arabian peninsula, and second, the image that emerges from the writings of French administrators and anthropologists working in the Maghreb. Both of these images result from what may be termed uncontextualized "snapshots," but they may serve to illustrate both the diversity of the African experience in the Mediterranean lands and the complexity of the issues involved.[95]

In the Arabian peninsula there are, or there have been until very recent times, considerable numbers of Africans of slave origin who seem to have been integrated into local society with fair success. Although in Arabia patrilineal descent is important as an indicator of social status, the adoption of a lineage through clientage has always been recognized as a legitimate way for a male to belong to a descent group, while for a female the "adoption" process came about more commonly, through concubinage or marriage. Both William Palgrave and Charles Doughty, traveling in the deserts and oases of Arabia in the 1860s and 1880s, respectively, remarked on the numerous communities of African descent, both pure and mixed, and were evidently surprised at the extent to which these ex-slaves had become "arabianized." Palgrave found that the treasurer of Faysal, the great Wahhābī ruler, was "jetblack, a negro, in fact, though not a slave, having obtained his freedom from Turkee, the father of the present king."[96] He also found in and around Riyād, the Wahhābī capital, a considerable number of men of mixed race known as *khuḍayriyya*, or "little green ones" ("green" being often in

Arabic a synonym of black), who were merchants, shopkeepers, and government servants, and he offered the following reflection on the situation of the emancipated African:

> The number of negro slaves in these provinces [southeastern and central Arabia] gives rise to a second stage of existence for the black, common in the East, though not equally compatible with his condition in the West. I mean that not of emancipation only, but of social equality also, with those around him—not by Act of Parliament or of Congress, but by individual will and public feeling. ... These new possessors of civil liberty soon marry and are given in marriage. Now, although an emancipated negro or mulatto is not at once admitted to the higher circles of aristocratic life, nor would an Arab chief of rank readily make his daughter over to a black, yet they are by no means under the ban of incapacity and exclusion which weighs upon them among races of English blood. Accordingly, negroes can without any difficulty give their sons and daughters to the middle or lower classes of Arab families, and thus arises a new generation of mixed blood here denominated "Khodeyreeyah" or "Benoo-Khodeyr," the which being interpreted means "The Greens" or "the sons of the green one." ... These "green ones" again, marry, multiply and assume various tints. ... Like their progenitors they do not readily take their place among the nobles or the upper ten thousand, however they do end by doing even this in the process of time; and I have myself while in Arabia been honoured by the intimacy of more than one handsome "Green-man," with a silver-hilted sword at his side, and a rich dress on his dusky skin, but denominated Sheykh or Emeer, and humbly sued by Arabs of the purest Ismaelitic or Kahtanic pedigree.[97]

Doughty also claimed that the position of the freed black in Arabia was a prosperous, even a favored, one for they were "rich men's children by adoption, where the poor disinherited Arabs must hire themselves to every man's task as day labourers."[98] Snouck Hurgronje also gave a glowing account of the situation of freed blacks in Mecca in the 1880s:

> There is hardly an office or position that is unattainable to such freedmen. They compete with the freeborn on a footing of perfect equality, and the result shows that they are not the worst equipped for the struggle as they are numerously represented among the influential burghers and the owners of houses and business establishments.[99]

These views of outsiders undoubtedly need to be compared with the view that Arabs of Arabia themselves held about their former slaves and the view those former slaves had of their own social and economic status, though in the present state of our knowledge, sources for such studies cannot readily be identified.[100]

The situation of the persons of slave ancestry in Morocco and Algeria is, or at least was in the recent past, somewhat in contrast to that of the reasonably integrated situation of the African freedmen of Arabia. Here we find distinct communities of black Africans, living in towns and oases. These communities are largely endogamous and continue to practice non-Islamic possession cults, such as the Hausa *bori* or the Songhay *holey*, or cults of purification and healing through sacrifice, such as those of the "Seven Springs" (*sab' 'uyūn*) in Algiers, the lightly Islamized pseudo-Ṣūfi cults of the Dīwān Sidi Bilāl in various Algerian locations, and the Gnawa cult of Morocco.[101] There are also Ṣūfi orders of a more recognizable variety, such as the 'Isāwa (Aissaoua) and the Hamādsha in Morocco that indulge in bloodletting and self-mutilation in a state of ecstatic frenzy. They are thought to owe some of their sacrificial practices to the influence of sub-Saharan African cults introduced by former slaves. These orders attracted large black memberships.[102] The existence of distinct and separate communities whose members continue to adhere to beliefs and rituals of their lands of origin, or who established or helped to promote essentially syncretic manifestations of the religion of former slave owners would seem to suggest that emancipation has not been accompanied by any great degree of social integration. Economically, too, blacks have tended to work in low status occupations—butchers, sweepers, unskilled laborers, jugglers, dancers, and street musicians. Only in exercising their talent as exorcisers of evil jinns do they find themselves respected by some members of the Berbero-Arab communities they live among and who acknowledge their skill in this art. The close connection between the oppression of slavery, the depressed social and economic state of the freedman, and the adoption of heterodox forms of religion has been summed up by Emile Dermenghem, who has also provided some of the most detailed eyewitness descriptions of the ceremonies of these cults:

> The cruel situation, at least as regards its origin, of the blacks of North Africa has favored the life of their brotherhoods and the maintenance of a Sudanic ritual adapted to Islam; and it is the liturgical activity of the brotherhoods which has favored the maintenance of racial consciousness and mutual self-help. The religious phenomena characterized by the words *zār* and *bori* (spirit possession) and by *diwān* (assembly) are widespread in Abyssinia, North Africa, Hausaland and among the Bambara and Songhay. ... Under the symbolism of the spirits the deeper goals, beyond the social effects, are a catharsis, a purification of the [psychic] forces, the curing of illnesses of nervous origin and the calming of the soul through ecstasy. This is the form which can easily be taken by the mysticism of an uprooted, exiled and oppressed minority which has accommodated itself to Islam in Africa, just as it did to Christianity in America.[103]

Although Dermenghem is one of the most recent writers to describe the black brotherhoods in North Africa, it is nevertheless over thirty years since he wrote. It would certainly be interesting to know how much of what he describes of these cults still exists and to what extent the creation of an independent and socialist-oriented Algeria has provided blacks with opportunities for upward social and economic mobility that would tend to break up the old communities.[104]

Some Concluding Observations

There is little point, given the present state of research in this field, in trying to make any generalizations. At the moment we still lack detailed studies of the institution of slavery as a whole in the lands of Islam,[105] and only when some steps have been taken in this direction shall we be able more clearly to discern the particular problems of the black slave and the black freedman within such societies. Nevertheless, in the nineteenth century, slavery and black slavery became synonymous—or almost so—in such areas as North Africa, Egypt, and the Arabian peninsula. In these areas it should be possible to undertake fruitful research on the black diaspora, not only because "slave" meant "black," but because the records are likely to prove far more abundant for the nineteenth century than for earlier periods. For many areas there are two kinds of records for much of the century: the correspondence and reports drawn up by colonial powers or European nations crusading for abolition, and the indigenous records—official and personal correspondence and, most important, the judicial records that document slave sales, taxes on slaves, runaway slaves, the enslavement of "free Muslims," the emancipation of slaves, and inheritance matters.[106] In addition, there is an extensive travel literature for North Africa and Egypt, as well as for the Sahara and those areas of sub-Saharan Africa from which the slaves were exported. Finally, there remains for the sociologist and the anthropologist a considerable field of inquiry among the surviving black communities of North Africa and Turkey in particular, and perhaps also Egypt and the Arabian Peninsula, though sensitivities over the issue of slavery and skin color in such countries present the researcher with inherent difficulties.[107]

In conclusion, let me draw attention to some of the salient features of slavery in the lands of Islam that may serve as points of comparison with other systems of slavery:

1. Slavery in the lands of the Mediterranean and the Near East during the Islamic era was a continuing phenomenon that had its

roots in remotest antiquity. Muslim scholars acknowledged the condition of slavery and regulated the institution.

2. Slaves in Muslim societies were from all races and colors. Islamic law recognized only two basic conditions: freedom, which is the basic assumption regarding the human condition, and slavery, which is a state of legal incapacitation (*hajr*) of limited duration. There were also two other related, but temporary, conditions: (a) being a slave whose eventual freedom had been guaranteed, either on the expiry of a stated term (*al-mu'taq ilā ajal*), or on payment of a certain sum (*al-mukātab*), or on the death of the owner (the case of the *umm walad* [slave mother] and the *mudabbar*); (b) being a client (*mawlā*) of one's former master after manumission. In theory this was perpetual, but in practice only lasted, at most, three generations.

3. Slaves' rights, disabilities, and exemptions were clearly defined in Islamic law. Although technically merely an item of property, the control of whose physical person was exclusively in the hands of his or her owner, the slave did have recourse to judicial authorities (the *muhtasib*) if he or she was grossly maltreated.

4. Plantation slavery, with its concomitant brutality and degradation, was comparatively rare. On the other hand, in certain times and places, military service was the forced lot of the male slave. Although this obviously exposed him to injury or death, it also allowed him some of the licence soldiers traditionally enjoyed and, if he were part of an elite bodyguard, he might have enjoyed considerable prestige and privilege.

5. The master's unrestricted right to cohabit with any or all of his unmarried female slaves looks, to late twentieth-century eyes, like the worst form of sexual exploitation. However, it should be seen against the context of a society and an age in which a free woman often had little say in whom she married and often met her husband for the first time on the wedding night. Furthermore, the slave woman who bore her master's child could not be disposed of, whereas the free woman could be unilaterally divorced.

6. Emancipation was an implicit assumption of the Islamic system, and many avenues were provided for it, some voluntary and some obligatory. Domestic slaves—males at least—might spend no more than a decade in bondage. Although this was obviously a boon to the individual already in slavery, it did help to create a continuing demand for more slaves, meaning that the cycle of violence and cruelty inherent in the capture of slaves in the African interior and their transportation to the Mediterranean lands was unending.

7. The notion of the inferiority and ultimately the enslaveability of "unbelievers" and in particular "pagans" (*mushrikūn*) was an implicit assumption of the Islamic theological-juridical system.[108] There was never any self-generated movement for the abolition of slavery from within the Muslim world, because slavery was considered an institution sanctioned by the holy law of Islam (the *shari'a*).[109]

The medieval law books such as the *Risāla* of Ibn Abi Zayd and the *Mukhtaṣar* of Khalil, from which I have drawn most of the points in my discussion of the legal position of slaves, are still considered fundamental textbooks of Islamic jurisprudence in Africa and are studied integrally in traditional Muslim teaching circles.

Finally, although I would wish to be proved wrong on this point, I believe that careful research would reveal that many of the old attitudes toward African (and in particular non-Muslim Africans), such as existed in the days when slavery was practiced, still survive in the Mediterranean lands of Islam.[110] But that is quite another subject.

NOTES

1. Ralph Austen, "The Trans-Saharan Slave Trade: A Tentative Census," in *The Uncommon Market: Essays in the Economic History of the Atlantic Slave Trade*, ed. H. Gemery and J. S. Hogendorn (New York: 1979), 23–76; "The Islamic Red Sea Slave Trade: An Effort at Quantification," *Proceedings 5th International Conference on Ethiopian Studies* (Chicago, 1979), 433–67.

2. Joseph E. Harris, *The African Presence in Asia* (Evanston: Northwestern University Press, 1971).

3. For overviews see Bernard Lewis, *Race and Color in Islam* (New York: 1971); "The African Diaspora and the Civilization of Islam" in *The African Diaspora*, ed. M. L. Kilson and R. I. Rotberg (Cambridge, Mass.: Harvard University Press, 1976), 37–56; Ibrahim K. Sundiata, "Beyond Race and Color in Islam," *Journal of Ethnic Studies* 6, 1 (1977):1–29; J. O. Hunwick, "Black Africans in the Islamic World: An Understudied Dimension of the Black Diaspora," *Tarikh* 5 (1978):20–40; 'Abduh Badawi, *al-Sūd wa 'l-ḥaḍārat al-'arabiyya* (Cairo, 1976); J. Comhaire, "Some Notes on Africans in Muslim History," *Muslim World* 46 (1956):336–41. The best general treatment of slavery in Islam remains the article "*Abd*" by R. Brunschvig in *The Encyclopaedia of Islam*, new ed. (Leiden: E. J. Brill, 1960–[hereafter *EI* (2), I:24–48. For further bibliography see Joseph Miller, *Slavery: A Comparative Teaching Bibliography* (Crossroads Press, 1971) and the journal *Slavery: A Worldwide Bibliography* (Milford, N.Y., 1985).

4. For *riqāb* / *raqaba*, see the Qur'ān, 2:177, 4:92, 5:49, 9:60, 58:2, 90:13. For "those whom your right hands possess," 4:2, 24, 25, 36; 16:71; 23:6; 24:31, 33, 58; 30:28; 33:50–55, 70:30.

5. Comhaire, "Africans in Muslim History," 336–37; Lewis, "The African Diaspora and the Civilization of Islam," 41. The term *Ethiopian* (*ḥabashi*) is, of course, very

imprecise and would include persons of many ethnic groups in the Horn of Africa, the Nile Valley, and the Red Sea hinterlands.

6. Muḥammad Bāqir 'Alwān, "Aghribt al-'arab," *al-Mawrid* 2, 1 (1973):11–13; Lewis, *Race and Color*, 11–15.

7. See 'Abduh Badawī, *al-Shu'arā' al-sūd wa-khaṣā'iṣuhum fī 'l-shi'r al-'arabī* (Cairo, 1973); Lewis, *Race and Color*, 11–15; Hunwick, "Black Africans in the Islamic World," 35–36.

8. Qur'ān, 4:36.

9. See W. Arafat, "The Attitude of Islam to Slavery," *Islamic Quarterly* 5 (1966):14, for a full list of Qur'ānic verses on the subject.

10. Abū Ḥāmid al-Ghazālī, *Iḥyā' 'ulūm al-dīn*, 5 vols. (Beirut: Dār al m'rifa, n.d.), II:219, trans. G.-H. Bousquet, "Des droits de l'esclave. Fragment extrait de l'Iḥ'yā' de Ghazālī," *Annales de l'Institut des Etudes Orientales* 10 (1952):420–22.

11. Aḥmad b. Khālid al-Nāṣirī, *Kitāb al-istiqṣā' li-duwal al-maghrib al-aqṣā* (Casablanca, 1955), V:133–44. The entire polemic is translated in Hunwick, "Black Africans in the Islamic World," 38–40.

12. See, for example, R. S. O'Fahey, "Slavery and the Slave Trade in Dār Fūr," *Journal of African History* 14 (1973):29–45; Leo Africanus (trans. A. Epaulard), *Description de l'Afrique* (Paris, 1956), II:480–81 for such practices in Borno, and Genéral Daumas, *Le Grand Désert*, 4th ed. (Paris, 1860), 199–215, for an example drawn from Katsina. See further Allan G. B. Fisher and Humphrey J. Fisher, *Slavery and Muslim Society in Africa* (London, 1970), 14ff.

13. J. R. Morell, *Algeria: The Topography and History: Political, Social and Natural of French Algeria* (London, 1854), 340–41; cf. al-Nāṣirī, *K. al-istiqṣā'* in Hunwick, "Black Africans," 39 for kidnapping in West Africa and 40 for the same in Morocco.

14. On these and other points of law in the discussion below, see Brunschvig in *EI* (2), I, 26–31. Reference will also be made to the following works of Mālikī jurisprudence: the *Risāla* of Ibn Abī Zayd al-Qayrawānī (d. 996), ed. and trans. Léon Bercher, 3d ed. (Algiers, 1949); the *Mukhtaṣar* of Khalīl b. Isḥāq (d. 1374), trans. G.-H. Bousquet, 4 parts (Algiers, 1956–62); the *Qawānīn Fiqhiyya* of Ibn Juzayy (d. 1340) (Beirut, 1974). See also the "Code de l'esclavage chez les musulmans" in *Le Grand Désert*, ed. Daumas, 319–344, based on Mālikī sources, and E. W. Lane, *The Manners and Customs of the Modern Egyptians*, 5th ed. (London, 1860), 100–102.

15. *Risāla*, 223–24; *Mukhtaṣar*, IV, 66–70; *Qawānīn*, 412–13.

16. Brunschvig in *EI* (2), I, 30; Terence Walz, "Black Slavery in Egypt during the Nineteenth Century as reflected in the *maḥkama* Archives of Cairo," in *Slaves and Slavery in Muslim Africa*, ed. J. R. Willis (London, 1985), II, 137–60.

17. Brunschvig in *EI* (2), I, 30; *Risāla*, 229; *Mukhtaṣar*, IV, 73–74; *Qawānīn*, 410–11.

18. Brunschvig in *EI* (2), I, 28; "Code de l'esclavage chez les musulmans," 328.

19. *Qawānīn* 408; Brunschvig in *EI* (2), I, 27.

20. Qur'ān, 2:177.

21. Qur'ān, 24:33.

22. On these various disabilities and exonerations see Brunschvig in *ĖI* (2), I, 27–29.

23. For the functions of the *muḥtasib* see Cl. Cahen and M. Talbi, art. *"Ḥisba"* in EI (2), III, 485–89; R. Levy, *The Social Structure of Islam* (Cambridge, 1957), 334–38; E. Tyan, *Histoire de l'organisation judiciare en pays d'Islam* (Paris, 1938–43), II:xxx. For a practical treatise, see Ibn al-Ukhuwwa, *Ma'ālim al-qurba fī aḥkām al-ḥisba*, text and abridged English trans. by R. Levy (Cambridge University Press, 1938, E. J. W. Gibb Memorial Series, new series, XII).

24. Ibn al-Ukhuwwa, *Ma'ālim al-qurba*, Arabic text, 27 (not in English summary).

25. On Jewish slave owning in medieval Egypt, see S. D. Goitein, *A Mediterranean Society*, vol. I, *Economic Foundations* (Berkeley: University of California Press, 1967), 130–47 et passim.

26. Lewis, *Race and Slavery*, 148, gives a translation of a fifteenth-century *fatwā* from North Africa that makes slavery a punishment for "unbelief": "slavery is a humiliation and a servitude caused by previous or current unbelief and having as its purpose to discourage unbelief."

27. On the sources of slaves and routes of the trade in medieval times, see M. Lombard, *L'Islam dans sa première grandeur* (Paris, 1971), 194–202.

28. The Muslims also bound themselves to send the Nubians a quantity of cereals and textiles as part of the agreement. See F. Lókkegard, art. *"Bakt"* in *EI* (2), I, 966.

29. See Harris, *African Presence in Asia*, 19–23; J. Burton Page, "Ḥabshī" in *EI*, 2, III, 14–16.

30. The pilgrimage to Mecca was also taken advantage of by West Africans for the sale of slaves. Such slaves were often sold in different locations to defray the expenses of the journey and to purchase goods to take back across the Sahara; see Taqī 'l-Dīn al-Maqrīzi, *Kitāb al-sulūk fī ma'rifat duwal al-mulūk*, trans. in *Corpus of Early Arabic Sources for West African History*, ed. J. F. P. Hopkins and N. Levtzion (Cambridge, 1981), 356 (examples from the years 1351, 1416, and 1439). See also Fisher and Fisher, *Slavery and Muslim Society in Africa*, 121–124, 128–29.

31. Leo Africanus, *Description de l'Afrique*, II, 480; Duarte Pacheco Pereira, *Esmeraldo de Situ Orbis*, trans. George H. T. Kimbel (London, 1937, Hakluyt Society, 2d ser., 79), 78, 92; G. R. Crone, ed. and trans., *The Voyages of Cadamosto and Other Documents on Western Africa in the Second Half of the Fifteenth Century* (London 1937, Hakluyt Society, 2d ser., 80, 17; G. F. Lyon, *A Narrative of Travels in Northern Africa in the Years 1818, 19 and 20* (London, 1821), 154; Morell, *Algeria*, 340.

32. Hans Vischer, *Across the Sahara from Tripoli to Bornu* (London, 1910), 148; A. A. Boahen, *Britain, the Sahara and the Western Sudan, 1788–1861* (Oxford, 1964), 158.

33. See J. Nicolaisen, *The Ecology and Culture of the Pastoral Tuareg* (Copenhagen, 1963), 439–46; Jeremy Keenan, *The Tuareg: People of Ahaggar* (London, 1979), 95–100. For a historical summary, see Priscilla E. Starratt, "Tuareg Slavery and the Slave Trade," *Slavery and Abolition* 2(1981):83–113.

34. Ibn al-Ukhuwwa, *Ma'ālim al-qurba*, 27; G. S. Colin and E. Lévi-Provençal, *Un Manuel hispanique de hisba, traité de Abū 'Abd Allāh Muhammad b. Abi Muhammad as-Sakatī de Malaga* (Paris, 1931), 47.

35. Colin and Lévi-Provençal, *Un Manuel hispanique de hisba*, 51.

36. See below, 313.

37. For a description of the slave market of Cairo, see Terence Walz, "Wakālat al-Ǧallāba: The Market for Sudan Goods in Cairo," *Annales Islamologiques* 13 (1977):217–45. For that of Istanbul, see Alan W. Fisher, "The Sale of Slaves in the Ottoman Empire; Markets and State Taxes on Slaves: Some Preliminary Considerations," *Boğazici Üniversitesi Dergisi* (Beseri Bilimler) 6 (1978):151–56.

38. C. Snouck Hurgronje, *Mekka in the Latter Part of the Nineteenth Century* (Leiden, 1931), 14.

39. Ibn Buṭlān, *Risāla fī shirā' al-raqīq wa-taclīb al-'abīd*, in *Nawādir al-makhṭūṭāt*, ed. 'Abd al-Salām Muhammad Hārūn, IV/6 (Cairo, 1954), 333–89. In the same volume is another treatise purely on the medical examination of slaves by a seventeenth or eighteenth-century writer, Muhammad al-Ghazālī, *Hidāyat al-murid fī taqlīb al-'abīd*, 391–410.

40. *Mukhtaṣar*, 164–65; *Risāla*, 196; comm. of al-Nafrāwī, *al-Fawākih al-dawāni* (Cairo, 1374/1955), II:96; Brunschvig in *EI* (2), I, 28.

41. Colin and Lévi-Provençal, *Un Manuel hispanique de hisba*, 50.

42. Ibid., 49–50; Ibn Buṭlān, *Risāla*, 376–84.

43. See Samuel W. Baker, *Exploration of the Nile Tributaries of Abyssinia* (Hartford, 1868), 533–34. On the Ethiopian slave trade in the nineteenth century see *Mordechai Abir*, "The Ethiopian Slave Trade and Its Relation to the Islamic World" in *Slaves and Slavery in Muslim Africa*, ed. J. R. Willis, II, 123–36.

44. Lane, *Modern Egyptians*, 183–84; G. Baer, "Slavery and Its Abolition," in his *Studies in the Social History of Modern Egypt* (Chicago, 1969), 163. An earlier version of this article was published in the *Journal of African History* 8 (1967):417–41.

45. Hurgronje, *Mekka in the Latter Part of the Nineteenth Century*, 109.

46. *Modern Egyptians*, 185.

47. G. Tournès, *Les Eunuques en Egypte* (Geneva: Imprimerie Vaney, 1869), 20–21.

48. H. R. Idris, *La Berbérie Orientale sous les Zirides* (Paris, 1962), 576, quoting the anon. *Kitāb al-istibṣār*, trans. E. Fagnan (Paris, 1900), 59–60.

49. J. L. Burckhardt, *Arabic Proverbs* (London, 1830), 176; Lane, *Modern Egyptians*, 38.

50. R. Hill, *On the Frontiers of Islam* (Oxford University Press, 1970), 183; J. L. Burckhardt, *Travels in Nubia*, 2d ed. (London, 1822), 301–302.

51. Muḥammad b. 'Abd al-Raḥmān al-Sakhāwī, *al-Ḍaw' al-lāmi' l-ahl al-qarn al-tāsi'*, 12 vols. (Cairo, 1353–55/1934–36).

52. Op. cit., III, no. 877 (customs collector); X, no. 684 (governor of Aden); VI, no. 839 (emissary to Ethiopia).

53. Ibid., III, no. 70.

54. For references to the use of black troops in medieval Egypt, see S. Lane-Poole, *A History of Egypt in the Middle Ages* (London, 1901), 63, 86–89, 132–33, 141, 145, 168, 192.

55. J. F. P. Hopkins, *Medieval Muslim Government in Barbary* (London, 1958), 72–73; Michael Brett (in *The Cambridge History of Africa*, vol. 2 [Cambridge, 1978], 529) argues that the terminology used in the sources does not distinguish the color of the slaves in the Aghlabid army in the early period and that they may just as easily have been Europeans. Only toward the end of the ninth century is there mention of *sūdān* ("blacks").

56. Idris, *La Berbérie Orientale sous les Zirides*, 530–31.

57. Hopkins, *Medieval Muslim Government*, 76.

58. Ibid., 78.

59. See Magali Morsy, "Moulay Ismā'īl et l'armée de métier," *Revue d'histoire moderne et contemporaine* 14 (1967):97–122; Allan Meyers, "The 'Abid al-Bukhāri: Slave Soldiers and State-Craft in Morocco, 1672–1790" (Unpublished Ph.D. diss., Cornell University, 1974).

60. Maurice Delafosse, "Les débuts des troupes noires au Maroc," *Hespéris* 3 (1923):1–12.

61. Some were evidently urbanized, see A. A. Batran, "The *'ulamā* of Fas, Mulay Ismā'īl, and the issue of the ḥarāṭin of Fas" in *Slaves and Slavery in Muslim Africa*, II, 1–15.

62. al-Nāsiri, *Kitāb al-istiqsā'*, VII, 76.

63. Moroccan sources (al-Nāsiri, *K.al-istiqsā'*, VII 61; Abū'-Qāsim b.Aḥmad al-Zayyāni, *al-Turjumān al-mu'rib 'an duwal al-mashriq wa 'l-maghrib*, ed. O. Houdas, Paris, 1886, 16) put the total of the *'abid al-Bukhāri* at 150,000 at their height, though this figure may include a large number assigned to public works as well as military duties. Allan Meyers in his article "Class, Ethnicity and Slavery: Origins of the Moroccan 'abid'" (*International Journal of African Historical Studies*, 10, 1977, 427–42) displays some uneasiness at this large figure, but seems to accept it *faute de mieux*. Lewis, *Race and Slavery*, 69, says they were "said to number 250,000," but it is not clear where he got this figure from or how much credence he gives it. Abdullah Laroui (*The History of the Maghrib*, Princeton University Press, 1977, 273) gives a figure of only "thirty to fifty thousand" for the size of the army at its height, though he does not indicate how he arrived at this. A figure of 150,000 sounds on the face of it exaggerated, though it

is said to be based on the ledgers (*kunnāshāt*) of the sultan's chief secretary. These ledgers—or at least some of them—are still preserved in Morocco and it is therefore possible that one day more accurate figures may become available.

64. Oscar Lenz, *Timbouctou: Voyage au Maroc, au Sahara et au Soudan* (Paris, 1886), II:355–56.

65. See T. Lockhart, art. "Aḥwāz" in *EI* (2), I, 305.

66. On the Zanj revolt, most recently, see the study of Alexandre Popovic, *La révolte des esclaves en Iraq au IIIe / IXe siècle* (Paris, 1976).

67. See W. Madelung, art. "Karmaṭi" in *EI* (2), IV, 664.

68. Baer, "Slavery and Its Abolition," 165–66.

69. Ibn Baṭṭūṭa, *Voyages* (*Tuḥfat al-nuẓẓār*): texte arabe accompagné d'une traduction par C. Defrémery et B. Sanguinetti (new edition with preface and notes by V. Monteil, Paris, 1969), IV, 378 (English trans. Said Hamdun and Noël King, *Ibn Battuta in Black Africa* [London, 1975], 23); René Caillié, *Travels through Central Africa to Timbuctoo* (London, 1830), II, 119; Lenz, *Timbouctou*, II, 73–74.

74. Ibn Baṭṭūṭa, *Voyages*, IV, 441 (Hamdun and King, *Ibn Battuta in Black Africa*, 58).

71. G. Wiet, art. "al-'Allāḳi" in *EI* (2), I, 418; see also L. E. Kubbel and V. V. Matveev, *Arabskiye Istochniki VII–X bekob* (Moscow, 1960), 41–42 (account of al-Ya'qūbi, d 897).

72. For a detailed study of eunuch terminology and of the Ṣaqāliba eunuchs, see D. Ayalon, "On the eunuchs in Islam," *Jerusalem Studies in Arabic and Islam* I (1979):67–124. On the making and employment of eunuchs in sub-Saharan Africa, see Fisher and Fisher, *Slavery and Muslim Society in Africa*, 143–48. See also art. "Khaṣi" by Ch. Pellat in *EI*, 2, IV, 1087–92.

73. Quoted in 'Abduh Badawi, *al-Shu'arā' al-sūd*, 203; see also A. J. Wensinck and J. P. Mensing, *Concordance et indices de la tradition musulmane* (Leiden, 1943), II, 38.

74. According to the Māliki school of law, a slave had to be freed if he or she were mutilated; see *Risāla*, 229; *Mukhtaṣar*, IV, 60; *Qawānin*, 408. See further Muḥammad b. 'Umar al-Tūnisi, *Tash'hidh al-adh'hān bi-sirat bilād al-'arab wa-Sūdān* (ed. Khalīl Maḥmūd 'Asākir and Muṣṭafā Muḥammad Mus'ad, Cairo, 1965), 233–34. Al-Tūnisi gives the title of an anticastration treatise by the Egyptian polymath al-Suyūṭi (d. 1505)—*Ḥurmat khidmat al-khiṣyān l-ḍariḥ sayyid wuld 'Adnān*—but I have been unable to locate a copy of it.

75. Lombard, *L'Islam dans sa première grandeur*, 196–97.

76. Ibid., map on 198, where a center of castration is also indicated near Cordoba, that is, in Muslim territory. According to Ibn Ḥawqal, *Opus Geographicum* (*K. Ṣūrat al-arḍ*), ed. J. H. Kramers (Leiden, 1939), 110, Jewish merchants were said to perform the operation in Andalusia in the tenth century.

77. Ibn Faḍl Allāh al-'Umari (d. 1349), trans. M. Gaudefroy-Demombynes, *L'Afrique moins l'Egypte* (Paris, 1927), 16–17.

78. Fisher and Fisher, *Slavery and Muslim Society in Africa*, 145–46.

79. See the anon. "Kano Chronicle" in H. R. Palmer, *Sudanese Memoirs* (Lagos, 1928), III:108–110. Kano began to appoint eunuch officials in the second half of the fifteenth century, and other West African kingdoms such as Songhay, Dagomba, Bagirmi, Darfur, and Borno later did so.

80. al-Zayyāni, *al-Turjumān al-mu'rib*, 15 (Arabic text). A late eighteenth-century European traveller in Morocco, and sometime physician to royal harems reported that the source of Moroccan eunuchs was the "kingdom of Bambara" (that is, the state based on Segu, a little upstream from the inland delta of the Niger) and he estimated that in 1789 they numbered no more than one hundred in the entire 'Alawid kingdom, see W. Lemprière, *A Tour from Gibraltar to Tangier, Sallee Mogadore, Santa Cruz. Tarudant and thence over Mount Atlas to Morocco*, 3d ed. (London, 1804), 357. Lenz, *Timbouctou*,

I, 395, reported that in nineteenth century Morocco some masters castrated their own slaves and used them as concubines.

81. Louis Frank, "Mémoire sur le commerce des nègres au Kaire et sur les maladies auxquelles ils sont sujets en y arrivant," *Mémoires sur l'Egypte* (Paris, 1800–1803), IV, 132ff.; O. Meinardus, "The Upper Egyptian practice of making eunuchs in the Eighteenth and Nineteenth Century," *Zeitschrift für Ethnologie* 94(1969):47–58; Tournès, *Les eunuques en Egypte*, 9ff.

82. N. Penzer, *The Harem* (London, 1936), 129. On these royal eunuchs, see also M. Izeddin, "Les eunuques dans le palais ottoman," *Orient* 6 (24)(1962):103–21; Ehud Toledano, "The imperial eunuchs of Istanbul: from Africa to the heart of Islam," *Middle East Studies* 20(1984):379–90; Alev L. Croutier, *Harem: the World of the Veil* (New York, 1989), 125–42, partly based on Penzer and other published sources, but with some personal and family reminiscences. A scathing denunciation of the black eunuchs of the Ottoman sultan's harem has been published in Cengiz Orhonlu, "Dervis Abdullah'in Darussaade Ağarli hakkinda bir Eseri. Risale-i Teberdariye fi ahvāl-i Dâru's-saade" in *Ismail Hakki Uzunçarsulu Armağani'ndan ayribasim* (Ankara: Turk Tarih Kurumi Basimevi, 1975), 225–49. I am grateful to Max Kortepeter for providing me with a summary translation of the document contained in this article.

83. On the physical appearance and character traits of eunuchs, see al-Jāḥiẓ, K. al-Ḥayawān, Cairo, 1938, I, 106ff.; Ibrāhīm al-Bayhaqī (fl.920), *K. al-mahāsin wa 'l-masāwi*, ed. Ibrāhīm Muḥammad Abū 'l-Faḍl (Cairo, 1961), II, 390–93; Sir Richard Burton, *Personal Narrative of a Pilgrimage to al-Madinah and Mecca*, Memorial ed., London, 1893, I, 372; Tournès, op. cit., 16–18; Hikmet and Félix Regnault, "Les eunuques de Constantinople," *Bulletin et Mémoires de la Société d'Anthropologie de Pais*, sér. V, 2 (1901):234–40.

84. J. L. Burckhardt, *Travels in Arabia* (London, 1829), 142–44. On the institution under the Mamlūks, see S. E. Marmon, "The Eunuchs of the Prophet: Space, Time and Gender in an Islamic Society," Ph.D. diss., Princeton University, 1990.

85. See, for example, *Letters Written during a Ten Years' Residence at the Court of Tripoli*, 3d ed., vol. I (London, 1819), 100, 174, 231; Palgrave, *Personal Narrative*, 271.

86. Morell, *Algeria*, 342; see also Walz, "Black Slavery in Egypt," quoting Emine F. Tugay, *Three Centuries: Family Chronicles of Turkey and Egypt* (London, 1963), to the effect that white slaves in the imperial service were customarily freed after nine years, while blacks were freed after seven. Shī'ī jurists recommended the freeing of a Muslim slave after seven years; see Brunschvig in *EI* (2), I, 31.

87. On the various paths to manumission according to Mālikī jurists, see *Risāla*, 220–29; *Mukhtaṣar*, IV, 59–72; *Qawānin*, 407–16; "Code de l'esclavage chez les musulmans," 340–44.

88. Walz, "Black Slavery in Egypt," 18.

89. Brunschvig in *EI* (2), I, 30–31; *Risāla*, 228–29; *Mukhtaṣar*, IV, 73–74; *Qawānin*, 410–11; Levy, *Social Structure of Islam*, 81.

90. Walz, "Black Slavery," 27.

91. *Race and Slavery*, 84.

92. Almost twenty-five years ago Leon Carl Brown remarked: "A disproportionately large number of black men are likely to be found, for example, working as unskilled laborers at a construction site or on a work-gang building a highway. ... The ill-defined and often ignored position of the black man in North Africa has been interpreted as indicating greater social mobility and less resistance along color lines than prevail in black–white relations in most of the world. Such an interpretation may be too optimistic—a kind of over-reaction to the more clear-cut segregation

pattern that characterizes white–black relations in the English-speaking world." See his "Color in North Africa," *Daedalus* 96 (1967):480n.12.

93. Up to seven times the price of an uncastrated male; see, by way of example, Magali Morsy, *North Africa 1800–1900* (London, 1884), 63, who gives figures for Tripoli in the 1820s; A. G. B. Fisher & H. J. Fisher, *Slavery and Muslim Society in Africa* (London, 1970, 164) who give figures for sales in the market of Kuka (Bornu) in the 1870s.

94. Louis Frank, a doctor who had experience of Egypt, remarking on the visibility of black Africans in Tunis, noted that this was because there was a lesser incidence of "plague" in Tunis than in Egypt and because the people of Tunis were in the habit of freeing their slaves and the latter generally preferred to remain in Tunis rather than return home where they might again be enslaved. See his *Tunis: Description de cette Régence* in *L'Univers pittoresque* (Paris, 1850), 116.

95. Not the least of these issues is the ideological framework within which the various commentators viewed the topic they were discussing. Even in the late nineteenth century there were those who were still ready to defend black slavery and claim it was a way of "civilising the savage." See Lewis, *Race and Slavery*, 82–84.

96. Palgrave, *Personal Narrative*, 272.

97. Ibid., 270–71.

98. Charles Doughty, *Travels in Arabia Deserta* (London: Jonathan Cape, 1923), I, 554.

99. Op. cit., 13.

100. An eighteenth-century African Muslim scholar, however, found cause to complain of Meccan attitudes, and he had never been a slave. Muḥammad b. Muḥammad al-Katsināwi al-Fullāni remarked: "In general the people of this land love no one—least of all those of our Sudanic race—unless it be of the satisfaction of some need of theirs, without any true affection or friendship. See his *al-Durr al-manẓūm wa-khulāṣat al-sirr al-maktūm fī 'l-sihr wa'l-talāsim wa 'l-nujūm* (Bombay, 1303/1885–86), 2; which he in fact wrote at the request of a Meccan scholar.

101. The essential reference on sub-Saharan religious influence in North Africa is Emile Dermenghem, *Le Culte des saints dans l'Islam maghrébin* (Pais, 1954), 253ff. Specifically on the *bori* cult in Tunis and Tripoli, see A. J. H. Tremearne, *The Ban of the Bori* (London, 1914), and the indignant polemic of Aḥmad b.Abi Bakr al-Tunbuktāwi, (1804), *Hatk al-sitr 'ammā 'alayhi sūdān Tūnis min al-kufr* in *Les Affinités culturelles entre la Tunisie, la Libye, le Centre de l'ouest de l'Afrique à l'époque moderne*, ed. Abdeljelil Temini, (Tunis: Publications de la Revue d'Histoire Maghrébine, 7, 1981); on the "seven springs" see J. D. Andrews, *Les Fontaines des génies (seba aioun). Coyances soudanaises d'Alger* (Algiers, 1903); on the Gnāwa, V. Pâques, *L'Arbre cosmique dans la pensée populaire et dans la vie quotidienne du nord-ouest africain*, (Paris, 1964), and her "Le monde des gnâwa" in *L'Autre et l'ailleurs: Hommage à Roger Bastide* (Paris, 1976) 169–82.

102. See René Brunel, *Essai sur la confrérie des Aissaoua au Maroc* (Paris, 1926); Vincent Crapanzano, *The Hamadsha: a Study in Moroccan Ethnopsychiatry* (University of California Press, 1973).

103. Emile Dermenghem, *Le Culte des saints*, 260. A recent doctoral thesis by Gerasimos Makris (London School of Economics, University of London, 1991) on the Tumbura cult in northern Sudan suggests that former slaves used this very adaptive possession and healing cult in support of their endeavor to cross boundaries from "paganism" to Islam, from non-Arabness to Arabness, and from "savagery" (as perceived by northern Sudanese Muslims) to "civilized" norms. Such cults, then, would represent less a revolt against a new culture forced upon the alienated or an attempt to hold on to a severed past, but the negotiation of an entry into a new identity.

104. A recent article indicates there has been little change in the Saharan regions of Algeria at any rate. See L. Blin, "Les noirs dans l'Algérie contemporaine," *Politique africaine* 30 (1988):22–31.

105. An exception is the recent monograph by Ehud R. Toledano, *The Ottoman Slave Trade and its Suppression* (1982), although as its title indicates its main emphasis is the trade itself and its abolition rather than the social and economic role of slaves before and after emancipation. Lewis, *Race and Slavery*, VI, comments on "the remarkable dearth of scholarly work on the subject. ... The documentation for a study on Islamic slavery is almost endless; its exploration has barely begun."

106. For different areas the volume and nature of local record will, of course, vary. For Egypt, Walz has observed: "The *maḥkama* archive holdings show that an in-depth study of slavery in Egypt can be—and deserves to be—written." See his "Black Slavery in Egypt," 137. For an example, albeit much more microcosmic, from a Muslim society south of the Sahara, see Alan Christelow, "Slavery in Kano, 1913–14: Evidence from the Judicial Records," *African Economic History*, 14 (1985):57–74.

107. Among the studies which do exist are the following: G. Zadowski, "Le rôle des nègres parmi la population tunisienne," *En Terre d'Islam* (1942):146–52; A. Lopashich, "A Negro Community in Yugoslavia," *Man* 58 (231)(1958):169–73; P. N. Boratav, "Les noirs dans le folklore turc et le folklore des noirs de Turquie," *Journal Societe des Africanistes*, 28, 1958, 7–23; Z. Komorowski, "Les descendants des soudanais en Algérie et leurs traditions," *Africana Bulletin* [Warsaw], 15 (1971):43–53; A. Destro, "Habs el 'Abid: il quartiere africano di Gerusalemme," *Africa* [Rome], 39 (1974): 193–212; Blin, "Les noirs dans l'Algérie contemporaine," (see above n104).

108. See P. de Moraes Farias, "Models of the World and Categorical Models: the 'Enslaveable Barbarian' as a Mobile Classificatory Label" in *Slaves and Slavery in Muslim Society*, ed. J. R. Willis, I 27–46; Lewis, *Race and Slavery*, ch. 8. See further above where the Moroccan historian al-Nāṣirī makes a careful distinction between random enslavement of Africans and the legality of enslaving persons captured in a *jihād*, although he points out that the requisite conditions no longer exist.

109. The impetus for abolition, first of the slave trade and then of slave owning, came from European powers (in particular Britain and France) who were in a position to put pressure on Muslim leaders in Africa and the Middle East. The reactions of local religious leaders to this phenomenon have not yet been the subject of detailed research, though Toledano, *Ottoman Slave Trade*, 272–78, gives a brief review of Ottoman reactions. See also a letter from the Moroccan sultan Mūlāy 'Abd al-Raḥmān b. Hishām to Consul General Drummond Hay (dated 18 March 1842), the text of which is given in Lewis, *Race and Slavery*, 156.

110. William J. Sersen, "Stereotypes and Attitudes Towards Slaves in Arabic Proverbs: A Preliminary View" in *Slaves and Slavery in the Muslim World*, I, 92–105, gives examples of Arabic dialects in which the word *'abd*—"slave" has become a generic word for "black African." See also Albertine Jwaideh and J. W. Cox, "The Black Slaves of Turkish Arabia During the 19th Century," *Slavery and Abolition* 9 (1988):45–59, who remark: "The distinction between *ḥurr* and *'abd* was binding and unalterable. It was a case of once an *'abd* always an *'abd* whether manumitted or not. And while not all *'abid* were black, the terms for negro and slave were used interchangeably," See also my remarks in my *West Africa and the Arab World: Historical and Contemporary Perspectives* (Accra: Ghana Academy of Arts and Sciences, 1991), 15, 17, 26.

18
Africans in Asian History*

Joseph E. Harris

HERE are virtually no published materials available in English or French about African communities in Iran, and I was unable to find an Iranian who knew of any such study in Arabic or Persian. However, Professor E. Bastani-Parizi of the University of Tehran has written several histories of Iran in which he briefly mentions African slaves and small settlements of African descendants. Some of the towns and villages he refers to are Zanjiabad ("village built by Africans"), Gala-Zanjian ("castle of Africans") in Baluchistan near a mountain called Mount of the Blacks, and Deh-Zanjian ("village of Africans") in Kerman Province.[1]

In Jiruft, an interior Persian entrepôt that relied on commerce with Hormuz, Minab, and Bandar Abbas, merchants from India, Ethiopia, East Africa generally, the Roman Empire, and other areas conducted a substantial trade that included African slaves. It is very likely that the inhabitants of the separate, black community near Jiruft are descendants of those African merchants and slaves. The inhabitants recall an African background and slavery and are sensitive to the suspicion with which they are regarded by other Iranians. Their general isolation has contributed to their dialect, which most other Iranians seem not to understand and which in part accounts for their "strangeness." There is another black community near the port of Bandar Abbas, and it seems to be composed of the descendants of African slaves who worked as dhow crewmen and laborers on nearby date plantations. Also, many of the present residents of Shiraz recall reports of African men and women slaves accompanying Iranian Muslims from the Hadj, but no separate

*Reprinted from Joseph E. Harris, *The African Presence in Asia: Consequences of the East African Slave Trade* (Evanston, Ill.: Northwestern University Press, 1971), 77–90, which also examines communities of African descent in Central India.

325

African community seems to exist in Shiraz today. Additional evidence of the African presence in Iran is the fact that the mother of the esteemed poet, Abu l'Makarim Mujir al Din, born in 1197, was an Ethiopian.[2] Very likely there are other cases of an African presence in Iran because so many sources refer to African slaves along the northern Persian Gulf, but this story must await additional research.

Although writers in India during the Middle Ages do not seem to have investigated the African origins of the Habshis, from time to time they refer to a unique or outstanding African in a particular Indian community. One of the earliest examples occurred in the thirteenth century, when it was reported that Queen Raziya, the sovereign of the sultanate of Delhi, became attracted to a Habshi slave named Jalal-ud-din Yaqut, whom she appointed to the post of royal stable master. There is no description of Yaqut's African background or the experiences he had en route to India. However, the noted Arab historian Ferista wrote that "a very great degree of familiarity was observed to exist between the Abyssinian and the Queen." They became so intimate that Yaqut would assist her onto her horse "by raising her up under the arms." The queen's father and the nobles not only protested that kind of behavior, but they later killed Yaqut.[3]

Another African in Delhi was Malik Sarvar, whom R.C. Majumdar describes as a eunuch, probably of "Negro" blood. He was a slave of Sultan Muhammad and in 1389 became the sultan's deputy, with the title of Khvaja Jahan. The sultan later conferred on him the title of Malik-ush-Sharq ("chief of the east") and appointed him governor of the eastern province, Malik-ush-Sharq left Delhi for Jaunpur in 1394 and eventually began to rule as an independent king. He was later succeeded by an adopted son whose name was Malik Qaranful ("clove"), a name commonly given to African slaves. Some observers assume, therefore, that he was African. His official title was Sultan Mubarak Shah. The next king in this line was Mubarak's brother, Ibrahim, who ascended to the throne as Shams-ud-din Ibrahim. His identity is more obscure. If he were in fact Mubarak's brother, he was probably African. Majumdar simply states that after Mubarak died in 1402 "the amirs raised his brother Ibrahim to the throne." The lack of a clearer identification of Ibrahim is most unfortunate, because it was during his rule that Jaunpur became famous and prosperous. It emerged as a center of learning, attracting renowned writers; it is also noted for its impressive architecture, especially the mosques. But whatever the ethnic identity of Ibrahim, it is likely that both Malik-ush-Sharq and Mubarak Shah were Africans. The three together made Jaunpur a prominent kingdom during the fifteenth century.[4]

During the second half of the fifteenth century, Africans in another part of northern India, Bengal, organized and asserted considerable political power. Rukn-ud-din Barbak, king of Bengal (1459–74) is said to have been the first Indian king to promote substantial numbers of African slaves to high rank. He maintained an estimated eight thousand African slave-soldiers in his army. In 1481 Barbak was succeeded by his son, who in turn was succeeded by his son. The last-named was deposed in favor of an uncle, Jalal-ud-din Fath Shah, who subsequently incurred the hostility of the African slave-soldiers. Thus, in 1486 a eunuch named Sultan Shahzada, commander of the palace guards, led the Africans in a successful usurpation of power, killed Fath Shah, and assumed the throne under the title of Barbak Shah. However, an African who was loyal to Fath Shah and was commander of the army, Amir-ul-Umara Malik Andil (Indil Khan), later murdered Barbak. At the request of Fath Shah's widow, he ascended to the throne under the title of Saif-ud-din Firuz. Some historians report that henceforth it became the rule in Bengal that he who killed the king's assassin had a right to the throne. In any case, Firuz's three-year reign restored a measure of discipline to the army and peace to the kingdom. When he died, Nasr-ud-din Mahmud, a minor whose ancestry remains in dispute, became king. Habesh Khan, another African, became Mahmud's regent.[5] When Habesh Khan assumed dictatorial power, Sidi Badr, an African guardsman, seized the throne in 1490. He ruled for over three years, under the title of Shams-ud-din Abu Nasr Muzaffar Shah. His army of 30,000 reportedly included 5,000 Abyssinians. After his assassination in 1493, the Africans in high posts were dismissed and expelled from the kingdom. This marked the end of the African dynasty in Bengal.[6]

The Siddis of Janjira

Janjira is said to be the Marathi corruption of the Arabic word *Jazira*, which means island. It is located off the west coast of India, about 45 miles south of Bombay. The first census of Janjira Island was taken in 1872 and reported a population of 1,700, of whom 258 were Siddis. Mostly relatives of the nawab (king), they were the principal landowners and civil servants and constituted the largest Muslim group on the island. Other religious groups included Hindus, Jews, and Christians. Until the British gained control of the island in 1879, a council of Siddi nobles chose the nawab, who was the head of state and religion (Islam). After consultation with the council, the nawab could appoint and dismiss state and religious officials.[7] How the Siddis obtained, preserved, and extended their power in Janjira and on the Konkan coast, just opposite the island, is explained largely by the role Janjira played in international trade.

In ancient times Janjira, the area around Bombay, and the Konkan coast participated in the profitable trade with Africa and Arabia. Pliny referred to the area as "the most frequented place on the pirate coast." One Indian writer, D. R. Banaji, has written that in ancient times "Siddis came to India only for the purpose of trade." Although there is very little evidence to confirm Banaji's statement, it is entirely possible that the ancient trade discussed in the Periplus did carry Africans to India's west coast. By the ninth century slaves are mentioned as being sent from the East African port of Sofala to ports in western India.[8]

According to one tradition, the Siddis arrived on Janjira Island around 1489, when an Abyssinian in the service of the nizam (king) of Ahmadnagar disguised himself as a merchant and took three hundred boxes of merchandise to the island. The "merchandise" included Siddi soldiers, who on command took possession of the island, appointed one of themselves king, and thus laid the foundation for the dynasties of the Siddi nawabs. The presence of Africans on Janjira prior to this time, however, can to a large extent be traced to the East African slave trade.

From about 1530 the Portuguese developed political and economic control over parts of the west coast of India, especially the Konkan coast, where many African slaves were imported. The number of slaves imported at any one time was small—between six and ten—but their arrival was fairly continuous to about 1740, when Portuguese maritime dominance was seriously challenged by the French and British. For the most part the slaves were from Mozambique, although the Portuguese also seized African slaves when they defeated the Muscat Arabs in Diu in 1670. The slaves were generally used by the Portuguese in businesses, on farms, in domestic positions, and in other menial jobs. Some of them were trained to be priests and teachers for religious schools, especially in Goa, which became Portugal's headquarters for its East African and Asian colonies.[9]

By the middle of the eighteenth century, therefore, Africans had established a long residence along India's west coast. Several observers noted the presence in this area of Abyssinian slaves, also known as Habshi Kafirs, with black skin and woolly hair.[10]

The most salient characteristic in the history of the Siddis of Janjira is the role they played from 1616 to about 1760 as prominent and successful naval guardians of the northwestern coast of India. When Malik Ambar, the African regent-minister in the Deccan, recovered the Konkan from the Mughuls in 1616, he appointed Siddi Ahmad Khan to command the area. From that point the Siddi seamen became a primary force on the Indian west coast. Malik Ambar did not exercise political or military control over Janjira; indeed, he recognized the Siddis' sea power and promised to direct trade to them in exchange for their refusal to ally themselves with the Mughuls.[11]

During the first half of the seventeenth century, British trade in the Arabian Sea increased to the point where the British East India Company sought to establish forts to protect and secure shelter for its company ships. As early as 1621 Malik Ambar attacked and inflicted a heavy loss on a British caravan.[12] The company thereupon sent Robert Jeffries to discuss the matter with Ambar, but the mission failed to gain either compensation or a promise of friendship. When subsequent negotiations with Ambar failed, the Siddis were tempted by bribes and subjected to force by company officials trying to separate the island from alliances with coastal rulers: "If wee cannot fairly obtaine it [Janjira], wee may forcibly" do so by considering Siddi interference with British shipping as piracy.[13]

This period was also marked by Mughul success in Gujarat. By 1636 Mughul armies had defeated the Marathas at Ahmadnagar, thereby becoming more dependent on an alliance with the Siddis of Janjira. (The Siddi agreement with Malik Ambar had terminated with his death in 1626.) As one Indian scholar has written:

> It is only when the Siddis of Janjira offered their services to the Moghals against the Maratha power on the sea that Aurangazib [the Mughul emperor] gave half hearted recognition to a fleet being organized on a reasonable scale. During 200 years of Moghal greatness, the Indian Sea was under alien control.[14]

The Mughuls recognized their need for a fleet in the Indian Ocean to divert the Maratha armies, to protect the Muslim pilgrims against attacks, and to guarantee the flow of trade into Mughul ports. They therefore agreed to subsidize the Janjira navy in order to achieve those objectives.[15]

From the middle of the seventeenth century, the power of the Marathas on the Konkan coast became a formidable force against Janjira. This was the time of the great Maratha hero, Shivaji, whose greatest achievement, according to one Indian military historian, was

> the welding of the Marathas into a nation ... and he achieved this in the teeth of the opposition of four mighty Powers like the Mughul empire, Bijapur [another Indian kingdom], Portuguese India, and the Abyssinians of Janjira.[16]

Of these several foes, the Siddis of Janjira were the most persistent and obdurate. Shivaji recognized the importance of allying his forces with or reducing the power of the Siddis. When he failed to do either, Shivaji created a strong navy to guarantee the flow of trade to his kingdom and to protect his subjects from periodic raids by the Siddis, who were regarded as "pirates alien by race, creed, and language." But the great Shivaji, in spite of long and gallant attacks on Janjira, never succeeded in capturing the island, which because of its impregnability came to be known as "the rock."[17]

The second half of the seventeenth century was also a time of great international rivalry in western India. There were conflicts between the Mughuls and the Marathas, and between both of them and the English, the Portuguese, and the Dutch, the last three of whom were competing for political and economic spheres of influence in western India as well as in East Africa. In 1665 the Portuguese ceded Bombay to the British government, which in 1668 transferred it to the East India Company; Janjira then became vital to the company as a base for protecting its maritime vessels. Attempting to exploit this situation, the Dutch in 1673 promised ships to the Marathas if they would attack Janjira and forestall British efforts to establish a base there, but the Marathas refused the offer.[18]

The Siddis were feared all along the western coast because of their frequent, indiscriminate raids on Indian and European vessels and towns. The only force capable of challenging them was the British, but they were reluctant to antagonize the Mughuls, with whom political and economic ties were regarded as necessary. But after a disagreement with the Mughuls in 1689, the British began capturing Siddi vessels supplying Mughul armies with provisions. Commander Siddi Kasim wrote several letters demanding that the English return the vessels; when that approach failed, he landed Siddi troops near Bombay, plundered the area, and then withdrew to Janjira.[19]

From the middle of the seventeenth century, when Mughul influence was dominate, Tegbakt, ruler of Surat, had acted as Mughul agent subsidizing the Siddi navy. Early in the eighteenth century, however, the Mughuls in Delhi began losing influence in Surat because of the increased flow of British money and arms to Tegbakt. The British hoped to persuade Tegbakt to transfer the subsidy from the Siddis to them. However, Tegbakt refused the appeal; he was suspicious of the British, whom he feared more than the Siddis. Thus rebuffed, the British sought agreements with Janjira. They succeeded in negotiating a treaty of alliance and friendship in 1733. The main articles of the treaty stipulated that, in case of war, Britain was to be the chief power (because of its greater resources and experience); if Bombay were attacked, Janjira was to contribute thirty small fighting boats and two thousand troops; if Janjira were attacked, Britain was to supply marines from Bombay. The two powers agreed to join against their enemies, and the consent of both governments was required for any peace settlements. The following year the East India Company agreed to subsidize the Janjira fleet as a further inducement to prevent them from aligning with "other forces hostile to English interests."[20]

Meanwhile, the Dutch continued their efforts to win Siddi support. They sought the cooperation of the Surat ruler and the Siddi fleet commander in an effort to secure a commercial monopoly at Surat. The fleet commander, Siddi Masud, seems to have cooperated with them, in spite of the treaty between Britain and Janjira. Although the details are not clear, between 1752 and 1756 Masud gained control of Surat with Dutch financial support; but when he was unable to maintain his control, the Dutch withdrew their aid, and control reverted to the Surat rulers.

In 1759 the British decided to eliminate Siddi influence in Surat completely. On 15 February 1759, they dispatched a large force of Europeans and Indians and several armed vessels of the East India Company's marine. On 4th March, the battle ended, with the British in command of Surat. The East India Company received a promise of the fleet subsidy that Surat rulers had been paying to the Siddis. Defeated, the Siddis were allowed to return to Janjira.[21]

Over the next century the influence of the Janjira Siddis declined perceptibly. Britain's political and economic stakes in India had risen to the point where she could not allow even the more powerful European countries to interfere; without a doubt, Siddi influence had to be eliminated. The defeat of the Siddis in 1759 represented the first and most important step in that direction. During the next three-quarters of a century the Janjira navy decreased to only a shadow of its earlier size and power. Then in 1834 the British government declared the island subject to British power; and later, in 1869, the first British resident officer was sent to Janjira. Although civil jurisdiction remained in Siddi hands, the resident officer had the power of review, and the Bombay government had veto power over the nawab's administration. In 1870 the nawab appealed for the return of Siddi authority; the Bombay government agreed to restore the nawab's authority if he would agree to reform his administration on the advice of the resident officer, defray all expenses of the British resident, maintain an efficient police force at a strength approved by the British, and formulate a code for revenue collection that would meet British approval. Preferential treatment of British trade was granted by the nawab, and in 1876 a British steamer began to sail between Bombay and Janjira. The final stroke against Siddi power in Janjira occurred when Siddi Ibrahim Khan died in 1879 and the British placed Siddi Ahmed Khan on the throne. There was much opposition from the Siddis, who felt that this action violated an important tradition. The great Siddi, Yacoot Khan, proclaimed on his deathbed that his family and Siddi nobles should choose a successor from among themselves. Therefore, although the Siddis were all equal candidates, it was their decision alone to choose a nawab. The action of the British denied them that prerogative and left no doubt about who the real power was in Janjira.[22] Today the Siddis' power and influence remain insignificant, though a Siddi is the ceremonial head of the island, which is a district in India.

Considering how small the Siddis were in number, their influence on Indian history is remarkable. It is unclear how they were able to wield such power over the several indigenous groups of the area. However, this was a region where Islam had been influential for centuries; and very likely it was this factor, along with the Siddis' maritime and military skills, that accounted for their success. It is no mean achievement that such a small, alien group exercised so much influence on the policies and actions of three European powers—England, Portugal, and the Netherlands—as well as local Indian powers. Furthermore, they achieved such a position without the advantage of a rich economy. Palm groves, salt, fish, timber, and some rice were the principal resources; and of those, only timber was in significant demand for export. The greatness of Janjira and the Siddis rested primarily on their strategic location in the Indian Ocean at a time when European maritime trade began to extend to South and East Asia, with India as a rich and crucial link. This phenomenon brought about European rivalry and, ultimately, British control.

Gujarat

Tradition holds that Africans were important in Gujarati armies as early as the thirteenth century, but it is likely that there were African mercenaries and slaves in Gujarat even earlier. However, by the sixteenth century Africans not only played significant roles in the armies but also rose to political and economic power. Although some of them no doubt descended from early African settlers in the region, many were also descendants of slaves and of Abyssinian prisoners taken by Arabs during the Muslim invasion of Ethiopia in 1527. Some of the latter were brought to Gujarat in 1531 by Mustafa bin-Bahram, a Turkish commander who was ordered by Constantinople to help defend Muslim India against Portugal. Mustafa's forces included Abyssinian prisoners, some of whom remained in Gujarat as merchants and mercenary soldiers. This seems to have been a principal base from which the subsequent Gujarati Habshi community emerged.[23]

There were several Habshis of particular note in the sixteenth century. When Mandal Dilawar Khan, a captain of Arab troops in Gujarat, was killed in battle in 1553, his deputy, an African named Yacut Sabit Khan Habshi, succeeded him as commander and received the honorary title of Ulugh Khan. Yacut was in turn succeeded by his son Khayrat Khan, who received the same honorary title and became a noted military commander. He was a patron of Hajji-ad-Dabir, a prominent author who wrote an Arabic history of Gujarat. Another Abyssinian, Jhujhar Khan, son of an earlier Habshi noble, was a commander who died in a battle near Diu in 1546 while protecting Gujarat from the Portuguese.[24]

In 1572 one of the important African nobles of Gujarat was Ikhtiyar-ul-Mulk, a commander of Habshi guards. Although he paid homage to the Mughul emperor Akbar, he deserted with his troops and rallied Afghans, Gujaratis, Rajputs, and Habshis in rebellion against Akbar. His rebel force eventually numbered about twenty thousand; although finally defeated by Akbar, he commanded the respect of Mughuls and Gujaratis alike.[25]

Sheik Sayeed al-Habshi Sultani was originally a Habshi slave who became a mercenary solider. On the death of his master, Mahmud III, around 1530, he joined Jhujhar Khan's army and served many years as a distinguished solider. When he retired, he acquired some land and became a wealthy noble, accumulating a large library that attracted scholars. He is said to have owned many horses, camels, and slaves. After having performed the Hadj, he became well respected, giving alms to the poor and feeding an estimated one thousand people daily.[26]

In 1573, just three years before his death, Sayeed (Sa'id) constructed a mosque in Ahmadabad. The chronogram for its construction reads: "For the sake of Allah he erected this mosque, and the builder is Sa'id." Known as Siddi Sa'id's mosque, it is simple in design with a roof built of arches. Its most beautiful features are the arched perforated windows with exquisite tracery and floral designs.[27] James Fergusson, noted authority on Indian and Eastern architecture, has observed of this mosque:

> It would be difficult to excel the skill with which the vegetable forms are conventionalized just to the extent required for the purpose ... but perhaps the greatest skill is shown in the even manner in which the pattern is spread over the whole surface. There are some exquisite specimens of tracery in precious marbles at Agra and Delhi, but none quite equal to this.[28]

The same expert, together with a colleague wrote:

> It is probably more like a work of nature than any other architectural detail that has been designed, even by the best architects of Greece or of the Middle Ages.[29]

Although the British colonials used the mosque for offices, British Consul Lord Curzon had it set aside as a monument. Today it occupies a square in the center of Ahmadabad. Commissariat wrote: "This lovely and world-famous mosque is the last noble specimen of the great creative period of the Muslim architecture of Gujarat."[30]

Siddi Bashire also built a mosque in Ahmadabad. The story behind this mosque is obscure. However, it is unique in that it has two shaking minarets, each comprising three stories. When one minaret is shaken, the vibration is carried to the other by the roof which joins them. Echoes are similarly carried from one to the other. This style is reported to have been an innovation at the time.[31]

The following lesser-known Africans are credited with constructing buildings and aqueducts in the vicinity of Ahmadabad: Ikhtiyar Khan, Oasim Khan, and Siddi Shamshir Khan, who were in the court of Ahmed Nizam Shah. There is also limited documentation to support oral accounts that the ruling family in the former state of Sachin was of African ancestry. In Surat, Jaffer Yab Khan, an Abyssinian slave in the family of the nawab, figured prominently in the 1758–59 invasion by the British, which ended in the restoration of Mecah [Atchund?] to the nawabship and the surrender of the castle at Surat to the English. For his participation on the side of the English, Jaffer's descendants received a pension from the British government.[32]

Richard Burton, who traveled extensively in Gujarat during the nineteenth century, reported that six hundred to seven hundred Africans arrived there annually. He also observed "several thousands" of African women inhabiting the region. In 1839 he saw a great number of African descendants in Karachi. "We meet them everywhere with huge water-skins on their backs, or carrying burdens fit for buffaloes." Unfortunately, Burton's curiosity did not lead him to investigate the background of this African presence in either of his studies.[33]

There are many persons of African descent in Gujarat's Gir forest and in Cutch. The proximity of this region to the Muslim provinces of Persia facilitated the migration of Africans from the Persian Gulf, where they had served as seamen and slaves. In fact, it is frequently said that Afro-Indians in western Gujarat are descendants of escaped slaves.

Wherever their origins, Africans in Gujarat played significant roles, not only in political and military matters, but also in cultural affairs.

Gujarat was very likely a gateway to India for many Africans from Muslim Persia, who brought with them cultural influences from the Persian Empire. This would account for the Muslim influences—dress, names, religious ceremonies, and architecture—evident in Afro-Indian communities in this part of India today.

NOTES

1. E. Bastani-Parizi, *Tarikh-e-Kerman* (Tehran: Bahman Press, 1961), 307, 476, translated for the author by Professor Boheni, English Department, University of Tehran, in September, 1967.

2. Bastani-Parizi, *History of the Saljuks and Goz in Kerman* (Tehran: Bahman Press: 1964) 12, 13, 15, 62, 176; and the oral testimonies of some United States Peace Corps Volunteers, Iranian professors at the University of Tehran and Paklovi University in Shiraz, and civil servants and merchants in Tehran, Isfahan, Shiraz, and Bandar Abbas during 1967.

3. Quoted in John Briggs, *History of the Rise of the Mohamedan Power in India* (Calcutta: Susil Gupta, 1958), I, 220.

4. R. C. Majumdar, *The History and Culture of the Indian People: The Delhi Sultanate* (Bombay: Macmillan, 1960), 186–87, 188, 698–702; and *The Cambridge History of India* (London: Cambridge University Press, 1937), III, 251–52.

5. Some observers believe Habesh Khan was Firuz's son, in which case he would have been African; others believe he was Fath Shah's son, in which case he would not have been African. See Majumdar, *History and Culture of the Indian People*, 214, 215.

6. R. C. Majumdar, *An Advanced History of India* (London: Macmillan, 1950), 345–346, and *Cambridge History of India*, III, 268–71.

7. Bombay, *Gazetteer of the Bombay Presidency*, Kolaba and Janjira (Bombay, 1883), XI, 409–23; and oral accounts.

8. D. R. Banaji, *Bombay and the Siddis* (Bombay: Macmillan, 1932), pp. x–xx; India, *Imperial Gazetteer of India, Bombay Presidency* (Calcutta: 1909), II, 488; and William Vincent, *Commerce and Navigation of the Ancients* (London: T. Cadell and W. Davis, 1807), II, 157. I have been unable to establish any connection between the Siddis of Janjira and Janjero in Ethiopia.

9. The Portuguese dispatched several military missions from Goa to East Africa. At least one African, Yusuf, son of Sultan Hasan of Mombasa, was educated in Goa by the Portuguese, who installed him on his father's throne under the name Don Jeronimo Chingula. This is a subject on which a good deal of additional research can be done, especially in the largely unused archives in Goa.

10. Bombay, *Gazetteer, Kolaba and Janjira*, 433.

11. Ibid., 434; R. V. Ramdas, "Relations between the Marathas and the Siddis of Janjira" (Ph.D. diss., University of Bombay, n.d.), 41.

12. William Foster, *English Factories in India, 1655–60* (Oxford: 1906), 208.

13. Ibid., 331.

14. K. M. Panikkar, *India and the Indian Ocean* (London: George Allan and Unvine, 1945), 8.

15. M. S. Commissariat, *A History of Gujarat* (Calcutta: Longmans, Green and Co., 1957), II, 173.

16. Jadunath Sarkar, *History of Aurangzib* (Calcutta: M. C. Sarkar, 1919), IV, 237–38. Note that Janjira is regarded as a "mighty Power."

17. Jadunath Sarkar, *Shivaji and His Times* (Calcutta: M. C. Sarkar, 1920), 251; and Mountstuart Elphinstone, *History of India* (London: J. Murray, 1905), 549–55.

18. Banaji, *Bombay and the Siddis*, 13–17.

19. Alexander Hamilton, *A New Account of the East Indies* (Edinburgh, 1927), I, 220–28; and J. A. Ovington, *Voyage to Surat in the Year 1689*, ed. II. G. Hawlinson (Oxford: Oxford University Press, 1929), 151.

20. Bombay, *Public Department Diary*, 5 (1732–33), 8 (1734–35), no. 33 (1759); and Bombay, *Surat Factory Diary* (March 1735–February 1736).

21. A. U. Aitchison, *Collection of Treaties, Engagements and Sunnuds* (London: Government of India, 1876), IV, 485–87; Bombay, *Gazetteer, Kolaba and Janjira*, 445–46; India, *Imperial Gazetteer, Bombay Presidency*, 126–27; and Commissariat, *History of Gujarat*, 172.

22. Bombay, Political Department, November, 1870, sec. A, 121–27; ibid., September, 1871, sec. A, 9–25; ibid., July, 1870, sec. A, 234–38; Aitchison, *Treaties*, 329–30; and Bombay, *Gazetteer, Kolaba and Janjira*, 449–52.

23. Commissariat, *History of Gujarat*, 470.

24. Ibid., 471.

25. Ibid., 508–24, 441–43, 448.

26. E. Dension Ross, *An Arabic History of Gujarat*, (London: John Murray, 1921), II, 640–43.

27. Ratnamanirao B. Jhote, *Ahmadabad* (n.p., n.d.), 16.

28. James Fergusson, *History of Indian and Eastern Architecture*, ed. James Burgess (Delhi: Munshiram Manoharlal, 1967), 236–37.

29. James Fergusson and Theodore Hope, *Architecture of Ahmadabad*, (London: John Murray, 1866), 86–87.

30. Commissariat, *History of Gujarat*, 505.

31. *Indian Express* (Bombay), 2 February 1968.

32. Radhey Shyam, *The Kingdom of Ahmadnagar* (New Delhi: Matilal Banarsidass, 1966), 372; Bombay, Foreign Department, 27 April 1855 37–40; India, Internal Department, December 1907, sec. B, 217.

33. Richard F. Burton, *Sindh and the Races That Inhabit the Valley of the Indus* (London: W.H. Allen, 1851), 253, 254, 256.

Return to
the Homeland

19

The Sierra Leone Krios: A Reappraisal from the Perspective of the African Diaspora

Akintola J. G. Wyse

HE African diaspora—the "expansion" of blacks of African descent to the New World, the Americas, and the Caribbean—emanated primarily from European contact with Africa, more especially from the economic and commercial system known as the *triangular trade*. Black men were seized from their homes and were exchanged for European goods and then transported as cargo to America, where they worked to produce the sugar, cotton, and other raw materials to supply the industries of Europe. After the cessation of the slave trade, many blacks remained in their homes of enforced adoption; others returned to their ancestral home in Africa, where their number was augmented by slaves rescued while being carried across the Atlantic. Some of these blacks formed a new society, the Krio Society of Sierra Leone.

This essay suggests that (1) the triangular trade must be seen not only in its economic context but also as a vehicle conveying persons, ideas, and foods; (2) the African diaspora can be examined from another dimension—the nineteenth-century transcoastal demographic movement, or internal dispersion, within the African continent itself. Two categories of settlers are considered. One group includes the New World returnees, the black poor from England, the Nova Scotians from Halifax, Canada, and the maroons from Jamaica. These settlers were rehabitated in Freetown and were joined by another group of Africans—the liberated Africans—Yorubas, Efiks, Igbos, Calabaris, Hausas, Popos, Congolese, Ashantis, and Mendes (Kossohs)—from along the Atlantic coast.

(There were other back-to-Africa groups in America, such as those promoted by the Afro-American Indian Paul Cuffe, 1811–71; but they had a marginal impact on the Sierra Leone settlement.) The interaction of these two categories of settlers gave rise to the evolution of the Krios. Even while their society was being formed, the "rescued Africans" began to move into other areas of Africa in the first half of the nineteenth century; Freetown also became a nodal point of dispersion, and the Krio diaspora began at this time.[1]

Our present knowledge of the Krio diaspora is limited, although some work has been done on it for some areas.[2] In this essay not much will be said about Krio immigrants in various parts of Africa. References will be made to them, of course, but specific comments will be limited to the Freetown Krios.

There is no lack of literature on the Krios of Sierra Leone,[3] but these people have not yet been satisfactorily discussed. As late as 1977, scholars raised doubts about the existence of a "cohesive group" called "Creoles" (Krios) before the middle of the present century.[4] What is important here, however, is to place the Krios within the context of the African diaspora. The study of these "new people in West Africa"[5] affords an opportunity to observe the forces at work in the general diaspora: the pulling of different cultures on the one hand and their coalescence on the other; the adjustments, for many, to strange environments; and the groups' contributions to, and impact on, the community in which they found themselves. The Krio dispersal was one within the larger African diaspora.

The history of the founding of the Sierra Leone settlement in 1787 for free blacks can be read in standard works on Sierra Leone history.[6] This essay will identify the major groups of immigrants.

The Making of a Community: Arrival, Resettlement, and Evolution

The Black Poor of London

The first group of immigrants to come to Sierra Leone were the black poor of London.[7] These were slaves who had escaped to London from overseas plantations or had accompanied their masters to the metropolis. Their freedom became more secure with the pronouncement of the famous Lord Mansfield judgement of 1772, which has popularly been interpreted as meaning that once a slave set foot on English soil he became a free man. Whatever the correct interpretation, this statement left many blacks without masters and so without protection. They became destitute and posed a social problem for the English government. It was initially to resettle these people that the Sierra Leone experiment was launched. As conceived, the experiment reflected the resurgent Christian evangelism of eighteenth-century enlightened Europe. There was also a growing interest in the study of human beings and their response to society, and one area of human endeavor that naturally received the attention of the humanitarians of the eighteenth century was the slave trade. This traffic in human beings began to be attacked in earnest during this period, and foremost in the ranks of the antislave trade lobby were philanthropists, evangelists, and liberal reformers like Thomas Clarkson, Granville Sharpe, William Wilberforce, Zachary Macauley, and Henry Thornton, that band of social reformers known as the Clapham Sect. In addition to mounting arguments against the slave trade, the Clapham Sect, by founding the settlement, made a positive gesture to expiate the wrongs that Europe had done to Africa through its direction of, and participation in, the odious commerce of humans for several centuries.[8]

But "the Province of Freedom," as the new colony was designated, was much more than this. Its sponsors, notably Granville Sharpe, hoped to provide a background, a launching pad for the evolution of a free, self-governing black community (with their tithingmen and hundredors),[9] enjoying and exercising all the rights and freedoms of Englishmen and equitably sharing the profits of their labor. It was meant to demonstrate that, given the opportunity and the encouragement, the black man could become as "civilized" as the white man. Also, the success for the project could be used to advantage in rebutting the claims of supporters of the slave trade that the only way to "civilize" black men was through the yoke of slavery.

The Sierra Leone peninsula was chosen as a settlement because of the glowing reports furnished by a British botanist, Henry Smeathman, on its agricultural potential. Between 1771 and 1774, Smeathman had collected specimens in the offshore Banana Islands. He himself had some ambitions of founding an agricultural settlement, and because his ideas were consistent with those of the humanitarians of the Committee for the Relief of the Black Poor (set up in 1786 under the chairmanship of Jonas Hanway), with whom he was in contact, the collaboration of these interested groups, supported by the British government, resulted in the mounting of an expedition to Sierra Leone. Four hundred eleven immigrants, including emancipated blacks and some white persons, left England in February 1787. They arrived in Sierra Leone on 14 May 1787.

A piece of land twenty square miles in area was secured from King Tom, a subchief of the Temnes who occupied the peninsula at that time. A site was cleared on the western tip of the peninsula near a watering place, and the settlers called it Granville Town. They elected their leaders according to the instruction of Granville Sharpe and proceeded to plan their settlement. That was the only positive achievement of this first batch of settlers, for from the outset the new settlement was plagued by a number of misfortunes: the weather, disease, the disappointing agricultural prospect, the hostile attitude of the local inhabitants, and a variety of other causes.

By 1791 only forty-eight of the original colonists remained, even though, at some expense to himself, Sharpe had sent supplies and another batch of colonists, mostly whites, in 1788. The ideal state Sharpe envisioned seemed to have died at birth, but significantly the project had not lost its relevance. Sharpe and his colleagues were still dedicated humanitarians. Another effort with a commercial flavor was now made to Sharpe's humanitarian ideals. Because some of the philanthropists were hard-nosed businessmen anyhow, and based their hopes on Smeathman's report on the agricultural possibilities of the peninsula, the humanitarians now decided to run the fledgling colony on a commercial basis. Their plans explained that Christian precepts and the humanitarians' civilizing aspirations would be put into practice. Under a benevolent Christian government, the settlers would be gainfully employed in agriculture. The trade that would derive from this occupation would be substituted for the trade in slaves, and the profits that would accrue would go to the Sierra Leone Company, which was chartered in July 1791.[10]

It is easy to be cynical about this profit motive of the company, but the sincerity of the humanitarians to establish a viable community that would become "civilized" and Christian, that would later spread the good points of European civilization to other parts of the continent, could not be questioned. This is the importance of the Sierra Leone experiment, although the vindication of these hopes was still about a quarter of a century away.

The Nova Scotians from Canada

While the directors in London were finalizing plans for the launching of the company and searching for immigrants to go to the settlement, an opportune incident occurred that was to give the colony renewed hope.[11] In 1791, an emancipated black man, Thomas Peters, risked a journey across the Atlantic to London to complain about the injustices meted out to his fellow blacks in Nova Scotia. He represented a group of black emancipated slaves who had fought on the side of the Union Jack during the American War of Independence. In gratitude for their help, and also in fear of reprisals being taken against them by the victorious Americans, the British government had offered these "black Loyalists" asylum in Nova Scotia, Canada. They had been promised many things, including free land, but these promises had not been kept. The cold climate of their new home was also not congenial, and among other things, these Nova Scotians resented the prejudices and slightly veiled contempt of their white neighbors.

While in London, Peters may have been put in touch with Granville Sharpe, the acknowledged friend of black men. It is not clear whether it was Sharpe or the chairman of the company, Henry Thornton, who suggested to Peters that Sierra Leone could be an alternative settlement for the Nova Scotians; but what is certain is that the Nova Scotians decided to emigrate to their ancestral home, Africa. Because the company needed black colonists, and the Nova Scotians wanted to emigrate, a mutually satisfactory arrangement was reached with the company. The company agreed to transport the Nova Scotians to Sierra Leone free and to allot to each man plots of land of specified sizes for agriculture. After overcoming a number of difficulties, Lt. John Clarkson, an ardent humanitarian and brother of Thomas Clarkson, one of the company directors, left Nova Scotia with 1,196 emancipees in January 1792. In March, the second major immigrant group in the colony arrived in Sierra Leone.

On landing, the Nova Scotians founded a site for a town near the first Granville Town and called it Freetown. There they were joined by the survivors of the earlier efforts at settlement. Within two years the town had been planned, with straight streets bearing the names of such famous contemporaries as Oxford, Westmoreland, Bathurst, Liverpool, Percival, Pultney, and Walpole. Stone houses began to appear. A local government of tithingmen and hundredors was established. Trial was by jury. A militia was created. In short, the makings of an administration were introduced within a very short time. Thus, the coming of the Nova Scotians actually began the colony of Sierra Leone.

This group set the pattern for the evolution of Krio society and bequeathed these attributes to their descendants; its high cultural attainments, its modern outlook, the sometimes ambiguous relationship with white men, its political consciousness, the continual struggle with authority, its religiosity, its litigiousness, its individuality, and that unfortunate capacity to fragment.[12] All these facets of the society that were to evolve had been established by the first years of the Nova Scotian presence in Sierra Leone. Many of the Nova Scotians were literate, and because most of them had been born in North America, they spoke only English. They were Christians who subscribed to a fundamentalist, antiauthoritarian Protestantism. They gave Freetown its Christian outlook. Their experiences in the American South and in Canada gave them a pioneer tradition. Living in an epoch of revolutionary fervor, and indeed having participated in a revolution (on the side of the British), they had acquired a high sense of political consciousness. As Paul Hair observed, "They were the first Africans to echo the slogans of modern world politics." And they reinforced these qualities with an independent spirit, hard work, and inventiveness.[13] In short, they imported Western civilization into Africa and implanted that Western tradition that still perplexes the foreign observer of past and present day Krios.

Not surprisingly, this literate and politically opinionated group soon ran afoul of a regime that granted minor concessions to articulate settlers but insisted on retaining ultimate authority in the hands of the company. The settlers resented white authority and challenged the company's rights to control the affairs of the settlement. They disputed the legality of the company's attempts to tax them, and indignantly cried, "No representation, no taxation." They staged a number of uprisings, without much success. The Nova Scotians were accused of having been tainted with the revolutionary dogma of the Americans; authorities ignored their claims for equality and called them ingrates. This conflict, arising from the African claim for political equality and regret felt by the British over their creation, is a theme that ran through Anglo-Krio relations in the colonial period.[14] The British maintained a consistent policy of using West Indian elements to counteract the claims and political agitation of "Sierra Leoneans" at specific periods in their history. The first successful use of the ploy was in 1800.

The Maroons

Difficulties with the company over taxation and misunderstandings over what had been promised the Nova Scotians came to a boil in 1799 when the company sought a legal basis for its rule. The charter that established authority was granted in July 1799, and it firmly entrusted power in the hands of a governor and his council and gave the latter judicial and administrative powers. A positive development was the establishment of a municipality, of a mayor's court, for civil cases, assisted by aldermen. Civil and criminal cases were to be tried by jury. But the charter took away rights that the Nova Scotians had cherished: for instance, their right to elect tithingmen and hundredors to influence the governor and the council.

Before the charter actually arrived, the Nova Scotians rebelled against the company. The forces of the company were almost at the point of being overrun when at this critical moment a ship arrived bringing about five hundred and fifty new immigrants, the maroons, accompanied by some troops. Although they had been expected, they could not have come at a more opportune time for the company. With these reinforcements the government forces were able to rout the Nova Scotians in October 1800. It was the first but certainly not the last time that violent African protest against European authority was suppressed by superior forces.

The colony's third group then arrived with a flourish. These maroons were descendants of slaves who originally came from Koromantee in the Gold Coast. They were reputedly Ashanti "warriors." And when they were taken to Jamaica, they proved to be the most intractable and ungovernable slaves; they ran away to the mountains (hence *Cimarons* = runaway slaves = Maroons) and waged a ceaseless war with the British authorities for many years. Finally, the British shipped them to Nova Scotia, but the disagreeable climate induced the British government to transfer them to the more congenial climate of Sierra Leone.[15]

The maroons brought their own subculture, such as music (the *talla*, a predecessor of the *goombay* music),[16] but they did not alter the society that was being formed. If anything, their relationship with the Nova Scotians was hostile at the beginning. Because the maroons had been used to frustrate the rebellion of the Nova Scotians, they were regarded by their neighbors with contempt as "barbarians" outside the pale of civilization. In time, however, the two groups fused into a more or less homogeneous community.[17]

By 1806, the hoped-for commercial success of the settlement still eluded the Sierra Leone Company for several reasons: the disappointing agricultural prospects, mainly due to the poor soil of the colony and the reluctance of the settlers to till the ground; the diversion to trade of individual settlers; the endless wrangling with the Nova Scotians; the attacks on the settlement by the French in 1794 (which nearly destroyed the colony); and the depredations of the local Temne people. Thus, in 1806 the company directors asked the British government, which had been providing handouts to the company since 1802, to take over responsibility of the colony. Thus, in 1808 Sierra Leone became a Crown colony. In the previous year the antislave trade lobby had succeeded in persuading the British parliament to abolish the slave trade,[18] and Sierra Leone, by virtue of its location and because of its antecedents, naturally became the base for the naval squadron that patrolled the West African coast to arrest violators of the antislave trade agreements. It also became the headquarters of the various admiralty courts that were set up to try slavers captured by the Royal Navy.[19]

The Liberated Africans

Abolition introduced the fourth and largest immigrant group, the liberated Africans, into the colony of Sierra Leone. The naval squadron and the admiralty courts were responsible for the recapture and rehabilitation in Sierra Leone of some sixty thousand slaves from 1808 to 1864.[20] These liberated Africans came from many parts of Africa, on the West and even from the East coasts.[21] They included the various subgroups of the Yoruba, Igbos, Hausas, Congolese, Popos, Ashantis, Calabaris, and Bambaras.[22] Of all these groups, the Yoruba were the largest; next came the Igbos.[23] Historians heavily emphasize the Yoruba elements and thus convey the impression that the bulk of the liberated Africans came from Yorubaland. There is also a tendency to ignore the many liberated Africans who were indigenous to Sierra Leone. I have argued in another essay that a large number of the liberated Africans were Mendes (Kossohs), Temnes, Limbas, and Susus, inhabitants of the interior of modern Sierra Leone. This evidence, of course, makes nonsense of the view held with some consistency even today that the Krios were foreigners.[24] The crucial point is that it was this fourth group, the liberated Africans, who had never seen the New World, who supplied the African face of the coin in this burgeoning colony; there are also documented cases of some Nova Scotians, like John Kizzell and John Gordon, who were able to trace their roots in Sierra Leone.[25]

Diffusion and Fusion

By 1800, the colony was a polyglot community, and it was made more variegated by successive additions of peoples from different social backgrounds in the subsequent decades of the first half of the nineteenth century. What were the chances then of such a community, about which an observer remarked eighty years later that it was "a good field for an anthropologist who desires to study the varieties of African men and races,"[26] welding itself into an identifiable ethnic group? That it did become one is not in question in this paper, but we must identify the factors that brought about its coalescence. Propinquity, shared experiences, and the British administration were certainly key factors. By declaring in 1853 that, together with earlier settlers, all liberated Africans were British subjects, the authorities distinguished these groups from the inhabitants of the interior, thereby conceding and acknowledging the evolution of an exclusive, if not exactly homogeneous, community. On the other hand, the administration favored one group over another at various times and failed even to choose a name for the community. Over time, various names were used to describe them; some of them were plainly pejorative: Sierra Leoneans, settlers, descendants of liberated Africans, colony-born, nonnative, a community of half-educated people,[27] and so forth. Such confusing terms hardly make identification less difficult.

Let us take the Nova Scotians first. They were Christians and had their own religious demonstrations of Methodists, Huntingdonians, and Baptist; they also had their own schools. Fully conscious of their political rights, their education, and their religiosity, they affected the mannerisms and assumed the attitudes of a middle-class elite.[28] This "effete" way of life, commented the Sierra Leone historian, A. B. C. Sibthorpe, eventually brought ruin to the Nova Scotians.[29] But Sibthorpe was a hostile commentator, and in any case, the maroons, a more "vigorous" and "industrious"[30] people, were sufficiently impressed to copy the postures and mannerisms of the earlier settlers. And notwithstanding their ambivalent attitude toward the settlers, the British encouraged them in their pretentions. The Nova Scotians then were a referent group to whose social ethics all subsequent groups had to subscribe, after an initial period of mutual hostility, if they were to become socially acceptable. In time the Nova Scotians began to intermarry with the maroons, and these two earlier groups intermarried with the liberated Africans, who, in their first years, were at the bottom of the social pyramid.[31]

So profound did this stratified status imprint itself on the society that the liberated Africans, even with their overwhelming numbers, did not destroy this Western infrastructure but merged into it. Still retaining their traditional beliefs and customs, the newcomers injected some color and variety into the community.[32]

It should be admitted, though, that the liberated Africans on arrival were not the most prepossessing sight. They were social outcasts. The early settlers taunted them with names like "willy foss niggers" and "new cruits."[33] Fergussen, the mulatto lieutenant-governor of Sierra Leone in 1840, said of them:

> The condition of a body of captive slaves on their arrival at Sierra Leone for liberation is the most miserable and wretched that can be conceived—emaciated, squalid, sickly looking, illfed, barbarous, confined in inadequate space, compelled to breathe an atmosphere hardly fit for sustenance of animal life —is it to be wondered that, in such circumstances, the faculties of the soul should be cramped and benumbed by the cruelties inflicted on the body? It is nevertheless from among such people and their descendants at Sierra Leone, their minds at length elevated by a sense of personal freedom and by the temperate administration of just and equable laws, that you are to look for the first practical results of your operation.[34]

The Acculturation of the Liberated Africans

For the first ten years after the recaptives had been freed from their dismal situation and fed and clothed, the rehabilitation of the liberated

Africans was not directed by any consistent policy. Policy varied from putting them to work on public works, to enlisting them in the army or apprenticing them to earlier settlers. But in 1814, when Sir Charles Macarthy became governor of Sierra Leone, a more positive policy was outlined. It developed into the parish system of 1817.[35] Briefly, Macarthy accepted the broad aims of the eighteenth-century philanthropists, to "civilize" and Christianize Africans, and to instill in them the appreciation of the supreme benefits of hard work. To include the liberated Africans in this grand design, he established local authorities in the villages founded for this purpose, where many liberated Africans were placed under the guidance of Church Missionary Society (CMS) clerics.

The CMS had begun to appear in Freetown in 1804, but its proselytizing efforts were directed toward the Susu in the interior. Disappointed in the Susu mission and urged by the government to cooperate with them in Christianizing the liberated Africans, the CMS began to concentrate on the newcomers.[36] Education and the direction of the civilizing process were to remain largely in their hands for the rest of the century, although the Methodist missionaries, who had begun work among the liberated Africans before CMS, also played a significant part.[37]

The missionaries, assisted by African catechists who had, at an early stage, showed an interest in evangelization, taught their pupils to read and write. The exercise may not have been an easy one, considering that many of the pupils were in fact adults; and there was a lot of backsliding, which incessantly despaired missionaries like the Reverend W. A. B. Johnson of Regent Village.[38] But many showed an aptitude to learn, and many adopted Christianity, "even enthusiastically."[39] A significant group of liberated Africans—mostly Yoruba, known in Sierra Leone as Aku—resolutely refused to abandon the Islamic faith to which they had recently been converted during the Fulani jihad of the nineteenth century. Sustained by Muslim itinerant traders and marabouts like the Susus, Foulahs, and Mandingos who frequently came to the colony and settled in the east end of Freetown, these Muslim-liberated Africans tended to live a cloister-like existence, much attached to their traditional way of life. But as recent studies have revealed, they did not cut themselves off from their Christian brothers; there were consanguinal links between them. They also showed the same thirst for education, even to the extent of nominally assuming Western names to seek admission in the missionary schools, and they remained part of the group, distinguished only by their religion. Today, they are referred to as Aku Mohamedans or Muslim Krio.[40]

The liberated Africans who became Christians did not eschew their traditional customs and rites. Some may have felt guilty in continuing to worship what the missionaries dismissed as idols, after they had become Christians. And their bewilderment should not surprise us. The almost pathological hatred some missionaries had for these African customs was enough to confound the African who was only just coming to terms with Christianity. John Peterson gives a number of stories of missionaries who denounced the *Egungun* or *Oje* cults and decried African drumming. On one occasion the Reverend Graf of Hastings wrathfully attempted to flog an *Egun*, only to find that he was flogging "a mass of empty *Egugu* clothes." Missionaries failed to appreciate that these cults—like *Oje*, the Hunting Society, *Gunugu*, and *Otta*—fulfilled a need and continued traditions that predated the liberated Africans' settlement in the colony.[41] And as Paul Hair, writing in 1964, has sermonized, the Krios do not need to feel guilty over the question of reconciling their adherence to Christianity with loyalty to African traditions "because Freetown Christianity is related on one side to one thousand and more years of Christianity in other continents and on another side to African traditions in religion; this does not mean that it ought to be treated as a false descendant of either or both."[42]

The ancestors of the Krios had anticipated this advice. They continued to absorb Western determinants of civilization, but they retained their traditional cultures. In time they were able to fuse these in a distinct culture that continues to fascinate or exasperate the foreign observer. Indeed, such was their ability to cooperate to better themselves, and to adapt traditional or benefit societies, such as the Seventeen Nations, to keep law and order among themselves, that more than one scholar has commented favorably on the liberated Africans' success at social mobilization.[43]

The liberated Africans were resilient, enterprising, inventive, and resourceful. This is clear from the success stories of many descendants of this group. To take one example, the constraints on agricultural development in the colony, and the poor planning by the government, rather than Africans' abhorrence of manual work, diverted the energies of the liberated Africans to trade, an occupation to which many were not strangers. Stories about recaptives combining their resources to buy salvaged ships in order to trade palm oil, fish, and timber along the coast, or to travel up the creeks and waterways of the hinterland of Sierra Leone as lone traders, blazing the trail for "civilization," are legion.[44]

Within thirty years of the arrival of the liberated Africans, a few of them had achieved substantial success to merit notice in society. Their wealth and education gave them a social standing in the Freetown community. They began to own property, competing successfully with the earlier settlers. Sibthorpe distinguished them in a graded scale from the mud houses of the most recent arrivals to the two-story houses with spacious piazzas of the established liberated Africans.[45] They began to send their children to England for further studies;[46] merchants like John Ezzidio, the Brights, Independent Grant, the Lewises, and many more became leaders of commerce and senior citizens in church and state. Christopher Fyfe's profile on four largely illiterate recaptives, Emmanuel Cline (Hausa), William Jenkins and James Godfrey Wihelm (Igbo), and William Johnson (Aku), who had established themselves in society within twenty years of their arrival, illustrates the success story of the liberated Africans as a group.[47]

As the material position of the liberated Africans improved, they became integrated into society. They turned themselves into a bourgeoisie, no different from their European counterparts in the outward manifestation of the Westernized modern society. This rise to prominence of children of low-status, liberated Africans reflected an open-ended society. Schools were established to give them an education superior to that of their parents: the Fourah Bay College in 1827 (from the earlier Christian Institution, founded in 1814); the CMS Grammar School (1845); and four years later its female counterpart, the Female Institution, rechristened the Annie Walsh Memorial School (1877). These schools, and the Wesleyan Methodist Boys' High School (1874) and the Girls' High School (1880), produced the first educated elite in West Africa. Those who were educated abroad vindicated the inherent abilities of Africans: Gurney Nicol, son of a recaptive Temne, became the first African graduate of Cambridge University in 1879.[48] Freetown could also boast of other determinants of Western modernism. It had a press dating from 1800, and by 1860 several of its newspapers were owned by Africans.[49] As the process of cultural fusion progressed, there was a pruning down of differences between the ethnic groups, though they still acknowledged their origins. Moreover, historical accident and practical realities began to fashion a form of speech referred to as patois but identified by Sibthorpe early in the nineteenth century as *Africo-German* or *Aku-English*. This speech form, drawing from its many African sources, later developed into the Krio language, based on English but having a syntax that is African and a grammar with its own regularity of form, diction, and etymology.[50]

By the middle of the century, a Krio society had been formed, and so successfully had it blended its adopted Western civilization and its inherited African culture that one scholar has commented:

> The way in which these Sierra Leoneans not only survived their traumatic experiences, but in a single generation mastered the language and skills of Europe so successfully that they became a prosperous and professional and merchant elite, is a major triumph of the human spirit.[51]

This view is reinforced by a look at another dimension of this example of the African diaspora, the outreach of the Krios, or the Krio dispersal, to other parts of Africa.

The Krio Dispersal

In a number of works this dispersal is interpreted as a Krio rejection of their own backyard.[52] Recent investigations make such a view untenable today, but at the same time one may concede that for many the pull coastward might well have been prompted by ethnocultural considerations.[53] However, the beginning of the move coastward is usually dated from 1839 (though there are indications that it might have started earlier), and the inspiration is traditionally attributed to the arrival in Freetown in 1839 of two Hausas/Mandingoes who declared that they were on their way to their homelands.[54] Many then realized that they might not be far from their own homelands. The idea that they could risk the voyage back caught the popular imagination. Some liberated Africans petitioned the colonial government to allow them to go to Badagry to establish a colony there. Their request was refused for a number of reasons, but the point that must not be missed is that the liberated Africans of their own volition and initiative wanted to go to their ancestral lands to take with them variables of Western civilization that they had imbibed in Sierra Leone. And despite initial official disapproval, they did brave the unknown to emigrate to other lands. It may have looked like cultural subimperialism, but in reality they were fulfilling the hopes of Granville Sharpe to be bearers of civilization, to be cultural frontiersmen; indeed, their project and the ideals it contained anticipated Thomas Fowell Buxton's own remedy for the slave trade that led to the Niger Expedition of 1841. In any case, once the liberated Africans began to return to their original homes, the dispersal generated itself. The story of the Egba shipowner, Captain Henry Johnson, may not be typical, but it gives a picture of how this dispersal was effected. Starting as a trader in the early 1830s, he was wealthy enough to buy a condemned slave ship for £205 in 1841. Two years later he bought another for £395. He sailed regularly back and forth between Freetown and Badagry taking emigrants and trade goods and returning with produce.[55]

By the first half of the nineteenth century, these immigrants, called Saros, were to be found in several places in Yorubaland among the various Yoruba subgroups. Their reception was not uniformly welcome. They were regarded as foreigners, but they had the skills that, as the European advance in African societies became more pronounced, were needed to meet this challenge. And because Sierra Leone at various times was the headquarters of the British settlements in West Africa, the services of these Westernized Africans were needed. Indeed, this need for minor officials gave an opportunity to the liberated Africans, or Saros, or Sierra Leoneans (these became interchangeable terms by this time) to follow, and sometimes to precede, the establishment of European civilization and administration. These Saros served as clerks, as missionaries, and even as secretaries for "native potentates" wherever they decided to settle.[56] Many raised their families in their new homes. A few may have rediscovered their kinsmen and then merged into the local setting. But quite a large number of the Saros retained their links with Sierra Leone, their "cradle of dispersion." They sent their children to schools in Freetown, visited their relatives in Sierra Leone, or returned to die there. Generally, they maintained a separate identity among the host peoples.

As the West African climate was still unkind to the European, the view gained currency that educated Africans could usefully be employed in responsible jobs. This led to the sponsorship of James Africanus Beale Horton, son of an Igbo recaptive, and Broughton Davies, an Aku descendant, to study medicine in Britain in 1855. These examples inspired Krio parents to do what they could to educate their sons as lawyers and doctors, who then joined the itinerant Saros and put their skills to use in various parts of Africa. These professions became the goals of many sons of merchant families. Many in the second half of the century were trained and qualified as lawyers and doctors.[57] This development has been seen as an important factor in the decline of the Krio commercial entrepreneurs of the nineteenth century because family businesses were not perpetuated by the white-collar sons of these merchants. But the examples of the Brights and Shorunkeh Sawyerrs, who retained their links with commerce, call for a qualification of that conclusion.

In the church, more than any other area, the descendants of the liberated Africans played prominent roles. The names that come readily to mind are those of Adjai Crowther (a recaptive himself), the first African bishop in the Niger, and the Reverend James Johnson, the radical clergyman from Sierra Leone.[58] The impact and the contributions of these and other Saros to the development of Nigeria and Ghana are too well known to need repeating here. "Sierra Leoneans," Krios, also went to work in many other parts of Africa as skilled artisans, teachers, lawyers, and doctors. They were to be found in the Congo, in South Africa, and in the French African territories.[59] It is hoped that studies of the Krio presence in these areas will be attempted.

Contemporaneous with the beginning of this dispersal was the government-directed emigration to the West Indies under the inden-

tured scheme to supply labor to the West Indian planters. Dr. J. U.
Aseigbu has observed that this scheme lasted only twenty-one years and
involved a small number of liberated Africans, but at least one researcher has suggested that the emigration caused a big drain on the
youth, skill, and potential of the Sierra Leone colony.[60]

With regard to the interior of Sierra Leone, Walker makes it clear in
his book on the Nova Scotians that from the earliest days the inhabitants
of the colony had some rapport, vague and imprecise as it was, with
interior inhabitants.[61] Deveneaux, Fyfe, and Ijagbemi have made references to Krio economic penetration of the northern parts of Sierra
Leone.[62] Krio men and women traded, settled, and interacted with
interior inhabitants. Churches were built in isolated areas, for example,
at Fourecai,[63] in what is now the northern province of Sierra Leone;
children from the hinterland were taught; and marriages between people in the interior and Krios took place. There are many Sierra Leoneans
today who are products of those unions. Many Krios stayed in the
protectorate even after the Hut Tax War of 1898 in which hundreds of
Krios were killed because they were regarded as agents of white
civilization and imperialism. This so-called Krio/countryman cleavage
is an overworked and overexaggerated theme in Sierra Leone history.[64]

Krio Baiting

By the middle of the nineteenth century, the Krios seemed to be
acting as "cultural vectors" in fulfilling the dreams of the original
conceivers of the Sierra Leone experiment. Yet is was precisely at this
time, in the 1860s, when the Krios were making important contributions
to West African societies and attaining important positions in the government, that doubts began to be raised about their achievements.[65]

Krio baiting was started by the mercurial Victorian adventurer,
Richard Burton, who, offended by the air of importance exhibited by his
Krio fellow passengers, was stung to disparage the whole group as
half-educated upstarts and degenerates. They were despised for aping
(badly, their detractors charged) the white man. They became the
scourge of the coast. One can forgive Burton and other Eurocentric
Negrophobes for having such opinions about the Krios, because they
were merely reechoing the growing racialism and intolerance toward
educated Africans in the period following Darwin's *Origin of the Species*.[66]
But African observers such as Dr. Edward Blyden, reputedly the most
distinguished black man in this period, and James Johnson himself,
were to repeat these opinions about the Krios. Emasculated by Western
influences, they were poor specimens when compared with their untu-

tored brethren in the hinterland—the pure and uncontaminated Africans.[67]

The Impact of the Krios

Because these views have a habit of repeating themselves over time, we must pause here to examine the society, the end product of the diaspora, by asking some pertinent questions and, it is hoped, supplying adequately plausible answers: Did the Krios execute and fulfill the hopes of the philanthropists as cultural agents of European civilization? Is there any validity in the disparaging remarks of observers from Burton to Ayandele who described the society as irrelevant, exclusive, with meaningless posturings, unable to come to terms with realities? Did the Krios, with an acquired culture, assume a superior attitude that frowned on manual labor; and was this attitude dominated by a white-collar ethic? In short, what is the relevance of the Krios for African diaspora studies?

David Skinner and Barbara Harrell-Bond have tried to answer these questions in a paper called "On Misunderstandings Arising from the Use of the Term 'Creole' in the Literature on Sierra Leone," as have A. J. G. Wyse and C. M. Fyfe in "Kriodom: A Maligned Culture."[68]

The term *Krio*, which has been used in this essay in place of the more widely known form "Creole," is now the acceptable term for people as well as their language. The work *Creole* (from the Spanish Criollo, that is, the children of aborigines and Spanish and Portuguese settlers born in Latin America) has been wrongly applied to the African colonists in Sierra Leone. For one thing the people called themselves Creeyo or Creo or Krio, and *Creole* may well be one of those over-compensations in the Krio language. The late Thomas Decker, an ardent cultural nationalist, suggested that the term *Creole* may have been imported by those "Africans who had sojourned in America and the West Indies" (the Nova Scotians and maroons?).[69] The term itself was first used by a colonial surgeon in Sierra Leone in 1843, and he explained it as meaning "children born in the Colony."[70] A more plausible origin of the current term is from the Yoruba verb *Kiri*, to walk about, and the adjective *Yo*, full or satisfied, contracted thus *Kriyo*. The liberated Africans, and their descendants the Krios, followed a pastime of visiting relatives and friends, especially after church service, and the Yoruba, whose cultural stamp seems to have been superimposed on Krio society, may have used this word to refer to their habit.[71]

The use of this form is not widespread, and many would want to contest the origins of Krio, but we "Kriolists" are satisfied about its antecedents, and when the completed work on a Krio dictionary by Professors Eldred Jones and Clifford Fyfe is published, greater currency will be given to it.

A superficial view of Krio society in the nineteenth and twentieth centuries would lend credence to the charge that they were "black Englishmen." Theirs was a genteel and bourgeois little "England in Africa" (and such was the intention of their sponsors, like Granville Sharpe), but it was a facade,[72] an outer shell that masked the deeper Africanness of the Krios. Like Africans from traditional societies, they have reverence and respect for their elders; they believe in a supreme being, have an understanding of the cycle of human life, and borrow liberally from Yoruba cosmology;[73] they observe *Komojade* or *pull na do* (the "bringing out" of the child) and *put stop* (engagement); they acknowledge the death cult or ancestor worship—three-day, seven-day, forty-day, and one-year commemorations of the death of a kinsman, celebrated in an *Awujoh* or big feast; and they follow elaborate traditional burial procedures.[74]

The Christian Krio, a senior member of his church and an important person in society, may also be a member of a Masonic lodge and a member of one or all of these Krio esoteric societies, imports from Nigeria: the *Egungun*, *Geledeh* or *Otts*, Hunting Society or *Ojeh*. These may have had religious or functional roles in their places of origin.[75] The Muslim Krio have also been influenced by Mende recaptives or immigrants in Freetown to participate in a female society, the *Bundo/Sande* society, an educational institution common in the hinterland of Sierra Leone.[76] The Krios have a fascinating corpus of proverbs and aphorisms. Indeed, their thought process and speech are dominated by proverbs with interesting images.[77] They also have their varieties of food, exclusive to them, in the wider polity of Sierra Leone: *foofoo* (a derivative of *cassava*), *abalah*, and various bean dishes, *ogiree*, their sauces (*piassas*), which only a few non-Krio could prepare with the requisite culinary excellence; their dances, *goombay* music (the descendant of the settlers' *Koonken* or maroons' *Talla*?); and their dresses, *cabaslot* (a long and loose-fitting dress), *print frock*, and embroidered carpet shoes (slippers). Like their language, drawn from African and European roots, the Krios have succeeded in producing a culture, culled from their experiences, that is neither entirely Western nor entirely African but a unique fusion of both. The Krio's success at cultural eclecticism is now slowly, if grudgingly, being acknowledged.[78]

The significance of the Krios is that out of a welter of disparate groups and tongues, collected from far and wide, they were able to produce something unique, identifiable, and viable, which in turn influenced other societies. Burton, Blyden, and others missed this point. Blyden and Holy Johnson, for all their denunciation of the "decadence" of the "coastal dwellers," for all their assumed African cultural nationalism, were never seen in any African costume but wore the Western garb for which they ridiculed the Krios.[79] But perhaps they reflected certain attributes of the society they condemned. They, too, were caught in the trap of Western civilization. it seems that the Krios have never been able to foreswear this Western outlook, nor for that matter should they because it is part of their history. The ridiculous extremes some Krios went to in referring to England as their home and wearing warm gabardine and woolen suits (the full regalia of tailcoats, vests, pocket watches, gold trinkets, spats, morning coats, and silk hats) have been commented on ad nauseam in many works. At this distance, removed from the situation, we can afford to laugh at them, but nineteenth-century Krios were much closer to the epoch; they were part of the Victorian order of things; and besides, they felt they owed everything to the British. S. J. S. Barlatt, a one-time mayor of Freetown and acting police magistrate, while conceding the minus points of British civilization, acknowledged that it had lifted him to a "higher plane than that occupied by my fathers."[80] Bankole-Bright, a solid nationalist of the 1920s and 1930s, the colonial administration's bête noire, and a much neglected figure in the history books, was proud of his slave ancestry and of his African name. Yet, he was a personification of the Edwardian dandy (his sartorial extravaganza was a byword), and he spoke consistently of his "organic connection with the British Crown."[81] This strong attachment to Britain and things British is condemned by some but must be seen in its proper perspective.

At the same time that British attitudes toward the Krios took a decidedly hostile turn in the second half of the last century, Krio reaction correspondingly took a questioning outlook. Assumptions on the British "antecedents" of the Krios were readjusted. One columnist, Rambler, in the *Sierra Leone Weekly News*, the foremost newspaper in West Africa at this time, declaimed in 1918; "Our admiration of the white man and his civilization is so great as to amount to superstition—graded superciliousness—England goners—masses—aborigines." And another castigated the "present generation of Creoles" for thinking

> that everything British is best, they don't seem to realize that there are abominations in European civilization and some of their system of thought and life are not good at all for the African. We long to see some intelligent

Creole girl of good family present herself at the hymeneal alter in a trousseau that shall be entirely *native style.*[82]

A. J. Shorunkeh-Sawyerr, a prominent lawyer and a highly respected politician, who had referred to "Sierra Leoneans" as "black Englishmen," was to chide a hostile commentator on the Krios thusly: "We Creoles are endowed with senses, sympathies, aversions and passions; the fact that they are unavailable to us under cramped conditions is not material."[83] These quotes indicated a dynamic people who are capable of taking an introspective look into their society, and with almost brutal frankness comment on the unattractive aspect of that society. The *Weekly News* issues of the early 1920s urged its readers to hold on to their African heritage; the idea was circulated that not everything European was good for the African.[84] Anglo-Krio relations were never at such a low ebb as in the early decades of this century.[85]

Spritzer commented on this decline in Anglo-Krio relations, and he cited the founding of the Dress Reform Society in 1887, and the spate of name changing that followed, as evidence of the changing attitude of the Krios toward their British mentors.[86] This is a simplistic way of looking at this phenomenon. Probably, the aristocratic Krios felt compelled to erect a rationale for this adherence to the African culture, but this could hardly be true for the large mass of Krios who were born with African names long before 1887, lived close to the traditional way of life, and regarded themselves as nothing but Africans. But then there seems to be an unfortunate tendency among writers to look at Krio society from the perspective of the *Aristo* Krios.

The contributions of the Krios to political and administrative development in the Gambia, the Gold Coast (Ghana), and Nigeria have been gratefully acknowledged in a number of works. The first-generation politicians in, for example, Nigeria either were Krios or had strong Krio connections. However, the practice of Nigerian academics to select some of these early Sierra Leonean elite and to adopt them as Nigerians and then regard others from the same group as foreigners is not helpful and can cause confusion.[87]

Krio relations with their hinterland—the key to the real impact of the Krios on the interior of Sierra Leone—have been a subject of much discussion, which would require an essay by itself. There is evidence of a much closer relationship between the Krios and the hinterland inhabitants. That there was a cleavage was the result of the political and cultural situation in the territory that was divided into two distinct administrative units; and British policy also deliberately fostered divisions between the two peoples. Furthermore, the Krios affected an unfortunate cultural arrogance toward the largely uneducated and illiterate protectorate dwellers.[88]

Facets of Krio Life: An Evaluation

Cultural ethnocentrism has been held against the Krios and blamed as the source of their preoccupation with white-collar jobs. But there is every reason to believe that the turn to a desk-bound job was simply a reaction to a situation. The British administration needed literate minor officials, and the Krios, a resilient and flexible people, acquired, often at great financial strain to their parents, the necessary recommendations for the job. Besides, their society was a progressive and dynamic one; liberated African parents were largely uneducated, but they had the natural ambition for their children to get the maximum education possible. At great cost to themselves, they gave their children the education available at the time. This is quite different from saying the Krios abhorred manual labor. On the contrary, the evidence indicates a comprehensive range in the job orientation of the Krios: seafaring, carpentry, black smithery, tailoring, farming, and furniture making, as well as the legal and medical professions. The following example also shows that Krio society did not necessarily frown on a person because of his occupation: Alimamy Bingia (Rainy Lumpkin), the sympathetic undertaker, was not a man with much formal education, but he numbered among his friends the "cream" of society; and he was wealthy enough to indulge in his exotic tastes and eccentricities, which included an annual feast, Awujoh, to celebrate his birthday![89]

The Krios were also preoccupied with agriculture, contrary to the view that the Krios abhorred the idea of working on the land. Articles in contemporary newspapers extensively discussed agricultural plans, and readers sent in many suggestions for the agricultural development of the country.[90] J. S. T. Davies, African assistant postmaster-general, discussed irrigation schemes, plant food, and scientific agriculture in a number of articles. Leading citizens like Sir Samuel Lewis and "Independent" Grant pursued agriculture on scientific and commercial lines.[91] Professor Abayomi Cole, a versatile genius, wrote treatises on agricultural produce and held classes on dietary variation for protectorate women; he planted ginger as a cash crop and produced recipes for making sugar, soap, and brandy.[92] S. B. Thomas, a wealthy Krio recluse, the "African Croesus," convinced of the positive good of agriculture, left about £54,958 to found an agricultural college for Krio boys at Mabang.[93] The building still stands at Mabang, a living testimony to the disappointed aspirations of this farseeing man. Last, agricultural societies were founded in 1907 and 1922 as pressure groups to stimulate interest in agriculture. The National Congress of British West Africa in its historic conference in 1936 discussed agriculture extensively and sent its recommendations to the colonial government. The latter was sufficiently interested to take note of these.[94]

Technical education was another area of interest for the Krios, who had been much criticized for their literary education, which, their detractors claimed (and still claim today), was irrelevant to a developing African society. The Krios valued action as well as pious ideas and advocated practical education.[95] As a result of the Krios' campaign for action, Adelaide Casely-Hayford established the Girls' Industrial School in 1923. Mrs. Casely-Hayford was the second wife of J. E. Casely-Hayford, a founder of the National Congress of British West Africa, the first protonationalist Pan-African political movement in British West Africa.[96] Two Krio doctors working in Lagos, Obadiah Johnson and J. K. Randle of Regent Village, Freetown, established a science chair at Fourah Bay College in 1926.[97] These are just a few examples of the Krios' emphasis on technical knowledge and its practical application.

Finally, the Krios contributed to the development of politics in West Africa. Education, the Christian religion, and association with the white man equipped the Krios with the necessary tools to understand European government and Western political ideology and to use their options, constricted as they undoubtedly were, to challenge the Europeans' ruling caste system. The first generation of educated Africans, the elite in other centers of European administration outside Freetown, contributed to such early protest movements and nascent polities like the Egba Board of Government, the Fante Confederation (1867), the Aborigines Rights Protection Society, and, in Sierra Leone, various ad hoc citizens' committees and associations, for example, the Sierra Leone Bar Association. Some, like the first two, aimed at combining the traditional basis of power with European concepts of political power to produce a polity that would harmonize with the society that was evolving.

The best example of all these early protest movements was the National Congress of British West Africa, founded in 1920. Its outlook, membership, and aspirations underlined the Pan-West African and cosmopolitan orientation of the contemporary elite. These early protesters did not overthrow European overrule because white power was then resilient and impregnable; and second, many did not want to drive Europeans away. What they asked for was equal treatment, a partnership, until the Africans were ready to take over the running of their own affairs. For the next fifty years, however, the British were not prepared to hand over power to the Africans, not even to share it with them, although political expediency advised minor concessions, such as membership of Africans in the legislative council.[98]

The history books have misrepresented the Africans who seemed to have held high posts under the colonial regime: Acting Principal Medical Officer, Dr. Awunor Renner; Colonial Chaplain, Reverend Gurney Nicol; African Assistant Director of Education, Reverend C. A. E. Macauley; and many judicial posts. Including these men, most of whom were Sierra Leonean Krios, in the establishment has been wrongly interpreted as evidence that the Krios enjoyed and exercised power under the colonial regime.[99] But when one looks closely at the operation of this privileged position, the discrimination, the poor salaries Africans earned compared with their white counterparts (which were calculated to inject an inferior status in the incumbents), and the fact that decision making remained with the colonial power, one must come to the conclusion that "power" was illusory. And this does not justify the claim that the "Creole therefore, enjoyed maximum participation in governing the Colony."[100] Of course, they were encouraged to believe that they would be the inheritors of British rule, and some convinced themselves that they would. But in the final analysis they lost.[101]

As developments progressed in Nigeria, the Gold Coast, the Gambia, and other parts where originally their services were needed, Krio immigrants found themselves pushed aside and thrown back to their little corner in Sierra Leone. Even there they were excluded from the center of power; they were excluded from the administrative cadre. Their disappointment was complete when the principle of "one man–one vote" ensured that they would never inherit the mantle of the British rule.[102] Although I disagree with Ayandele on several points, I do agree with his idea that they were "deluded" aspirants.[103] They were criminally naive.

From a global perspective, to take such a depressingly negative view of Krio contributions to the development of West Africa would hardly be fair to their efforts and achievements. They largely fulfilled the aspirations of the founders of Sierra Leone "that the colony of Sierra Leone would not only permit the displaced persons of the Atlantic slave trade to evolve a society of their own, but might prove an agency for the social and spiritual regeneration of the whole negro world."[104] J. F. A. Ajayi endorses the vindication of this hope when he observes:

> The dispersal of people from Sierra Leone to different parts of West Africa, the Gambia, Gold Coast, Lagos, the Niger, Calabar, Fernando Po, Victoria— gave rise to a class of educated Africans with relations all over West Africa, and thus giving a certain reality to West Africa as the political basis of their nationalism.[105]

They bequeathed an inheritance of political agitation to, and inculcated some sense of cosmopolitanism into, educated West Africans. That this cosmopolitan ideal did not survive beyond the 1940s was due to a number of causes: the rise of regional nationalism, the differences between ideals and realities, and the policy of the imperial power. Also the grand design of a super West African polity was overoptimistic. Still there are some intangible, if not familiar, links between the former British West African colonies.

In conclusion, Krio society, evolving from many strands, successfully blended these to bring out a unique and identifiable community that showed its dynamism and readiness to change, as it faced the many traumas and challenges that presented themselves. With particular reference to the African diaspora, the Krios are a living example of the dimensions of this phenomenon, the meeting of cultures and their fusion.

NOTES

1. K. L. Little, "The Significance of the West African Creole for Africanist and Afro-American Studies," *African Affairs* 49, 197 (1950):308–19; J. D. Hargreaves, "African Colonization in the Nineteenth Century: Liberia and Sierra Leone," *Sierra Leone Studies* 4 (1960–62); George Shepperson, The African Abroad or the African Diaspora," in *Emerging Themes of African History*, ed. T. O. Ranger (London: Heinemann, 1968), 152–76; Paul Hair, "Africanism: The Freetown Contribution," *Journal of Modern African Studies* 4 (1967):521–39; C. Fyfe, "Reform in West Africa: The Abolition of the Slave Trade," in *History of West Africa*, J. F. A. Ajayi and M. Crowder (London: Longman, 1974) 2:30–56; Richard West, *Back to Africa: A History of Sierra Leone and Liberia* (New York: Holt, Rinehart and Winston, 1970).

2. K. A. B. Jones-Quartey, "Sierra Leone's Role in the Development of Ghana, 1820–1930," *Sierra Leone Studies* (1958):73–83; J. F. A. Ajayi, *Christian Missions of Nigeria 1841–1891: The Making of a New Elite* (Chicago: Northwestern University Press, 1965); J. H. Kopytoff, *A Preface to Modern Nigeria: The Sierra Leoneans in Yoruba, 1830–1890* (Madison: University of Wisconsin Press, 1965); E. A. Ayandele, *The Missionary Impact on Modern Nigeria, 1842–1914* (London: Longman, 1960); Pauline H. Baker, *Urbanization and Political Change: The Politics of Lagos, 1917–1967* (Berkeley: University of California Press, 1974); S. J. S. Cookey, "West African Immigrants in the Congo, 1885–1896," *Journal of the Historical Society of Nigeria* 3, 2 (December 1965).

3. Basic texts on the Krios include C. Fyfe, *A History of Sierra Leone* (London: Oxford University Press, 1962); John Peterson, *Province of Freedom: A History of Sierra Leone, 1787–1870* (London: Faber and Faber, 1969); C. Fyfe and E. D. Jones, *Freetown: A Symposium* (Sierra Leone University Press, 1968); Arthur Porter, *Creoledom: A Study of the Development of Freetown Society* (London: Oxford University Press, 1963); L. Spitzer, *The Creoles of Sierra Leone: Responses to Colonialism, 1870–1945* (Madison: University of Wisconsin Press, 1974); A. B. C. Sibthorpe, *The History of Sierra Leone* (London: Frank Cass, 1970); J. J. Crooks, *A History of the Colony of Sierra Leone, Western Africa* (reprint ed., London: Frank Cass, 1972). These are old books but very useful on background material. Articles and pamphlets on the Krios are too numerous to list here.

4. David Skinner and Barbara E. Harrell-Bond, "On Misunderstandings Arising from the Use of the Term 'Creole' in the Literature on Sierra Leone," *Africa*, 47, 3

(1977):305–19.

5. Thomas Decker, "The Krios of Sierra Leone," *African World* (July 1948):9–10.

6. See note 3.

7. J. U. J. Asiegbu, *Slavery and the Politics of Liberation, 1787–1861: A Study of Liberated African Emigration and British Anti-Slavery Policy* (London: Longman, 1969).

8. Ibid.

9. Ibid. This was a system of government romantically linked to that of the English Frank—a pledge under King Alfred of England—and to that in Israel under the judges. Every ten householders formed a tithing; every ten tithings equaled a hundredor. The latter then elected from among themselves a headman for the town.

10. Asiegbu, *Slavery and the Politics of Liberation.*

11. Ibid; G. Haliburton, "The Nova Scotian Settlers of 1792," *Sierra Leone Studies*, o.s., 9 (1975):16–25; Hair, "Africanism," 521–39; A. P. Kup, "John Clarkson and the Sierra Leone Company," *Journal of African Historical Studies*, 5, 2 (1972):203–20.

12. Ellen Gibson Wilson, *The Loyal Blacks* (New York: G. P. Putnam's Sons, 1976) and James W. St. G. Walker, *The Black Loyalists: The Search for a Promised Land in Nova Scotia and Sierra Leone 1783–1870* (London: Longman, 1976) are two books that treat the Nova Scotians exhaustively. They have superseded all previous works. In this section references will be made to other works only if a special point needs emphasizing. However, see this writer's review of Walker's book in *Journal of the Historical Society of Sierra Leone*, 2, 1 (January 1978):80–82; Asiegbu, *Slavery and the Politics of Liberation*, 19.

13. "Hair, Africanism, 524; Asiegbu, *Slavery and the Politics of Liberation*, 18.

14. West, *Back to Africa*, 49–73.

15. See sources cited in notes 3 and 12 for background accounts.

16. Sibthorpe, *The History of Sierra Leone*, 28.

17. C. Fyfe, *Africanus Horton* (London: Oxford University Press, 1972), 5; Hair, 25–26.

18. Fyfe, "Reform in West Africa," 30–56.

19. W. E. F. Ward, *The Royal Navy and the Slavers: The Suppression of the Atlantic Slave Trade* (London: George Allen and Unwin, 1969); Asiegbu, *Slavery and the Politics of Liberation*, 24ff.

20. D. A. Vonque Stephen, "A History of the Settlement of Liberated Africans in the Colony of Sierra Leone during the First Half of the Nineteenth Century" (M.A. thesis, Durham University, 1962).

21. Fyfe, *Africanus Horton*, 7.

22. Decker, "The Krios of Sierra Leone," 9–10; T. R. Griffith, "On the Races Inhabiting Sierra Leone" (Pamphlet in Sierra Leone Collection, Fourah Bay College Library, 1886); S. W. Koelle, *Polyglotta Africana* (1854, reprint ed., University of Sierra Leone, 1963).

23. J. F. A. Ajayi, "The Aftermath of the Fall of Old Oyo," in Ajayi and Crowder, *History of West Africa*, 129–56, especially infra, 156.

24. A. J. G. Wyse, "Search Light on the Krios of Sierra Leone: An Ethnographical Study of a West African People," mimeographed.

25. Wilson, *The Loyal Blacks*, 242.

26. Griffith, "On the Races Inhabiting Sierra Leone," xx; interview with Chris During, a Krio "culture propagandist," 1975.

27. Cardew to Chamberlain, 28 May 1898, CO267/438/13266.

28. Hair, "Africanism," 524.

29. Sibthorpe, *The History of Sierra Leone*, 28, 50.

30. Griffith, "On the Races Inhabiting Sierra Leone," Africanus Horton.

31. Porter, *Creoledom*, chap. 31; Mary Louise Clifford, *The Land and People of Sierra Leone* (New York: J. B. Lippincott Co., 1874) for an example of a prejudiced account sprinkled with a few penetrating insights; M. Crowder, "An African Aristocracy," *Geographical Magazine* 31, 4 (August 1958):183–90.

32. Crowder, "An African Aristocracy," 183–90.

33. Stephen, "A History of the Settlement of Liberated Africans," passim; Robert Clarke, *Sierra Leone: A Description of the Liberated Africans with Observations upon the Natural History of the Colony and a Notice of the Native Tribes, etc.* (James Ridgway, 1843; reprint ed., 1969), especially pp. 22–60 and chap. 6; Sibthorpe, *The History of Sierra Leone*, 52–57; Spitzer, *The Creoles of Sierra Leone*, 9.

34. J. A. B. Horton, *West African Countries and Peoples* (Edinburgh: Edinburgh University Press, 1969), 54.

35. Stephen, "A History of the Settlement of Liberated Africans," 22–144; Porter, *Creoledom*, 36–50.

36. A. P. Kup, "Sir Charles Macarthy (1768–1824), Soldier and Administrator, *Bulletin of the John Rylands University Library of Manchester* 60, 1 (Autumn 1979):56–94.

37. Nathalie I. K. Eleady-Cole, "Education in Sierra Leone, 1787–1914" (M.A. thesis, University of London, 1967); E. S. Sawyer, "The Development of Education in Sierra Leone in Relation to Western Contact" (M.A. thesis, McGill University, 1969), 1.

38. W. A. B. Johnson, *Memoir of the Reverend W. A. B. Johnson, Missionary of the C.M.S., Regents Town, Sierra Leone, A.D. 1816–1823* (London: Seeleys, 1852).

39. C. Fyfe, "The Foundation of Freetown," in Fyfe and Jones, *Freetown* 4–5; P. E. H. Hair, "Freetown Christianity and Africa," *Sierra Leone Bulletin of Religion* 6, 2 (December 1964):13–21.

40. Peterson, *Province of Freedom*, passim; Spitzer "The Sierra Leone Creole: A Reappraisal," in Fyfe and Jones, *Freetown*, 100–15; Porter, *Creoledom*, 12–13; David E. Skinner and Mary Berkley Skinner, "The Introduction of Islam in Sierra Leone" (Paper presented at Sierra Leone Symposium, University of Ontario, Canada, 7–9 May 1971) give some examples of government persecution of Muslims. Harun al Rashid, a Muslim, entered the CMS grammar school as Henry Valesius King and later went to study at Futa Djallon and Fez. He became the first Sierra Leonean pilgrim to Mecca. On his return he taught Arabic at Fourah Bay College. This example is not an isolated one. See Sawyerr, "The Development of Education," 46–47.

41. Peterson, *Province of Freedom*, especially pp. 252–69; A. J. G. Wyse and Christopher Fyfe, "Kriodom: A Maligned Culture" (Paper presented at Culture Seminar, Ahmadu Bello University, Zaria, April 1977).

42. Hair, "Freetown Christianity," 13–21.

43. Asiegbu, *Slavery and the Politics of Liberation*, 29; C. R. A. Cole, "A History of Local Government and Voluntary Association in the Rural Areas of Sierra Leone from 1905 to the Present" (M.A. thesis, Durham University, 1963).

44. J. D. Hargreaves, *A Life of Sir Samuel Lewis* (London: Oxford University Press, 1958); Gustav K. Deveneaux, "The Political and Social Impact of the Colony in Northern Sierra Leone, 1821–1896" (Ph.D. diss., Boston University, 1973); Christopher C. Fyfe, "European and Creole Influence in the Hinterland of Sierra Leone before 1896," *Sierra Leone Studies*, n.s., 4 (June 1955); C. Fyfe, "Four Sierra Leone Recaptives," *Journal of African History* 2, 1 (1961):77–85; Asiegbu, *Slavery and the Politics of Liberation*, 29–30. The *Sierra Leone Weekly News* did a series on "Notable Sierra Leoneans in the Past" in 1899. See issues for 7 January and 10 June 1899.

45. Sibthorpe, *The History of Sierra Leone*, 52–57.

46. Ibid., 42.

47. C. Fyfe, "Four Sierra Leone Recaptives," 77–85. See also works by Peterson, Fyfe, Porter. For views by European observers, often sneeringly and grudgingly given, see H. C. Luke, *A Bibliography of Sierra Leone* (London: Oxford University Press, 1925), 14–18; W. G. A. Ormsby-Gore, *Report on His Visit to West Africa during the Year 1926* (London: H.M.S.O., 1926), 22–23, 153–54; T. F. Buxton, "The Creole in West Africa," *Journal of the African Society* 12 (1912–13):385–94.

48. Fyfe, *A History of Sierra Leone*, is the most competent authority on this achievement aspect of Krio history.

49. C. Fyfe, "The Sierra Leone Press in the Nineteenth Century," *Sierra Leone Studies* (June 1957); C. Fyfe "The Sierra Leone Press in the Nineteenth Century—A Revision," *Journal of the Historical Society of Sierra Leone* 2, 1 (January 1978):62–64; G. Deveneaux, "Public Opinion and Colonial Politics in Nineteenth Century Sierra Leone," *International Journal of African Historical Studies*, vol. 2 (1970).

50. Sibthorpe, *History of Sierra Leone*, 28; Decker, "The Krios of Sierra Leone," 9–10. For views on the Krio language see A. T. von Bradshaw, "Vestiges of Portuguese in the Languages of Sierra Leone," *Sierra Leone Language Review* 4 (1965):5–27; E. D. Jones, "Some Aspects of the Sierra Leone Patois or Krio," *Sierra Leone Studies*, n.s. (1936):97–107; Fyfe, "Mid-Nineteenth Century Evidences of a Sierra Leone Patois," *Sierra Leone Language Review* 1 (1962):19–26; Christopher Fyfe, "Languages Reflecting the Thought of an African People: The Case of Krio" (University Colloquium on Black Civilization and Education, Fourah Bay College, March 1975)

51. Elizabeth Isichei, *The Ibo People and the Europeans: The Genesis of a Relationship to 1906* (London: Faber and Faber, 1973), 91.

52. For instance, Spitzer, *The Creoles of Sierra Leone*, chap. 3.

53. Conclusions to these investigations in several articles by this writer that are still in mimeo; see also T. S. Johnson, *The Story of a Mission: The Sierra Leone Church, First Daughter of the CMS* (London: S.P.C.K., 1953), 83.

54. Eleady-Cole, "Education in Sierra Leone," 49; Carl Campbell, "John Mohammed Bath and the Free Madingoes in Trinidad: The Question of Their Repatriation to Africa, 1831–1838," *Journal of African Studies* 4 (Winter 1975–76):467–95.

55. Asiegbu, *Slavery and the Politics of Liberation*, 29; Fyfe, *Africanus Horton*, 17; Fyfe, "Four Sierra Leone Recaptives," 78–83; Ajayi and Crowder, *History of West Africa*, 47–52; and works by Ajayi, Ayandele, and Kopytoff. There is an article on Captain Henry Johnson, who was so wealthy that he used to "dry money," in *Sierra Leone Weekly News*, 1 June 1899.

56. Ayandele, *Missionary Impact*, passim; E. A. Ayandele, *Holy Johnson: Pioneer of African Nationalism, 1836–1917* (London: Frank Cass, 1970); Baker, *Urbanization and Political Change*, 17–27, 49–57.

57. Fyfe, *Africanus Horton*, passim, and Fyfe, *History of Sierra Leone*, passim.

58. Ajayi, *Christian Missions*; Ayandele, *Missionary Impact* and *Holy Johnson*.

59. *Sierra Leone Weekly News*, 25 May 1901, announced the founding of a West African Club by Sierra Leone immigrants in the Cape of Good Hope, South Africa; Eleady-Cole tells us that Sierra Leoneans also worked on the Panama Canal, in "Education in Sierra Leone," 380.

60. Eleady-Cole, "Education in Sierra Leone" 379–80.

61. Walker, *The Black Loyalists*; Wilson, *The Loyal Blacks*, 280ff, 368.

62. See above; Ijagbemi, "The Freetown Colony and the Development of 'Legitimate' Commerce in Adjoining Territories," *Journal of the Historical Society of Nigeria* 5, 2 (June 1870):247–65.

63. *Sierra Leone Weekly News* 22 February 1913; Eleady-Cole, "Education in Sierra Leone," 165, cites an example of Krio educational effort in Tikonko, in present-day Southern Province.

64. A. J. G. Wyse, "Some Thoughts on Themes in Sierra Leone History," *Journal of the Historical Society of Sierra Leone* 2 (January 1978):65–73.

65. Fyfe, *A History of Sierra Leone*; Hair, "Africanism," 521–39. For example, John Ezzidio, in 1863, was nominated as the first African to sit in the reconstituted legislative council in Sierra Leone, having been elected by his colleagues in the commercial world; Horton was a surgeon major in the British Colonial Army; Crowther was a bishop. For a Critical assessment of the evolution of the Krio elite in a wider context of West Africa, see G. Deveneaux, "Some Historical Consideration Concerning Elites in Africa," *Journal of the Historical Society of Sierra Leone* 2, (1 January 1978):33–56.

66. R. F. Burton, *Wanderings in West Africa from Liverpool to Fernando Po* (London: Tinsley Bros. 1863) 1:193; see West's views on Burton in *Back to Africa*, 189–97; Graham Greene, *Journey without Maps* (New York: Doubleday, Doran, and Company, 1936), 34.

67. Edward W. Blyden, *Christianity, Islam and the Negro Race* (London, 1887); Hollis R. Lynch, *Edward Wilmot Blyden: Pan-Negro Patriot, 1832–1912* (London: Oxford University Press, 1967); idem; "The Native Pastorate Controversy and Cultural Ethnocentrism in Sierra Leone, 1871–1874," *Journal of African History* 5, 3 (1864):395–413. Much more critical assessment of Blyden's attitudes are A. Fajama's review of Lynch's biography on Blyden, *Journal of African History* 5, 3 (1970):447–48; Robert W. July, "Nineteenth Century Negritude, Edward Blyden," *Journal of African History* 5, 1 (1964):73–86; H. Osman Newland, *Sierra Leone: Its People, Products and Secret Societies* (New York: Negro University Press, 1916; reprint ed., 1969), 184ff. On Johnson's views, see Ayandele, *Holy Johnson*.

68. See notes 4 and 41.

69. *Daily Guardian*, 13 September 1939; V. E. J. Buckle, "The Language of the Sierra Leone Creeo," *Sierra Leone Studies* 22 (September 1939):2024.

70. R. Clarke, *Manners and Customs*, 33–38.

71. Wyse, "Search Light on the Krios of Sierra Leone," and Charles K. Olumokun Nicol, "Origins and Orthography of the Kriyo Language," *West African Review* (August 1949).

72. Wyse and Fyfe, "Kriodom"; R. J. B. Thompson, "Western Education as a Formative Factor in the Social Attitudes of the Creoles in Sierra Leone" (Dip. Ed. thesis, Durham University, 1962), especially 2–5; T. S. Max-Peters, "A Critical Examination of the Creole of Sierra Leone, and the Effects of Their Religion, Traditions and Customs on the Education of their Children" (Dip. Ed. thesis, Durham University, 1962); T. C. Luke, "Some Notes on the Creoles and Their Land," *Sierra Leone Studies*, o.s. 21 (1939):53–66. The quote is from L. Probyn, "Sierra Leone and the Nations of West Africa," *Journal of the African Society* 6 (1906–1907):250–58.

73. J. Omosade Awololu, *The Yoruba Philosophy of Life* (Paris: Presence Africaine, 1970).

74. See the following for elucidation: Harry Sawyerr, "Ancestor Worship: A Discussion of Some of the Problems Inherent in the Phrase," *Africa* 23 (1953): 25ff; Sawyerr "A Sunday Graveside Libation in Freetown after a Bereavement," *Sierra Leone Bulletin of Religion* 9, 2 (1967):41–49; H. S. Wilson and S. L. Proudfoot, "Changing Social Functions of a Creole Feast," *African Affairs* 58, 231 (April 1959):135–50; Abner Cohen, "The Creole Way of Death" (Paper presented at Sierra Leone Symposium, University of Ontario, Canada, 7–9 May 1971): C. Magbaily Fyfe and Isabella Horoe, "Krio Traditional Beliefs," *Africana Research Bulletin* 7, 3 (1979):3–26.

75. Wyse and Fyfe, "Kriodom," 12–15; Peterson, *Province of Freedom*, 250–69; Cohen, "The Creole Way of Death," makes much of Krio membership in Masonic lodges. I think he tends to exaggerate the statistics, p. 7. See also Abner Cohen, "The Politics of Ritual Secrecy," *Man* 6 (1971):427–628.

76. Peterson, *Province of Freedom*, 265; Personal communication from Gribril Cole, an honors student working on the Muslim Krios at Foula Town and Fourah Bay, Freetown, May 1979.

77. Christopher Fyfe, "Thought of an African People" (Colloquium, Fourah Bay College. March 1975). A handsome collection of Krio proverbs can be found in *The Journal of the Krio Literacy Society* 13, 1(1972).

78. Fyfe, "Reform in West Africa," 49; Spitzer's confused discussion in *The Creoles of Sierra Leone*, chap. 4.

79. Lynch, "The Native Pastorate Controversy," 395–413. Curiously enough for one who was an African cultural nationalist, Holy Johnson abhorred "idolatory" worship. See Ayandele, *Holy Johnson*, 23; Peterson, *Province of Freedom*, 254–56.

80. *Memorial of the Jubilee of Her Majesty's Reign and of the Centenary of Sierra Leone* (London: W. B. Whittingham and Co., 1887), 104–105.

81. A. J. G. Wyse, "Research Notes on Dr. Bankole-Bright (1883–1958): His Life to 1939," *Africana Research Bulletin* 5, 1 (1974):3–27.

82. *Sierra Leone Weekly News* issues for 1910. Quotes are from issues of 3 July 1915 and 18 May 1918; *Daily Guardian*, 27 and 28 April 1949.

83. Skinner and Harrell-Bond, "Misunderstandings Arising from the Use of the Term 'Creole,'" 313; *Sierra Leone Weekly News*, 12 September 1914, and *Sierra Leone Weekly News*, 16 March 1893, for an interesting comment on Sawyerr's statement. The columnist observed: "Of course, as a literal fact, there can be no such being as a 'Black Englishman.' If Sierra Leoneans are the abnormal beings which such a phrase implies, then they will soon share the fate of the 'Black Americans' (Read Nova Scotians and Maroons) who preceded them in that Peninsula and gave place to the recaptives, in giving place in their turn to the normal population who were found here by both settlers and recaptives. Black Englishmen must die out. . . ." In a rather Burtonesque way, the writer was emphasizing the African side of the Krios.

84. *Sierra Leone Weekly News*, 3 July 1915; 31 March 1917.

85. This was illustrated by two events, the 1919 and 1926 strikes, treated by this writer, in "The 1919 Anti-Syrian Riots: A Krio Plot?" *Journal of the Historical Society of Sierra Leone* 3, 1–2 (1979):1–14 and "The 1926 Railway Strike and Anglo-Krio Relations: A View Point," *The International Journal of African Historical Studies*, 14, 1 (1981):93–123.

86. Spitzer, *The Creoles of Sierra Leone*, chap. 4.

87. Ibid., Ayandele, *Holy Johnson*.

88. See for example, A. J. G. Wyse, "Sierra Leone Creoles, Their History and Historians," *Journal of African Studies* 4, 2 (Summer 1977):228–40, and Wyse, "Search Light on the Krios"; C. Clapham, *Liberia and Sierra Leone: An Essay in Comparative Politics* (London: Oxford University Press, 1976), especially chap. 3.

89. Greene, *Journey without Maps*, 37–38, and Spitzer, *The Creoles of Sierra Leone*, have brief references on Bungie. This writer has a short biographical sketch on him that appears in *The Encyclopaedia Africana*. See *Sierra Leone Weekly News*, 1 December 1917 for Bungie's annual invitation to an *Awujoh*, and an advertisement of his business.

90. *Sierra Leone Weekly News*, 10 September 1906; 27 December 1919; 24 January 1920; 14 October 1922.

91. Hargreaves, *A Life of Sir Samuel Lewis*.

92. "Pen Portrait of Dr. Abayomi Cole," *African World Supplement* (June 1926); biographical sketch by this writer in *The Encylopaedia Africana*; *Sierra Leone Guardian and Foreign Mail*, 12 April 1981; *Sierra Leone Weekly News*, 3 September 1904; 14 January 1904.

93. Slater to Amery, 28 September 1925, CO267/610/45993; *Sierra Leone Weekly News*, 25 May 1901; *Colonial and Provincial Reporter*, 22 April 1916.

94. A. J. G. Wyse, "Politics in Colonial Sierra Leone: The Example of the Sierra Leone Branch of the National Congress of British West Africa, 1918–1940" (Public lecture given to the Historical Society of Sierra Leone, 25 October 1978); and Wyse "Search Light on the Krios".

95. Wyse, "Politics in Colonial Sierra Leone"; Eleady-Cole, "Education in Sierra Leone," 197ff; Sawyerr, "Development of Education in Sierra Leone," 40ff.

96. *Sierra Leone Weekly News,* 22 May 1920; 19 June 1920; 26 June 1920; and 16 January 1922; Louise Metzger, "Three Female Sierra Leonean Teachers," *Teaching Today* 3 (January 1973):47–53.

97. *Aurora,* 16 April 1921; 11 June 1921; 22 October 1921; *Sierra Leone Weekly News,* 23 February 1929; Heisler to Manley, 23 January 1923, G3A1/O Folio 12 (CMS Archives, Waterloo Road, London); T. J. Thompson, *The Jubilee and Centenary Volume of Fourah Bay College, Freetown, Sierra Leone* (Freetown, 1930), 153–54.

98. Discussion of these points can be found in major works on West African history by D. Kimble, *A Political History of Ghana: The Rise of Gold Coast Nationalism, 1850–1928* (London: Oxford University Press, 1963); M. Kilson, *Political Change in a West African State: A Study of the Modernization Process in Sierra Leone* (Cambridge: Harvard University Press, 1966); Kimble "The National Congress of British West Africa, 1918–1935," in *Protest and Power in Black Africa,* eds. Robert Rotberg and Ali Mazrui (London: Oxford University Press, 1970), 571–88; J. Ayodele Langley, *Pan-Africanism and Nationalism in West Africa, 1900–1945* (Oxford: Clarendon Press, 1973); "The Gambia Section of the National Congress of British West Africa," *Africa* 39, 4 (October 1969):382–95; G. Olusanya, "The Lagos Branch of the National Congress of British West Africa," *Journal of the Historical Society of Nigeria* 4, 2 (June 1968):321–33. See also works by Ayandele, Ajayi, Baker, Isichie, cited above. Articles discussing specific aspects of the activities of Africans in the colonial period include Yaw Twumasi, "Press Freedom and Nationalism under Colonial Rule in the Gold Coast (Ghana)," *Journal of the Historical Society of Nigeria* 7, 3 (1974):499–520; Arif Hussain, "The Educated Elite; Collaborators, Assailants, Nationalists: A Note on African Nationalists and Nationalism," ibid, 485–97; Fred Omu's review of Langley's *Pan-Africanism,* ibid., 510–11; Tekena H. Tamuno, "Some Aspects of Nigerian Reaction to the Imposition of British Rule," *Journal of the Historical Society of Nigeria* 3, 2 (December 1965):271–94; O. Adewoye, "Sapara Williams: The Lawyer and the Public Servant," *Journal of the Historical Society of Nigeria* 6, 1 (December 1971):47–65; C. Wyse, "The Sierra Leone Section of the National Congress of British West Africa," mimeographed; for fairly sympathetic studies on the African elite, see Hans Kohn and Wallace Sokolsky, *African Nationalism in the Twentieth Century* (London: Van Nos Reinhold, 1965); W. Arthur Lewis et al., *Attitude to Africa* (Middlesex: Penguin Books, 1951); J. W. de Graft Johnson, *Toward Nationhood in West Africa: Thoughts of Young Africa Addressed to Young Britain,* New impression with introduction by F. K. Drah (1928; London: Frank Cass, 1971); Magnus Sampson, *Makers of Modern Ghana,* vol. 1 (Accra, 1969).

99. Kilson, *Political Change;* J. Cartwright, *Politics in Sierra Leone, 1947–1967* (Toronto: University of Toronto Press, 1970); P. O. Esedebe, "The Independence Movement in Sierra Leone," *Tarkh* 4, 1 (1971):15–26; G. Allen, *Constitutional Change, 1863–1967* (Pamphlet in FBC Library, Freetown, Sierra Leone). An honors role of past Fourah Bay College students and their postcollegiate careers is in Thompson, *Jubilee of Fourah Bay College,* 157ff. This myth that the Krios had been a pampered, privileged minority gained currency in the 1950s over the constitutional crisis of 1947. The following typified the mood: George Padmore, "Democratic Advance in Sierra Leone," *Crisis* 64, 3 (March 1957):149–52; cf. with his more favorable account in Padmore, *How*

Britain Rules Africa (London, 1936), chap. 4; Padmore, *Pan-Africanism or Communism? The Coming Struggle for Africa* (London, 1956), 15; "Political Prospects in Sierra Leone," *World Today* 4 (1953):206–17; J. D. Hargreaves, "Western Democracy and African Society," *International Affairs* 21, 3 (1955):327–34; and issues of *West Africa* for 1947. See also Henry Harold Gaffney, Jr., "Administration and the Administrative Service in Sierra Leone" (Ph.D. diss., Columbia University, 1967); cf. R. S. Jordon, "The Creoles and the Civil Service in Sierra Leone, 1957–1969," *Sierra Leone Symposium*, University of Ontario (Canada, 7–9 May 1971).

100. Dick Simpson, "Ethnic Conflict in Sierra Leone" in *The Politics of Cultural Sub-Nationalism in Africa: and the Problem of "One State, Many Nationalisms,"* ed. Victor A. Olorunsola (Garden City, N.Y.: Doubleday and Co., 1972), 153–88.

101. E. W. Blyden, III, "Sierra Leone: Pattern of Constitutional Change, 1924–1957" (Ph.D. diss., Howard University, 1959); Roy Lewis, *Sierra Leone. Experiment in Democracy in an African Nation* (New York: University Press, 1970), especially p. 7. For a plaintive and indignant protest, see Ahmed Alhadi, "The Re-emancipation of the Colony of Sierra Leone" (Pamphlet in Sierra Leone Collection, Fourah Bay College Library, Freetown, 1956); Slater to Thomas, 17 June 1924, with enclosures, CO267/604/32100.

102. D. J. R. Scott, "The Sierra Leone Election, May 1957," in *Five Elections in Africa*, ed. W. J. W. Mackenzie and Kenneth E. Robinson (Oxford: Clarendon Press, 1960), 168–268; Hair's review of Fyfe's *History of Sierra Leone* in *Sierra Leone Studies*, n.s. 17 (June 1963):281–96; Haw, "Africanism," 571–39; Baker, *Urbanization and Political Change*, 53ff.

103. E. A. Ayandele, *The Educated Elite in the Nigerian Society* (Ibadan: Ibadan University Press, 1974). Although the title refers to Nigerians, the subject matter had a lot to say about the Krio or "Saro" as they were known in Nigeria. Cf. Deveneaux, "Some Historical Consideration Concerning Elites in Africa," 73–86.

104. Hargreaves, *A Life of Sir Samuel Lewis*, ix.

105. J. F. A. Ajayi, "Origins of Nigerian Nationalism," *Journal of the Historical Society of Sierra Leone* 2, 2 (1967):196–210.

20
The Role of
African American Women in
the Founding of Liberia

Debra Newman Ham

D
URING the nineteenth century, the West African coast underwent tremendous change as a result of pressure in Western nations for the termination of the African slave trade. The United States Constitution provided for the abolition of the African slave trade by 1807, and England called a halt to the trade in the same year. Western political leaders were concerned not only with the economic repercussions, cruelties, and inhumanity of the trade but also with the future status of the huge black population in the Western Hemisphere.

Some individuals were opposed to slavery and developed the idea of the resettlement of blacks in Africa. In 1787, therefore, a group in Britain founded Sierra Leone. Blacks who had participated in the American Revolution on the side of the British and some runaway slaves who refused to be brought under British control emigrated to Sierra Leone, where they joined others from Jamaica, Canada, and England. In 1815, Paul Cuffe, a prosperous black shipowner who had become disenchanted with opportunities for blacks in the United States, took a small group of blacks from the United States to Sierra Leone at his own expense after unsuccessfully petitioning Congress for aid.[1]

Some Americans who had envisioned that additional free blacks could be sent to Sierra Leone were disappointed when poor relations with Great Britain after the War of 1812 seemed to make such a venture impractical. An uneasy coalition of American abolitionists and negrophobes joined in December 1816 to form the American Colonization Society (ACS), an organization designed to finance the return of willing free American blacks to Africa. When negotiations to settle blacks from the United States in Sierra Leone failed, ACS officials purchased land south of Sierra Leone in 1822 and called the new settlement Liberia. During the course of the nineteenth century, about eighteen thousand blacks emigrated to Liberia. About half of the emigrants were women, who generally emigrated with their families, kin groups, and friends from plantations or hometowns, or, occasionally, alone. Many blacks settled in Liberia because they were freed from slavery only on the condition that they emigrate.[2]

The black male emigrants to Liberia were primarily interested in establishing lucrative trading ventures. As the slave trade drew to a close, Western shippers were eager to establish "legitimate" trade with Africans and settlers on the West African coast. Palm oil and coffee beans were profitable exports for a time, but competing world markets and the innovations of the Industrial Revolution often kept prices low or decreased the demand for tropical products. Liberians with farms large enough to support themselves and their families were often more financially secure than those who speculated in commerce. There was a great deal of competition for the few jobs ACS offered to the colonists. With paid employment so scarce, women who needed to work—the vast majority of all settler women—generally found that only the land offered them a livelihood.[3]

More than eight thousand black women from the United States emigrated to Liberia during the 1800s, as well as a small group— about 150 women—from Barbados. Joining these women were fifteen hundred recaptive females (African women who were rescued from slave ships and subsequently settled in Liberia). Male and female settlers established about a dozen villages along the Liberian coast during the century. The indigenous Africans among whom the emigrants settled were the Deys who lived in the immediate region of Cape Mesurado, where Monrovia was founded. The area to the north of the Cape was populated by the Via, and the southern coastal strip was occupied by the Bassa, Kru (Kroo), and Grebo. The most populous interior group was the Kpelle, and the strongest groups politically were the Vai, the Gola, and the Mandingo. The Mandingo, who specialized in trade, were interspersed among the Gola, the Vai, and other ethnic groups such as the Kissi, Gbandi, Dan (Gio), Krahn, Loma (Buzzi), Mano, Belle, and Mende, all of whom were groups living in the Liberian interior.[4]

African and settler women in Liberia generally did the same type of work but tended to conceptualize their tasks in quite different ways. African women played a primary role in traditional society as agriculturalists, traders, and homemakers. Although they rarely held political power, women were often influential as leaders of the Sande female initiation society. Free African women could exercise a degree of independence if they were successful traders or belonged to wealthy or powerful families. However, even these women were usually in positions subordinate to men. Whether women were free or enslaved, they represented wealth to their husbands, owners, or headmen. Because of their value to the society, women were sometimes kidnapped or captured in battles to increase the number of their captors' wives or to be sold as slaves. African women were aware of their value to their families and communities and sought protection by moving into male family members' villages.[5]

Many of the tasks of African men and women were complementary. Men cleared the land for the rice fields, while women did the planting and harvesting. After the harvest, men gathered the bundles of rice from the fields and brought them back to the village. Men erected the frames and thatched the roofs of houses, and women daubed the walls with mud. Women picked cotton and spent hours spinning it into thread, but it was often the men who wove the thread into cloth. Both men and women dyed cloth and made pottery. In the markets, goods produced by men and women were generally sold by women.[6]

African women were usually industrious and eager to take advantage of opportunities for trade. Many simply "made small market" in their own villages. There they would sell their surplus produce and craft items to neighbors and travelers. Other women who lived near trade routes would set up their wares along the most traveled paths.[7] It was at periodic markets, however, that women appeared in great numbers both to buy and to sell. Daniel Whitehurst, an 1834 traveler to the Liberian interior and an observer of the Bopulu market, reported that about five hundred women with their children and more than two hundred men traveled for miles to sell their products or to procure goods at this important market. Whitehurst remarked that the market was a world in itself where people from many ethnic groups bought and sold items from a leaf of tobacco to a thimble full of salt. Most of the sales, he observed, were made by women with children on their backs. These women sold palm oil, palm nuts, and palm butter, various fruits and vegetables, and smoked meat. Expensive items such as hides, gold, ivory, and slaves were generally owned by men, although women sometimes did the selling for their husbands who stood in the background quietly overseeing the bargaining.[8]

Although local markets were important, probably the most significant economic activities performed by African women during the nineteenth century were the manufacture of salt and the production of palm oil. Salt was used as a medium of exchange throughout much of West Africa, and palm oil was purchased by the settlers for export to Europe. Salt production was usually done by African women during the dry season. The men built long sheds for the women on the beach, where they used several methods to extract salt. One way was to boil the sea water in iron pots until the salt, which was black in color, crystallized on the sides of the pans. Another method was to dig shallow holes near the ocean where the tide water could drain into them. The water would then evaporate in the heat of the sun, leaving a saline crust residue that was removed and dissolved again in a mixture of warm salt water and wood ashes. The solution was poured into a conical basket with a little sieve at the top to prevent the sand from getting into the salt. The salt was dried in large, shallow brass pans called "neptunes," which were imported from Europe.[9]

The women then took strips of bamboo about three feet long and formed them into cylinders about three inches in diameter. Salt was packed into the cylinders, which were then covered with several layers of leaves to protect against dampness or rain during transport. These "salt sticks" were taken inland, usually to Bopolu, and exchanged for ivory and other products that netted the manufacturers an amount equivalent to about seventy-five cents to one dollar per gallon. One observer at Bopolu, commenting on the importance of the salt sticks, simply said, "Salt is their gold."[10]

Palm oil, which was extracted by the women from the nut of the oil palm tree, was almost universally used in Liberia as a sauce over rice and as fuel for oil light. Several methods of oil production were described by nineteenth-century observers. Bassa women usually dug a large square pit in the ground that was then filled with ripe palm nuts. The women would trample the nuts to press the oil out of the shell until the nut and the oil formed one mass. Water was then poured into the hole to separate the oil, which was removed with a dish or with the palm of the hand and put into a calabash (gourd). Another mode of oil production was to bury the nuts in the ground until they were very soft. Then they were taken out and put into a mesh cloth, melted with hot water, and strained into a container filled with water so that the oil could rise to the surface and be removed.[11]

An ACS agent wrote about the uses of this oil:

> Palm oil, until six months old, answers every purpose of olive-oil, as used for culinary purposes in the south of Europe. Butter and lard have all of their uses fulfilled, and perhaps with advantage to the health of the people.[12]

Many of the settler women, particularly those from the United States and Barbados, distinguished themselves from the African women in whose midst they lived by refusing to do the same type of work as the African women or, at least, by refusing to perform the work in the same way. If African women chopped and carried wood, settler women tried to avoid this chore by hiring African women to do it for them.[13] If they were forced by poverty to do such work, settler girls rather than women were sent to perform it. The settler women, who saw themselves as an enlighted group whose example would teach African women how to better themselves, believed that their influence would be compromised if they were engaged in activities like producing salt and palm oil or other tasks that might suggest equality between the two groups. While they were still in the United States, both free and enslaved black women had learned to feel superior to the African slaves who came into their midst. African newcomers to America knew little about the English language, Christianity, or Western ways. This, coupled with ideas of racial superiority learned from the whites among whom they had lived in America, caused the settlers to arrive in their African homeland laden with biases.

In reality, settler women could not afford to be choosy about work because outside of agrarian pursuits there were few ways for them to earn a living. Less than five percent of the settler women came to Liberia with money earned in business or inherited from former masters. Although settler women did not actively engage in the export trade in Liberia, they sometimes accumulated wealth through hired male agents who conducted business for them. A small number of women were financially able to invest in real estate. Nevertheless, rich and poor women alike had to turn to various aspects of farmwork for their subsistence. In the first few decades after founding Liberia, the ACS was very concerned about the settlers' preoccupation with trade and neglect of agriculture, so the society offered monetary awards to Liberians for outstanding agricultural achievements. The fact that one of the recipients of a ten-dollar prize was a settler woman named Peggy Hope, who had cultivated an acre and a half of peanuts, demonstrates that women were active—and successful—as agriculturalists in the early years of the settlement.[14]

Emigrant letters and missionary and travelers' accounts indicate that most women worked on comparatively small holdings. For example, Charlotte Herring devoted several hours a week to cultivating a small garden on one-sixteenth of an acre of stony soil. In 1865 she earned twenty-five dollars from selling the garden's produce; in 1866, she earned twenty-eight dollars; and in 1867 she made thirty-one dollars in seven months. All of her proceeds were in cash (usually United States or European money), which was highly valued because Liberia produced no currency of its own. In reference to Herring's agricultural successes, the editors of the *African Repository*—the ACS monthly journal—asked, "Can a single woman in any other country, on the same amount of land, do any more?" An educated woman seemed equally enthusiastic about her Liberian labors. In an 1839 letter she described the Millsburg settlement as a delightful place for anyone disposed to work. She discussed the availability of timber and the fertility of the soil.[15]

Women also raised farm animals. Martha Harris Ricks, one of the wealthier members of nineteenth-century Liberian society, reported in 1858 that she owned turkeys, ducks, sheep, and hogs. She remarked in a letter, "I milk my two cows every day, I have my oxen. If people perish here, they perish because they will not work." Ricks was able to hire one man to help her with the farmwork after the death of her first husband. Another woman, P. D. Harris, had raised dozens of ducks and chickens by 1849. She had started with six birds, and by the time they multiplied to one hundred, she and her family were able to have fried chicken or roast duck whenever they felt like it and still have many birds left over. Even Jane Roberts, the wife of the first Liberian president, Joseph Jenkins Roberts, applied herself to a few farm tasks. An ACS agent, who dined at Roberts's home in 1845, wrote that he was served a "fine fat turkey raised by the Governor's lady, and served up in a handsome style."[16]

It was possible to achieve a degree of prosperity if both the husband and the wife or other family members contributed to the family income. For example, Nicey Harrison—an old woman who had emigrated from the Cherokee Nation where she had been a cook at a mission station—had vegetable and flower gardens. Her husband, Simon, cultivated a number of coffee trees. Another family, the Steels, consisted of eleven members. Catharine Steel, a fifty-year-old widow who lived in New Georgia, was listed in the 1843 Liberian census as the owner of five acres of land and a thatched-roof house. Her family included two grown children: a son, aged twenty-six, and was a farmer, and a daughter, aged twenty-eight, who was a washwoman. The Steels had a total of four acres cultivated: one acre of Indian corn, one acre of potatoes and yams, and two acres of cassava. The value of their farm was estimated at twenty-five dollars.[17]

In 1863, a settler reported the names of several dozen settlers who had prosperous sugar cane and coffee farms, products that had a lively Western market for several decades, from the 1840s through the 1870s. There were five women on the list. At the Virginia settlement Mrs. M. M. Jordan had three acres of sugar cane, and Mrs. Dangerfield owned four thousand coffee trees. Two women who lived at the Kentucky settlement—Mrs. T. Outland and Mrs. Mimi Young—had two thousand coffee trees each. Mrs. Gray at the New York settlement owned two hundred coffee trees and six acres of sugarcane. The Reverend Alexander Crummell, a British-educated black scholar and theologian who emigrated to Liberia in 1853, commented that one of the more prosperous women of Grand Bassa, the wife of a merchant, had started a coffee farm on the Benson River and "unassisted by anyone built her own house" and spent most of her time there planting coffee.[18]

Jobs available to unskilled women in Liberia were limited. Of the sixty-one women listed as heads of families in the 1843 census, twenty-three were laundresses, ten were seamstresses, eighteen were nurses, and one was a huckster (peddler). Only one of the female heads of families lived alone. Four lived with one other person, and the rest headed households of from three to fourteen persons, often including some people who were not kin. Unfortunately, no other censuses were taken during the nineteenth century, and the accuracy of this one is subject to question.[19]

Laundresses generally worked for the wealthier settlers or earned money by doing the laundry of the sailors on passing ships. Governor John Russwurm reported in 1837 that after the visits of one British and two American warships, the women were kept busy doing the sailors' laundry for several days, and some of the other colonists were able to sell a large amount of produce to the ships' galleys.[20]

Some women found jobs as housekeepers. The only information known about Sally Taylor, a twenty-eight-year-old single woman, who worked as the housekeeper at the ACS emigrant shelter in Caldwell, was that she was killed when the house was struck by lightning in 1826. In 1850, Mrs. Ralph Moore, who was the "matron" of the ACS shelter at Robertsport, received a compliment from a white visitor who found the facility in perfect order:

> The house was kept clean and well-ventiated, the table arrangements were very simple, plain and good; personal cleanliness was most rigidly enforced, often to the great annoyance of the new emigrants.[21]

Martha Ann Cassell was the matron of St. Mark's, the Protestant Episcopal Church hospital, and the superintendent of the church's orphan asylum, both of which were in Cape Palmas. Cassell was a household manger who "exercised a mild but firm government." Part of her job was to request necessary supplies. A letter she wrote in 1869 to the Protestant Episcopal headquarters in the United States asking for a list of medicines "very much needed for the asylum" provides some evidence of the type of duties she performed. Lucinda Arnet was employed by the Muhlenberg mission that was located on the St. Paul's River. In 1866, the mission school had forty-five children. Arnet was the "overseer of the culinary and washing departments," and she also taught. A few women were housekeepers in the homes of wealthier settlers.[22]

Although the second Liberian president, Steven Benson, mentioned in a message encouraging immigration that women in Liberia could work as milliners and dressmakers, only a small number of women made money by sewing. One missionary teacher said that some of the older girls were able to occasionally earn "a trifle by their needle." A white visitor to Liberia described some of the shops in Monrovia and said she met a stylish black woman who had recently emigrated from the United States for the purpose of establishing a millinery shop. However, the sad truth was that few settlers could afford to have others sew for them.[23]

Women who were employed as "nurses" attended to the needs of the sick or cared for young children. These were generally unskilled women who today would be called maids, companions, or babysitters. Only wealthy settlers or missionaries could afford the services of nurses. One female missionary was cared for by Mrs. Carroll, a nurse in Cape Palmas. When the missionary became ill, she took a cruise to Monrovia with the hope that the trip would improve her health. The missionary commented that on the journey her "poor nurse was so dreadfully seasick" that she was useless. Consequently, the missionary had to be cared for by the African crew on the boat. However, after they had arrived in Monrovia, the missionary remarked that her nurse took good care of her, "packing and unpacking and taking sole charge of everything for me."[24]

Several women also set up "cook shops," or restaurants, and trading establishments; a few ran illegal "bawdy houses" and bars. The census indicated that some women worked as hucksters or peddlers. One traveler to Liberia met an old woman in Clay Ashland who had a table of cakes, biscuits, and beer for sale. Her stand was situated under a tree to protect herself from the blazing sun. In the 1843 census, Catharine Jacobs listed her occupation as "huckster." She supported a family of four with her income.[25]

Women who had many different domestic skills were able to display their talents at periodic fairs that were held in Liberia. The purpose of the fairs was to encourage agricultural production and domestic and industrial arts among the Liberian settlers. The ACS appropriated five hundred dollars a year for several years to be used as prize money for the participants in the fair. The First National Fair, which took place in Monrovia from 14 to 21 December 1857, was held on the premises of the Methodist Episcopal Mission. Large rooms were filled with articles for exhibit, while outdoor enclosures were used for cattle, pigs, sheep, and goats.[26]

Numerous female exhibitors won prizes for produce such as arrow-root, oranges, potatoes, papaya, and cotton. Processed foods or food products for which prizes were awarded to women were butter, pickles, catsup, papaya preserves, lily starch, "double extract of feverbush," bar soap, sage, prepared chocolate, and corned beef. One woman won a second prize for a ram she had raised. Women exhibited slippers, socks, handbags, collars, coats, pants, bonnets, cushions, quilts, fringes, under-sleeves, baby clothes, and chair covers. Most of the prizes awarded to women were for needlework.[27]

In the report of the Committee on Adjudication of the National Fair, the members commented that the exhibits by the female contributors were worthy of special notice and especially commended the fancy needlework, which they thought was both tasteful and well made. The report mentioned that many of the articles were the contributions of young women who "evinced a degree of taste and ability to work" that they hoped would "keep pace with the increase of years." The commit-tee members wrote that the articles exhibited demonstrated that the women of the Republic could produce cheaply many of the articles that were being imported from abroad at very high prices.[28]

Of the 128 persons receiving prizes, 30 were women. Most of the monetary prizes were valued between fifty cents and three dollars. However, one of the three ten-dollar prizes went to Mrs. Henry Williams for a cloth that she wove from African cotton. The committee members commented that the quality of the cotton was good and that they were eager to see a more extensive cultivation of cotton in the country. They further stated their belief that if more women dedicated themselves to weaving, they could supply the country with at least part of its demand for cloth.[29]

Fairs continued to be popular in Liberia until the early 1860s. Spurred by the example of Mrs. Williams and other women weavers at the first and second fairs, numerous women in Liberia began to develop an interest in weaving. Martha Harris Ricks, who was very nationalistic, wrote to an ACS official in 1859 that her young nation was still ascending and that soon Liberia would be able to "walk, run, and fly," because of its progress in the area of domestic manufacturing. She also noted that many women were spinning and weaving. Another writer mentioned that several looms were in operation.[30]

The idea of domestic production of cloth did not take hold, however, because in 1868 the *African Republic* reported that there were no "manufactures" where women could be employed. In the article, the author suggested that women could become self-employed by weaving baskets, making mats, or plaiting straw for hats and bonnets. Some of the poorer women, the writer suggested, could be taught by teachers and missionaries to preserve fruits for the foreign market. The author concluded that "hundreds of girls and women would find it to their advantage to be occupied in labors of the kind suggested," but the author offered no practical plan for the commencement of such activities. Although many settler women remained in poverty because there were few unskilled jobs available to them other than agricultural work, the fairs demonstrated that the women were skilled in the production of domestic goods.[31]

It was in daily life that settlers, Africans, and recaptives influenced each other the most. The regular encounters that were a part of life's vital activities—marriage and divorce, buying and selling, working and playing—brought all segments of Liberian society together continually. Africans worked in settler homes and lived with them in their settlements. Settler men traveling into the interior developed liaisons with African women, and it was not uncommon that the children of these unions came into settler homes as wards. They were sometimes referred to as "outside children" and were usually treated as inferiors in the settler households. Through this means, however, many African girls and boys were reared in the midst of settler society.[32]

Another means of cultural assimilation between settler and African women was through interaction in business. African women brought goods to marketplaces in settler communities and were exposed to their language and life-style. Other African women acted as porters. An ACS agent wrote in 1831 that the porters he hired to carry baggage to a nearby village were of both sexes and a variety of ages and sizes. He commented that the women with children on their backs could still carry from fifty to seventy pounds on their heads. Often African women were paid twenty-five cents for bringing wood for use in settler homes. A colonization agent criticized the settlers for paying this amount because they "felt above such work" but were "suffering from pecuniary embarrassments."[33]

The African and recaptive women and girls who were most affected by the settler life-style (and vice versa) were those who lived in the homes of the colonist. The Reverend A. D. Williams, for example, raised two African girls who were teenagers by 1835. Both of them were members of Williams's Methodist church. Williams wrote, "It fills me with joy to hear them tell of the goodness of God and to shout forth his praise...." An 1841 obituary for one of these females, Eliza Jones, indicates that she married a settler.[34]

Some African female workers in settler homes were indentured. An indenture certificate for Louisa White, an African orphan, dated 12 June 1838, says that Louisa "voluntarily and of her own free will" consented to be apprenticed to Malvina White, a seamstress, who lived in Monrovia. Malvina pledged to teach Louisa to be a seamstress; to provide her with sufficient food, clothing, and lodging; and to give her two years of schooling during the nine years that she was bound. In return, Louisa was called on to serve her mistress faithfully and to protect her reputation and property. The indenture certificate also provided that Louisa should not "absent herself day or night...without leave, nor haunt tipling shops or taverns or any other places of ill fame." The certificate was signed with Louisa's "X" and Malvina's husband's signature.[35]

Sometimes African girls and women who served in settler homes were mistreated, and some were considered to be inferior. Yet, there were instances where real affection developed between the servant and those served. Many settlers felt that their treatment of the Africans and recaptives who lived in their homes demonstrated the depth of their Christian commitment. Jane Rose Roberts took on the task of educating some of the recaptive children who stayed in her household. When a gentleman visited the Roberts, Jane Rose called in a little boy who had been named Benjamin Coates. The child entered, bowed gracefully to the guest, and then repeated the Ten Commandments and the Apostles' Creed from memory. Urged on by Jane, he ended his presentation by singing "I Want to Be an Angel."[36]

Although the settler women drew Africans into their culture by many means, the most important and beneficial avenue was education. About one-third of the settler females were literate, but only a small percentage worked at the only professional job available to them—teaching. Most of the educated women formed a part of the Liberian elite. Some of the teachers also had administrative or housekeeping duties, but it was their role as instructors and their regular salaries that elevated them to the Liberian elite. During the most of the first decade of the Liberian colonization venture—the 1830s—only freeborn blacks were allowed to emigrate from the United States. Freeborn blacks tended to be better educated than emancipated slaves because slaves were often forbidden by law to acquire literacy skills. Moreover, freeborn blacks generally had more material possessions than did slaves. In the United States, free women sometimes had the opportunity to join churches and women's benevolent and charitable organizations, consequently finding some other avenues for education and training.

Some of these educated women became the day and Sunday school teachers in Liberia. They taught children from all of the cultures that converged on the Liberian coast. They were basically elementary education teachers who emphasized reading, writing, and arithmetic and who always included Christian principles and biblical instruction. Christianity was the primary purpose that some of these settlers emigrated to Liberia. The number of settler women who became day school teachers during the nineteenth century was probably not greater than one hundred. A greater number of them, however, were involved in Sunday schools. At that time the Sunday school curriculum generally included reading and writing as well as religious training. Both day and Sunday schools were important in the process of cultural assimilation.

There were some extremely well-qualified settler women who helped shape the minds of Liberian youths. Most of these women had dual motives: they desired to "civilize and Chirstianize the heathen," and they wanted to provide both African and settler children with sound educational foundations. They believed that the best preparation for potential young Christians was a thorough education in Western letters and values. Eunice Sharpe Moore, a well-educated settler from New York City, typified the attitudes of most of the nineteenth-century female teachers. From Monrovia in 1839, she wrote to the members of a female missionary society in New York, explaining that she taught pupils ranging in age from three to twenty "who were not as advanced in learning as they . . . [were] in years." Moore's desire to evangelize her students as well as give them a rudimentary education comes out clearly in the following excerpt from a letter that is interspersed with biblical quotations. Writing of her love and aspirations for her students, she stated:

> I have some very interesting little girls, who have endeared themselves to me by a thousand tender ties. I have watched them from the alphabet to more interesting things, I have seen them trying to point out the different countries on the map; . . . but all this was not half so entertaining to me as when I saw them crowding to the alter of God. Surely, Oh God! Out of the mouths of babes and sucklings thou has perfected praise.[37]

There were ethnic and sexual biases and language barriers in the classrooms of Liberia. When schools were established, the ideal was to build separate schools for boys and girls and separate ones for black American settlers, recaptives, and Africans. Although this type of segregated educational environment was desired, often there were not enough teachers or adequate money to support separate schools, so the children were either educated together, in separate classes in the same school, or at different sessions during the day.[38]

In Monrovia, by 1826, there was a girls' school with about twenty pupils. It was taught by Miss. E. Jackson, who received a salary of twelve dollars a month. Jackson taught reading, writing, spelling, the principles of religion, and needlework. The students were charged a tuition of fifty cents a month, but those who were unable to pay were given financial aid by the ACS or by concerned Liberian and United States citizens. That same year, a school for recaptive girls under the age of fourteen had also been established. Each weekday evening these girls received three hours of instruction, learning to read and spell English words. The instructor of the recaptive girls, Mrs. Williams, received a salary of eight dollars a month. She received four dollars less than the teacher of the settler girls because greater value was placed on educating the settlers and because she spent less time in the classroom.[39]

The Ladies Liberia School Association of Philadelphia (originally called the Ladies Association Auxiliary to the ACS) was founded in 1831 to sponsor the education of some settler and African girls. The first teacher at the Ladies Association girls' school in Monrovia was a settler named Elizabeth Mars Thompson. This woman became one of the most important educators in nineteenth-century Liberia. She was born in Connecticut in 1807 and was educated at the expense of several acquaintances in Philadelphia. She emigrated to Liberia in 1833 with her first husband, William Johnson, but he died soon after their arrival. She later married James Thompson, an immigrant from the West Indies.[40]

Observers commented that Elizabeth Mars Thompson's school in Monrovia was conducted in a manner highly creditable to her. In 1833, she taught a total of fifty-seven girls: fourteen girls were under age five; eighteen were between the ages of five and ten; twenty-two were between the ages of ten and fifteen; and three were older than fifteen. She taught them arithmetic, spelling, reading, writing, geography, and grammar. Thompson taught in Monrovia for two years, sometimes holding classes in her home. In 1835 she and her husband moved to Cape Palmas in southern Liberia, where the couple worked with the Protestant Episcopal mission. When her second husband died in 1838, Thompson continued the school she had established at the Cape, although she suffered periodic bouts of illness. In an 1840 letter she wrote that her girls' school had twenty-two pupils, including both settler and African girls. An 1843 report on missionary influence in Liberia commented on Thompson's work:

> Of female missionaries and teachers in Liberia, let us inquire who among the many intelligent, accomplished and pious ladies that have solemnly devoted themselves to this hazardous field of labor, possess the physical ability, or has evinced that capacity for the instruction of the native youths, as Elizabeth Thompson.[41]

A singular situation reflects Thompson's commitment to her work in Liberia and perhaps reflects the dedication of all the Liberian teachers—about whom far less is known. In 1846, Thompson visited her hometown of Hartford, Connecticut. During her stay she received the unexpected word that she would not be reassigned to the Protestant Episcopal mission in Cape Palmas. This information threw her into "deep anxiety and regret having been engaged, and deeply interested in the mission since early in the year 1836." She stated that she taught the first school for Africans in Cape Palmas and supported the growth of other Protestant Episcopal mission efforts in Cape Palmas while loved ones and colleagues succumbed to tropical diseases. Thompson also noted that her children, who knew the Grebo language, had been consecrated to the mission by their father, and with adequate education "would become efficient laborers in the work among the heathen." She stated that she would immediately pursue another opportunity for African service because she had no desire to remain in the United States.[42]

Thompson received an appointment from the Maryland Colonization Society, and in a letter from Hartford dated 30 March 1846, she wrote that she accepted the offer with reluctance. It seems that Thompson served only a short time with the Maryland Society because soon after her return to Liberia, the Protestant Episcopal mission opened a school for settler girls and appointed her as the head teacher. In 1856, war broke out between the colonists of Cape Palmas and the Grebos, and Elizabeth Thompson's home was destroyed. She lost everything but her clothes. Her furniture, bedding, books, linen, and household articles, which she had been gradually accumulating for twenty years, were all lost. Her school was also burned. Thompson, her family, and her adopted children then moved into another nearby mission station. Although Thompson was able to teach again for several years after the war, her health worsened progressively. By 1861 she was brought to the Liberian coast, where she served as the matron of St. Mark's Hospital until her death in 1864 at age fifty-six. During the decades of her service in Africa, she helped with the education of many colonists and Africans, especially orphans, sometimes using her own home as the classroom and offering her own substance to maintain others.[43]

In spite of dedicated teachers, such as Elizabeth Mars Thompson, women's education in Liberia suffered, especially after the primary level. A few high schools for girls were established, but none of them enjoyed a long life, and many of the primary schools lasted only as long as the teacher endured. Nevertheless, many Liberians received a fundamental education at the hands of these dedicated women. Of all of the contribtuions made by settler women, their role in educating the youth of Liberia was probably the most important. Some settler women lived sacrificially so that they could share their knowledge with the children of the growing Republic. True, settler women were guilty of cultural biases and of feelings of superiority toward the Africans they taught, but that did not usually hinder them from acting as dedicated and conscientious teachers.

Educated women formed mutual aid societies, sewing circles, missionary societies, temperance clubs, savings and burial organizations, and societies for the purpose of aiding the needy. The contributions of settler women through these organizations were extremely important for the development of Liberia. These groups became effective agents of assimilation, and educated and Christianized African women subsequently formed branch groups of their own to minister to members' needs, support African churches or missions, and aid African villagers who were poor or sick.

Assimilation was a painful necessity for African nations that had already been ravaged by the slave trade for several centuries at the hands of those who were technologically superior. Failure to find some grounds on which to compete with Western nations would continue to leave Africa at the mercy of the West. Although the work performed by African women in Liberia during the nineteenth century and later was more vital to the nation's economy than that of settler women, the work of settler women was necessary for building national foundations for the twentieth century. Unfortunately, the attitudes that settler women brought with them sowed seeds of discontent that would yield a crop of bitter fruit in the future. Working women as a group, however, both settlers and Africans, proved to be laborers who were able and willing to sow the seeds and reap the harvest for the development of the Liberian nation.

NOTES

1. Two general histories of the rise of the colonization movement in the United States are P. J. Staudenraus, *The African Colonization Movement, 1816–1865* (New York: Columbia University Press, 1961), and Early Lee Fox, *The American Colonization Society* (Baltimore: Johns Hopkins Press, 1919).

2. For information about the colonization movement from the perspective of the settlers on the West African coast, see Tom W. Shick, *Behold the Promised Land* (Baltimore: Johns Hopkins University Press, 1980), and Debra L. Newman, "The Emergence of Liberian Women in the Nineteenth Century" (Ph.D. diss. Howard University, 1984).

3. See Newman, chap. 4.

4. See Shick, Introduction and chap. 1; Newman, chap. 1.

5. James C. Riddell, "The Gbannah Ma (Mano) in Two Economies: Dynamics of Finite-Labor Economics" (unpublished, University of Liberia Library, Monrovia), 5–10; Ester Boserup, *Women's Role in Economic Development* (New York: St. Martin's Press, 1970), 15–41; *African Repository* (hereafter *AR*) 28 (January 1852):13; Caroline H. Bledsoe, *Women and Marriage in Kpelle Society* (Stanford, Calif.: Stanford University Press, 1980);

Jewell Taylor Gibbs, "Life in a Liberian Village," *Radcliffe Quarterly* 42 (November 1958):20–23.

6. David F. Lancy, "Work, Play and Learning in a Kpelle Town" (Ph.D. diss., University of Pittsburgh, 1974), 134–35.

7. Ibid., 135–43; Benjamin K. Anderson, *Narrative of a Journey to Musardu* (Reprint, London: Frank Cass, 1971), 64.

8. *AR* 12 (September 1836):273, 276–77.

9. Ibid.; *AR* 42 (November 1866):339; *AR* 31 (August 1855):247, Harriette G. Brittan, *Scenes and Incidents of Everyday Life in Africa* (New York: Pudney and Russell, 1860), 174; Abayomi Kranga, *History of Liberia* (Liverpool: D. W. Twe, 1926), 80; Alexander M. Cowan, *Liberia As I Found It in 1858* (Frankfort, Ky.: A. G. Hodges, 1858), 26.

10. Ibid.

11. *AR* 28 (October 1852):317.

12. Cowan, *Liberia*, 101–102.

13. Ibid., 122.

14. *AR* 17 (July 1841):215; *Twenty-Fourth ACS Annual Report, 1841*, 11.

15. *AR* 44 (April 1868):115; *AR* 15 (August 1839):215.

16. *AR* 25 (August 1849):230–31; *AR* 21 (November 1845):340.

17. *Role of Emigrants Sent to Liberia by the American Colonization Society and Its Auxiliaries, to September, 1843, and Census of the Colony of Liberia, September, 1843*, Senate Document 458, 28th Congress, 2d Session, volume 9, part 150.

18. *AR* 39 (October 1863):310–11; *AR* 46 (September 1870):280.

19. Census of 1843.

20. Penelope Campbell, *Maryland in Africa: The Maryland State Colonization Society, 1831–57* (Chicago: University of Illinois Press, 1971), 143.

21. *AR* 3 (November 1827):276; *AR* 33 (December 1837):362.

22. Alfred B. Williams, *The Liberian Exodus* (Charleston, South Carolina: The News and Courier Book Presses, 1878), 45; *AR* 47 (June 1871):189: *AR* 41 (April 1865):99; Martha A. Cassell to Reverend Kimber, Bible House, 13 March 1869, Liberia Correspondence, Archives of the Episcopal Church, Austin, Texas; *AR* 42 (October 1866):303.

23. Brittan, *Every-Day Life* 224; Mary B. Merriam, *Home Life in Africa* (Boston: A. Williams, 1968), 52.

24. Brittan, *Every-Day Life*, 224.

25. Republic of Liberia vs. Charles and Julia Harmon, n.d., Maryland County Court of Quarter Sessions and Common Pleas. The Harmons were accused of keeping a "bawdy house," of promoting "lewdness," and of "corrupting public morals." Hearing concerning ownership claims of Mrs. Joseph Williams, n.d. This was a case involving a man who was a trading agent for his wife. The transcript also mentions that the man's first wife ran a "cook shop." Land Records, vol. N/N, Liberian National Archives; Census of 1843; Cowan, *Liberia*, 77.

26. *AR* 34 (May 1858):150–53; *Seventeenth Maryland Colonization Society Annual Report, 1858*, 9: *Forty-Second ACS Annual Report, 1859*, 14–15; *Forty-Third ACS Annual Report, 1860*, 11–12.

27. Ibid.

28. Ibid.

29. Ibid.

30. *AR* 36 (January 1860):1, 7.

31. *AR* 44 (February 1868):48–49.

32. See Debra L. Newman, "The Emergence of Liberian Women in the Nineteenth Century," (Ph.D. diss., Howard University, 1984), 336–62.

33. Alexander M. Cowan, *Liberia, As I Found It* (Frankfort, Ky: A. G. Hodges, 1858), 122.

34. *AR* 12 (March 1836):96; Obituary of Eliza Jones, 1 January 1841, *African Luminary.*

35. Indenture Papers, 12 June 1838, Land Records, Liberian National Archives, Ministry of Foreign Affairs, Monrovia.

36. *AR* 39 (April 1863):111.

37. *AR* 14 (March 1838):73.

38. *AR* 3 (May 1827):95–96.

39. Ibid.

40. *First Annual Report of the Ladies Liberia School Association* (Philadelphia: Lydia R. Bailey, 1833) 1–8; *AR* 40 (November 1864):334–35.

41. *AR* 10 (May 1834):89; *AR* 8 (December 1832):299, 303; *Third Annual Report of the Ladies Liberia School Association, 1835* (Philadelphia: Lydia R. Bailey, 1935), 7.

42. Elizabeth M. Thompson to the Reverend P. P. Irving, 24 March 1846, Liberia Correspondence, Archives of the Episcopal Church; Brittan, *Every-Day Life,* 78–79.

43. Elizabeth M. Thompson to the Reverend P. P. Irving, 25 March and 30 March 1846, Archives of the Episcopal Church; *Maryland Colonization Journal* 4 (July 1847):2; *AR* 33 (May 1857):145–46; *AR* 34 (May 1858):139: *AR* 39 (October 1863):289; *AR* 40 (November 1864):334–35.

21

Afro-American Influence in Colonial Malawi, 1891–1945

Kings M. Phiri

ISTORIANS of Africa have been aware, since the early 1960s at least, that the scope of their discipline ought to be extended to include the extent to which peoples of African descent abroad have participated in and contributed to African history.[1] The importance of this awareness, arising so early in the development of modern African history, was nevertheless, not widely felt until the mid-1970s. Of the few pioneers, George Shepperson of Edinburgh University in Scotland, has been perhaps the most committed. Writing for the newly launched *Journal of African History* in 1960, he effectively underlined the crucial role that Afro-Americans and other diaspora Africans played in the emergence of African nationalism during the first half of this century.[2]

Later scholars in this field have sought to broaden our understanding of relations between Africa and the African diaspora and the extent to which the history of Africa had been influenced by Africans abroad. For example, in his address to the Second International Congress of African Historians held in Dar es Salaam in 1965, Joseph Harris noted that Afro-Americans had helped to shape the course of events in central and southern Africa and that the story of how this was done had to be investigated.[3] This challenge has in recent years been assumed by a number of scholars. For example, Walton Johnson has investigated the role of Afro-American missionaries in southern Africa during the early colonial period, while Richard Ralston has traced the early career of southern African students who studied in America before 1940. Taken together, these studies have gone a long way to demonstrate that Afro-Americans were extensively involved in central and southern Africa during the colonial period and that contact with black America was an important episode in the education and development of several modern African leaders.[4]

It is the aim of this chapter to add to this growing fund of information on relations between Africa and Africans abroad. In particular, it will seek to draw attention to the different facets of interaction that existed between Afro-Americans and the people of colonial Malawi and to improve on the very fragmentary approach to this subject in the existing literature.[5] It will show that Afro-Americans were involved in colonial Malawi as potential colonists, Christian missionaries, sponsors of young Malawians who studied in black colleges in the United States, and brokers of educational and racial ideologies spawned in their part of the world. The chapter also serves as a guide to the possibilities of further research in this area.

The sources, both written and oral, of this chapter are located in archives in three continents. There are those that are housed in the National Archives of Malawi in Zomba, and others in the Public Records Office and other archival institutions in Britain. To these must be added records in the United States of the different Afro-American organizations or societies that had contacts with the peoples of Malawi and central Africa. An effective consultation of all these archives would call for more time and money than has been available for this particular exercise.

Oral sources also exist in the form of reminiscences of those who were exposed to Afro-Americans or their ideas. Such reminiscences come from mission-educated, elderly persons. These persons are scattered throughout Malawi, so that a considerable amount of time would be required to interview them profitably. However, enough research has been conducted to provide a basis for this seminal study.

The beginnings of Afro-American contact with south-central Africa and with Malawi in particular can be traced to the last quarter of the nineteenth century. This was a time when, in spite of the colonial domination in Africa, the Afro-American was quite excited about the back-to-Africa movement.[6] There were those Afro-American leaders who thought in terms of a mass exodus of blacks from the United States to Africa and others who thought that the best approach was to sponsor missionary projects through which a few Afro-Americans at a time would be returned to Africa as carriers of Christianity to their African brethren. It was this kind of mood within Afro-America that men like Dr. Albert Thorne, an arch exponent of Afro-American colonization of Africa, tried to exploit.

Albert Thorne was a native of Barbados but spent much of his youth in Edinburgh, Scotland, where he studied medicine. While there, between 1894 and 1897, he began to work on a scheme through which he hoped to bring Afro-Americans and other New World Africans to Malawi (then British Central Africa) as colonists. It was his firm conviction that Africans of the diaspora rather than the European colonists would best fulfill the noble mission of redeeming Africa spiritually and industrially. Thorne was obviously not pleased about British, French, and Belgian imperial expansion in Africa. His choice of New World Africans as a substitute rested on other important beliefs that the black race in the Caribbean and North America had acquired skills that would be useful to African development; that the harsh conditions under which they lived in the New World afforded them little scope for the full development and use of those skills; and that being of African descent they would be more humane as colonizers than the Europeans with their lust for colonial profits. Finally, Dr. Thorne chose the area around Lake Malawi (Nyasa) as an experimental field for his scheme because it was an area with which Scotland, his adopted home, was already involved.[7]

Thorne's colonization scheme came to nothing. It was undermined by the reluctance of his would-be Scottish supporters to support a scheme that would have involved the establishment of a black republic in what was already a European (British) colony. Malawi was, after all, the only colony in Africa that an independent Scotland would have had. It had been explored for European settlement by Scottish missionaries between 1858 and 1891. It is, nevertheless, of interest to gauge how the people of Malawi would have reacted to the establishment of the proposed Afro-American colony.

Local newspapers, such as the *Central African Planter*, in early colonial Malawi suggest that such schemes were discussed among educated Malawians of that time, particularly in the Shire Highlands. Joseph Bismarck, a product of the Church of Scotland Mission at Blantyre, was stirred enough to air his honest opinion about the proposed colonization schemes. He retorted: "Will these Negro American Christians do anything good in our country? Won't they sit down in their houses and read their books when they come out here, and make us poor Bantu do their work instead of themselves?"[8] In other words, to Bismarck, a colonist was basically an exploiter of the indigenous people, the color of his or her skin notwithstanding. While Bismarck's rhetoric may well have been representative of what educated Africans felt about the issue, the bulk of the African population in Malawi in the 1890s were left too dazed by the wars of colonial occupation to have a considered opinion about such matters.[9]

Although Afro-Americans never came to Malawi as colonizers, in subsequent years a few of them came as Christian missionaries. They were encouraged in this mission by John Chilembwe, a native of

Chiradzulu District in southern Malawi. In 1897, the Reverend Joseph Booth, a radical English missionary, who then conducted an industrial mission at Mitsidi near the modern city of Blantyre, took Chilembwe to the United States to be trained for the ministry. Booth left Chilembwe with some Afro-American Baptists in New York and Philadelphia. They in turn sent him to Lynchburg Seminary in Virginia. Shepperson and Price have offered a sensitive analysis of how Chilembwe's personality was transformed as a result of his connections with the Afro-American world.

Before his departure for the United States, the young Chilembwe had the kind of trust in white men that was rare among his people. He had, on more than one occasion, helped his mentor, Joseph Booth, to dispel the belief then current among the Yao, Chilembwe's ethnic group, that Europeans were cannibals who bought slaves in Africa for the sake of their human flesh. After nine years of contact with Afro-Americans, and perhaps as a result of his mental maturity, however, Chilembwe turned into a critical observer of European rule and activity in his part of Africa.[10] His developing sense of grievance against British colonial rule in Malawi eventually induced him to lead the famous Native Rising of 1915, which briefly rocked the country's colonial administration.

The making of a radical out of Chilembwe has been traced back to his student days in the United States, which in the words of Shepperson and Price, "coincided with a period of intense reaction to white discrimination against Negroes." Although little is known of Chilembwe's movements in the United States, it is nevertheless argued that he was exposed to the bitter racial strife between whites and blacks that prevailed then in some parts of American cities; that he witnessed the carefully planned disenfranchisement of many blacks who had received the vote under the liberal state constitutions of the Reconstruction Era; that he enjoyed the patronage and occasional company of at least a few "Ethiopian-minded" Afro-American Baptist leaders; and that he must have been privy to firsthand accounts of how self-conscious Afro-Americans had resisted slavery and racial exploitation.[11] Above all, as far as his future career in Malawi was concerned, he was associated with one or two Afro-American missionary projects for the development of Africa.

Thus, when Chilembwe returned to central Africa in 1900, it was as "a John the Baptist making a path for American Negro missionaries." Back in his own home district of Chiradzulu, southern Malawi, and in anticipation of support promised him by the National Baptist Convention of America (NBC), Chilembwe purchased ninety-three acres of land at Mbombwe for his Providence Industrial Mission (PIM). Within two years, he was joined by two Afro-American missionaries, the Reverend

Landon N. Cheek and Miss Emma B. Delaney, whom the NBC sent out to assist him. With the help of funds from the NBC headquarters in Louisville, Kentucky, the three missionaries, one local and two American, were able to expand the PIM's network of churches and schools not only in the Shire Highlands of southern Malawi but into parts of Mozambique as well. In addition, they were able to organize homecraft classes for women and to embark on the commercial farming of coffee, cotton, pepper, and rubber at the central station.

One of the most obvious effects of the Afro-American missionary presence at Chilembwe's mission at the time was the attempt to establish an educational curriculum that represented a radical departure from anything attempted in the various educational programs of the orthodox missionary societies. It was a curriculum modeled on that of Booker T. Washington's Institute at Tuskegee, Alabama, and it is possible that Cheek and Delaney were the architects of it. The kind of education it provided was meant to transcend mere proficiency in the three Rs by including aspects of industrial and agricultural training. The long-term goal of such an educational program was "to build up a clean, neatly dressed community, with industrious and sober habits."[12]

Another impact of Afro-American missionaries was the appetite for self-improvement through education that it whetted among the Mbombwe young men who came into regular contact with the Afro-American missionaries. This did not become clear until much later. On their return to the United States, both Cheek and Delaney encouraged young members of Chilembre's church to follow them. The story of at least one such young man Daniel Sharpe Malikebu to take up the offer, will be discussed later.

Cheek and Delaney were practical missionaries who did all in their power to help Chilembwe and his followers until 1906, when the time came for them to return to the United States. Even then, they did not escape the malevolence of the neighboring Scottish missionaries and British colonial administrators. This was because Cheek was critical of what he saw of race relations in the Shire Highlands, the part of Malawi that proved most attractive to white settlement. He observed, among other things, that the native population was deliberately kept poor and ignorant so as to serve the interests of the white settlers. The suspicion that the administration had of the Afro-American missionaries at Chilembwe's PIM was aggravated by the presence, thirty miles away, of other Afro-American missionaries who were made even more suspect than Cheek and Delaney. These were Thomas Branch, his wife, and their three children. They arrived in Malawi from Pennsylvania in April 1901 to open the Seventh Day Adventist Mission at Plainfield (Malamulo) in Thyolo District.[13]

Thomas Branch soon ran into difficulties with the administration because it was feared that he, as well as Chilembwe's Afro-American assistants, were attempting to introduce the nationalistic, Ethiopian brand of Christianity with its war cry of "Africa for Africans." Indeed, before the end of his first year in Malawi, Branch was accused of inciting the indigenous péople to understand that their land had been raped by the white man.[14]

In the year that followed, Branch not only suffered the indignity of being distrusted by the colonial administrators and settlers near his mission, but he also lost the confidence of his headquarters in the United States. The general conference, as the mission board of his church was termed, accused him of having acted too independently and of having established a poor image of the Seventh Day Adventists by not acting according to the demands of the local situation. The result was that in 1907 he was replaced as head of the mission by Pastor Joel Rogers, a white American missionary, and subsequently forced to resign from the mission field. From then onward, Afro-Americans were excluded from positions of high authority in the service of the Seventh Day Adventists Mission in Malawi.[15]

The difficulties that the early Afro-American missionaries to Malawi had with the Europeans in their neighborhood made it unlikely that Chilembwe's experiment of inviting them into the country would be encouraged. Afro-Americans, no matter what their background, were in colonial Malawi a tolerated but not desirable class of immigrants. As things turned out, however, it was Chilembwe himself who gave the colonial administration of that time an appropriate excuse for disallowing further Afro-American involvement in Malawi. Beginning from about 1912, Chilembwe, who was then also haunted by a host of personal problems, saw it as his prime task to oppose any government measures that he deemed an affront to the dignity of his people; the oppression and exploitation of those who worked on European estates; the alienation of the most arable land in the country; racial discrimination; and the employment of Africans in colonial wars. In January 1915, after the administration had ignored several of the petitions concerning these grievances that he signed on behalf of his followers, he decided to mastermind the bloody but brief uprising of the local population in the Shire Highlands against British rule.[16]

Chilembwe's revolt may be said to have brought to an end the first and, undoubtedly, most pronounced phase of Afro-American involvement in Malawi. The commission of inquiry, which the governor appointed to investigate the cause of the rising, concluded that Chilembwe had imbibed dangerous political notions from his Afro-American connections and that his attitude toward race relations had been inflamed by "a certain class of American Negro publications" that he had been importing on a regular basis.[17] This meant, by implication, that direct Afro-American involvement in colonial Malawi would not have official approbation.

After 1915, Afro-Americans continued to be involved in Malawi, primarily through their indirect contacts with certain categories of Malawians. These contacts took many forms. There was the continued Afro-American sponsorship of specific missionary projects; their moral and financial support of young Malawians who went to the United States in search of higher education; and their educational as well as racial outreach.

In spite of this observation, one must also admit that we know very little about Afro-American contacts with the people of Malawi in what may be described as the post-Chilembwe period. Yet, such contacts appear to have been important to the activities of a number of educated Malawians of the time. It was through such contacts, for example, that support from Afro-American churches reached affiliated Christian congregations in Malawi. Several local evangelists and educators tried to serve their own people with this kind of external support.

The first one that comes to mind is the Reverend Hanock Msokera Phiri, who established the African Methodist Episcopal Church (AME) in Malawi in 1924. Phiri had been a migrant worker in Rhodesia (now Zimbabwe) and South Africa when he was introduced to the AME.[18] In 1923, together with his nephew Hastings Kamuzu Banda, he had an interview in Johannesburg with Bishop L. T. Vernon, then in charge of the AME's fifteenth District (South Africa). At Vernon's bidding, Phiri returned to Malawi to open a branch of the church in 1924.

Back in Malawi, Phiri applied for and was granted permission to establish a mission in Kasungu, his home district. In an interview granted to this writer in 1971, Phiri indicated that what attracted him to the AME was its belief in African or Negro autonomy and economic self-reliance. "I was impressed," he declared, "by the prospect that with their help, we too in Nyasaland (Malawi) would control our own educational system, economic enterprises and send out our own missionaries."[19] It is also possible, however, that Phiri was influenced by the not too remote example of those who had successfully established branches of the AME in Zimbabwe and South Africa.[20] Independency, thus seems to have motivated Phiri in his beginning a missionary career. In later years, however, he was to underplay this fact, maintaining instead that like all the other missionaries, he opened his mission "in order to evangelise and civilise his people."[21]

In subsequent years, Phiri and his supporters managed to expand the evangelical and educational program of their mission. At Mdabwi, the main station, a church and school were built and a big garden opened. The church and school were staffed by African teachers whom Phiri enticed away from the neighboring Livingstonia Mission of the Free Church of Scotland. The garden was apparently intended to play a key role in the industrial training program of the mission, but eventually it served only the mundane function of producing food for the teachers and boarders at the school. By 1934, it was producing maize, beans, upland rice, and sugar cane for this purpose.[22]

The problem of funds, which plagued almost every independent African church movement in Malawi,[23] is one that also inhibited the progress of Phiri's church. Much of the church's financial support came from school fees, from donations received from members of the church at work in Zimbabwe and South Africa, and after 1928, from government grants-in-aid to those schools that had been approved. These were slender sources even in terms of the mission's meager budget. Phiri, thus, conducted his church with an ever-soaring budget deficit. These were years when some of the teachers in charge of the "bush" schools complained of working for as long as nine months without receiving their pay.[24] To his frequent mention of these financial difficulties, leaders of the AME in South Africa advised Phiri that his church would have to be completely self-supporting then or in due course. Their extramural assistance to him would be limited. They were prepared to educate young Malawians who would then return to play key roles within the church in Malawi. At one time in the 1930s, they also suggested to Phiri that he should collect curios from all over Malawi. They would then have them transported to America, where sympathizers and well-wishers were willing to pay a good price for them. This was viewed as a less humiliating way of raising funds for the work of the AME in Malawi than was begging.[25]

None of these offers seems to have had much appeal to Phiri. He, therefore, remained frustrated over the issue of financial assistance from the parent body in the United States. He was also frustrated in another area: his ambition to visit the United States as a delegate to one of the general conferences of the AME. This was never realized. The main reason was that the parent organization stuck to the policy that leaders of the church in Africa had more to gain from interaction with other African delegates at regional conferences held, for the most part, in South Africa or Zimbabwe. Given these frustrations, Phiri later adopted a bitter tone in his correspondence with his superiors. Writing to the bishop of the Seventeenth District (central Africa) in 1964, he complained of how the mother body in America had neglected him financially. He reminded the bishop of his long service in behalf of the church, which included establishing the church in Malawi, extending its influence into eastern Zambia and the Katanga (Shaba) province of the Belgian Congo (Zaire), and baptizing 30,000 people in the name of the AME.[26]

It should be noted, in fairness to the parent body that Phiri criticized, that in the United States funds for the support of mission work overseas were not forthcoming, particularly in the 1930s and 1940s. The economic depression of the 1930s made the situation very desperate indeed. This was clearly reflected in the subsidies that the AME sent to its African districts. For example, in 1941, exclusive of salaries for the bishops and their secretaries, only $700 was received for the Fifteenth and Seventeenth Districts (south and central Africa, respectively).[27]

In spite of the difficulties that obviously surrounded his effort, it is to Phiri's credit that he not only consolidated the work of his mission in Malawi but also managed to extend it into neighboring parts of Northern Rhodesia (Zambia), where he founded stations at Fort Jameson (Chipata) and Abercorn (Mbala).[28]

Another Malawian evangelist and educator who received Afro-American sponsorship in the post-Chilembwe period was Daniel Sharp Malikebu. In 1922, the National Baptist Convention appointed Malikebu to succeed Chilembwe as leader of the Providence Industrial Mission in Chiradzulu. Malikebu had just completed his studies in the United States. Together with his wife, Flora Ethelwyn, who was Afro-American, Malikebu was given the task of reopening the PIM in Malawi. After some misunderstanding with the colonial administration in Malawi that involved four years' delay, the Malikebus were given permission to reopen the mission in 1926.[29]

The NBC expected them to evangelize the local people, to educate them, and to provide basic medical services. Like the Reverend Phiri, however, Malikebu found himself without sufficient funds for implementing this program of his mission. It is clear from the correspondence that was exchanged between him and the NBC headquarters that the parent organization had very little money to spare for him. This is clearly reflected from the slender support that he received from the United States for the most important undertakings of his mission during the first decade of its resurrection: the construction of the large, brick-walled, and corrugated iron-roofed church at Mbombwe from 1929 to 1933, and the construction as well as furnishings of Dr. Malikebu's surgery facility in the years that followed.[30] Furthermore, the Malikebus labored alone during the first twenty years of their mission. Until 1945, Dr. Malikebu was the only pastor in this mission field. This made it almost impossible for him to ask for leave or to enjoy occasionally the kind of rest that would have led him to reassess his work. In his own words, he had "labored with the odd feeling that all would be at a loss if something tragic befell him."[31]

What we know of the relations that the Reverend Phiri and Dr. Malikebu had with their Afro-American sponsors raises a number of questions to which the attention of future investigations could profitably be drawn. There is, for example, the need to know the extent to which these local missionaries could be guided by their Afro-American sponsors and to assess the amount of financial and material support that they actually received from the sponsors.

The second type of contact between Malawi and Afro-America in the post-Chilembwe period was provided by young Malawians who traveled to the United States to study in Afro-American colleges. Although Malawi could boast of several young men who made such journeys before 1945, the limelight usually centers on only two of them, Daniel Sharpe Malikebu and Hastings Kamuzu Banda, primarily because both of them later made a great contribution to the welfare of their people.[32] Through his work at the PIM and its interest to the National Baptist Convention of America, as well as through his marriage to an Afro-American, Malikebu was an obvious link in the relations between Malawians and Afro-Americans. The same cannot be said with great assurance of Banda, whose connections with Afro-America may have been diluted during his long stay in Great Britain after 1937.

Daniel Malikebu traveled to the United States in 1908 at the invitation of his former school teacher at Chilembwe's PIM, Emma Delaney. With her support and the backing of certain Afro-American Baptist leaders in New York and Ohio, he was sent to school in North Carolina. Later, he studied at Selma College in Alabama and then at Meharry Medical College in Tennessee, where he was certified in 1917.[33]

During his fourteen years' stay in the United States. Malikebu established a far-flung network of contacts—with the medical staff at Meharry, YMCA staff workers in several parts of the United States, and Baptist leaders. For this and other reasons, Malikebu would later refer to the United States as "home."

Hastings Kamuzu Banda, now life president of Malawi, could have been an even greater contact for Afro-American ideas and influences in Malawi than Malikebu had other factors not intervened. According to his late uncle, the Reverend Hanock Msokera Phiri, the AME bishop who sponsored his travel to the United States hoped that he would later qualify as an educationist, lawyer, and medical doctor for service with a self-supporting AME mission in Malawi. It was undoubtedly Banda's own deportment, even in the 1920s, that determined the interest the AME leaders developed in him. Almost all accounts of him suggest that young Banda had a tenacity of purpose and a burning desire for success that must have greatly impressed those with whom he came into contact. E. S. Munger, whose short biography of Banda is the only one that is readily available in Malawi, maintains that he wanted to become as learned and articulate as Dr. J. E. Kwegyir Aggrey, whose inspiring addresses to black and white South Africans Banda attended in 1921.[34] It is essentially the same impression that we get from the reminiscences of Banda's own uncle:

> Kamuzu (Banda) had searched for the church of Negro Americans for four years. In 1923 he wrote me saying that he had established contact with this church. He sent me £4.00 so that I could travel from Livingstone (Zambia) and meet him in Johannesburg. ... There was a big meeting of the AME in Johannesburg which he and I were requested to attend. They introduced us as Nyasalanders who had come to join the AME. We were led to Bishop L. T. Vernon who asked us what plans we had. We told him we had come all the way from Nyasaland—thirty days' footing—with one intention: to be educated. The Bishop then said that he would take Kamuzu to America for further education. ... In 1925, we told the Bishop that Banda had saved £75 from his wages and by selling his German made flute, for his travel to America. He said it was enough since Kamuzu would be issued a concession ticket for his travel. So Kamuzu went to America in July 1925.[35]

In the United States, Banda was initially sent to Wilberforce Institute in Ohio, a school that was established to help peoples of African descent in America to gain knowledge and build character. At Wilberforce, both liberal and industrial education received equal attention and emphasis, and it was under that kind of educational system that Banda earned his high school diploma. Thereafter, he proceeded to Indiana University and the University of Chicago, where he received his bachelor of philosophy degree in 1931. Up to that point, the majority of his benefactors appear to have been Afro-Americans, including the AME. If this thesis is true,[36] then his economic fortunes, and perhaps his attitude toward Afro-America as well, changed somewhat after his admission to Meharry Medical College in 1932. The bulk of his financial support then was derived from white philanthropists. Apparently, one of his most enthusiastic supporters at this time was Walter B. Stephenson, president of Delta Electric Company in Marion, Ohio. By that time, Banda was in a strong position to make a critical assessment of his American environment and to appreciate the severe limitations that white racism imposed on the development of black character and initiative.

There can be little doubt, on the whole, that Banda left the United States in 1937 with a wider perception of problems that faced the African race in both America and Africa. Besides what his contacts with Afro-Americans taught him, he also had the opportunity to exchange views on a variety of issues affecting colonial Africa and the African race with fellow African students such as A. B. Xuma and J. R. Rathebe, both of whom came from South Africa and whom Banda met while in the United States. These episodes must have been useful to him later when he decided to assume a leadership role in the struggle for African independence and constitutional rights in central Africa after World War II.[37]

The third type of Afro-American contact was through the spread of their educational and racial ideologies. Mention has already been made of how Booker T. Washington's philosophy of education was sown at Chilembwe's Providence Industrial Mission in the first decade of this century. According to this philosophy, the ideal educational system had to be relevant to the environment of the people it was meant to serve, cultivate both the mind and ordinary skills of its pupils, and train people for self-employment afterward.[38] Besides Chilembwe, Charles Domingo, one of the most outspoken independent African church leaders of the early colonial period in Malawi, also tried to adopt it as the guiding principle of his schools. Between 1907 and 1912, he wanted to build a central boarding school at Chipata, the main station of his Seventh Day Baptist Church in Mzimba district, which he hoped would grow into an African College.[39]

In the 1920s, the Reverend Hanock Phiri also tried to apply this philosophy to the educational work of his mission in Kasungu. At Mdabwi, the central station, the pupils divided their time between the classroom and working in the garden mentioned earlier. Phiri, it should be noted, was exposed to Booker T. Washington's philosophy of education quite early in his life, at a time when he was a student at Livingstonia's Overtoun Institute, the most famous school in east-central Africa then, during the first decade of this century:

> I studied at Kondowe (Overtoun Institute) from 1903 to 1910 when I completed the course in Theology. While there, I learned a great deal about the education provided by the American Negroes from Mr. Edward Boti Manda who was a teacher from Tongaland. Mr. Manda used to receive letters from two teachers at Tuskegee, Booker T. Washington's school. These teachers were Morton Luther and Miss Amanda. They had an interest in the education of Africans and their letters spoke of the educational opportunities which existed in America and of the progress they were making at Booker T. Washington Institute.[40]

In applying the spirit of Tuskegee to the work of his mission, Phiri was perpetuating a tradition that was already established as an integral part of the educational schemes of several local missionaries. The adoption of this philosophy was an appropriate move at the time because colonial settlers were generally opposed to the immediate advancement of the native population, while very few employment opportunities existed for Africans with a liberal education per se.

Finally, mention must be made of the impact that the Garvey movement had in Malawi during the interwar period. The racial philosophy of the movement's Jamaican-born leader, Marcus Garvey, made a strong impression on educated Malawians of the time—teachers, evangelists, and civil servants.[41]

Garvey's successful organization of the Universal Negro Improvement Association (UNIA) and the emotions that his movement evoked among black peoples all over the world have been given a simple but adequate analysis by, among other writers, David Cronon.[42] In his words, Garveyism "suddenly emerged as a movement of world significance, with a spiritual power that reached deep down into the colored peoples of the world." The appeal of Garvey's movement rested on its distrust of white leadership and financial support; its emphasis on black racial pride and economic self-reliance; and its call for the redemption of Africa from colonial rule. But while the bulk of support for the movement in the United States came from the urban proletariat, in Malawi it was frustrated, mission-educated men who found in Garveyism a reinforcement for their own convictions. According to the Lindens, this was because such men found themselves without influence under the colonial system and were generally despised by the white ruling class, in spite of their many accomplishments.[43]

Indeed, Garveyism found its most fertile ground among graduates of Livingstonia's Overtoun Institute, the most advanced school in east-central Africa at the time. In the words of one of these men, Charles Chidongo Chinula, "In those days [the 1920s], we read Marcus Garvey's newspapers and learned that many American Negroes would be carried back to Africa in ships. We believed that Garvey was a great man and that he was there to help all of us."[44] Like Phiri, Chinula had been a pupil at Livingstonia, felt the call to serve God in a special way, and ended up establishing his own church, *Eklesia Lanangwa* (the Gospel of Freedom), in the early 1930s. Partly because of the difficulties he had with the Livingstonia missionaries, his original employers, he seems to have developed an aversion to being controlled by Europeans or anyone else for that matter.[45] For this reason, he once sharply rebuked the Reverend Phiri for submitting to being under Afro-American bishops whom Chinula dismissed as "black Europeans."

Chinula later emerges as a tough but protean figure in African nationalist politics in Malawi. His writings and speeches then closely paralleled those of Marcus Garvey at an earlier date. There was the same emphasis on "Africa for Africans" and pride in the black idiom.

For example, in urging the chiefs in his own home district, Mzimba, to take up the fight against imposition of the Federation of the Rhodesias and Nyasaland that would strengthen the position of whites in central Africa, Chinula presented the following arguments. Africans had to oppose federation because their interests were not the same as those of the Europeans who wanted it. Second, Africa was for the Africans, just as Scotland was for the Scots. Therefore, it was up to the Africans to decide their own future. Third, God was pleased to create a black man and to give him the African continent saying "Here is your own country!" Turning to the argument that Nyasaland (Malawi) would derive certain economic benefits from federation, he simply dismissed this by saying that it was better to be poor but free and independent than to be rich and yet a slave of someone else.[46]

Such views were shared by many graduates of Livingstonia. That some of them could be traced to the influence of the Garvey movement is not easily proved. However, several of these men subscribed or had friends abroad who subscribed to Garvey's newspaper, the *Negro World*. They included Edward Boti Manda, the most famous of them all, at Livingstonia; Yesaya Zelenji Mwasw at Chinteche; Charles Chidongo Chinula in Mzimba; Hanock Msokera Phiri at Kasungu; and George Simeon Mwasw in Lilongwe. The impression that Garveyism made on these men was compounded by the political awakening underway among educated Africans in Malawi during the interwar period. Everywhere in the country, educated men formed political pressure groups through which they were able to air their grievances and to address some of them to the government for redress.[47]

Leaders of these pressure groups were generally literate persons enjoying a recognizable status in the community. In spite of this, they made constant if usually ineffective appeal to the less literate in order to broaden their impact. The result was that their message was often popularized and even distorted by their illiterate followers. Garvey's message was subject to this process as it was passed from mouth to mouth. The written word in the *Negro World* was distorted rather grotesquely as it was translated into the language of an oral culture. Hence, by the late 1920s, fantastic stories were spread about what Afro-Americans were planning to do by force to redeem Africa from colonial rule. Rumors told of an Afro-American invasion in which the Europeans would be driven out, of American-made bombs that would select and strike only white people, and of planes that would bring Afro-Americans in thousands.[48]

To gauge the real impact of Garvey's ideas in Malawi, however, one should concentrate on those who attempted a fruitful application of them to their local situation. George Simeon Mwase was one of them.

He originally came from Nkhata-Bay District in northern Malawi, where he was educated at Livingstonia. In the 1920s, however, he moved to Lilongwe in the central part of Malawi, where he presided over the Central Province Native Association. A regular subscriber to the *Negro World*, Mwase tried to instill the spirit of economic independency among his fellow associationists. He wanted them to operate their own trading enterprises, to adopt cash-crop farming on an extensive scale, and to be completely independent of European and Asian capital in so doing.[49]

Another close follower of the Garvey movement in Malawi was the Reverend Yesaya Zelenji Mwase, who also came from Nkhata-Bay District. Mwase was one of the first three African pastors to be ordained by the Livingstonia Mission in 1914. After many years of frustrations with the derogatory manner in which his white missionary counterparts treated him, Mwase sought independence through the control of his own churches and educational institutions. Garvey's ideas must have offered him a sure anchor, for in 1932, Mwase formally broke away from the Livingstonia Mission in order to found his own church, the Black-man's Church of God. Two years later, he proclaimed that the hope of the African race lay in self-help through the establishment and control of not only independent churches, but schools, colleges, and hospitals as well. In line with this view, he submitted plans for a Black Man's Educational Society in "Malawi." The society was to collect funds from members of the black race within and outside Malawi for the building of a college and hospitals, and training of teachers.[50]

In later years, Mwase tried to raise funds from Malawians who were at work in Northern Rhodesia and Katanga, but his scheme, like those of Garvey himself, eventually collapsed. There was too much opposition to it from the government and from fellow educated Malawians who resented his boisterous ambition.

Conclusion

Today, when thousands of Afro-Americans are returning to Africa, albeit temporarily, in search of their roots, it may not be easy to appreciate the significance of their earlier, sporadic contacts with Africa, which has been the subject of this chapter. It may also be misleading to think, as Walton Johnson has done, in terms of how these earlier contacts affected the course of events within Africa.[51] The continent of Africa and its people were not readily accessible to Africans of the diaspora during the colonial period because of the state of penury in which most diaspora Africans found themselves in their countries of adoption and because of the restrictive migration laws that the various colonial regimes in Africa enforced with great efficiency.

The conclusion to draw from this chapter is that Afro-Americans, even under the most restrictive conditions of the colonial period, were aware of their historical connection with Africa and particularly keen to support missionary and educational projects that would benefit their brethren on the continent. By supporting native evangelists and educators such as the Reverends John Chilembwe and Hanock Msokera Phiri in Malawi, or inviting young Malawians such as Daniel Sharpe Malikebu and Hastings Kamuzu Banda to the United States to pursue their dreams for higher education, they did answer the need of persons in the "motherland" for whom colonialism had closed the avenues of opportunity.

NOTES

1. See Joseph E. Harris, "Introduction to the African Diaspora," and George Shepperson, "The African Abroad or the African Diaspora," in *Emerging Themes of African History*, ed. T.O. Ranger (London: Heinemann, 1968), 147–76.

2. George Shepperson, "Notes on Negro American Influences on the Emergence of African Nationalism," *Journal of African History* 1, 2 (1960): 299–312.

3. Harris, "Introduction to the African Diaspora," 149.

4. Walton Johnson, "The Afro-American Presence in Central and Southern Africa, 1880–1905," *Journal of Southern African Affairs*, 4, 1 (1979): 28–42; and Richard D. Ralston, "American Episodes in the Making of an African Leader: A Case Study of Alfred B. Xuma (1893–1962)," *International Journal of African Historical Studies*, 6, 1 (1973):72–93.

5. For example, the work of George Shepperson on the Reverend John Chilembwe and the Providence Industrial Mission is a monument in this field but is confined to the period before 1915. Shepperson agrees that researchers should now turn their attention to the period after 1915.

6. A. Meier and E. Rudwick, *From Plantation to Ghetto: A History of Afro-Americans* (New York: Hill and Wang, 1966), particularly 177–200; and also Arnold H. Taylor, *Travail and Triumph: Black Life and Culture in the South since the Civil War* (London: Greenwood Press, 1976), 50–52.

7. For a summary of Dr. Albert Thorne's proposed colonization scheme and its fate, see M. M. Mapuranga, "Dr. Albert Thorne's Unsuccessful Attempt at Setting up a Black Colony in Malawi, 1894–1923," *Malawi Journal of Social Science* 5 (1976):44–56.

8. *Central African Planter* 13, 2 (March 1897). Bismarck was also reacting against the Reverend Joseph Booth's proposal to invite Afro-Americans to Malawi to help him in the task of uplifting the indigenous inhabitants through a scheme of his own making, the African Christian Union.

9. H. H. Johnson, *British Central Africa* (London: Methuen and Company, 1897), 80–151.

10. G. Shepperson and T. Price, *Independent African: John Chilembwe and the Origins, Setting and Significance of the Nyasaland Native Rising of 1915* (Edinburgh: Edinburgh University Press, 1958), 85–89.

11. Ibid., 93–109.

12. Ibid., 146.
13. C. K. Khanje, "The Impact of Malamulo Mission in Southern Thyolo, 1902–1972" (Student Research Paper, Chancellor College, University of Malawi, Zomba, 1972/73); and Shepperson and Price, *Independent African*, 134–35.
14. *Central African Times*, no. 34, 25 May 1901.
15. F. E. Wilson, director of the South-East Africa Union of Seventh-Day Adventists, Blantyre, Malawi, in a letter to this writer, 29 May 1979.
16. Bridglal Pachai, *Malawi: A History of the Nation* (London: Longmans, 1973), 214–24; also Robert I. Rotberg, "The Rise of Nationalism: The Case of East and Central Africa," *World Politics* 15 (1962–63):85–86.
17. "Report of the Commission Appointed by His Excellency the Governor to Enquire into Various Matters and Questions Concerned with the Native Rising within the Nyasaland Protectorate." in *Supplement to the Government Gazette*, 31 January 1916.
18. The AME in South Africa had been growing since the 1890s, when Bishop Henry McNeal Turner visited that country and made the most of the black South African Christian desire for independence from white-controlled churches.
19. The Reverend Hanock Msokera Phiri to this writer, Mdabwi Mission, Kasungu, Malawi, 2 April 1971.
20. One of them was the Reverend Magkatho, who had established a large farm and network of schools near Bulawayo by 1925; see T. O. Ranger, *The African Voice in Southern Rhodesia 1898–1930* (London: Heinemann, 1970), 41–43.
21. H. M. Phiri to the District Education Officer, Kasungu, 16 February 1967, in *The Hanock Msokera Phiri Papers* (National Archives of Malawi, Zomba).
22. J. Chule Nyirenda, teacher to the Reverend H. M. Phiri, 8 January 1934, in *The Hanock Msokera Phiri Papers*.
23. I am grateful to Fr. J. C. Chakanza for this information. He has made an extensive study of independent African church movements in Malawi.
24. This is strongly indicated in the correspondence of the 1940s in *The Hanock Msokera Phiri Papers*.
25. *The Hanock Msokera Phiri Papers*.
26. H. M. Phiri to Bishop H. I. Bearden, 4 December 1964, in *The Hanock Msokera Phiri Papers*.
27. J. R. Coan, General Superintendent, "Message to the Presiding Elders, Ministers and Laymen of the 15th Episcopal District of the African Methodist Episcopal Church" (Transvaal: Wilberforce, 15 May 1941).
28. R. J. Macdonald, "The Rev. Hanock Msokera Phiri and the Establishment in Nyasaland of the African Methodist Church," *IJAHS*, 3 (1970):75–88; also J. Parratt, "Religious Independency in Nyasaland: A Typology of Origins" (Staff Seminar Paper, Department of Religious Studies, Chancellor College, Zomba, 1979), 11.
29. R. J. Macdonald, "Rev. Daniel Sharpe Malikebu and the Reopening of the Providence Industrial Mission 1926–1939." in *From Nyasaland to Malawi*, ed. R. J. Macdonald (Nairobi: East African Publishing House, 1975), 216–30.
30. Following the death of Dr. Malikebu in March 1979, there has been an argument among his followers at the PIM as to how much of the mission's property was Malikebu's personal property, acquired with the help of his Afro-American friends. The winning side holds the view that all the major developments were financed out of local effort, since very little support came from the United States.
31. D. S. Malikebu to Dr. J. H. Jackson, president, Foreign Mission Board, NBC, 29 February 1968. Copy of this letter is in the National Archives, Zomba.
32. Pachai, *Malawi*, 267–88; and Emily Nyamazao Maliwa, "The History of Nationalism and Intellectual Movements in Nyasaland" (M.A. thesis, University of Chicago, 1961), 60–82.

33. Macdonald, "Reverend Daniel Sharpe Malikebu," 216–19; also Shepperson and Price, *Independent African*, 142.
34. E. S. Munger, *President Kamuzu Banda of Malawi: Bridgebuilder of Africa* (American Universities Field Staff Reports, 1969), 6.
35. The Reverend Phiri to writer, 3 April 1971.
36. Dr. Banda himself has so far said or written little about this phase of his life. Hence, what others have written about it tends to be conjectural and may well be misleading. In casual conversations with some of his close followers in Malawi between 1958 and 1964, Banda would simply remark that he had been friends with a number of good people while in the United States. See Aleke K. Banda, "Dr. Banda's Day: A Public Address" (Malawi Congress Party Headquarters, Limbe, Malawi, 6/7/60).
37. Munger, *President Kamuzu Banda* 7; and "Biography of the President Dr. H. Kamuzu Banda" (Mimeographed paper, Research Office, Blantyre).
38. Booker T. Washington, *Up from Slavery* (New York: Dell Publishing Company, 1965), 154–224.
39. J. McCraken, *Politics and Christianity in Malawi, 1875–1940: The Impact of Livingstonia Mission in the Northern Province* (London: Cambridge University Press, 1977), 214.
40. The Reverend Phiri to writer, 3 April 1971.
41. M. L. Chanock, "The New Men Revisited: An Essay on the Development of Political Consciousness in Colonial Malawi," in *From Nyasaland to Malawi*, 235; Maliwa, "The History of Nationalism and Intellectual Movements," 117.
42. E. David Cronon, *Black Moses: The Story of Marcus Garvey and the Universal Negro Improvement Association* (Madison: University of Wisconsin Press, 1969), 41–72.
43. J. Linden and I. Linden, "John Chilembwe and the New Jerusalem," *Journal of African History* 12, 4 (1971): 629–51.
44. The Reverend Charles Chidongo Chinula to this writer, Sazu Home Mission, Mzimba, 8 April 1971.
45. D. D. Phiri, *Malawians to Remember: Charles Chidongo Chinula* (Lilongwe: Longman Malawi, 1975), 14–22.
46. C. C. Chinula, "How Will You Defend Your Country from Federation?" (Address to the Chiefs and Leaders) in *The Charles Chidongo Chinula Papers*, 1930–1962 (National Archives, Zomba).
47. Jan van Kelsen, "Some Early Pressure Groups in Malawi," in *The Zambesian Past*, ed. E. Stokes and R. Brown (Manchester: University Press, 1966). 376–411.
48. George Shepperson, "Myth and Reality in Malawi" (Fourth Melville J. Herskovits Memorial Lecture, Northwestern University, 13 April 1966), 7–11.
49. Chanock, "The New Men Revisited," 251–53.
50. Y. Z. Mwasi, "My Essential and Paramount Reason for Working Independently" (Sanga, Chintechi, 12 July 1933). Original manuscript edited by J. K. Parratt, Department of Religious Studies, Chancellor College, Zomba, February 1979.
51. Johnson, "Afro-American Presence in Central and Southern Africa," 28–29.

22

The Presence of
Black Americans in
the Lower Congo
from 1878 to 1921

Kimpianga Mahaniah

HIS work deals with the presence of black Americans in the Lower Congo and their impact on the history of the Belgian Congo up to 1921, the year that the politicoreligious movement of Simon Kimbangu erupted.

Geographically, the Lower Congo, of the former Belgian Congo, is at the mouth of the Congo River. It was once part of the coastal state of the Kongo. Its inhabitants are referred to as *Bakongo* (the plural) and *Mukongo* (the singular). In this essay they will be referred to as the *Kongo*.

The Kongo people have been in contact with Europeans since 1482, when the Diego Cao and the Portuguese expedition landed at the mouth of the Congo River. Contact with the Portuguese from the fifteenth century to the end of the nineteenth century was dominated by both *legitimate* trade and the slave trade. Many Kongo were brought to the New World through the slave trade.

The year 1877 ended the first phase of Kongo contact with Europe. Indeed, Stanley's crossing from the east to west Atlantic coast demonstrated the possibility of penetrating central Africa via the Congo River. In 1877, central Africa was dominated by intense and continual contact with Europe and America and by the effective occupation of Africa by European colonial powers. Indeed, as part of the politics of balkanization of Africa drawn up at the Conference of Berlin in 1884 and 1885, Kongoland was divided into four entities: Belgian Congo, Cabinda, the

Portuguese colony of Angola, and the French Congo. The Lower Congo, the subject of this study became part of the Congo Independent State, which became the Belgian Congo in 1908.

To occupy central Africa effectively, the Belgian authority was forced first to occupy the Lower Congo, which is the entrance. Before the end of the nineteenth century, the region was evangelized by four Protestant missions and three Catholic congregations. The missionaries built mission stations, hospitals, and schools that grouped many people together. The colonial administration and businesses built towns and cities such as Leopoldville (Kinshasa), Kasangula, Kisantu, Thysville (Mbanza-Ngungu), Kimpese, Matadi, Boma, Tshela, and Luozi. Two of these are international ports: Matadi and Boma. However, without a railroad, the penetration of central Africa through the mouth of the Congo River would have been very difficult, if not impossible. Indeed, Stanley was well aware of this when he said that the Congo was not worth a penny without a railroad.

The local population worked in the building of the colonial infrastructure fostered by missionaries, administrators, and businesses. The colonialists also brought people from all over the world to work in the Lower Congo.[1] For this reason, the Lower Congo had intensive contact with Europe throughout the colonial period, which ended in 1960 with the political independence of the Belgian Congo.

One of the groups with which the Kongo made contacts was black Americans. In this essay black Americans include all those of African descent living in the Americas.

Some black Americans were missionaries with Protestant mission societies in the Lower Congo; others were passing through to work in the interior of the Belgian colony. The Kongo also made contact with black Americans working as sailors in boats that docked at Matadi and in industries in cities such as Leopoldville.

In addition, the Kongo made direct contact with black Americans in the New World. In the early stages of evangelization, many Kongo boys and girls were taken to Europe and America by missionaries who used them as showcases for the home churches in order to solicit more funds. These young people also helped missionaries translate English literature into the Kikongo language. While in Europe and America, the Kongo young people received training in various institutions.

Indeed, the first university-trained Kongo, Stephen Mvemba, graduated in 1894 from Shaw University, Raleigh, North Carolina, a black American school. Another young Kongo man, Mfumu Lutunu, visited Belgium, Great Britain, and the United States. In New York he made contact with a black American who spoke to him in the Kikongo language. The black American invited Mfumu Lutunu to his home, but the missionary group that brought this young man declined the invitation.[2] Mfumu and other young Kongo men who saw black Americans in the New World brought back many versions of their experiences in America.[3]

These contacts and stories were sources of information for the Kongolese about black Americans in the world. The black American image in the Kongo was well described by my Kongo informants, who in 1973 gave me the following version of the slave trade and the African presence in the New World:

> The white men dumped these Africans on a big island where they abandoned them. After many centuries of isolation, the African descendants, who came to be called black Americans, developed a prosperous industrial country with a strong army. When the white men came back, they were surprised to see that the black Americans had developed an industrialized society. Before such a reality the white men were forced to accept them as equals. When some black Americans came back to Africa, the white men told them that they could not go back because the Africans did not want them to come back.[4]

This version led many Kongolese to believe that the black American had a strong nation with a strong army. They believed that the black American was completely free from white men. Indeed, he was regarded as so powerful and strong that white men feared him. During the colonial period of the Belgian Congo, from the end of the nineteenth century to 1960, many Kongolese yearned to be free men in the image of the black American.

Indeed, the black American was believed to be not only physically and intellectually imposing but also a freedom fighter for black men everywhere. A black man, such as he who had beaten the white man at his own game, would come back to liberate the Kongolese from Belgian colonialism. The Belgian authorities and the missionaries made it very difficult for black Americans to come to the Belgian Congo and cause tension and disruption among the Kongolese.

Black American Missionaries in the Lower Congo

As early as 1886, black American missionaries were working in the Lower Congo with the Livingstone Inland Mission Society, a British society that was transferred in 1884 to the American Baptist Foreign Mission Society (ABFMS).[5] The arrival of black American missionaries in the Lower Congo, however, brought racial tension and conflict to the surface.

The attitude of the early Protestant missionaries in the Lower Congo toward their black colleagues was no more enlightened than that of their white countrymen at home. On the subject of the renomination of the Afro-American Lulu Fleming to Mpalabala, Charles Harvey wrote in 1895:

> I knew Miss Fleming very well when she was out here before and in some respects admired her for her energy and ability. She showed a sincere desire to do good work amongst the people, particularly the women, some of whom were a good deal influenced by her. Nevertheless, I should not like to see her come back to Mpalabala for the following reasons: (1) separatist tendency (2) her being away from the mission field too long (four years of medical studies). Miss Fleming exhibited a strong separatist tendency when she was out here before. Her aim was to make her work a distinct one and not to allow it to be identified with the general Mpalabala work.

On the nomination of another black missionary, James Dawes, Charles Harvey wrote:

> As regards Mr. Dawes, seeing that both Mr. Richards (of Mbanga-Manteke) and Mr. Hoste (of Lukunga) are strongly against his going to their stations, there seems to be no opening left for him. Most certainly that work at Mpalabala would be better without him and he is not the man for Matadi; therefore, I do not feel in the interest of the work that I ought to petition you to keep him in it. He is not without ability but he is not sufficiently civilized to stand the wear and tear of Congo Mission life without great danger of social and moral deterioration. I am hoping that the day will come when the old fallacy will be completely exploded that for a rough uncivilized country rough men will do, for just the reverse is true, the wear and tear is too true for a mere veneer of Christian civilization to endure long under such conditions.[6]

Catherine Mabie, a medical missionary, in voting in 1904 against reopening the field to black missionaries, observed:

> The American Negro is not in my humble judgment yet sufficiently toughened in the fiber of his character to be subject to the exigencies of African missionary life with all its perplexing problems, requiring the nicest moral distinctions and judgment of no mean order. It isn't because he is black but because as yet he has proven himself far from being thoroughly furnished. For his own sake as well as that of the mission, I think it is far better that we should not as yet encourage his perilous experimentation with life in the Congo.[7]

To many white missionaries, the return of black missionaries was an intolerable interference in the God-given mission of the Anglo-Saxon race. This attitude was expressed frankly by Charles Harvey who, aside from writing more than almost any other missionary, seems to have been the spokesman for the missionaries in the field writing to the executive board. In addition, he wrote frankly and freely:

> I must say that I agree with you in reference to the colored brethren. Speaking of them generally they have not stamina to lead and not grace and humility to follow. Moreover, they are so hyper-sensitive that it is very difficult to get along with even the best of them. The slightest difference of opinion or clash of judgment is liable to be attributed to color prejudice on the part of the white man. The African, I nearly believe, has a great part to play in the regeneration of his own country but it is rather the native-born African (who is after all the only real African) who is developed from the soil and cultivated under natural conditions. In the very nature he is not fit by nature and gifts. ... I think it must be argued, too, Divine Providence has evidently placed the Anglo-Saxon (perhaps Teuton) race in the forefront of the battle to be pioneers of the Gospel and if that is so and God has manifestly given them that distinctive work to do. He depends upon it when others enter into the same labors who are so definitely called and fitted. He will speak again on the survival of the fittest and the character of the work accomplished.[8]

Under such conditions, some black missionaries suffered emotional breakdowns in the field. A Dr. Jackson of Kukunga beat a missionary colleague who called him a liar.[9] James Dawes of Mukimvika made an assault on a Mr. Cadman, a missionary colleague.[10] Some, such as Dr. Jackson, resigned after only a short time. Before the policy of excluding black missionaries was instituted, some European missionaries believed that the black missionaries should have their own station. Suggestions were made for Irebu, an isolated station in the Upper Congo, and Mukimvika, a dying station in Portuguese Angola. Charles Harvey and John Duncan advocated the establishment of a separate field:

> We have been negotiating with the colored people of the South to assume the support of Mukimvika and man it with their own men. Nothing, however, may come of this and so we shall aim to retain Mukimvika as a purely mission station.[11]

Having thus failed to find a solution, the policy of simply not appointing any black missionaries was adopted, and after 1897 no more black appointments were made.

It is our policy not to send out any more colored people after all the experiences we have had and I am refusing all such applications. Should we ever change our policy it would be to have a station entirely manned with colored people.[12]

As late as 1928, the "white missionary only" policy of the ABFMS had not been reversed. In reply to an inquiry from Dr. W. E. B. Du Bois, C. M. Albaugh, then an assistant secretary of the ABFMS, said that the society had at that time fifty missionaries in the Belgian Congo and that "no American Negroes are now working under our Board. Throughout the past fifty years a total of fourteen American Negroes have been missionaries under our society."[13] All fourteen, he might have added, had been appointed before 1897.

The attitude of the European missionaries in the field and later that of the board at Boston contradicted the aims of the American Baptist Missionary Union (ABMU), which was part of the Northern American Baptist Convention. In 1813, the Baptist Church of America was split into northern and southern branches. The southern branch of the Baptist church adopted its name of ABMU in 1841 and no longer accepted slavery, which it condemned as an un-Christian practice. Therefore, it no longer accepted church members who were owners or sellers of slaves.[14]

The northern branch already supported several mission stations in Burma, Siam, and China, and among the Indian population of North America. Originally interested in the return of black Americans to Africa as a possible solution to the slavery question, the union sent its first missionary to Liberia in 1820 to found a colony for emancipated black Americans.[15]

In sending those blacks who had been enlightened by Christianity and Greco-Latin civilization, the church tried to solve the double problem of internal American racial difficulties and the duties of evangelization and civilization in Africa at the lowest possible cost. It was generally believed in the nineteenth century that black people, although they had lived in the Western world for generations, were the only ones who could successfully penetrate the interior of Africa. With African blood in their veins, these blacks were supposed to be able to resist the tropical climate and diseases, whereas Europeans could not. This myth was exploded, of course, as the black missionaries fell prey to the same diseases as their white colleagues.

The aims of using black missionaries in the Lower Congo were never realized. The two groups in the mission field had preconceived racial prejudices and so did not trust one another. The refusal of the pioneering missionaries to work with black missionaries shows that many of them were culturally and racially biased. Some pioneering missionaries in the Lower Congo used the policy of divide and conquer to prevent the influence of any rebellious black American missionaries who might have made Africans aware of spiritual and political white domination. For a long time, there was a feeling expressed in the Lower Congo, especially before the explosion of the prophetic movement of Simon Kimbangu in 1921, that the black brothers of the Africans, the black Americans, would return with a strong army and throw out all the white men from Kongoland. The same story was given to Maquet-Tombu, a Belgian author, who questioned one of the deported prophets who said that "the black Americans will soon come and conquer the Congo."[16]

The influence of black Americans did not contribute toward giving the Kongo a solution for their situation, but the black missionaries did inform world opinion about the atrocities committed against the Kongolese by King Leopold II's regime. Reverend William Sheppard, a black missionary and one of the first two missionaries of the Southern Presbyterian Church to open in 1890 a mission field in Kasai, was one of the first missionaries to speak out against the Congo Independent State and the first to write articles in American and European newspapers exposing atrocities committed in the collection of rubber and taxes. The increased sensitivity of world opinion and the internationalization of the problem led to the movement for reform, which aimed at protecting the welfare of the Kongolese.[17]

Black Americans and the Emergence of the Kimbangu Movement in 1921

Simon Kimbangu was born between 1881 and 1891 at Nkamba village, near Ngombe-Lutete (Wathen), the oldest Baptist Mission Society mission in the Lower Congo. His father was named Kuyela, and his mother was Lwezi. After his mother died during his childhood, Kimbangu was raised by his aunt, Mama Kinzembo, who adopted him as her son.[18] The father was a *nganga-gnombo*, a diviner. As a child, Kimbangu witnessed his father's work divining perpetrators (*ndoki or nkuyu*) of disease, death, or natural disaster.

In his childhood Kimbangu was blessed by the Reverend Cameron, a pioneering missionary of BMS, as was reported in a letter to Cameron from two Protestant catechists explaining why they became followers of Simon Kimbangu.

As for the person (Kimbangu) concerning whom these matters arose, he was the son of the woman who gave you water at that time when you were in danger of being killed, when you, Mr. Cameron, were chased on the Ntontani-Nkamba road, when your donkey was hit by a bullet. The woman who gave you water was the mother of the man through whom these things came about. Her name was Kinzembo. You said to her, "Kinzembo, thank you for the help you have given me in this trouble by giving me water; may God bless you in everything." When you had said that you said, "Let us pray," and you prayed. You blessed her son by saying that your God has a great mission and things for your son to do.[19]

As an adolescent Kimbangu led a normal, traditional life. He studied four years at a village school and at the Ngombe-Lutete mission station. After converting to Protestantism at the mission, he began to work as a catechist teacher of the BMS, but he was very soon "dismissed from the church and any work he had as school teacher." By the time Kimbangu received his call, he was no longer a BMS catechist. He had spent some time as a tobacco trader, an occupation that took him to villages and markets all over his region. On his travels Kimbangu witnessed all the misery of the Lower Congo, a region that was being devastated by an epidemic of influenza that came from Europe. The Kongolese, who lacked adequate medical care and nourishment, died by the thousands.

In 1913, Kimbangu married Mama Marie Mwilu, who bore three sons: Charles Kisolokele (1914), Solomon Kiangani Dialungana (1916), and Joseph Diangienda (1918).

Simon Kimbangu began to show signs of charisma before 1921, the year his prophetic movement became public. One night, between 1918 and 1921, while resting on his mat in his village of Ngombe-Kinsuka, near Nkamba, he heard a voice but refused to respond to the call. To escape this voice and to earn money, Kimbangu went to Ndolo-Kinshasa, a suburb of Leopoldville, where he worked as a domestic for Europeans and as a laborer at the Huileries du Congo Belge, a British-established company. But in Ndolo-Kinshasa nothing went right for him. At the end of the month when he went to collect his salary, his employer told him that there was no salary for him. The voice calling him to a new vocation grew louder and more threatening. If Kimbangu did not go to the village and accept his new vocation he would die, the voice reportedly said. Everything that Kimbangu undertook in Ndolo-Kinshasa failed, so he returned to his village.

While in his village Kimbangu continued to have dreams and visions calling him to serve God. On 6 April 1921, while in his village of Ngombe-Kinsuka (Nkamba), Kimbangu heard the loud scream of a dying woman and felt compelled to go inside the house to heal her. He laid his hand on her and began to pray and to tremble, overcome by the spirit of God. The woman recovered. She grew frightened: Was Simon a sorcerer? Had he cast a spell on her only to retract it later?

Kimbangu was influenced not only by the traditional Kongo ethos and the evangelization of the Protestant mission in the area of Ngombe-Lutete but also by urban life in Ndolo-Kinshasa where various ideologies and forces were at work. It is important to understand the daily life of the Kongolese in Ndolo-Kinshasa and other urban centers where people accommodated colonialism and became acculturated. It is also important to note the Afro-American link and the early efforts of the Kongolese to counteract the dehumanizing effects of urban life.[20]

The exact date of Kimbangu's arrival at Ndolo-Kinshasa and the length of his stay have not been established. It is certain, however, that Kimbangu worked at Ndolo-Kinshasa as a domestic to some European families and that he worked at the Huileries du Congo Belge in 1920. Ndolo-Kinshasa, a suburb of Leopoldville and Brazzaville, was the capital of the French Congo colony; it is twelve kilometers from Leopoldville, the Belgian Congo's capital. Around 1900, Ndolo-Kinshasa had only twelve European residents, but by 1919 it had five hundred and by 1921 it had seven hundred who spoke French, English, German, Portuguese, and even Italian. All these expatriates had one thing in common: the desire to get rich as quickly as possible. Kinshasa had a population of twenty thousand Kongolese by 1920. All these Kongolese went to Kinshasa for work to provide the income needed to live in the monetized colonial society.

As in all colonial centers of the Belgian Congo, the European and African populations were segregated. The Kongolese living areas were known as "camps belges" or, in Kikongo, *belezi*. To stabilize the working population, each individual worker was given a piece of land, measuring four hundred square meters, where he built his own house and cultivated a garden for his family's food. However, the immigration of workers increased so rapidly that Kinshasa's facilities could not accommodate them by 1920. Water, housing, and food shortages became serious. Murder, prostitution, theft, violence, and arrest became part of the daily experience. Unemployment soared.

The Kongolese population was divided into three groups: the small Kongolese elite, the working group, and the marginal group. The small Kongolese elite were clerks, chiefs of personnel in foreign companies, and headwaiters. They were mostly graduates of the mission schools. They separated themselves from people of their own race. They spent their money futilely trying to live the life of the Europeans. The second group were mostly recent immigrants who did not have a job or who practiced a trade. Their population totaled between five thousand and six thousand. The third group consisted of seven thousand laborers who worked long hours in companies or firms of Ndolo-Kinshasa.

To protect their own interests, the Europeans formed a syndicate of employers, Syndicat des Employeurs de Kinshasa (SEK), intended to prevent strikes and to fix workers' salaries. Every worker was given an identity card. He paid a fine of thirty cents if he left his job without his employer's permission and could be put in jail for deserting his job and physically punished at the whim of his employer. The Kongolese elite soon discovered that neither their improved material position nor their training entitled them to acceptance by the Europeans. The intellectual and material means at their disposal were not sufficient for a European life-style. For the colonial Europeans, the Kongolese were simply laborers.

With this background it is understandable that, like rural Kongolese, the urban populations turned to ideas and actions whose aims were to help them to interpret their lives in the colonial situation. The first Kongolese to try to channel the Kongolese sentiment in Ndolo-Kinshasa was André Yengo. Yengo, a Kongo, was a Baptist and a graduate of the BMS mission school. He founded a hierarchical organization called "Congomen," which aimed to implement the liberation of black people from European domination with firearms if necessary and to found a national black church.

Another organization in Kinshasa, headed by a black American* called Wilson, was formed by black Americans who worked at the Huileries du Congo Belge where Kimbangu also worked. This group was Garveyist in its ideology and read materials such as the *Negro World* sent by the headquarters of the Universal Negro Improvement Association. The ideas of Garvey penetrated not only Yengo's organization but also the minds of workers who came into contact, directly or indirectly, with the black Americans.

Efraim Andersson, a Swedish missionary in central Africa, writing on the influence of black Americans in bringing about the prophetic explosion of 1921, suggests that the ideas of Marcus Garvey, the founder of the Universal Negro Improvement Association, and those of W. E. B. Du Bois, one of the founders of the National Association for the Advancement of Colored People, had some influence. Even though the two leaders opposed each other bitterly on how to relieve the exploitation of blacks, they were not far apart in their ideas about Africa. Marcus Garvey wanted blacks to return to the motherland of Africa, establish a black nation with the ideology of Africa for Africans, and expel all colonialists. Du Bois, while fighting for complete economic and political equality between white and black in the United States, also cherished

---

* More recent research identifies Wilson as a Sierra Leonean. Ed.

the thought of liberating Africa and founding a great central African state based on the former German Africa and Belgian Congo.[21] These ideas and even pamphlets could be found in some sections of Boma, Matadi, and Kinshasa, where Simon Kimbangu was employed at the Huileries du Congo Belge before he became a charismatic leader. The Reverend Reynolds, a Protestant missionary teaching at the Kimpese Pastor and Teacher Training School during the prophetic movement of 1921, was convinced that politics and Pan-African ideas entered into the movement. He also reported the popular belief circulating in the Lower Congo about a ship that would "be seen coming up the Congo at Manyanga," after which the white people would leave the colony. This ship was the result of the echoes created by the Black Star Line, created by Marcus Garvey to take black Americans back to Africa.

The existence of these organizations was noticed by colonial security on 20 March 1921, when a dossier was taken from a Kongolese clerk. This dossier, which contained information about life in Kinshasa and in the Belgian Congo from a Kongolese point of view, was sent by Emmanual Johan, later Kimbangu's secretary, to his brother, John Panda Farnana, a Kongolese living in Brussels. Farnana was to use it in the defense of the Kongolese cause in Belgium. At that time Johan was a twenty-five-year-old graduate and a clerk of a BMS pastor of Kinshasa, whose mailbox he used.

John Panda Farnana studied at Brussels and then at the school of colonial agriculture at Nogent-Sur-Marne (l'Ecole d'Agriculture Coloniale de Nogent-Sur-Marne). After his studies he returned to the Belgian Congo for a year and then went back to Brussels, where he made his home. In ideology he was a Garveyist. He participated in the colonial congress in Brussels every year and founded the Union Congolaise de Bruxells (Congolese Union of Brussels), which he also called "Societé de secours et de developpement moral et intellectuel de la race congolaise" (The Society for the Help and Intellectual and Moral Development of the Congolese Race). Farnana's association sought to develop the intellectual and moral values of the Kongolese and encourage participation in the politics and administration of the colony. The Kongolese could develop only when there was an end to prejudice against the abilities and intelligence of Kongolese and an end to social and economic discrimination. At a conference in the fall of 1920, Farnana warned the Belgian public that if the Belgian government did not change its policies and methods in its colony, there would be a revolution.

Kimbangu could not help being influenced by the trends in Belgian Congo urban life. At his trial he admitted being in direct contact with the group of André Yengo and the black Americans:

Kimbangu avoue également avoir ete en rapport, a Leopoldville, avec un noir american. Le Kimbanguisme se rattacherait donc sur le vaste mouvement pan-negre dont d'autres colonies africaines ont eu a souffrir?[22]

Kimbangu, like most Kongolese, was not, as the Belgians would have wished, isolated from the ideas of Pan-Africanism that were circulating in America and Europe. Through reading and personal contacts, many ideas from Africans in the diaspora filtered into the Belgian Congo, and the Lower Congo in particular.

It is also important to observe that it was not only the know-how of black Americans that impressed the Kongo but also their physical power and their casual attitude toward Europeans. Indeed, the Kongo admired black Americans in their rebelliousness toward Europeans. The contacts with black Americans helped the Kongo to counter the effects of feelings of inferiority cultivated by the colonial situation. Thus, the Kongo began to see Europeans as humans and not as superbeings. This is substantiated by a description on the impact of black Americans that was given to me in 1972 by an informant:

Makidi Kuntima, one of my informants, reports that as a child he heard his paternal uncle Massamba cursing people in a foreign language when he became angry. When Mr. Makidi learned English, he discovered that his uncle had been speaking English. This uncle worked at the Huileries du Congo Belge for many years beginning around 1920. He was so much influenced by black American culture that he could speak pidgin English. Even his temperament was affected. He respected no one, even Europeans, with whom he had many fights at the Huileries who came under the influence of black Americans. The black American was seen as heroic and was very much admired for challenging Europeans.[23]

Conclusion

Black Americans were physically present in the Lower Congo through mission fields and in other colonial infrastructures. It has been established through the study of colonial and Belgian literature that Simon Kimbangu, the protonationalist leader in Belgian Congo, was in direct contact with black Americans and influenced by Marcus Garvey's movement. The impact of black Americans in Kongolese history is not a matter of doubt. Historians have not yet dealt seriously with this aspect of Kongolese history. However, a complete study should compile statistics on black Americans who worked in the Belgian Congo from 1878 to the present and examine how the black Americans were employed in the system that took them there. The impact of black Americans on the resistance movement should also be investigated, but this is possible only if the researcher investigates oral tradition, interviewing people about the myths, images, and echoes that they possess about black Americans. Some black Americans wrote diaries; in these diaries they explained their conflicts with the system that employed them and about their attitudes toward the Kongolese. A thorough study should investigate the archival material in both America and Europe and the oral traditions that the average Kongolese (now Zairean) has about black Americans and their experiences in the diaspora. It is here that one sees the need for cooperation between researchers in Zaire and in the United States.

Biographical Information on
Black American Missionaries in Lower Zaire[24]

Clinton Caldwell Boone, M.D. was born on 9 May 1883, in Winston, North Carolina, and was baptized in 1893. He was a member of Philips Church of Winston. Educated at Richmond Theological Seminary (Virginia Union University), Richmond, Virginia, and at Water Normal Institute, Winston, he arrived in the Belgian Congo in 1901. On 16 January 1901, he married Eva Roberts Coles and earned the commendation and support of the Lott Cary Convention. While in the Belgian Congo he worked at Mpalabala, where his wife died on 1 December 1902. He resigned from the Belgian Congo mission (ABFMS) in 1911 and on 6 February 1913, he was sent to Liberia by the Lott Cary Convention.

James Christopher Dawes joined the mission field in 1890 and worked at Mpalabala until 1894, when he resigned from mission service.

Lulu Cecilia Fleming, M.D., was born on 28 January 1862 at Hibernia, Clay County, Florida, and was baptized on 14 January 1877 in Jacksonville. Educated at Shaw University, Raleigh, North Carolina, she was appointed to the Congo mission service on 10 January 1886 and arrived there on 16 May 1886. She served at Mpalabala from 1886 to 1891 when she returned to Boston, where she received her medical degree. Four years later, she returned to the Belgian Congo and was stationed at Irebu. She returned again to the United States in 1899 and died in Philadelphia on 20 June 1899.

Joseph J. France was from Accra, West Africa; he was an African lay missionary. On 11 April 1877, he arrived in the Congo, where he worked as lay assistant in Matadi and Mpalabala and assumed responsibility of the mission store. He resigned from missionary service in 1889 to take up the study of medicine at Shaw University in Raleigh, North Carolina.

Bessie E. Gardner was born on 26 September 1865 in Madison, Virginia. She was a member of the Roxborough Baptist Church in Philadelphia and was educated at Wayland Seminary, Washington, D.C. She was appointed for Congo mission service in 1890 and arrived 6 January 1893. She was stationed at Lukunga and returned to the United States in 1895; she resigned from mission service in 1897.

Nora A. Gordon was born in 1867. She was educated at Spelman Seminary, Atlanta, Georgia, and was appointed on 21 January 1889; she arrived at Banana on 13 May 1889. She married The Reverend S. C. Gordon, BMS missionary in the Congo in 1895, and worked at Mpalabala and Lukunga. She died in January 1901.

Rev. William A. Hall was born in 1857 in Jamaica. He was ordained on 14 September 1884 at Roncerverte, West Virginia. He was educated at Coloba College, Jamaica, and at Richmond Theological Seminary (Virginia Union University), Richmond, Virginia. He was appointed on 1 June 1888 and arrived in the Congo in 1889. In November 1893, he married Elizabeth Garland. He was stationed at Mpalabala, Matadi, Irebu, and Mukimvika stations. Mr. Hall resigned from mission service in November 1916. He was a cashier and bookkeeper in Jamaica and taught school for five years before being appointed by the English Baptist Society as a missionary to Cameroon, but the station was destroyed by the Germans.

Clara H. Howard was born in 1865 in Atlanta, Georgia. She was trained at Spelman Seminary, Atlanta, and was appointed missionary to the Belgian Congo on 9 September 1886; she arrived on 28 June 1890. Miss Howard was stationed at Lukunga and Mukimvika stations. She resigned from the mission service 3 May 1897 and became a member of the faculty at Spelman Seminary in 1899. As late as 1917 she was still employed there.

George Henry Jackson, B.D. and M.D. was born in Natick, Massachusetts, on 28 February 1863. He was baptized in 1884 in Natick and was ordained on 29 June 1887. He received his MA at Shaw University, Raleigh, North Carolina, in 1891. In 1887, he studied at Hamilton Theological Seminary, and between 1887 and 1891 he studied at Yale Divinity School, where he received his B.D. in 1892; he later received his M.D. from Yale Medical School. His mother was white and his father was black. He was appointed by the ABFMS for the Congo mission on 9 May 1892 and arrived on 3 September 1893. He was stationed at

Lukunga and resigned from mission service on 1 January 1895. From 1887 to 1893 he did pastoral work in the United States at Immanuel Church, New Haven, Connecticut. After his return in 1895 he was an assistant instructor at Yale until 1897. He was an American consul in France from 1897 until 1923, and after 1925 did some work in literacy and religious welfare. He died on 13 November 1943 in Los Angeles.

Stephen E. Jackson was a brother of Dr. George H. Jackson. In 1893 the brothers went together to the Congo, where they were stationed at Lukunga until their resignation in 1895.

NOTES

1. Rene J. Cornet, *La bataille du rail: la construction du chemin de fer de Matadi au Stanley Pool* (Brussels: Edition L. Cuypers, 1947) 213–15.
2. Albert Thys, the head of the Matadi-Kinshasa Railroad Company, recruited three hundred West Indians from Barbados and the English Antilles and five hundred Chinese from Macao in 1891.
3. Z. Nlemvo, who worked on the composition of a grammar and dictionary of Kikongo for many years, went to England in 1884 with W. H. Bentley. He accompanied the British Baptist Mission Society's missionaries in order to work intensively with Mr. and Mrs. Bentley on the manuscript of the dictionary and grammar. Robert Walker, Francis and Margaret Rattray, Nkebani, Stephen Mvemba, Nkoyo, Edith, Lukoki and Frank Ileva, all from Mpalabala, lived and studied for several years in England and America as early as 1881. These young people were brought by various missionaries of the Livingston Inland Mission Society, a British mission society.
4. Jeanne Maquet-Tombu, *Le siecle marche: Vie du chef Lutunu* (Brussels: Office de Publicite, 1952).
5. Jackson Mahaniah Kimpianga I, interview on the coming of missionaries in the Manianga region, Sundi Lutete (Lower Zaire), 23–27 September 1972. The interview was in Kikongo. At the time of the interview the informant was over seventy years old.
6. Charles Harvey (Mpalabala) to Duncan, 9 February 1895, American Baptist Foreign Mission Society Archives, American Baptist Convention Headquarters, Valley Forge, Pa.
7. Charles Harvey (Mpalabala) to Duncan, 11 October 1893, American Baptist Foreign Mission Society Archives, American Baptist Convention Headquarters, Valley Forge, Pa., 3–4.
8. Catherine Mabie (Mbanza Manteke) to Huntington, 26 April 1902, American Baptist Foreign Mission Society Archives, American Baptist Convention Headquarters, Valley Forge, Pa., 4.
9. Charles Harvey (Matadi) to Duncan 11 October 1895, American Baptist Foreign Mission Society Archives, American Baptist Convention Headquarters, Valley Forge, Pa., 4.
10. Dr. Jackson (Lukunga) to Duncan, September 1894, American Baptist Foreign Mission Society Archives, American Baptist Convention Headquarters, Valley Forge, Pa., 1.
11. Charles Harvey (Matadi) to Duncan, 18 May 1894, American Baptist Foreign Mission Society Archives, American Baptist Convention Headquarters, Valley Forge, Pa., 3.

12. Duncan (Boston) to Charles Harvey, 18 March 1893, American Baptist Foreign Mission Society Archives, American Baptist Convention Headquarters, Valley Forge, Pa., 2.

13. Duncan (Boston) to Charles Harvey, 6 April 1893, American Baptist Foreign Mission Society Archives, American Baptist Convention Headquarters, Valley Forge, Pa., 1.

14. D. M. Albaugh (Boston) to Dr. Du Bois, 12 September 1928, American Baptist Foreign Mission Society Archives, American Baptist Convention Headquarters, Valley Forge, Pa. The last black missionary of this society left Zaire in 1916. From 1897 to 1962 there was no appointment of black missionaries. Bufford Washington, a medical doctor, was appointed in January 1962. He and his wife Carrie were stationed at the hospital of IME Kimpese, Lower Zaire. They stayed there for one term (four years) and resigned. The Reverend Joseph Tyler, Jr., and his wife Maggie were appointed to the Kinshasa station in June 1973 and resigned in August 1974. The Reverend Gerald Davis and his wife Laverne arrived at Kinshasa in July 1977 and left the mission field in June 1978.

15. Mrs. H. Grattan Guiness, *The New World of Central Africa* (London: Hodder and Stoughton, 1890), 36.

16. Henry C. Vedder, *A Short History of Baptist Missions* (Philadelphia: Judson Press, 1927), 268.

17. Efraim Andersson, *Messianic Popular Movements in the Lower Congo*, trans. Donald Burton et al. (Uppsala, Sweden: Studia Ethnographia Uppsalensia, 1958), 255.

18. Stanley Shaloff, *Reform in Leopold's Congo* (Richmond: John Knox Press, 1970), 195.

19. D. Desanti, *Le Kimbanguisme a 50 ans* (Paris: Edition Continent 2000, 1971), 8–9 and Pierre K. Luzolo, *Zola kwa Nzambi* (Nkamba: E.J.C.S.K., Siege Administratif, 1958), 19–20.

20. Cecilian Irine, "The Birth of the Kimbanguist Movement in Lower Zaire 1921," *Journal of Religions in Africa* 6 (1974): 74.

21. Most of the information in this section came from Damasco Feci, "La vie cachee et vie publique de Simon Kimbangu selon la litterature coloniale et missionaire belge," *Cahiers du Cedaf* 9–10 (1972): 11–62.

22. Andersson, *Messianic Popular Movements*, 253.

23. Makidi ku Ntima, interview on the impact of black Americans in Zaire: Philadelphia, Pa., 5 May 1972. Mr. Makidi was at the time of the interview a Ph.D. student at Temple University.

24. Biographical data on black American missionaries in the Lower Congo came from individual files found in the archives of the American Baptist Foreign Mission Society, American Baptist Convention Headquarters, Valley Forge, Pa.

23
Brazilian Returnees
of West Africa

S. Y. Boadi-Siaw

THE phenomenon of African former slaves returning to their original homes has so far not received the attention it deserves. Pierre Verger has done much work on the relationship between Brazil and West Africa. Others like Antonio Olinto and Raymundo Souza Dantas, two Brazilian diplomats, have observed and written about the "Brazilian" communities in West Africa. More recently, the scholar Jerry M. Turner deals directly and fully with these "Brazilians" in his doctoral thesis, "Les 'Bresiliens'—The Impact of Former Brazilian Slaves upon Dahomey" (Boston University, 1975). Jean Herskovits Kopytoff, in *A Preface to Modern Nigeria* (Madison, 1965), and A. T. Porter, in *Creoledom* (London, 1963), examine the phenomenon of the returnees in their respective areas. But more needs to be done to clarify the motivations and the influences that determined their attitudes and reactions on their return to their home areas.

This essay examines the Brazilian returnees to West Africa in the nineteenth century. It seeks to provide some answers to the question of why they behave the way they did on their return by looking at their attitudes, occupations, and contributions to West African society. Their stay in Brazil so affected them that they behaved more like Brazilians than like Africans on the West African coast. Thus, in this essay they are called *Brazilians*.

The term, however, is not completely accurate because the *Brazilian* communities included people of different origins, some having had little or no connection whatever with Brazil. Some were former Portuguese fort and factory officials who remained on the coast and had their children by local women. Others were Brazilian, Portuguese, and even Spanish slaveship crewmen who were left on the coast after their ships

421

had been seized and destroyed by British patrols. By far the most numerous, however, were the former slaves who returned to West Africa when they secured their freedom or were deported from Bahia (Brazil) because of their supposed involvement in the slave revolt of 1835. Other West Africans who never went outside Africa have become identified with the group because they were slaves and servants to some well-to-do original Brazilians in West Africa.[1]

The Arrival

Some Brazilians came to West Africa even before the nineteenth century. They usually arrived at Whydah, where the Portuguese had built a fort in 1721. But their growth as a separate and numerically important group dates from the early nineteenth century. In spite of the expulsion of the governor of the Portuguese fort and its abandonment at the end of the eighteenth century, the slave coast continued to attract large numbers of Portuguese and Brazilian ships and nationals. Some minor officials of the fort indeed chose to remain after the expulsion and engaged in trade. These and other Brazilian traders who came and settled on the coast became the nucleus of the Brazilian community in the nineteenth century. Newcomers attached themselves to this group. One of the more famous of this early group was "Xaxa" Francisco Felix de Souza, a minor Brazilian official of the Portuguese fort who remained to become a rich, independent slave trader.

Significant numbers of the Brazilians began to arrive in West Africa in the first decades of the nineteenth century. In 1835, an uprising of the black population—slave and free—in Salvador, Bahia, shook the authorities so much that they took measures forcing many former slaves to leave for West Africa. Local authorities placed severe restrictions on people of African descent, including fines and deportations of those who in any way were "suspected of trying to provoke slaves into insurrection." Under these restrictions, many freed Africans left seeking a more congenial life elsewhere. Many eventually came to West Africa, which they regarded as home. Thus, the Brazilian community in Accra, after whom a street is named (Brazil Street) in James Town, dates its arrival to this period (1836).[2]

Throughout the nineteenth century, more immigrants continued to come as they acquired freedom and money to pay their passage. The final abolition of slavery, which occurred in Brazil in 1888, provided another impetus for former slaves to migrate to West Africa. Many of those who had been sent to Brazil as young people nurtured the remembrances of their homes in Africa and longed to return. The total abolition of slavery opened the way for them to attempt to fulfill this longing. Many thus found money and boarded ships coming to the West African coast in the period immediately after 1888 and even later. They risked the uncertainties of the voyage and reception to come to Lagos, Whydah, Badagry, and other port cities of West Africa. The most recent estimates put the number that left Brazil at approximately three thousand for the whole of the nineteenth century.[3]

The arrival date of individuals in West Africa significantly affected their fortune. Those who arrived in the period before 1851 seem to have had better fortune than those who arrived later. Whereas some of the earlier arrivals like de Souza, Jose Domingos Martins, and Joaquim d'Almeida, and others established powerful and wealthy independent commercial houses and exercised great political and social influence, no later arrivals achieved such commercial, political, and social success in the nineteenth century, mostly because the Europeans were more active as traders or as representatives of their governments after 1851. The establishment of the British in Lagos in 1851 and the French in Porto Novo soon after meant the incoming Brazilians worked at a disadvantage if they sought to establish commercial enterprises. In addition, many of those Brazilians of the earlier period became rich because they engaged in the slave trade to Brazil that allowed slaves to be imported until 1850, though legally the trade had been abolished in 1831 in Brazil. As a result, to this day the families established by the pre-1851 arrivals enjoy a higher social standing in the Brazilian communities than those of the post-1850 immigrants.[4]

The Situation in Brazil

The Brazil that these people were leaving provided both the reasons for their departure and the background for an understanding of their behavior and attitudes. Nineteenth-century Brazilian society greatly influenced the former slaves and determined their economic activities and their social aspirations when they came to West Africa.

The Brazilian society from which they came was a stratified one based on birth, race, and wealth. The emperor (until 1889) sat at the top of the pyramid with his family. Next came various titled men and their families, dukes, counts, and viscounts, who were descended from the older Portuguese colonists and controlled large estates and, consequently, had considerable economic and political influence. Next to them came the various professional people—lawyers, doctors, merchants, and the managers of various nonagricultural enterprises. They aspired to nobility and often intermarried with the landed elite. The people in these top classes almost wholly originated from European countries.

Below them came the artisans, small traders, and other independent craftsmen who earned enough to live on and care for a family, but not sumptuously. Again, they were mainly white but included a sprinkling of the mixed peoples—mulattoes, mestizos—and even some blacks. Next came the free blacks and mulattoes who practiced various callings that brought in something to live on, but barely. They were cooks, bakers, washermen and washerwomen, carpenters, sailors, water carriers, porters, sweets sellers, cattle herders, and so on. A few whites belonged to this group. In the period up to 1888, the slaves formed the bottom section of the Brazilian society.

In the early nineteenth century, Africans—free and slave—formed a majority of the population. Out of the total estimate of 3,817,000, about 2,515,000 had African blood. They provided the labor that gave the wealth and comfort to the privileged minority. As some of the Brazilian aristocrats admitted, "Brazil owed its civilization to Africa.... [T]he African provided the leisure for the aristocracy to pursue the arts and to govern. Consequently, the civilization that had developed in Brazil rested squarely on the black's labor."[5]

Two main divisions of the slave population can be made—the plantation and mine slaves and the urban slaves. The plantation slaves generally had harder lives than their counterparts in the city. They came directly under the control and disposition of their owners, patriarchs who ruled their isolated plantations with a strong hand. Not even the representatives of central authority could challenge them, and—on an isolated plantation—slaves could not even take advantage of the national laws passed to mitigate the harshness of slavery. Brutal means of punishment were commonly employed on the plantation: the horsewhip, wooden or iron stocks in which arms and legs could be held, iron collars put on necks, and chains and iron weights that could be attached to the feet of slaves even while they worked.[6]

Slaves supplied the labor for the production of cash crops such as coffee, sugar, and cotton on large and small estates. A nineteenth-century observer said:

On the plantation, everything or almost everything is the product of the black man: it is he who has built the houses; he has made the bricks, sawed the boards, channeled the water, etc.; the roads and most of the machines in *engenho* (mill) are, along with the lands cultivated, the products of his industry. He has also raised cattle, pigs and other animals needed on the *faxenda* (plantation).[7]

The needs of the plantation and its inhabitants occupied the slaves from four in the morning until ten or eleven at night during certain periods. Only short breaks for early lunch, snacks or coffee or *cachaca* (a strong drink made from sugar cane), and the evening meal, all taken at the place of work, provided some rest. Variations existed, but the pattern was the same on the large plantations that produced most of Brazil's exports.[8]

Such a hard life produced the wealth that the aristocratic families spent lavishly. Two American ministers of religion saw the plantation life of a Silva Pinto family and described it this way:

> At dinner we were served in a large dining-room. The *Comendador* (title of the owner) sat at the head of the table, while his guests and the various free members of his family sat upon forms, the *feitors* (overseers) and shepherds being at the lower end. He lives in true baronial style.[9]

Guests apparently often stayed with the owner, who delighted in serving them "long repasts" in costly chinaware and silver and gold bowls. The Silva Pinto family had its own chapel attached to the "big house." They also had their own orchestra consisting of "fifteen slave musicians" and a choir of slaves who had been trained to read music and play the various musical instruments—violins, flutes, bugles, trombones, and others—for the entertainment of the *comendador* and his family and guests.

Other slaves worked for small farmers, who usually had limited resources and land. Often, those farmers treated their slaves with some consideration. They supervised them personally, and in some cases, labored alongside them, even sharing with them the poor food and living quarters. Relations of affection could therefore develop between master and slave. But the small farm was the exception in nineteenth-century Brazil when the main cash-crop-producing unit was the large estate. The numbers involved in the smaller farms, therefore, formed an insignificant proportion of the slave population.[10]

The slave not only was worked hard and harshly treated, but he also was the object of racial prejudice and abuse. The planters generally regarded the African as an inferior being who had to be harshly disciplined, closely supervised, and constantly kept under surveillance; otherwise, he would not work, since he was "by nature the enemy of all regular work." On the whole, therefore, the African—slave or free—remained at the bottom of the economic and social scale in nineteenth-century Brazil because of the "prevalence of prejudices, the effects of routinism, and the absence of scientific knowledge," as Stein puts it. Some planters and town dwellers did not share the prejudices, but the general belief in the inferiority of the African remained and determined the harsh treatment meted out to the black offender, the unwillingness of managers of nonagricultural industries to train them for employment, and the unwillingness of the government to suppress discriminatory practices or mitigate the cruel treatment given African slaves.[11]

The hard labor and condition of life on the plantations contrasted somewhat with the situation of the slaves who worked in urban areas. These slaves normally worked in their masters' houses as domestics: cooks, cleaners, nurses to children, bodyguards, and companions to their masters and their wives. Others worked outside in artisan jobs as apprentices or junior partners to carpenters, masons, shoemakers, blacksmiths, and so on. Some worked as independent artisans who brought a certain portion of their gain to their masters. Many sold sweets, vegetables, cakes, bread, and fruits that they carried on their heads or displayed in kiosks situated at vantage points. Others carried water from the sources to sell in houses or hired themselves out to work for individuals or carried loads to and from the ports. Some slaves living and working on their own, had masters who interested themselves only in the money their slaves brought them at the end of the week. Many Brazilians indeed lived on such earnings their slaves brought them.[12]

These slaves, de ganho, as they were called, formed an elite among the slaves, hardly distinguishable from the free blacks. They not only enjoyed more freedom but, because of the nature of their work, had more opportunity to free themselves through purchase. Indeed, the city slaves in general were able to purchase their own freedom more frequently than their counterparts on the plantations. With the opportunities they had, they could save enough money to meet the purchase price set by their masters. City slaves also had more opportunities for knowing their rights under the laws that regulated such self-purchase than their counterparts on the isolated plantations under the control of the all-powerful patriarchs.

African Contributions to Brazil

Whatever the attitudes to and treatment of the African in Brazil, he contributed significantly to the society and economy. The economy of Brazil, in fact, lay on his shoulders. He supplied the labor that produced all the exports; mainly coffee, sugar, rubber, cotton, and some minerals. Coffee alone accounted for two-thirds of the exports in 1889.[13] The only exceptions were the few small industries that began to appear during the 1850s and employed local white labor and European immigrants. The labor of blacks in personal services and in all types of enterprises made them indispensable to the economic growth of Brazil.

But the African contributed more than his labor. His presence helped mold the physical characteristics, personality, language, dress, and general quality of life of the Brazilian. In color, facial looks, eye color, hair, and physique, many Brazilians show marked African features. Indeed, the African presence in the population transcends the approximately forty percent listed as black or colored (pardo or mulatto) in the 1950 census—the last to list people by color. Thus, a former minister of state, diplomat, senator, and a respected professor and writer, Snr. Afonso Arinos de Melo France, has described his country as "one of the largest African countries."[14]

African influences, particularly West African, also abound in Brazilian life. The large colorful dresses of the Bahian *acarajé* (our *akara*) sellers and many of the ornaments, tunics, long gowns, and skirts worn by many in Brazil show African traits. Various art works and crafts, like the religious figurines used in the *candomblé* and *macumba* shrines and festivals and the wooden and iron figurines sold, for instance, at the model market on the seashore of Salvador, are clearly African. Many colonial churches with fine interior and exterior decorations in gold, silver, stone, and wood bear testimony to the capabilities of the Africans who worked them. The best known of these artists was Antonio Francisco Lisboa, "O Aleijadinke" (little cripple), a son of an African slave woman and a Portuguese immigrant. His soapstone carvings and other decorations of church buildings in Minas Gerais that date from the eighteenth century continue today to attract thousands of admirers each year.

More important, Brazilian religious life shows the pervasive influence of African (particularly Yoruba, Ewe, and Fon) practices and beliefs. Almost pure forms of West African worship and practices remain in the *candomblé, orixás,* and *macumba* found in may parts of Brazil, especially in Bahia, Pernambuco, Rio de Janeiro, and Minas Gerais. In spite of attempts in the nineteenth and the early twentieth centuries to suppress them through public campaigns and police action, they have persisted and have maintained their vitality through contacts with their West African sources.

Apart from the purely West African religious houses and cults, popular beliefs and practices of professing Roman Catholics also show the influence of African religions. Syncreticism has resulted, for example, in the identification of African gods with Roman Catholic saints and their worship as such. This began in earlier periods when slaves, expected to be Catholics and unable to worship African gods freely, gave them Roman Catholic saint names and worshiped them. Thus, *Xangó,* the Yoruba god of thunder and lightning became St. Jeronymo; *Oxossi,* the god of hunting, became St. George; *Yemanjá,* the goddess of the sea, became Our Lady of Mercy and of Rosary. In the worship of the god-saints, the African elements are thoroughly mixed with Roman Catholic ones, in both the cult houses and the churches.

Other influences show in the diet of Brazilians. Through their work as cooks, domestic servants, and nurses, Africans introduced new foods into the diet of their masters and mistresses. The use of palm oil, hot pepper, guava, okra, and others thus came into Brazil. Whole new dishes like *vatapa* (a seasoned preparation of cassava flour cooked with chicken or fish); *angu* (a corn dough meal very similar to *banku*; *acarajé* (bean cakes fried in palm oil) (our *akara*); *ofo* (a composition of shrimps, greens, hot pepper, and palm oil); *caruru* (okra stew with onion, pepper, and shrimps); as well as others became part of the Brazilian menu.[15]

African influences also show in the Portuguese spoken in Brazil, especially in the inflections, simplifications of form and morphology, and vocabulary. Brazilian Portuguese borrowed extensively from African languages: *angu, giló, fubá vatapa, quliombo* (village), and *caruru* came directly from Africa. Music and dancing have been influenced by Africa. The popular samba music and dance, the tango, the *congadas* and *reisadas* (dramatic dances at Epiphany celebrations), and *batuque* have demonstrable African origins. In folklore also the African influence shows itself, as the studies of Edison Carneiro and others have revealed.[16]

Return to West Africa

Thus, the Brazil the former slaves and others left had a large African input. On the other hand, they also took with them vestiges of their stay, which they revealed in the way they viewed things, in their social aspirations, and in their economic activities in West Africa. They came mainly because they saw West Africa as the home to which they wanted to return, at least to die. But they came as nineteenth-century Brazilians of African origin. For a long time they remained as a separate, alien group in West African societies—belonging to two places and to none.

The influence of their Brazilian stay showed particularly in their attitude toward land ownership. Many of them aspired to own land on a large scale, setting up a plantation to produce a cash crop with a large house, many servants, and slaves. Thus, those who were economically successful in West Africa set up palm oil plantations, built large houses, owned slaves and servants, and had many children and dependents on the pattern of a Brazilian patriarchal plantation owner. The only difference was that these immigrants built their wealth through trade—something the Brazilian landowners never soiled their hands with, depending, rather, on the labor of their slaves and servants on their lands.

A good example of a Brazilian patriarch in West Africa, "Xaxa" Francisco Felix de Souza, had land in Whydah that he developed into a palm oil plantation with large numbers of slaves and servants. He also owned several large houses built on the pattern of the colonial Latin American *casa poblado*[17] in the cities along the coast in which the master lived regally. Jose Domingo Martins, another Brazilian trader, similarly established plantations and built "big houses" along the coast. So also did Joaquim d'Almeida, a returned former slave. These Brazilians, even the former slaves, willingly enslaved others. With nineteenth-century Brazil as the pattern, they loved being the masters and members of an elite.[18]

The situation in West Africa in the nineteenth century, however, often determined the activities of the Brazilian returnees. Also others, like the Sierra Leonean emigrants, did similar things. But the Brazilians constantly looked back to Brazil and always referred to their Brazilian experience in any situation.

Indeed, these people never forgot the Brazil they had left. According to John Duncan, those who were deported to West Africa looked to Brazil as "a place where they had spent their happiest days." Not only these but many others, even the immigrants, felt the same. After the end of slavery in Brazil, some returned to live in Brazil. Others traveled between Brazil and the West African coast and sent their children to be educated in Bahia and sometimes to settle there. The division of the Alakija family between Bahia, Lagos, and Abeokuta resulted from this phenomenon.[19]

Their stay in Brazil also influenced the kinds of economic activities they involved themselves in when they returned to West Africa. The most important occupation was trading. This came almost naturally to the Brazilians. In Brazil, little opportunity existed for the former slaves who had no skills or money to invest in land or other enterprises. Thus, many had taken to petty trading, retailing small items they received on credit from large firms. Many others sold food items they made themselves or obtained from others. Others sold fruits, vegetables, and corn that they raised on small rented plots near the cities. This kind of trading became a common way many of the returnees used to make a living. They generally sold small items at first for others (usually earlier arrivals). Later, they obtained goods on credit from European trading firms at the coast. Some, therefore, became quite wealthy and owned their own stores from which they sold or supplied small retailers. Antonio Olinto portrays this well in his book *Casa d'Agua*, an historical novel based on the experiences of some returnees to Lagos.

Some of the free Africans in Brazil engaged in intercontinental trade in bulk goods—an experience some carried to West Africa. Jerry Turner tells of a number of merchants who carried on trade between Bahia and the West African coast. Two of these Africans, Antoino de Costa and Joao Monteiro, chartered a British ship, *Nimrod*, to transport 160 freed men to West Africa in the face of the restrictions on and persecutions of the community conducted by the local authorities following the 1835 revolt. Such merchants did profitable business, bringing tobacco, sugar, *cachaca*, and salted beef to West Africa and carrying back palm oil, kola nuts, drums, Yoruba cloth, pepper, beads, and so on.[20]

Some of these merchants and others who built their wealth in other ways after settling on the West African coast became the organizers of the commerce with Europe and Brazil. Such were the de Souzas, Jose Domingos Martins, Joaquim d'Almeida, Francisco Olympion o Silva, and Mama "Sabino" Vieyra. Such traders, who made big fortunes and established big houses and families, came mainly in the period before 1851. After 1851, the economic and political conditions gave them less opportunity to occupy such a middle position between the local people and Europeans.[21]

In the period immediately before and after 1851, British, French, and German firms established agents in the coastal towns to act as suppliers of European goods and buyers of local export products. The greater involvement of the agents of the European firms like Victor Regis, Thomas Hutton, Banner Brothers, Stewart and Douglas, and O'swald and Company in the exchange of goods with the local peoples challenged, and in the end eliminated, the Brazilians as large-scale merchants and middlemen. Using their ability to control the sources of the European trade goods, their ownership of the means of transportation, that is, ships, and their home governments' political presence or influence, these firms gradually pushed out the Brazilians (and Sierra Leoneans). The Brazilian traders were reduced to taking goods from these firms on credit or to becoming agents for them if they wanted to maintain their trading activities. A few, however, continued to trade on their own with Bahia, which had diminished after the effective abolition of the slave trade in Brazil in 1851.[22]

The next important occupation of the Brazilians was artisanship or the practice of various trades that were learned while in Brazil. Many slaves were apprenticed to master carpenters, masons, goldsmiths, blacksmiths, bakers, shoemakers, tailors, and others. With these skills they worked to earn more money than they would otherwise have made for their masters and themselves. Many freed themselves by what they earned through such skilled work and continued the same work as freed men. Those who had no skills when freed often apprenticed themselves to others to learn. Thus, among the slaves in 1872, there were 40,766 seamstresses, 13,196 textile workers, 5,599 carpenters, 2,163 shoemakers,

1,379 tailors, 1,858 artists, and 808,401 plantation hands.[23] The skilled slaves had great market value, which masters proudly advertised whenever they wanted to sell such slaves. For instance, ads in newspapers of nineteenth-century Brazil read: "For sale: a mulatto of 22 years of age, a good tailor and a good herdsman; also a black of the same age; there is also a young girl who cooks very well and bakes too. Her conduct is very good. There is another black woman 22 years old who is a very good cook. Location: Livramento street No. 4"; and, "A very young slave girl, with a beautiful figure is for sale. She knows how to cook and starch and iron clothes. She is a perfect dressmaker, ideal for any seamstress. Location: The dispensary of Joaquim Ignacio Ribeiro Jnr. on Boa Vista Square."[24]

Many of those who returned to the West African coast, thus possessed skills with which they could earn a living. Opportunities for large-scale trade were necessarily limited. Retail trade and hawking were not attractive to most. Nor was farming very feasible because the system of landholding in the family or community in West African societies made it difficult for outsiders to obtain land. Many, therefore, had to fall back on their skills. Thus, the founder of the Paraiso family of Porto Novo and Agoue, Jose Paraiso, arrived in about 1850 and served as a barber to the established slave trader compatriot Jose Domingos Martins.

Marcus Augusto Jose Cardoso, skilled in carpentry and joinery, arrived in Lagos with his father in 1869. He built a number of religious and educational facilities in Lagos, Cotonou, Ibadan, and Ebutemetta. He became famous in the area for his leadership in various religious and educational undertakings, including the construction of the first Roman Catholic cathedral in the area, the Holy Cross of Lagos. Another former slave, Martiano do Bomfin, worked as a carpenter and brick mason on the same cathedral with a respectable pay of two shillings and sixpence a day, and later returned to Bahia. Another, Paulo Fretias, worked as a carpenter in Nigeria for twenty years (1890–1910) and then returned to Bahia where he died in 1918.[25]

The skills of the former slaves had special value in the second half of the nineteenth century in West Africa. The Europeans had begun to establish themselves, but not well enough to have trained the necessary artisans for constructing the various government and trade buildings they needed. The carpenters, masons, joiners, tailors, and barbers arriving from Brazil were god-sent, and the incoming Europeans recognized this. Thus, a French official at Porto Novo urged his government to act and establish a French protectorate there because, "although there was not a sizable European population resident in the town, the presence of this creole community with its links to western civilization should encourage the French to act." Similarly, J. Chapman, one of the (CMS) missionaries in Lagos, wrote to his counterpart in Sierra Leone that "the influx of these men [the Brazilians], all of whom must have something of European civilization among them (though doubtless alloyed with European vices and much error for many of them are Roman Catholics) together with the return of so many from Sierra Leone, must have a most important influence for good upon the interior of Africa." Another British resident in Lagos observed that the Brazilians had among them "master masons, carpenters, painters, cabinet makers and master-smiths.... On the women's side proficiency in bakery...laundry and dressmaking distinguished the Agudas."[26]

As a result of the value of their skills, those returnees received good wages, especially in Lagos where the Europeans were more numerous. Thus, even as early as 1845 the missionary Charles A. Gollmar warned his group from Lagos that "we must be prepared for a greater expense...than I anticipated." He blamed the Portuguese slave traders for the fact that "carpenter work is paid 300 percent higher than at Badagry." But the obvious explanation was that the many different groups—missionaries, British government officials, the different trading company representatives—all placed a high demand on the few artisans available. The demand continued high in the coastal towns like Lagos and Porto Novo throughout the nineteenth century. Thus, a carpenter could earn two shillings and sixpence a day in the 1880s, quite an attractive wage considering that in the 1890s a Nigerian official of the Prisons Department who had years of experience and overseas training earned about four shillings a day (six pounds a month). In Accra, Brazilians were greatly respected for their skills in building, tailoring, and farming.[27]

Other areas showed the Brazilian influence in the contributions of the immigrants. Agriculture in West Africa was affected by the Brazilians. Most of them had to abandon the hope of reaching the Brazilian ideal of a lordly life when they came to West Africa, but some managed to acquire land either through gifts by local rulers or through purchase. Thus, "Xaxa" Souza received a land grant from King Guezo of Dahomey to make a plantation. On part of this land he built a luxurious two-story house for his descendants but made a plantation of palm trees on which his many slaves and servants worked. On the other hand, the father of the Bahian Snr. Maxwell Porferia Assumpcao Alakija bought land soon after his arrival in Abeokuta. He "was the first person in that city to own a cotton gin" for processing the cotton he had planted. Jose Domingos Martins also owned a number of palm oil plantations and other farms on which he raised cattle near Porto Novo.[28]

Other immigrants had small pieces of land, often given to them by their better-off compatriots like de Souza. On these "they raised food items for the supply of their needs and those of their community." These small farmers became more easily absorbed into the local community, and greater interchanges of ideas took place as a result. Thus, John Duncan commented in several places on the knowledge of agriculture that the former slaves had and that they used in cultivating "several very fine farms about six or seven miles from Whydah." He added that the cultivation of crops "in drills" in places beyond Abomey had resulted from "the instruction of returned slaves from the Brazils." The Brazilians in Aara received gifts of land on which they made gardens, planting mangoes, coconuts, many varieties of beans, and manioc, which became known as cassava.[29]

The Brazilian returnees derived their skills in farming not only from their experiences on plantations but also from their previous practices in Africa. Also, some of them had practiced truck farming near cities in Brazil. On many Brazilian plantations the owners also allotted small plots of land to the slaves. On these, in their free time, they raised food crops to supplement their meager daily allowance and some cash crops to raise money to purchase goods and, in some cases, their own freedom. Subsistence farming, however, was nothing new to these people who had been farming in West Africa long before the Europeans arrived in the fifteenth century. But plantation agriculture and the raising of crops far beyond the needs of a family represented new experiences for the slaves and freedmen in Brazil. These practices suited a country preoccupied with supplying the demands of foreign countries for raw materials.

These experiences with Brazilian agriculture became useful in nineteenth century West Africa, where Europeans similarly had started demanding more and more raw materials. West Africans had not concentrated on producing cash crops for outside markets, and the Brazilians' experience was helpful. The palm oil plantations of the richer Brazilians in Porto Novo, Whydah, and other places were geared toward meeting the European demands. How far the decision of the Dahomean state to go into plantation production of palm oil and nuts was prompted by the example and advice of the Brazilians has not been investigated. I venture to propose that the Dahomeans took to cultivating palm oil in plantations through the influence of the Brazilians who had such direct experience.[30]

The Brazilians also exerted influence in education. They had seen in Brazil that education could raise one's status and earning power. Some had indeed acquired education in parochial schools or in the homes of their masters and ladies. However, not many schools existed for the education of the population as a whole. At independence in 1822, few schools existed, and the educational system had not recovered from the expulsion of the Jesuits in 1759. Under the empire (1822–89), primary education came under local and municipal authorities who had little interest in the spread of education to the populace. In fact, even in Europe, popular education began to interest politicians only in the second half of the nineteenth century.

Thus, only the children of the landed aristocratic families, rich merchants, and professionals received any measure of education. The vast majority of the population—eighty percent by C. H. Haring's estimate, which included almost all the Africans—remained illiterate. According to another estimate, out of a slave population of 1,509,403 in 1872, only 1,403 had some education—about 0.09 percent.[31]

In West Africa, however, the Brazilians sought to educate their children so that they could better their status. They knew the advantages Western education could give a person in the increasingly European-dominated society of coastal West Africa of the nineteenth century. Indeed, those who had some education gained advantages over others right away. They became scribes, interpreters, and advisers to local chiefs and thus acquired a place in the society. Moreover, those who took to trading had an opportunity to use their education to advantage in their dealings with the Europeans (Portuguese was for a long time the trade language along the coast). In the period of greater European presence from 1851 on, those with education served as interpreters, negotiators, and advisers to both local rulers and the Europeans, especially in the inevitable clashes between the two. During the European takeover and under the colonial administrations, the educated had a secure place—as interpreters, court clerks, postal clerks, and so on. In Dahomey, the French relied heavily on the Brazilians, and even in Lagos the British used their services.[32]

The Brazilians rose to positions of importance under the colonial regimes despite their initial problem of language because they led the drive for education. The first European schools in Dahomey opened in the abandoned Portuguese fort in Whydah and in Brazilians' homes. The Brazilians were the first to send their children to the mission schools opened by the French and British. In fact, they demanded schools from the missionaries.[33] We have noted the efforts of the Brazilian Marcos Cardoso in organizing and building schools in Dahomey and Nigeria in the late nineteenth century. Their early recognition of the advantages of education and their seizure of the opportunities offered by the incoming European officials and missionaries enabled the Brazilians to gain a disproportionate prominence among the elite of the West African coastal states, Togo, Benin, and Nigeria.

In the architecture they contributed to West Africa, the returnees also showed the influence of Brazil. The masons, carpenters, joiners, and others used their skills in constructing private and public buildings in the coastal cities and inland. José Cardoso contributed as a carpenter and joiner in the construction of various chapels, school buildings, and cathedrals. Other skilled returnees contributed in constructing those and other buildings as carpenters and masons. Having learned their skills in Brazil, they naturally tried to copy the architectural styles of the buildings they had seen or helped build in Brazil. In this way, they influenced the architecture of West Africa, especially since not only fellow Brazilians but also Europeans and local people relied on their skills.

In Porto Novo, Whydah, Ague, and other places, Brazilian Muslims also constructed religious houses. Thus, the first Imam of Ague, one Saidon, a Brazilian former slave, initiated the construction of a mosque in 1850. In 1883, the Imam of Whydah, Abdullahi Alechou, the son of a Brazilian former slave, began building the biggest mosque of the town at the time.[34]

When the wealthy Brazilians built individual houses, they modeled them after the houses they had seen in Brazil. Many such houses still stand in the areas where the Brazilian communities lived in the various towns in West Africa. As the Reverend G. K. Nelson, himself a descendant of Brazilian immigrants, wrote in 1963, "Some houses which the Brazilians constructed are still standing, some of those having served, until recently, as residences (palaces) of some tribal chiefs of Accra."[35] The Brazilian paper, *Brazilian Report*, in 1962 carried a picture of a neoclassic building in Salvador, Bahia, with an explanation that the houses of the Brazilians in Lagos and other places resembled buildings in Bahia.[36] A more detailed scholarly study of the buildings on the two sides of the Atlantic would clarify such Brazilian influences on West African architecture.

Finally, in religion the Brazilians helped spread Christianity and Islam in West Africa. All slaves had to receive baptism before setting foot on Brazilian soil. This the slave traders usually did by having their human cargo baptized en masse before they went into the ships. In Brazil itself, each slave owner had to provide for the Roman Catholic religious education of his slaves. Many plantations, therefore, had their own chapels with resident chaplains. Each morning and evening, prayers for all the residents on a plantation took place. So, in theory, all became Roman Catholics; and in practice, many became committed to Roman Catholicism. At least, they became, like most Latin Americans, attached to the external forms and ceremonials.

Others, however, retained their traditional beliefs and practices, often disguising these under Roman Catholic worship and forms. Some others kept their Islamic faith in spite of the hostility they faced in the strongly Catholic country. Indeed, those who came in the first half of the nineteenth century to Bahia had such a strong attachment to Islam and such missionary zeal that they converted others to their religion there. According to Jerry Turner, they even set up an imamate in Salvador and had *qadis* in the provinces. They are reputed to have provided the leadership for various revolts in Bahia, culminating in the famous one of 1835 that some writers have consequently considered an extension of the jihads of West Africa.[37]

Most Brazilians, however, professed Roman Catholicism when they returned to West Africa, which helped to distinguish them. As Jerry Turner shows in his dissertation, they welcomed the first Roman Catholic missionaries to the area, provided the first congregations, contributed to the needs of the missions, and helped to build the first churches and schools. Their enthusiasm arose from their desire for material things like schools and a desire to maintain the cultural inheritance from Brazil that helped give them a separate identity. But they proved to be generally poor Catholics in the eyes of the missionaries because they tended to be attached more to the outward ceremonials and festivals (especially those they had celebrated in Brazil) while they showed indifference toward Roman Catholic rituals and personal morality. This earned them the censure of the European missionaries, whose initial enthusiasm toward them quickly waned. But the Brazilians supplied a ready congregation and the necessarily support and encouragement for the mission. Their contribution to the building of churches and schools and the zeal of some helped establish Roman Catholicism in many places in West Africa.[38]

The Muslims among them also continued in their beliefs and practices. They joined the Muslim communities in the coastal towns and other places. In these, some became spokesmen on occasion. For example, the French lieutenant-governor of Dahomey in 1902 chose Ignacio Paraiso as a Muslim representative of his central Committee of Public Instruction.[39] Some like Saidon of Ague (c. 1850) and Abdullahi Alechou (c. 1883) of Whydah, indeed exercised the functions of Imam for the Muslim communities in these towns. The influence these Muslims exercised was necessarily limited. Islam had been in West Africa far longer than in Brazil, and leaders for the local communities came more from the indigenous groups. Besides, under the French and British they found little opportunity for leadership in the Westernized atmosphere that favored their Roman Catholic counterparts.

Conclusion

Socially and economically, therefore, the roles the Brazilians played in West Africa, in large measure, came from their experiences and training in Brazil. Underprivileged, despised, and ill-used, they managed to leave an impact on the economy and culture of the society. Through living in nineteenth-century Brazil, they also acquired certain values and skills that they carried to West Africa. Generally, they left Brazil because the society was hostile to them, and they thought it offered them fewer opportunities for attaining a respectable place, economically or socially.

In West Africa, most had to abandon their high goals, and some became disappointed, but on the whole, the Brazilians bettered themselves. Through diligence and the use of their experiences and skills acquired in Brazil, they achieved reasonable and, in some cases, great wealth. Socially, though an alien group in what they had regarded while they were in Brazil as "home," they achieved a respectable place denied them before. Indeed, though regarded sometimes as half-baked Europeans, their possession of a measure of European culture and skills gave them an advantage over those who had never left the coast, when the Europeans established their rule over West Africa. This explains the high positions they achieved in colonial and postcolonial West Africa, socially, economically, and even politically.

NOTES

1. John Duncan, *Travels in West Africa in 1845 and 1846* (reprint ed., London: Frank Cass Co., 1968) 1:101, 113, 138, 185–86.
2. Jerry M. Turner, "'Les Bresiliens'—The Impact of Former Brazilian Slaves upon Dahomey" (Ph.D. diss., Boston University, 1975), 43–51, especially 45; Duncan, *Travels* 185; R. Souza Dantas, *Africa Dificil* (Rio de Janeiro, 1965) 44–48.
3. Turner, "Les Bresiliens," 70–73, 77–78, 85.
4. Ibid., 83.
5. E. Bradford Burns, *A History of Brazil* (New York: Columbia University Press, 1970), 180; R. K. Kent, "African Revolt in Bahia: 24–25 January 1835," *Journal of Social History* (Summer 1970), 335.
6. Stanley J. Stein, *Vassouras: A Brazilian Coffee County 1850–1900* (New York: Atheneum 1970), 134–38.
7. Quoted in Stein, *Vassouras*, 165.
8. Burns, *A History of Brazil* 136–37; Stein, *Vassouras*, 161–65.
9. J. C. Fletcher and D. P. Kidder, *Brazil and the Brazilians* (Philadelphia: American Museum Science Books, 1857), 440–42.
10. Stein, *Vassouras*, 139.
11. Ibid., 133.
12. Mary Karash, "Rio's Black Brazilerias," in *The African in Latin America*, Ann Pescatello (New York: Knopf, 1975), 168–72; Fletcher and Kidder, *Brazil and the Brazilians*,

132–37; Mahommah G. Baquaqua, "Recollections of a Slave's Life," in Pescatello, *The African in Latin America*, 186ff.

13. E. Bradford Burns, *Latin America: A Concise Interpretive History* (Englewood Cliffs, N.J.: Prentice-Hall, 1972), 132.

14. Afonso Arinos de Melo France, interview in November 1973 in his house in Rio de Janeiro.

15. S. Y. Boadi-Siaw, "The Development of Relations between Brazil and African States, 1950–1973" (Ph.D. diss., University of California, Los Angeles, 1975), 8, note 13.

16. Ibid., 10; Edison Carneiro, *O Folklore Nacional* (Rio de Janeiro, 1954).

17. Professor James Lockhart defines a *casa poblada* as a "peopled house,... a large house,... a table where many guests were maintained, Negro slaves, a staff of Spanish and Indian servants, and a stable of horses. The *casa poblada* was the largest single element in the dream of a lordly life which all Spaniards shared." *Spanish Peru 1532–1560: A Colonial Society* (Madison: University of Wisconsin Press, 1974), 21.

18. Turner, "Les Bresiliens," 93–95, 103–5, 115–16; David Ross, "The Career of Domingo Martinez in the Bight of Benin, 1833–64." *Journal of African History* 6 (1965):79–90; Duncan, *Travels*, 102–3, 137, 278.

19. Duncan, *Travels*, 201–2; Lorenzo Turner, "Some Contacts of Brazilian Ex-slaves with Nigeria West Africa," *Journal of Negro History* 27 (January 1942):65; Turner, "Les Bresiliens," 101.

20. Turner, "Les Bresiliens," 50–63; Turner, "Some Contacts of Brazilian Ex-slaves with Nigeria West Africa," 59–60; Pierre Verger, *Flux et Reflux* 358–62.

21. Turner, "Les Bresiliens," 89–120.

22. Colin W. Newbury, *The Western Slave Coast and Its Ruler: European Trade and Administration among the Yoruba and Adja-Speaking People of South Western Nigeria, Southern Dahomey and Togo* (London: Oxford University Press, 1961), 56ff, 81.

23. Robert Conrad, *The Destruction of Brazilian Slavery, 1850–1888* (Berkeley: University of California Press, 1972), 299.

24. Gilberto Freyre, *O Escravo nos Anuncios de Jornais Brasileiros do Seculo XIX* (Recife, 1963), opposite pp. 58, 60.

25. Turner, "Les Bresiliens," 121–23; Turner, "Some Contacts of Brazilian Ex-slaves with Nigeria West Africa," 60–64.

26. Turner, "Les Bresiliens," 222–23; Jean H. Kopytoff, *A Preface to Modern Nigeria* (Madison: University of Wisconsin Press, 1965), 87, 98.

27. Lorenzo Turner, "Some Contacts of Brazilian Ex-slaves with Nigeria West Africa," 63; E. A. Ayandele, "An Assessment of James Johnson and His Place in Nigerian History, 1874–1917—Pt. II, 1890–1917," *Journal of the Historical Society of Nigeria* 3, 1 (December 1964):84; Dantas, *Africa Dificil*, 46.

28. Turner, "Les Bresiliens," 94; Turner, "Some Contacts of Brazilian Ex-slaves with Nigeria West Africa," 65; Ross, "The Career of Domingo Martinez," 83–84.

29. Duncan, *Travels*, 138–39, 185–86, 278: Dantas, *Africa Dificil*, 46.

30. The time of the growth in importance of the plantations—the early decades of the nineteenth century—coincides interestingly with the time of the growing influence of "Xaxa" de Souza in Dahomean affairs, especially after the accession of Guezo. Also, plantations of coffee, coconut palms, and rubber in Togo were begun mainly by Brazilians before the German colonial government promoted them seriously in the late nineteenth century. And when the French colonial government wanted, in the 1890s, to promote agriculture, it unsuccessfully sought to bring in former slaves from Brazil and other places to accomplish it. See Newbury, *The Western Slave Coast*, 150–55.

31. Clarence H. Haring, *Empire in Brazil: A New World Experiment with Monarchy* (Cambridge: Harvard University Press, 1958), 108–10; Conrad, *The Destruction of Brazilian Slavery* 297.

32. Turner, "Les Bresiliens," 213ff.

33. Ibid., Chap. 4 gives more details on this.

34. Turner, "Some Contacts of Brazilian Ex-slaves with Nigeria West Africa," 60–64; Jerry M. Turner, "Escravos Brasileiros no Daome," in *Afro-Asia* 10–11 (1970):14–15.

35. Quoted in Dantas, *Africa Dificil* 46.

36. *Brazilian Report* (Salvador) 2, 3 (July–August 1962):1.

37. Ibid., 35ff; R.K. Kent, in "African Revolt" argues against such a view.

38. Turner, "Les Bresiliens," 103, 155ff., 168–69, 181–90.

39. Ibid., 207.

24
Garvey and
Scattered Africa

Tony Martin

IN the last few days of the First African Diaspora Studies Institute (FADSI), a debate over the word *diaspora* spontaneously developed. Before I begin my discussion of Garvey I would like to make a simple, straightforward suggestion that the term *diaspora* be deleted from our vocabulary, because the term *African diaspora* reinforces a tendency among those writing our history to see the history of African people always in terms of parallels in white history. On this model of thinking Garvey is called a "black Zionist"; George Padmore, a "black revolutionary"; and Du Bois, a "black titan." There are parallels between black history and white history, of course, but it is unfortunate that blacks do not see our history primarily in its own right. We always seem to be looking for parallels in the experience of other peoples to shape our history. In the old days, other peoples told us we had no history at all; now they acknowledge that we have a history, but only in terms of other peoples' history. So, we should do away with the expression *African diaspora* because we are not Jews. Let us use some other terminology. Let us speak of the African dispersion, or uprooted Africa as somebody suggested, or scattered Africa.

During FADSI, we heard scholars speak about the development of Pan-African consciousness dating back at least to the eighteenth century. They have spoken of slaves and their yearnings to reunite with their African homeland; of persons who helped found Liberia and Sierra Leone; of early Pan-Africanists, like Edward Wilmot Blyden the greatest intellectual figure in the African world of the nineteenth century. They also spoke of Africans from the continent—people like John Chilembwe of Malawi and Kwame Nkrumah of Ghana—who reciprocated this kind of Pan-African activity.

441

Marcus Garvey comes out of this Pan-African tradition. But Garvey was unique in the history of Pan-Africanism in that he reached heights others did not achieve. Garvey did something crucial that those who came before him and those who came after him were unable to do. He was able to gather up all of this Pan-African sentiment, both overt and latent, and channel it into a single, massive, worldwide, highly disciplined organization. Here we have the genius of Marcus Garvey and what stands him apart from other Pan-Africanists, as important as they all are. No one else was able to exploit to such a degree that Pan-African sentiment that has always been manifested among African peoples. I have heard people refer to the Pan-African manifestation as a minority element in Afro-America, for example. I disagree with this. The yearning for a Pan-African relationship has always existed in the Afro-American population as well as in black populations elsewhere. The largest mass movements in the history of Afro-America have had a Pan-African element: the Garvey movement; Elijah Muhammad's movement; the Liberian Exodus Association of South Carolina, which in 1877 attracted some sixty-five thousand freedmen in a matter of three months.

Garvey, then, was able to channel this latent and ever-present Pan-African desire into organization in a very short space of time. And what an organization it was. He appeared in the United States in 1916, and by 1919 he was a world figure. By the mid-1920s he had built an organization that had over 1,100 branches in over forty countries. There is hardly a nook or cranny of the African universe that was not directly organized by the Garvey movement. There were over seven hundred branches in the United States, and, contrary to popular opinion, the place where the Universal Negro Improvement Association (UNIA) branches proliferated most was not in northern cities but in the South. Of the top thirteen or so states, in terms of number of branches per state in the United States, ten were in the South. Louisiana alone had seventy-four branches. Mississippi, West Virginia, Virginia, and North Carolina each had over forty branches. The West Indies had branches in almost every island of any significance. Spanish-speaking areas such as Cuba, Puerto Rico, and the Dominican Republic had branches; the Anglophone West Indies—Trinidad, Jamaica, Antigua, Barbados, St. Thomas, and St. Croix —had branches; the Dutch-speaking Caribbean—Surinam and other islands—had branches; and the French-speaking Caribbean—places like Haiti—had branches.

In South and Central America, too, the UNIA was thoroughly established with well over forty branches in Panama; numerous branches in Costa Rica, Nicaragua, and Guatemala; and one branch each in Brazil, Venezuela, and Ecuador. And on the African continent itself, UNIA was well established. Many people are surprised to discover that in South Africa UNIA had at least eight branches in the 1920s. Namibia had two.

Branches were scattered throughout much of West Africa—Liberia, the Gold Cost (Ghana), and Sierra Leone. Garveyites thrived in the Belgian Congo (Zaire), Kenya, and Uganda. There was hardly a place where black people lived that the Garvey movement did not take root in an organizational form. UNIA established itself even among the small black community in Europe, where branches sprang up in England, Wales, and France. There was even a branch of UNIA as far away as Australia. There were about twelve branches in Canada. So when I say that there was hardly a nook or cranny of the African universe where UNIA did not take root, I am speaking almost literally. That is how Garvey distinguished himself from other Pan-Africanists. He was able to take that Pan-African sentiment and channel it into a massive organization.

Not only was UNIA spread all over the world, it was a Pan-African organization in every sense. At headquarters in Harlem, for example, one could find not only African Americans but persons from a variety of African, West Indian, and other countries. In 1922, Garvey sent a delegation to the League of Nations to plead on behalf of the Africans in Namibia and Tanganyika and the other German colonies. This delegation consisted of four persons—a Haitian, a Sierra Leonean, a Jamaican, and an African American. And this is just a random example, symptomatic of UNIA's real Pan-African nature. In fact, many branches in Afro-America had leaders who were from South Africa, Haiti, and a variety of other places. So this was, indeed, a Pan-African organization in every sense of the word.

And Garvey proved by building this organization that black people, no matter where they lived, were susceptible to a common ideology. They could be organized around a common political program. This is very important. We all know that there are peculiarities and local differences among black communities in different places, but Garvey proved that despite these differences there was an underlying unity—historical, racial, and to some extent cultural—among African peoples.

The three main elements of Garvey's program for organizing black people can be briefly summarized. First, there was the question of race first. Garvey told black people that they must put their racial self-interest first and foremost. Garvey was not a racist. He was simply being realistic. He argued that other races put their own racial self-interest first and foremost. Garvey argued that the white person in America, be he Republican, Democrat, or Socialist, was first and foremost a white person and that if "push came to shove" he would defend his racial interest. Black people would have to do the same, to mobilize themselves along racial lines. In the 1920s, this was a message that black people everywhere wanted to hear and wanted to implement.

The second major plank of Garvey's ideology was that black people should be self-reliant. He was saying this at a time when the race was subjugated everywhere. In Africa, it was a question of the recent conquest as a result of the European scramble for the continent; in Afro-America, it was the recent revival of Jim Crow and the loss of the franchise; in the West Indies, it was discrimination of all kinds. African people everywhere were eager for Garvey's message. Garvey argued that an oppressed people must free itself. Garvey never accepted white philanthropy and amazed his rivals in the United States by obtaining more money from black people than other groups like the NAACP could obtain from their rich philanthropic associates of other races. So black people rallied behind this cry of self-reliance.

Garvey's third major plank—the idea of nationhood—was equally successful in appealing to African people regardless of where they lived. Garvey argued that Africa, the focal point of his nationhood, must be strong and must develop a strong nation. Garvey urged African peoples everywhere to rally behind this plea for African nationhood.

Garvey argued that no race will ever be respected until it is strong. He argued that a strong Africa would lend diplomatic, economic, and moral support to Africans struggling elsewhere. He used to tell a story about Jack Johnson, the heavyweight boxing champion, who went to Australia—and he beat the white man in Australia—and then came back to America—and he beat the white man in America. No matter where he went, Garvey said, Jack Johnson was strong. So if Africa were strong, then Africans, no matter where they lived, could benefit from that strength.

This is the reason why Garvey spent so much time, energy, and money trying to establish a foothold in Liberia especially, and in Africa in general. He wanted Africans to recapture their resources. For Garvey knew full well that Africa was among the world's richest continents in terms of its natural resources. And concomitant with a strong Africa was Garvey's eventual desire for a United States of Africa; that was the term Garvey used. In fact, he once wrote a poem—Garvey was a prolific poet—called "Hail, United States of Africa," in which he mentioned all the countries of Africa. His dream was a strong and united African continent that would be respected in the community of nations.

In building this movement, Garvey had a tremendous impact on nationalist struggles everywhere. It is one thing to say that Garvey's organization had over 1,100 branches in over forty countries, but he actually touched the lives of major African nationalist figures everywhere. Many of the major nationalist figures from the 1930s onward served their apprenticeship, so to speak, in the Garvey movement. In South Africa, for example, Garveyites worked in the hierarchy of the country's two major African organizations of the 1920s—the African National Congress (ANC), formed in 1912, and the Industrial and Commercial Workers Union (ICU), founded by Clements Kadalie in 1919. The chairman of the Industrial and Commercial Workers Union was a Garveyite and a trustee of the Cape Town division of UNIA. Many of the executive committee members of the ICU throughout the 1920s were Garveyites. The ANC newspapers, *African World* and *Abantu Batho*, were major vehicles for the dissemination of Garveyism in South Africa.

In many of the other African countries, too, Garvey had a great influence on nationalist figures. In Kenya in the early 1920s, Harry Thuku, an early pioneer in the Kenyan nationalist movement, was one of those who found inspiration in Garvey and corresponded with him. Jomo Kenyatta, then quite young and radical, was similarly affected and later wrote that he considered himself a Garveyite in the 1920s. In Nigeria, the secretary of the Lagos UNIA in the early twentieth century was Ernest Ikoli, later a well-known figure in the Nigerian Youth Movement and other nationalist organizations.

Garvey's influence was equally felt among African nationalists in America and other countries. Elijah Muhammad, a major figure in the nationalist movement among African Americans from the 1930s to the 1970s, began his political career inside the Garvey movement. Muhammad was a member of UNIA in Detroit, Michigan, in the 1920s. Some of his earliest work for the Nation of Islam, the organization he founded, was done from Liberty Halls, the meeting places of UNIA, in Chicago and Detroit.

In the West Indies, too, Garvey had a similar impact on the early nationalist struggle. In Trinidad, the most important early nationalist movement was the Trinidad Workingmen's Association (TWA). Most of those in TWA were also in the Garvey movement. In 1919, this organization led the workers' struggles in Trinidad. The TWA made Garvey's editorials from his newspaper, the *Negro World*, part of its weekly meetings.

Back in the United States, even Malcolm X was brought up in a UNIA household. His father, as he mentions in his autobiography, was a UNIA organizer in Lansing, Michigan, and in other places. Kimpianga Mahaniah has mentioned the Kimbangu case in the Belgian Congo and the influence of UNIA on Kimbangu. In the Gold Coast, one of the major nationalist figures, J. E. Casely-Hayford, who edited the popular newspaper the *Gold Coast Leader*, also kept in contact with Garvey and frequently praised the Garvey movement in his newspaper. In an article in the *Gold Coast Leader*, Casely-Hayford actually expressed a preference for the Garvey movement over the Pan-African Congress, the movement led by W. E. B. Du Bois.

These are only some of the major figures in the history of nationalism among our people everywhere who were influenced by Garvey. I do not think that there is a single figure who spread his influence as widely, who mobilized as many people, or who directly or indirectly influenced as many important people as did Garvey.

One of the ways of gauging Garvey's impact on the African dispersion was his impact on the imperialists who rallied to form a Pan-Africanism of their own. Garvey's Pan-Africanism called on the mass of African people striving for nationhood and freedom. But to counter Garvey, the imperialists had to come together on an international scale as well. The National Archives of the United States and the Public Record Office in London contain reams of correspondence between the British and the American governments; between the South African and the Belgian governments; and between the French and British governments. There was not a single imperialistic government that was not alarmed by the success of the Garvey movement.

One of the interesting things about Garvey was the depth of his Pan-African background. He was supposed to have been a descendant of the maroons in Jamaica—Africans who escaped slavery and defied the slavery regime for hundreds of years. In his own travels—and Garvey traveled very widely—he lived in many black communities. He traveled all over Latin American and the West Indies and in about eight countries in Europe. He also published in Duse Mohamed Ali's *Africa Times and Orient Review*, one of the major Pan-Africanist journals of the day. Garvey wrote for this journal in London. Another little-known aspect of Garvey's Pan-African background was his wide reading of Pan-African topics. He was an avid reader of African history, and one of his great heroes in terms of historical writings was Edward Wilmot Blyden, the West Indian-born West African statesman and scholar. I have a quotation written in 1915 before Garvey came to the United States, in which he praises Blyden as a historian. In speaking to an audience of Afro-Jamaicans, he said:

> You who do not know anything of your ancestry will do well to read the works of Blyden, one of our historians and chroniclers, who has done so much to retrieve the lost prestige of the race, and to undo the selfishness of alien historians and their history which has said so little and painted us so unfairly.[1]

In terms of Garvey's Pan-African background, he also had direct contact with several leading Pan-Africanists. One of his early mentors was Dr. J. Robert Love, a physician and politician in Jamaica. Love was a man who had studied medicine in the United States, where he had been a very good friend of Henry McNeil Turner, the famous Pan-Africanist bishop of the African Methodist Episcopal Church. Love later moved to Haiti and worked with Bishop James Theodore Holly, another well-known Pan-African figure. Garvey also had very close contact with a sadly neglected, yet important African American figure, John Edward Bruce, who befriended Blyden and corresponded with an amazing array of personalities throughout the African world.

I will end this short discourse with a quotation from Garvey on the question of Africa. This quotation epitomizes Garvey's view of African liberation:

> The white world may despise us;
> The white world may scoff and spurn the idea of
> A free Africa because they say: "How dare you talk
> About Africa when Africa is in the possession of England,
> When Africa is in the possession of France,
> When Africa is in the possession of Spain?"
> What logic have you, Mr. White Man?
> Have you not before you the pages of history
> Recording the rise and fall of peoples, of races and of nations?
>
> White Man, can you not learn by experience?
> Why talk about the permanency of Great Britain in Africa?
> Why talk about the permanency of France in Africa?[2]

NOTES

1. Tony Martin, *Race First: The Ideological and Organizational Struggles of Marcus Garvey and the Universal Negro Improvement Association* (Westport, Conn.: Greenwood Press, 1976), 82.
2. Ibid., 110.

*Toward a
Synthesis*

25
Diaspora Studies and Pan-Africanism

St. Clair Drake

THOSE persons who may have read an article of mine published some years ago in the *Black Scholar* on "The Black Diaspora in Pan-African Perspective" can rest assured that despite the similarity of titles, I shall not simply rehash the ideas presented there and inflict them on you again. It does seem appropriate, however, for me to begin by noting that although the title of that article refers to *the* black diaspora, I pointed out that there had been several diasporas out of sub-Sahara Africa during the past ten thousand years, although I planned to discuss only one in detail—and that is the same one with which I am concerned now. Professor Joseph E. Harris, whose foresight and energy brought us together in 1979 at Howard has, as you know, fascinated us with his publication about the African impact on the subcontinent of India. Professor Frank Snowden has shared his wealth of information about black people living in ancient Greece and Rome and early Christian and "pagan" North Africa. We are, of course, familiar with Ivan Van Sertima's pioneering work on the evidence of a pre-Columbian African impact on the Americas; at the FADSI he discussed the diaspora into Europe, presumably beyond the Mediterranean area. Most of the papers presented at the Diaspora conference, however, dealt with the African diaspora in the Western Hemisphere, and it is to that geographical area that I shall confine my remarks. I shall resist the temptation to talk about Africans and West Indians living in the British Isles about whom I wrote my doctoral dissertation in anthropology many years ago. Professor Folarin O. Shyllon from Ibadan University in Nigeria has given us a comprehensive account in his chapter, "Blacks in Britain: A Historical and Analytical Overview."

Some Parameters of African Diaspora Studies

The term *diaspora* began to gain currency during the mid-1960s among English and American scholars who were studying the black experience as an aspect of African history. Several serious students of the fate of Africans after their dispersal into the Western Hemisphere began to define a subfield within the broader field of African studies. The comprehensive statement of this trend toward giving scholarly recognition to these interests under the rubric "diaspora studies" is the classic paper that Professor George A. Shepperson of Edinburgh read to an international congress of Africanists in Dar es Salaam in 1965. This word of Greek origin that originally referred to the first Babylonian exile of the Jewish people and was later applied to their subsequent tragic dispersions became a popular designation of the fate of sub-Saharan Africans. As we shall mention later, the study of this dispersal into the Western Hemisphere, without the application of the name, had begun within the North American black community in the early nineteenth century and was associated with their struggle to maintain their sense of worth under an oppressive system of chattel slavery. Ironically, it was also a struggle against well-meaning "friends" who opposed slavery but were not willing to accept black men and women as equal partners in the antislavery movement. A genre of literature that might be called "vindicationist," that asserted the capacity and dignity of black men and the worth of their cultures, involved the constant use of historical and social studies of the diaspora as well as of Africa.

After 1791, Haiti became the kind of key symbol in the diaspora that Ethiopia was in Africa and one where "real" history was available for inspiration instead of mythic history. Toussaint L'Ouverture became a hero to black people in the United States, which achieved its independence only twenty-five years before Haiti. Occasional papers (nos. 18 and 19) of the American Negro Academy, published in the 1890s, were on *The Message of St. Domingo to the African Race*. When American marines invaded the country during World War I, the National Association for the Advancement of Colored People mounted a protest movement. And Howard University's distinguished historian, Dr. Rayford Logan, who was honored last night,* numbers among his many works a volume published by the University of North Carolina Press in 1941, *The Diplomatic Relations of the United States in Haiti*. It was among the intellectuals of Haiti during the 1920s that the literary movement, with a

---

*The honorees at the FADSI were Rayford W. Logan and Mercer Cook, Professors Emeriti, Howard University; Dorothy Porter, Librarian Emerita, Howard University; St. Clair Drake, Professor Emeritus, Stanford University (Ed.).

magazine named from the West African bards, *Griots,* under the leadership of Drs. Jean Price-Mars and Duvalier, first sounded the call for a black aesthetic that later assumed the name *negritude.* Haiti, even more than Liberia and Ethiopia—and there were only these three until Ghana became independent in 1957—was the treasured symbol of black sovereignty. It has a special place in the design of diaspora studies taking shape as an aspect of traditional Pan-African activity. Why Haiti has never realized its full potential despite its immense contributions to black liberation would be one important inquiry.

Both the phrasing of my topic and the theme of the sessions held at the FADSI on conceptual and contextual parameters imply that some diaspora studies are carried out within other frames of reference than the one that I am proposing to define as traditional Pan-African activity. A concept of the black world is necessary in defining Pan-African activity. It would include all of those areas where the population is actually black in a phenotypic sense, that is, Negroid, or where the people think of themselves as black despite considerable miscegenation, or where they are so defined by others. For almost a century, a conscious and deliberate movement has been developing within various parts of the black world to increase cultural contacts between its diverse segments and to unite them in the pursuit of common interests. I refer to this as traditional Pan-African activity. *For diaspora studies to be considered an aspect of this activity, an aspect operating in the cultural sector of it, they must contribute toward maintaining and reinforcing black consciousness and must be oriented toward the goal of fostering understanding, solidarity, and cooperation throughout the black world.* Some diaspora studies make no such contribution.

Pan-African apolitical activity can be traced back into the eighteenth century, but Pan-African political activity has been concentrated between the years 1900 and 1958—a terminal that I shall discuss later. During that span of years, Pan-African political activity developed as a series of local, highly specific struggles against discrimination based on race and color, sometimes overt, sometimes covert, and against material and psychological legacies of the slave trade. *What makes the activity Pan-African is the conceptualization on the part of the participants in these local struggles of their being part of a larger worldwide activity involving black people everywhere, with the various segments having obligations and responsibilities to each other.* This concept is certainly not dead as witness the relatively high level of support from within the Afro-American community for the Patriotic Front in Zimbabwe or the organization of Trans-Africa to coordinate Afro-American support for completing the struggle against white supremacy regimes in Africa and for aid to independent African states that express a need for it. On 3 April 1980, for instance, the New Jersey Coalition of Black Student Organizations held a conference on southern Africa at Princeton University around the theme Black America—Southern Africa: Same Struggle, Same Fight. The United Nations ambassador from Ghana attended.

The most sophisticated of what I am calling the traditional Pan-Africanists see their struggles as not only involving black people everywhere but also as being organically related to Third World struggles generally and to the worldwide struggle of proletariat and peasantry regardless of race. But they visualize the struggle of black people as organically related *to*, not subsumed *under*, these other struggles. This is the difference between the courageous and dedicated Martinican, Frantz Fanon, who chose to operate at the more general level and wrote *The Wretched of the Earth* while immersed in the fight for Algerian independence, and the Trinidadian George Padmore, who became an advisor to Kwame Nkrumah and chose his battleground in "black" Africa. Both men would have agreed, however, that black people need to maintain a high level of race consciousness in their local situations, Fanon stressing the temporary, tactical nature of such consciousness raising. Both would have cautioned against allowing black consciousness to degenerate into reverse racism, black chauvinism, and xenophobia hiding behind race solidarity. Above all they opposed the use of race solidarity as a shield for black exploiters. Neither saw any need to apologize for race solidarity, although Fanon was much more concerned than Padmore about the eventual complete working out of the dialectical paradigm implicit in his *Black Skin, White Masks*, namely, "White 'brain-washing' can only be overcome by acceptance of *negritude*, the black antithesis to a white thesis, thus negating the negation. But eventually there should be a movement from the point of negativity toward a synthesis, a point when one says, 'I do not want to be either black nor white, but only a human being.'"

As long as an educated and wealthy Nigerian can be "Jim Crowed" in Johannesburg on his own ancestral continent or can still see a Ku Klux Klan cross burning in Mississippi, or until Africans have their proportionate share of posts on the great corporations that control their economies, or until one sees a few black faces among the top elites throughout the Arab world and in Hispanic America and Brazil where they are more rare now than in the racist United States, mobilization *as blacks* is still necessary. In 1966, I published an article entitled "Hide My Face? An Essay on Pan-Africanism and Negritude." I preceded it with words from a spiritual, "I ran to the rocks to hide my face and the rocks cried out 'No hiding place!'" I had just read about some Afro-American tourists being physically attacked by youths in Rome who shouted at them, "This is for murdering our nuns in the Congo!" These could have been some very conservative anti-Lumumba, pro-Tshombe black Americans. To the Italian youths, however, they were only symbols of generalized blackness. With mobs screaming in Notting Hill and Brixton "Keep Britain White," with Chinese men attacking African students for consorting with Chinese girls, and with the great battle against racism in South Africa yet to come, not to mention the "blacklash" in the United States, demobilization of international black solidarity, such as it is, would seem to be very premature. Worldwide black consciousness is a psychological reserve that can be mobilized to achieve local ends as well as to aid others as the liberation process continues on. This consciousness has not been awakened primarily by deliberate propaganda campaigns of Pan-African organizations. The sights and sounds conveyed by the mass media for the ends of others arouse black consciousness as a by-product. And so the collectively shared symbols of the black world have come to include a Steve Biko, a Malcolm X, and a Martin Luther King, Jr., as well as the poets of the Harlem Renaissance and of negritude. And within the pop culture there is a galaxy of greats ranging from Muhammed Ali and the magnificent track stars of East Africa, to Arthur Ashe and Yannick Noah in the tennis world, to the singers of jazz and gospel and the blues, of reggae, calypso and the high life, and brilliant performers on Africa's drums in both the Old World and the New.

Cultural Interpenetration

Diaspora studies should, of course, include an analysis of the processes and implications involved in the mutual interpenetration of homeland cultures and diaspora cultures. Our cultural leaders continuously remind us that the conservation of black music and dance, song and folklore, and written literature does not serve only political ends. Cultural products, expressing as they do the "soul" of ethnic groups, have a *raison d'etre* of their own; they also contribute to what Senghor calls "the civilization of the universal." People express themselves because they like to, because they enjoy doing so. Cultural products do not have to be justified by their contribution either to black survival or to black liberation, but they also have functions in relation to these ends that should not be ignored. The debate between cultural nationalists and revolutionary nationalists that has proceeded not only in Harlem but also at conferences in Africa where Senghor's words have been pitted against Sekou Toure's needs sober evaluation, but its very existence is a healthy phenomenon. It signifies that culture is deemed relevant. It has surfaced in another form in Castro's Cuba, where charges have been made that African culture is being gradually strangled in favor of a revolutionary culture that finds no place for it. Analysis of the controversy provides a challenge for diaspora studies, as does the charge that the Brazilian establishment favors traditional African culture as exemplified by *candomblé* and *macumba* because it is a barrier against revolution in the *favelas*. Scholars from these Western Hemisphere nations working with African counterparts might assess the allegations and evaluate the findings from several perspectives, including the Pan-African perspective.

From a Pan-Africanist perspective, intellectual work is not always given the important role that we assign to it. A freedom fighter on his stomach slithering through the mud in Namibia tonight might not have much sympathy with our deliberations at this conference. A Soweto school boy fleeing to the Botswana border after the great rebellion might look askance at his school fellows whose only concern was securing high grades. All of us are indebted to the courage and the sacrifices of the freedom fighters, but many factors determine how we fight and also determine temperament and intellectual inclinations that make us one kind of person or another. Also, time, place, and context are important in assessing the social importance of any kind of intellectual activity. There is, in addition, a necessary division of labor in the field of traditional Pan-African activity, and those who have assumed the cultural tasks need not apologize for their disciplined devotion to those pursuits. Commitment is expressed by them through choice of problem and style of work, not dexterity with weaponry.

The Black Scholar as Craftsman: Comparative Biography

Not all African scholars and scholars of African descent wish to carry out diaspora studies that are directly related to traditional Pan-African activity. This is certainly their right, but their studies nevertheless often contribute toward Pan-African goals by the very nature of their subject matter and the use to which what they produce is put. Other scholars in the diaspora have concentrated on studies of the homeland, not of the diaspora in which they live and work. For some of these, their traditional Pan-African activity takes place outside of the framework of their scholarly work, and their life histories provide significant data for students of Pan-Africanism in the diaspora. A most distinguished example is Professor Elliott P. Skinner, who was born in Trinidad but emigrated to the United States at an early age. His doctoral dissertation in anthropology was a valuable study of village life in Guyana that illuminates the nature of relationships between persons of East Indian descent and those of African descent. He then decided to enter the field of African studies and has given us two outstanding books, *The Mossi of Upper Volta* and *A Glorious Age in Africa*, as well as a reader, *Peoples and Cultures of Africa*. Dr. Skinner served as United States ambassador to Upper Volta and then returned to become the Franz Boas Professor of Anthropology at Columbia University. He will be remembered by Pan-Africanists, however, for two activities that are indirectly related to his own research or diplomatic career. He founded an organization for mobilizing financial assistance to the West African nations that were ravaged by the drought in the Sahel, and he helped to organize African-American Scholars, Inc., an agency for assembling funds to make it possible for African and Afro-American scholars to carry out joint research projects in Africa that contribute toward African development as well as for some Afro-American scholars to pursue such research alone. At this conference, Professor Skinner is assisting us in clarifying our conceptual apparatus for carrying out diaspora studies, drawing, in part, on his own detailed study of "stranger" groups within Africa itself. I cite Professor Skinner's work at some length because I want to make very clear my own belief that the field of diaspora studies involves the cooperation of scholars who are interested in Pan-African activity—or they would not be here—although the major focus of their own scholarly work may not be diaspora studies. Their careers merit study and presentation as models for youth throughout the black world.

A number of black scholars in the Caribbean segment of the diaspora have combined research teaching in Africa with similar pursuits in the diaspora. One who would certainly not claim to be working within the framework of traditional Pan-African activity but whose work has had a profound effect on those activities is Sir Arthur Lewis, one of the world's outstanding Keynesian economists, a native of the West Indian island of St. Lucia and the first black man to hold a university chair in Britain, the prestigious post in economics at the University of Manchester. He is now on the faculty at Princeton University in the United States. At one point he served as theoretician for the British Labor Party, but he also paid his Pan-African dues on numerous occasions. He served twice in Ghana drawing up development plans and took time out to serve as head of the Caribbean Development Bank when the nations of that area inaugurated that cooperative venture. He also served as vice chancellor of the University of the West Indies during the period when a decision was made to carry out a sympathetic study of the problems of the Rastafarians. Are there possibilities, as time goes on, of academic figures at African universities playing similar roles in relationship to the study of implementation of development plans in the Caribbean?

The amazing career of that elder statesman of the black left, C.L.R. James, includes the writing of a substantial volume on the history of the Russian revolution, the definitive translation of Souvarine's biography of Stalin, as well as the work Pan-Africanists all know and treasure, *The Black Jacobins*. And he wrote a novel before entering politics and still remains an expert on cricket. It is sometimes forgotten that C.L.R. James was a member of the official family that administered the short-lived Federation of the British West Indies. Advanced in age, he sounded the call for the Sixth Pan-African Congress that met in Tanzania in 1974. In thinking of Caribbean personalities to whom the youth of Africa might eventually be exposed as a result of publications emanating from a conference such as this, Walter Rodney, a native of Guyana, also comes to mind. He wrote a doctoral dissertation that destroyed some of the myths about the slave trade in Upper Guinea. Later, while teaching at the University of the West Indies, he wrote a book called *Groundings with My Brothers*, in which he introduces the novel but sensible idea that black consciousness and black power in the Caribbean should not refer only to the people that colonial systems designated as black, but to all of the colored who are exploited—the East Indians, the mulattoes, and whatever other disinherited people would accept the "black" identity. Still later, he taught at the University of Dar es Salaam and wrote the influential book, *How Europe Underdeveloped Africa*. Recently he was associated with the Working Peoples Alliance in Guyana that is bringing together East Indians, blacks, and Native Americans in a movement demanding democratic socialism. Black political leaders may have considered Rodney a thorn in the flesh, but the peasants and workers of Jamaica, Tanzania, and Guyana knew he stood for their welfare.

Finally, mention might be made of a Barbadian, Edward Braithwaite, who spent twelve years as an education officer in Ghana and then earned his doctoral degree from the University of London, where he wrote a dissertation on Creolization in Jamaica. His great contribution to the Pan-African aspect of diaspora studies has come through his poetry, a trilogy, *Masks, Islands*, and *Rights of Passage*. In "Journeys," a poem in the latter volume, he wrote:

> Soft winds
> to San Salvador, Christoph-
> er, Christ, and no Noah
> or dove to promise us, grim
> though it was, the simple sal-
> vation of love. And so it was Little
> Rock, Dal-

las, New Orleans, Santiago
de Cuba, the miles of
unfortunate islands....
Then Capetown and Rio....

Braithwaite is frankly and aggressively Pan-African in the traditional sense; Rodney's Pan-Africanism is tempered more by the Third World orientation that life in Guyana or Trinidad imposes; Arthur Lewis prefers to work in a mainstream where his unusual talent has opened up unusual opportunities.

Comparative biography should be an important component of diaspora studies. The diverse and fascinating personalities are spread over a vast area of time and space. There are problems of devising criteria of significance, economy in choice, and format of presenting that present a challenge. It might be noted that Professor Harris, who convened this conference, has produced a very readable short biography of an East African personality. The *Encyclopedia Africana* represents a cooperative effort at assembling biographical details on prominent persons of the past. There are less prominent but significant individuals in local situations that need to be written about by scholars. A similar task is facing students of the black diaspora, especially for Hispanic America and Brazil.

What Is "Traditional" Pan-African Activity?

Ethos of the Tradition

Up to this point I have been using the expression *traditional Pan-African activity* without explaining what I mean by *traditional*. I am implying that there is some kind of Pan-African activity that is not traditional and that I am not discussing that kind of activity. All of us are, of course, familiar with the term *Pan-African*, which, over the years, has come to be associated with the activities of such individuals as Dr. W. E. B. Du Bois, the Afro-American scholar; Blaise Diagne of Senegal, French deputy during the time of World War I without whose aid the 1919 Pan-African conference could not have been called; or Kwame Nkrumah, who gave the term such wide currency after World War II. Although it has become a dirty word in some leftist circles, such as the Fourth International Spartacists, it still has high positive emotional effect for most politically conscious Africans and people of African descent.

When I use the term *traditional* to describe the variety of Pan-Africanism about which I am speaking, I am referring to the central focus of Pan-Africanism prior to the mid-1950s and especially before the publication of a very influential book that was published in England in 1955, George Padmore's *Pan-Africanism or Communism*? (That question mark was behind the title in the original Dobson edition.) This book constituted the ideological base for Nkrumah and Padmore in developing the philosophy underlying two conferences that met in Ghana in 1958, the First Conference of Independent African States in April and the All-African Peoples Conference in December. Kwame Nkrumah was at the height of his popularity and influence and was considered the virtual symbol of Pan-Africanism as Afro-Americans and West Indians understood the term. His country had achieved independence in 1957 after six years of partial self-government, during which he achieved high visibility. I remember the occasion of his visit in June 1951 when he delivered the convocation address at Lincoln University and received an L.L.D. degree. At the reception his old classmates almost lifted him from the floor as they rejoiced. His doctoral citation stated that "You have twisted the lion's tail. The British may call you Leader of Government Business but you are Prime Minister to us." He was made prime minister a short period thereafter. Then, between the two conferences in 1958, I heard him speak in the U.S. Armory in Harlem to almost ten thousand people, inviting them to come to Africa as teachers and technicians. He was presented with a silver bowl on behalf of the people of Harlem as a symbol: "the vessel that has caught the tears of all the mothers of Africa weeping as their children were torn from them and sent across the ocean." A few months later, at the All-African Peoples Conference, Nkrumah said with great warmth that he was glad to see so many West Indians and Afro-Americans present:

> We take their presence here as a manifestation of their keen interest in our struggle for a free Africa. We must never forget that they are part of us. These sons and daughters of Africa were taken from our shores and despite all centuries which have separated us they have not forgotten their ancestral links.... Many of them have made no small contribution to the cause of African freedom. Names which spring immediately to mind in this connection are Marcus Garvey and Dr. W. E. B. Du Bois.

A year after Nkrumah's Harlem visit and his speaking these words, George Padmore died. I sat and watched and listened as Nkrumah delivered the funeral oration from a verandahlike portion of Christianborg Castle high up over the Gulf of Guinea where the surf was relentlessly pounding in as it had done for centuries. Down below were the dungeons where slaves had been held while awaiting shipment out through that surf and across the ocean. Nkrumah recited the history of Padmore's life and spoke of his first meeting with him that developed into the indescribable relationship that exists only between brothers. Then Nkrumah made a statement that was part of one of the most moving scenes I ever witnessed during a decade of intermittent residence in Africa:

> Who knows but from this very spot his ancestors were carried out across the ocean there while the kinsmen stood weeping here as silent sentinels. We have brought his ashes "home to rest."

The plaque beneath the urn reads: "He loved Africa more than life. Requiescat in pace." Dr. Du Bois died in Ghana a few years later and after a state funeral was buried just outside the walls of the castle. These gestures were not just personal idiosyncrasies of one African nationalist leader. Laden with multiple layers of meaning, they symbolized the culmination of the historic trend that I am referring to as *traditional Pan-Africanism*—unity of sentiment and action between individuals in Africa and the diaspora. Similar gestures will never occur again, for they signaled the end of an epoch.

I saw one more such gesture—in 1966, at the First Festival of Negro Arts in Dakar—that was even more significant because it crossed barriers of language as well as space and time. The event was a reception given by President Leopold Senghor for the participants in the festival. The Afro-American dancer, Katherine Dunham, had been employed as an adviser on choreography to the Senegal government. She escorted the ninety-one-year old Haitian founder of the Society of African Culture, the spiritual father of *Presence Africaine* and the festival, the venerable Jean Price-Mars, to be received by the poet-president, Senghor. The symbolism was not lost on the assembled throng. The festival occurred eight years after the two conferences. Why, then, do I say that an epoch in traditional Pan-Africanism was ending? In the first place, the period of uncomplicated united struggle to secure independence from the white oppressor ended for each colony as it became a nation. Diaspora blacks had to decide which of various political factions, if any, within the new nations they would support. Second, a coup in Nigeria in 1966, followed soon thereafter by one on Ghana that overthrew Dr. Nkrumah's regime and sent him into exile, began a parade to the seats of power of military men who had no allegiance to the kind of sentimental Pan-Africanism described above and who were without any previous experience in dealing with West Indians and Afro-Americans. Finally, the shift toward armed struggle in southern Africa posed problems for many Afro-Americans who had enthusiastically supported Nkrumah's "nonviolent positive action." The festival of 1966 signaled the fact that *cultural* Pan-Africanism would henceforth provide a broader basis of identification and cooperative endeavor in the black world than *political* Pan-Africanism and that the initiative for both aspects had passed completely from the diaspora to Africa.

The stories I have related about Kwame Nkrumah and the First Festival of Negro Arts illustrate the ethos of *traditional* Pan-Africanism, a phenomenon that has been accorded a more accurate designation, perhaps, in the subtitle to Hollis Lynch's biography of Edward Wilmot Blyden. He refers to him as a "Pan-Negro patriot." Traditional Pan-Africanism was the attempt by those who had been defined by others in a derogatory and demeaning way as the blacks, les noirs, sale negre, and niggers, as speakers of pretoguese instead of Portuguese, to assert their dignity and their defiance. Most of them lived in the African heartland, in sub-Saharan Africa stretching southward from the savannah land the Arabs had named *bilad al Sudan, land of the blacks*. But millions were also scattered throughout the Western Hemisphere, constituting what the great Jamaican who tried to organize the whole black world called "the beloved and scattered millions" and what in more recent years we have been calling the peoples of the black diaspora. Traditional Pan-Africanism consciously and deliberately attempts to create bonds of solidarity based on a commonality of fate imposed by the transatlantic slave trade and its aftermath. The initiative originally came from "the beloved and scattered millions" because it was they who needed the psychological reinforcement of identification with a homeland most. However, from the 1890s on through the 1920s, initiatives from South Africa seeking various kinds of support from Afro-Americans became important. Professor Shepperson and his students are engaged in exciting pioneering scholarship on Afro-American contacts with southern and eastern Africa over this span of years.

The term *Pan-Africanism* gained currency during the first half of the twentieth century because of the spread of knowledge in Africa, the West Indies, Paris, London, Brussels, and Lisbon about a series of conferences that were convened at the initiative of a group of black intellectuals in the Anglophone areas of the Western Hemisphere. The first conference was convened in London in 1900 by a lawyer from Trinidad, Sylvester Williams. It had a continuation committee that functioned more to keep consciousness alive than to make protests. Then in 1919, Dr. W. E. B. Du Bois, a United States citizen, persuaded the National Association for the Advancement of Colored People to finance a meeting at Versailles. It ran concurrently with the peace conference after World War I that is often called the first Pan-African conference. In 1921 came a third, convened by Dr. Du Bois, and then a fourth in 1927 that he called and that the National Association of Colored Women of the United States paid for. This one was held in New York. These conferences were political in intent; they produced manifestos and protest delegations asking for the elimination of racial discrimination on the basis of race and color everywhere and for the gradual movement toward self-government in the Caribbean and Africa. They did not challenge imperialism and capitalism directly nor the principle of interracial cooperation.

The term *Pan-Africanism* is usually restricted to this group of conferences associated with Sylvester Williams and W. E. B. Du Bois, but it was quite arbitrary not to include the older black nationalist political tradition with which the names Martin Delany and Edward Wilmot Blyden are associated, as well as the emigrationist, Paul Cuffe, of the early nineteenth century. This variety of Pan-Africanism culminated during the 1920s in Marcus Garvey's Universal Negro Improvement Association (UNIA). These black nationalist leaders did not challenge capitalism as a system for organizing production, and some of them were willing to cooperate with American and European imperialists in realizing their goals. Garvey, however, insisted on "Africa for the Africans at Home and Abroad." Blyden was a defender of African cultures although he preferred them in an Islamic form. Garvey exhibited very little appreciation for contemporary African cultures, although the glories of ancient Egypt and Ethiopia assumed great symbolic import for the UNIA movement. What all of these leaders had in common was their insistence on unity among Africans, West Indians, and Afro-Americans in the struggle against racial derogation and for some degree of autonomy from white control, not a common admiration for African cultures.

Pan-Africanism with a "small p"

An extension of the term *Pan-Africanism*, even beyond the boundaries of political and quasi-political activity led by race-conscious intellectuals, has been suggested by Professor George Shepperson, who in a seminal article that appeared in 1962 in the journal *Phylon*, published by Atlanta University, suggested that we not ignore the Pan-Africanism with a small *p* that antedated organized political Pan-Africanism by at least a century and perhaps more, and flourished between their sporadic conferences. He was referring to the activities of individuals and groups that kept alive the memory of African origins, to churches in North America that sent missionaries to Africa, and to informal activities of various sorts. *Indeed, this FADSI conference in which we are participating is one expression of Pan-Africanism with a "small p"—it has ends that are not political and is part of a people-to-people approach to transatlantic relations among black people.* Any convocation of black scholars from Africa, the West Indies, and the United States constitutes in itself one aspect of traditional Pan-African activity and, insofar as it will be discussing diaspora studies, is an important continuation of an activity with roots that have considerable antiquity.

Some Characteristic Features of Traditional Pan-Africanism

Given the very restricted base on which the Pan-African conferences of 1900, 1919, 1921, 1923, and 1927 rested and even the very small number of people involved in the International African Service Bureau that George Padmore, T. Ras Makonnen, and Jomo Kenyatta kept alive in Britain between 1935 and 1945, it is evident that pan-Africanism with the small *p* has had greater sociological significance than the small groups of intellectuals and politicians, as important as they were in carrying forward the African revolt against imperialism. It was the widespread existence in South Africa and the United States of a church-based ideology that is called "Ethiopianism" that created the apperceptive mass to which Garvey was able to appeal during the 1920s. The Universal Negro Improvement Association secularized Ethiopianism. It is not without significance that the anthem of UNIA was called "The Ode to Ethiopia" and that speakers from the Liberty Hall platforms in various cities frequently quoted the psalm, "Princes shall come out of Egypt and Ethiopia shall soon stretch forth her hands unto God." The black church in the United States can be analyzed as having institutionalized a form of pan-Africanism early in the nineteenth century without ever calling it that.

Pan-Africanism with the small *p*, like political Pan-Africanism, had its origins in the Western Hemisphere, and until the mid-eighteenth century, found expression primarily in symbolic affirmations of an African identity, usually expressed in ethnic terms, a clinging to the selfhood of being Ibo or Yoruba or Congo or Angola or Coromantee, while elaborating institutions that were syncretistic in a double sense, merging customs of many ethnic groups into something called African that, in turn, had absorbed European cultural elements. From the mid-eighteenth century to the mid-nineteenth, the antislavery movement included some free blacks and mulattoes in its ranks, but at the same time, some individuals in these groups were beginning to develop relations with Africans and people of African descent outside of their own homelands.

The years between the freeing of the slaves in the United States and the outbreak of World War I involved extensive relations between Africans and Afro-Americans under the auspices of the African Methodist Episcopal Church; the African Methodist Episcopal Church, Zion; the National Baptist Convention, U.S.A.; the National Baptist

Convention, Inc.; the Lott Carey Baptist Convention, and several white mission boards. Black colleges and universities also became the meeting ground for African and Afro-American students. Tuskegee, Hampton, Lincoln, Fisk, Howard, Wilberforce, and Livingstone made a significant contribution toward the training of young Africans during these years. This was Pan-African activity, as was, too, the sending of individuals to Africa by Tuskegee during the early years of the twentieth century to teach cotton growing.

World War II marked the end of this long period, during which the impact of North American blacks on Africa was greater than the impact of Africans on Afro-Americans. I think it can be demonstrated that this reversal of influence began with the emergence of independent African states, when African students and visitors were less dependent on blacks, and white America discovered Africa.

No comprehensive synthesizing volume on pan-Africanism with the small *p* can be written until the impact of West Indians on British and French African colonies has been studied with the kind of detail that Professor Shepperson and the Edinburgh scholars have given to the Afro-American impact, and until we have a clearer picture of relations between blacks in Hispanic Africa and Brazil with Africa during and after slavery.

The most distinctive characteristic of traditional Pan-Africanism has been its emphasis on fostering solidarity between all black people everywhere. Both cultural and political activity have always been present, with the former reinforcing the latter. Essien-Udom, the Nigerian political scientist, speaks in one of his perceptive articles about the vanguardism of Afro-Americans prior to World War II, and Leopold Senghor has given them the credit for inaugurating negritude, even though they did not use the term. Since 1945, African nationalist leaders have been in the forefront of the movement toward *continental* Pan-Africanism but much of the institutional expression of traditional Pan-Africanism has come from a talented and energetic group of French-speaking scholars from both Africa and the Caribbean, who organized the *Society for African Culture*, convened conferences of black writers in Paris and Rome, and founded *Présence Africaine*. Alioune Diop, editor of that journal, has stated that these proponents of negritude saw the need to reaffirm on the international level, "the presence of ethos of the black communities of the world and to defend the originality of their way of life and the dignity of their culture." Senghor has emphasized the point repeatedly that this culture must be viewed as having a distinctive contribution to make to the culture of the universal, which is made up of many diverse strands. The solidarity, in the final analysis, has to be based on common interests not common values, for diversity of tribe, class, religion, and culture abounds. Yet all of the peoples of the diaspora and most of those in the homeland have been on the receiving end of racial discrimination, and this has generated some common responses. But what Senghor calls negritude refers to life-styles and symbolic statements handed down from generation to generation as African groups have migrated about the continent, dividing and subdividing, modifying the original culture inheritance, but never destroying its basic core of values. The peoples of the diaspora carried these values and customary behavior that embodied them across the Atlantic where further modification occurred. During the twentieth century (and occasionally even before that) black intellectuals have stressed the existence of what they consider a unique Negro way of confronting the world as an aid to increasing solidarity for action. Anthropologically trained scholars insist that persistence and spread of negritude is entirely a matter of cultural transmission, that genetic inheritance has nothing to do with the matter at all.

The cultural component in traditional Pan-African activity is easier to organize and sustain than the political component. Even that, however, has its dilemmas and contradictions, as the Festival of African and Black Arts (FESTAC) in Nigeria during 1978 revealed. There were those who thought Arabs should not participate; they had no negritude to offer. There was a dispute over the Brazilian deputation that included whites and insisted that a paper with a strong black thrust not be accepted for the colloquium. Yet, the significant point is that Nigeria, the largest African nation, sponsored the festival and gave it a Pan-Negro emphasis even though other racial groups participated. FESTAC was significant because the elites in the new independent African states do not have the same need for moral and financial support from diaspora black peoples that their nationalist leaders sometimes had before attaining power, and they do have to work for continental unity. Pan-African political activity, as opposed to cultural activity, is made more difficult, too, by the ideological differentiation on the continent since 1966. The rise of left-wing and right-wing dictatorships has confused and alienated many friends of Africa in the diaspora. Most can avoid making a political commitment of an ideological sort, however, when participating in an event like FESTAC. They can, too, in participating in a conference like this one or in working for the institutionalization of diaspora studies in Africa and continued contacts between intellectuals in the homeland and the diaspora. But scholars, as well as artists, are working within a quite different climate from that of pre-1966 Africa, prior to the era of the coups, when traditional Pan-Africanism was given higher value by influential African elites than it is today.

As diaspora studies take root in the homeland, some division of labor may be necessary. Some types of research, teaching, and public education about blacks in the Western Hemisphere will be feasible and/or appropriate in some political contexts and not in others. (Indeed, at times, some scholars may have to work in exile, not at home, and those at home may have to work under self-imposed restraints.) I can think of some African countries, not represented at the FADSI conference, where diaspora studies involving blacks in North America will probably be subject to considerable monitoring and may have to "tow an official line." This is not a conference at which discussion of this topic is appropriate. It should not, however, be forgotten. At a subliminal level we must remember Abdias Nascimento of Brazil, Ngugi wa Thiong'o of Kenya, Walter Rodney of Guyana, and Manigat of Haiti as well as many others in both the diaspora and the homeland, including even people like Frank Yerby, Richard Wright, and Willard Motley, black Americans who did not feel that they could live and work in the United States. We are not discussing any of our exiled, detained, imprisoned, or silenced intellectuals, but there is an obligation on us to keep their names alive in our footnotes at least. They must not be forgotten as living examples of some aspects of black history—diaspora and homeland—working themselves out over centuries.

Another distinctive characteristic of traditional Pan-Africanism, one that has been under question since the middle of the 1960s, was a willingness to cooperate with people of all races in intellectual and political endeavors if they did not attempt to hamper the development of black leadership or try to "lay down a line" as to what goals and strategies were proper for black liberation. Black people would have their own organizations but would also belong to other interracial organizations of their choice. They would also choose as collaborators white people with congenial ideas and attitudes. For instance, the membership of the American Society of African Culture (AMSAC) was made up of "men and women of culture of African descent," but the pages of its journal, *African Forum*, were open to contributors without regard to race. The conference from which the publication *Pan-Africanism Reconsidered* was derived had white as well as black participants, but it was an AMSAC conference. Carter Woodson had established this principle when he founded the *Journal of Negro History* in 1916, and it was the policy of *Phylon*, a scholarly journal founded by Dr. Du Bois at Atlanta University. *Présence Africaine* had a few French savants on its board of editors when it was established. This pattern of interracial participation was denounced as integrationist by the black nationalists of the 1960s, but this seems to have been only a stage—and perhaps a necessary one—in the North American Afro-black mobilization process.

Traditional Pan-Africanism included within its ranks individuals of diverse political orientations, and this involved some degree of participation by Pan-African leaders in other movements that were interracial. In England, George Padmore worked with Maxton's Independent Labor Party, and C.L.R. James worked with groups affiliated with the Fourth International, both there and in the United States. Other members of the Pan-African Federation inner circle were close to the Fabian society, the Labor Party, and the movement for Colonial Freedom. Marcus Garvey represented the other extreme that repudiated any kind of close ties with nonblack political organizations, particularly if they were socialist in outlook, but he was willing to seek support from the Ku Klux Klan in the United States in carrying out a program of parallel action that would help to secure federal assistance for Afro-Americans wishing to emigrate to Africa.

During the 1970s the polarization among Pan-Africanists in the diaspora became extreme with one group of black nationalists taking a "plague on all your Marxist houses" position while Amiri Baraka (LeRoi Jones) moved to the position of calling for the organization of an "interracial communist party" based on Marxist-Leninist Mao Tse-tung thought. Middle-class Afro-Americans, trying to take a middle position, had already been bewildered and dismayed when Nkrumah said in a book written from his exile in Guinea that:

> The African revolutionary struggle is not an isolated one. It not only forms part of the world socialist revolution, but must be seen in the context of the Black Revolution as a whole. In the U.S.A., the Caribbean and wherever Africans are oppressed, liberation struggles are being fought.... The total liberation and the unification of Africa under an All-African socialist government must be the primary objective of all Black revolutionaries throughout the world. It will at the same time advance the triumph of the international socialist revolution and the onward progress toward world communism.

Diaspora studies must include an analysis of these significant ideological shifts and their implications for those in the diaspora who claim to be traditional Pan-Africanism. How wonderful it would be if Professor Essien-Udom could write a book for us on the transformation of the Black Muslims into the world community of Islam in the West.

Up to this point I have not described the kind of Pan-Africanism that I am contrasting with traditional Pan-Africanism. It is the kind whose entry onto the stage of history was heralded by Padmore's book *Pan-Africanism or Communism?* and that took on actual political content at the First Conference of Independent African States in April 1958. It is the dominant type of Pan-Africansim today and has placed traditional

Pan-Africanism in the political sphere very much on the defensive. It should never be forgotten that when that conference was called, there were only eight independent African states, exclusive of South Africa, which Africans did not consider African. Four of these did not consider themselves black nations—Egypt, Libya, Morocco, and Tunisia; only two were indubitably black—Ghana and Liberia; two were ambivalent and undecided—Sudan and Ethiopia. Black people who did not reside in Ethiopia had always made it their key symbol of black independence and sovereignty, but the Solomonic dynasty did not always accept that designation with enthusiasm. If securing unity of action of the eight was an objective, Nkrumah and Padmore were not going to attain it with black solidarity slogans. In fact a negritude ideology was dysfunctional to that continental unity to which Nkrumah gave priority. It is no accident that projecting the African personality, not expressing negritude, was the stated aim of the conference. The ground had been prepared for this in Padmore's 1956 book when he defined an African as anyone regardless of race, color, creed, tribe, or nationality who believed in one man, one vote, and economic, political, and social equality. *In my own writing about these matters during the 1960s I suggested that the term* racial Pan-Africanism *be used to refer to what I am now calling* traditional Pan-Africanism *and the term* continental Pan-Africanism *be used for efforts to unite all Africans in Africa.* Racial Pan-Africanism and *continental* Pan-Africanism are not always compatible. There is a constant dialectical interplay between them that sometimes results in contradictions that must be resolved. A case in point was the Sixth Pan-African Congress in 1974, meeting in Dar es Salaam.

Nkrumah had always been adept at keeping continental Pan-Africanism central but not neglecting what he conceived of as the legitimate concern of Africans for the fate of people in the diaspora. The organizers of the Sixth Pan-African Congress had to face problems he had never had to deal with. Delegates from the diaspora thought that the conference had downgraded its racial responsibilities too much when it passed a resolution criticizing skin color politics and seated white delegates from Cuba. Many were furious, too, when they were rebuked for not making overtures to white workers in the United States. It was clear that an enclaved black minority within the most powerful capitalist nation on earth where racism was rampant within the working class was not seeing problems from the same perspective that representatives of sovereign states, especially those with a Marxist orientation on a continent that was predominantly black were.

The leaders of the African sovereign states had voiced an expression of concern for the fate of Afro-Americans at the founding conference of the Organization of African Unity. That was not enough, however, for those Pan-Africanists who stressed the unity of the entire black world and for whom Africa was home. Tom Mboya once, when speaking in Harlem, created considerable hostility in the audience when he suggested that Afro-Americans should not fantasize about a return to Africa. The legislature in his country, Kenya, voted down a bill to bestow automatic citizenship on immigrants from the West Indies and on Afro-Americans. The full implications of the emergence of African states and of *continental* Pan-Africanism for the continued viability of *racial* Pan-Africanism merit careful study.

"The Return" as a Pan-African Theme

Traditional Pan-African activity has always involved attempts of some people in the diaspora to make contact with the ancestral homeland, either to return there to stay, to visit temporarily, to take back to it what they assume are some of the benefits they have secured in the diaspora, or to seek aid for their own projects of various sorts. The idea of an actual return of some or all of the scattered people has been a persistent one in the black diaspora. Professor Shepperson and his students at Edinburgh have been involved in some very exciting explorations into the details of the reverse flow of people and ideas from the Western Hemisphere to Africa. In doing so, they are giving implicit recognition to the fact that the term *diaspora* is both metaphor and paradigm abstracted from the experience of the Jewish people who constituted the classical case. The term was applied in its Greek form to the first Babylonian captivity when a portion of the Jewish people were carried off as slaves into Mesopotamia. One of the most beautiful of the psalms, Psalm 137, contains the classical lament:

> By the rivers of Babylon,
> There we sat down,
> Yea, we wept when we remembered Zion.
> We hanged our harps upon the willows
>   in the midst thereof,
> For there they that carried us away captive
> Required of us a song:
> And they that wasted us required of us mirth,
> Saying,
> Sing us one of the songs of Zion.
> How shall we sing the Lord's songs
> In a strange land?
> If I forget thee Oh Jerusalem,
> Let my right hand forget her cunning;
> If I do not remember thee,
> Let my tongue cleave to the roof of my mouth....

This nostalgia, coupled with the concept of the return, is an integral part of the paradigm of a diaspora. It was also an integral part of what I am calling traditional Pan-Africanism, varying in intensity with time, place, and social status. As might be expected, it was most pronounced during American slavery, which extended from the early sixteenth century until past the mid-nineteenth century.

What proportion of the Jewish exiles in Babylon "hanged their harps on the willow tree" and what proportion bowed down to the alien sounds of the psalters, the sackbuts, the dulcimers, and the harps of ten strings that were seducing them into heathen ways we shall never know. Those who refused to make mirth and to sing may have been a minority compared with those who were settling down in the strange land, singing strange songs and composing new ones. Certainly in every subsequent Jewish diaspora there has been the constant pull between traditionalists and assimilationists. But a remnant always preserves the memories of the homeland, and on some occasions, as in Zionism today, the myth of the return grips a much larger part of the people and becomes a powerful force. Obviously the fit between the paradigm of the return and the black experience is a very loose one, but the myth of the return has been important in diaspora history and has had implications for the history of the continent, not only through Sierra Leone and Liberia but for less thoroughly researched situations, too.

The desire to return home was strong among the first generation of Africans who were landed in the Western Hemisphere, and there was a first generation always present somewhere from the year 1518 over the ensuing 340 years, that is, until the slave trade was completely suppressed. New documentation of abortive attempts to get back home is always turning up, and we have documented statements in the forms of petitions from Massachusetts in 1773, in Trinidad, and perhaps from many other areas, petitions of slaves or recently freed Africans asking to be repatriated. But even more impressive are the folklore and the folk customs. Throughout the West Indies old people handed down to their children the idea that when they died their spirits returned to "Guinea" to join the spirits of the ancestors there. In some places corpses were buried facing east and west, not north and south, to facilitate the journey across the Atlantic. Slave holders' accounts are constantly blaming suicides among the first generation on the deep-seated belief that through death they are making the return. The stuff of poetry and drama is at hand for literary students of the diaspora. A study of comparative folklore may be rewarding, too, for those who become interested in this theme. The New Beacon Books publishing company in London published a small volume in 1971 by Petronella Breinburg, entitled *The Legends of Suriname,* which was described as "beautifully reconstructed folktales based on the Afrocentred tradition of Suriname." The naked lady has turned a little boy into a toad. He had heard that on one night every year, the night of the Emancipation Celebration, July 1, one could see what people called "the flying slaves." In the final story the little boy persuades the sorceress to transform him into a bird so that he can see if this is true. Finally, he sees three men flying. "Their black skins shone as if carefully greased." One of the men tells him a story of why they return every year to shout and warn people through the hooting of the owl that they cannot fly:

> It was a long time ago, many years before Emancipation, that word had gone round that those of us who could stop eating salt would be able to fly back to Africa. So we all went on a salt-free diet. But our wives and children were forced to eat food in the houses where they worked. So it became clear that it would be mostly us men who could fly back. Our children did not want to lose us.

The remaining portion of the story is not clear. I leave it to the folklorists to interpret the tale and its meanings for us. I simply use it to point out the persistence of a tale about returning to Africa. Folklorists will want to discover how widespread variants of the legend of the flying slave are throughout the diaspora, too. Professor Lawrence W. Levine has given us a magnificent volume, *Black Culture and Black Consciousness: Afro-American Folk Thought from Slavery to Freedom*, although it does not contain the tale of the flying slave. It would be interesting to know if some other legend played a similar role in the total body of North American black folklore.

The extent to which the myth of the return to Africa after death is still retained in the Western Hemisphere has not been thoroughly studied. I was told, during a field trip to Jamaica in 1968, that a belief persists that unless graves are dug facing east and west, the spirit cannot return to Guinea, that is, to Africa. I was not able to investigate the prevalence of the belief. Metraux does not report any such beliefs in his study of the voodoo religion of Haiti, and he reports that the use of the term *Guinea* no longer refers to Africa, saying that "the loa, or at any rate the most important ones, live in Guinea. This name has for long been without real geographical meaning, for Guinea is a sort of Valhalla, not situated anywhere." Questions such as these need clearing up.

While Africa was assuming the character of a mythical land of the ancestors for most slaves, it was being continuously given concreteness whenever new increments of slaves were landed. It was also always a goal for emigration in the minds of some even unto the third and fourth generation. The black Zionist aspect of Marcus Garvey's Universal

Negro Improvement Association in the 1920s is evidence that historian August Meier is on sound ground when he contends that a strong minority interest in emigrating to Africa has always existed in the North American diaspora, rising and falling in its appeal in response to economic, social, and political conditions. The pre-Civil War situation is well documented, and one peak was reached just before the Civil War when even free blacks who had opposed emigration began to support it. The story of Martin R. Delany is one that would appeal to African children. A black man in North America led an exploring party to Nigeria and signed treaties with Yoruba obas for the coming home of exiles who would embark on cotton growing along with Africans.

Hope engendered by the Civil War killed off emigrationist sentiment. It surfaced again strongly in Oklahoma after hopes for political power were dashed in the early twentieth century. A Gold Coast African, Chief Sam, organized the emigrants, who actually made it across the Atlantic in 1914. Such movements in North America reached their apogee with the Garvey movement in the wake of the race riots of 1919 and the oppression of 1921. Research on such movements in other parts of the Western Hemisphere has not been systematically carried out. It is hoped it will be eventually.

There has been no mass back-to-Africa movement in North America since Garvey organized the Black Star Line in the 1920s. With the rise of independent African states since World War II, however, interest in Africa among Afro-Americans rose dramatically. One result of this re-Africanization process has been a stream of individuals making the return as visitors, as isolated individuals working in Africa for short periods of time, as government and business representatives, and as soldiers of fortune. A few have gone permanently and taken out African citzenship, but only a very few. It is probable that, proportionately, a larger number of people from the Caribbean have gone to the new Africa and on a more permanent basis. Of much wider extent has been the psychological return, the emergence of a positive identification with Pan-African implications among large segments of a middle class that once preferred to forget Africa. The modern return can have its sinister aspects, too, as a few blacks from the diaspora ally themselves with exploitative neocolonialist business interests that do not have the welfare of Africans at heart. These are the modern equivalents of ex-slaves from the diaspora who sometimes settled on the West Coast and became slave traders themselves or allies of slave traders. Among such might be placed the Afro-American public relations expert who accepted a six-figure advertising account to try to sell the puppet state Transkei to the American public when not a nation on earth except Malawi and Rhodesia would recognize the apartheid fraud. Other more problematic cases are the ardent supporters of moderate solutions in southern Africa where probably only radical solutions can benefit the black masses. The postwar return should be the subject of diaspora studies, and African scholars should take on the task of evaluating the impact. Afro-Americans need the benefit of their frank appraisal.

The most dramatic case of devotion to the myth of the return in the contemporary black world is that of the Rastafarian Brethren of Jamaica. So restless were they in the land of their birth, they dubbed Babylon, and so anxious to return to Africa that a study of their history, social condition, and aspirations was carried out by the University of the West Indies when the highly respected economist Arthur Lewis was vice chancellor. A well-known Jamaican anthropologist, M. G. Smith, headed the research team, and on the basis of the recommendations, a delegation was sent to Africa by the government to see if a repatriation venture could be arranged. This is an example of diaspora studies functioning as one aspect of Pan-African activity. This was action-oriented research, not a study of the Rastas for purposes of testing theories about messianism or to produce one more book on a colorful religious movement. It should be noted that neither of the scholars mentioned thought that he was jeopardizing his reputation by becoming involved in the study. Both were making contributions in areas of their academic disciplines far removed from the subject of this study—which incidentally has been published and is readily available for students of the African diaspora in the New World.

I cannot leave the subject of the Rastas without noting that not only was it not possible to arrange for any settlements in Africa, but also there has been some degree of accommodation with the present black government on the island. But even as Rasta music becomes assimilated into the pop culture of the world, its ethos remains close to the classical paradigm of the diaspora. MRR Records of Kingston, Jamaica, is now selling an album by Count Ossie and the Mystic Revelation of Ras Tafari that contains a rendition of "By the rivers of Babylon did we sit down." It had been previously released in a version recorded by the Melodians as a part of the soundtrack for Jimmy Cliff's moving picture *The Harder They Come.* I might state in passing that a comparative study of popular music in the West Indian islands would be of some interest, to isolate contrasting themes and to measure the extent to which Christian religious elements enter into it and where such elements can be found. Given the large populations of East Indian ancestry in Trinidad and Guyana, some Muslim and some Hindu, their thread can be woven into the fabric. There is a group in Barbados called the Consolers who sing a brand of gospel music that contrasts sharply with the music of the

Rastafarians; it is a cross between Afro-American gospel music and Southern white church music.

Discussing Barbados leads to a wider area of inquiry than music, that is, differences in island national character, reflected in type of music but also in other ways. From 1627 until the present, Barbados has never been under the cultural influence of any European power other than England. It has had no Spanish of French leavening to reinforce African gaiety as in most of the other islands. And the result helps to confirm the argument of anthropologists who insist that there is nothing genetic about negritude or soul. Intriguing questions arise as to why Trinidad has produced a number of distinguished Marxist intellectuals while Jamaica seems to be the seedbed of black nationalism and Barabados has produced policemen, doctors, businessmen, and lawyers. Perhaps I may be permitted this oversimplification that seems a bit pejorative, for my father is a "Badian," and I am criticizing as a partial insider. My mother was from Virginia. I am therefore a Pan-African diaspora product.

Fortunately the Caribbean was spared an invasion by American anthropologists trying to define the basic personality of each island with TAT and Rorschach tests during the 1950s. The field is clear for friendly African scholars using less offensive research tools to discuss variations in ethos and temperament among various segments of the black diaspora and to evaluate the implications. It will have to be done with a more scholarly and sensitive hand than Dr. Nkrumah used when he berated the West Indian heads of state for dissolving the federation of the British West Indies in 1961, accusing them of taking a step backward from the Pan-African path to unity. He felt justified in doing so as one black political leader to another. Not all of his fellow black leaders in the Caribbean thought that it was any of his business. Surrounded by West Indians who had made the return and become a part of his official family, Nkrumah was not prepared to see the Atlantic as any more of a significant barrier to black unity than the Sahara.

A study of the return, in relation to the dilemmas and contradictions in the North American black experience, could profit from a fresh look by African students of the diaspora. During the period of the Revolutionary War and the religious Great Awakening of the latter half of the eighteenth century, the few free blacks in North America seem to have been integrationists who not only believed but hoped that the Christian preachers and the Declaration of Independence meant what they said about brotherhood and equality. They were rudely disillusioned in 1787 when the Constitution of the United States recognized slavery and northern churches proved to be bastions of Jim Crow and racism. The free black leaders, rebuffed, began to build their own institutions, and the choice of names for them is significant: *African* Methodist Episcopal Church; *African* Methodist Episcopal Zion Church; *African* Lodge No. 459 of the Prince Hall Scottish Rite Masons; the *African* Grove Theater of New York; and scores of Baptist congregations and self-help clubs including *African* in their name. The affirmation of an African identity was accompanied by a striving to realize the ideals of white middle-class society. To mention Shango or Ogun in an African Methodist Church would have been sacreligious. But Africa was not forgotten. All of these churches immediately began to send missionaries to "Christianize" and to "civilize" their "heathen" brothers and cousins. They were ashamed of their "backwardness" and "paganism." But there was never any racist insinuation in this "uplift" idealogy as there was in the white missionary effort. And from the outset these black missionaries were interested in developing trade relations with their converted brethren. Such concepts formed an apperceptive mass within the membership of Afro-American churches that was there for Garvey to appeal to. And in some AME quarters, a strong emigrationist movement flourished under the leadership of Bishop Henry McNeal Turner, who appealed not for a few missionaries to make the return but wanted to lead large groups of settlers. While all of this was going on, there was fierce resistance to the American Colonization Society and other whites who, until after the Civil War, wanted to deport all free blacks to Liberia, which they founded for such a purpose. Much has been written about all of this, but not from a African perspective. It needs evaluation as well as description and analysis and some discussion of how it should be presented to African children as they are introduced to diaspora history. And we might begin with that remarkable little Senegalese girl who was sold into Massachusetts slavery at the age of eight but who, in her teens, won international renown as a poet. Phyllis Wheatley highlights all of the contradictions of that epoch but also touches our hearts as well as our minds.

The Scope of Diaspora Studies

Interpretation and Reinterpretation
Within the Pan-African Framework

Diaspora studies as an aspect of Pan-African activity have, for the past 180 years, proceeded concurrently with diaspora studies motivated by various other reasons. Indeed, the first studies of Africans in the New World diaspora were incidental by-products of what, today, we would call sponsored research with Native Americans as the objects. The Spanish crown insisted—half honestly and half hypocritically—that it was greatly concerned about the souls of the Indians. The Catholic church insisted that this was the only reason for which it was prepared to sanction rape and murder by the conquistadores or the exploitation of the encomienda system. So, from the outset, it commissioned priests to study the languages and cultures of the Indians in the West Indies in order to facilitate conversion. Some of the holy fathers were astute observers and diligent recorders of what they saw. Some of them, like Fathers Labat and De Tertre, did their assigned job but also devoted considerable attention to describing the slaves. They have left valuable documentation of the seventeenth century. From their time until the nineteenth century we have to depend on travelers' tales or the writings of various groups with axes to grind, planters, or the religious sectarians and humanitarians who opposed them. When the British parliament decided to consider abolishing the slave trade, commissioned studies appear again, this time for use by the government agencies in London. All of this material has become grist for the mill of those contemporary scholars who, for the past two decades, have been recasting the entire picture of slavery in the Americas. Black scholars have been critical about the unbalanced amount of attention that has been given to slavery as compared with other periods in black history, but still the surface has only been scratched. Some African scholarly work would be welcome.

Insofar as we are concerned with the Western Hemisphere diaspora, we are concerned with only one branch of the great African tree. The media and the television screen have sensitized the United States, and some other portions of the world, too, to the theme of roots during the past few years. The roots and the trunk are firmly positioned in sub-Saharan Africa. The American branch and the fruit it has borne have caught the imagination of novelists and poets and challenged the intellect of historians and social scientists. For almost two centuries these novelists and poets have exploited the drama and the romance involved in the story of millions of Africans and their descendants gradually spreading, over a 460-year period, throughout the Western Hemisphere and forming communities from Nova Scotia to Argentina, from the Atlantic to the Pacific. Over time the Africans' bodies have become multihued from mixture with many varieties of white men and Indians, and their customs developed into a blend in varied proportions of things African they have been able to retain—or have wanted to retain —while their labor has been exploited and their citadels of the self have been assaulted by the descendants of Spaniards and Portuguese, Englishmen, Dutchmen, Frenchmen, and Danes during the period of enslavement and thereafter. Their music and their dancing have never ceased to fascinate people whose motivations were on the side of exoticsm and voyeurism, and sometimes a desire to co-opt and commercialize it all. For us, it has had a different meaning. The Afro-American poet Langston Hughes expressed the contrast in points of view from the perspective of one diaspora group. He wrote during the 1920s:

> Because my mouth is wide with laughter
> And my throat is deep with song,
> You do not know I suffer
> I've held my pain so long.

The African poet-philosopher Léopold Senghor, in an address to the First Festival of Negro Arts in Dakar in 1966, reminded us that the singing of the songs was a crucial element of survival in the diaspora, not merely a negative holding back of pain. Interestingly, in Catholic Brazil, in a context quite different from that which produced the jazz that Langston Hughes spoke of and the "sorrow songs" that Du Bois wrote about, the singing has been used in a distinctive form of vindication at the folk level. It is almost inconceivable that in Mississippi, white and black balladeers would sing to each other this way with an audience hanging on their words, as in Brazil:

> BLACK SINGER: This color business is silly;
>   White is vanity;
>   A man shows himself only
>   Through his ability,
>   Proper speech
>   And by his morality.
>
> WHITE SINGER: You really cannot deny
>   That your race is a terrible thing;
>   Cursed as it has been
>   Ever since the time of Cain.
>
> BLACK SINGER: You talk to me about Cain?
>   That really beats me up!
>   This black race of ours
>   Has never had a traitor;
>   Judas was a white man
>   He was the one
>   Who betrays our Lord.

What were the processes that gave us cultures so different as those of the United States and those of Brazil, even though both were compelled to grapple with the meaning of being black? Diaspora studies seek an answer.

The African diaspora into the Western Hemisphere, viewed in its full amplitude, involved the massive dispersal of more than 10 million men, women, and children from a homeland in sub-Saharan Africa, between 1500 and 1850, a period of 350 years. Most of them were used as forced labor by agricultural producers within the framework of an expanding capitalist system in its mercantilist phase, for the enrichment of Western European nations who were fighting each other for hegemony. After 1850, as industrial capitalism gained momentum in those countries, with England in the lead, Africans were no longer exported to the Americas. Rather, they were exploited on their own native soil. In the lands of the diaspora, caste and class systems emerged in which shade of color became salient and racist myths that had sanctioned slavery were now used to sanction the subordination of black people who were used as underpaid marginalized forces of production.

The experience of black people in the Americas brought new systems of exploitation into existence. Slavery was at least as old as the Neolithic Revolution in the Middle East, but never before had racial slavery been justified by the dogma that some one variety of mankind was born to be the servant forever of others. There was nothing new about color prejudice either, but never before had it been institutionalized to fix the status of men decisively and irrevocably until plantation slavery began in the New World. Nor had any systems of subordination ever developed a doctrine of racism teaching that some varieties of men had defective brains and emotions that doomed them and their descendants to low status forever. This refinement was reserved to the late nineteenth century and first half of the twentieth century in the countries that claimed to have dethroned superstition by science. The desire to defend the slave trade and to convince black men and women of their own inferiority led to a monstrous prostitution of science that eventually boomeranged with Hitler's racial theory in the center of Europe itself.

During the sixteenth century in the newly found western lands, the pink Europeans who called themselves white used firepower and firewater to annihilate some or reduce to peonage the indigenous population—men who looked red. A new variety of mankind was created in the process: the mestizo. A Catholic priest, Father Las Casas, suggested that Africans be imported to save the Indians of the Caribbean from extinction, and he lived to repent the advice he gave the Spanish sovereign. When sugar became king, white indentured labor was doomed in the Caribbean, and African manpower was imported on a massive scale. Mulattoes grew in number along with the profits from sugar. In the continental areas of New Spain and New Grenada where Indians formed the basic labor force in rural areas, Africans worked in urban areas and mines, and out of their relations with Indians came the *zambos*, who, mixing with mulattoes, began to produce the kaleidoscope of physical types in many parts of Hispanic America. Scholars interested in the broad sweep of comparative history and in testing generalizations about race, culture, and social stratification—and in speculating about the future—have produced a voluminous amount of literature. A few of these scholars have been black men and women of the diaspora. Their ranks increase each year. How much richer the insights would be if now a group of African scholars could join in this collective enterprise, and if some of them would work from a Pan-African perspective.

For centuries the interpretation of diaspora history ws dominated by racists, first by those who believed in biological determinism and genetic deficits, and more recently by those who blend a brand of cultural determinism or geographical determinism with doctrinaire Freudian or Jungian psychology. While ethnopsychology is more scientific than biological racism, it carries a racist potential that cannot be ignored, whether it is used to bolster white supremacy or negritude. Obviously, interpretations of African adjustment in the Western Hemisphere must be grounded in geographical studies, taking into account that the movement of people from tropical Africa into tropical America involved a less traumatic readjustment than their introduction into the snow and ice of North America. Yet, they did not die out there as was often predicted, and there is poetic justice in the fact that a black man in his parka, Matt Henson, drove the dogsled that carried Admiral Peary to the North Pole in 1909. Professor Klein, in his comparative study of Cuba and Virginia, has suggested that geography and climate may have been of crucial importance in explaining patterns of resistance. He notes that it was much more difficult for runaways to survive during winter months in North America than in the West Indies. The geography and geopolitics of black history in the Western Hemisphere should not be ignored in developing diaspora studies but should, of course, be closely articulated to economic studies. A broad Marxist historical matrix that takes account of environmental differences has been, for me, the most useful base in which to ground sociological and anthropological analyses.

The combined endeavors of scholars of all races, approaching the same phenomena from varied perspectives, has resulted in an overarching framework that most diaspora studies use. It focuses on what social scientists call acculturation and miscegenation, the former sociological, the latter biological with sociological implications. For the past decade some scholars have been emphasizing a previously neglected point, namely, that for peoples of African descent in the diaspora, these processes have always taken place under conditions of economic and political domination, in situations defined by the holders of power in terms of a racist theory of white supremacy rationalized by biological and theological dogmas of white racial superiority. The names of two anthropologists, Melville Herskovits and Roger Bastide, have been associated most prominently with hemispherewide studies of acculturation and miscegenation involving African peoples of the diaspora; Sidney Mintz, John Szwed, and Norman Whitten have led the movement in North America toward emphasizing the context of economic subordination within which these processes occur. I would like to emphasize that acculturation and miscegenation involving black and white people have occurred in other times and places where the relations were not interpreted in terms of race nor so highly charged with emotions tied up with color consciousness as in the Western Hemisphere diaspora. Such situations are of importance in studying diasporas from a global perspective.

Enough preliminary work has been done in the fields of history, sociology, economics, and anthropology to give rewarding results to efforts at simple descriptive integration. A comprehensive synthesis of the whole diaspora story in a single volume is yet to be done. It is a dramatic story and an intensely human one, but perhaps only fragments can be placed together into patterns now. It is the story of an enslaved people acting as enslaved people everywhere have done, often showing a double face, one for master and another for family and friends; sometimes fawning and flattering, but occasionally poisoning and cutting oppressive masters' throats. Some slaves ran away, and some rebelled. We treasure their stories and use them to refute charges of supine acquiescence. The rebels reflected in their total personality what was a part of every slave's personality, although not all were of a heroic mold. Most slaves worked at the tasks assigned to them with varying degrees of enthusiasm. Like human beings everywhere, they sized up what kind of behavior was required for survival and for the benefit of self and kinsmen. Some acquired privileged positions, and the "Queen Esther syndrome" was not unknown. A woman who shared the bed of the man who wielded power could, sometimes, lend protection to her people. There were rapes and sexist sadism, too, but masters and mistresses were also seduced by slaves who were pleasant of manner and sexually powerful. Others acted like Joseph in the house of Potiphar and resisted the seduction of women in power. There was no single pattern of adjustment.

Wherever possible, groups of Africans and their descendants used beliefs and customs from the homeland syncretized with those of Europeans to achieve group ends, and individuals used them for survival, self expression, and mobility. Comedy was present in the diaspora experience; some observers from the outside have emphasized it to the exclusion of the tragic element that was always present and was the dominant mood. A committed Pan-Africanist can recognize the comic relief and even appreciate it; but neither laughter, detachment, nor exoticism can ever be more than a passing mood. Tragedy that generates anger as well as compassion is the dominating ethos of a Pan-African perspective.

Honesty demands the admission that the diaspora story involves some scoundrels as well as some heroes, and some black opportunists as well as the dedicated individuals. The sixteenth and seventeenth centuries reveal a long list of unknown leaders of revolts against slavery and founders of communities of runaways, maroon communities; but it also has a record of black men in Brazil helping the Paulistas steal land from the Indians and in Peru exploiting Indians "on their own" in areas remote from Lima. A few centuries later, Brazilian slaves who had bought their freedom turn up as slave traders along the coasts of what are now Benin and Togo. Black "buffalo soldiers" were proud of their role in helping white men to bring the Native Americans under subjection in the North American West, while others fought side by side with Native Americans of Florida in the so-called Seminole wars. Cuba had its Maceo heroically leading the fight for freedom against the Spaniards, but thousands of slaves in the western part of the island refused to rally to his call. The bald facts of caution, cowardice, and perfidy that sometimes appear in the diaspora record must be neither suppressed not overemphasized but placed into a meaningful framework of interpretation. Mine is an oversimplified one. I simply say, "Black people are just like all other people."

Pan-Africanist interpretation, like nationalistic interpretation, always involves the process of revaluation, one aspect of which is the refusal to accept a double standard when dealing with violence and villainy. The murder and rape that accompanied the revolt of the slaves in Santo Domingo must not be written off as savagery while the behavior of Bolivar's troops in the fight for South American independence is lauded as heroism. When ruffians threw rocks at the British soldiers on the Boston Common in 1770 and were fired on, a black man died and became a legend: "Crispus Attucks was the first to spill his blood for American independence—a black man." Both black and white Americans praise these patriotic hoodlums. In other diaspora cases, black freedom fighters are downgraded. One source says that "30 to 40 percent of the patriot army that General San Martin brought across the Andes to liberate Chile seem to have been Negroes" but then comments that "for all their bravery, these fighting men of colors were pawns, driven on by interests more of less alien to their own." Professor Morner must be questioned. "Were they any different from any other rank and file soldiers in those armies?" "How can you prove that they felt no investment in the struggle?" The blacks who fought with Marti and Maceo in Cuba did. Ultimately, however, the acts of men in such historic struggles are not to be evaluated by their subjective intentions but by their objective results. It is irrelevant whether either John Brown or Dessalines was a psychiatric case. Each played a part in black liberation, and that is what counts. All of diaspora history needs revaluation in terms of this norm.

Descriptive Integration of the Pan-African Perspective

Approaching the task of descriptive integration from a Pan-African perspective will immediately focus attention on problems, personalities, and details that are either overlooked from other points of view or considered insignificant. For instance, a fitting preface to the whole diaspora story has been supplied by Ivan Van Sertima, a Guyana-born anthropologist teaching at Rutgers University in the United States. His book, *They Came Before Columbus,* is controversial, but it cannot be ignored by any serious student of the diaspora. In fact, its publication highlights the fact that the work of a distinguished Harvard student of linguistics who opened up this question decades ago *was* ignored by his fellow academics. Dr. Du Bois was one of the few scholars who ever referred to it even in a footnote. Dr. van Sertima had the motivation, the scholarly training, and the writing skill to pull together the evidence from a wide variety of disciplines in tackling this question that Professor Wiener had approached from too narrow a base to be convincing. Professor van Sertima provides the evidence for supplanting extravagant fantasies about ancient black transatlantic explorers with very plausible hypotheses.

When Columbus did come, one El Pietro Negro was a pilot on one of his ships. It was only the so-called Negro history school that considered the fact significant enough to point to year after year during Negro history week.[1] Eventually articles appeared in the *Journal of Negro History* that pointed to an impressive group of explorers accompanying the conquistadores before slavery in the Americas became established. Such ideas having been kept alive were picked up in the 1960s, when black studies became fashionable and a white scholar, John Upton Terrell, produced a very readable popular account in 1968 of one of these. His *Estevanico the Black* is a fascinating account of an African who led two expeditions into what is now the southwestern portion of the United States. Some of these sixteenth-century figures were Ladinos who had adopted Spanish of Portuguese culture and came directly from Africa. We are being told in standard works, now, of Ladinos who came to the Indies and Mexico, made their fortunes, and retired to Spain!

The illumination of facets of history that others might neglect is nowhere more vividly illustrated than in the number of books that have appeared in the last five years about Sally Hemings, usually referred to as the *alleged* or *reputed* black mistress by whom Thomas Jefferson had five children. Black scholars and journalists were discussing Sally without the words alleged or reputed for decades before Professor Winthrop Jordan became the first white scholar with the courage to deal openly with this subject in his book, *White over Black*, published in 1968. When black scholars first opened up the discussion of subjects such as these, they did so as an aspect of traditional Pan-African activity. They had a vindicationist purpose in mind as part of the antiracist struggle.

Since the mid-1960s, a few black scholars have been insisting that diaspora scholarship can be purged of the implicit and unconscious racism that suffuses much of it only if an actual substitution of new terms for old processes takes place that reflects the historic subordination and violence that "neutral" terms mask. Thus, they would argue that *miscegenation* should really be replaced by the terms *racial genocide* and *racial suicide*. They would replace the term *acculturation* with *co-optation* or *brainwashing*. Most Afro-American scholars have not felt the need for such drastic revisions in concept and terminology but do insist on looking at diaspora phenomena from "a black perspective" as well as from other perspectives. The phrase "diaspora studies as an aspect of traditional Pan-African activity" is one formulation from a black perspective. Using the conventional sociological and anthropological concepts and terms, I focus on their operation and that of several subprocesses that I define, operating over long spans of time, in specifically defined geographical areas. I search for factors that have led to:

1. Attenuation, dilution, and in some cases obliteration of Africanity, in both culture and physique;
2. Persistence of Africanity and analysis of how it functions in routinized life-styles as well as in times of crises.

These basic processes and subprocesses can be observed ecologically by noting the extent of persistence of African customs and of Africans as a visible people, in various areas, decade by decade and century by century. They can be observed in social space by noting the extent to which class systems emerge in which shade of color is a status indicator, and the extent to which Africanity is altered with upward social mobility. The differential allocation of power and prestige by shade of color and its implications for the solidarity of peoples of African descent is a crucial research problem.

It might be relevant here to cite a few cases that sharpen the distinction between a traditional Pan-African frame of reference and an approach dominated by other interests. One of the first published works that attempted to view the African presence in the diaspora as a whole was Sir Harry Johnston's *The Negro in the New World*. Extremely interesting and well documented with plenty of photographs, it was, however, very opinionated. Here was the black experience seen through the eyes of a British imperialist with an appreciation for many aspects of French culture. He had faith in the educability of black people and was hostile to the antiscientific bias that he believed missionaries were imposing on New World blacks. The objectives and tone of the book were those of the civilizing mission under the *Pax Britannica*. It is a very useful research aid when used critically. Appearing four years later was W. E. B. Du Bois's book, *The Negro* (revised years later as *Black Folks Then and Now*, which, although the focus was on Africa, counterposed a different diaspora perspective to Johnston's in the sections on the Americas.

Between 1915 and World War II, diaspora studies were an important component in the research, publication, and educational work of an influential complex of institutions founded and nurtured by a remarkable man and functioning here in Washington, D.C., I am referring, of course, to the Association for the Study of Negro Life and History,[2] founded in 1915 by a Harvard-trained black historian, Dr. Carter G. Woodson, and a small group of friends and coworkers. The next year, the Association founded the *Journal of Negro History*, whose pages were open to scholars of ali races but whose editorial direction was firmly in the hands of Afro-Americans. Eventually, the Associated Publishers was formed and made available works as diverse as Woodson's textbook for American schools, *The Negro in Our History*, a book by Maurice Delafosse on Africa, and Arthur Ramos's *Negroes in Brazil*. The annual observance of Negro history week led to the publication of the *Negro History Bulletin* and preparation of packets of educational materials containing photographs of prominent black men. Around Woodson an intellectual community developed that Robert W. Fogel and Stanley L. Engerman dubbed "the Negro school" in their controversial study of slavery in the United States called *Time on the Cross*. They emphasize its importance to American historiography not only by opening up for research neglected and underemphasized themes but also for using kinds of documentation not previously used to a great extent, such as wills and bills of sale in studies of the plantation area.

The annual meetings of the Association for the Study of Negro Life and History provided a platform from which a wide variety of black and white scholars presented the results of their research and speculation. Among those who did so frequently during the 1920s was an anthropologist, Melville J. Herskovits, who over a period of two decades became the outstanding authority on the impact of African cultures on cultural development in the Americas; his research culminated in the publication of *The Myth of the Negro Past* in the 1940s. In his autobiography, Kwame Nkrumah favorably cited Herskovits's work as lending support to Pan-African ideology and activity. But Herskovits always saw himself as a professional anthropologist using the New World as a laboratory for testing hypotheses about culture and for refining his concepts of acculturation, retention, reinterpretation, and syncreticism, not as a stimulus to political activity. He hoped, however, that one result of his scientific work would be to replace error with truth and thus to increase respect for Africans and people of African descent. Herskovits considered a passionate commitment to Pan-African goals to be an impediment to honest scientific research but never recognized the built-in biases of liberal humanitarian reform and the so-called objectivity associated with it. (He once scornfully referred to Jomo Kenyatta's *Facing Mt. Kenya* in a conversation with me as the work of a "half-baked anthropologist.") Until very late in his career he avoided accepting black students for serious anthropological training, but by that time he had dropped his extreme cultural relativism, too, and was serving on the State Department task force of academics advising on how to deal with a resurgent Africa.

Perhaps no anthropologist has made a more significant contribution to diaspora studies than the French savant Roger Bastide. In addition to his massive work on African religions in Brazil, he also attempted to integrate data covering both hemispheres in a study of the processes of acculturation. Some of his work done during a period of teaching in Sao Paulo shows deep concern for the socioeconomic conditions of black people and reveals his distress over discrimination against mulattoes and blacks. Yet, Bastide's psychoanalytic bias obtrudes itself so often into his thinking that his work is flawed. Numerous other anthropologists have contributed to our understanding of the black diaspora in what might be called Catholic America, but their preoccupation with the esoterica, and particularly with African religious survivals, places them far outside the ken of traditional Pan-African studies. Nevertheless, they are useful and interesting and intellectually stimulating. There is a dearth of anthropological literature dealing with the English-speaking

Caribbean but a plethora of sociological and psychological literature dealing with blacks in North America.

Two examples of scholars whose command of detail about black people in the diaspora is remarkable, but who espouse a point of view that is certainly not Pan-African, are the Swedish historian Magnus Morner and the Dutch sociologist Herman Hoetinik. Magnus Morner thinks it unfortunate that Africanism, indigenism, *mestizaje*, and *Hispanidad* are gaining strength at the very time that "the individual's racial characteristics are beginning to lose their importance in society." His optimistic misreading of the signs of the times not only places him in opposition to Pan-African activity but is also not shared by many of his white colleagues who foresee an increase in racial prejudice and discrimination in some Latin American areas as they industrialize and absorb immigrants from South Africa, Angola, and Rhodesia (Zimbabwe). Herman Hoetinik, on the other hand, is so convinced that dark skin color will remain a stigma that he can see social peace only in what he calls homogenation, a stepped-up degree of miscegenation that will eliminate the Negro as a physical type. Without saying so explicitly, he supports the dream of Jose Vasconcellos of a great cosmic race composed of European, Indian, and Negro ancestry emerging in the New World. Without questioning their sincerity or accusing them of covert racism, as is sometimes done, and certainly accepting their empirical research as valuable, it is still important to make clear that their research is not a part of traditional Pan-African activity.

The work of some nonblack scholars comes very close, however, to being a part of that activity in their selection of problems, in a willingness to collaborate closely on an egalitarian basis with black scholars, and in the absence of either liberal humanitarian or assimilationist preachments. Some of these scholars are participating in this conference. I would like to single out for comment the role of Professor George Shepperson and his colleagues at the University of Edinburgh. In addition to such important contributions as Shepperson and Price's *Independent African* and Professor Shepperson's articles referred to in this essay, a number of African and Afro-American graduate students have carried out research under the auspices of the Edinburgh group.

Cultural Tasks in the Context of Political Change

In February 1961, when Lumumba was murdered, Adlai Stevenson was about to make his maiden speech as United States ambassador to the United Nations. A black nationalist contingent from Harlem created such a commotion of protest in the balcony over Lumumba's assassination that the assembly had to be suspended. Within a day or two I received a phone call from the publisher of a well-known liberal magazine asking me to write an article pointing out that Africans did not feel they had anything in common with American blacks and that, therefore, they were making fools of themselves in taking such strong stands about Congo issues. I declined the invitation. Soon articles appeared in two magazines attempting to make this point. Both stressed problems that arose when African men took Afro-American wives back to Africa and oversimplified a variety of complex issues involving relations between Africans and Afro-Americans.

Soon after the request to write the article, I received a telephone call from a university that had a government contract to prepare area handbooks for use in military and paramilitary operations in various parts of the world. I was told that it was urgent that such a handbook be prepared for Ghana and was offered the usual consultant's fee if I would agree to participate. I declined. That first quarter of 1961 was a very busy one. I soon had another call, this time from the University of California at Berkeley. The newly organized Peace Corps had asked that institution to set up a training program to prepare a group of secondary school teachers for work in Ghana. When I was convinced that Nkrumah wanted those teachers very much, I decided to participate in the project of training them for work in Ghana, doing so during the summers of 1961, 1962, and 1964. I saw no conflict between this and my Pan-African commitments. During the second summer, while assisting Peace Corps teachers to settle in, I cooperated with the Ministry of Social Welfare of Ghana in carrying out the first conference of West African social workers, the report of which was later published with Dr. Peter Omari of Ghana and me as coauthors. (The conference itself was a brainchild of Dr. Adelaide Cromwell, Director Emerita of the Afro-American Studies Center at Boston University.)

During 1963, I attended the Kenya independence celebrations as a guest of the newly installed African government, having been active for a number of years in Kenya student welfare activities during the Mau Mau liberation war. On my way home I stopped in Ghana and spent some time with Nkrumah. He was very disturbed over the recent assassination of President Kennedy. The meaning of "positive nonalignment" was given dramatic expression as we sat under a portrait of Lenin that Nkrumah had received on a state visit to Moscow, when he stressed the understanding that John F. Kennedy had of African problems and Kennedy's willingness to support African states even if they were trying to develop socialist societies. During 1964, it became increasingly clear that the death of Kennedy marked the end of an era in relations between Afro-Americans and Africans.

Relations between Nkrumah and black Americans were unusually close, and the euphoria between African nations and the United States was also generally pronounced during the Kennedy years. During 1963, the Organization of African Unity (OAU) was established. It passed a resolution expressing "the deep concern aroused in all African peoples and governments by the measures of racial discrimination taken against communities of African origin living outside the continent and particularly in the United States of America." But that same resolution voiced an "expression of appreciation for the efforts of the Federal Government of the United States of America to put an end to these intolerable malpractices which are likely seriously to deteriorate relations between the African peoples and governments on the one hand and the people and government of the United States of America on the other." To dismiss this as mere rhetoric is to underplay the importance of repeated ritual commitment in creating a backlog of favorable sentiment that can be drawn on in future Pan-African activity. It is to ignore, too, the fact that the Kennedy regime was using black Americans in a number of prominent positions in and out of Africa and was contributing in various ways to African economic and technical development on a scale far greater than in the past. The assassin's bullet in November 1963 did not end all of this, but the euphoria gradually diminished and the strings placed on aid became more restrictive. Pan-African relations were affected by these changes.

Ideology and Afro-American Class Relations

Ideological divisions that began during the early Kennedy years over the Congo crisis became more entrenched as the Rhodesian liberation movement and guerilla warfare in the Portuguese territories mounted in intensity. Afro-American opinion gradually became divided between radical and moderate positions and the United States government took an increasingly conservative position on southern African questions. The civil war in Nigeria further polarized Afro-Americans or caused many of them to draw back in bewilderment from African political issues. As the black power upsurge took place in the United States, an age variable became important, with young black nationalists espousing a radical Pan-African position and older Afro-Americans assuming a more cautious stance. The peak of middle-class Afro-American organized activity oriented toward Africa came within the four-year period after the death of Kennedy and while the United States was groping for a policy that would encourage an end to the Congo conflict and could deal with problems posed by the Unilateral Declaration of Independence in Rhodesia. The American Negro Leadership Conference on

Africa (ANLCA), which had been founded in 1962, however, preferred not to embark on a program of mobilizing opposition to Tshombe and Ian Smith, and instructed its full-time lobbyist in Washington to spend a great deal of his time trying to arrange for Nobel Peace Prize laureate Martin Luther King, Jr., to mediate between Biafra and Nigeria. These efforts ceased with the assassination of Dr. King in the spring of 1968. The ANLCA went out of existence the next year. The American Society for African Culture (AMSAC) participated actively in the First Festival of Negro Arts in Dakar in 1966, and its journal, *African Forum*, carried political comment as well as articles on literary matters. It, too, went out of existence during the early 1970s.

With the demise of the American Society for African Culture and the American Negro Leadership Conference on Africa, middle-class interest in African affairs took on a more official form. The Congressional Black Caucus became a major agency in expressing a black viewpoint on African issues and had the kind of clout a single lobbyist for the American Negro Leadership Conference never had. More recently, TransAfrica has been organized to coordinate the interests of the Afro-American community in African affairs, and the NAACP dispatched a task force to Africa in 1977 that prepared a comprehensive report. It seems clear that the established leadership whose point of view is expressed through these organizations (and through the activities of the Reverend Leon Sullivan, a member of the board of General Motors) favors a moderate solution of southern African political problems in which black governments with a substantial measure of white participation will emerge, creating a favorable investment climate for multinational corporations through whom a transfer of technology and a gradual rise in the standard of living of black populations will take place. Socialist solutions are definitely not favored. Extensive participation of Afro-Americans in the African branches of corporations and in the diplomatic and quasi-diplomatic service of the United States is foreseen. The established leadership does not see this as imposing an American solution to African problems, or themselves as supporters of neocolonialism. Rather, this leadership is convinced that far-sighted, responsible Africans favor solutions such as these and are cooperating with them. Black radicals everywhere denounce this view, but Gulf Oil still pumps oil in Angola, and Sekou Toure still seeks new investments.

While this Afro-American middle-class consensus about African affairs was developing during the 1970s, a much more radical sector of Afro-American opinion also found organizational expression. An African Liberation Support Committee (ALSC) arose on a black nationalist base mobilizing support for freedom fighters in Guinea-Bissau, Angola, Mozambique, Zimbabwe, Namibia, and South Africa (Azania). By 1973, the ALSC was able to involve ten thousand people in a street demonstration in Washington, D.C., where Congressman Charles Diggs spoke on behalf of the Congressional Black Caucus. By 1975 the ranks of the African Liberation Support Committee had been fractured in a right-left split between *continental* Pan-Africanists and *racial* Pan-Africanists and between those who supported black nationalist solutions and those who were willing to support Cuban and Soviet aid for specific sides in African disputes. The various segments of the African Liberation Support Committee—under varied names—still remain a vigorous grassroots force for focusing attention on African problems, providing a forum for African visitors who espouse their own points of view, and fostering cultural events. The lack of unity may, itself, be contributing toward a more realistic view of Africa by Afro-Americans and may be drawing them away from a more naive form of sentimental Pan-Africanism. Meanwhile, these activities exert pressure on the establishment-oriented organizations of the black middle class to act.

The Black Studies Movement

During this period when black Americans were extending their hands outward toward the homeland through a variety of activities under the auspices of AMSAC, ANLCA, ALSC, and many other organizations including individual churches and voluntary associations, research and publishing about Africa had no firm base in any black institution of higher learning. Black scholars were being trained in most African studies programs organized during the late 1950s and early 1960s at several of the major universities. Howard University and Lincoln University (Pennsylvania) tried to sustain existing programs, with very meager support from the philanthropic foundations. In addition to my activities in AMSAC and ANLCA, I played a minor part, along with two other black scholars, E. Franklin Frazier of Howard and Lorenzo Turner of Roosevelt University, in the establishment of the African Studies Association in 1958 and in the Area Training Fellowship Program of the Ford Foundation before that. It is no disparagement of the contributing foundations and the African Studies Association, the African-American Institute and the well-established African studies programs to say that they definitely were not an aspect of traditional Pan-African activity. Some of us used these structures to help push forward such activity, but that was not their *raison d'être*. Today, however, there are institutional structures devoted to scholarly endeavors that do have such an aim. It is these, in collaboration with African university departments, research institutes, and similar ones in the West Indies, that offer a challenging new opportunity for a rapid expansion of diaspora studies. I refer to the black studies programs or African/ Afro-American studies programs that have come into being since 1968. It is in these institutional increments rather than in the major African studies programs that diaspora studies have their best chance of flourishing as a cooperative activity between Afro-American, African, and West Indian scholars and those nonblack scholars who wish to be associated with them.

The black studies movement is, itself, an important aspect of diaspora studies. When Dr. King was assassinated in the spring of 1968, the response of youthful blacks all over the United States was to destroy commercial property as the symbol of white exploitation. The response of youthful blacks at predominantly white colleges and universities was to strike and to seize buildings and to demand the hiring of more black faculty, the recruiting of more black students, the expression of more concern for the welfare of the black employees who contribute to the comfort and cleanliness of faculty and students, but above all, the immediate establishment of black studies programs. Relevant education was the battle cry. Black studies meant courses about black people everywhere—their history, their institutions, their culture—with emphasis on the preparation of black people to liberate themselves from oppression but also to appreciate the music, song, and dance, as well as the written literature they had produced. A preference for black teachers was expressed when black subjects were being taught and for black student-faculty committees to administer such programs. Courses about Africa were nearly always demanded. In many programs, courses on the Caribbean were integrated into a diaspora component to complement one on Africa.

After the passage of a decade, there are over two hundred programs now existing in black studies, African studies, Pan-African studies, or African/American studies at American colleges and universities. Many give a first degree in black studies. Some, including the Afro-American institutions, Howard and Atlanta; Harvard, Yale, and Cornell; and at least one or two of the institutions in the state university systems of New York and California and the city system of New York, plan to concentrate on graduate work and research during the next decade. Some institutions have very distinctive programs, although they have not been widely publicized, such as the Five Colleges Consortium based on the University of Massachusetts at Amherst or the graduate program at Ohio State oriented toward combining black studies with social work and education. At some institutions, the program is small, but individual professors of some distinction are on the faculty. These programs offer the possibility for one-to-one exchanges with research institutes in Africa, Latin America, and the Caribbean, as well as for individual faculty exchanges between members of departments in institutions where individuals may be doing significant research. Black studies programs constitute the single most important academic structure in the United States for initiating and consolidating cooperative relations with African, Caribbean, and Latin American institutions interested in developing diaspora studies as an aspect of traditional Pan-African activity. And the black studies movement has developed its distinctive publications, such as the *Journal of Black Studies* (SUNY at Buffalo), *Africana Studies* (University of Cincinnati), *Western Journal of Black Studies* (Washington State–Pullman), *Umoja* (University of Colorado at Boulder), and *Black Lines* (University of Pittsburgh). The National Council of Black Studies, which has been in existence for several years, serves as an integrating agency.

Certainly a large volume of the cooperative work in diaspora studies will proceed under the auspices of African studies programs in the United States and Latin American studies programs. But these agencies cannot fulfill the function that I am referring to as the development of diaspora studies as an aspect of traditional Pan-African activities. They have constraints on them that would make a Pan-African orientation difficult. Administrators of such programs certainly understand the necessary division of labor that means that some tasks are not effectively carried out by black studies programs, and at some institutions, cooperation between the two types of programs is both routine and fruitful. For instance, the University of California at Los Angeles recently held a symposium on the economy of the black world, sponsored by the Center for Afro-American Studies but with the cooperation of the African studies program. African studies programs prior to 1970 were not inclined to support activities that might have a Pan-African thrust, but after the painful confrontation at Montreal in 1969 between black power militants and the officials of the African Studies Associations (ASA) of Canada and of the United States, it was recognized that the ASA would have to incorporate some anti-imperialist activities into its program if African scholars of the homeland and diaspora were to be associated with it. It was also recognized that there was a need for an organization wholly committed to Pan-African interests such as the African Heritage Studies Association that had been founded by Professor John Henrik Clark and others, as well as the newly organized black studies programs. African scholars, like Afro-American scholars, will sometimes wish to belong to both types of organizations; others will not.

One result of the black studies movement has been to bring a number of African scholars into close, continuing contact with Afro-American professors and students. These are individuals who have been teaching regularly in black studies programs. African studies programs had previously brought a few African scholars into American academia, too. Both types of programs now have African professors whose experience with the diaspora would seem to make invaluable links with African institutions in the process of institutionalizing diaspora studies in Africa—both through their publications and as visiting professors. Outstanding among these has been Dr. S. O. Mezu from Nigeria, who founded the Black Academy Press in Buffalo, New York. His book of verse, *Tropical Dawn*, contains a poem to the civil rights martyr Medgar Evers that reveals his own Pan-African identification: "Medgar is dead but is ever here/Evers is gone but is everywhere/The branch shall grow again." He has also coedited a book on *Black Leaders of the Centuries*. But his reputation rests on his published work on Senghor and negritude and the fact that he holds a Ph.D. in Romance languages.

A decade after the founding of the Black Academy Press, Dr. Francis Botchway from Ghana, serving as chairman of the Afro-American Studies Program at the University of Cincinnati, founded the very impressive quarterly journal *Studia Africana*. Its international editorial board, in addition to Afro-Americans, included professors from Université du Benin (Togo), University of Ife, University of Nairobi, and the University of Ghana! The inaugural issue contained an article on "Multiple Images and Complex Realities: Pan-Africanism in Perspective" (Spring 1977).

The papers being presented at the conference cover a wide range of interests, and the theme of the return seems to have been one that attracted the interest of a number of African scholars. This is evidence that for some participants the conference is perceived as having some relevance to Pan-African activities if only through keeping memories alive by historical research. However, the conference itself falls within the historic tradition of Pan-African activity as expressed through non-political activities of educators and scholars. During the thirty-five years between the end of the Civil War and the turn of the century, an increasing number of African students enrolled at black schools in the United States. In 1895, Gammon Theological Seminary of Atlanta University held a conference on Africa that attracted a number of eminent scholars, white and black. Its aim was to attract attention to the African mission field. Two years later, Alexander Crummell, who had been associated with Liberia College but had decided to return to the land of his birth in the United States, founded the American Negro Academy. He had taken a degree from Cambridge in England in 1853, and now he had the dream of organizing a group of younger blacks who would apply scholarly attention to the task of elevating the black people. The membership was to be limited to forty, and William M. Ferris, author of *The Negro Abroad*, in an account of the founding, states that Crummell "communicated with colored scholars in America, England, Hayti and

Africa." Only two Africans seem to have been elected to the academy before it expired in 1920, however, including Fadumah Orishatukeh from Sierra Leone (M.A.,1908), and J. E. Kwegyir-Aggrey of the Gold Coast, then a professor at Livingstone College in North Carolina and later to become an internationally known African educator. One of the aims of the academy was "the defense of the Negro against vicious assaults." The Association for the Study of Negro Life and History, founded in 1915, established branches at the major black colleges and universities that numbered African students among their members. Its founder, Carter G. Woodson, in his own writing, by publishing Delafosse's work, and through the pages of the *Journal of Negro History* and the *Negro History Bulletin*, carried on a constant campaign of vindication that included popularization of African history. Dr. W. E. B. Du Bois, through his book published in 1913, *The Negro*, challenged the detractors who defamed Africa and, later through the columns of the magazine *Crisis*, carried on a never ceasing campaign in adult education on African affairs. At Howard University, Dr. William Leo Hanberry, through his impact on successive cohorts of students, African and West Indian as well as Afro-American, helped to create a tradition at Howard in the field of history, while Dr. Alain Locke was doing the same in art for the appreciation of African cultures.

During the late 1930's, Kwame Nkrumah and a group of African students at Lincoln laid the foundations for what became an African studies program at that institution and helped to get one under way at the University of Pennsylvania as well. African students became increasingly exposed to diaspora studies throughout the 1930s, 1940s, and 1950s at black universities in the United States, where courses in Afro-American history and literature were regularly given. By what anthropologists call participant observation, African students became familiar with the black experience in the United States. Ojike's *I Have Two Countries*, Nkrumah's *Ghana: An Autobiography*, and Mugo Gatheru's *A Child of Two Worlds* give some glimpses of what this kind of learning meant.

Some Urgent Intellectual Tasks

I assume that most of us at this conference are primarily concerned with teaching and research about diaspora institutions generally. While at Stanford University, I introduced a course on "Race and Culture Contact in the Caribbean." This required retooling after fifteen years as an Africa specialist. In addition to two six-month trips to the Caribbean, it meant becoming familiar with the bibliographies and the few integrating volumes as well as a mass of monographic literature and journal articles. And, because I wanted to teach the course from a black perspective, I embarked on reading novels, poetry, and journalism to get the feel of the area's most sensitive spokespersons. My own experience leads me to believe that one of the most important aids to the development of diaspora studies will be the provision of resources for released time and vacation travel and study for teachers who are adding diaspora studies to present specialties, and fellowships and exchange professorships for some who wish to pursue various aspects of diaspora studies in depth. No matter what the perspective of the educator who is just entering this field, or expanding his or her knowledge of it, these resources are essential, and it is hoped that some foundations will recognize this need, especially for our African collaborators.

From the perspective of forwarding the goals of traditional Pan-African activity through diaspora studies, the dissemination of the findings of research assumes even greater importance than the carrying out of new research projects. Diaspora studies are well enough developed now to warrant some concentrated attention on the development of delivery systems. I would visualize these kinds of activities as crucial:

1. Preparation of comprehensive annotated bibliographies about diaspora peoples for secondary and elementary school teachers;
2. Analysis of standard works on Africans in the diaspora to isolate omissions, distortions, stereotypes, insensitive and offensive comments, and failure to point out alternative interpretations of controversial issues in textbooks and media presentations
   (a) of Africans for American readers,
   (b) of Africans for other diaspora readers,
   (c) of Afro-Americans for African readers,
   (d) of Afro-Americans for other diaspora readers,
   (e) of Caribbean and Latin American peoples for Africans,
   (f) of Caribbean and Latin American peoples for Afro-Americans;
3. Preparation of readers and anthologies beginning, perhaps, with comparative folklore and comparative literature for various grade levels in schools of Africa and the diaspora;
4. Preparation of a series of biographies of prominent individuals in the diaspora for use at various grade levels (note Professor Harris's publication on East African personalities);[3]
5. Preparation of definitive supplementary textbooks on the social and cultural history of the diaspora viewed as a whole.

Audiovisual aids should also be prepared for African schools on diaspora historical themes and personalities, folklore, drama and music, and scripts and scenarios written for mass-media productions. A handbook should be prepared on how to use these teaching aids for two purposes: (1) to carry on historic vindication tasks that still remain in the fight against racism and the derogation of black people and (2) the goal of intercultural understanding. A similar monograph should be prepared for use in approaching educators and textbook publishers.

The stress up to this point has been on the processing of scholarly material for use by consumers of research, the nonscholars—children in schools, students in extramural and adult education classes, and television and radio viewers generally. This task is the least complicated one in diaspora studies but perhaps the one involving the most sheer drudgery and financial outlay for middle-level personnel. These activities feed directly into another goal that has political and administrative implications and complications—persuading decision makers in government and educational institutions, as well as publishers, to use such material, to integrate data on Africans in the diaspora into the textbooks and syllabi, the curricula, and even the list of examination subjects.

In trying to carry out any of these tasks, the question arises as to what the most effective means might be. It might be useful to review the activities that have brought Africans and the people of the diaspora into contact during the centuries:

1. Noninstitutional activities of individuals—visits by friends, travelers, sailors, and correspondence, including pen pals;
2. Relations between officials and representatives of black churches or blacks sent to Africa by white boards;
3. Relations between officials and representatives of black voluntary associations;
4. Relations fostered by black educational institutions in the diaspora;
5. Interstate relations between nations with large black populations.

Two new possibilities that have come with the organizations of African nations are (1) relations initiated by African educational institutions and (2) relations initiated by African scientific and educational societies. The existence of the United Nations also offers opportunities through UNESCO of securing assistance in the carrying out of some of the above tasks, but Pan-Africanist scholars would insist that design, administration, and evaluation of research and teaching projects be in the hands of Africans and peoples of African descent. They would do so in the spirit of Frederick Douglass who, when he insisted on an antislavery paper controlled by blacks as well as the interracial *Liberator*, wrote: "It is evident that we must be our own representatives and advocates, not exclusively but peculiarly—not distinct from, but in connection with, our white friends. The man struck is the man to cry out."

Possible Research Related to Pan-African Objectives

Although I have stressed the urgency of beginning to plan for the dissemination of what we now know about the diaspora among the peoples of Africa who, up to this point, have not had access to such information in the way in which the Negro history movement and the black studies movement and the Afro-American press have brought it to the North American segment of the diaspora (including history taught in Schenley Whiskey ads!), participants in the FADSI conference will, of course, also give high priority to research.

Before proceeding to define concrete research proposals, we should, perhaps, provide a broad context in time to match the context in space by first experimenting with the periodization of Western Hemisphere black history from a black perspective. It is conventional in writing U.S. history, for instance, to use important presidential regimes as distinctive markers in the time flow, as in the Age of Jackson. I could conceive of defining an Age of Christophe as a high point in diaspora history, the last figure in a great triumvirate that runs Toussaint-Dessalines-Christophe in Haiti. The basic assumption is that the Haitian revolt that began in 1791 had great historic implications for the whole diaspora—that facts, fears, and fancies about San Domingo influenced relations everywhere between black people and whites, mulattoes, and Indians. The thirteen-year war against the French, British, and Spaniards resulted in the founding of the second independent state in the New World—Haiti—in 1804, adding to the mythical Ethiopia a symbol of black sovereignty. Christophe's reign brought all of this to a climax. Certain other periods have already become standard such as the Harlem Renaissance, which should be renamed as the period of the black power upsurge, for Garvey's rise coincided with the literary movement. Somewhere high on the list should be a meticulous analysis, using all forms of documentary sources, as well as oral documents, of the decade preceding the Fifth Pan-African Congress when a small group of intellectuals in London formed, first, the International African Service Bureau (Padmore, James, Kenyatta, and others) and then the Pan-African Federation in 1944 with T. Ras Makonnen as a moving force. This English-speaking group had some contact with a francophone group in Paris. Someone with a flare for this kind of intellectual activity or a consortium of African studies and black studies programs should take on the task of preparing a framework into which the social and political movements, the Haitian regime, and the diaspora new nations are fitted, and within which smaller discrete problems can be defined. Incidentally, one of these subproblems might be a thorough evaluation of the role of four defunct Afro-American post-World War II organizations—American Society for African Culture, American Negro Leadership Conference on Africa, Council on African Affairs, and African Liberation Support Committee—and the monitoring of the performance of TransAfrica and any future organizations of this type that come into existence. Assessment and monitoring of diaspora activity oriented toward Africa would be particularly appropriate.

In addition to large-scale cooperative projects such as one for Brazil, it is possible to define a number of discrete problems that merit some attention if research is being designed to approach diaspora studies from a traditional Pan-African perspective. These could provide subjects for master theses or doctoral dissertations:

1. A comparative study of *voluntary* emigration from Africa to Guyana, Trinidad, Brazil, Jamaica, and North America in historical perspective;
2. A comparative study of relations between the peoples of the African diaspora and the East Indian diaspora in Trinidad, Martinique, Jamaica, and Guyana;
3. A study of reasons that account for the persisting high proportion of phenotypically black people at the bottom of the social structure in Hispanic America and Brazil as well as in other cultures that make a tripartite division of the population into white, colored, and black;
4. The impact of Caribbean emigrants on economic and political development in West Africa before and after independence, comparing French and British areas;
5. Afro-Americans as a factor in the *underdevelopment* of Liberia as compared with Sierra Leone;
6. The so-called Hausa Revolts in the early nineteenth century in Brazil and their Pan-African implications.

I assume that some joint research projects will be set up eventually in which African institutions will be participating in cooperation with diaspora institutions. From the perspective of traditional Pan-African activity, a topic that merits considerable attention is the attempt to ascertain the full implications of the distinctive form of race relations that exists in Brazil. This country has always attracted the attention of anthropologists who have been intrigued by the retentions and syncretisms involving Yoruba, Congo, and Gold Coast religious beliefs and practices. One of the most scholarly and insightful of all the diaspora studies carried out by anthropologists is Roger Bastide's *Religions of Brazil*. But from a Pan-African perspective, some other questions are more relevant than Congo religions in rural areas. One of these is why, given a Brazilian population visibly of African descent that is as large as that in the United States, its influence on the black world has been so small by comparison. We have a Pele to match Jack Johnson but no one to pair with W. E. B. Du Bois.

There was a black presence in Brazil as early as 1531 in the one important city of that time, Bahia, and in its hinterland. This was almost a century before the first Africans became a part of a permanent settlement in English-speaking North America. It is a project of comparison and contrast between peoples of African descent in Brazil and in the United States that I propose as one having great significance for diaspora studies carried out as one kind of Pan-African activity. Since the twenty Africans were landed by a Dutch ship at Jamestown in Virginia in 1619, the Afro-American population has grown to over 25 million in the continental United States. The people classified as black and mulatto in Brazil would, if combined, constitute a population somewhat larger than that called black in the United States. The Afro-Americans or blacks are about 11 percent of the total population in the United States; the comparable group in Brazil is about a quarter of that nation's population. The poverty of the *favelas* is more severe, in some ways, than that of the ghettos, and there is no strong clear voice stating the aspirations and needs of black Brazilians. Some scholars attribute this to the fact that race and color are not salient in analyzing social problems in Brazil, that only economic class is relevant. What is the truth of the matter?

Brazil is the Portuguese variant of the Latin American pattern of race relations that has the effect of weakening black solidarity within a country and consequently making the problem of Pan-African solidarity more complicated. Throughout Latin America since the sixteenth century, there has been a custom, sometimes backed up by law, of drawing a distinction between blacks and mulattoes of varied degrees of mixture, and between both groups and the dominant whites. This is in contrast to what some anthropologists call the dual caste system of the North American English-speaking colonies and the United States, where people were classified as black if they had *any trace* of African ancestry. The Latin American system of classification was coupled with a much more relaxed attitude toward interracial sexual relations than among Puritan Anglo-Saxons.

It is apparent that over a period of four centuries, African genes are spread all through that part of the population in Latin America classified as white. Castro was obviously serving political ends when he defended his Angola venture by saying, "The blood of Africa flows through all Cubans," but there was also much truth in his exaggerated rhetoric. Three countries, Mexico, Panama, and Costa Rica, report less than 150,000 blacks and mulattoes combined in their populations, with equal numbers of each. Once there were many more. Physical absorption of black people in Mexico and Panama has been very pronounced, much of it via Indian-African admixture.

If we examine seven other countries, the one reporting the largest number of people of African descent, about 2,500,000—Colombia—enumerates less than half a million of these as black. Of course, how they look and what they are called may not coincide. The flight from Africanity and from blackness, the constant attempt to attenuate blackness or to deny it, becomes the goal of everyone striving to move up in the social system—or to smooth the way for children to raise their status. They call it cleansing the race. The word translated as "whitening" became a part of the vernacular. The Dominican Republic, adjacent to Haiti, most of whose people are classified as black, enumerates 130,000 blacks and 1,500,000 mulattoes. In Puerto Rico, 50,000 blacks are listed along with half a million mulattoes, and in Cuba 670,000 blacks are registered to 800,000 mulattoes. Some Latin American scholars use the same word for the gradual disappearance of Africanity that they use for the transformation of Indians into something else—*mestizaje*. The Dutch sociologist Hoetinik has stated at some length where he thinks the process of whitening is leading when he calls it, with approval, *homogenization by miscegenation*. The Hispanic American scholar Vasconcellos invests the process with a romantic aura when he suggests that it will result in a new and highly desirable cosmic race. For both men, the persistence of clusters of Africanity and Negroidness in these areas is an impediment to progress and national unity, but they are sure both will eventually disappear. In Cuba there is ambivalence—pressure for a new revolutionary culture on one hand and some quasi-official exaltation of the divine mulatto on the other, but now the newfound African identity has come. Is there any possibility that in Cuba or elsewhere whitening as a value would ever disappear? Does Pan-Africanism carry with it a preference for a specific desired outcome in both the short-run and the long-run of the processes of acculturation and miscegenation? Both proceed irrespective of the will of intellectuals or politicians. Can the factors that determine the speed be isolated and statements of probability be made about them?

Brazil, although Latin, is not Hispanic, and although its people, too, exhibit similar attitudes toward Africanity and blackness, they are significantly different. The most fruitful comparison within Latin America is with Cuba, for both countries absorbed large numbers of Africans as slaves until after the middle of the nineteenth century, and West African religions have persisted in both with astonishing vitality.

In comparing the Pan-African implications of the black experience in the diaspora, I think the hypotheses can be validated that wherever diaspora black people have become involved in a struggle for their own rights, for their own dignity within a country, or where they have been the objects of colonialism, Pan-Africanism emerges as a reinforcement to their own struggle. There have been such struggles in Cuba. Black people in Brazil have never been involved on a large scale in such a struggle. There was no equivalent of North America's Civil War or the Ten Years War. Brazilian blacks have never felt a need to identify strongly with Africa in a political sense. Yet, paradoxically, a sense of Africanity at the cultural level has remained much stronger in Brazil than in North America. There are striking similarities but also very great differences in the history of black people in these two vast nations. The parameters along which race relations developed were laid down during the seventeenth century. As a pedagogical device, I suggest the selection of Brazil as the centerpiece with its dramatic stories of runaways and maroon settlements, including the Palmares Republic that lasted over seventy years, with the British colonies in Barbados, Jamaica, and North America presented for comparison. Haiti would take the spotlight in the eighteenth century and North America in the early nineteenth as diaspora history developed. Brazil was unique throughout these centuries, and the story should be brought in a comparative framework that helps explain why its Pan-African role has been so limited in a political sense.

During the first half of the eighteenth century there was a very rapid population buildup in North America as well as in Jamaica and Barbados. Britain had broken the Dutch preeminence in slave trading and was organizing the transatlantic exportations for stocking sugar plantations in the Caribbean and the rice, indigo, and tobacco plantations of North America. In none of these groups during the first half of the century does any significant group of literate Africans or people of African descent emerge, and the brutal nature of slavery evoked considerable insurrection. In Brazil, on the other hand, a few mixed-blood individuals had appeared as men of letters occupying positions of high status in the late seventeenth century, and their numbers multiplied in the eighteenth century. Bahia continued to be a cultural center as it had in the past with a class split between a mulatto elite group standing between an exclusive Portuguese top that claimed to be white and a bottom that was African in culture as well as in color. Attenuated Africanity became the characteristic of upward social mobility. Two new urban centers had become important. In one of these, Rio de Janeiro, African religious institutions were preserved by an artisan class that though enslaved worked on its own, had a peculium, and saved money for the purchase of the freedom of its members. They mobilized themselves by the preservation of their African institutions. In the other city, the wealthy center of the mining region of Minas Gerais, a very different pattern prevailed. Here, both Africans and mulattoes found scope for skill and reward for it. But a very definite rift was institutionalized between people who were oriented toward and cherished African culture and mixed-blood, upwardly mobile people who were regarded as Brazilian not black. In North America the great scholar Machado Assis would have been defined as a "great *Negro* man of letters." There he was a "great Brazilian." But such men did not supply leadership to an evolving black community after emancipation in 1888. They were skimmed off by integration. North America could not tolerate such a system.

Friendly white scholars in Brazil who have suggested that black people need to organize *as blacks*, such as Professor Fernandes of Sao Paulo, have been harassed by the government as enemies of Brazil's racial democracy. Yet, some black people as early as the 1930s were expressing a desire for such organization. It would be interesting to find out if the roots extend much farther back and, if so, what hampered their growth. There is need for research, too, on the several abortive efforts to organize blacks as blacks in Brazil during the 1930s and for dissemination in English and French of the documents existing in Portuguese about the National Negro Convention that met in Sao Paulo in 1945 and in Rio de Janeiro in 1946; the National Negro Conference that met in 1949; and what has been called the First Congress of the Brazilian Negro that met in 1950. Five years later, a Semena do Negro, or Negro week, was held. The driving force behind these conferences was Abdias do Nascimento, who won government disfavor for his efforts. It is to the credit of the University of Ife in Nigeria that it provided him with a temporary base from which to carry on his scholarly work during the 1970s. The official Brazilian government position is that given time, all social and economic differences between blacks and other Brazilians will disappear, and so will blacks as a visible group. Why stir up racial trouble in the meantime?

The making of the North American comparison with respect to Pan-Africanism inevitably leads to the asking of more general questions about the contemporary Pan-African activity of Brazilian black people. Some tantalizing glimpses of the activities of Angola intellectuals after World War II were provided by Professor Gerald M. Moser of Pennsylvania State in the spring 1967 issue of *African Forum*, AMSAC's special issue on "The Negro in Brazilian Literature." After referring to Lisbon as a point of contact between intellectuals from Portuguese Africa and Brazil and the fact that a number of Portuguese-speaking African writers lived for a while in Brazil, he wrote:

> Like the rest of the continent, Portuguese Africa has been stirred by a socio-literary movement whose first impetus came from more advanced but less sizable mulatto and Negro groups in the Americas. In the case of Portuguese Africa, influences from Brazil naturally played an important part, as well as negritude ideology from France.

This whets our appetite for more—knowledge of personalities and their specific works and translations from Portuguese of Brazilian poetry with a Pan-African thrust into other languages. But also we would want a discussion of why there were no Frantz Fanons and George Padmores operating in Angola, Guinea-Bissau, and Mozambique. Did the Pan-African interest remain entirely cultural? And where are the leaders of this tendency now?

I first became aware that there was a Brazilian problem about twenty-five years ago when I was a visitor in London and went to dinner one evening with a highly educated black Brazilian and a Ghanaian. The Brazilian intellectual began to explain to us the virtues of what I now recognize as Professor Vasconcellos's concept of the cosmic race, stating that if miscegenation could be speeded up, one Brazilian race—part black, part Indian, part white, with a touch of Japanese—would eventually result. "Now we have two problems," he said, "a race problem and a class problem. Then we'd have only one. The rich could fight it out with the poor." My Ghanaian friend was incensed. "Are you asking me to agree that it would be good if all black people disappeared from your country? That we should voluntarily commit race suicide so the nation could simplify its problems?" The Brazilian friend answered, "Well there wouldn't be any white people left either." The Ghanaian answered, "But you'd be absorbing us, not us you. That wouldn't be any equal blending," I managed to divert the subject into a discussion of African religious survivals and away from the miscegenation question that would prevent our remaining friends for the rest of the evening.

The next time I thought about Brazil was when I read that Katherine Dunham and Irene Diggs had faced discrimination in public places in Brazil, and that this did not coincide with a view that Professor E. Franklin Frazier and Lorenzo Turner, Afro-American scholars, had reported. I decided to read a bit about Brazil and became even more confused, despite the fine work of Marvin Harris and Charles Wagley under UNESCO auspices designed to clarify what was not the simple problem some North Americans thought it was. Organizing my thinking in a comparative frame of reference seemed most fruitful.

Then, in 1966, when I attended the First Festival of Negro Art in Dakar, I noted that one aspect of Brazilian participation paralleled that of the United States. Official emphasis was placed on a cultural indebtedness to Africa. The Brazilian government had produced a beautifully designed and illustrated booklet describing the extent to which Brazilian culture was *Afro*-Lusitanian not just Lusitanian. Music, song, dance, and folklore as well as cuisine were cited. The United States had facilitated the participation of Duke Ellington's band, several gospel choruses, and dance groups.

I did not know at the time that the editor of AMSAC's *African Forum* was preparing, at the same time, a special issue on Negro and Brazilian literature with the assistance of Professor Antonio Olinto of the Federal University of Rio de Janeiro. We were very proud to devote most of volume 2, number 4, spring 1967, to Brazil. One of the most impressive articles was "The Negro Theater in Brazil," by Abdias do Nasciemento, economist, playwright, actor, director, and founder of *Teatro Experimental do Negro* (TEN). It was an eye opener. He mentioned that he attended a seminar on economics in Lima, Peru, in 1941 and decided to go to see a performance of a play written by a white American about a black man, entitled *The Emperor Jones*. It was a play that Paul Robeson made famous. Nasciemento wrote:

> The role of the hero was played by a white actor in blackface.... Why a white man made up as a Negro? I asked myself. For lack of a Negro actor? I remembered, however, that in my own country, where at that time there were 20 million Negroes out of a total population of 60 million, I had never seen a play in which the leading role had been played by an actor of my race. Could it be therefore that Brazil was not a real racial democracy?

He resolved to found a theater that "would open the role of protagonist to the Negro, enable him to rise from the status of a secondary or folkloric character to become the subject and hero of plays in which he appeared." By 1944 he had such a theater in existence and was being called a subversive for having organized TEN.

It was not until I read Nasciemento's article that I knew that the Foreign Ministry of Brazil had refused to authorize TEN to send a group with the Brazilian delegation to present one or more of its plays. Does history repeat itself? A decade later at FESTAC in Nigeria, a Brazilian delegation was also present. Nasciemento was, by then, in self-imposed exile teaching at the University of Ife in Nigeria. He prepared a paper on racism in Brazil. The government of his country threatened to withdraw from FESTAC if Nasciemento participated. His paper was not read. Between the two festivals, I had embarked on a program of trying to educate myself about race relations in Brazil. I have increasingly come to the conclusion that any organized program of diaspora studies would devote special attention to this country.

Brazil highlights the problem of the role of people of African descent who are enclaved within a white nation as that nation develops inter-state relations with African nations. As the Brazilian government rolls out the welcome mat for white settlers who once lived in Angola and Mozambique as well as Rhodesia, and who bring their racist attitudes with them, what is the role of Brazilian blacks and mulattoes to be? What are the implications of the developing economic relations with Nigeria, and can these be used as leverage to improve the lot of blacks *within* Brazil? If so, how? What of Brazilian relations with South Africa? Diaspora studies concerned with the international relations aspects of Pan-Africanism will certainly be interested in pursuing these problems. I suspect that African scholars will find it easier to embark on such research than Afro-American scholars. But, in any event such studies are crucial. Some years ago Professor Biobaku of Nigeria, who was then at the University of Ife, opened up relations with the University in Bahia for cooperative cultural studies. It is likely that incountry studies in Brazil will have to be nonpolitical.

The type of institutions that black people in the United States elaborated during the nineteenth and twentieth centuries contributed toward the development of a type of Pan-African relationship that reached its most complete fulfillment during the 1960s. These were relations between a university-trained stratum of black Americans of all shades of color with African leaders of all political persuasions and diverse ethnic and acculturational experiences. The former close ties between Afro-American churches and Africans became of diminishing importance as did black community relations within the United States with students from the new African nations. The type of institutions that black people have developed in Brazil may provide the basis for another type of relationship during the 1980s—the religious organizations of the illiterate, samba clubs of the urban youth, and the nascent protest organizations of intellectuals, particularly if the democratizing trend continues.

In comparing the relatively restricted level of Pan-African activity in Brazil with that of the Afro-American population in the United States, two quite separate kinds of questions must be raised. One involves a kind of research that any interested scholar could carry out; the other would have to be the work of the committed Pan-African scholar. The first is the simple straightforward analysis of *why* the lines of development have been so different. This is an important and fascinating comparative study for understanding the dynamics of black communities and of race relations. But there is another question, too, at another level of analysis, a question in the realm of value judgments, a philosophical question—*Should* an effort be made to draw black Brazilians into the network of Pan-African relations, or should their more parochial mode of living black be accorded a legitimacy in its own right? Some Brazilians have raised this question themselves.

In addition to fact-finding and hypothesis testing, there is also the need occasionally to step back from the details that obscure the issue. We need integration of facts about black diasporas on the global scale as well as in smaller areas. The question always becomes one of timing, of assessing when enough spade work has been done, when enough monographic literature is available, when closure is not unreasonably premature. The concept of diaspora history as an extension of African history, and treated as an extension of African history, is perhaps worth a trial monograph even now. A fascinating chapter could be written on the so-called Hausa revolts in Brazil, which have been interpreted as extensions of conflicts going on in the Hausa states in the homeland. For the past decade I have been attempting another type of integration, involving only the diaspora peoples' societies and culture, and trying to assemble all the data bearing on two questions:

1. Where and with what intensity have African cultural forms and values persisted in various areas of the Western Hemisphere, and why the differences from area to area?
2. How have images of Africa, African cultural elements and cognitive styles, and Pan-African contacts entered into routine survival adjustments as well as into mobilization for protest and rebellion against oppression during 480 years of Western Hemisphere diaspora history?

Conclusion

I spoke at the beginning of Nkrumah and Azikiwe as two individuals who were interested in the scholarly dimensions of Pan-African activity. Each expressed this by trying to encourage the universities in their respective nations to use some Afro-American and West Indian personnel where possible and by dramatic symbolic acts involving Afro-American professors. Dr. W. E. B. Du Bois had wished for many years to edit what was at first called a Negro encyclopedia. An American foundation made possible the production of a small preliminary volume, but no foundation was willing to supply the funds for the black radical scholar to produce an encyclopedia on the scale Du Bois envisioned. As soon as Ghana became a republic, in the year 1960, Dr. Nkrumah invited Du Bois to come to Ghana and begin editing *Encyclopedia Africana*. Du Bois was then ninety-three. Nkrumah said, in effect, "The white philanthropists wouldn't support your important project. Our independent African nation will." The old man died a few years later. By then he had become a citizen of Ghana, and his adopted nation gave him a state funeral. The ashes of George Padmore, the West Indian adviser, had been placed in the Christiansborg Castle wall in 1959; now Du Bois, the Afro-American, was buried just outside the castle wall. The symbolism was quite clear in both cases.

For many years, William Leo Hansberry tried unsuccessfully to secure foundation support for his studies of ancient Ethiopia, the current Republic of Sudan. There was extreme skepticism among white establishment scholars about many of his findings, which are now taken for granted. His students at Howard University not only learned from him but were inspired by him, and Nnamdi Azikiwe, particularly, was impressed by Dr. Hansberry's knowledge of African history. When the university was established at Nsukka under the patronage of Dr. Azikiwe, the African Studies Institute was named for Dr. Hansberry, who was invited there on a visiting professorship.

Both the Hansberry and Du Bois cases are cited as unique events not as precedents to be followed. Nkrumah and Azikiwe were of the first generation of African nationalists, those who had won the victory, engaged in settling old scores and in setting the record straight. These kinds of gestures were very appropriate for that time period. The present and the future dictate less highly personal and dramatic affirmations of Pan-African solidarity. Our meeting together is an act of exploring new ways to engage in one variety of Pan-African activity and in a form appropriate to our own time and to a new situation. West Africa now abounds in universities and not only has the personnel to staff the faculties but also intellectuals who can accept posts in African programs and black studies programs in the United States and the West Indies. Twenty years have resulted in dramatic change. Professor Kenneth Dike was a distinguished professor of history at Harvard; Professor Mezu has not only enriched our Afro-American studies programs but also established the Black Academy Press; and I could go on naming African scholars who have come to us as some of us were going to Africa to teach during the 1950s and 1960s. May this two-way traffic continue, and may the older Caribbean stream continue, both ways, too. The relatively new field of diaspora studies, as it develops in Africa, will profit from it.

When Dr. Du Bois died, another Afro-American, Dr. Alpheus Hunton, who was once on the faculty of Howard University, took up his work with the *Encyclopedia*. After the coup in Ghana, Hunton moved on to Zambia. When he died there, Kenneth Kaunda and the political party, UNIP, gave him a state funeral. I cite his case to emphasize the fact that Afro-American involvement with the emerging African states was not confined just to West Africa; and there are many other examples.

One additional research project that might provide an opportunity for African students to write theses at the master level would be the assembling of monographic studies about Afro-Americans and West Indians who contributed to the new nations during their first decade. This is not to foreclose the production of some important theses on the diaspora rascals and sharpies who appeared on the scene, too.

As I contemplate the metaphor of the root and the stem and the branches with which I began, and I think of the past cooperation between Africans and peoples of the diaspora, my mind comes to rest on the Jamaican emigrant to New York whose poetry is often included in accounts of the Harlem Renaissance, Claude McKay. One of his poems about black Americans and the 1919 race riots became famous because Churchill quoted it during the Battle of Britain: "If we must die let it not be like hogs/Hunted and penned in some inglorious spot." But this one is about the tree, and it is very apropos at this moment, apropos to this meeting where we are considering our past and our future, the follies and the glories, that is the truth about the black experience:

> So would I live in rich imperial growth,
> Touching the surface and the depth of things,
> Instinctively responsive unto both,
> Tasting the sweets of being, fearing no stings,
> Sensing the subtle spell of changing forms
> Like a strong tree
> Against a thousand storms.[4]

NOTES

1. Renamed and extended to Black History Month.
2. Now the Association for the Study of Afro-American Life and History.
3. *Recollections of James Juma Mbotela* (East African Publishing House, Nairobi, Kenya, 1977); *Abolition and Repatriation in Kenya* (Historical Association of Kenya, Nairobi, Kenya, 1977).
4. "Like a Strong Tree," in *The Passion of Claude McKay: Selected Poetry and Prose, 1912–1948*, ed. Wayne F. Cooper (New York: Schocken Books, 1973), 127.

SELECTED BIBLIOGRAPHY

Journal Articles and Book Chapters

Bastide, Roger. "Dusky Venus, Black Apollo." *Race* 3 (1961):10–18.
Cross, Malcolm. "Colonialism and Ethnicity: A Theory and Comparative Case Study." *Ethnic and Racial Studies* (January 1978):37–59.
Drake, St. Clair. "The Black Diaspora in Pan-African Perspective." *Black Scholar* 7 (September 1975):2–14.
——. "Hide My Face, on Pan-Africanism and Negritude." In *The Making of Black America*, edited by August Meier and Elliott Rudwick, 66–90. New York: Atheneum, 1969.
——. "Negro Americans and 'The African Interest.'" In *The American Negro Reference Book*, ed. John P. Davis, Englewood Cliffs, N.J.: Prentice-Hall, 1966.
Kent, R. R. "Palmares: An African State in Brazil." *Journal of African History* 6 (1965):169–75.
Lynch, Hollis R. "Pan-Negro Nationalism in the New World, before 1862." In *The Making of Black America*, edited by Meier and Rudwick, 42–65.
Mazrui, Ali. "Negritude, the Talmudic Tradition and Intellectual Performance of Blacks and Jews." *Ethnic and Racial Studies* 1 (January 1978):19–36.
Ofuatey-Kodjoe, W. "The Ideological Triangle: Reciprocal Ideological Influences among Afro-West Indians, Afro-Americans and Africans." *Studia Africana* 1 (Spring 1977).
Rodrigues, Jose Honorio. "The Influence of Africa on Brazil and of Brazil on Africa." *Journal of African History* 3 (1962).
Shepperson, George. "The African Diaspora—or the African Abroad." *African Forum: A Quarterly Journal of Contemporary Affairs* 2 (Summer 1966):76–93.
——. "Notes on Negro-American Influences on the Emergence of African Nationalism." *Journal of African History* 1 (1960):309–10.
——. "Pan-Africanism and 'pan-Africanism,' Some Historical Notes." *Phylon* 23 (1962):353–54.
Stuckey, Sterling. "Through the Prism of Folklore: The Black Ethos in Slavery." *Massachusetts Review* 9 (Summer 1968).

Collections of Articles and Essays

Huggins, Nathan I., Martin Kilson, and Daniel M. Fox, eds. *Key Issues in the Afro-American Experience*. New York: Harcourt, Brace, Jovanovich, 1971. Contains articles mostly concerned with North America by twenty-seven scholars, about a third of which are black. Philip Curtin presents a comprehensive background article on "The Slave Trade and the Atlantic Basin: Intercontinental Perspectives," and a valuable demographic discussion is contributed by Herbert S. Klein in "Patterns of Settlement of the Afro-American Population in the New World." Nathan Huggins and Houston Baker suggest fruitful conceptual parameters for analyzing the Afro-American experience. Articles of special relevance to the theme of this chapter are Edwin S. Redkey, "The Flowering of Black Nationalism: Henry McNeal Turner," and E. U. Essien-Udom, "Black Identity in the International Context." St. Clair Drake wrote the concluding essay entitled "Prospects for the Future."

Whitten, Norman E., Jr., and John R. Szwed, eds. *Afro-American Anthropology: Contemporary Perspectives*. New York: Free Press, 1970. Includes twenty-two research reports on peoples of African descent in Haiti, Brazil, Ecuador, Guyana, Honduras, Tobago, Nevis, Antigua, and various parts of the United States by twenty-three scholars, two of whom were black. The editors evaluate the work of Herskovits and put forward their own frame of reference for study in the introduction. Sidney Mintz contributes an excellent theoretical essay. An article by Roy Bryce-LaPorte makes a significant contribution to the study of the marginalized black populations from the West Indians *within* the diaspora.

World Encyclopedia of Black Peoples, Vol. 1. St. Clair Shores, Mich.: Scholarly Press, 1975. Includes among twenty entries by African and Afro-American scholars the following: James A. Hefner, "The Economy of the Black Americas"; George Kent, "Literature of the Black People of the Americas"; Cedric Robinson, "Social Conditions among the Black People of the Americas"; Leslie B. Rout, Jr., "History of the Black People of Spanish America"; Sterling Stuckey, "History of the Black Peoples of America" [USA].

Young, Carlene, ed. *Black Experience: Analysis and Synthesis.* San Rafael, Calif.: Leswing Press, 1972. Contains eighty-four selected readings, many quite brief, by both white and black authors, organized around themes and concerned primarily with the United States. The compiler provides a perceptive introductory essay entitled, "The Black Ethos: What Is It?" and St. Clair Drake contributes a concluding essay on "The Black Experience in Black Historical Perspective."

Collected Works of Single Authors

Harris, Joseph E., ed. *Pillars in Ethiopian History* and *Africa and Africans as Seen by Classical Writers: The William Leo Hansberry African History Notebook.* Vols. 1 and 2. Washington, D.C.: Howard University Press, 1974, 1977. Dr. Hansberry was on the faculty of Howard University and devoted most of his scholarly career to a study of the interrelationships between ancient Ethiopia (i.e., Nubia or Kush) and the surrounding areas in Africa as well as with the classical world. Dr. Hansberry pioneered during a period when scant recognition was given to the peoples and cultures of that area as compared with the intensive concentration on Egyptology.

Herskovits, Melville J. *The New World Negro.* Bloomington: University of Indiana Press, 1966. A collection of papers edited by his wife, Frances Herskovits. (Includes several papers read before the Association for the Study of Negro Life and History.) Discussions of religious syncretisms in Brazil and Haiti based on his fieldwork are a valuable contribution to diaspora studies.

Mintz, Sidney W. *Caribbean Transformations.* Chicago: Adline, 1974. Author notes that the chapters were "originally written during a period stretching over two decades." All have been "considerably revised and rewritten here." "Afro-Caribbeana: An Introduction" suggests an original conceptual framework and states the author's view that "Afro-Caribbean and the Afro-United States are becoming more alike in spite of vast historical differences." Plantation economies and peasant societies are contrasted: Jamaica, Haiti, and Puerto Rico are the special cases emphasized.

Books with a Pan-African Perspective

Adams, C. C., and Marshall A. Talley. *Negro Baptists and Foreign Missions.* Philadelphia: Foreign Missions Board of the National Baptist Convention, USA, 1944.

Azikiwe, Nnamdi, *Liberia in World Politics*. London: Negro Universities Press, 1962.

Barrett, Leonard E. *Soul-Force: African Heritage in Afro-American Religion*. New York: Doubleday, 1974.

Bertley, Leo W. *Canada and Its People of African Descent*. Pierrefond: Bilongo Publishers, 1977.

Blassingame, John W. *The Slave Community: Plantation Life in the Antebellum South*. New York: Oxford University Press, 1972.

Blyden, Edward Wilmot. *A Voice from Bleeding Africa on Behalf of Her Exiled Children*. Monrovia, Liberia: 1956.

———. *Vindication of the Negro Race*. Monrovia, Liberia, 1957.

Brown, William W. *The Rising Sun, or, The Antecedents and Advancement of the Colored Race*. Reprint. London: Negro Universities Press, 1970.

Casley-Hayford, J. E. *Ethiopia Unbound: Studies in Race Emancipation*. Reprint. London: Frank Cass, 1969.

Crummell, Alexander. *The Relations and Duties on the Free Colored Men in America to Africa*. Hartford: 1861.

Dark, Philip J. C. *Bush Negro Art: An African in the Americas*. London: Alec Tiranti, 1954.

Davis, John A., ed. *Africa from the Point of View of American Negro Scholars*. Paris: Présence Africaine, 1958.

DeCosta, Miriam, ed. *Blacks in Hispanic Literature*. Port Washington, N.Y.: Kennikat Press, 1977. A collection of papers from a conference held at Howard University.

Delany, Martin R. *Official Report of the Niger Valley Exploring Party*. New York: 1861.

———. *The Condition, Elevation and Destiny of the Colored People of the United States*. Reprint. New York: Arno Press, 1968.

Drake, St. Clair. *Black Religion and the Redemption of Africa*. Chicago: Third World Press and Institute of the Black World, 1971.

Du Bois, W. E. B. *The Negro*. New York: Henry Holt, 1975.

Elder, Jacob, *Evolution of the Traditional Calypso of Trinidad and Tobago*. Ph.D. dissertation, University of Pennsylvania, 1966.

Essien-Udom, E. U. *Black Nationalism: A Search for an Identity in America*. Chicago: University of Chicago Press, 1962.

Garvey, Amy Jacques, ed. *The Philosophy and Opinions of Marcus Garvey*. Reprint. New York: Humanities Press, 1968.

Geis, Gilbert, and William Bittle. *The Longest Way Home*. Detroit: Free Press, 1964.

Holly, James T. *A Vindication of the Capacity of the Negro Race for Self-Government*. New Haven: Yale University Press, 1857.

James, C. L. R. *The Black Jacobins*. New York: Viking Press, 1938.

Jenkins, David. *Black Zion: The Return of Afro-Americans and West Indians to Africa*. London: Wildwood House, 1975.

Lynch, Hollis R. *Edward Wilmot Blyden: Pan-Negro Patriot*. London: Oxford University Press, 1967.

Malcolm X. *The Autobiography of Malcolm X*. New York: Grove Press, 1965.

Martin, Tony. *Race First: The Ideological and Organizational Struggles of Marcus Garvey and the Universal Negro Improvement Association*. Westport, Conn.: Greenwood Press, 1976.

Miller, Floyd J. *The Search for a Black Nationality: Black Emigration and Colonization, 1787–1863*. Urbana: University of Illinois Press, 1975.

Moses, Wilson J. *The Golden Age of Black Nationalism: 1850–1925*. Hamden, Conn.: Archon Books, 1978.

Nkrumah, Kwame. *Ghana: An Autobiography*. Edinburgh: Oxford University Press, 1959.

Padmore, George. *Pan-Africanism or Communism?* London: Dobson, 1956.

Payne, Daniel A. *History of the African Methodist Episcopal Church.* Reprint. New York: Arno Press, 1969.

Price-Mars, J. *Ainsi parla l'oncle.* Paris Imprimatur de Compiègne, 1928.

Redkey, Edwin S. *Black Exodus: Black Nationalism and Back-to-Africa Movements, 1890–1910.* New Haven: Yale University Press, 1969.

Richards, Henry J., ed. *Topics in Afro-American Studies.* Buffalo, N.Y.: Black Academy Press, 1971. A collection of twelve essays by a Trinidadian professor of foreign languages at the State University of New York (SUNY), Buffalo, and published by the press founded by an African professor, Dr. S. O. Mezu, at the same institution. Three other African scholars and another West Indian contributed essays. The editor noted that "This anthology is dedicated to the thirty-three students at the State University of New York at Buffalo who spent the academic year studying and developing with me a program in Afro-American Studies." Dr. Felix Okoye, chairman of the Black Studies Department at SUNY, Brockport, wrote on "The Afro-American and Africa."

Rodrigues, Jose Honorio. *Brazil and Africa.* Berkeley: University of California Press, 1968. Rodrigues concludes that "Brazil is, like Cuba, more Africanized than any of the American states except Haiti."

Shepperson, George, and T. Price. *Independent African.* London: Edinburgh, 1958.

Smith, M. G., Roy Augier, and Rex Nettleford. *The Ras Tafarian Movement in Kingston.* Jamaica: University of the West Indies, 1962.

Sterling, Dorothy, *The Making of an Afro-American: Martin Robinson Delany, 1812–1885.* Garden City, N.Y.: Doubleday, 1971.

Stuckey, Sterling, ed. *The Ideological Origins of Black Nationalism.* Boston: Beacon Press, 1972. Contains R. A. Young's "The Ethiopian Manifesto," Walker's "Appeal," Martin R. Delany's "The Political Destiny of the Colored Race," and other documents, including a scholarly introduction by the editor.

Tulloch, Headley. *Black Canadians: A Long Line of Fighters.* Toronto: North Carolina Press, 1975.

Turner, Lorenzo D. *Africanisms in the Gullah Dialect.* Chicago: University of Chicago Press, 1949.

Uya, Okon E. *Black Brotherhood.* Lexington, Mass.: Heath, 1971.

Other Books and Special Publications

African Forum: A Quarterly Journal of Contemporary Affairs 2 (Spring 1967) provides a special issue on "The Negro and Brazilian Literature." See especially Zora Seljan's article on "Negro Popular Poetry in Brazil," which includes the ballad cited in the chapter and Abdias do Nasciemento, "The Negro Theater in Brazil," by the leading exponent of negritude and black power in Brazil.

de Azevedo, Thales. *Les Elites de Coleur dans une Ville Bresiliene.* Paris: UNESCO, 1953.

Bastide, Roger. *Les Ameriques noires, les civilisations africaines dans le nouveau monde.* Paris: Payot, 1967. A hemisphere-wide synthesis.

Bastide, Roger. *The African Religions of Brazil: Toward a Sociology of the Interpenetration of Civilizations.* Baltimore: Johns Hopkins Press, 1978. An English translation by Helen Sebba of a book originally published in 1960 in French.

Blassingame, John, ed. *Slave Testimony: Two Centuries of Letters, Speeches, Interviews and Autobiographies.* Baton Rouge: Louisiana State University Press, 1977.

Bowen, J. W. E., ed. *Africa and the American Negro.* Facsimile ed. New York: Arno, 1896. Papers delivered at a conference at Gammon Seminary.

Brotz, Howard. *The Black Jews of Harlem*. New York: Free Press, 1964.

Degler, Carl. *Neither White nor Black: Slavery and Race Relations in Brazil and the United States*. New York: Macmillan, 1971.

Engerman, Stanley L., and Eugene D. Genovese, eds. *Race and Slavery in the Western Hemisphere: Quantitative Studies*. Princeton: Princeton University Press, 1975. See especially " History and Anthropology: A Brief Reprise," by Sidney W. Mintz and "Comments on the Study of Race and Slavery," by Stanley L. Engerman, as well as articles breaking new ground: Colin A. Palmer, "Religion and Magic in Mexican Slave Society, 1570–1650" and Mary Karasch, "From Porterage to Proprietorship in Rio de Janeiro, 1808–1850."

Harris, Marvin. *Patterns of Race in the Americas*. New York: Walker, 1964.

Herskovits, Melville. *The Myth of the Negro Past*. New York: Harper, 1941.

Hoetink, H. H. *Caribbean Race Relations: Two Variants*. London: Oxford University Press, 1971.

Huggins, Nathan I. *Black Odyssey: The Afro-American Ordeal in Slavery*. New York: Pantheon Books, 1977.

Jordan, Winthrop. *White over Black: American Attitudes toward the Negro, 1550–1812*. Baltimore: Penguin Books, 1968.

Knight, Franklin S. *Slave Society in Cuba during the Nineteenth Century*. Madison: University of Wisconsin Press, 1970.

Labat, Pere. *Nouveaux voyages aux Isles de l'amerique*. The Hague: P. Husson, 1724.

Lowenthal, David. *West Indian Societies*. New York: Oxford University Press, 1972.

Maquet, Jacques. *Africanity*. New York: Oxford University Press, 1972.

Memoires de l'Institut Français d'Afrique Noire (Dakar, Senegal) no. 27 (1953). Special issue, "Les Afro-Americains."

Morner, Magnus. *Race Mixture in the History of Latin America*. New York: Little, Brown and Co., 1967.

Mullin, Gerald W. *Flight and Rebellion: Slave Resistance in Eighteenth Century Virginia*. New York: Oxford University Press, 1972.

"The Present Status of Afro-American Research in Latin America." *Daedalus: Journal of the American Academy of Arts and Sciences* (Spring 1974).

Price, Richard. *Maroon Societies*. New York: Doubleday, 1973.

Szulc, Tad. *The United States and the Caribbean*. New York: Spectrum Books, 1971.

van den Berghe, Pierre. *Race and Racism*. New York: Wiley, 1967. Brazil, Mexico, South Africa, and the United States used as case studies.

Wagley, Charles, ed. *Race and Class in Rural Brazil*. Paris: UNESCO, 1952.

——, and Marvin Harris. *Minorities in the New World: Six Case Studies*. New York: Columbia University Press, 1958.

Wood, Peter H. *Black Majority: Negroes in Colonial South Carolina from 1670 through the Stono Rebellion*. New York: W. W. Norton, 1974.

Contributors

S. Y. Boadi-Siaw is a historian at the University of Cape Coast in Ghana. His research and publication interests are: relations between African countries and Brazil, Africans in Latin America and Afro-Brazilians in West Africa.

Roy Simon Bryce-Laporte is MacArthur Professor of Sociology at Colgate University. He formerly served as Director, Research Institute on Immigration and Ethnic Studies, Smithsonian Institution. He has published many articles and the following books: *Contemporary Perspectives of Alienation* (New York: Praeger, 1978) with Claudewell S. Thomas; and *Sourcebook on the New Immigration*, 2 vols. (Transaction Books, 1979).

St. Clair Drake, Sociologist Emeritus at Stanford University, taught at the University of Liberia and the University of Ghana, authored many articles and the following books: *Black Metropolis* (New York; Harcourt, Brace, Jovanovich, 1945) with Horace R. Clayton; *Black Religion and the Redemption of Africa* (Chicago: Third World Press, 1971); *Black Folk Here and There* (Los Angeles: Center for Afro-American Studies, 1978 and 1990), 2 vols.

Debra Newman Ham is the Afro-American Specialist at the Library of Congress. She has published a number of articles and the following book: *Black History: A Guide to Civilian Records in the National Archives* (Washington, 1984).

Joseph E. Harris is Professor of History at Howard University. He has authored several articles and the following books: *The African Presence in Asia: Consequences of the East African Slave Trade* (Evanston: Northwestern University Press, 1971); *Africans and Their History* (New York: New American Library/Penguin Books, 1971); *Repatriates and Refugees: The Case of Kenya* (Washington: Howard University Press, 1987).

John Hunwick is Professor of History and Religious Studies at Northwestern University. He has published many articles and the following books: *Shari'a in Songhay* (1985), *Religion and National Integration in Africa* (Evanston: Northwestern University, 1992).

Angela Jorge is Associate Professor of Spanish Language and Hispanic Literature and Culture at the State University of New York at Old Westbury, New York. She specializes in Afro-Hispanic culture, African religions in Hispanic communities, and has written extensively in Puerto Rican studies.

Ibrahim Baba Kaké has published a number of articles on various topics in African history. He also has authored the following books: *Historie de l'Afrique Centrale* (Paris: Presence Africaine, 1972) and *Les Noire de la Diaspora* (Paris-Libreville: Lion, 1978).

Muzong W. Kodi taught at the University of Nairobi, Kenya before joining the Association Banques Centrales Africaines, Centre Africain D'Etude Monetaires in Dakar, Senegal.

Lawrence W. Levine, Professor of History, University of California at Berkeley, is a MacArthur Fellow. Among his many publications are: *Defender of the Faith: William Jennings Bryan, The Last Decade, 1915–1925* (1965); *Black Culture and Black Consciousness: Afro-American Thought from Slavery to Freedom* (New York: Oxford University Press, 1977); *Highbrow-Lowbrow: The Emergence of Cultural Hierarchy in America* (1988).

J. Kimpianga Mahaniah taught for a number of years at the Université Nationale du Zaire and at the Faculte de Théologie Protestante du Zaire. A researcher at the Centre d'Etudes des Religions Africaines, Catholic Theological Faculty in Kinshasa. He has written a number of articles on Christianity in Zaire and on therapeutic medicine.

Tony Martin is Professor of Black Studies at Wellesley College in Massachusetts. His many publications include: *Race First: The Ideological and Organizational Struggles of Marcus Garvey and the Universal Negro Improvement Association* (Westport: Greenwood Press, 1976); *Marcus Garvey, Hero: A First Biography* (New Marcus Garvey Library, 1983); *The Pan-African Connection: From Slavery to Garvey and Beyond* (New Marcus Garvey Library, 1984).

Guerin C. Montilus is Professor of Anthropology at Wayne State University. Among his publications are several articles and *Dompim: The Spirituality of African Peoples* (1990).

Colin A. Palmer is William Rand Kenan Professor of History, University of North Carolina at Chapel Hill. He has authored a number of articles and the following books: *Human Cargoes: The British Slave*

Trade in Spanish America, 1700–1739 (University of Illinois Press, 1981); *Slaves of the White God: Blacks in Mexico, 1570–1650* (Harvard University Press, 1976).

Kings Mbacazwa Phiri is Professor History at the University of Malawi. His research and articles have concentrated on oral history, methodology, precolonial economic and political change in Malawi.

Adell Patton, Jr., is Associate Professor of History at Howard University. His research and published articles have concentrated on African resistance, the frontier in African history, and physicians in African history.

Albert J. Raboteau is Henry W. Putnam Professor of Religion and Dean of the Graduate School at Princeton University. In addition to a number of articles, he has authored the following book: *Slave Religion: The Invisible Institution in the Antebellum South* (New York: Oxford University Press, 1980).

George Shepperson is Professor Emeritus of History, University of Edinburgh, Scotland; and has taught in American, African, British, and Canadian universities. He has published extensively in American, African, African American, and Scottish history, in addition to his pioneer book, *Independent African* (Edinburgh, 1958) with T. Price.

Folarin Shyllon, Senior Research Fellow at the Institute of African Studies, University of Ibadan, Nigeria, has published many articles and the following books: *Black Slaves in Britain* (London: Oxford University Press, 1974); *James Ramsay: The Unknown Abolitionist* (Edinburgh: Canongata, 1977); *Black People in Britain, 1555–1833* (London: Oxford University Press, 1977).

Thomas E. Skidmore is Professor of History and Director of Ibero-American Studies at the University of Wisconsin. In addition to articles, his books include: *Politics in Brazil, 1930–1964* (Oxford University Press, 1967); *Black Into White: Race and Nationality in Brazilian Thought* (1974); *The Politics of Military Rule in Brazil, 1964–1985* (Oxford University Press, 1990).

Elliott P. Skinner is Franz Boas Professor of Anthropology at Columbia University and former United States Ambassador to Burkina Faso. He has published many articles and the following books: *The Mossi of Upper Volta* (Stanford, 1964); *African Urban Life: The Transformation of Ouagadougou* (Princeton, 1974); *African Americans and U. S. Policy Toward Africa, 1850–1924* (Washington: Howard University Press, 1992).

Filomena Chioma Steady is Professor of Women's Studies at the California State University at Sacramento and Consultant at the United Nations. She has published a number of articles and the following book: *The Black Woman Cross-Culturally* (Schenkman Books, 1981).

Okon Edet Uya is Professor of History at the University of Calabar, Nigeria, and former Nigerian Ambassador to Argentina. Among his many publications are: *Black Brotherhood: Afro-Americans and Africa* (Lexington: Heath, 1971); *From Slavery to Public Service: Robert Smalls, 1839–1915* (Oxford University Press, 1971); *The African Diaspora and the Black Experience in New World Slavery* (Okpaku Communications, 1992) also published in Spanish.

Akintola J. G. Wyse is Professor History at the University of Sierra Leone. He has published a number of articles and the following books: *Dr. Bankole Bright and the Politics of Colonial Sierra Leone* and *The Krios of Sierra Leone: An Interpretive History* (Howard University Press, 1991).

Index